德國建築藝術在中國

Torsten Warner 華納

DEUTSCHE ARCHITEKTUR IN CHINA
Architekturtransfer

GERMAN ARCHITECTURE IN CHINA
Architectural transfer

德國建築藝術在中國
建築文化移植

Ernst & Sohn

Umschlag/Cover:
Chinesische Perspektive von Quingdao, um 1908
Bird's eye perspective of Quingdao, around 1908

Übersetzung ins Englische/English translation:
Chris Charlesworth, London; Susan Cox, Dublin
Übersetzung ins Chinesische/Chinese translation:
Fang Wang, Darmstadt; Weiwei Wang, Darmstadt;
Yanzhi Shi, Darmstadt
Herstellung/Production: Annika Preyhs

Satz deutsch und englisch/English and German
typesetting: Ditta Ahmadi, Berlin
Satz chinesisch, Reproduktion, Druck und Bindung/
Chinese typesetting, reproduction, printing and
binding: Everbest Printing Co., Ltd., Hongkong

© 1994 Ernst & Sohn
Verlag für technische Wissenschaften
und Architektur GmbH, Berlin
Ernst & Sohn ist ein Unternehmen der
VCH Verlagsgruppe
Ernst & Sohn is a member of the
VCH Publishing Group

Alle Rechte vorbehalten, besonders die der
Übersetzung in fremde Sprachen.
All rights reserved, especially those of translation
into other languages.

ISBN 3-433-02429-4

INHALT
CONTENTS 目錄

Geleitwort Preface	7	序言
Vorwort Introduction	9	前言
Architekturtransfer Architectural transfer	10	有關城市及其德國建築
Beijing (Peking)	22	北京
Beidaihe (Peitaiho)	52	北戴河
Tianjin (Tientsin)	56	天津
Hongkong	80	香港
Shanghai (Schanghai)	84	上海
Wuhan (Hankou. Hankow)	140	武漢
Shandong (Provinz Schantung. The province of Shantung)	154	山東
Jinan (Tsinanfu)	178	濟南
Qingdao (Tsingtau. Tsingtao)	194	青島
Dank Acknowledgements	304	鳴謝/致謝
Anhang Appendix	306	插圖附錄

GELEITWORT

Das Buch von Torsten Warner erscheint zu einem günstigen Zeitpunkt: auf einer internationalen Konferenz über die Erhaltung des architektonischen Erbes beeindruckte mich kürzlich die Feststellung, daß überall auf der Welt eine wachsende öffentliche Strömung zu erkennen sei, die Bauten der Vergangenheit nicht nur im Interesse einer ästhetisch empfindenden Minderheit, sondern auch auf Wunsch aller Bevölkerungsteile zu pflegen und zu restaurieren. Und zwar nicht allein die Prachtbauten, sondern auch die Häuser der Bürger und einfacher Menschen, weil die Bewahrung der architektonischen Leistungen der Vergangenheit das Gefühl der eigenen historischen Identität stärkt. Das KSZE-Symposium über das kulturelle Erbe in Krakau im Mai-Juni 1991 formulierte sogar, daß eine vollständige Dokumentierung dieses Erbes eine der wichtigsten Hinterlassenschaften für zukünftige Generationen sei.

Es mag widersprüchlich erscheinen, daß der Transfer westlicher Baukunst nach China – und gerade deutscher architektonischer Vorbilder – in der Epoche der »ungleichen Verträge«, durch die die chinesische Souveränität von den fremden Mächten geknebelt wurde, heute in China als Teil der Geschichte der eigenen modernen Architektur und damit als kulturelles Erbe empfunden wird. Die Ausländer bauten sich ja größtenteils ihre öffentlichen Gebäude und Wohnhäuser, um Elemente ihrer heimatlichen Umgebung nach China zu verpflanzen und sich damit von der fremden Umwelt zu isolieren. Aber es gehört zum Genie des chinesischen Volkes, fremde Einflüsse aufnehmen und assimilieren zu können, um damit – trotz des eigenen kulturellen Reichtums – selbst bereichert zu werden.

Die Wiederverwendung architektonischer Merkmale aus der Zeit des westlichen Architekturtransfers nach China in der heutigen chinesischen Bauweise, wie sie Torsten Warner besonders für Qingdao nachweist, ist ein Beispiel für diese fast spielerische Stärke der

PREFACE

The time is ripe for the publication of this book by Torsten Warner: at a recent international conference on the conservation of the architectural legacy, I was particularly impressed to observe the growing world-wide interest in the care and restoration of old buildings. This interest does not merely reflect the aesthetic sensibilities of a minority but the concerns of all sectors of society, and applies not only to particularly majestic buildings but also to the houses of the bourgeoisie and lower classes. The reason behind this development is that the preservation of past architectural achievements helps reinforce the feeling of historical identity. The CSCE symposium on the subject of cultural legacy in Cracow in May-June 1991 went as far as identifying the comprehensive documentation of this tradition as one of the most important legacies for future generations.

The fact that the introduction of Western architecture to China – and particularly of German architectural models – during the time of the »unequal treaties«, which the foreign powers used to suppress Chinese sovereignty, is today seen in China as part of the history of indigenous modern architecture and, thus, a cultural legacy, may seem somewhat contradictory. For the most part, the foreigners erected their own official buildings and private residences in order to import elements of their home environment to China, and in this way protect themselves from their foreign surroundings. However, it is characteristic of the Chinese spirit to assimilate foreign influences for the purpose of enrichment, despite the wealth of the existing indigenous culture.

The use of architectural features from this period of Western architectural transfer in contemporary Chinese architecture, as illustrated by Torsten Warner, particularly in the case of Qingdao, is an example of the almost playful confidence of Chinese culture, which is so totally pervaded by a sense of its own superior-

序言

由托爾斯頓・華納撰寫的本書可謂逢時而出。在前不久召開的國際建築遺產保護會議上，本人目睹了世界各國對保護及修復古建築的興趣與日俱增，感受尤深。此熱趣不止於數學者審美之敏感，更源於社會各層人士之關注，而其保護對象不只是個別富麗堂皇的建築物，而且是中、下層社會公民的住宅。這一發展傾向源於保護古建築可以加深人們對其自身歷史個性的歸屬感之功效。而一九九一年五月至六月在克拉克召開的，由歐洲安全及合作會議所主辦的有關文化遺產問題的學術交流會甚至於認定：對這些古舊建築的全面考証及記錄存檔將是今人能夠留給後人的最重要的遺產之一。

西方建築藝術，特別是德國建築風格被引入中國時，正是外國列強以"不平待條約"干涉中國主權時期，而今中國人卻將這段時期的建築看作其本土建築史中現代建築遺產的一部份，亦即其文化遺產的一部份。這一事實似乎自相矛盾，其實不然。外國人在中國建造顯示其民族特色的商業、行政辦公以及居住建築，在很大程度上是為了將其故國環境的片段移植到中國，從而獲得安全感且了卻異國思鄉之情。而中華民族雖具源遠流長之文化歷史，卻始終以融合外來民族的文化以豐富自身為其精神特性。

中國某些當代建築對這一時期的建築語言加以引用之事實(如托爾斯頓・華納在考察青島建築時所述)是中國文化近乎於玩娛的自信心——一種優越感極強的自信心的寫照。頑固地排斥外來影響往往掩蓋著已經意識到自身的弱點，但又不願意承認的自卑心理。

托爾斯頓・華納以近乎於偵探的縝密查明了德國建築師在中國於十九世紀末二十世紀初設計的眾所周知及鮮為人知的建築。本書展示了中德文化交融的歷史瞬間，其豐富的內容甚至使曾長年僑居中國的人也眼界大開。這一極有膽識的研究將有助於中德雙方的相互理解。

前德意志聯邦共和國大使
斐培誼博士

von ihrer eigenen Überlegenheit so durchdrungenen chinesischen Kultur. Nicht trotzige Abwehr des Fremden, hinter der sich in der Regel nicht eingestandenes Bewußtsein eigener Schwäche notdürftig verbirgt, sondern stolze Aneignung und Einschmelzung dessen, was befruchtend ist.

Torsten Warner hat mit geradezu detektivischer Akribie bekannte und unbekannte Bauten deutscher Architekten der Jahrhundertwende aufgespürt und dokumentiert. Dabei ist selbst für denjenigen, der lange Jahre seines Lebens in China verbracht hat, Neues zu Tage getreten. Entstanden ist ein Werk, das einen kurzen Augenblick gemeinsamer deutsch-chinesischer kultureller Erfahrungen in das allgemeinere Blickfeld rückt. Gerade in einer schwierigen Phase der beiderseitigen Beziehungen kann dieses Unterfangen hilfreich sein.

Professor Dr. Per Fischer
Botschafter a.D.

ity. There is no stubborn rejection of foreign influence that usually camouflages, and shows an unacknowledged awareness of, indigenous weaknesses, but a proud appropriation and integration of worthwhile features.

Torsten Warner has traced and documented familiar and unknown examples of German turn-of-the-century architecture in China with a detective-like meticulousness. The result is a revelation, even to one who has spent many long years in China, and a work which succeeds in bringing a short period of the common German-Chinese cultural experience into a more general light. This achievement can only be of great help, particularly in a time characterised by difficulties in relations on both sides.

Professor Dr. Per Fischer
Former Ambassador to China

VORWORT

Während einer Exkursion der Meisterklasse für Architektur der Hochschule für Angewandte Kunst in Wien im Mai/Juni 1989 nach Nordchina kam mir die Idee zu dieser Forschungsarbeit. Ich war von Shanghai fasziniert, dieser Weltstadt europäischen Formats in Ostasien – eine Metropole, die noch heute reich ist an schönen Bauten der klassischen Moderne, der Art deco und des Expressionismus.

Diese Arbeit untersucht eine der jüngsten Phasen der 4000jährigen chinesischen Architekturgeschichte: den Transfer von westlicher Architektur nach China. Es stellt die deutsche Kolonialgeschichte anhand der Architektur dar.

Ich habe mich durchgängig für die Pinyin-Schreibweise entschieden, die seit den 70er Jahren als amtliche Umschrift der chinesischen Schriftzeichen in lateinische Buchstaben angewandt wird. Bei der jeweils ersten Erwähnung in den Kapiteln wird die früher verwendete Umschrift in Klammern hinzugefügt.

Um die Jahrhundertwende und dann in den 30er Jahren gab es in China bereits eine Expansionsphase der Städte, in der viele Gebäude verloren gingen. Mit dem Ende der 80er Jahre beginnt eine neue Welle der Expansion und damit des Abbruchs. Einige der in diesem Buch vorgestellten Bauten wurden während meines Aufenthaltes in den Städten abgetragen. Ihre Grundstücke waren zu wertvoll geworden. Alle Gebäude sind ein Teil der chinesischen Architekturgeschichte. Sie sind Elemente europäischer und amerikanischer Zivilisation, die nach China verpflanzt wurden. Ihre Stadtviertel und Gebäude sind es wert, auch künftigen Generationen erhalten zu bleiben. Es ist mein Wunsch, daß dieses Buch dazu beiträgt.

Hamburg, im Mai 1993

Torsten Warner

INTRODUCTION

The idea for this study came to me during an excursion to China in May/June 1989 for senior architecture students from the University of Applied Art in Vienna. I was fascinated by Shanghai, this cosmopolitan European city in Asia, a metropolis which today still has many of the most beautiful examples of buildings from the period of Classical Modernism, Art Deco and Expressionism.

This study examines one of the most recent phases in the 4000-year history of Chinese architecture, the migration of Western architecture to China, and examines the history of German colonialism from an architectural perspective. The descriptions of the buildings also include an account of the background to their construction.

I have used the Pinyin phonetic system, the official transscription of Chinese characters into the Roman alphabet, which has been in use since the 1970s. The former versions of the transscription are, however, also provided with the first reference to the place names in each chapter.

Around the turn of the century and again in the 1930s, cities in China underwent a period of expansion and many buildings were replaced. Similarly, the end of the 1980s marked a new era of expansion and, thus, removal. Some of the buildings described in this book were torn down during my stay in the cities. The sites on which they stood had become too valuable. All of the buildings are part of Chinese architectural history. They are also part of European and American civilisation as it was imported to China. It is worth every effort to preserve these buildings and the areas in which they stand for future generations, and it is my hope that this book will contribute towards the achievement of this aim.

Hamburg, May 1993

Torsten Warner

前言

一九八九年五月至六月間，我隨維也納工藝美術大學的建築學高班到中國進行學術考察，途中所觀覽的中國數城給我印象極深。尤其是上海，這座具有歐洲風貌的亞洲都市至今仍擁有折衷主義、現代主義、裝飾派藝術、以及表現主義等勝行時期極優秀的建築典例，身臨其境更使我流連忘返。做這項研究的念頭不禁萌生。

本書所探討的只是中國四千年建築史中近代階段的一個片斷：即西方建築藝術在中國的移植，並從建築學的角度看德國殖民史。本書對所述諸建築之建造的歷史背景均有詳實的描寫；各章節亦以有關省市的殖民史為引子。本書採用中國官方自七十年代以來實行的漢語拼音方案。當某地名首次出現時，其後括號內總注有其舊名的拼音。

十九世紀末二十世紀初以及本世紀三十年代，中國城市規模幾經擴展，許多建築物被拆毀翻新。與此類似，八十年代末中國各城市經歷了又一次拆舊建新的擴充。數座納入本書的建築便在筆者逗留中國期間被拆除，其原因是這些建築所處地段地價暴漲，使建築本身的價值顯得微乎其微。然而，所有這些建築物，不僅是中國建築史的一部份，而且是西方文明史的一部分。保護這些古建築及其城區將值得每份不遺餘力的苦作。筆者謹此獻上本書。

一九九三年五月於漢堡

ARCHITEKTURTRANSFER

»Im gotischen Dom: Streben, Bewegung, Übermaß, Höhe, Enge, Raumlosigkeit, Unruhe, hinauf in immer steilere schwindelnde Lüfte, von der Erde hinweg ins leere Blau des Abstrakten, des Jenseits, – hier im chinesischen Palast: Erdbewußtsein, Ruhe, unendliche Räume in der Breite und Tiefe gegliedert, die Zeit als Raum, das große, vornehme Wartenkönnen, behagliche Wirklichkeit ausgebreitet auf der sicheren Erde, gelb und stark in Farben leuchtend, darüber als Ahnung sich wölbend und Bedeutung verleihend der große, erhabene, blaue Himmel: Einheit von Himmel und Erde, die Ewigkeit konkret in der Zeit erscheinend, das Erhabene im Diesseits.«[1]

Seit der Mitte des 19. Jahrhunderts trafen in den Hafenstädten und christlichen Missionsstationen Chinas zwei Kulturen aufeinander und erzeugten eine noch heute erlebbare Spannung. Doch so einfühlsam und verständnisvoll wie Richard Wilhelm im Jahre 1926 beschrieben damals nur wenige Europäer die chinesische Architektur. Man bemängelte die Einförmigkeit der Städte mit ihren eingeschossigen Hofhäusern, das Fehlen von Türmen und anderen vertikalen Elementen im Stadtbild. Es wurde kritisiert, daß es keine öffentlichen Stadtparks gab. Das vorhandene Grün war hinter grauen Mauern verborgen. Die Ausländer wußten natürlich von den Schönheiten der chinesischen Gärten, doch der Zugang blieb ihnen verwehrt.

Chinas Kunst und Kultur war während des Rokoko (1730–1780) in Europa sehr in Mode. Friedrich der Große ließ sich 1754/57 in Sanssouci in Potsdam ein chinesisches Teehaus erbauen. Die englischen Chippendale-Möbel standen im Zeichen dieser Chinoiserie. Doch die europäische Architekturgeschichte des 19. Jahrhunderts vernachlässigte China; man konzentrierte sich auf die eigene Geschichte. Entsprechend unvorbereitet waren dann auch die Europäer bei der Eröffnung der ersten Handelsniederlassungen in China, als

ARCHITECTURAL TRANSFER

Since the mid-19th century, China's ports and Christian missions have been witness to the collision of two cultures, giving rise to a tension still palpable today. Sinologist Richard Wilhelm wrote of this impression in 1926:

»In the Gothic cathedral: striving, movement, excess, up into the ever steeper vertiginous airs, away from the earth into the empty blue of the abstract, the hereafter. Here in the Chinese palace: awareness of the earth, tranquillity, unlimited spaces aligned in width and depth, time as space, the great refined ability to wait, contented reality spread out on the secure earth, yellow and strong shining through colours; above, a presentiment, the great elevated blue sky spans and lends meaning: unity of sky and earth, eternity a concrete appearance in time, the sublime on this side of the great divide.«[1]

However, few Europeans at the time were able to look at Chinese architecture with the understanding and sensitivity shown by Richard Wilhelm. Criticism is levelled at the monotony of the cities with their single-story courtyard house, the absence of towers and other vertical elements in the city skyline and the lack of city parks is also criticised. Any green areas were hidden behind grey walls. The foreigners were, of course, aware of the beauty of Chinese gardens, but they were denied access to them.

During the period of Rococo in Europe (1730–1780), Chinese art and culture were extremely modern. In 1754/57 Frederick the Great built a Chinese Tea House in Sanssouci in Potsdam. The popularity of English Chippendale furniture was another example of this chinoiserie. However, 19th-century European architectural history neglected China; the emphasis was on the ancient world. Thus, Europeans were completely unprepared when they came into contact with Chinese architecture in the first of the concessions established in China.

Heinrich Hildebrand was the first German en-

有關城市及其德國建築

十九世紀中葉，東西方文化在中國沿海城市以及西方基督教傳教站交鋒了。這一差異的交鋒所導致的張力至今仍顯而易見。一九二六年漢學家衛禮賢曾對此感受加以敍述："哥特式大教堂：奮爭向上，拔地而起直刺雲天，拋開華麗的堆砌，穿過嶙峋剔透、陡峭凌空的拱勝，升騰到飄渺的虛無之中：中國宮殿：腳踏實地，平展舒張，殿宇無盡，伏地伸延，靜穆而舒適，從容不迫。宮殿燦燦之黃色琉璃瓦與冥冥之藍色天穹相輝映，渾然一體。永恆寓於現實中，超脫蘊於塵世間".〈1〉
當時能象衛禮賢這樣以如此洞察力來描述中國建築藝術的歐洲人曲指可數，大多數則只是抱怨在中國城市裡只見清一色四合院平房：不見任何諸如尖塔聳立的樓房，更無公園。草木蔥蘢的庭園只隱藏於高牆深院之中。外國人對玲瓏別致的中國園林雖有所耳聞，卻無緣目睹。
在洛可可時期一七三零至一七八零，中國的藝術風靡歐洲。弗里德里希一世於一七五四至一七五七年間在波茨坦的逍遙宮中建了一座中式茶樓。當時流行於世的英國奇彭代爾家具式樣亦是這一時期受中國工藝美術影響的產物。但是，十九世紀歐洲建築史只注重對古希臘、羅馬的研究，卻完全忽略了對中國建築藝術的研究。所以當歐洲人在中國開設商行時，對中國的建築藝術惊異不已，嘆為觀止。
德國工程師海因里希·錫樂巴是對中國建築進行深入研究的第一人。他於一八九七年發表了一篇有關位於北京近郊大覺寺的論文。〈2〉建築師因斯特·比希曼於一九零六年至一九零九年之間在中國作旅行考察，曾系統地研究並滿懷深情和贊嘆地著書介紹中國的建築藝術。由於第一次世界大戰的緣故，這些圖文並茂的著作被擱延至二、三十年代才得以陸續出版。〈3〉
在中國幾座沿海城市辟為通商口岸後，外國商人及傳教士便接踵而至。而這些先行者首先面臨的問題便是尋找一種適合當地氣候環境，使室內保持涼爽，宜於健康生活的建築形式。同時，大多數外國人不願意也不可能放棄其文化習俗和生活方式。英國商人將在其印度殖民地頗為成功的一

sie mit der chinesischen Baukultur konfrontiert wurden.

Heinrich Hildebrand war der erste deutsche Ingenieur, der genaue architektonische Studien durchführte. 1897 veröffentlichte er die Untersuchung über den Tempel Dajue Si bei Beijing (Peking).[2] Zu einer wirklich systematischen Erforschung der chinesischen Baukunst führten die Studienreisen des Architekten Ernst Boerschmann in den Jahren 1906 bis 1909. Durch den Ersten Weltkrieg verzögert, erschienen seine Bild- und Architekturbücher erst in den 20er und 30er Jahren.[3] Seine Werke über die chinesische Architektur sind einfühlend und voller Bewunderung.

Zunächst kamen Kaufleute und Missionare nach China. Diese Pioniere mußten, um die gesundheitlichen Risiken zu mindern, Bautypen entwickeln, die ständig Kühle in den Gebäuden hielten. Auch wollten und konnten die meisten Ausländer ihre gewohnten Lebensweisen nicht aufgeben, waren ihrer Heimatkultur verbunden. Steigende Grundstückspreise in den ausländischen Handelsniederlassungen führten bald zum Bau von mehrgeschossigen Häusern, bei denen jede Etage von solch einer schattenspendenden Veranda umgeben war. Der Stil dieser praktischen Gebäude wurde ironisch als »Compradorstil« bezeichnet – nach den chinesischen Mittelsmännern der europäischen Kaufleute. Wie alle ausländischen Gebäude damals sahen auch die Bauten der deutschen Gemeinden aus: der 1901 eingeweihte deutsche Club Germania in Hongkong, das 1884/85 erbaute deutsche Generalkonsulat in Shanghai oder das 1899 erbaute Geschäftshaus der Firma Carlowitz & Co. in Shanghai. Auch in Qingdao (Tsingtau) wählte man bei den frühen Gebäuden diesen Typus.

Nur wenige der in China lebenden Ausländer suchten bewußt die Auseinandersetzung mit der chinesischen Lebensweise und wohnten in chinesischen Hofhäusern. Victor Segalen, der zwischen 1913 und 1914 in Beijing lebte, gehörte zu ihnen: »Ich habe im Hof gegessen, unter der rechteckigen Dämmerung des

gineer to complete a detailed architectural study of China. In 1897, he published a study on the Dajue Sie temple near Beijing (Peking).[2] However, the first really systematic study of Chinese architecture was compiled by the architect Ernst Boerschmann during study trips from 1906 to 1909. However, Boerschmann's architectural and picture books were not published until the 1920s and 30s on account of the First World War.[3] His books about Chinese architecture are perceptive and full of admiration for what he saw there.

The first Europeans who went to China were traders and missionaries. In an attempt to reduce health hazards, these pioneers were forced to develop building methods which maintained low temperatures in the buildings. Most foreigners could not, and moreover did not wish to, give up their customary life styles and were strongly bound to their native cultures. The British traders introduced a type of building to the foreign concessions in China which had long proven successful in India: the bungalow surrounded by a veranda. The increase in the price of land in the foreign concessions, however, soon led to the construction of multi-storey houses; each floor had its own shady veranda to provide protection from the sun. This practical style of building was ironically labelled the »comprador style« after the Chinese middlemen who worked with the European traders. The German community lived and worked in the same types of buildings as the other foreigners, as is illustrated by the architecture of the Club Germania in Hongkong, which was opened in 1901, the consulate in Shanghai, built in 1884/85, and the business premises of the company Carlowitz & Co. also built in Shanghai in 1899. This style was also used for early buildings in Qingdao (Tsingtao).

Few of the foreigners living in China consciously sought exposure to the Chinese way of life and lived in Chinese courtyard houses. One of these was Victor Segalen who lived in Beijing between 1913 and 1914: »I ate in the

種建築形式搬到中國，該建築平面為四面設敞廊的單層佈局。隨著地皮價格上漲，外國商業區內逐漸出現多層建築。每層均有遮蔭的敞廊環繞。該建築式樣被戲稱為"買辦建築風格"，得名於與外商合作的中國中間商。當時德國的建築亦均仿效了這一形式，如：一九零一年在香港落成的德國格瑪妮娜俱樂部；一八八四年至一八八五年建成的上海德國領事館；一八八九年竣工的禮合公司商業樓以及青島的早期建築。

只有很少一部份外國人有意識地去體驗中國人的生活方式並擇四合院而居。於一九一三年至一九一四年僑居北京的維克多·賽加倫為其中之一："我在天井裡用餐，頭頂是一方蒼茫的暮色。..........在四合院的環抱中，我愜意地享受這安寧的氣氛。"[4]於一九零九年至一九一一年任職於成都領事館的德國公使馬丁·菲舍爾曾寫道："這種陌生且別有風味的生活習俗對一個來自另外一種完全不同的文化的異國人來說魅力無窮。中國的起居習俗之妙處在於與自然息息相通。歐洲的建築形式為了迎合現代化的需要，使人與自然的交融性喪失貽盡"[5]

建於北京的公使館均為中國式的建築，其原因是因地制宜、就地取材、使用當地工匠及其所諳熟的施工方法來得較為簡便。許多建築為中國原有建築的擴建，而房屋之間相對位置卻沒有按照中國傳統方式排列。青島的德國市政廳至一九零六年均在中國一巡撫前私邸——多進式四合院中辦公。當然，此為特例。

自從九座通商口岸開埠後，外國人獲得在特定區域內購地置房的權力。幾年內，這些外國人區便漸具與中國城區大相徑庭的歐洲風貌。成為留居於此的外商第二故鄉。這些身處異鄉的人們在工作之餘尋找輕鬆安逸的娛樂場所，尋找與家鄉有關聯之物，他們定期舉行文化活動，如排練劇目等，以了卻思鄉之情。然而，各國僑民還是僅與其本國人交往；各國均各自開設俱樂部；僑民子女就讀其本國僑校，各國獨特的建築風格也日趨明顯。在租界成形的最初的幾十年內，僅有中西兩種建築形式差異。至二十世紀初，則出現各國力圖以其獨特的建築風格表現其民族特色的趨勢。[6]

11

Himmels. (...) Ich genieße in Geborgenheit die geometrische Ruhe meines Hauses.«[4] Der deutsche Gesandte Martin Fischer schrieb während seines Aufenthalts in Chengdu (Provinz Sichuan) in den Jahren 1909/11: »Der fremde und ungewohnte Lebensstil hatte manches, was auch den ansprach, der aus einem ganz anderen kulturellen Milieu kam. Was die chinesische Wohnkultur auszeichnete, war ihre Naturnähe, die bei unserer Bauweise in Europa durch die Erfordernisse der modernen Zivilisation oft ganz geopfert werden mußte.«[5]

Die ersten in Beijing erbauten Gesandtschaften waren Gebäude in chinesischer Bauart, da es zunächst das Einfachste war, mit ortsüblichen Materialien und in einem den chinesischen Handwerkern bekannten Stil zu arbeiten. Man nutzte bestehende chinesische Häuser und erweiterte sie durch Anbauten. Lediglich die Zuordnung der Gebäude untereinander erfolgte nicht nach der chinesischen Bautradition. Auch in Qingdao arbeitete die deutsche Stadtverwaltung bis 1906 in den um mehrere Höfe gruppierten Häusern der früheren Residenz des chinesischen Generals. Doch dies waren die Ausnahmen.

Nach der Öffnung einiger Küstenstädte für den Handel mit dem Ausland konnten Ausländer dort in genau festgelegten Gebieten Land erwerben und wohnen. Im Laufe der Jahre entstanden hier ausländische Stadtteile, die am europäischen Städtebau orientiert waren und sich deshalb von den chinesischen Vierteln unterschieden. Die Kaufleute bauten sich hier eine zweite Heimat auf. In dieser anstrengenden, fremden Welt Chinas suchte man nach Bekanntem, nach Orten der Erholung, in denen man seine Kräfte regenerieren konnte. Hierzu gehörte auch eine regelmäßige kulturelle Orientierung, Rückbesinnung auf seine europäische Herkunft, wie zum Beispiel gemeinsames Theaterspiel. Gleichzeitig grenzten sich die Ausländer voneinander ab: Es gab nationale Klubs und nationale Schulen für die Kinder. Auch in der Architektur wurden die kulturellen Unterschiede

courtyard under the rectangle of the twilight sky. (...) Safe and sound, I enjoy the geometric tranquillity.«[4] The German envoy Martin Fischer wrote the following account during his stay in Chengdu (Sichuan province) where he lived in from 1909 to 1911: »The foreign and unaccustomed life style had some elements that were attractive, even to those coming from a completely different cultural milieu. The exemplary feature of the Chinese way of life was its proximity to nature, an aspect which has been completely sacrificed in European architecture due to the demands of modern civilisation.«[5]

The first legations built in Beijing were Chinese-style buildings, as to begin with it was easier to work with local materials in the style familiar to Chinese tradesmen: existing Chinese buildings were used and extensions added on to them. The only aspect that differed from Chinese architectural tradition was the arrangement of the buildings in relation to each other. Until 1906 the German municipal administration in Qingdao also worked in the houses of Chinese General's former residence which were grouped around several courtyards. This was, however, an exception. Following the opening of several coastal towns to foreign trade, foreigners were allowed to acquire and reside on land in specific areas. In the course of the years, foreign quarters were established which were based on European urban planning concepts and were, thus, completely different to the Chinese quarters. The traders built themselves a second home. They sought something familiar, places where they could recover from the difficult and alien world of China. Regular cultural orientation and reference to shared European origins were a part of this and took, for example, the form of a common theatre. Despite this, however, the individual groups of foreigners tended to keep to themselves: there were national clubs for the adults and national schools for the children. The architecture also came to reflect the cultural differences between the foreigners. Whereas du-

上海的第一座具有典型德意志風格的建築是由德國建築師海因里希·貝克設計的德國康科迪亞總會。一九零四年，他以具有德國文藝復興式復古風格的設計方案在該建築招標中一舉奪魁。該建築的轉角塔樓高四十八米，至二十年代止，它一直為上海外灘最高的建築。貝克也由此一舉成為上海德僑的首席建築師。他以同樣的手法設計了德國花園俱樂部，眾多的商業大樓和別墅，以及德華銀行分別在上海濟南和北京的分行。德僑視此種風格為既適應亞洲之地理氣候且體現德意志民族精神的理想之作。此外，德國在經濟上日益崛起，在遠洋貿易方面也與英國並駕齊驅。建築外觀不免刻意標新立異。具有德國文藝復興古風格的建築形式便成了德意志精神以及德國在中國殖民地經濟實力的象徵——如當時某國際博覽會所示，這些建築是德國民族風格對群英薈萃的世界建築競賽的獨特貢獻。[7]

一八九七年，德國海軍佔領了膠州灣，並立即著手興建青島——東亞唯一由德國創建的城市。德國終於如願將之建成一座純德國式城市。幾年之內，青島便成了"德國文化和城市建設藝術的展覽館"。[8]對新城內建築風格的選定在當時曾引起頗多爭議。德國總督都沛祿文認為新城市應強調德國民族特性：強調與中國城市的差異：新城內的建築應具有現代風格。這一意見在當時廣為接受。[9]起初德國建築師因為對中國的氣候特點知之甚少，在設計時未能脫出英國殖民地式建築套路，多採用這種當時在亞洲頗受青睞的建築形式。然而不久這一現象便速然改觀：出現傾斜陡峭的德國式屋頂與高聳的塔樓高低相襯，錯落有致。中國流行的青磚被紅磚所取代。後期建造的建築其外牆均以灰漿抹面後塗以明快的色彩。由於建築法規禁止用瓦楞鐵皮鋪頂，紅瓦屋頂便成了青島獨有的景色。花崗石在青島一帶價格低廉，加之當時在德國國內風行花崗石裝飾構件，所以在青島花崗石便成了當時典型的建築材料。這種採自嶗山地區的花崗石最初僅被用作建築基座。一九零六年竣工的總督官署的三個主立面均完全以花崗石板飾面。一九零七年落成的總督別墅和一九一零年建造的基督教堂均用表面鑿成凸凹

der Ausländer immer deutlicher. Während in den ersten Jahrzehnten der Niederlassungen nur zwischen westlicher und chinesischer Architektur unterschieden wurde, forderte man seit der Jahrhundertwende von den Architekten typische Gebäude in nationalen Baustilen.[6]

Das erste Gebäude Shanghais in einer typisch deutschen Architektursprache wurde von dem in Shanghai lebenden Architekten Heinrich Becker erbaut. Er gewann den Wettbewerb für den deutschen Club Concordia im Jahre 1904 mit einem Entwurf in der Art der deutschen Neorenaissance. Becker wurde zum Hausarchitekten der deutschen Gemeinde in Shanghai. Er baute im gleichen Stil den deutschen Gartenclub, mehrere Geschäftshäuser, Villen und die Bankhäuser der Deutsch-Asiatischen Bank in den Städten Shanghai, Jinan (Tsinanfu) und Beijing. Damit war ein Baustil für Asien gefunden, mit dem die deutsche Gemeinde ihre nationale Identität verband. Deutschland war wirtschaftlich immer wichtiger geworden, holte auch im Überseehandel gegenüber Großbritannien weiter auf. Man wollte sich von den Konkurrenten jetzt auch äußerlich absetzen. Gebäude im Stil der deutschen Neorenaissance wurden Zeichen der nationalen Identität und des wirtschaftlichen Erfolgs in den internationalen Handelsniederlassungen Chinas. Sie repräsentierten, wie auf einer Weltausstellung, »den deutschen Beitrag zu einem architektonischen Völkerwettkampf.«[7]

Im Jahre 1897 besetzte die deutsche Marine die Bucht von Jiaozhou (Kiautschou). Man begann dort mit dem Bau der Stadt Qingdao (Tsingtau), der einzigen deutschen Stadtneugründung in Asien. Dies bot nun endlich die Chance, unbeeinflußt von anderen ausländischen Mächten und ohne Rücksicht auf die bestehende chinesische Bebauung, eine rein deutsche Stadt anzulegen. Qingdao wurde innerhalb weniger Jahre zu einem »deutschen Kulturmuseum« und einer »deutschen Städtebauausstellung«.[8] Während der ersten Jahre stritt man innerhalb der deutschen Ge-

ring the first decades of the concessions the only distinction in architectural style was between Western and Chinese buildings, after the turn of the century demand grew for typical buildings in national styles which could be recognized as such.[6]

The first buildings in Shanghai to be constructed in typical German national style were designed by the German architect Heinrich Becker. Becker won the competition for the German Club Concordia in 1904 with a design in German neo-Renaissance style. The building consisted of a 48-metre-high corner tower which made it the highest building on the embankment road, the Bund, in Shanghai until the 1920s. Becker became the »house architect« for the German community in Shanghai. He designed the German Garden Club, several office buildings, villas and branches of the German-Asian Bank in Shanghai, Jinan (Tsinanfu) and Beijing. An architectural style was thus established for Asia which linked the Germans with their national identity. Economically, Germany had grown from strength to strength and was quickly catching up with Great Britain in the area of foreign trade. The Germans now needed to distinguish themselves externally from their competitors. Buildings in German neo-Renaissance style became a symbol of national identity and economic success in the Chinese foreign concessions. Like exhibits in a World Exposition, they were »the German contribution to the architectural competition of the nations.«[7]

In 1897 the German navy occupied the Bay of Jiaozhou (Kiaochow) and work was begun on the construction of the city of Qingdao (Tsingtao), the only new city to be founded by the Germans in Asia. This was finally an opportunity to build a completely German city free from the influence of other foreign powers and the necessity of integrating Chinese buildings. Within a few years, Qingdao became a »German cultural museum« and a German »urban design exhibition«.[8] During the initial years there were disputes within the

不平、頗具立體感的花崗石作牆體。

威廉二世執政時期，許多建築，尤其是邊遠地區的一些建築多以花崗石為主要建築材料。一九一零年由建築師施偉希頓以羅馬式復古風格為的威廉二世設計的波茨南皇宮便是一例。阿爾豐斯‧派克偉特將該皇宮雄偉的氣勢與青島德國總督府邸相類比。〈10〉威廉二世式建築在當時流行極廣、影響極大，在中國的德國建築師多諳熟這種風格，有些建築師還將其作為設計范例。〈11〉一八九七年於科布倫芝的萊茵河與摩澤爾河交匯處的德意志之角落成的威廉二世坐騎全身雕像，其質感粗樸的花崗石面加工手法以及其人物、動物雕像很可能是青島總督府邸裝飾細部的淵源。

具有羅馬式復古風格的天津德國康科迪婭總會及其附近的羅蘭德雕像可謂威廉二世式建築風格流行時期在中國的典例。裝點著武漢德國領事館樓頂翅擁球宇的雄鷹雕像亦可見於威廉二世在柏林的新行宮南翼的裝飾。常見於青島辦公建築的在威廉二世時期極為流行的羅馬式復古風格與較為現代的德國青年派風格之間有不難尋覓的關聯。與洛可可風格一樣，德國青年派從亞洲的藝術中吸取創作靈感，並以其為母題。當時青島最美觀的建築均揉凝羅馬式復古風格與青年派風格於一體。天津法租界內的建築則是裝飾更為繁褥的法國新藝術風格，其影響亦可見於天津德租界內的一些建築。

在家鄉為小鎮名士的德國建築師在中國則被視為德國文化的使者。他們不得不在深受外來影響的陌生工作環境中力圖保持德國建築高質量標準。他們不僅如願以償，有些建築甚至在質量上與當時德國本土建築相比有過之而無不及。同時，在中國的德國建築更有其獨特風采，原因是中國工匠雖然照圖施工，但卻難免將其傳統經驗和文化背景知識摻和在細詳實施中。例如濟南哥特式復古風格教堂的卷葉花飾看上去如片片雲彩，恰如中國式建築常用的裝飾題材。

與其非洲殖民地相比，德國在中國殖民地的建築質量要高很多。原因何在？是因為各國建築師在中國的激烈競爭，還是因為中國人為稱道廣為記載的機敏善學，或是因為中國工匠建築技巧嫻熟、觸類旁通，

meinde noch über den zu wählenden Baustil, doch setzte sich die Ansicht des deutschen Gouverneurs Truppel durch, daß man im Europäerviertel eine moderne deutsche Stadt mit modernen Häusern entstehen lassen und nicht im chinesischen Stil bauen sollte.9 Die Bauten der ersten Jahre zeigten auch den englischen Einfluß. Die deutschen Architekten kannten das Klima der Region noch nicht und behielten diesen in Asien bewährten Stil zunächst bei. Doch schon bald wurden die Dächer der deutschen Häuser steiler, und Türme betonten die Asymmetrien. Anstelle der in China üblichen dunkelgrauen Ziegelsteine verwendete man rote. Spätere Bauten wurden verputzt und hell gestrichen. Berühmt wurden die mit roten Dachziegeln gedeckten Dächer Qingdaos – Wellblech war im Europäerviertel durch die Bauordnung verboten. Granitstein war in der Region ein relativ preisgünstiges Baumaterial und wurde damals in Deutschland bei repräsentativen Gebäuden häufig verwendet. So wurde Granit zum charakteristischen Gestaltungsmittel in der Stadt. Er kam aus den nahegelegenen Laoshan-Bergen und wurde zuerst nur für die Sockel der Bauten verwendet. Die drei Hauptfassaden des 1906 fertiggestellten Gouvernements-Dienstgebäudes waren dann vollständig mit Granitplatten verkleidet. Bei der neuen Gouverneursvilla 1907 und der evangelischen Kirche 1910 wurde Granitrustikamauerwerk in sehr plastischer Form verwendet.

Granit war ein prägendes Baumaterial einer Vielzahl von Gebäuden im Deutschen Reich während der Regierungszeit Kaiser Wilhelms II., besonders auch in seinen damaligen Randgebieten. Dazu gehört beispielsweise das Kaiserschloß in Posen, das 1910 im neoromanischen Stil von Franz Schwechten erbaut wurde. Alfons Paquet verglich die Monumentaliät des Schlosses mit der des Gouverneurswohnhauses in Qingdao.10 Wilhelminische Bauten wurden häufig publiziert und waren den deutschen Architekten in China bekannt, wurden bei einigen Gebäuden direkt

German community as to the architectural style to be chosen. In the end, the opinion of the German Governor, Truppel, prevailed and it was decided to build a modern German city in the European quarter which would be reflected in the style of the houses. The necessary concessions would, of course, be made for climatic requirements.9 The buildings erected during the initial years, however, still showed a British influence. The German architects were not yet familiar with the climate in the region and chose for the meantime to stay with the style that had proven successful in Asian conditions. However, it was only a matter of time before the roofs of the German houses became more steep and towers began to appear which gave the buildings asymmetrical proportions. Red brick began to replace the dark grey brick normally used in China. Later buildings were rendered and painted in bright colours. Qingdao became famous for its red roofs – the use of corrugated sheet iron was prohibited in the building regulations for the European quarter. Granite was a relatively cheap building material in the region and was also fashionable in Germany at the time. Thus, granite became the predominant building material used in the city's buildings. It originated from the nearby area of the Laoshan mountains and was initially only used for the bases of the buildings. The three main façades of the Government building completed in 1906 were completely clad in granite. An extremely plastic form of rough textured granite masonry was used in the new Governor's residence which was constructed in 1907 and in the Protestant church of 1910.

Granite was the main material used in a number of buildings constructed during the German Empire and the reign of Kaiser Wilhelm II, particularly in the outposts. The neo-Romanesque style of the Kaiser's Palace in Posen, designed by the architect Franz Schwechten and built in 1910, was an example of this. Alfons Paquet compared the monumentality of the palace with the Governor's residence in

對西方的工藝駕輕就熟？若將中國與非洲同一時期的殖民建築相比較，非洲的該類建築在造型結構上要簡易得多。[12]殖民列強瓜分非洲，彼此之間無甚關聯，各行其政，加之非洲傳統建築水平與中國的也無法相提並論。非洲傳統的粘土建築物對建築師來說雖頗具異國情調，卻絲毫不能勾起任何與之全力相爭的興趣。[13]相反，中國這一具幾千年歷史的文明古國，其城市、宮殿及其復雜的結構工程建造技術為人嘆服。西方建築師不禁要與之較量，爭個高低，以證實西方技術的優勢。建築藝術和城市設計是一個國家工業實力和產品質量的象徵，中國人對此深為關注。為贏得在中國市場的地位，各國的工程師和商人在競爭中不得不力爭以其最佳的設計和產品取勝。

德國建築師為現實所迫，盡力適應中國的建築傳統。山東省境內由德國營造的兩條鐵路線的火車站便是中西合壁的例證。青島至濟南沿淺中小車站均採用中國式屋頂。天津至南京（津浦線）北路段上的車站雖形式各異，卻多少都夾雜著中國傳統手法，如至今仍保存完好的泰安車站即為一佳例，其屋檐下起支撐和裝飾作用的斗拱為中國傳統卻由花崗石鑿成。青島由魏瑪傳教會所建的中國男童學堂以及其為中國人開的花之安醫院均完全採用中國傳統平面形式——四合院以便使活動於此的中國人不致對環境感到陌生。聖言會在山東建的教堂均無塔樓以尊重中國習俗。因為根據風水經，擇址佳劣與興衰相關聯。高聳的建築若未像中國寶塔那樣由風水先生為其擇址定向，總歸凶多吉少。傳教士們務必體察此情，以避免使其教堂成為中國當地居民的眼中釘。德國典型的桁架結構建築將木支架相互交叉以起穩固作用。但由此構成的叉形在中國是忌諱的。一八九九年竣工的總督私邸和同年奠基的水師飯店的立面仍以這種外露的木構架為主要的裝飾手法，其後便消聲匿跡。人們放棄這種裝飾手段，在建造桁架結構時只以垂直和水平的木支架作裝飾，其原因是漢字"X"表示錯誤的意思，不吉利。根據風水經，樓梯應避開大門入口。德國建築師卡爾·培迪克在設計武漢德國工學院教學樓時注意到這一點，因而將樓梯安排在入

zum Vorbild.¹¹ So könnten die rustikalen Granitsteinarbeiten und Tierskulpturen am Sockel des Reiterstandbilds von Kaiser Wilhelm I., auf dem Deutschen Eck in Koblenz 1897 errichtet, Vorbild für die Details am Gouverneurswohnhaus in Qingdao gewesen sein. Der deutsche Club Concordia in Tianjin, mit seinen neoromanischen Formen und der Rolandskulptur in unmittelbarer Nähe, war vielleicht das charakteristischste Gebäude dieser Ära in China. Auf dem Dach des deutschen Konsulats in Wuhan (Hankou) ließen die Architekten einen über der Weltkugel schwebenden Adler montieren, entsprechend dem Schmuck, der am Wohnsitz Kaiser Wilhelms II. in Postsdam den Südflügel des Neuen Palais zierte.

In Qingdao findet man häufig eine Verbindung zwischen dem in der wilhelminischen Ära bei Regierungsgebäuden beliebten neoromanischen Baustil und dem Jugendstil. Dieser verwendete, wie bereits das Rokoko, Motive aus der asiatischen Kunst. Die schönsten Gebäude in Qingdao wurden in der Verbindung von Neoromanik und Jugendstil erbaut. In Tianjin prägte der dekorativere französische Jugendstil die französische Niederlassung und beeinflußte Bauten in der dortigen deutschen Niederlassung.

Architekten, von nur lokaler Bekanntheit in Deutschland, wurden in China zu Kulturvermittlern. Sie hatten eine schwierige Aufgabe zu bewältigen, denn sie wollten unter fremden Einflüssen und neuen Arbeitsbedingungen die aus der Heimat gewohnte Qualität erzeugen; und das gelang ihnen. Die deutschen Gebäude in China halten den Vergleich mit dem damals in Deutschland Üblichem stand, einige sind qualitativ hervorragend. Trotzdem unterscheiden sich die Gebäude von den Vorbildern ihrer Heimat. Denn es waren chinesische Handwerker, die zwar nach gezeichneten Vorlagen arbeiteten, doch bei der Umsetzung ihre Erfahrung und ihren kulturellen Hintergrund miteinbrachten. An vielen Details läßt sich das ablesen. Die Krabben an der neogotischen Kirche in Jinan (Tsinanfu) Qingdao.¹⁰ The Wilhelminian buildings were well publicised at the time; the German architects in China were familiar with them and some used them as models in their own designs.¹¹ Thus, the rough textured granite masonry and animal sculptures used in the equestrian statue of Kaiser Wilhelm I on the Deutsches Eck in Koblenz of 1897 could have been the inspiration for the details of the Governor's residence in Qingdao.

The German Club Concordia in Tianjin with its neo-Romanesque forms and nearby sculpture of Roland was perhaps the most »typical« building of this period in China. There was an eagle suspended over a globe on the roof of the German consulate in Wuhan (Hankow), a detail corresponding to the decorations on the south wing of the Neues Palais in Potsdam, Kaiser Wilhelm II's residence.

It is possible to observe many links between the neo-Romanesque style of the government buildings of Qingdao popular in the Wilhelminian era and a quite modern style, that of Jugendstil. Like Rococo, this style used motifs from Asian art. The most beautiful buildings in Qingdao were built on the basis of this link between neo-Romanesque and Jugendstil. In Tianjin, the characteristic style of the buildings in the French settlement was the more elaborate French Art Nouveau, and its influence can be seen in the buildings in the German settlement there.

Architects who were mere local celebrities in Germany were elevated to the status of cultural ambassadors in China. They faced an enormous task in their quest to reproduce the quality familiar from home under foreign influences and in new working conditions. However, they succeeded in achieving this aim. The German buildings in China stand up to comparison with the buildings in Germany at the time, and some are even superior in quality. Despite this, however, the buildings in China create a rather different impression to those in the homeland. The reason for this is that, despite working to drawn-up specifica-

口兩側。進門後向左或右轉方見樓梯。青島德國俱樂部，客人則需繞半圈——如同繞過的中國式的"照壁"才進入廳房，而樓梯則設在廳房盡頭。

如外國人試圖尊重並學習中國傳統習俗一樣，清朝皇室在一九零一年敗北八國聯軍後也企圖改革。至一九一一年秋清政府倒台，對西洋建築的仿效初見端倪，一九零五年，慈禧太后在北京南海畔令建了不少中西合璧式殿宇。〈14〉德國工程師羅克格於一九一零年至一九一一年在北京為海軍大臣恭親王載洵（音譯）建了一所具有歐洲風格的私邸。大清銀行總裁陳漢樸（音譯）和清道台永滔（音譯）也聘請羅克格在北京為其設計私宅；由於辛亥革命爆發，這些計劃未能實施。一九一零年在北京營建一座純歐洲式的國會大廈的計劃為這一熱潮之巔。該計劃設想其會議大廳的座位排列將仿效柏林的帝國大廈而其規模則倍之。然而中方的委託人由於對現代建築術語無甚知曉，難以為國會大廈確定合適的規模和形制，完全依賴外國行家的指點。羅克格受託在一九一一年被燒毀的北京東華門的舊址上仿建一座勃蘭登堡門式的城門。出於其美學觀點，他婉言推卻了這一委託。〈15〉

七十年代中，中國建築師再次開始了對歐洲建築輸入中國的歷史的研討。他們諳熟遺留下來的歐洲建築的特點也深知其存在價值。一九七六年秋，天津地震后，為承延天津市城建傳統，所有新建的六層樓房立面皆以法國傳統古典復興式圖案加以裝飾，有些沿街立面屋頂還飾以欄牆。一八六二年至本世紀四十年代，法國在天津佔有大片租界，當時形成的建築風格至今仍決定著天津的城市個性。

德國式的建築則是青島的"靈魂"。花崗石在德國撤離青島後七十年再次流行。與後現代主義思潮在歐洲的出現相平行，青島重新發現了自身獨特的建築史及其本土的"現代主義"。六、七十年代所建房屋均延用傳統風格，市中心基本上保持原貌。八十年代新建的那些千篇一律的樓房則幾乎將青島變成中國許多毫無個性的城市之一，青島北部新城區便是如此。新建的房均須與青島特有的五種顏色相協調：紅瓦屋頂，黃色的海灘和建築立面，綠

sehen nicht wie blattförmige Verzierungen aus, sie ähneln kleinen Wolken – einem in China häufigen Ornament.

Anders als in den afrikanischen Kolonien Deutschlands waren die in China errichteten deutschen Gebäude qualitativ hochwertiger. Die Bauten in Afrika sind zwar im gleichen Zeitraum entstanden, doch in ihrer Gestaltung und Detaillierung viel einfacher.[12] Afrika war unter den Kolonialmächten aufgeteilt. Jede verwaltete ihren eigenen Staat. Es gab nur wenig Konkurrenz zwischen den einzelnen Mächten. In China dagegen lebte die Mehrzahl der Ausländer in den Niederlassungen der Großstädte. Afrikas Bautradition hatte eine andere Qualität als die chinesische. Die afrikanischen Lehmbauten galten zwar als exotisch, doch stellten sie für die Kolonisatoren keine architektonische und kulturelle Herausforderung dar.[13] China war dagegen ein anerkanntes Kulturland mit einer jahrtausendealten Geschichte. Seine riesigen Städte und Paläste, die historische Ingenieurbaukunst, all dies rief größte Bewunderung bei den Ausländern hervor. Angesichts dieser Voraussetzungen wollte man die Überlegenheit der westlichen Kultur beweisen. Gleichzeitig war die chinesische Bautechnik auf die Arbeit mit westlichen Techniken besser als in Afrika vorbereitet. Das Geschick und die Lernfähigkeit der chinesischen Handwerker wurden in den Berichten der deutschen Ingenieure regelmäßig betont. Architektur und Städtebau der Ausländer in China wurden zu Musterausstellungen, in denen man Industrieprodukte vorstellte. Diese Qualität wurde von den Chinesen anerkannt. Die ausländischen Ingenieure und Kaufleute suchten die geschäftliche Zusammenarbeit mit China und versuchten, sich dabei gegenseitig zu überbieten.

So gab es auch Gründe für die deutschen Architekten, sich der chinesischen Bautradition anzupassen. Die Landbahnhöfe der beiden deutschen Eisenbahnlinien in der Provinz Shandong (Schantung) erbauten sie in einem chinesisch-europäischen Mischstil. Die klei-

tions, the Chinese tradesmen drew on their experience and cultural background in the realisation of the plans. The crockets on the neo-Gothic church in Jinan (Tsinan) do not look like leaf-shaped decorations but like small clouds – a common ornament in Chinese art.

Why are the German buildings in China of better quality than those in the German colonies in Africa? Was it the competition between the various foreign national groups working in China? Was it the Chinese tradesmen, whose skills and ability to learn new techniques are praised in all the reports? Had their own architectural tradition prepared them to work better with Western building techniques? Contemporaneous African buildings were much more basic in their design.[12] Africa was divided between the colonial powers. Each power administered its own state and there was little competition between the individual powers. In addition to this, the architectural tradition in Africa was of a quite different quality to that in China. African clay buildings were seen as exotic, but did not represent a challenge to be bettered.[13] China, on the other hand, was an ancient culture with a history spanning thousands of years. Its enormous cities, palaces and buildings based on complex engineering structures were deeply admired by the foreigners: this had to be matched if they wanted to present a convincing case for Western technology. Architecture and urban design took the role of exhibitions for the presentation of industrial products. And this quality was recognised by the Chinese. Foreign engineers and traders were constantly trying to outdo each other in their quest for business with China.

Thus, the German architects had plenty of reasons to try and adapt to the Chinese architectural tradition. The rural train stations on both of the German railway lines in Shandong province (Shantung) were built in a mixture of the Chinese and European styles. The small rural train stations along the railway line from Qingdao to Jinan had traditional Chi-

樹：湛藍的天空，碧藍的大海。這些色彩對到過青島的人來說代表著一種令人心曠神怡的異鄉情調。保持這五種色彩的特色無異於保持青島的個性及魅力。青島自始是中國海軍的基礎之一，城市內許多地域至今仍為軍隊所管轄。大片地域內禁止建造居住區。管轄區內許多建築因此在文革時期免遭破壞。新的建築法規要求所有的新建築用紅瓦鋪頂。由於城市居民人數激增而空間有限，人們在通常為兩、三層高德國式別墅上增建樓層。為使五、六層達到與從前類似的比例關係，增建的頂層外牆以瓦覆蓋，建成蒙莎頂。這樣使行人能看到屋頂，達到與原有建築相類似的外觀效果。當年蒙莎頂的出現是因為這種屋頂形式既符合規定的檐高又保證頂層的層高不低於其他樓層的高度。如今這一原則的逆推在青島得到運用。青島的城建法規激發了建築師的創作靈感。十九世紀風行德國的文藝復興式復古及羅馬式復古建築風格在青島復蘇，有些建築附有矮壯的角塔：有些採用了巴羅克風格的山牆裝飾：有些甚至以瓷磚鋪鑲出模仿木構架立面效果的圖案。有些則有以花崗石作線角的窗子隨意裝點著立面，如建於一九零七年的總督私邸的外牆所示。青島建築外牆主要以黃色——帝王黃粉刷。一九八九年落成的青島市政府辦公樓將這一發掘運用德國建築師在二十世紀初建設青島時所採用的建築手法的熱潮推升到新的熱度。該建築外觀完全照抄原總督府行政辦公樓，兩建築彼此對崎如若鏡影。這一始於八十年代的青島建築風格復興的現象是二十世紀中國建築史上別開生面的一頁。

nen Landbahnhöfe der Eisenbahn, die von Qingdao nach Jinan führte, trugen traditionelle chinesische Dächer. Die Landbahnhöfe im Nordabschnitt der Tianjin-Nanjing-Bahn (Tientsin-Pukow-Bahn) waren alle unterschiedlich gestaltet und mit chinesischen Stilelementen versehen. Eines der besten Beispiele stellt der heute noch gut erhaltene Bahnhof in Tai'an (Tai-an-fu) dar. Das typisch chinesische hölzerne Konsolenkapitell wurde in Granit nachgebildet als Verzierung unter der Traufe verwendet. In Qingdao waren lediglich zwei Gebäude in chinesischer Bauart errichtet worden: die Schule der Weimarer Mission für chinesische Jungen und das Faber-Hospital für chinesische Patienten. Um den Einheimischen das Einleben zu erleichtern, hat man diese Bauten in der für sie gewohnten Hofhausstruktur errichtet. Bei den Missionskirchen der Steyler Missionsgesellschaft in Shandong wurde bewußt auf hohe Türme verzichtet. Die Missionare nahmen damit Rücksicht auf die chinesische Bautradition. Denn nach den Gesetzen des »fengshui«, d.h. der Geomantik, können Kraftfelder positiv und negativ beeinflußt werden. Hohe Bauwerke sind grundsätzlich störend, wenn sie nicht wie Pagoden von Geomanten genau plaziert werden, um dann positive »Kraftströme« an das richtige Ziel zu lenken. Die christlichen Missionare mußten auf diese Tradition Rücksicht nehmen, sollten ihre Kirchtürme nicht als »Unglücksbringer« in der Bevölkerung gelten. Das aussteifende Holzkreuz deutscher Fachwerkbauten war in seiner Zeichenhaftigkeit in China ebenfalls mißverständlich. Bei dem 1899 erbauten Gouverneurswohnhaus oder dem Seemannshaus (Grundsteinlegung 1899) war es ein wichtiges Element in der Fassadengestaltung, danach fehlte es völlig. Der Grund dafür liegt in der Bedeutung des chinesischen Schriftzeichens »X« = »falsch«. Man verzichtete in der Folge auf diese Dekoration und errichtete Fachwerk nur noch aus senkrechten und waagerechten Hölzern. Treppen sollten nach den Regeln des chinesischen »fengshui« möglichst nie in

nese roofs. The train stations in the northern section of the Tianjin-Nanjing railway (Tientsin-Pukow railway) were all designed differently with elements of the Chinese style. One of the best examples is the railway station in Tai'an (Tai-an-fu) which is well preserved. The typical Chinese wooden bracket capital was used in granite as a decoration under the eaves. The only buildings designed in Chinese style in Qingdao were the buildings for the Weimar Mission School for Chinese Boys and the Faber Hospital for Chinese patients. These buildings were designed in the customary courtyard arrangement to facilitate their use by the native population. The mission churches of the Steyler Missionary Society in Shandong did not have a high steeple. In this the missionaries expressed their respect for the laws governing the Chinese architectural tradition and particularly the »fengshui«, i.e. geomancy, according to which fields of force can be influenced positively and negatively. High buildings are fundamentally disruptive if they are not, like pagodas, precisely located by geomancer so that the positive »flow of force« is directed to the correct destination. The Christian missionaries had to respect this tradition if their church steeple was not to be seen by the local population as a »source of bad luck«. The symbolism of the wooden crosses in German buildings was also misleading in China. In 1899 it was still prominent in the design of the façade of the Governor's residence or the seamen's club (foundation stone laid in 1899), but was completely absent hereafter. The reason for this is the similarity with the Chinese character »X« which means »wrong«. Thus, this form of decoration was dispensed of and after this only half-timbered structures made up of vertical and horizontal elements were used. In accordance with the rules of Chinese »fengshui«, stairs should not, if possible, be located on the axis of the entrance to a house or building. German architect Carl Baedecker observed this rule in the second college building he designed in China. Thus, the two stairways of the Ger-

man-Chinese college in Wuhan (Hankow) were at the sides of the entrance. One entered the hall and then turned right or left to access the stairways parallel to the entrance. In the Tsingtao Club also, visitors are led around the corner (like a Chinese »wall of spirits«) before they enter the hall, at the end of which there is a staircase.

Just as the foreigners became more open to Chinese influences, the Imperial Chinese court also showed itself more open to reform following its defeat in the war against the Allies in 1901, and they began to experiment with Western architecture until the Qing dynasty was overthrown in autumn 1911. In 1905, the Empress Dowager Cixi (Ts'u-hsi) built houses for herself on the southern lake of Nanhai in Beijing in a mixture of European and Chinese styles.[14] In 1910/11 German architect Curt Rothkegel designed a large private house in European style for the Minister of the Marine Prince Zaixun (Tsai-hsün) in Beijing; the director of the Chinese Imperial Bank, Chen-han-pu, and the Taotai Yung-tao also had houses designed by Rothkegel, which, however, due to the revolution in 1911, were not built. The high point of European influence on Chinese architecture, however, was the planned construction of a parliament building in Beijing in 1910. This building was to have a purely European character, the seating order was identical to that in the Berlin Reichstag, but the Chinese version was nearly twice its size. However, the Chinese client had difficulties finding the correct scale and expression for this modern building to be built in a foreign architectural idiom and was dependent on good advice. Rothkegel was commissioned to build a gate building similar to the Brandenburg Gate to replace the eastern city gate of Beijing, Donghua Men (Dunghua-men), which was burned down in 1911; Rothkegel refused this commission on aesthetic grounds.[15]

The mid-1970s saw the beginning of a new phase in China's preoccupation with European architectural history. Chinese architects

Eine neue Phase der Auseinandersetzung mit der europäischen Architekturgeschichte in China begann Mitte der 70er Jahre. Chinesische Architekten kannten die Besonderheit und den Wert der alten europäischen Bauten. So wurden nach der teilweisen Zerstörung der Stadt Tianjin 1976 durch ein Erdbeben

alle sechsgeschossigen Neubauten nach französischem Vorbild mit neoklassizistischen Mustern an den Fassaden verziert. Manche erhielten sogar Balustraden. Man hatte sich auf die Tradition der Stadt berufen. In Tianjin bestand zwischen 1862 und den 1940er Jahren eine große französische Handelsniederlassung. Ihr Baustil prägt noch heute die Stadt.

Qingdaos unverwechselbare Stimmung bildeten die deutschen Gebäude. 70 Jahre nach dem Ende der deutschen Besetzung kam es zu einer Renaissance der Granitarchitektur. Zeitparallel mit der Postmoderne in Europa fand die Wiederentdeckung der eigenen »Moderne« und der einzigartigen Architekturgeschichte der Stadt Qingdao statt. Nur wenige Neubauten hatten in den 60er und 70er Jahren das Stadtzentrum verändert. In den 80er Jahren drohten gesichtslose Häuser auch Qingdao zu einer der tausenden gleichaussehenden Städte Chinas zu machen, sowie es in seinen nördlichen Stadterweiterun-

were aware of the special nature and value of the old European buildings. Thus, following the destruction of the city of Tianjin in 1976 as the result of a severe earthquake, the façades of all new six-storey buildings were decorated with neo-classical patterns based on the French tradition. Some were even given balustrades at the street edge of the flat roof. This was a reference to the city's architectural tradition; there had been a major French concession in Tianjin from 1862 to the 1940s. The architectural style developed then is still characteristic of the town today.

The »genius loci« of Qingdao were the German buildings. Seventy years after the end of German occupation there was a renaissance in granite architecture. The rediscovery of the native »Modernism« and the unique architectural history of the city of Qingdao occurred parallel to the emergence of Post-Modernism in Europe. The city centre had only been marginally changed by the addition of a few new buildings in the 1960s and 70s. During the 1980s, faceless buildings were threatening to transform Qingdao into another of a thousand identical Chinese cities, and this was already happening with the northern expansion of the city. Yet, it did prove possible to rescue this unique city. It was decided that new buildings had to be limited to the five traditional

gen bereits geschehen war. Doch das Typische des Stadtbildes konnte gerettet werden. Man beschloß, Neubauten den fünf traditionellen Farben der Stadt unterzuordnen: Rot der Dächer, Gelb des Strandes und der Fassaden, Grün der Bäume sowie zwei Blautöne für Meer und Himmel. Politisch durchsetzbar war diese die Bauten verteuernde Gestaltungsordnung, da die Stadt als Sommerfrische genutzt wurde. Alle, die hier einmal Urlaub gemacht hatten, verbanden diese Farben mit Erholung und einer gewissen Exotik – dieses für den Tourismus wichtige Stadtbild wollte man bewahren. Gleichzeitig war Qingdao ein chinesischer Marinestützpunkt. Dem Militär gehören noch heute viele Immobilien in der Stadt, Bauten, die während der Kulturrevolution vor Beschädigungen geschützt waren, und Grundstücke, die bis heute nicht für den Massenwohnungsbau zur Verfügung standen. Die neuen Baugesetze in Qingdao schreiben seit 1985 hohe rote Ziegeldächer für alle Neubauten vor. Die deutschen Villen waren nur zwei bis drei Stockwerke hoch. Heute muß wegen der zunehmenden Bevölkerungsdichte und des knappen Raumes höher gebaut werden. Um ähnliche Proportionen bei einem fünf- bis sechsgeschossigen Gebäude zu erhalten, wird das letzte Stockwerk als Mansarddach ausgebildet, indem man die Fas-

colours in the city: red for the roofs, yellow for the beach and the façades, green for the trees and the two blues of the sky and sea. It was possible to impose this rule as the city was used as a summer resort. Anyone who had been here on holiday associated these colours with relaxation and a certain exoticism – it was aimed to preserve these associations. At the same time, Qingdao was a Chinese navy base, many of the sites in the city were property of the military as were buildings which were protected from destruction during the Cultural Revolution and sites which had not hitherto been made available for large-scale residential complexes. The new building regulations for Qingdao prescribed high red tiled roofs for all new buildings. The traditional German villas were only two or three storeys high. Nowadays however, due to increasing population density it is necessary to build taller buildings on the available space. To achieve similar proportions in a five to six-storey building the top storey is built as a mansard roof by covering the façade with roof tiles. Thus the »roof surface« is visible from the pedestrian perspective and the proportion of wall to roof surface corresponds to that of the German models. The mansard roof is based on the idea that despite the prescribed eaves height it is still possible to fit

sade mit Dachziegeln verkleidet. Das macht die »Dachfläche« aus der Fußgängerperspektive sichtbar, und das Verhältnis zwischen Wand- und Dachfläche entspricht dem der deutschen Vorbilder. Das Mansarddach entstand seinerzeit aus der Überlegung heraus, daß dadurch trotz festgelegter Traufhöhe noch ein weiteres vollwertiges Stockwerk gebaut werden konnte. Heute findet dieses Prinzip in Qingdao seine Umkehrung. Durch die Bauordnung der Stadt war die Kreativität der Architekten gefordert. Die deutsche Neorenaissance und Neoromanik des 19. Jahrhunderts erwachen am Ende des 20. Jahrhunderts zu neuem Leben. Neubauten haben wieder gedrungene Ecktürme oder neobarocke Giebel; man findet sogar Wandfliesenmuster, die Holzfachwerk imitieren; Fenster werden mit Granit eingefaßt oder grob behauene Granitsteine spielerisch frei auf der Wandfläche verteilt, wie man es vom Gouverneurswohnhaus von 1907 kennt. Überwiegende Farben des Fassadenputzes sind Gelbtöne – Kaisergelb. Der vorläufige Höhepunkt der »Qingdaoer Renaissance« war im Jahre 1989 die Verdoppelung des 1906 erbauten Gouvernements-Dienstgebäudes, der Neubau für die Qingdaoer Stadtregierung entstand als sein Spiegelbild direkt dahinter. Die »Qingdaoer Renaissance«, die in den 80er Jahren begann, ist für Chinas Architektur des 20. Jahrhunderts einzigartig.

in another full storey. The principle is now being reversed in Qingdao today and the building regulations promoted the creativity of the architect. 19th century German neo-Renaissance and neo-Romanesque are waking up to a new life. New buildings once again have squat corner towers, some have neo-Baroque gables; there are even wall-tiling patterns that imitate the old style half-timbering; windows are bordered using granite, or granite, masonry is freely distributed on the façade in a playful manner as in the Governor's residence of 1907. The predominant colours of the plastered façades are tones of yellow – imperial yellow. The contemporary high point of the »Qingdao renaissance« was in 1989 when the double of the government building, built in 1906, was erected in mirror image opposite the original; the new building houses the Qingdao municipal administration. The »Qingdao renaissance« which began in the 1980s represents a unique stylistic development in 20th century Chinese architecture.

BEIJING

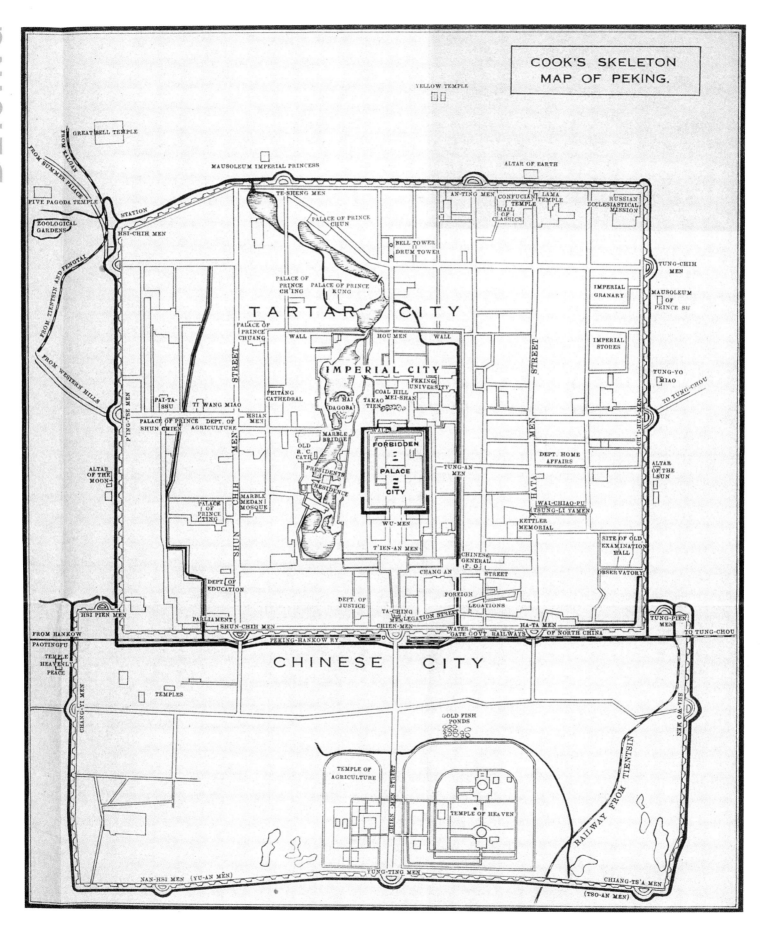

BEIJING (PEKING)

»Niemand kann bestreiten, daß Peking ein Meisterwerk geheimnisvollen Schaffens ist. So richtet sich der dreifache Plan seiner Städte nicht nach den Gesetzen eingeschlossener Menschenmassen, noch nach den Wohnbedürfnissen von Leuten, die essen und sich vermehren. Die Hauptstadt des größten Reiches unter dem Himmel ist um ihrer selbst willen gewollt worden – gezeichnet wie ein Schachbrett, ganz im Norden der gelben Ebene, umgeben von geometrischen Wällen, durchzogen von breiten Straßen, in rechten Winkeln zerschnitten von Gassen und dann bebaut in einer einzigen monumentalen Anstrengung.«[16]

Durch den zweiten Opiumkrieg 1856 bis 1858 hatten sich England und Frankreich auch die Rechte auf eine Gesandtschaft in Beijing erkämpft. Als sich die chinesische Regierung weiterhin weigerte, fremde Gesandschaften zuzulassen, zogen 1860 englische und französische Truppen von Tianjin (Tientsin) nach Beijing und zerstörten den alten Sommerpalast Yuanming Yuan.

Die chinesische Regierung versuchte, die Ausländer von der Stadt fernzuhalten, und bot ihnen den Park des zerstörten Sommerpalasts und andere Gebiete außerhalb der Stadtmauer für den Bau der Gesandtschaften an. Doch die Unterhändler bestanden auf Grundstücken innerhalb der Stadt.

Das riesige Häusermeer Beijings, ohne vertikale Elemente wie Kirchtürme oder mehrgeschossige Häuser, nur eingerahmt von einer hohen Stadtmauer, wird in den meisten Berichten von Ausländern als einförmig beschrieben. Den Grundriß der Stadt bildete ein großes Rechteck, ein Teil war die Mandschustadt (Tatarenstadt), von einer 12 Meter hohen und 20 Meter starken Stadtmauer umgeben.[17] Innerhalb dieser lag die Kaiserliche Stadt; sie umfaßte in einem Mauerrechteck den Kohlenhügel, die Seen und die Verbotene Stadt. Der Kaiserpalast in ihrem Zentrum – die Verbotene Stadt – war wiederum von ei-

BEIJING (PEKING)

»There is no denying that Peking is a masterpiece of mysterious creation. Thus, the threefold plan of its cities is not based on the laws of enclosed masses, but the living needs of people who eat and procreate. The capital of the greatest empire on earth was wanted for itself – laid out like a chess board – to the far north the yellow area, surrounded by geometrical embankments, with wide streets intersected at right angles by alleys and then built on in one single monumental effort.«[16]

Great Britain and France had fought for the right to an legation in Beijing during the Second Opium War of 1856 to 1858. In 1860, when the Chinese government persisted in its refusal to allow foreign legations, British and French troops from Tianjin (Tientsin) moved to Beijing and destroyed the old Summer Palace Yuanming Yuan.

The Chinese government, however, continued its efforts to keep the foreigners out of the city and offered them the park of the demolished Summer Palace (and later other areas outside the city wall) as sites for the construction of their legation. However, the negotiators insisted on being allocated sites within the city and finally the Europeans were given sites east of the six ministries »The six boards« on the east of Tian-an-men Square. The Ministry of Foreign Affairs »Tsungli Yamen«, which was built in 1860 for the sole purpose of dealing with the new legations, was located approximately one kilometre away from the new diplomatic quarter in a side street off Hatamen street in the east of the city.

Most reports by foreigners describe Beijing's sea of buildings which were devoid of vertical elements, such as church spires or multi-storey buildings, and enclosed by a high city wall, as monotonous. The city plan forms a large grid, one part being the Manchu City (Tartar City) which was surrounded by a 12-metre high and 20-metre thick city wall.[17] The Imperial City was enclosed by this wall; it in-

北京

"誰也不能否認北京城是巧奪天工之作。北京三重城牆的格局根本沒有顧及在其中居住的芸芸眾生衣食住行的需求。天下第一國的國都是為了自身的需求而建的。從地圖上看北京像一只置於華北平原北部的棋盤，為一長方形的城垣環繞，寬闊的大街與細窄的巷道縱橫交錯。北京城是耗費了巨大的人力，物力才建起的。"〈16〉

一八五六年到一八五八年間英法兩國以第二次鴉片戰爭要挾大清政府以使其同意外國公使在京設立公使館，遭中方一再拒絕一八六零年英法聯軍從天津出發，在北京放火焚毀了夏季宮苑圓明園。

中國政府欲把洋人擋在城外，把燒毀了的圓明園的地域，後來又將城外的其它地段割讓與英法兩國。然而談判代表堅持要在城內設公使館，並最終獲得了天安門東端"六部"官署所在地段的使用權。清政府為加強與外國公使館的聯系於一八六零年成立了"總理衙門"總理衙門位於城東哈德門大街一條橫馬路上，距使館區約一公里。

鳥瞰北京城只見一片茫茫的房海，為高高的城牆所環繞，卻不見類似教堂帶有尖塔的多層建築。許多外國人的報導都把這一景象描述為單一乏味。北京城的平面呈長方形。滿族人所住的內城城牆高十二米寬二十米。〈17〉皇城在滿族城內，為一矩形的城垣所環繞。皇城內是紫禁城、三海和景山。紫禁城位於皇城的中心，亦築有一道長方形的城牆。北京所有的大街道均為南北、東西走向。滿族區的南端與漢人區毗鄰。在漢人區內有天壇，先農壇等名勝。一九一一年北京約有人口一百萬。〈18〉

外國公使館位於內城普通的居住區內。外國官員及眷屬住在設有傳統的中國庭園的四合院。荷蘭、美國和德國的公使館位於公使館街的南面，在滿族城城牆內沿處。北京當時的生活與歐洲人的生活習俗大不相同。夜裡實行宵禁，關閉城門，火車站與城內的路也截斷。城裡沒有公園，街道旁沒有樹木遮蔭，路面既沒有鋪石板也沒有用石子加固。

北京的主街道上店鋪鱗次櫛比。住宅都建在彎曲狹窄的胡同裡。這些單層住宅通常為高牆所環繞，使人看不到裝飾雅緻的內

nem Mauerrechteck umgeben. Alle größeren Straßen verlaufen hier in Nord-Süd- und West-Ost-Richtung. Südlich an die Mandschustadt schloß sich die chinesische Stadt an. Die sie umgebende Stadtmauer faßte eine breite rechteckige Fläche ein, innerhalb der auch der Himmelstempel lag. Im Jahre 1911 hatte Beijing etwas über 1 000 000 Einwohner.[18]

Die Gesandtschaften befanden sich in einem gewöhnlichen Wohnviertel der Mandschustadt. Man bewohnte chinesische Hofhäuser mit den traditionellen Gärten. Die südlich der Gesandtschaftsstraße gelegenen Grundstücke der holländischen, amerikanischen und deutschen Gesandtschaft grenzten an die Innenseite der Stadtmauer. Das Leben in Beijing unterschied sich damals sehr vom europäischen Leben. Nachts wurden die Stadttore Beijings geschlossen, damit war die Verbindung zum Bahnhof unterbrochen. Es gab keine öffentlichen Stadtparks oder Bäume entlang den Straßen, die sich damals in einem sehr schlechten Zustand befanden; denn sie waren weder gepflastert noch mit Schotter befestigt.

Die Hauptstraßen Beijings wurden von einer endlosen Kette von Geschäften gesäumt, die Wohnhäuser lagen dagegen an schmalen und verwinkelten Seitengassen (Hutongs). Diese in der Regel eingeschossigen Wohnhäuser waren alle mit Mauern umgeben, die den Blick in die schön gestalteten Innenhöfe und Gärten verwehrten. Lediglich Details wie ein besseres Eingangstor oder eine Mauer aus großen Ziegelsteinen ließen erahnen, was sich dahinter verbarg.

Doch plötzlich drohte den ausländischen Gesandtschaften in Chinas Hauptstadt Gefahr. Um 1895 hatten sich auf dem Land Selbstschutzvereinigungen gegen das Räuberunwesen gebildet. Sie nannten sich »Faust zum Schutze der öffentlichen Ordnung«. Durch Zaubersprüche hielten sich ihre Mitglieder für unverwundbar.[19] Von der Provinz Shandong breitete sich die Bewegung nach Norden aus, nun »Gesellschaft der großen Messer« oder

cluded the Coal Hill, the lakes and the Forbidden City in a square walled enclosure. The Imperial Palaces in the centre – the Forbidden City – was also surrounded by a square walled enclosure. All of the major streets run in a north-south and west-east direction. The Chinese city was located to the south of Manchu City. The city wall surrounding Chinese city enclosed an orthogonal area within which was the Temple of Heaven and the Altar of Agriculture. In 1911, Beijing had just over 1 000 000 inhabitants.[18]

The legations were situated in a normal residential quarter of Manchu city. The foreign diplomats lived in Chinese courtyard houses with traditional gardens. The grounds of the American, Dutch and German legations to the south of the legation street bordered on the inner side of the city wall. Life in Beijing at the time was very different to the life to which the Europeans who lived there were accustomed. Beijing's city gates were locked at night with the result that the connection to the railway station was cut off. There were no public parks or trees lining the streets, which at the time were in very bad condition as they were not surfaced or covered with roadstone. Beijing's main streets were lined with an endless line of shops; the houses were on the narrow crooked side alleys (Hutongs). These mostly one-storey houses were all surrounded by walls which blocked the view of the beautifully laid-out courtyards and gardens. Only minor details, such as a better quality entrance or a wall of large bricks, gave any indication of what lay behind. The courtyard houses of poor and very affluent families stood side by side in the same alleys; there was no particularly exclusive neighbourhood within Manchu City.

The foreign legations in China suddenly found themselves under threat in the late 19th century. Around 1895, vigilant associations were founded in rural areas to provide protection against robbery. They called themselves the »Fist for the Protection of Public Order«. Their members believed themselves to be invin-

院和花園。只有顯赫氣派的門戶和磚石砌築的高牆讓人去想象牆後的秀色。普通人家和達官貴人的四合院都建在同一條胡同里，在滿族城區沒有高級住宅區。

十九世紀末在京的外國使節的生命安全突然受到了威助。一八九五年間以農民為主體自發創辦了自衛抗匪組織，號稱"維護公共秩序的拳頭"。這個組織的成員自稱通過咒語可以"刀槍不入"。[19]這一運動源於山東省後席卷北部地區，稱為大刀會和義和拳。其鋒芒直指外國傳教士和中國的基督教徒。許多人被謀害，其中包括兩名德國傳教士。一九零零年五月這股排外抗教會的風潮愈演憲烈，聲勢浩大，參與者甚至四處清拆鐵軌。而清政府對此卻態度暧昧，剿撫兼施。少數政府武裝甚至參與了義和團運動。然而參戰的人數總共不超過幾千人。北京市民持中立態度。[20]一九零零年六月二十日德國公使克林德在去總理衙門的路上被殺害。在這之後外國公使館被義和團和政府軍幾個部系圍困了五十五天之久。一九零零年八月十四日八國聯軍從天津北上解救了公使館區的九百名外國人和三千名華人教徒。八國聯軍將北京城洗劫一空。德國軍隊從觀象台劫取了幾台天文儀器作為戰利品，曾在波茨坦的宮苑展出。一九二零年根據凡爾賽條約才完璧歸趙。[21]

義和團運動之後外團公館區大大地擴展了。一九零一年公使館區東、北、西三面用開闊的緩衝地帶，南面借助於十二米高的城牆防護起來。每個公使館均有自己的衛隊並建有兵營。公使館區有糧庫和軍械庫，有獨立的司法財政權，管理機構和供電系統，北京城內成了一個自成體系的獨立區域。公館區的守衛部隊共有一千三百五十名士兵和五十一名軍官。他們分別來自十個國家：英國、法國、德國、意大利、奧匈帝國、美國、日本、俄國、荷蘭和比利時。其它的部隊駐守在天津鐵路沿淺，以保證與海相連的陸路暢通無阻。

隨着政局逐漸穩定公使館的守護部隊也逐漸撤離。一九零九年初德國衛隊只有一百二十名士兵和四名軍官。比利時、美國和奧地利的公使館以西洋風格建起了新的樓房。在公使館區具有哥特式復古風格的聖·米歇勒（音譯）天主教堂於一九零三年

»Boxer« genannt. Sie richtete sich gegen christliche Missionare und chinesische Christen, viele von ihnen wurden ermordet, im Jahre 1897 auch zwei deutsche Missionare. Im Mai 1900 verstärkte sich die fremden- und christenfeindliche Bewegung zunehmend, Eisenbahnlinien wurden unterbrochen. Doch die chinesische Regierung verhielt sich uneinheitlich gegenüber den Boxern. Es gab vereinzelt Regierungstruppen, die sich dieser Bewegung angeschlossen hatten, doch waren nie mehr als einige tausend Personen an den Kämpfen beteiligt. Die Einwohner Beijings blieben neutral.[20] Am 20. Juni 1900 wurde der deutsche Gesandte Clemens von Ketteler auf dem Weg zum Außenministerium ermordet. Anschließend belagerten die Boxer und einzelne Verbände der Regierungstruppen 55 Tage lang die Gesandtschaften. Am 14. August 1900 befreiten internationale Truppen, die aus Tianjin angerückt waren, das Viertel. 900 Ausländer hatten sich dort zusammen mit 3 000 chinesischen Christen verschanzt gehalten. Beijing wurde darauf durch die ausländischen Truppen geplündert. Die Deutschen nahmen einige astronomische Instrumente aus dem Observatorium als Kriegsbeute mit. Diese wurden im Schloßpark von Potsdam aufgestellt, nach dem Versailler Vertrag 1920 mußten sie wieder zurückgegeben werden.[21]

Die Grundstücke der Gesandtschaften wurden nach dem Boxerkrieg erheblich vergrößert. Im Jahre 1901 befestigte man das Gesandtschaftsviertel dreiseitig durch ein Glacis, im Süden war es durch die 12 Meter hohe Stadtmauer geschützt. Jede Gesandtschaft besaß eine Gesandtschaftsschutztruppe, für die Kasernen gebaut wurden. Es gab große Lebensmittel- und Waffenlager. Das Gesandtschaftsviertel wurde zu einem eigenen Stadtteil innerhalb Beijings mit juristischer und steuerlicher Hoheit, einer eigenen Stadtverwaltung und eigener Stromversorgung. Die Schutzwache des Gesandtschaftsviertels umfaßte insgesamt 1350 Mann und 51 Offiziere aus zehn Ländern: England,

cible on the basis of magic spells in their possession.[19] The movement spread from the province of Shandong to the north and became known as the »Society of big knives« or »Boxers«; its activities were directed against Christian missionaries and Chinese Christians, many of whom were murdered, including two German missionaries in 1897. In May 1900, the anti-Christian and anti-foreigner movement heightened and some railway lines were cut. The Chinese government was somewhat ambiguous in its treatment of the Boxers. Individual groups of government troops had joined the movement, but there were never more than a few thousand participants in the fights: Beijing's population remained neutral.[20] On 20 June 1900, the German ambassador Clemens von Ketteler was killed on his way to the Ministry of Foreign Affairs. The legations were then besieged for 55 days by the Boxers and individual groups of government troops. On 14 August 1900 international troops, who had advanced from Tianjin, liberated the quarter. 900 foreigners together with 3 000 Chinese Christians had barricaded themselves in the quarter. Beijing was then attacked and plundered by the foreign troops. The Germans took some astronomical instruments from the observatory as spoils of war. These were set up in the palace gardens in Potsdam, but had to be returned to China after the Treaty of Versailles in 1920.[21]

After the Boxer Rebellion, the sites allocated to the legations were extended. In 1901 three sides of the diplomatic quarter were fortified by a glacis and it was protected to the south by the 12 metre-high city wall. Each legation had its own defence troops and barracks were built to house the troops. Large warehouses were also built to store food and weapons. The diplomatic quarter became an independent area within Beijing, with legal and fiscal sovereignty and its own municipal administration and power supply. The defence forces for the diplomatic quarter included a total of 1350 soldiers and 51 officers

對在京的外國人開放，此教堂至今仍保存完好。[22]在公使館區有旅館、商店和醫院，街道也保養得很好。因為北京沒有外國商業租界權，那些對外國人來說必不可少的服務性商行能設在公使館區。只有傳教士、受僱於中方的醫生和教師可以住在公使館之外，建築師羅克格與家眷住在北京東北隅一座豪華四合院府邸裡。府邸的花園內迭石假山散置於曲廊亭榭之間，瀑布噴泉淙淙有聲，景色幽深秀麗。

在北京的歐洲人非常懷念故鄉城市的文化生活。外國的劇團和樂隊很少到北京演出。[23]因為歐洲人喜好郊游。在盛夏時節常去北京西郊群山游憩。西山地區多有廟寺，其中大覺寺[24]是德國公使館的工作人員和其他外國人偏好的去處。大覺寺位於暘台山麓。寺院內樹木蔥翠。枝葉繁茂。從寺內可以遠眺山下的平川。德國公使館的衛隊每年夏天在"戒台寺租房消夏"。每次可以有四十五到五十人在那兒休息三周。公使館給士兵的訓令強調他們的客人身份，要求他們待人謙遜、盡心合作。[25]

鐵路的鋪設改變了人們的生活條件。一八九七年北京與北部海域通車，北戴河由此成為華北地區最受青睞的海濱浴場。許多外國家庭在那兒建造別墅。[26]自一九零八年起德國公使館在北戴河也建有兩幢別墅以及衛兵宿舍。

一八九七年北京車站仍設在距北京南門"永安門"三公里處的"馬家鋪"。自一九零零年春西門子公司的電車行駛於車站和永定門之間，從永定門到公使館區還有三公里之遙。一九零二年義和團運動之後，火車站被遷到前門東側公使館區附近。一九零五年前後前門對面的京漢線火車站竣工啟用。[27]

一九一四年到一九一五年間人們開始鋪建有軌電車道。[28]為了將北邊的滿族城區與南邊的漢人城區貫通起來。唯一的辦法是在前門的城牆上打開豁口作電車通道，因為電車軌的走向與其它各城門的城牆相平行。交通部委托德國建築師羅克格規劃改建前門的方案，以改善前門一帶的交通狀況。於是呈半圓形的城門兩側的城牆被拆除了。城樓被改建為帶有觀景平台的博物館。為了便利交通，為有軌電車開道，在前門的城牆又增開四個通道。

Frankreich, Deutschland, Italien, Österreich-Ungarn, Amerika, Japan, Rußland, Holland und Belgien. Weitere ausländische Truppen waren entlang der Bahnlinie nach Tianjin stationiert, um die Verbindung mit dem Meer zu sichern.

Mit der fortschreitenden politischen Entspannung reduzierte man die Gesandtschaftswachen. Im Frühjahr 1909 bestand die deutsche Wache nur noch aus 120 Soldaten und vier Offizieren. Einige Gesandtschaften, wie die belgische, amerikanische und österreichische, errichteten sich neue Gebäude im westlichen Stil. Für die in Beijing lebenden Ausländer wurde 1903 im Gesandtschaftsviertel die heute noch sehr gut erhaltene katholische Kirche St. Michel im neogotischen Stil eröffnet.[22] Es gab dort Hotels, Geschäfte und Krankenhäuser. Da Beijing nicht den rechtlichen Status einer ausländischen Niederlassung hatte, durften sich die zur Versorgung der Ausländer notwendigen Geschäfte ausschließlich im Gesandtschaftsviertel ansiedeln. Außerhalb dieses Viertels konnten nur Missionare und die ausländischen Ärzte und Lehrer wohnen, die in chinesischen Diensten standen. Zu ihnen gehörte auch der Architekt Curt Rothkegel, der mit seiner Familie im Nordosten Beijings wohnte. Die in Beijing lebenden Ausländer vermißten vor allem ihr europäisches Kulturleben; selten besuchten vertraute Theater- oder Konzertgesellschaften die Stadt.[23] Zur Erholung unternahmen die Europäer vor allem Exkursionen in die Umgebung. In den Westbergen bei Beijing befanden sich zahlreiche Tempel – ein beliebtes Ausflugsziel für die Städter während des heißen Sommers. Der Tempel Dajue Si (Tachüeh-sy), »Tempel des großen Erkennens«,[24] wurde von den Mitarbeitern der Deutschen Gesandtschaft und anderen Ausländern gerne besucht. Man konnte dort von den Mönchen Zimmer mieten und sich während der heißen Sommermonate einige Wochen erholen. Der Tempel liegt am Fuß eines Berges inmitten eines Parks mit schönen Bäumen und einem weiten Blick über die

from ten countries: Britain, France, Germany, Italy, Austria-Hungary, America, Japan, Russia, Holland and Belgium. Additional foreign troops were stationed along the railway line to Tianjin to secure the link with the sea.

The legation troops were gradually reduced in number as progress was made in political détente. In spring 1909 the German defences had been reduced to 120 soldiers and four officers. Some of the legations – Belgian, American and Austrian – erected Western style buildings. In 1903, the neo-Gothic Catholic church of St. Michele was built in the diplomatic quarter for the foreigners living in Beijing: this church still stands and is in very good condition.[22] There were hotels, shops and hospitals in the diplomatic quarter and the roads were well maintained. As Beijing did not have the legal status of a foreign settlement, shops selling provisions for the foreigners could only be opened in the diplomatic quarter. The only foreigners who lived outside the quarter were missionaries, doctors and teachers who worked for the Chinese. Curt Rothkegel, an architect, was an exception; he lived with his family in a courtyard palace in the north east of Beijing which had a park with hills, bridges and pavilions, a waterfall, lake and fountains.

The foreigners living in Beijing missed the cultural life they were accustomed to in European cities: the city was seldom visited by foreign theatre or music groups.[23] The Europeans' main source of entertainment took the form of excursions in the surrounding countryside. There were numerous temples in the mountains to the west of Beijing – a popular resort for city dwellers during the hot summer. Diplomats from the German legation and other foreigners particularly liked to visit the Temple Dajue Si, »The Temple of Great Perception«.[24] It was possible to rent rooms from the monks and spend a few weeks recovering from the city in the hot summer months. The temple is at the foot of a hill in the middle of a park with beautiful trees and has an extensive view over the surrounding

Ebene. Für die deutsche Gesandtschaftsschutzwache wurden jeden Sommer Räume im Kloster Jietai Si (Tje-tai-tze) gemietet. Bis zu 50 Personen konnten sich hier für jeweils drei Wochen erholen. In den Befehlen an die Soldaten wurde ausdrücklich darauf hingewiesen, daß sie lediglich Gastrecht genössen und sich zuvorkommend und bescheiden zu verhalten hätten.[25]

Mit dem Bau der Eisenbahn veränderten sich die Lebensbedingungen. Ab 1897 gab es zwischen Beijing und dem Meer eine Bahnverbindung. Dadurch konnte sich Beidaihe (Peitaiho) zum beliebtesten Seebad Nordchinas entwickeln. Viele ausländische Familien bauten dort ihre Sommerhäuser.[26] Auch die deutsche Gesandtschaft besaß ab 1908 zwei große Villen und Unterkünfte für die Gesandtschaftsschutzwache in dem Seebad.

1897 lag Beijings Bahnhof noch in Majiapu (Matschiapu), drei Kilometer vor dem Südtor Yongding Men (Yung-ting-men). Zwischen Bahnhof und Stadttor verkehrte seit dem Frühjahr 1900 eine elektrische Bahn der Firma Siemens und Halske, von dort aus waren es noch etwa drei Kilometer zum Gesandtschaftsviertel. Nach dem Boxerkrieg wurde der Bahnhof verlegt. Ab 1902 befand er sich östlich vom Stadttor Qianmen und damit in der Nähe der Gesandtschaften. Um das Jahr 1905 wurde auf der gegenüberliegenden Seite des Stadttores der Bahnhof der Beijing-Wuhan-Linie (Peking-Hankou-Linie) eröffnet.[27]

Im Jahre 1914/15 wurde in Beijing der Bau von Straßenbahnlinien geplant.[28] Um die nördlich gelegene Mandschustadt mit der südlichen Chinesenstadt zu verbinden, mußte die Straßenbahn am Stadttor Qianmen die Stadtmauer durchqueren. Hier bestand die einzige Möglichkeit, denn an allen anderen Stadttoren liefen Eisenbahngleise parallel zur Stadtmauer. Die halbkreisförmige Torburg der Stadtmauer wurde abgetragen und das danach freistehende vordere Stadttor zum Museum mit Aussichtsterrasse umgebaut.

countryside. Every summer rooms were rented in the Jietai Si monastery for the German legation troops and 45 to 50 people could spend three relaxing weeks there. The soldiers' orders stressed that they were strictly guests there and were to behave with the utmost co-operation and modesty.[25]

The construction of the railway brought about a marked change in living conditions. From 1897, Beijing was linked to the sea by rail. As a result, Beidaihe (Peitaiho) became the most popular seaside resort in north China and many foreign families built summer houses there.[26] The German legation had two large villas and accommodation for the legation troops in the resort from 1908.

In 1897 Beijing's railway station was still in Majiapu, three kilometres beyond the Yongding Men southern gate. From spring 1900 an electric railway built by Siemens and Halske linked the station and the city gate, from which it was only about three kilometers to the diplomatic quarter. After the Boxer Rebellion the station was moved. From 1902 it was located to the east of the Qianmen city gate and, thus, quite close to the legations. The station for the Beijing-Wuhan line (Peking-Hankow line) was opened on the other side of the city gate in 1905.[27]

Work commenced on the construction of the tramlines in Beijing in 1914/15.[28] In order to link the northern Manchu city with southern Chinese city the tramline had to cross the city wall at the Qianmen city gate. This was the only possible course as there were railway lines running parallel to the city wall at all of the other city gates. In 1914 German architect Curt Rothkegel was commissioned by the Chinese Ministry of Transport to draw up plans for the conversion of the area around the Qianmen gate to improve the traffic situation there. The semi-circular city wall gate fortress was dismantled and the then freestanding exterior city gate was converted to a museum with a viewing terrace. Four additional passages were built through the city wall to facilitate the extra traffic and the tramlines.

Beijing

CH'IEN-MEN, KAISERLICHES STADTTOR
CH'IEN-MEN, THE IMPERIAL CITY GATE

Heutige Funktion. Current use
Qianmen, Ausstellungsgebäude
Qianmen Dajie (Chien-men-Straße),
Beijing (Peking)
Qianmen, exhibition venue
Qianmen Dajie (Ch'ien-Men Street),
Beijing (Peking)

Architekt. Architect
Curt Rothkegel

Bauleitung. Site architect
Gertrud Rothkegel

Kosten des Umbaus. Building costs
etwa 324 000 Goldmark
approximately 324 000 gold marks

Bauherr. Client
Verkehrsministerium
Chinese Ministry of Transport

Planungszeit. Planning phase
1914

Bauzeit. Construction time
Juni 1915 – 1916
June 1915 – 1916

Zustand. Condition
Das Bauwerk ist sehr gut erhalten.
Very well preserved.

Stadtor Qianmen mit Torburg.
Vor dem Umbau, um 1910
Südansicht, 1991
Qianmen city gate with gate fortress prior to
conversion; around 1910
View from the south, 1991

Das Qianmen wurde als südliches Stadttor der Mandschustadt Beijings 1419 erbaut. Während des Boxerkrieges zerstörte es ein Feuer,[29] doch baute man das Tor in den folgenden Jahren wieder auf. Als der Straßenverkehr innerhalb Beijings immer mehr zunahm und gleichzeitig eine Straßenbahn geplant wurde, beauftragte das Verkehrsministerum den Architekten Curt Rothkegel, das Konzept für eine neue Verkehrsplanung im Bereich des Qianmen zu entwickeln.[30] Rothkegel ließ die halbkreisförmige Mauer abreißen, die das äußere und das innere Stadttor miteinander verband und so einen Hof bildete. Durch die Stadtmauer wurden vier je 9,5 Meter breite Durchfahrten gebrochen, zwei davon für die Straßenbahn.[31] Das freigestellte äußere Stadttor des Qianmen baute Rothkegel zu einem Museum und öffentlichen Aussichtspunkt um. Auf der Nordseite des äußeren Stadttors wurden zwei großzügige, für die traditionelle chinesische Architektur völlig untypische zweiläufige Treppen mit Zwischenpodesten errichtet, über die die Besucher auf die zur Aussichtsplattform umgestaltete Mauerkrone in 13 Meter Höhe hinaufgehen konnten.[32] Die Aussichtsplattform führte Rothkegel als einen 1,60 Meter breiten Balkon um das gesamte äußere Stadttor herum. Von hier oben hat man den besten Blick über die lange Straßenachse der Qianmen Dajie.

Der weiße Balkon, der an die Brüstungen der Terrassen der Verbotenen Stadt oder des Himmelstempels erinnert, war ein Fremdkörper an diesem mächtigen Bauwerk. Um eine optische Verbindung zu der glatten, grauen Oberfläche des Stadttores zu erhalten, ließ Rothkegel halbkreisförmige, weiße Gesimsbänder über zwei der drei Fensterreihen, den früheren Schießscharten, anbringen, die sehr plastisch wirken.[33] Diese »modische Verzierung« des ansonsten schlichten Stadttores war damals umstritten: »Die Fensteröffnungen wurden mit geschwungenen Gesimsbändern überdacht, in der einigermaßen verfehlten Absicht, dem Stadttor dadurch ein

The Qianmen was built in 1419 as Beijing's Manchu city southern gate. It was completely destroyed by a fire during the Boxer Rebellion,[29] but was rebuilt during the subsequent years. When the volume of traffic in Beijing increased and there were plans for a tram network, the transport ministry commissioned the architect Curt Rothkegel to develop a new traffic concept for the Qianmen area.[30] Rothkegel pulled down the semi-circular wall that connected the outer and inner city gate and formed a courtyard. Four 9.5 meter-wide passages were broken through the city wall, two of which were intended for the trams.[31] Rothkegel then converted the free-standing outer Qianmen gate into a museum with a public viewing platform. Two large double staircases with intermediate landings, quite untypical of traditional Chinese architecture, were constructed on the northern side of the outer gate. These staircases made it possible for visitors to climb to the top of the wall (13 metres), which had been converted into a viewing platform.[32] The viewing platform took the form of a 1.6 metre balcony which went right around the outer city gate. The long street axis of Qianmen Dajie could be viewed for the first time from this platform.

The white balcony, which was detailed in the same manner as the parapets on the terraces of the Forbidden City or the Temple of Heaven, was out of place on this monumental construction. To create an optical link with the flat grey surface of the gate, Rothkegel designed semi-circular white plaster panels over two of the three rows of windows, the former embrasures, which were very plastic in their effect.[33] This »fashionable decoration« of the otherwise plain city gate was controversial: »curving canopies have been allied over the loopholes with the somewhat inexpedient intention of making them look like palace windows. The transformation of this outside tower is indeed one of the most deplorable features in the refashioning of Ch'ien men, and it is hard to find any practical excuse or reason for it.«[34]

改建前的帶有半圓形城牆的前門，攝於一九一零年左右。
南立面，一九九一年。

前門、皇城城門

現用途：前門展覽館
地址：北京前門大街
建築師：羅克格
工程指導：格特魯德‧羅克格
改建造價：約三十二點四萬金馬克
業主：交通部
規劃期：一九一四年
建造日期：一九一五年六月至一九一六年
現狀：樓體保存完好

北京的南城門前門建於一四一九年。義和團運動期間一場大火使前門夷為平地，此後又按照原樣復建。〈29〉由於北京的交通越來越擁擠，鋪設電車軌道的工程迫在眉睫。交通部委托德國建築師羅克格重新規劃前門地段的交通路線。〈30〉

羅克格被授權設計。其方案建議拆除連接內外城門的半圓形城牆，以開闢交通廣場。〈31〉人們按照他的設計在城牆上開了四個九點五米寬的豁口，其中兩個用於鋪設電車軌道，並將外城門改建成展覽館的公共觀景點。外城門的北邊建起了兩條氣勢宏偉卻與中國建築風格毫不相同的歐式階梯。沿此設有休息平台的曲尺型雙梯可登上十三米高的城牆頂端，即觀景平台。〈32〉所謂觀景台就是一道一點六米寬圍繞外城門而建的平台。在觀景台上可憑杆眺望前門大街的全景。平台上的白色護欄形同故宮和天壇的漢白玉欄杆，玲瓏秀美，但和巍峨雄偉的城門卻不相稱。羅克格讓人用半圓形的裝飾線將城門上的箭窗連接起來。這種實用美觀的裝飾線使灰色的城牆平添了生氣。當時對這種把西洋花飾用於古樸城樓的嘗試眾說紛紜："建築師滿以為在箭窗的上沿添幾條波浪形裝飾線就能使城門變得像宮殿一般。事實證明，改建外城門是該計劃中永遠無法補救，因而最令人痛心的失誤，任何由此獲得的實用效益都與此失誤無法相比。"〈34〉然而聘請歐洲建築師改建中國城門勢必導致中西建築手法並用。城門本是一種防禦設施，經改建成為展覽館和觀景台。兩形式與功能極不相稱。由此可見，新的功能也要新的建築手段。

在中國人眼里羅克是一位可信賴的優秀建

BEIJING

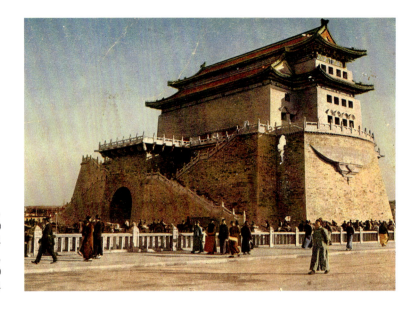

Nordwestansicht,
Postkarte, um 1920
Modell, 1914
View from the north-west,
postcard, around 1920
Model, 1914

palastartiges Aussehen zu verleihen. Der Umbau dieses äußeren Stadttores ist in der Tat einer der beklagenswertesten Züge der Umstrukturierung des Ch'ien men, und es ist schwer, dafür irgendwelche konkreten Entschuldigungen oder Gründe zu finden.«[34]
Der Umbau eines chinesischen Stadttores durch einen europäischen Architekten mußte zwangsläufig zu einer Verschmelzung von europäischer und chinesischer Architektur führen. Das ursprüngliche Stadttor hatte den klaren Ausdruck eines Wehrbaues, durch den Umbau wurde es zu einem Museum mit Aussichtsterrasse. Die hinzugefügten fremden Stilelemente waren Ausdruck einer neuen Funktion.
Curt Rothkegel (1876–1946) hatte sich in chinesischen Kreisen den Ruf eines guten und zuverlässigen Architekten erworben. 1908 errichtete er für die chinesische Regierung in Xiamen (Amoy) ein Empfangsgebäude für die amerikanische Flotte. 1910 wurde er beauftragt, das Parlament für Beijing zu bauen. Zu-

When a European architect is commissioned to design the conversion of a Chinese city gate, what results is, of course, a mixture of Chinese and European architecture. The defence function of the original city gate was clearly reflected in its architecture; after its conversion it became a museum and viewing terrace and the new foreign elements reflected its altered function.
Curt Rothkegel (1876–1946) enjoyed a reputation as a good reliable architect in Chinese circles. In 1908 he built a reception building for the American fleet for the Chinese government in Xiamen (Amoy). In 1910 he was commissioned to design the parliament building in Beijing. He also built the provisional parliament building. He built a European-style villa for the Minister of the Marine, Prince Zaixun (Tsai-hsün) and produced a design for a building for the Ministry of the Marine. He designed the Chinese-style Chinese Empire pavilion for the public health exhibition in Dresden in 1911.[35] This was followed in 1912 by

設計模型,一九一四年。
西北面外觀,明信片圖片,約一九二零年。

築師。一九零八年,他受中國政府之托在廈門設計了美國海軍招待所。一九一零年,他再次受聘在北京設計國會大廈和臨時國會大廈。羅克格為海軍大臣,皇子載洵(音譯)設計了一幢西式別墅並幫助規劃籌建海軍部大樓。一九一一年在德累斯頓的醫療衛生展覽會上,羅克格按中國建築風格設計了大清帝國展覽廳。〈35〉一九零二年,他改建慈禧太後的寢宮—儲香宮。(音譯)(慈禧太后逝於一九零八年)一九一四年,他在中南海的中華民國臨時大總統袁世凱的稱帝加冕儀式設計了"政事堂(音譯)"。羅克格在這些設計中均使用了傳統的中國手法——單層結構以及北京流行的總灰色磚瓦。

一九一四年秋,羅克格在保衛青島,抵抗日軍的戰鬥中被俘,在日本俘虜營里囚禁六年之久。其夫人格恃魯德、羅克格一八八一至一九七八年接替他的工作。一九二零年,羅克格返抵中國,在北京的天津從事建築設計活動。一九二四年,羅克格遷居沈陽並在此設計了許多大工廠的廠房、俱樂部大樓,以及德國領事館和法國紅衣主教的住宅。一九二九年在中國工作了二十五年之久的羅克格返回德國。〈36〉

Stadttor Antingmen mit Torburg
Ostfassade,
Entwurfszeichnung, 1914
Gesimsbänder, 1991
Atingmen city gate with gate
fortress
East façade, drawing, 1914
Eaves panels, 1991

sätzlich plante er ein provisorisches Parlamentsgebäude. Für den Marineminister Prinz Zaixun (Tsai-hsün) erbaute er eine Villa im europäischen Stil in Beijing und projektierte ein Marineministerium. Er entwarf den Pavillon des chinesischen Kaiserreichs auf der Hygieneausstellung in Dresden 1911 im chinesischen Stil.[35] 1912 folgte der Umbau des ehemaligen Wohnpalais »Schwe wu Sche« der 1908 verstorbenen Kaiserin und 1914 der Bau des Krönungspalais Zhengshi Tang (Dschang sche tang) für den Präsidenten Yuan Shikai im Seepalast-Viertel der Kaiserstadt. Diese Gebäude wurden im chinesischen Stil erbaut. Sie waren eingeschossig und aus den in Beijing üblichen schwarz-grauen Ziegeln.

Im Herbst 1914 geriet Rothkegel bei der Verteidigung Qingdaos gegen die Japaner in japanische Kriegsgefangenschaft, die sechs Jahre währte. Seine Ehefrau, Gertrud Rothkegel (1881–1978), führte die Arbeiten fort. 1920 kehrte Curt Rothkegel nach China zurück, war in Beijing und Tianjin tätig, verlegte 1924 seinen Wohnsitz nach Shenyang (Mukden), wo er mehrere große Fabriken, Klubgebäude, das deutsche Konsulat und die Residenz des französischen Bischofs baute. 1929 kehrte Rothkegel nach 25jähriger Tätigkeit in China nach Deutschland zurück.[36]

the conversion of the former residential palace »Schwe wu Sche« of the Empress Dowager who had died in 1908, and the construction in 1914 of the Crown Palace Zhengshi Tang for the President Yuan Shikai in the Sea Palace quarter of the Imperial City. All of these buildings were designed in Chinese style. They had one floor and were built using the black-grey bricks characteristic of the buildings in Beijing. In Autumn 1914, Rothkegel was taken prisoner by the Japanese during the defence of Qingdao against the Japanese and was imprisoned for six years. His wife, Gertrud Rothkegel (1881–1978) continued his work. In 1920 Curt Rothkegel returned to China and worked in Beijing and Tianjin. In 1924 he moved to Shenyang (Mukden) where he designed several large factories, club buildings, the German consulate and the French Bishop's residence. In 1929 Rothkegel returned to Germany having worked for 25 years in China.[36]

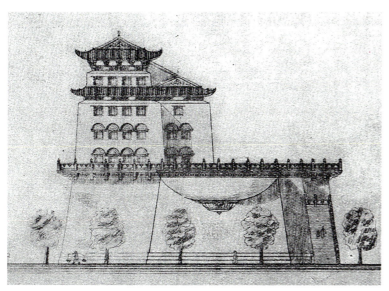

帶有半圓城牆的安定門。
東立面，一九一四年繪制的設計圖。

裝飾線，一九九一年。

BEIJING

CHINESISCHES PARLAMENTSGEBÄUDE
CHINESE PARLIAMENT BUILDING

Jianguomennei Dajie/Jianguomenbei Dajie, Beijing (Peking)

Architekt. Architect
Curt Rothkegel

Geplante Baukosten. Estimated cost
etwa 5 400 000 Goldmark
approximately 5 400 000 gold marks

Entstandene Baukosten. Final cost
etwa 990 000 Goldmark
approximately 990 000 gold marks

Ausführung. Contractors
Telge & Schroeter, Peking, Tientsin, Hamburg

Bauherr. Client
Kaiserliche chinesische Regierung
The Imperial Chinese Government

Bauzeit. Construction time
1910 – Herbst 1911, dann Baueinstellung
1910 – autumn 1911, building then discontinued

Zustand. Condition
Die Fundamente waren komplett und 4 800 Kubikmeter Mauerwerk fertiggestellt. Nach der Revolution 1911 wurden die Arbeiten nicht fortgeführt.
The foundation and 4 800 cubic metres of wall were completed. Work on the building was not continued after the revolution of 1911.

Deutscher Reichstag, Entwurfszeichnung von Paul Wallot, 1882
German Reichstag, drawing by Paul Wallot, 1882

Curt Rothkegel bezeichnete sein Parlamentsgebäude als einen Bau von »etwa der doppelten Größe des Reichstags-Gebäudes in Berlin«[37], das 1894 fertiggestellt worden war. Die Perspektivzeichnung Rothkegels zeigt das chinesische Parlamentsgebäude aus dem gleichen Winkel, wie Wallots Ansicht des Reichstages vom Königsplatz aus.[38] Rothkegels Entwurf für Beijing ist viel breiter gelagert und trägt – entsprechend der geplanten Regierungskonstitution – drei Kuppeln: Kaiser, Unterhaus und Oberhaus. Die beiden äußeren Kuppeln sind etwas zu flach proportioniert.

Der *Ostasiatische Lloyd* veröffentlichte im Jahre 1910 eine ausführliche Beschreibung des Parlamentsprojekts: »In der äußersten Südostecke der Tatarenstadt auf dem Gelände, auf dem früher nördlich unterhalb der Pekinger Sternwarte die alte Prüfungshalle (…) lag, wird nun das Wahrzeichen des modernen Chinas, das Parlamentsgebäude, erstehen, gleichsam als Eingangspforte zu dem konstitutionellen China. (…) Als massiven rechteckigen Granitbau werden wir das neue Parlamentsgebäude erstehen sehen, mit der Front nach Westen, der Tartarenstadt (Kaiserliche Stadt, d. Verfasser) zu. Vier Straßen führen vom Osten der Stadt senkrecht auf die Hauptfront des Gebäudes hin, die in der Mitte, gerade über dem großen Eröffnungssaal, eine gewaltige, das Ganze überragende Kuppel krönt, die ihren Abschluß in der sogenannten Laterne erhält. Große, breite Wandelhallen stellen die Verbindung des Mittelkuppelbaues mit den beiden seitlichen Flügeln her, in denen die beiden Plenarsitzungssäle des Ober- und des Unterhauses liegen. Auch sie sind nach außen hin ebenfalls durch einen Kuppelbau kenntlich gemacht, wenn auch diese Kuppeln wesentlich niedriger als die Hauptkuppel gehalten sind. Nach den beiden Enden fällt weiter in den seitlichen Polizei- und Stallgebäuden usw. der Monumentalbau immer mehr ab. Der ganze große Gebäudekomplex ist ringsum mit einer hohen Mauer umschlossen (…). Der

Curt Rothkegel described his parliament building as a building »approximately twice the size of the Reichstag building in Berlin«[37] which was completed in 1894. Rothkegel's perspective shows the Chinese parliament building from the same angle as Wallot's view of the Reichstag from the Königsplatz in Berlin.[38] Rothkegel's design for Beijing was far more extensive and had three domes which reflected the planned form of government with the Emperor, upper and lower houses. The two lateral domes are somewhat flat in their proportions.

The *Ostasiatische Lloyd* published the following detailed description of the parliament project in 1910: »In the far south-east corner of the Tartar City, the symbol of modern China, the parliament building, the gate – so to speak – to constitutional China, will be built on the site on which the old examination hall used to stand, to the north of the site just below the Peking observatory. The new parliament building will take the form of a massive rectangular granite building with its façade facing west to the Imperial City. There are four roads leading directly from the east of the city to the main façade of the building which is crowned at the centre right above the great inauguration hall, by a dome which terminates at the so-called »lantern«. Large, wide foyers provide the links between the central dome building and the two side wings which house the assembly halls for the upper and lower houses. These are also represented on the exterior of the building by domes which, however, are considerably lower then the main cupola. This monumental building spreads sideways in both directions to the police and stable buildings. The entire complex is surrounded by a high wall which is interrupted at the main façade by a monumental group of five gates and at the sides and back by several individual gates. (…) The square on which the parliament building is to be erected is approximately 550 metres long and 300 metres wide. (…) Just as there is a large open square at the front of the building,

羅克格曾預計北京國會大廈將是一八九四年竣工的柏林國會大廈的兩倍。〈37〉瓦洛特從帝國廣場的角度繪制了帝國大廈草圖，羅克格繪制的中國國會大廈也採取了同樣的視角。〈38〉但羅克格設計的國會大廈將更加雄偉。預計的政府組閣形式的皇上、下議院和上議院。國會大廈有三個穹頂，兩側的圓頂較之正中的圓頂偏低，因而顯得有些比例失調。

《德文新報》於一九一零年發表文章對國會大廈的建築方案做了詳盡的描寫：—"在內城的東南角，北京觀象台前以北，即在以前的科舉考場舊址上將要矗立起象徵中國步入立憲制，走向現代化的國會大廈。新的國會大廈將為長方形的花崗石建築，面朝西，正對著皇城。四條大街從城市的東部一直延伸至國會大廈。氣勢宏偉的主圓拱形頂端設有塔式天窗，下面是議會大廳。寬闊的迴廊門廳橫貫主樓和兩側的上、下議院會議廳"兩邊側樓的拱頂體現了上、下議院與皇族內閣之間的隸屬等級關係。與主穹頂相比，側樓拱頂顯得過於低矮。從總體來看，議會大樓中間高起，兩翼越來越低，大廈的兩端分別為衛護處和馬廄。大廈四周將高築圍牆。正面是宏偉的正門，後面及兩側均設有通道。整個建築群佔地面積長五百五十米，寬三百米。大廈前後均開辟寬闊的廣場。正門前計劃建一條十寬闊的行車坡道，後面則准備修建三條供皇帝，文武大臣和外國使節使用的坡道……國會大廈的中軸線上是坡道，露天平台，門廳和能容納八百人的議會大廳，接著就是皇帝的御座，皇帝和群臣朝政議事的處所。這裡與後面的坡道連接。從正面的廣場，沿著坡道，穿過露天平台進入門廳和會議廳直至皇上的御座准備鋪設五道層層向上的階梯，每道階梯由七個台階組成……國會大廈進口處是一間開敞的迴廊門廳，正中的穹窿有三層樓高，迴廊連接著中間和兩側的議院大廳……兩側議廳之間的總長為一百多米。〈39〉根據政府建築當局的要求，中央會議大廳的座位參照柏林國會大廈的模式設置……兩側的旁廳各容納四百五十名議員，座位的設置呈扇形。側大廳長二十七米，寬二十一米……根據計劃，中央的大圓頂用銅鐵鍛制。但具體的細節尚未確定。大

保爾·瓦洛特繪制的德國帝國大廈透視圖，一八八二年。

北京、中國國會大廈

地址：北京建國門內大街（建國門北大街口）
建築師：羅克格
預計費用：約五百四十萬金馬克，二百萬兩銀子
實際費用：約九十九萬金馬克
建築：特格·施洛特公司，北京，天津，漢堡
業主：大清政府
建造日期：一九一零年秋至一九一一年，此後施工中斷
現狀：地基部份完工，四千八百立方米的牆體砌築完畢。一九一一年辛亥革命後工程中止。

Chinesisches Parlamentsgebäude,
Blick von Westen,
Perspektivzeichnung, 1910
Chinesisches Parlamentsgebäude,
Hauptgeschoß, 1911
Chinese Parliament Building,
view from the west,
perspective drawing, 1910
Chinese Parliament Building,
main floor, 1911

Platz, auf dem sich das Parlamentsgebäude erheben wird, ist etwa 550 Meter lang und 300 Meter breit. (…) Wie vor der Vorderfront sich ein großer freier Platz ausdehnt, so ist auch ein rückwärtiger großer Platz mit drei Auffahrten für den Kaiser, den kaiserlichen Hof und die Diplomaten vorgesehen. (…) Die Disposition im Innern des Gebäudes ist, wie gesagt, die, daß die linke Seite für das Ober-, die rechte für das Unterhaus vorbehalten ist. Getrennt sind sie in der Mitte durch die große Auffahrt, die Freiterrasse und eine große Eintrittshalle mit dem darauf folgenden Eröffnungssaal, der ungefähr 800 Personen Platz bietet. Daran schließen sich nach hinten Hofräume an, in der Mitte für den Kaiser und den kaiserlichen Hof und in der Mittelachse weiter rückwärtig Vorräume zu den Hofräumen, endlich die große Auffahrt für den Kaiser und den kaiserlichen Hof. Vom Hauptplatz in der Folge der erwähnten Gebäudeteile, über die Auffahrt, Freiterrasse, Eintrittshalle und den Eröffnungssaal zum Kaiserthron steigen in regelmäßiger Reihenfolge fünf mal sieben Stufen an. (…) Hinter dem Haupteingang kommt man in eine große Wandelhalle, die sich in der mittleren Rotunde durch drei Stockwerke des Hauses erhebt. (…) die Gesamtlänge der Wandelhalle mit Eröffnungshalle vom Eingang eines Sitzungssaales zum anderen beträgt über 100 Meter. Der Wandelhalle gegenüber befindet sich der große Sitzungssaal, in dem die Anordnung im einzelnen nach dem Muster des Deutschen Reichstages getroffen sind, eine Vorschrift des Bauamtes für den Architekten. (…) Die in den beiden Sitzungssälen für je 450 Abgeordnete[39] vorgesehenen Sitzreihen verlaufen strahlenförmig, die Säle selbst sind je 27 Meter lang und je 21 Meter breit. (…) Die große Mittelkuppel wird wohl, wie bisher geplant ist, aus Eisenmaterial bestehen. Jedoch ist Genaues darüber noch nicht bestimmt. Ihre Gesamthöhe wird 75 Meter betragen. Die Länge des Gebäudes ist auf 240 Meter, die Tiefe auf 120 Meter berechnet. (…)«[40]

Die Kaiserinwitwe Cixi (Tz'u-hsi), die eigentli-

there is also a large square at the back of the building with three driveways for the Emperor, members of the Emperor's court and diplomats. A large wide ramp leads to the main entrance at the front. (…) The layout of the interior is, as already mentioned, with the left side reserved for the upper house and the right for the lower house. The two wings are separated in the middle by the large drive, the open terrace and a large entrance hall which leads to the inauguration hall which will accommodate approximately 800 people. At the back of this room at the centre there are reception rooms for the Emperor and his court and these are followed along the central axis to the back by the lobbies to the reception rooms, and then finally the large driveway for the Emperor and his court. There are five flights of stairs, each with seven steps, leading from the main square to each of the parts of the building mentioned – the drive, the open terrace, the entrance hall and the inauguration hall to the imperial throne. (…) Behind the main entrance there is a large foyer which extends upwards through three floors of the building under the central dome. The foyer represents the link between the central building and the two side wings which house the two assembly halls. (…) the total length of the foyers and the inauguration hall from one assembly hall to the other is over 100 metres. The large assembly hall is at one end of the foyer and the arrangement here mirrors that of the German Reichstag in every detail in accordance with the building authority regulations. (…) The seating arrangement in both halls is radial and they are intended to accommodate 450 representatives,[39] the actual rooms are each 27 metres long and 21 metres wide. (…) It is planned to use iron to build the great centre dome, but the details have yet to be finalised. The dome will be 75 metres high. The length of the building is calculated as 240 metres, its width 120 metres. (…)«[40]

The Empress Dowager Cixi (Tzu-hsi), the actual ruler of China, had imprisoned political

中國國會大廈西面透視圖，一九一零年。

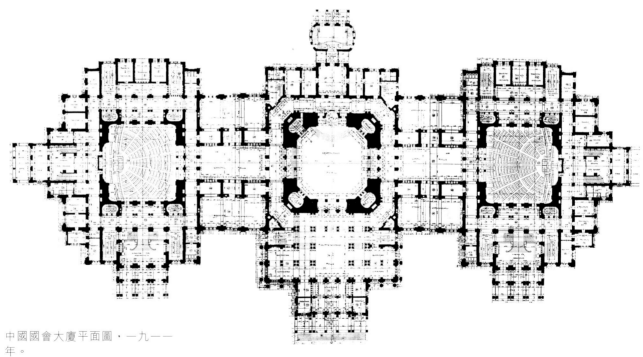

中國國會大廈平面圖，一九一一年。

che Herrscherin Chinas, hatte 1898 politische Reformer und mit ihnen ihren Neffen, den jungen Kaiser, verhaften lassen, doch nach der Niederlage Chinas im Boxerkrieg wurde sie selbst zur politischen Reformerin. 1905 reiste eine Kommission ins Ausland, um in verschiedenen Staaten die unterschiedlichen konstitutionellen politischen Systeme zu studieren. 1908 wurde ein Neun-Jahres-Programm zur Umstellung in eine konstitutionelle Monarchie bis zum Jahr 1917 verkündet. Am 14. November 1908 starb der junge Kaiser, einen Tag darauf die 74jährige Kaiserinwitwe; der Reformprozeß setzte sich dennoch fort. 1909 kam es zu den ersten Wahlen von Provinzversammlungen.[41] Der Architekt Rothkegel wurde mit dem Bau eines Parlaments beauftragt, am 7. April 1910 unterzeichnete er den Vertrag mit dem Bauamt.[42] Vertreter der Provinzversammlungen und des Kaiserhauses trafen sich im Herbst 1910 in Beijing und forderten eine frühere Einberufung des Parlaments, die daraufhin vorgezogen und mit Kaiserlichem Edikt für das Jahr 1913 festgesetzt wurde.[43]

Im Herbst 1911 stürzte die Revolution die Qing-Dynastie. Die Republik China stoppte das gigantische Bauvorhaben, obwohl bereits fast 20 Prozent der Planungs- und Baukosten entstanden waren. Noch ausstehende Honorare versuchten Rothkegel und das Bauunternehmen auf diplomatischem Weg unter Einschaltung der Gesandtschaft in Beijing zu erhalten. Zunächst schien es so, als ob die Republik China das Parlamentsgebäude fertigstellen wolle.[44] Im Januar 1914 lautete der Kompromiß: Wenn das Bauunternehmen oder der Architekt das Geld für den Parlamentsbau – über eine Anleihe – besorgen, werde das Parlament doch gebaut. Schließlich wurde der Vertrag annulliert.[45] Der repräsentative Neubau war der jungen Republik zu aufwendig. Als Versammlungsort wurde das sogenannte Provisorische Parlamentsgebäude genutzt, das ebenfalls von Rothkegel stammt.

reformers with her nephew, the young Emperor, in 1898. However, following the defeat of the Chinese in the Boxer Rebellion, she herself became a political reformer. In 1905 a commission was sent abroad to study constitutional systems in different states. In 1908, a nine-year programme was announced for the conversion of China to a constitutional monarchy by 1917. The young Emperor died on November 14th 1908 and was followed one day later by the 74-year old Empress Dowager; the reform process was, however, continued. The first elections were held for the provincial assemblies in 1909.[41] Rothkegel was commissioned to design the parliament building and he signed the contract with the building authorities on April 7th 1910.[42] Representatives of the provincial assemblies and the imperial court met in Beijing in autumn 1910 and demanded that the opening of parliament be brought forward. The opening was brought forward and set for the year 1913 in an imperial edict.[43]

In autumn 1911 the Qing dynasty was overturned by a revolution. The Chinese Republic stopped the gigantic construction project although almost 20 percent of the planning and building costs had already been incurred. Rothkegel and the contractors tried to obtain outstanding fees through the German legation in Beijing. Initially it appeared that the Chinese Republic would agree to go ahead with the parliament building.[44] The following compromise was announced in 1914: if the building contractor or the architect managed to obtain the money to complete the parliament building (through a loan), it could be built. Finally, however, the contract was cancelled.[45] The great edifice was too lavish for the young republic and the so-called »provisional« parliament building, also designed by Rothkegel, was then built to house the assemblies.

廈總高七十五米，寬二百四十米，長一百二十米。⁽⁴⁰⁾

中國真正的統治者，慈禧太后於一八九八年下令逮捕、軟禁政治改良派和支持變法的年輕皇帝。然而義和團運動後，她自己也主張政治改革。一九零五年，慈禧曾派一代表團到國外考察各國不同的政體。一九零八年，又公佈了一個預備立憲的九年計劃，到一九一七年要將中國變成君主立憲制。一九零八年十一月十四日，年輕的皇帝駕崩，一天之後，七十四歲的慈禧太后也去逝。然而改革已是勢不可擋。一九零九年，中國出現第一次選舉諮議局代表。⁽⁴¹⁾建築師羅克格受托設計議會大廈。一九一零年八月七日，他與建築局簽訂了設計合同。⁽⁴²⁾一九一零年秋，政資院和諮議局議員聚會北平。立憲派屢屢請願，皇上下諭縮短預備期，定於一九一三年召開國會。⁽⁴³⁾

一九一一年秋，辛亥革命推翻的清朝政府。那時設計、預算和施工已耗費了百分之二十的建造資金。由於經濟的原因，國民政府意欲中止這一龐大的建築工程。羅克格的建築公司力爭通過德國大使館使用外交手段追回未付的酬金。⁽⁴⁴⁾中華民國政府開始似乎也不希望國會大廈工程半途而廢。一九一四年元月達成的協議是：如建築公司或羅克格能通過貸款籌措到資金，國會大廈工程便可繼續進行。然而由於種種原因，合同最終還是被取消。⁽⁴⁵⁾這座象徵性的建築物對年輕的共和國來説價格太昂貴。由羅克格設計的所謂臨時國會大廈就成了國會議政的場所。

中國國會大廈地基，一九一三年。
中國國會大廈南北角，一九一一年。

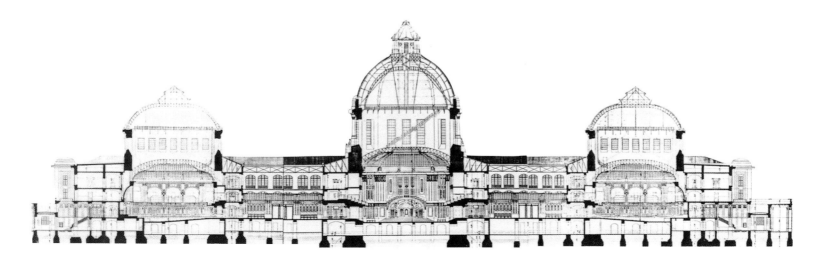

39

北京

BEIJING

PROVISORISCHES PARLAMENTSGEBÄUDE
'PROVISIONAL' PARLIAMENT BUILDING

Heutige Funktion. Current use
Freizeitzentrum für alte Menschen
Xuanwumen Dongdajie, nördlich der Xinhua
News Agency, Beijing (Peking)
Leisure centre for old people
Xuanwumen Dongdajie, Beijing (Peking)

Architekt. Architect
Curt Rothkegel

Baukosten Neubau. Building costs
etwa 108 000 Goldmark
approximately 108 000 gold marks

Inneneinrichtung. Cost of interior fittings
etwa 36 000 Goldmark
approximately 36 000 gold marks

Bauherr. Client
Republik China
Republic of China

Bauzeit. Construction time
Herbst 1912 – April 1913
autumn 1912 – April 1913

Zustand. Condition
Das Gebäude ist gut erhalten.
Well preserved.

Haupteingang, Südansicht, 1993
Ehem. Provisorisches
Parlamentsgebäude, 1993
Main entrance, south side, 1993
Former Provisional Parliament
Building, 1993

Im Gegensatz zum großen Parlamentsgebäude wählte Rothkegel für das Provisorische Parlament chinesische Baumaterialien. »Der Sitzungssaal des ›Provisorischen Parlaments-Gebäudes‹ hingegen stand wieder in streng chinesischer Umgebung und mußte daher in schwarzem Ziegelrohbau gebaut werden. Im Stil etwa der anliegenden Gebäude.«[46] Es entstand ein dreigeschossiges, überraschend niedrig wirkendes Gebäude mit klassizistischen Zügen und einer harmonisch gegliederten Fassade.

Zur Eröffnung des Parlaments gibt der *Ostasiatische Lloyd* eine Beschreibung: »Heute erhebt sich in der Nähe des Chien men ein schmucker in grauem Backstein gehaltener Rotundebau, der mit dem Gebäude der früheren Finanzschule und dessen Neben- und Hintergebäuden durch einen langen, überdachten Gang verbunden ist. Der Bau macht von außen keinen besonders gewaltigen Eindruck. (...) Der Sitzungssaal ist in weißer Farbe gehalten. (...) Der Sitz des Präsidenten ist nicht, wie früher der des Prinzregenten im Beratenden Ausschuß, erhöht angebracht, sondern befindet sich in gleicher Höhe wie die Sitze des Präsidenten des Hauses und seiner beiden Sekretäre, offenbar damit die republikanische Gleichheit auch äußerlich gewahrt ist. (...) Im Parterre sind 650 Sitze, vor denen je ein kleines Pult steht für die Abgeordneten und daneben etwa 300 Sitze für die Senatoren für den Fall, daß beide Häuser des Parlaments in wichtigen Fragen (...) zusammen tagen. Die Galerie faßt 350 Plätze, die mittleren Logen sind für das diplomatische Korps gedacht. (...) Außer der Sitzungshalle gibt es noch eine Reihe kleiner Säle. Für den Präsidenten ist ein geschmackvolles Zimmer, dessen Möbel aus Deutschland stammen, eingerichtet worden; ferner ist je ein Erholungszimmer für die Minister und Regierungsvertreter und für die Abgeordneten vorhanden. (...)«[47] Bis 1924 tagte hier das chinesische Parlament.

Unlike his design for the large parliament building, Rothkegel opted to use Chinese building materials for the provisional parliament building. »The assembly hall of the ›Provisional parliament building‹ was again, by contrast, in a strictly Chinese environment and the structure had to be built in brick, in roughly the same style as the neighbouring buildings.«[46] It was a three-storey building, which nevertheless managed to look very low, with classical features and a well designed façade.

The *Ostasiatische Lloyd* describes the opening of parliament: »Today, a decorative rotunda in grey brick, which is linked to the former finance school and its auxiliary buildings by a long covered path, has raised its head near the Chien men. The building is not particularly imposing from the outside. (...) The assembly hall is painted white. (...) The President's seat is not raised the way in which the Prince Regent's was when participating in consultancy committees, but is on the same level as the seats of the president of the house and his two secretaries. The intention is obviously to ensure that Republican equality is also maintained in external matters. (...) There are 650 seats on the ground floor and in front of each seat there is a small lectern for the representatives. Beside these seats there are a further 300 seats for the senators, should both houses meet together to discuss important issues. The gallery has 350 places and the central boxes are intended for the diplomatic corps. (...) In addition to the assembly hall there is a series of smaller rooms. A tasteful room with furniture from Germany has been designed for the president; there is also a recreation room for the ministers and government representatives and for the parliamentary representatives. (...)«[47] The Chinese parliament met in this building until 1924.

臨時國會大廈

現用途：青年人娛樂活動中心
地址：宣武門東大街
建築師：羅克格
建築造價：約十點八萬金馬克
內部裝修：約三點六萬金馬克
業主：中華民國政府
建造日期：一九一二年秋至一九一三年四
　　　　　月
現狀：樓體保存完好

與造國會大廈不同，在建造臨時國會大廈時羅克格選用了中國傳統的建築材料。"臨時國會大廈的四周都是中國式的樓房。為了與這些建築風格相協調，國會大樓外牆用大青磚砌造"〈46〉臨時國會大廈有三層樓，但看上去並不顯得很高。大廈顯示了古典主義的風采，立面的布局勻稱美觀。

《東亞時報》對臨時國會大廈的落成做了如下報導："前門附近新崛起了一座外形美觀的青磚建築，它就是臨時國會大廈。一條沒有頂蓬的長廊將大廈、舊財政學校的主樓、側樓及後樓連接起來。從外表上看，該樓並不顯得碩大無比⋯⋯會議廳內粉刷成白色。總統的座位與攝政王的軍機部不同，不是高高在上，而是與眾議院主席和他的兩名秘書的座位平起平坐。座位設置的用意顯然在於體現共和國人人平等的原則⋯⋯正廳中央和後排有六百五十個座位，每個座位前有一張供議員使用的小台桌。上、下議院如有要事共商，上議院則使用旁側的三百個座位。大廳樓上的三面設有樓座三百五十個，正面的樓座供外交官員使用。除了正廳還有許多小型廳室。議會主席的專用房間布置得尤其雅緻，室內家俱均為德國制造。此外，部長們、政府代表以及議員可在各自專門的房間休息"〈47〉直到一九二四年，中華民國的國會都在這座大廈裡執行議會職權。

南立面主入口，一九九三年。
當年的臨時國會大廈，一九九三年。

KAISERLICH DEUTSCHE GESANDTSCHAFT
IMPERIAL GERMAN LEGATION

Dongjiaomin Xiang
(Gesandtschaftsstraße/Sodenstraße),
Beijing (Peking)
Dongjiaomin Xiang
(Legation Street/Soden Street),
Beijing (Peking)

Architekt. Architect
Ernst Ohlmer[48]

Bauherr. Client
Auswärtiges Amt
Ministry of Foreign Affairs

Bauzeit. Construction time
1875–1879, spätere Umbauten
1875–1879, later converted

Zustand. Condition
Das Gebäude wurde im Sommer 1985 abgetragen, Neubau des Capital Hotels.
Building was pulled down in summer 1985 and replaced by the Capital Hotel.

Die Gebäude der deutschen Gesandtschaft wurden in einem europäisch-chinesischen Mischstil errichtet. Das Wohnhaus des Gesandten und das gegenüberliegende Kanzleigebäude waren eingeschossig. Der Eingang zum Grundstück war chinesisch gestaltet, steinerne Löwen bewachten das Torgebäude. Ein Merkmal vieler chinesischer Bauwerke ist die im Innenraum sichtbare Dachkonstruktion. Beim Wohnhaus des Gesandten war die Dachuntersicht mit einer Kassettendecke verkleidet, die abwechselnd mit dem deutschen Reichsadler und dem chinesischen Drachen bemalt waren. Europäische und chinesische Möbel statteten die Repräsentationsräume der Gesandtschaft aus.[49]

Das Grundstück wurde südlich durch die hohe Stadtmauer der Mandschustadt begrenzt, die damals in diesem Bereich nur von Europäern betreten werden durfte. Gesandtenwohnhaus, Kanzleigebäude und das Kommandeurswohnhaus lagen an der Nordgrenze des Grundstücks, der Gesandtschaftsstraße. Die deutsche Gesandtschaft besaß einen sehr schönen Garten.[50] Im Osten schlossen die heute noch gut erhaltenen Gebäude der 1902/04 erbauten Belgischen Gesandtschaft an das Grundstück an. Bereits vor dem Ersten Weltkrieg forderte man einen Neubau. So schrieb der *Ostasiatische Lloyd* 1911: »Während dann nach dem Boxerjahr fast alle Gesandtschaften neue große Paläste errichten ließen, hat die deutsche Gesandtschaft sich auch seitdem mit den alten Gebäuden begnügt. (…) Wiederholt sind mehr oder weniger umfangreiche Ausbesserungen notwendig geworden; jetzt aber dürfte endlich auch das Deutsche Reich sich zu einem angemessenen, würdigen Umbau entschließen müssen.«[51]

The German legation building was built in a mixture of European and Chinese styles; the ambassador's residence stood opposite the legation chancellery and both were single-storey buildings. The entrance to the site was Chinese in style with stone lions »guarding« the gate building. A feature of many Chinese buildings is the way that the roof structure is visible in the interior. In the ambassador's residence, the underside of the roof was covered by a coffered ceiling which had alternating pictures of the German imperial eagle and the Chinese dragon. The reception rooms of the legation were fitted with both European and Chinese furnishings.[49]

The site was bordered to the south by the high city wall of Manchu City. The ambassador's residence, chancellery and commander's residence were on the northern border of the site. The German legation had a beautiful garden.[50] The grounds were often photographed from the city wall, to which only Europeans had access at the time. The site was bordered to the east by the Belgian legation buildings which were built in 1902/04 and are still in very good condition.

Requests for a new building for the German legation had been made even before the First World War. In 1911, the *Ostasiatische Lloyd* had the following to say on the topic: »Whereas after the Boxer year almost all of the legations built new premises, the German mission has made do with the old building. (…) More or less extensive improvements have had to be made to the building on several occasions; it is about time, however, that the German Empire embarked on an appropriate conversion of the building.«[51]

大德國欽差公署

地址：北京東交民巷（使館街，鹽場大街）
建築師：恩斯特·奧爾默⟨48⟩
業主：外交部
建造日期：一八七五年至一八七九年
現狀：一九八五年夏拆除，新建新僑飯店

德國公使館的建造使用了中西結合的建築手法。大使的住宅和辦公室均為平房。公使館的大門前依照中國的風格習慣立了一對石獅。中國建築室內的木梁架暴露在外的特點被採用。大使住宅內的天花板是由繪著德國鷹徽和中國彩龍圖案的花格鑲板裝飾起來的。公使館的會客廳擺設著歐式和中式家俱。⟨49⟩

公使館的南端是高高的內城城牆。大使的住宅、辦公處以及武官的住宅均在北端使館街上。德國公使館有一座美麗別緻的花園。⟨50⟩對歐洲人來說，德國公使館是攝影取景的最佳背景。德國公使館的東面是一九零二年到一九零四修建的比利時公使館。這座建築至今仍保存完好。

早在第一次世界大戰之前就有人建議重建公使館。一九一一年，《德文新報》作了如下報導："義和團運動之後，几乎所有的公使館都在大興土木。唯有德國公使館對那些舊房子還戀戀不捨……盡管大修小補不斷，現在也該下決心改建舊房，使之無愧於德意志帝國。"⟨51⟩

公使的住宅，約一九零一年。

德國公使館內觀，攝於一九零五年左右。
使館大門入口，約一九零一年。

KETTELER-DENKMAL
KETTELER MONUMENT

Chongwenmennei Dajie (Hatamen Street, vor dem Lockhart Hospital), Beijing (Peking)
Chongwenmennei Dajie (Hatamen Street, in front of the Lockhart Hospital), Beijing (Peking)

Bauherr. Client
Kaiserlich chinesische Regierung
Imperial Chinese government

Bauzeit. Construction time
26. Juni 1901 – 18. Januar 1903
26 June 1901 – 18 January 1903

Zustand. Condition
Seit 1919 neuer Standort im Zentralpark (Zhongshan Gongyuan). Das Denkmal ist gut erhalten, die Inschriften wurden verändert.
At its new location in the Central Park (Zhongshan Gongyuan) since 1919 and is well preserved; the inscription has been changed.

*Dieses Monument
ist auf Befehl Seiner Majestät des Kaisers von China errichtet worden.
Für den an dieser Stätte
durch ruchlose Mörderhand
am 20. Juni 1900 gefallenen
Kaiserlich deutschen Gesandten
Freiherr Clemens von Ketteler.
Zum ewigen Gedächtnis an seinen Namen,
zum bleibenden Beweise für den Zorn
des Kaisers ob dieser Freveltat,
Zur Warnung für Alle.*[53]

*This monument
was built by order of His Majesty Emperor of China.
For the German Ambassador
Freiherr Clemens von Ketteler
brutally murdered on this site on 20 June 1900.
To the eternal memory of his name,
as a permanent expression of the anger
felt by the Emperor at this deed,
as a warning to all.*[53]

Der Ehrenbogen, chinesisch Paifang (Pailou), war ein typisches Denkmal chinesischer Städte. Aus Holz oder Stein gefertigt, überspannte er die Straße und erinnerte an außergewöhnliche Persönlichkeiten.
Das Ketteler-Denkmal wurde von Prinz Chun (Tschun) im Januar 1903 eingeweiht. Verwendet wurde weißer Marmor, die Gesamtbreite beträgt 17,50 Meter, die Höhe des mittleren Daches etwa 11 Meter.[52] Das Denkmal trug in den Sprachen Deutsch, Chinesisch und Latein über den Durchgängen die nebenstehende Inschrift.
Über die Errichtung des Denkmals schrieb der *Ostasiatische Lloyd*: »Das Denkmal wird im Stile der bekannten chinesischen Ehrenpforte aus massiven Steinen gebaut; (…) zum Transport eines einzelnen Blockes waren etwa 150 Pferde notwendig. Alle Steine wurden erst auf dem Bauplatz behauen. Nachdem die Steinmetze ihre Tätigkeit beendet haben, ist der Aufbau im Gange. (…) Zum Bau des Gerüstes, welches zeitweise eine enorme Last tragen muß, sind ausschließlich Stangen von etwas mehr als Armdicke verwendet; zehn bis fünfzehn solcher Stangen sind mit Tauen zusammengebunden und ersetzen so die notwendigen Strebebäume.«[54]
Der Standort des Denkmals, die Hatamen-Straße war eine der Hauptverkehrsstraßen Beijings in Nord-Süd-Richtung und von vielen Ehrenbögen überspannt. Sie führte in die Nähe des Außenministeriums in der Oststadt und zum Lama-Tempel im Norden. In ihrem südlichen Abschnitt begrenzte sie auf der östlichen Seite das Gesandtschaftsviertel.
Am Ende des Ersten Weltkriegs wurde das Denkmal an der Hatamen-Straße abgetragen und am Eingang des damaligen Zentralparks wiederaufgebaut. Die Inschrift wurde geändert in eine lateinisch und chinesische: »Dem Sieg des Rechts.«[55] Seit 1953 trägt es die Inschrift: »baowei heping« (Verteidigt den Frieden) in der Handschrift des Dichters Guo Moruo. An Clemens von Ketteler erinnern heute Denkmäler in seiner Geburtsstadt Münster in Westfalen.

The commemorative arch, Chinese *Paifang* (P'ailou) was a common monument in Chinese cities. Made of wood or stone, it spanned the street and was erected to the memory of exceptional persons.
The Ketteler memorial was inaugurated by Prince Chun (Tschun) in January 1903. It is made of white marble and is 17.5 metres wide, the height of the highest point of the arch is approximately 11 metres.[52] The monument bore an inscription in German, Chinese and Latin above the passages, given in the margin.
The *Ostasiatische Lloyd* published the following commentary on the erection of the monument: »The monument is built of massive stone in the style of the famous Chinese commemorative arch; (…) Some 150 horses were needed to transport just one stone. All of the stones were hewn on the construction site. When the stonemasons had finished their work, construction got under way. The scaffold, which at times must bear enormous weights, is made solely from poles little thicker than a human arm; ten to fifteen of these poles are tied together with ropes and thus replace the necessary bracing.«[54]
The street where the monument stands, Hatamen Street, was one of Beijing's main north-south thoroughfares and was spanned by numerous honorary arches. It passed near the Ministry of Foreign Affairs in the east city and further on to the Lama Temple in the north.
The southern section of the street formed the eastern boundary of the diplomatic quarter.
At the end of the First World War the monument was removed from Hatamen Street and erected at the entrance of the then Central Park. The inscription was changed in Latin and Chinese: »To the Victory of Right.«[55] Since 1953 it bears the inscription »*baowei heping*« (Defend the peace) in the handwriting of the poet Guo Moruo. There are other monuments marking the memory of Clemens von Ketteler in his birthplace Munster in Westphalia, Germany.

克林德紀念碑

地址：北京崇門外大街；原哈德門大街，同仁醫院前面。
業主：大清政府
建造日期：一九零一年六月二十一日至一九零三年一月十八日
現狀：一九一九年遷移至中央公園（中山公園）保存完好，碑文已改動

牌坊是中國典型的紀念性建築，分石制、木制兩種。在城鎮里，牌坊巍然跨越街道的兩端，紀念那些傑出的人物。
一九零三年，皇太子（載淳）主持了克林德紀念牌的落成典禮儀式。這座漢白玉牌坊寬十七點五米，中央門樓高十一米。(52)碑文分別用德語、漢語和拉丁文三種文字鐫刻於正樓的額坊上：
謹尊聖旨建樹此牌坊
茲紀念一九零零年六月二十日被謀殺之德意志帝國公使，克林德公英名與牌坊永存
立此牌坊告誡天下之臣民，聖皇不恕天下之罪行。(53)
《德文新報》對紀念牌坊的建造作了如下報導："紀念牌坊按照中國著名的凱旋門風格用石塊建成。運輸這樣的一塊巨石要用一百五十四馬。石塊的雕鑿加工均在建築工地上進行。經石匠精雕細琢後堆砌安裝。令人贊嘆的是，中國工匠的極其簡單的工具縣吊起沉重的石塊。他們用比胳臂稍粗的竹筒搭建支架，以此承受巨石的負荷。十至十五根竹筒用繩索扎結在一起就可代替建築支架必不可少的支撐柱。"(54)
紀念牌坊位於南北走向的交通干道崇文門內的大街上。崇文門大街東至外交部，北抵雍和宮，南達使館區，沿街立有多間牌坊。第一次世界大戰後，克林德紀念牌坊被拆除。此後移址當時中央公園的入口處並改名為"公理戰勝牌坊"碑文只用了漢語和拉丁語。(55)一九五三年，牌坊再度改名為"保衛和平"石牌坊。詩人郭沫若題詞，鐫刻於正樓額坊上。人們在克林德的故鄉，威斯特法倫的明斯特爾城又為他立了一塊紀念碑。

克林德紀念碑，約一九零五年。
位於中山公園的保衛和平紀念碑，一九九二年。

DEUTSCHES GARNISONS-LAZARETT
GERMAN GARRISON HOSPITAL

Nördlich der Dongjiaomin Xiang (Yorkstraße),
Beijing (Peking)
North of Dongjiaomin Xiang (York Street),
Beijing (Peking)

Bauleitung. Site architect
Ludwig, Garnisonsbauinspektor[56]
Ludwig, garrison building inspector[56]

Bauherr. Client
Ostasiatische Besatzungs-Brigade
East Asia Occupying Brigade

Bauzeit. Construction time
um 1905–1906
approximately 1905–1906

Zustand. Condition
Das Gebäude wurde um 1985 abgetragen.
Heute steht dort ein modernes Krankenhaus.
Pulled down around 1985 and replaced
by a modern hospital.

Das Lazarett war wie die benachbarte Deutsch-Asiatische Bank in der Art der deutschen Neorenaissance erbaut. Giebel an den Seiten und in der Mitte des Gebäudes gliederten die Südfassade. Mit Granitstein und Rustikamauerwerk waren Teile der Fassade verkleidet und die Gebäudekanten hervorgehoben. Ursprünglich sollte das Lazarett einen Turm erhalten. Militärische Überlegungen sprachen dagegen, da bei einem erneuten Angriff auf das Gesandtschaftsviertel ein Turm der feindlichen Artillerie das Einschießen wesentlich erleichtert hätte.[57]

Der zweigeschossige Bau mit Veranden vor den Krankenzimmern, lag abseits der Gesandtschaftsstraße, hinter dem deutschen Offizierskasino und den Wohnhäusern der Offiziere. In enger Zusammenarbeit mit dem Lazarett stand eine Poliklinik für chinesische Patienten.[58] Für ihre erfolgreichen Behandlungen erhielten die deutschen Ärzte von ihren Patienten Ehrentafeln, die sie im Flur aufhängten.[59]

Like its neighbour the German-Asian Bank, the garrison hospital was built in German neo-Renaissance style. Gables at the side and centre of the building provided the alignment for the south façade. Parts of the façade were covered in granite and rough-textured masonry popular among German architects at the time; the quoins were also emphasised. It was originally planned to give the hospital a tower. However, this decision was reconsidered for military reasons; such a tower would have made work much easier for the enemy artillery in the case of another attack on the diplomatic quarter.[57]

The two-storey building with verandas in front of the wards was located off Legation Street, behind the German Officers' Casino and the officers' residences. A clinic for Chinese patients worked in close co-operation with the garrison hospital.[58] The doctors received plaques from their patients in gratitude for successful treatment which were hung in the hospital hall.[59]

Deutsches Lazarett, Südansicht, um 1910
German Garrison Hospital, view from the south, around 1910

德國野戰醫院

地址：北京東交民巷；原江米巷
建築指導：路德維希，衛戍部隊建築總監〈56〉
業主：東亞戰領軍兵團
建造日期：約一九零五年至一九零六年
現狀：一九八五年樓房被拆除，現為國仁醫院

野戰醫院的建造與接鄰的德華銀行一樣，應用了德國文藝復興復古的建築手法。正中和兩側的山牆使主立面的輪廓更加分明、清晰。建築師運用不同的石料點綴立面，以粗石勒腳，用大理石砌築牆角。按照最初的設計，野戰醫院設有塔樓。然而，從戰略上考慮建造塔樓不妥當，因為當敵人進攻時，高聳的塔樓最容易被炮火擊中。〈57〉
野戰醫院有二層樓，沿著病房外圍是券式外廊。醫院離大使館街不遠，在軍官俱樂部和住宅的後面。為中國病人開設的診所與野戰醫院配合默契。〈58〉診所的走廊里高懸著各式各樣的金匾，中國病人以這種方法來讚揚德國醫生妙手回春的醫術。〈59〉

德國野戰醫院的南立面，約一九一零年。

Beijing

DEUTSCH-ASIATISCHE BANK
GERMAN-ASIAN BANK

Dongjiaomin Xiang
(Gesandtschaftsstraße/Scharnhorststraße),
Beijing (Peking)
Dongjiaomin Xiang (Legation Street/
Scharnhorst Street), Beijing (Peking)

Architekten. Architects
Becker & Baedeker, Shanghai[60]

Ausführung. Contractors
F.H. Schmidt, Altona, Hamburg, Tsingtau

Bauherr. Client
Deutsch-Asiatische Bank, Berlin
German-Asian Bank, Berlin

Bauzeit. Construction time
1906–1907

Zustand. Condition
Das Gebäude wurde im Januar 1992
abgetragen.
Pulled down in January 1992.

Die Deutsch-Asiatische Bank war ein gutes Beispiel für einen deutschen Neorenaissancebau – und damit für Beijing äußerst ungewöhnlich. Man plante 1991, den Bau unter Denkmalschutz zu stellen, doch das Abbruchunternehmen kam den Behörden zuvor. Der dreigeschossige Turm mit hoher Dachhaube betonte die Gebäudeecke und machte die Bank zu einem der höchsten Gebäude im Gesandtschaftsviertel. In einem Schreiben der Ostasiatischen Besatzungs-Brigade an die deutsche Gesandtschaft erinnerte das Militär an die Gefahr, daß ein solcher Turm feindlicher Artillerie das Einschießen wesentlich erleichtern würde und die direkt daneben befindlichen Offizierswohnungen und Mannschaftsbaracken (Waldersee Kasernen) dadurch gefährdet wären. Aus diesen Gründen hatte man bei dem Garnisons-Lazarett und einem Wasserreservoir auf einen Turm verzichtet. Obwohl die Bank in einem Schreiben an den Gesandten vom Bau eines Turmes absah, wurde er dennoch errichtet.[61]

In die Putzfassade waren feine Scheinfugen eingeritzt, die Natursteinquader imitierten. Eine hölzerne Veranda im ersten Obergeschoß schloß das Gebäude nach Osten ab. Unterhalb der Traufe ließen die Architekten männliche Masken mit Bart und riesigen Ohren modellieren, ebenso auf den Schlußsteinen der Bogenfenster. In Shanghai hielten chinesische Betrachter diese Dekorationen für die Hausgötter der Ausländer. Die hier verwendeten Fratzengesichter, Maskarone – in Europa in der Spätrenaissance und im Barock verwendet –, gehörten zu den ganz wenigen noch erhaltenen europäischen Menschenskulpturen an chinesischen Gebäuden. Die chinesische Kupfermünze mit ihrem quadratischen Loch in der Mitte verwendeten die Architekten an den Zaunpfosten als Symbol für das Bankgebäude.

Die Deutsch-Asiatische Bank in Beijing war das Schwestergebäude des deutschen Club Concordia in Shanghai. Beide Bauten sind von denselben Architekten entworfen worden.

The German-Asian Bank was an excellent example of a building in German neo-Renaissance style, and as such was a very unusual building for Beijing. It was planned to put a conservation order on the building in 1991, however, those wishing to tear down the building succeeded in submitting their plans to the officials first. The three-storey tower with its high roof emphasised the corner of the building and made the bank one of the highest buildings in the diplomatic quarter. In a letter to the German legation, the East Asia Occupying Brigade drew attention to the fact that a tower of this nature would make it easier for enemy artillery to strike and would, thus, endanger the nearby officers' residences and barracks (Waldersee barracks). For this reason, it had been decided not to add a tower to the garrison hospital and a building for a water reservoir. Although the bank agreed not to build the tower in a letter to the Ambassador, it was built in the end.[61]

The plastered brick façade had artificial joints which were intended to give a natural stone effect. A wooden veranda on the first floor terminated the building to the east. Grotesque male faces with beards and enormous ears decorated the keystones of the arched windows and under the eaves. Chinese observers in Shanghai believed these decorations to be the foreigners' house gods (josses). These grotesque faces or mascarons, which were common in Europe during the late Renaissance and Baroque periods, were one of the few surviving examples of Western human sculptures on Chinese buildings. The Chinese copper coin with its square hole in the centre mounted on the fence posts as a symbol for a bank building.

The German-Asian Bank in Beijing was the twin building of the German Club Concordia in Shanghai. Both buildings were designed by the same architects.

德華銀行

地址：北京東交民巷；原使館街（沙恩霍斯特街口）
建築師：貝克·培迪克，上海
施工：漢堡阿爾托納區F·H·施密特公司
業主：德華銀行
建造日期：一九零六年至一九零七年
現狀：一九九二被拆除

德華銀行是成功地運用德國文藝復興式復古風格的范例。在北京是一幢不同凡嚮的建築物。一九九一年，人們計劃把樓房列入國家文物保護對象，但拆建公司搶先一步，走在文保單位之前。銀行大樓屬使館區最高的建築物之一，圓頂的塔樓有三層樓高。東亞佔領軍駐華兵團在給德國使館的一封信中申稱這樣的高塔易招引敵方炮兵的轟擊，會殃及附近的兵營。正因為考慮到這一點，當年在建造野戰醫院和水庫時，建造塔樓的計劃被放棄了。盡管銀行也寫信給使館表示不建塔樓，而實際上卻沒有遵守諾言。在立面的混水牆面上鑿出類似接縫的方形凹槽，使立面看上去就像用天然方石鑲飾一樣。大樓東面是木制敞廊，屋檐下及券窗上沿裝點著蓄胡大耳的人臉雕飾。上海人把這種頭像看成是外國人的家神臉譜。文藝復興後期及巴洛克時期的建築常用這種怪臉像做裝飾。這種怪臉人物像在中國現存的西洋建築物上已不多見。該建築用仿中國銅錢的石刻裝點柵欄入口，以表示其銀行身份。北京德華銀行和上海德國總會康科迪婭總會出於同一建築師之手，可謂是姐妹樓。

德華銀行西南角，一九零七年。
使館街上的主入口，一九零七年。
怪臉頭像，攝於一九九二年元月。

PEKING CLUB/INTERNATIONAL CLUB

Heutige Funktion. Current use
Standing Committee of Beijing Municipal Peoples Congress
Taiji Chang 8 (Marco Polo Street), Beijing (Peking)

Architekt. Architect
Curt Rothkegel

Baukosten. Building costs
etwa 216 000 Goldmark
approximately 216 000 gold marks

Bauherr. Client
International Club Peking

Bauzeit. Construction time
März 1911 – Oktober 1912
March 1911 – October 1912

Zustand. Condition
Das Gebäude ist gut erhalten, die Innenräume sind verändert.
Well preserved; the interior has been altered.

Ehem. Peking Club, Westansicht, 1992
The former Peking Club, view from the west, 1992

Der ehemalige International Club ist ein zweigeschossiges, relativ unauffälliges Gebäude mit Veranden auf der West- und Südseite. Das Walmdach ist flach geneigt und hat einen weiten Dachüberstand. Ein großer Jugendstilgiebel sitzt auf dem Dach über der Westfassade. Der Architekt verzichtete bewußt bei diesem internationalen Gebäude auf deutsche Stilmerkmale. Die innere Organisation des Gebäudes entspricht dem ebenfalls von Rothkegel erbauten deutschen Club Concordia in Tianjin.

Zur Einweihung des Klubgebäudes veröffentlichte der *Ostasiatische Lloyd* eine Beschreibung des Gebäudes: »Im Erdgeschoß befinden sich außer den Umkleidezimmern und den Toiletten die große Halle, das Kneipzimmer, die behaglich-vornehm eingerichtete Bibliothek. Längs der ganzen Südfront läuft eine 3,75 Meter breite Veranda. Im ersten Stock haben wir außer mehreren kleinen Eßzimmern für Privatgesellschaften, die auch (...) als Spielzimmer dienen können, und den dazu gehörigen Toilettenräumen, den großen Gesellschafts (Ball)-Saal und den Theatersaal, dessen Bühne eine Ausdehnung von 10 zu 9 Metern hat. (...) Im zweiten Stock liegen die Wohnung des Geschäftsführers, Küche und Vorratsräume. Alle Räume haben Zentralheizung (...)«[62]

Seit 1860 gab es die ersten Gesandtschaften in Beijing, wenige Jahre später wurde der Peking Club gegründet. Zuerst diente er lediglich Sportzwecken wie Pferderennen. Während es in den anderen ausländischen Niederlassungen Chinas jeweils mehrere nationale Klubs gab, stand dieser allen Ausländern Beijings offen. Im Winter wurde auf dem Grundstück des Klubs eine Eisbahn errichtet, im Sommer Tennis gespielt. Das erste Klubhaus befand sich bis zum Boxerkrieg auf dem Grundstück der deutschen Gesandtschaft, das zweite in der Thomannstraße.

The former International Club is a two-storey, relatively modest building with verandas on the west and south sides. The hipped roof is quite low and the roof overhang is wide. There is a large Jugendstil gable structure on the roof over the west façade. The German architect consciously elected not to use any elements of German style on this international building. The interior organisation of the building is reminiscent of the German Club Concordia in Tianjin, which was also designed by Rothkegel.

The *Ostasiatische Lloyd* published the following description of the building on the occasion of the official opening: »In addition to the changing rooms and toilets, the ground floor houses the large hall, the bar and the elegant and comfortable library. There is a 3.75 metre-wide veranda along the entire south façade. In addition to several small dining rooms for private parties, which can also (...) be used as games rooms, and the accompanying cloakrooms, the first floor contains the large function (ball) room and the theatre which has a 9 × 10 metre-wide stage. (...) The director's apartment, the kitchen and storerooms are on the second floor. All rooms are centrally heated. (...)«[62]

The first legations were established in Beijing in 1860 and the Peking Club was founded a few years later. Initially it was used solely for sporting purposes and organised horse-racing events. Whereas the other foreign settlements in China had several national clubs, all foreigners in Beijing met at this club. An ice-rink was built in the grounds during the winter and in summer there were tennis courts. Up to the Boxer Rebellion, the first club house was in the grounds of the German legation; the second was in Thomann Street.

前北平俱樂部西立面，一九九二年。

北平俱樂部／國際俱樂部

現用途：人民代表大會常務委員會辦公樓
地址：北京台基廠大街八號
建築師：羅克格
建造費用：約二十點六萬馬克
業主：北平國際俱樂部
建造日期：一九一一年三月至一九一二年十月
現狀：樓體保存完好，內部有所改變

當年的國際俱樂部不起眼的兩層樓房在西、南兩側設敞廊屋頂坡度平緩，屋檐伸出很遠，西面的屋頂是具有輕年派風格的山牆頂樓。德國建築師考慮到俱樂部的國際性，有意識地捨棄了德國典型的建築風格。內部結構佈局與天津的出於同一建築師之手的德國康科迪婭總會相似。《德文新報》就俱樂部的落成作了如下評論："一樓是更衣室，廁所，大廳，酒吧和舒適高雅的圖書館。一條三點七五米寬的券式外廊橫貫於南西樓面。二樓有許多供私人聚會的小餐廳，這些小餐室也可用作遊戲室，此外還有廁所，巨大的交誼舞廳和劇場。劇場舞台面積為十乘九平米……三樓是俱樂部經理住宅、廚房和儲藏室。俱樂部大樓設置中央供暖設備。"〈62〉

一八六二年北京就有了外國公使館，北平俱樂部成立在這之後幾年，最初旨在組織各種體育活動，如賽馬等。各國的租界區內均設有其各自獨立的俱樂部。而北平國際俱樂部卻向所有外國人開放。冬季，俱樂部開設溜冰場，夏季可以打網球。義和團運動前國際俱樂部在德國使館的地界上，後來遷至托曼大街（音譯）

BEIDAIHE

GESANDTSCHAFTS-SOMMERHÄUSER
LEGATION SUMMER RESIDENCES

Heutige Funktion. Current use
Erholungsheim des Zentralkomitees der kommunistischen Partei
Xihaitan Lu/Xiyi Lu (Landstraße von Rocky Point nach Westend), Beidaihe (Peitaiho)
Holiday home of the Central Committee of the Communist Party
Xihaitan Lu/Xiyi Lu (Land Street from Rocky Point to Westend), Beidaihe (Peitaiho)

Architekt. Architect
E. Herold[63]

Bauleiter. Site architect
Ludwig, Garnisonsbauinspektor
Ludwig, Garrison building inspector

Baukosten. Building costs
78 000 Goldmark
78 000 gold marks

Bauherr. Client
Auswärtiges Amt, Deutsches Reich
Ministry of Foreign Affairs

Bauzeit. Construction time
1907–1908

Zustand. Condition
Das Gebäude ist sehr gut erhalten.
Very well preserved.

Chinesinnen im Seebad Weihai, Karikatur, 1912
Chinese women at the seaside resort of Weihai, cartoon, 1912

Das ehemalige Gesandtenhaus und das Beamtenhaus stehen relativ nahe beieinander, auf einem etwa sechs Meter hohen felsigen Geländesprung mit Blick über das südlich vorgelagerte Bohai-Meer. Nördlich und westlich davon lagen die Gebäude der deutschen Offiziere und Mannschaften der deutschen Gesandtschaftsschutzwache.[64] Von der Terrasse des Gesandtenhauses führten zwei halbkreisförmige Treppenläufe hinab zum Strand.

Ungewöhnlich war bei diesem Bau die Kombination von Arkaden eines Sommerhauses mit einem Fachwerkgiebel im deutschen Heimatstil. Das Dach war mit chinesischen Ziegeln gedeckt und besaß auch die typisch chinesischen dreieckigen Entlüftungsöffnungen am Giebel. Das Beamtenhaus lag leicht versetzt dahinter. Auch hier wurden Fachwerkgiebel und luftige Arkaden kombiniert. In dem internationalen Seebad Beidaihe wollte man sich durch die typisch deutschen Giebelformen von den Bauten der anderen Ausländer unterscheiden.

Der *Ostasiatische Lloyd* beschreibt das Anwesen anläßlich der Einweihung durch den Gesandten Graf von Rex im Sommer 1908: »Eine langgestreckte Meeresbucht, landwärts von mächtig ragenden wildgezackten Felszügen umgeben, das Ufer an den beiden Enden mit europäischen Villen bedeckt, das ist das Seebad Peitaiho, in dessen Mitte in erhöhter Lage die Häuser erbaut sind, die dem deutschen Gesandten in Peking und seinen Beamten im Sommer die Erholung bieten sollen, die das (…) Klima Pekings (…) nicht zu geben vermag. (…) Jetzt stehen die beiden Häuser aber vollendet da, keine prunkhaften Luxusbauten, aber ein würdiges Unterkommen für die Gesandtschaft, das durch die geschickt ausgewählte Lage inmitten der Seekolonie den ganzen Strand beherrscht. So dicht am Meere, daß das Rauschen der Wellen ununterbrochen zu ihnen dringt, und dabei doch so erhöht, daß die breite Terrasse des Gesandtenhauses einen weiten Ausblick auf die See, den Strand und die den Hinter-

The former ambassador's residence and officials' residence are relatively close to each other on an approximately 6-metre high cliff-like jump with a view over the Bohai sea. The accommodation for the German officers and legation troops were located to the north and west.[64] There were semi-circular stairways leading from the terrace of the ambassador's house to the beach.

An unusual feature of this building was the combination of typical summer house arcades and the latticework gable in the German vernacular style. The roof was of Chinese tiles and also had the typical Chinese ventilation openings on the gable. The officials' residence was beside the ambassador's house, slightly lower down on the site. Half-timbered gables and airy arcades were also used here. The typical German gables used here in the international sea resort of Beidaihe were, no doubt, an expression of the desire on the part of the émigrés to present themselves as a nation. The gables also functioned as a souvenir of home. Holiday architecture – homesick architecture?

The *Ostasiatische Lloyd* describes the scene on the occasion of the official opening presided over by ambassador Count von Rex in summer 1908: »The sea resort of Peitaiho consists of an elongated cove surrounded on the land side by powerful overhanging rugged cliffs, with both ends of the shore populated by European villas. In the middle of all this, there are houses built on elevated sites which will provide holiday recreation for the German ambassador in Peking and his officials in summer, which (…) Peking's climate (…) does not afford. (…) The two houses now stand completed, not extravagantly luxurious edificee, but fitting accommodation for the legation staff, and thanks to the cleverly selected location they stand right in the middle of the resort and have a command of the entire beach. The two houses are so close to the sea that it is possible to hear the uninterrupted roaring of the waves and they are so high up in the cliffs that the wide ter-

當年的公使別墅與外交官員的別墅相距不遠，座落於一個高於周圍地面約六米的岩石坡上。站在坡頂上，南面的勃海風光可盡收眼底。在使館別墅的北側和西側是德國使館警衛隊官兵的住房。〈64〉使館別墅的平台前兩條半圓形的階梯通向海灘。別墅的建築風格別具匠心，券柱式外廊與具有德國鄉土風情的顯露式木構山牆珠聯璧合，屋頂鋪設中國瓦，山牆上裝飾著典型的中國式三角氣窗。公使別墅的斜後方是外交官員的別墅。這幢建築物也兼用了德國式山牆與中國式通風拱廊。在北戴河這一國際性的海濱浴場採用典型的德國式山牆表達了德僑對本民族的推崇及其思鄉的情感。別墅是避暑消夏之所，亦是寄托鄉情之處？

《德華新報》就德國公使馮‧雷克斯伯爵一九零八年夏參加公使館別墅落成儀式典禮一事作了報導："千姿百態的岩石環繞坦蕩的海灣，海灣兩端沿岸別墅星羅棋布，這就是北戴河，為避開北京的炎夏，德國公使館在海灣中央的高地上為公使和外交官員建造別墅。……現在這一工程已大功告成，雖數不上豪華型建築，然而與使館的身份卻相配無疑。兩幢房子座落在北戴河的中心，引人注目的地段。面向大海，站在公使別墅的平台上可耳聞喧嘩的海浪，鳥瞰美麗的海灣，眺望連綿的群山。"〈65〉

北戴河在過去和現在都是僑居中國北方的歐洲人浴場。鐵路的鋪設給北戴河的交通提供了便利，從天津乘火車僅二百四十五公里；北京則有三百八十五公里，從火車站到海濱渡假區只有八公里的路程。一八九六年，北戴河大約只有二十座別墅，到一八九九年已發展到近百幢。〈66〉一九零四年，德國大使馮‧牧姆為興建德國使館避暑別墅在北戴河置地約六萬五千平米。

在北海浴場的中國婦女，漫畫，一九一二年。

德國使館別墅

現用途：中共黨中央委員會療養院
地址：北戴河西海灘路（西一路口）
建築師：E赫洛爾特〈63〉
工程指導：路德維希‧衛戎軍團建築總監
建築費用：七點八萬金馬克
業主：德意志帝國外交部
建造日期：一九零七年至一九零八年
現狀：保存完好

BEIDAIHE

Treppe zum ehem. Gesandtenhaus, 1992
Gesandtenhaus, Südwestansicht, 1908
Beamtenhaus, Südwestansicht, 1908
Steps to the former ambassador's residence, 1992
Ambassador's residence, view from the south-west, 1908
Residence of a civil servant, view from the south-west, 1908

grund abschließende Gebirgskette gestattet, liegen die beiden Häuser da (…).«[65]

Beidaihe war und ist noch heute das Seebad der in Nordchina lebenden Europäer. Mit dem Bau der Eisenbahn wurde der Ort bequem erreichbar. Er liegt etwa 245 Bahnkilometer von Tianjin und 385 Kilometer von Beijing entfernt. Vom Bahnhof waren es noch 8 Kilometer bis zu der Feriensiedlung am Strand. 1896 gab es bereits um die 20 Sommerhäuser, 1899 waren es fast 100 Sommerhäuser.[66] 1904 hatte der deutsche Gesandte von Mumm das etwa 65 000 m² große Grundstück zur Einrichtung eines Sommerquartiers für die deutsche Gesandtschaft gekauft.

race of the ambassador's house commands a panoramic view of the sea, the beach and the mountain range in the background (…).«[65]

Beidaihe was and still is the resort favoured by Europeans living in northern China. The construction of the railway made it easier to reach. It is approximately 245 kilometres by train from Tianjin and 385 kilometres from Beijing. The railway station is 8 kilometres away from the beach resort. As early as 1896, there were approximately 20 summer houses, and by 1899 the figure had reached almost 100.[66] In 1904 the German ambassador von Mumm purchased the approximately 65 000 m² site for the construction of a summer residence for the German legation staff.

北戴河
公使別墅西南角‧一九零八年。
外交官員別墅西南角‧一九零八年。
通往前公使別墅的台階‧一九九二年。

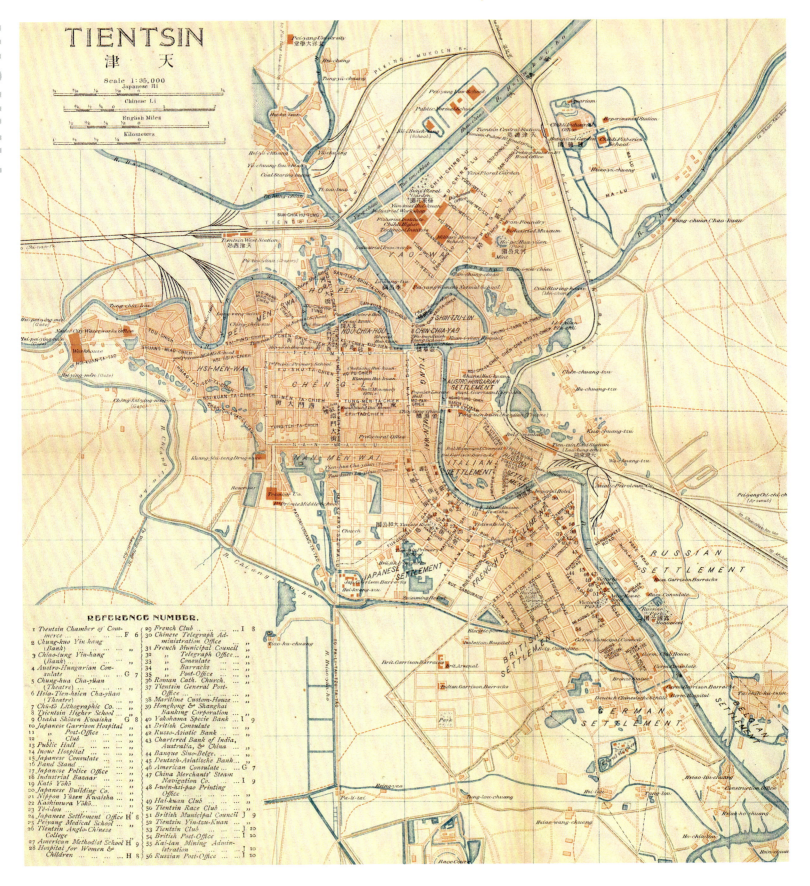

TIANJIN (TIENTSIN)

Das Handelszentrum Tianjin war der Kreuzungspunkt wichtiger Wasserstraßen. Die Stadt liegt 50 km vom Meer entfernt und ist von dort über den Hai He-Fluß (Hai-Ho, Peiho) mit Dampfschiffen erreichbar. Sie war der Seehafen Beijings, das 130 km entfernt und mit der Stadt über den Hai He und einem weiteren Kanal verbunden ist. In Tianjin endete der aus dem Süden Chinas kommende fast 1800 km lange Kaiserkanal.

Das chinesische Stadtzentrum Tianjins hatte einen rechteckigen Grundriß und war bis 1901 von einer 10 Meter hohen Mauer umgeben. Mehrere Vororte lagen vor allem nördlich davon, wo auch der Kaiserkanal in den Hai He mündete, sich also ein großer Warenumschlagplatz befand. Die ausländischen Niederlassungen wurden südlich der chinesischen Stadt angelegt, flußabwärts am Ufer des Hai He. Tianjin ist auf flachem Gelände erbaut. Die Umgebung bestand aus Sumpfland. Das Gelände, auf dem die Niederlassungen entstehen sollten, mußte erst trockengelegt und aufgeschüttet werden, bevor mit dem Bau von Häusern und Straßen begonnen werden konnte. Die Niederlassungen waren vom Meer aus bei Flut mit Schiffen mit einem Tiefgang von bis zu fünf Metern zu erreichen.[67] Ursprünglich betrug die Entfernung zwischen Tianjin und Dagu (Taku) am Meer 77 km, doch zwischen 1901 und 1919 wurde der Hai He mit vier Durchstichen begradigt, so daß auf dem Fluß nur noch 45 km zurückgelegt werden mußten.

Im Jahre 1905 wurde mit dem Bau von elektrischen Straßenbahnen begonnen, die ursprünglich als Transportmittel für die Arbeiter geplant waren. Sie führten um die innere chinesische Stadt und durch die japanische und französische Niederlassung, über Brücken auf der anderen Seite des Hai He zum Bahnhof der Beijing-Shenyang-Eisenbahn (Peking-Mukden) und durch die russische, italienische und österreichisch-ungarische Niederlassung. Die von ihnen erschlossenen Stadtteile

TIANJIN (TIENTSIN)

The trading centre Tianjin was at the intersection of important waterways. The city is 50 km from the sea and could be reached by steamship via the Hai He river (Hai-Ho, Peiho). Tianjin was the seaport for Beijing which is 130 km away and linked to the city by the Hai He and another canal. The almost 1800 km-long Imperial Canal from south China ended in Tianjin.

Tianjin's Chinese city centre had a grid-iron plan and up to 1901 it was surrounded by a 10 metre high wall. There were several suburbs mainly to the north where the Imperial Canal entered the Hai He and where there was a large goods distribution centre. The foreign settlements were set up south of the Chinese city, down river on the bank of the Hai He. Tianjin is built on flat land and is surrounded by a marsh. The area on which the settlements were built had to be reclaimed before building work could start on the houses and streets. At high tide the settlements could be accessed from the sea by boats with a draught of up to 5 metres.[67] The distance between Tianjin and Dagu (Taku) was originally 77 kilometres, but between 1901 and 1919 four cuts were made to straighten the Hai He, and it was then only 45 kilometres.

Work commenced on the construction of the tramlines in 1905. The trams were originally planned as a means of transport for the workers and the lines went around the Chinese city centre and through the Japanese and French concessions, across bridges to the other side of the Hai He to the railway station of the Beijing-Shenyang railway (Peking-Mukden) and through the Russian, Italian and Austro-Hungarian concessions. The areas of the city accessible by tram became better developed than the remoter areas. There was talk about extending the tram lines through the British and further on to the German concessions, but this plan was never implemented.

天津

天津既是重要的水路交通樞紐，又是經濟貿易中心之一。天津距海岸線五十公里，從那裡乘船沿海河可直達天津。天津是始於杭州全長近一千八百公里的大運河之終點。運河和海河將天津和北京連接起來。天津距北京一百三十公里，是北京通往海道的重要門戶。

天津中心地區呈長方形，一九零一年以前一直由一道十米多高的城牆所環繞。城北有許多小集鎮。那裡是運河與海河的交匯處，因而也是大規模的貨物集散地。外國租界位於舊城南部，沿著海河，順流向東伸延。天津地勢平坦，四周是沼澤地帶。在沼澤地開闢租界，建造房屋和街道，首先要對其加以治理，即排水填土。漲潮時可乘吃水不超過五米深的小船直達租界區。〈67〉天津和大沽的距離原先是七十七公里，一九零一年到一九零九年間進行的四次截彎取直改道工程，使兩地的水道距離縮短為現在的四十五公里。

一九零五年天津開始鋪設有軌電車鐵道。為了方便工人上下班，電車環繞著舊城，穿過日法租界，越過海河大橋到對岸的北京──沈陽車站（老龍頭車站），再開過俄、意、匈、奧租界。靠電車線路近的城區要比離得遠的城區發展得快。將電車線經英國租界延長到德國租界的計劃，雖得以商議，但未能付諸實施。天津周圍地區發得較早。由於鋪設鐵路的天津周圍地區開發得較早。一八八八年從天津經由唐山到開平煤礦的鐵路正式通車。這條鐵路線一直通到沈陽。〈68〉

一八九七后，天津與北京之間的鐵路也已竣工，次年，這條鐵路由單軌擴建為雙軌。一九零八年到一九一二年英德工程師承包天津到南京的鐵路工程。〈69〉津浦線車站設於舊城區北部。

第二次鴉片戰爭後天津闢為通商口岸，一八零六年，英法軍隊進犯北京，摧毀了具有巴洛克風格的皇家花園──圓明園。迫使中方接受"天津條約"。〈70〉此后外國人在北京有租界權，在天津有商業貿易租界權。一九零一至一九一七年，在天津有租界的八個國家是英、法、德、日、俄、奧、意大利、比利時。〈71〉各國租界之間

entwickelten sich besser als die abgelegenen. Zwar wurde die Möglichkeit diskutiert, die Straßenbahnlinie durch die englische weiter bis zur deutschen Niederlassung zu verlängern, doch gelangte dieser Plan nie zur Ausführung.

Bereits sehr früh wurde die Umgebung Tianjins durch Eisenbahnen erschlossen. Im Jahre 1888 eröffnete man die Bahnlinie von Tianjin nach Tangshan zu den Kaiping-Bergwerken. Diese Bahn verlängerte man weiter in Richtung Shenyang (Mukden).[68] Seit 1897 war Tianjin außerdem durch eine Eisenbahn mit Beijing verbunden, die bereits nach einem Jahr auf zwei Spuren erweitert wurde. Zwischen 1908 und 1912 bauten englische und deutsche Ingenieure die Eisenbahnlinie von Tianjin nach Nanjing (Pukow).[69] Ihr Bahnhof in Tianjin lag nördlich der inneren chinesischen Stadt.

Der zweite Opiumkrieg zwang China, auch Tianjin für den ausländischen Handel zu öffnen. 1860 waren englische und französische Truppen nach Beijing gezogen und hatten den kaiserlichen Barockgarten Yuanming Yuan zerstört, um so den »Vertrag von Tientsin« durchzusetzen.[70] In der Folge wurden ausländische Gesandtschaften in Beijing eröffnet und Handelsniederlassungen in Tianjin. Zwischen 1901 und 1917 besaßen 8 verschiedene Staaten in dieser Stadt Niederlassungen: England, Frankreich, Deutschland, Japan, Rußland, Österreich-Ungarn, Italien und Belgien.[71] Es bestanden keine Grenzen zwischen den Niederlassungen der einzelnen Nationen, aber dennoch waren es voneinander unabhängige, selbstverwaltete Gebiete mit eigenem Rechts- und Steuerwesen und einer eigenen Polizei. Im Jahre 1914 wurde die chinesische Einwohnerzahl von Tianjin mit 750 000 Menschen angegeben, hinzu kamen nur 5 400 ausländische Zivilisten und bis zu 6 000 Soldaten.[72] Die Zivilisten konnten in Tianjin in jeder der 8 Niederlassungen wohnen; es herrschte weder eine Trennung nach Nationalitäten, noch waren Chinesen davon ausgeschlossen.[73]

Tianjin was accessible by railway from a very early stage. In 1888 a railway line was opened that went from Tianjin to the Kaiping mines at Tangshan. This railway line was later extended in the direction of Shenyang (Mukden).[68] Tianjin was also linked by rail to Beijing from 1897. After only one year of operation an additional track was added to this line. Between 1908 and 1912, British and German engineers built the railway line from Tianjin to Nanjing (Pukow).[69] The station for the Tianjin-Nanjing railway (Tientsin-Pukow railway) lay to the north of the Chinese centre.

The Second Opium War forced China to open Tianjin to foreign trade. In 1860, British and French troops set out for Beijing and destroyed the imperial Baroque garden Yuanming Yuan in order to implement the »Treaty of Tientsin«.[70] After this, foreign legations were established in Beijing and the concessions in Tianjin. Between 1901 and 1917 eight different states had concessions in this city: England, France, Germany, Japan, Russia, Austria-Hungary, Italy and Belgium.[71] There were no spatial boundaries between the individual concessions, but they were independent, self-administered areas with their own legal and fiscal systems and their own police forces. In 1914, the Chinese population of Tianjin was 750 000 and there were only 5 400 foreign civilians.[72] The latter could live in any of the eight foreign concessions in Tianjin because there was no division according to nationality; the Chinese were not excluded either.[73]

The oldest two concessions, the British and the French were located to the south of the Chinese city on the bank of the Hai He. They became the economic centre of the city and the other concessions never quite managed to overtake their 35-year lead. In 1895, Germany acquired its own concession in Tianjin. Three years later Japan was able to establish its concession in an area that directly bordered the Chinese city and was, thus, in the centre of the city.

The main commercial street, the first street

沒有界線，然而各行其政，有自己的司法、財政和保安機構。一九一四年，天津的居民人數是七十五萬，外國僑民是五千四百人。[72] 外國人可任意在各租界居住，中國人也可以住進外租界。[73]

英、法租界是最早的租界，位於舊城南海河河畔，也是天津的經濟中心。三十五年后，其它國家才相繼開闢租界，人們對英法租界的經濟優勢只能望洋興嘆。一八九五年德國在天津設立租界。三年後，日本在於舊城毗鄰的地段，既市中心也建了租界。天津的商業貿易大街與海河的沿河大街平行，在法租界的地段上稱法蘭西路，越過英租界時又稱維克多利亞路，向南延伸到德租界稱威廉街，這裡也是商業街的盡頭。所有大銀行的貿易商行的營業部均設在法蘭西路和維多利亞路。一九零七年德華銀行在英租界的商業街上設立分行。直到一九一一年，德領館一直設在英租界。與上海、武漢不同，這的沿河大街上沒有什麼重要建築物，只有輪船停泊裝御貨物於此。

一九零一年法國、英國和德國的租界進一步擴大。在海河對岸又設立了四個國家的租界：奧匈租界正對著舊城區，向南是意大利租界，俄國租界，最後是占地不多的比利時租界。這些租界的興建工程進展遲緩。與此同時，人們拆除了環繞舊城的護城牆，鋪設了一條寬闊的大街。

義和團運動期間一九零零至一九零一年，天津再次為歐洲軍隊的京作戰的大本營。日本、俄國、美國、法國、美國、德國、意大利和奧地利八國的軍隊集結在天津，營救在北京被圍攻的公使館區。一九零零年八月十四日，八國聯軍解放了被圍困的人們。德國陸軍元帥瓦德西為八國聯軍統帥，一九零零年九月二日率兵九萬抵達天津。一九零一年一月，外國軍隊撤離北京和河北省，只有一千三百五十人做為使館警衛部隊繼續留駐北京。[74]

義和團運動之後外國軍隊均駐扎在天津的外國租界裡。各國軍隊均有自己的兵營，當時在天津常常可以看到不同國籍的外國官兵。[75]

隨著形勢的變化駐京的軍隊人數也在波動。義和團運動之后，軍隊一直在撤離，一九零八至一九零九年外國軍隊已裁減到

Die ältesten beiden Niederlassungen, die britische und die französische, lagen südlich der chinesischen Stadt am Ufer des Hai He. Sie entwickelten sich zum wirtschaftlichen Zentrum der Stadt. Der 35jährige Entwicklungsvorsprung konnte von den später gegründeten Niederlassungen der anderen Länder nicht aufgeholt werden. Deutschland erhielt 1895 eine eigene Niederlassung in Tianjin. Drei Jahre später konnte Japan seine Niederlassung auf einem Gebiet gründen, das direkt an die chinesische Stadt grenzte – also im Zentrum der Stadt lag.

Die repräsentative Hauptgeschäftsstraße, die erste Parallelstraße zur Uferstraße, führte als Rue de France und Victoria Road durch die französische und die englische Niederlassung und endete im Süden als Wilhelmstraße in der deutschen Niederlassung. Alle wichtigen Banken und Handelsgesellschaften besaßen im englischen und französischen Abschnitt dieser Straße ihre Geschäftshäuser. Noch 1907 baute die Deutsch-Asiatische Bank ihr neues Geschäftshaus in der englischen Niederlassung. Auch das deutsche Konsulat lag bis zur Fertigstellung eines Neubaus 1911 in der englischen Niederlassung. Anders als in den Städten Shanghai und Wuhan (Hankou) standen an der Uferstraße in Tianjin keine repräsentativen Gebäude. Hier legten Schiffe an und wurden Waren in die Lagerhäuser transportiert.

Im Jahre 1901 kamen zusätzlich zu den »Extra-Concessions« für Frankreich, England und Deutschland vier neue Niederlassungen auf der gegenüberliegenden Seite des Hai He hinzu. Direkt gegenüber der chinesischen Stadt lag die österreich-ungarische Niederlassung, südlich daran anschließend die italienische, dann die große russische und schließlich noch eine kleine belgische Niederlassung. Ihr Ausbau erfolgte meist sehr langsam. Zu dieser Zeit wurde die Stadtmauer um die innere Stadt abgetragen und eine breite Straße angelegt.

Während des Boxerkrieges (1900–1901) wurde Tianjin ein zweites Mal zum Ausgangsparallel to the embankment road passed through the French and British concessions as the Rue de France and Victoria road respectively and terminated in the south as Wilhelm Strasse in the German concession. All of the important banks and business houses had their offices in the British and French sections of this street. In 1907 the German-Asian Bank built its new building in the British concession and until a new building was completed in 1911, the German consulate was also located in the British concession. Unlike Shanghai and Wuhan (Hankow), there were no important buildings along the embankment road in Tianjin. The ships anchored here and the goods they brought were transported to the stores.

In 1901 with the acquisition of »Extra-Concessions« by France, England and Germany, four new concessions were established on the opposite bank of the Hai He. The Austro-Hungarian concession was directly opposite the Chinese city, this was bordered to the south by the Italian concession and then the large Russian concession and the small Belgian concession. This area developed very gradually. Around this time the wall around the Chinese city was demolished and a wide street built in its place.

During the Boxer Rebellion (1900–1901), Tianjin was used for the second time as a base for the European military effort against Beijing. Troops from eight countries – Japan, Russia, Great Britain, France, America, Germany, Italy and Austria – assembled here to advance to Beijing to liberate the besieged diplomatic quarter in Beijing. On 14 August 1900, the troops achieved their goal and liberated the besieged quarter. On 2 September 1900, General Field Marshal Count von Waldersee, who was the Commander-in-Chief of the International Force, arrived in Tianjin with some 90 000 soldiers. By September 1901, all of the foreign troops had left Beijing and the province of Hebei; the legation troops with 1 350 soldiers were left behind.[74]

少於四千人。〈76〉一九一一年秋，辛亥革命後，軍隊又劇增。一九一二年，在中國北部地區有駐軍一萬人，僅天津一地就有六千人。〈77〉

德國、法國和俄國支持"馬關條約"，從而鉗制日本。由此德國也有了租界。〈78〉德國商業租界面積約是零點六九平方公里，遠離中國人的貿易區。租界雖然沿著海河岸延伸長達一千六百米，但卻都不適於開設鋪店或建造庫房。所以租界內僅陸續出現了些住房。〈79〉在德國獲得租界的四年後，即一九一九年，德國人才不緊不慢地開始填海造地，鋪設街道。其原因是德國商人可以在英、法租界內舒舒服服地過日子。

德國租界分成三個部分。"北部區域"發展得最早。一九一一年辛亥革命後開始開發"南部區域"。一九零一年向中國政府無期限地租賃另一面積約一點五二平方公里的"擴展租界區"百分之十的地段地勢被墊高。十年後人們才開始在此修建馬路。至一九一六年擴展租界區。〈80〉最初三個區場由德國領事管理。到一九零六年地方協會接管"南北區域"，並成立了租界行政管理機構，而審判權仍歸屬領事館。〈81〉

是由外交部還是由帝國海軍部來管理租界直接影響到租界的發展進度。比較德國在天津的租界和德國一手興建的新城青島，不難看出青島的建設步伐要快得多。青島由帝國海軍部管轄時德國軍用開支大量資金被用於青島基本設施建設。相反，天津的德租界靠租界稅收來支付各項開支和貸款利息。所以大部份德國人不住在德國租界，而散住在其它國家的租界裡。促成作出這種決擇的因素往往是住房的質量和費用，而不是充滿家鄉氣息的居住環境。〈82〉

德租界在穩步發展。一九零一年十二月，為德國信仰基督教的官兵而建的教堂落成。一九零五年，"北部區域"開始供電。一九一二年後，在"南區"也相繼供電。一九一三年，"威廉學堂"以及在德國租界內為中國學生開設的一所德華中學相繼創辦，此時還計劃建一所與上海、武漢類似的德中工程學院。德租界街道兩側先後種有楊樹和金合歡，沿河地段形成景色宜人的林蔭大道。

貨倉和碼頭均集中在離中國商城較近的其

punkt eines europäischen Militäreinsatzes gegen Beijing. Truppen aus 8 Nationen – Japaner, Russen, Briten, Franzosen, Amerikaner, Deutsche, Italiener und Österreicher – sammelten sich hier, um das belagerte Gesandtschaftsviertel in Beijing zu befreien. Am 14. August 1900 erreichten die Truppen ihr Ziel und befreiten die Eingeschlossenen. Am 2. September 1900 traf Generalfeldmarschall Graf von Waldersee in Tianjin ein, der das Oberkommando über die ausländischen Truppen erhalten hatte. Mit ihm kamen rund 90 000 Soldaten. Bis September 1901 räumten alle ausländischen Truppen Beijing und die Provinz Hebei, zurück blieb eine 1350 Mann starke Gesandtschaftstruppe.[74]

Nach dem Boxerkrieg stationierte man ausländische Truppen in den Niederlassungen Tianjins. Jede Nation besaß ihre eigenen Kasernen. Die zeitweise recht hohe Zahl von Truppen prägte damals das Stadtbild.[75] Entsprechend der politischen Situation veränderte sich die Zahl der in Nordchina stationierten Soldaten. Nach dem Boxerkrieg waren sie kontinuierlich reduziert worden. In den Jahren 1908/09 war die Anzahl der fremden Truppen auf weniger als 4 000 Mann gesunken.[76] Doch nach der Revolution vom Herbst 1911 wurde sie wieder stark erhöht, und 1912 betrug die Truppenstärke in Nordchina wieder etwa 10 000 Mann. Davon waren allein in Tianjin 6 000 Mann stationiert.[77]

Deutschland hatte seine Niederlassung in Tianjin 1895 erhalten, nachdem es sich gemeinsam mit Rußland und Frankreich für den »Frieden von Shimonoseki« eingesetzt hatte.[78] Die Größe der deutschen Handelsniederlassung betrug etwa 0,67 km². Sie lag am weitesten von der chinesischen Geschäftsstadt entfernt und war deswegen trotz einer Uferlänge von 1600 Metern zur Anlage von Geschäfts- und Lagerhäusern ungeeignet. So entwickelte sie sich in den folgenden Jahren vor allem zu einem Wohnviertel.[79] Mit dem Ausbau der Niederlassung, der Aufschüttung des Sumpflandes und der Anlage von Straßen begann man erst im Jahre 1899, vier

After the Boxer Rebellion, the foreign troops were stationed in Tianjin's foreign concessions. Each country had its own barracks. The, at times, considerable number of troops present very much forged the image of the city.[75] The number of troops stationed in north China changed according to the political situation. After the Boxer Rebellion the numbers were continually reduced and by 1908/09, the number of foreign troops had been reduced to under 4 000.[76] However, after the revolution of autumn 1911 they were reinforced again considerably, and in 1912 the number of troops in north China had reached 10 000, of which 6 000 were again stationed in Tianjin.[77]

Germany maintained its concession in Tianjin after it had joined forces with Russia and France in supporting the »Treaty of Shimonoseki«.[78] The German concession was approximately 0,67 km² in area. It was situated far away from the Chinese city and because of this was unsuited as a location for business premises and warehouses despite its 1600 metre embankment. Thus in subsequent years it became a predominantly residential area.[79] Building in the area began in 1899 four years after the marshland was reclaimed and the streets laid out. There was no great hurry, as the German businessmen enjoyed a comfortable life in the already built-up British and French concessions.

The German concession was subdivided into three areas, the »North area« was the first to be developed; after the Chinese revolution in 1911, the »South area« was built. In 1901 the additional 1.52 km² »Extended Settlement« was leased from the Chinese government »forever«. But it was not until a decade later that construction and laying of streets began in this area. By 1916 only 10 percent of the land in the »Extended Settlement« had been reclaimed.[80] All three areas were initially administered by the German consulate. In 1906 the »North and South Area« were awarded the status of a local authority and a concessions authority was established for the admin-

它外國租界。德國租界內無碼頭。有些德國人希望在江邊建一個火車站，鋪設一條與津浦線連接的鐵路支線，以此彌補地段上的劣勢。另一些人則設想把津浦干線建在德國的租界擴展區，然而中國方面卻決定把鐵路鋪設在中國商業區北部。

中國居民區最初規劃建在離海河岸較遠的"南區"西半部，其面積約占租界區總面積的百分之二十。一八九八年，當排外風潮波及中國各地時，中國人被禁止住近"北區"。〈83〉一九零五年以後，外國人對中國人的態度有所轉變。他們千方百計地從文化意識上對當地中國人施加影響。增進相互之間的友好往來，以圖在近期或將來得益於此。小心翼翼地避免一切與種族差異有關的話題，以博得中方的好感。〈84〉因此一九一一年秋，清朝政府垮台後，許多富有的滿州家族攜金銀細軟逃到租界以求得外國法律的庇護。

一九一二年五月，德國領事克尼平致信德國總理疾呼："我們對中國人應一視同仁，允許他們在租界居住。"〈85〉幾個有房地產的德國人在辛亥革命後將"北區"的房子連同地皮一起賣給中國達官貴人和商賈。事後，領館才得到其外交部的復函："只有出自政治原因才能讓中國人遷入'北區'。"〈86〉房地產交易便隨之活躍起來。〈87〉

Jahre nachdem man die Niederlassung erhalten hatte. Es bestand keine Eile, bequem leben konnten die deutschen Kaufleute in den bereits ausgebauten englischen und französischen Niederlassungen.

Die deutsche Niederlassung unterteilte sich in drei Gebiete. Zunächst wurde das »Nordareal« ausgebaut, nach der chinesischen Revolution 1911 folgte dann die Bebauung des »Südareals«. 1901 war zusätzlich die »Erweiterte Niederlassung« mit einer Größe von 1,52 km² »für ewige Zeiten« von der chinesischen Regierung gepachtet worden. Doch erst ein Jahrzehnt später begann man auch dort mit dem Ausbau und der Anlage von Straßen. Bis 1916 waren erst 10 Prozent der Fläche der »Erweiterten Niederlassung« aufgeschüttet.[80] Alle drei Gebiete wurden zunächst durch das deutsche Konsulat verwaltet. 1906 wurde dem »Nord- und Südareal« das Recht eines Kommunalverbandes verliehen und eine Niederlassungs-Gemeinde als Verwaltung eingerichtet.[81] Die Gerichtsbarkeit des deutschen Konsulats blieb weiterhin bestehen.

Die Verwaltung durch das Auswärtige Amt oder das Reichsmarineamt wirkte sich auf die Entwicklung der Siedlungen aus. Vergleicht man die deutsche Niederlassung in Tianjin mit der deutschen Stadtneugründung Qingdao (Tsingtau), so stellt man fest, daß Qingdao wesentlich schneller ausgebaut wurde. Die Stadt Qingdao stand unter der Verwaltung des Reichsmarineamts, und es konnte sehr viel Geld aus dem deutschen Militärhaushalt in die Infrastruktur der Stadt investiert werden. Dagegen mußte die deutsche Niederlassung in Tianjin ihre Ausgaben durch eigene Steuereinnahmen finanzieren. Daher wohnte die Mehrzahl der Deutschen hier auch nicht in der deutschen Niederlassung. Man wohnte über alle ausländischen Niederlassungen verteilt. Wohnungsqualität und Kosten waren die einzigen Kriterien, nicht das nationale Umfeld.[82]

Langsam schritt der Ausbau der deutschen Niederlassung voran. Die evangelische Garni-

istration of the area.[81] The German consulate's jurisdiction was still valid.

Whether or not a concession or protectorate was administered by the German Ministry of Foreign Affairs or the German Admiralty greatly affected the speed of development. A comparison of the development of the German concession in Tianjin and the new city of Qingdao (Tsingtao) reveals that Qingdao developed at a far more rapid pace. The city of Qingdao was under the administration of the German Admiralty (Reichsmarineamt). Thus, a lot of money from the German military finances was invested in the development of municipal infrastructure in Qingdao. In contrast, the German concession in Tianjin had to finance its expenditure, including interest, through its own fiscal revenue. The majority of Germans did not live in the German concession; the quality and cost of accommodation and not the national environment were the criteria on which they based their choice of residence. The different nationalities were spread across the different foreign concessions.[82]

The development of the German concession progressed slowly. The German Protestant Garrison Church was officially opened in December 1901; the »North area« received its electricity supply in 1905, but the »South area« had to wait until after 1912; in 1913, the Kaiser Wilhelm School was opened. There was also a German-Chinese intermediate school for Chinese students in the German concession. It was also planned to establish a German-Chinese school of engineering as had been done in Shanghai and Wuhan. The streets in the German concession were lined with shadowy trees, initially poplars and later Chinese acacias. An attractive promenade was built at the German Bund, the embankment road.

As the warehouses and docks were in the other foreign concessions nearer to the Chinese commercial centre, there was no harbour activity in the German concession and it was hoped that the building of a new railway

sionskirche wurde im Dezember 1901 eingeweiht; Stromversorgung erhielt das »Nordareal« bereits 1905, das »Südareal« erst nach 1912; die Kaiser-Wilhelm-Schule wurde 1913 eröffnet. In der deutschen Niederlassung befand sich schließlich auch eine Deutsch-Chinesische Mittelschule für chinesische Schüler. Der Bau einer Deutsch-Chinesischen Ingenieurschule wie in Shanghai und Wuhan war geplant. Die Straßen der deutschen Niederlassung hatte man mit schattenspendenden Alleebäumen, zuerst mit Pappeln, später mit chinesischen Akazien, bepflanzt. Am deutschen Bund, der Uferstraße, war eine reizvolle Promenade angelegt worden.

Da sich die Lagerhallen und Schiffsanlegeplätze in den anderen, näher an der chinesischen Geschäftsstadt liegenden ausländischen Niederlassungen befanden, gab es in der deutschen Niederlassung keinen Hafenbetrieb. Mit dem Bau eines Hafenbahnhofs und eines Anschlußgleises an die Tianjin-Nanjing-Bahn hoffte man, den Standortnachteil ausgleichen zu können. Außerdem gab es Überlegungen, den Bahnhof dieser von deutschen Ingenieuren geplanten Bahn in der »Erweiterten Niederlassung« zu errichten. Doch der chinesische Bauherr der Bahnlinie entschied sich für einen Standort im Norden der chinesischen Geschäftsstadt.

In der ursprünglichen Planung der deutschen Niederlassung hatte man nur die vom Flußufer entfernt liegende Westhälfte des »Südareals« zur Errichtung von chinesischen Wohnhäusern vorgesehen, etwa 20 Prozent der Niederlassungsfläche. Im »Nordareal« sollten keine Chinesen wohnen dürfen. Diese konservativen Bestimmungen stammten noch aus der Zeit um 1898, als es fremdenfeindliche Bewegungen in China gab.[83] So wie sich die Haltung der Chinesen gegenüber den Ausländern nach dem Boxerkrieg verbesserte, beeinflußte der Sieg Japans im russisch-japanischen Krieg 1905 das Verhältnis der Europäer gegenüber den Asiaten positiv. Die »allgemeine Anschauung der Fremden gegenüber den Chinesen begann sich zu

station at the docks and a branch line of the Tianjin-Nanjing railway would compensate for the disadvantages of its location. In addition, there were plans to locate the station for this railway, which had been planned by German engineers, in the »Extended Settlement«. However, the Chinese client opted for a site in the north of the Chinese city.

In the original plans for the German concession, Chinese housing was only planned for the western half of the »South area«, which was not close to the embankment and represented approximately 20 percent of the area of the concession. These conservative plans originated from the period around 1898, when there was widespread racist feeling in China.[83] From as early as 1905, there was a change in the »general Chinese resentment against the foreigners. There was fierce competition among the foreigners to see who could exercise most cultural influence on the natives and be closest to them personally in the hope of gaining direct advantages in the near or more distant future. (...) Efforts to avoid emphasising racial differences were almost embarrassingly assiduous as a part of the desire to stay in the favour of the Chinese.«[84] Thus, in 1911, when the Qing dynasty was overthrown, many affluent Manchu families fled to the foreign concessions where they placed themselves and their property under foreign protection.

In May 1912, the German Consul Knipping pleaded in a letter to the Imperial Chancellor »that we can no longer differentiate between foreign and Chinese nationals (...) in the population of our concession.«[85] After the revolution, some of the Germans sold houses and sites in the »North area« to high-up Chinese officials and business men and were given authorisation to do so in retrospect by the German Foreign Office, which »authorised the access of the Chinese to the North area only for political reasons«.[86] These deals livened up the property market considerably.[87]

wandeln. Die Fremden streben in regem Wettbewerb danach, die Landesbewohner kulturell zu beeinflussen und ihnen persönlich näher zu kommen, in der Hoffnung auf mittelbare Vorteile in der näheren oder weiteren Zukunft. (…) Man vermeidet mit fast peinlicher Aufmerksamkeit noch irgend welche Rassenunterschiede zu betonen, um in dem Rennen um die Gunst der Chinesen nicht zu kurz zu kommen.«[84] So flüchteten viele wohlhabende Mandschu-Familien im Herbst 1911 nach dem Sturz der Qing-Dynastie in die Niederlassungen, wo sie sich und ihr Eigentum unter den Schutz des Auslands stellten.

Der deutsche Konsul Knipping fordert im Mai 1912 in seinem Schreiben an den Reichskanzler, »daß wir in der Besiedlung unserer Niederlassung (…) einen Unterschied zwischen Fremden und Chinesen nicht mehr machen dürfen.«[85] Einige der deutschen Grundbesitzer hatten nach der Revolution Häuser und Grundstücke des »Nordareals« an ehemalige hohe chinesische Beamte und Geschäftsleute verkauft und erhielten dazu nachträglich auch die Genehmigung des Auswärtigen Amtes, das »den Zuzug von Chinesen in das Nordareal nur aus politischen Gründen zuließ«.[86] Der Immobilienmarkt wurde durch diese Geschäfte kräftig belebt.[87]

CLUB CONCORDIA

Heutige Funktion. Current use
Tianjin Xietong Construction Centre
Jiefang Nanlu/Bengbu Dao
(Wilhelmstraße/Rohrscheidtstraße),
Tianjin (Tientsin)

Architekt. Architect
Curt Rothkegel

Baukosten. Building costs
etwa 405 000 Goldmark
approximately 405 000 gold marks

Ausführung. Contractors
F. H. Schmidt, Altona, Hamburg, Tsingtau

Bauherr. Client
Club Concordia Tientsin

Bauzeit. Construction time
Mai 1905 – Juli 1907
May 1905 – July 1907

Zustand. Condition
Das Gebäude ist gut erhalten,
besonders die Innenräume. Der Südturm
wurde beim Erdbeben 1976 zerstört.
Well preserved, particularly the interior;
the southern tower was destroyed in the
earthquake of 1976.

Kaiser Wilhelm II. bevorzugte den neoromanischen Stil, und so wurden während seiner Amtszeit viele öffentliche Gebäude in diesem Baustil errichtet. Diesen nationalen Architekturstil wählte man auch für den Club Concordia, dem kulturellen Zentrum der deutschen Niederlassung. Im Erdgeschoß des Klubneubaus befanden sich die Bar mit einer rustikalen Holzbalkendecke, ein Billardsaal sowie ein Lesezimmer. Im ersten Stock waren ein Theatersaal mit Bühne und der Speisesaal untergebracht, hier gab es eine umlaufende Terrasse auf der Süd- und der Westseite. Im Dachgeschoß lag die Küche, über einen Speiseaufzug war sie mit den darunterliegenden Stockwerken verbunden.[88] Sehr gut erhalten ist die Halle mit der großzügigen Treppenanlage im Nordteil des Gebäudes. Zentrales Schmuckstück dort ist ein großer Kamin. Im Garten gab es früher Tennisplätze. Bereits 1895, im Jahre der Eröffnung der deutschen Niederlassung, wurde der Klub gegründet.[89] Die Räume befanden sich zunächst in der englischen Niederlassung in der Victoria Road, gegenüber dem englischen Klub. Betrachtete man die nationale Zugehörigkeit der Mitglieder, so war der Club Concordia eigentlich kein deutscher Klub. Etwa 20 Prozent der Mitglieder waren Ausländer, lediglich der Vorstand mußte Deutsch sprechen können.[90] Durch den Neubau erwartete man eine »Vergrößerung des Verkehrs in der etwas abseits gelegenen Niederlassung«.[91] Eine lateinische Inschrift an der Flurwand im Obergeschoß erläuterte seinen Namen: »Concordia parvae res crescunt; discordia maximae dilabuntur«[92]

Kaiser Wilhelm II favoured the neo-Romanesque style and, thus, many public buildings built during his reign were designed in this style. This national architectural style was also chosen for the Club Concordia, the cultural centre of the German concession. The ground floor of the club building housed the bar with rustic wooden rafters, a billiard room and a reading room. On the first floor there was a theatre with a stage and the dining room. This floor had large balconies on the west and southern sides. The top floor housed the kitchen which was connected to the lower floors by a dumbwaiter.[88] The hall with its generous staircase was located in the northern part of the building and is very well preserved. The decorative focus is a large fireplace. There used to be tennis courts in the garden.

The club was founded in 1895, the year that the German concession was founded.[89] The club was originally located in the British concession in Victoria Road opposite the British club. If one considers the nationality of its members, the Club Concordia was not really a German club. Approximately 20 percent of its members were foreigners; only the club committee had to be able to speak German.[90] The new building was expected to give rise to an »increase in traffic in the rather remote settlement«.[91] A Latin inscription on the wall in the corridor on the upper floor explained the name of the club: »Concordia parvae res crescunt; discordia maximae dilabuntur«.[92]

康科迪婭總會

現用途：天津協同設計中心
地址：天津解放南路（蚌埠道口），原威
　　　廉街（羅爾賽德街口）
建築師：羅克格
建造費用：十五萬兩白銀，約四十點五萬
　　　　　金馬克
施工：漢堡阿爾托納區F‧H‧施密特公司
業主：康科迪婭俱樂部
建造日期：一九零五年五月至一九零七年
　　　　　七月
現狀：樓體，尤其是內部結構保存完好，
　　　一九七六年南角塔由於地震倒塌。

威廉二世酷愛新羅馬風式的建築風格。在他執政期間，許多公共設施都是用這種建築形式修建的。作為德國租界中心的康科迪婭總會也選擇了這種建築風格。總會的一樓是裝飾著造型粗樸的欄柵平板酒吧，台球房及閱覽室。二樓是，設有舞台的劇場的餐廳，南北兩面各是平台，頂樓為廚房。升降機可將飯菜送到一、二層樓。〈88〉樓北部的大廳保存完好，廳內的梯氣勢華貴軒昂，一只巨大的壁爐起著畫龍點睛的作用。花園里設有網球場。
總會成立於一八九五年與德國租界的建立同年。〈89〉總會的活動室在原處英租界維多利亞太街上的美國俱樂部的對面。若僅以總會員的國籍而論，康科迪婭根本不算德國總會。約百分之二十的成員來自其它國家，只不過是總會的董事必須會說德文。〈90〉新建總會意在活躍地處偏遠的租界內的文化生活，促進人際交往。〈91〉二樓的走廊牆壁上鐫刻著一段拉丁文，用於解釋總會名稱的含義：同心同德則盛，離心離德則衰。〈92〉

康科迪婭總會西側，一九零七年。
西面外觀，一九九二年。
西側入口大廳內景，一九九二年。

KAISERLICH DEUTSCHES KONSULAT
IMPERIAL GERMAN CONSULATE

Jiefang Nanlu/Pukou Dao
(Wilhelmstraße/Denkmalstraße),
Tianjin (Tientsin)

Ausführung. Contractors
F. H. Schmidt, Altona, Hamburg, Tsingtau

Bauherr. Client
Auswärtiges Amt
Ministry of Foreign Affairs

Einweihung. Opening
1911

Zustand. Condition
Das Gebäude existiert nicht mehr.
No longer exists.

Deutsches Konsulat, Südansicht.
Im Vordergrund das
Kriegerdenkmal, 1911
German Consulate, view from
the south. In the foreground the
War Memorial, 1911

Erst 1911, 16 Jahre nach dem Erwerb der Niederlassung, bezog das deutsche Konsulat ein Gebäude in der deutschen Niederlassung. Es lag an der Nordecke des achteckigen Wilhelmplatzes, dem Zentrum der Niederlassung. Der Neubau wirkte ungünstig proportioniert: Ein klassizistisches Eingangsportal wurde mit vier Krüppelwalmdächern im deutschen Heimatstil kombiniert.

Zuvor befand sich das deutsche Konsulat in der britischen Niederlassung. 1908 berichtete der *Ostasiatische Lloyd*: »Das alte Konsulat (…) entspricht den Anforderungen schon lange nicht mehr. Für einen Neubau ist in der deutschen Niederlassung ein großes Grundstück vorgesehen; die Mittel für den Bau sollen aus dem Verkauf des alten Grundstücks genommen werden.«[93] Doch die Budgetkommission des Reichstags hatte die Forderung nach einem Neubau am 28. März 1908 abgelehnt.

Bis Ende 1905 wurde die gesamte deutsche Niederlassung in Tianjin durch das Konsulat verwaltet. Als der deutschen Niederlassung durch den Reichstag das Recht eines Kommunalverbandes verliehen wurde, teilten sich die neu gegründete Niederlassungsgemeinde und das Konsulat die Verwaltung der »alte Konzession«, die in ein Nordareal und ein Südareal gegliedert war. Der Konsul führte den Vorsitz bei den Gemeindeversammlungen, konnte gegen Beschlüsse Einspruch erheben, sich aber nicht bei Abstimmungen beteiligen und konnte auch nicht in den Gemeinderat gewählt werden. Beim Erwerb von Grundstücken durch Nicht-Deutsche mußten sich diese dem Konsulat gegenüber zur Unterwerfung unter die deutsche Gerichtsbarkeit bereiterklären. Die 1901 zusätzlich von China erworbene Fläche, »Erweiterte Niederlassung« genannt, wurde bis zu ihrer Auflösung 1917 alleine durch das Konsulat verwaltet.[94]

It was not until 1911, 16 years after its acquisition of the concession, that the German consulate moved into a building in the German concession. The building was on the northern corner of the octagonal Wilhelm Square, the centre of the concession. The new building seemed out of proportion: a classical entrance portico was combined with four half-hipped roofs in the German vernacular style.

The German consulate had previously been located on a site in the British concession. In 1908, the *Ostasiatische Lloyd* reported: »The old consulate (…) has failed to meet its requirements for some time now. A large site in the German concession has been selected for the erection of a new building; the new building is to be financed by the funds raised in the sale of the old site.«[93] However, the Reichstag financial commission rejected the request for a new building on 28 March 1908. Until the end of 1905, the entire German concession in Tianjin was administered by the consulate. When the German concession was awarded the right of a local authority by the Reichstag, the newly-founded concession authority and the consulate shared the administration of the »old settlement«, which was subdivided into a north and south area. The Consul presided at the local authority meetings and could object to decisions, but had no vote and could not be elected to the council. Any non-Germans who acquired land in the concession had to sign a declaration of subjugation addressed to the consulate. The additional land obtained from China in 1901, which was known as the »Extended Settlement«, was administered solely by the consulate until its dissolution in 1917.[94]

大德國領事館

地址:天津解放南路(浦口道:原威廉大街碑石路口)
施工:漢堡阿爾托納區F‧H‧施密特公司
業主:外交部
落成儀式:一九一一年
現狀:樓房已不存在

一九一一年,直到德國得到租界權十六年后,領事館才遷入租界。新領館座落在長方形的威廉廣場的東北隅,租界的中心地段。新建的領事館細部組合欠協調。古典式門樓與四個典型的德國坡屋頂并用顯得牽強附會。

領事館最初設在英國商業租界。一九零八年的《德華新報》報導:"英租界內的舊領館已不能滿足各方面的需求。人們計劃在德租界內徵用土地,建新領館,打算用出售英租界那塊地皮的錢作為建造新領館的資金。"〈93〉然而,帝國議會財政預算委員會於一九零八年五月二十八日否定了關於撥款籌建新領事館的申請議項。

直到一九零五年,天津德租界均由領事館統一管理。自從帝國議會授權租界成立地區聯合會以后,新建立的租界機構與領事館一起分管南區和北區的租界的行政事物。領事擔任租界全體居民行政會議主席,有權對大會的決議提出異議,但沒有表決權,也不得參加租界工部局代表的競選。凡欲購置德國租界土地人員必須在領事館簽署恪守德國法律的聲明。一九零一年從中方租借的地段稱作"擴展租界"。
一九一七年契約解除,這以前擴展租界由領館單獨管理。〈94〉

德國領事館南側及館前陣亡將士紀念碑,一九一一年。

KRIEGERDENKMAL
WAR MEMORIAL

Jiefang Nanlu/Pukou Dao (Wilhelmplatz),
Tianjin (Tientsin)

Entwurf. Design
Professor Freiherr von Uechtritz, Berlin

Bauherr. Client
Ostasiatische Besatzungsbrigade
East Asia Occupying Brigade

Einweihung. Opening
17. Juni 1905
17 June 1905

Zustand. Condition
Das Denkmal wurde 1918/19 durch englische und französische Truppen abgetragen.
Pulled down by British and French troops in 1918/1919.

Kriegerdenkmal, Nordansicht.
Nach der Einweihung 1905
War Memorial, view from the north.
After the inauguration in 1905

Der Wilhelmplatz war der Endpunkt der Hauptgeschäftsstraße, die sich von der französischen über die englische bis in die deutsche Niederlassung erstreckte, und bildete das Zentrum der deutschen Niederlassung. Hier wurde 1901 die deutsche evangelische Garnisionskirche[95] und 1911 das deutsche Konsulat errichtet. Am 17. Juni 1905 fand die Enthüllung des Kriegerdenkmals auf dem Wilhelmplatz statt. Es erinnerte an die norddeutschen Rolandsäulen[96] und war den »Angehörigen der deutschen Land- und Seestreitkräfte in Tientsin« gewidmet, die an den Kämpfen in den Jahren 1900–1901 in China beteiligt waren.

Im *Ostasiatische Lloyd* wurde das Denkmal beschrieben: »Der Entwurf dieses Denkmals, dessen Ausführung dem Bildhauer Professor von Uechtritz in Berlin übertragen ist, zeigt (…) auf einem Sockel, um den sich ein Kranz der Wappen aller deutschen Bundesstaaten zieht, neben einem mit ausgebreiteten Flügeln zur Abwehr bereiten Adler die Figur eines geharnischten Deutschritters mit Schwert und Schild, dessen Panzerhemd mit dem eisernen Kreuz und den Reichsadlern in ähnlicher Weise, wie es die deutsche Kaiserstandarte ist, geziert sind. Den Schild schmückt der Reichsadler, das Schwert ist kraftvoll von der vorgestreckten Rechten auf den Boden gestemmt, der Blick des wachehaltenden Ritters schweift forschend geradeaus. Die Figur erinnert auffallend an ein bekanntes Bild SM des Kaisers, das als Schlußvignette Georg Franzius' bekanntes Buch ›Kiautschou, Deutschlands Erwerbung in Ostasien‹ schmückt.«[97]

The Wilhelmplatz square was at the end of the main business street which extended from the French, through the British to the German concession and constituted the centre of the German concession. The German Protestant Garrison Church[95] was built on the square in 1901 and in 1911 the German consulate was also built here. The war memorial on Wilhelmplatz was unveiled on 17 June 1905. The memorial was reminiscent of the north German Roland columns[96] and was dedicated to the German army and navy in Tientsin who had taken part in the struggles of 1900–1901 in China.

The memorial was described in the *Ostasiatische Lloyd* as follows: »This memorial, which was designed by the sculptor Professor von Uechtritz in Berlin, has (…) a German knight in armour with sword and shield standing on a pedestal, around which is wound a wreath bearing the coats of arms of the Federal German States. There is an eagle with its wings spread out in defence beside the knight. The knight is wearing a coat of mail decorated with the Iron Cross and the German Eagle, in accordance with the Imperial German Standard. The shield is also decorated with the Imperial eagle, the sword is powerful and pointing downwards in the outstretched right arm of the knight on guard whose eyes pierce straight ahead. The figure is conspicuously reminiscent of a well known picture of the Kaiser which appears as the closing vignette in Georg Franzius' famous book ›Kiautschou, Deutschlands Erwerbung in Ostasien‹« (›Kiaochow, Germany's Acquisition in East Asia‹).[97]

陣亡將士紀念碑

地址：天津解放南路（浦口道）原威廉廣場
設計：馮・於希特利茨男爵，教授，柏林
現狀：一九一八年至一九一九年被英法軍隊拆毀

威廉廣場是始於法租界，途經英租界終抵德租界的一條主要商業大街的盡端，也是德租界的中心。一九零一年，在此為德軍官兵營建了基督教堂〈95〉一九一一年，德國領館也遷至威廉廣場。一九零五年六月十七日，廣場上舉行了陣亡將士紀念碑的揭幕儀式。紀念碑的雕像與在德國北部集市廣場上常見的身披鎧甲，手持戰劍的騎士雕像相似。〈96〉這座紀念碑是為了紀念一九零零年至一九零一年在中國陣亡的曾駐扎天津的陸、海軍將士。

《德文新報》對紀念碑的描寫如下：＂紀念碑的設計和雕塑均委托柏林的雕刻家馮・於希特利茨教授。紀念碑的雕像是一個手持長劍和盾牌全副武裝的德國騎士。雕像的基座四周裝飾著由各個州州徽組成的浮雕花環。雕像旁是一只展翅飛翔的雄鷹。騎士鎧甲上繪有與皇旗一樣的裝飾圖案：十字架與象徵著德意志帝國的雄鷹。在騎士的盾牌上也同樣鐫刻著雄鷹圖案。騎士高高舉起的右臂將劍有力地插在地上，雙眼警覺地審視著前方。這尊雕像令人聯想到皇上的名畫。這張騎士畫像作為封底裝點著格奧爾格，弗蘭茨吾斯的名著《膠州，德國在東亞的領地》。＂〈97〉

陣亡將士紀念碑北立面，攝於一九零五年落成典禮後。

DEUTSCH-ASIATISCHE BANK
GERMAN-ASIAN BANK

Heutige Funktion. Current use
Geschäftshaus
Business premises
Jiefang Beilu 108 (Victoria Road),
Tianjin (Tientsin)

Architekten. Architects
Becker & Baedecker, Shanghai[98]

Bauleitung. Site architect
Karsten Hermann Suhr, Tientsin, Shanghai

Ausführung. Contractors
F. H. Schmidt, Altona, Hamburg, Tsingtau

Bauherr. Client
Deutsch-Asiatische Bank, Berlin
German-Asian Bank, Berlin

Bauzeit. Construction time
1907–1908

Zustand. Condition
1976 wurde das Dach durch ein Erdbeben zerstört und durch ein Flachdach ersetzt.
The roof was destroyed by an earthquake in 1976 and replaced by a flat-roof.

Ähnlich den anderen ausländischen Banken in der Victoria Road, gliedern Säulen die Straßenfassade der Deutsch-Asiatischen Bank. Das Dach dagegen ist, wie bei modernen Geschäftshäusern damals in Deutschland üblich, als hohes Mansardwalmdach ausgebildet und nicht wie bei vielen der Nachbar-

gebäude als Flachdach. Der Mittelrisalit wurde durch einen Schmuckgiebel betont, ebenso die Eingänge an den Seiten. Im Erdgeschoß des Gebäudes befanden sich Schalter- und Diensträume, im Obergeschoß die Wohnung des Bankdirektors.

Die italienische Neorenaissance war damals der von Banken in Europa bevorzugte Baustil. Die meisten Banken in der Hauptgeschäftsstraße Tianjins, der Rue de France und der Victoria Road, wurden in diesem Stil erbaut. Deshalb wählten die Architekten der Deutsch-Asiatischen Bank wohl auch nicht den Baustil der deutschen Neorenaissance, in dem sie die Filiale in Beijing erbaut hatten, sondern eine moderne Mischform, die sich durch ein charaktervolles Dach auszeichnete.

As is the case with the other banks on Victoria Road in the British concession, the order of the street façade of the German-Asian Bank is provided by columns. As was standard for modern business premises in Germany at the time, on the other hand, the building had a mansard roof, unlike many of the flat-roofed neighbouring buildings. The central projection was emphasised by a decorative gable, as were the entrances at the short sides of the building. The counters and service rooms were on the ground floor and the upper floor housed the bank director's apartment.

The popular style for bank buildings in Europe at the time was Italian neo-Renaissance. Most of the banks in Tianjin's main business street, the Rue de France and Victoria Road, were designed in this style. It was most likely for this reason that the architects of the German-Asian Bank did not chose German neo-Renaissance, which had been used for the Beijing branch, but opted instead for a modern hybrid style whose distinctive feature was the unusual character of the roof.

Deutsch-Asiatische Bank,
Ostansicht, 1991
Ostansicht, 1908
German Asian Bank,
view from the east, 1991
German-Asian Bank,
view from the east, 1908

德華銀行

現用途：商業辦公大樓／商店
地址：天津解放路一百零八號；原維克多
　　　利亞路
建築師：貝克・培迪克，上海⁽⁹⁸⁾
工程指導：卡斯泰・赫爾曼蘇爾　天津
　　　　　　　　　　　　　　　上海
施工：漢堡阿爾托納區F・H・施密特公司
業主：德華銀行　柏林
建造日期：一九零七年至一九零八年
現狀：一九七六年地震時樓頂倒塌，現為
　　　平頂

德華銀行和英租界維克多利亞路上的其它銀行一樣，立面以錯落有致的廊柱裝飾，顯得極有韻律。按照當時德國流行的商業辦公大樓的式樣，銀行的樓頂為高陡的復折四坡屋頂，而四周的樓房建築大都是平頂。銀行正面和側面的裝飾山牆強調中間的突出立面和側立面上的入口。底層是設有營業窗口的大廳和業務洽談室。銀行主任的住宅設在二樓。當時歐州銀行多採用意大利文藝復興式復古建築手法。天津的商業主要街道，法蘭西大街和維克多利亞大街上的銀行就採用了這種建築風格。因而在建造德華銀行時，建築師沒有採用德國式的文藝復興式復古手法，而採用了折衷的形式。別具一格的銀行樓頂就體現了這種兼收并蓄的手法。德華銀行在北京的分行則是德國式文藝復興復古手法建造的。

東立面外觀，一九九一年。
德華銀行東面外觀。

TIANJIN

WESTBAHNHOF
WEST STATION

Xizhan Qianlu, Tianjin (Tientsin)
Entwurf. Design
Deutsche Ingenieure
German engineers
Ausführung. Contractors
Tientsin-Pukow Eisenbahngesellschaft
Tientsin-Pukow Railway Company
Bauherr. Client
Chinese Government Railways
Eröffnung. Opening
14. Dezember 1910
14 December 1910
Zustand. Condition
Das Gebäude ist gut erhalten, die Neubauten zu beiden Seiten sind stilistisch und farblich an den Bahnhof angepaßt.
Well preserved; the new buildings on both sides blend well with the original station building in terms of both style and colour.

Westbahnhof, Südansicht, 1991
West Station, view from the south, 1991

Die Wartehalle im erhöht liegenden Erdgeschoß besitzt einen großen, halbkreisförmigen Vorbau auf der Bahnsteigseite, von dem aus man den Betrieb auf dem Bahnsteig beobachten kann. Der Maßstab dieses Gebäudes entspricht dem Standard damaliger deutscher Bahnhöfe, dagegen ist seine Fassade trotz ihrer Mittelsymmetrie sehr unruhig und überladen. Wahrscheinlich war dieser europäische Stadtbahnhof für einen Standort nahe der ausländischen Niederlassungen entworfen worden. In der chinesischen Umgebung der nördlichen Vorstadt Tianjins wirkt er heute noch sehr fremd.

Der 625 km lange Nordteil der Eisenbahnlinie Tianjin-Nanjing war durch deutsche, der 375 km lange Südteil durch englische Ingenieure erbaut worden. Für die Bahnhofsgebäude des Nordteils gab es kein einheitliches Gestaltungskonzept, jedes wurde von einem anderen Architekten entworfen. Man kann jedoch feststellen, daß sich die Bahnhofsentwürfe deutscher Ingenieure immer nach ihrer Umgebung richteten. Die Stadtbahnhöfe in Tianjin und Jinan wurden in einem modernen europäischen Baustil errichtet, während man bei Landbahnhöfen Mischungen von europäischer und chinesischer Architektur wählte.

Seit dem Beginn der Vermessungsarbeiten 1904/05 für diese Bahnlinie gab es Verhandlungen um den zukünftigen Standort des Bahnhofs in Tianjin. Die ausländischen Geschäftsleute forderten einen Bahnhof im Südwesten der chinesischen Stadt und damit in unmittelbarer Nähe zur französischen und englischen Niederlassung. Diese Verbesserung der Infrastruktur hätte die Niederlassungen wirtschaftlich erheblich belebt. Gleichzeitig gab es von deutscher Seite Bemühungen, den Bahnhof in der »Erweiterten Niederlassung«[99] anzusiedeln, oder zumindest ein Anschlußgleis mit Hafenbahnhof wie in Wuhan zu erhalten. Schließlich wurde der Bahnhof im Norden der Stadt, nahe der Mündung des Kaiserkanals in den Hai He und damit in großer Entfernung zu den europäischen Niederlassungen errichtet.[100]

The waiting room in the raised ground floor has a large semi-circular projecting balcony structure on the platform side from which it is possible to observe the activity on the platform. The scale of this building corresponds to the standard for German railway stations at the time; in contrast however, the façade is extremely overwrought, despite the central symmetry. This European-style urban station was probably designed for a location near the foreign concessions. Standing as it does in the Chinese surroundings of the northern suburb of Tianjin, it still looks very out of place today.

The 625 km-long northern section of the Tianjin-Nanjing railway line was built by German engineers, the 375 km long southern section by British engineers. There was no standard design approach for the railway buildings in the northern part, each was designed by a different architect. It is however, possible to see that the designs for the stations produced by the German engineers were always influenced by the station environment; the city stations in Tianjin and Jinan were built in modern European style, whereas a mixture of European and Chinese styles was used for the rural stations.

Negotiations about the future location of the station in Tianjin had been under way since the surveying had been started for the railway from Tianjin to Nanjing in 1904/05. The foreign business community wanted a station in the south west of the Chinese centre and thus right next to the British and French concessions. This improvement in infrastructure would have brought a considerable increase in activity to the concessions. At the same time efforts were made on the German side to have the station located in the »Extended Settlement«[99] or at least a branch line and a harbour station as in Wuhan. The station was finally built in the north of the city near where the Imperial Canal entered the Hai He and as far as possible away from the European concessions.[100]

津—歸線　天津西站

地站：天津西站前街
設計：德國工程師
施工：津浦線鐵路公司
業主：中國政府鐵路局
通車日期：一九一零年十二月十四日
現狀：樓體保存完好，兩側所建房屋在建築風和上和色彩上均與火車站諧調一致。

候車室設在一樓，由一個半圓形的高台與月台連接。站在高台上可觀察到月台上人來車往的情景。這座建築物的形制規模和比例與當時德國火車站的標準一致。車站的立面雖有正中對稱的軸線，然而因裝飾繁縟，顯得並不協調。這個歐化的火車站也許當初是為某一個外國租界為背景而設計的，如今卻顯得與天津北郊的中國式建築群格格不入。

津浦線六百二十五公里長的北干線由德國工程師負責設計，三百七十五公里長的南線則由英國工程師承擔。沿北線的各個車站在造型上沒有統一的格式，各由不同的建築師設計。然而有一點是一致的：由德國工程師設計的車站總是先考慮到環境的因素。天津、濟南的火車站采用了現代歐洲的建築手法，而鄉鎮火車站則是中西手法兼而有之。一九零四至一九零五年，自從天津鐵路測量工作完成後，火車站的選址工作就開始了。外國商人建議把火車站造在中國居住區的西南部，即與英、法租界接鄰的地段。因為基本設施的改善能促使租界經濟繁榮起來，德國方面卻力爭讓車站建在德國租界的擴展區，〈99〉或者至少能象武漢一樣鋪設一條與港口車站相連接的鐵路支線。火車站的地址最終確定在天津北部大連運河與海河匯處的附近，離各國租界最遠的地方。〈100〉

天津西站南立面，一九九一年。

WOHNHAUS
RESIDENCE

Jiefang Nanlu 252/Zhengjiang Dao
(Wilhelmstraße/Schreyerstraße),
Tianjin (Tientsin)

Bauzeit. Construction time
zwischen 1903 und 1914
between 1903 and 1914

Zustand. Condition
Das Gebäude ist gut erhalten,
jedoch ohne Turmdach.
Well preserved; the roof of the
tower is missing.

Wohnhaus, Ostfassade, vor 1914
Blick von Osten, 1991
Residence, eastern façade,
before 1914
View from the east, 1991

Die Baukörper dieses Wohnhauses wirken wie aus einem Katalog zusammengestellt.[101] Der Turm mit spitzem Dach betont den Eingang an der Ecke, ein hoher Giebel mit Krüppelwalmdach die Ostfassade an der Wilhelmstraße. Zu diesen typisch deutschen Bauteilen kamen Formen, wie man sie sonst in Tianjin an den Gebäuden der italienischen oder französischen Niederlassung fand. Ein weiter Dachüberstand überschattet die Fassaden, und der südliche Gebäudeteil entlang der Zhengjiang Dao ist mit einem von Balustraden eingefaßten Flachdach gedeckt. Die Fassade besteht aus zweifarbigem Ziegelsichtmauerwerk; die Steine sind in verschiedenen Rauten- und Punktmustern verlegt. Nach dem Erdbeben im Jahre 1976 wurden an der Fassade stabilisierende Ringanker befestigt.

Die 1902 gegründete Tientsin-Baugesellschaft, Besitzerin eines großen Teils der Grundstücke der deutschen Niederlassung, vermietete Häuser an deutsche Offiziere. In ihrem Geschäftsbericht schrieb sie: »Waren auch die Mieten seit dem, mit der Verminderung der deutschen Truppen 1906 einsetzenden Mietsturz, nicht wieder auf ihre alte Höhe zurückgelangt, so hat sich dafür eine rege Nachfrage nach Wohnungen in unserer zwar langsam, aber doch erfreulich aufblühenden deutschen Niederlassung geltend gemacht.«[102]

Put together, the elements that make up this residence are like something from a building catalogue.[101] The tower with its pointed roof emphasises the entrance at the corner, a high gable with a half-hipped roof emphasises the east façade on Wilhelm Strasse. These typical German elements were combined with features common in buildings in the French or Italian concessions in Tianjin. For example, a wide roof overhang provided shade for the façade, and the southern wing of the building along Zhengjiang Dao has a flat roof with balustrading. The façade consists of two-coloured fair-faced clay brickwork; the stones are set in different rhomboid and dotted patterns. After the earthquake in 1976, supporting ring beams were attached to the façade.

The Tientsin Building Company, which was founded in 1902, owned most of the sites in the German concession with houses rented to German officers. The following observation is recorded in its business report: »Rents may not have completely recovered since the plunge resulting from the reduction in German troops in 1906, however, there is a healthy demand for accommodation in our somewhat slow, but happily, blossoming German concession«.[102]

住宅

地址：天津解放南路（鎮江道口）；原威廉路
現狀：樓體保存尚好，塔頂已不存在

這所住宅就象是從建築構件樣品集錦中信手選了几種風格不同的模式，依樣建造，然後拼湊起來的一樣。〈101〉拐角上的尖頂塔樓下是住宅的進出口，高高的山牆和歇山頂裝飾著威廉大街上的東部立面。這些典型的德國建築手法又與天津的意大利、法國租界流行的建築風格滲合在一起。寬大的屋檐遮擋陽光的照射，位於鎮江大道上的住宅南翼還有一個帶護欄的屋頂。立面是用兩種顏色的磚石砌成的菱形和點狀圖案的清水牆。一九七六年地震後，外牆用圈樑加固。

一九零二年組建的天津建築公司占有德租界的大部分地皮。公司將房子出租給德國軍官。在公司的工作報告中有如下記載："一九零六年，德軍開始撤退，房租猛跌。現在盡管租金的數額已達不到原有的高度，然而在逐步興旺，繁榮的租界裡對住宅的需求量仍然很大。"〈102〉

住宅東角一瞥，一九九一年。
住宅東立面，一九一四年前。

WOHNHAUS
RESIDENCE

Xuzhou Dao 29, (Mummstraße, zwischen Wilhelmstraße und Taku Road), Tianjin (Tientsin)

Xuzhou Dao 29, (Mumm Strasse, between Wilhelm Strasse and Taku Road), Tianjin (Tientsin)

Architekt. Architect
vermutlich Curt Rothkegel
probably Curt Rothkegel

Bauzeit. Construction time
zwischen 1906 und 1914
between 1906 and 1914

Zustand. Condition
Das Gebäude ist gut erhalten, an der Südfassade sind die Loggien verändert. Nach dem Erdbeben 1976 wurden Ringanker an der Fassade angebracht.
Well preserved, the loggias on the south façade have been changed; ring beams were attached to the façade following the earthquake in 1976.

Im Grundriß ist dieses Wohnhaus mit vier Wohnungen axial symmetrisch, die beiden Eingänge befinden sich an den Seiten des Gebäudes. Die Türflügel zieren hölzerne Katzenköpfe mit überlangen Zungen. Solche geschnitzten Tiermotive finden sich häufig bei Gebäuden des Architekten Rothkegel.

Der Eingang des Mehrfamilienhauses ist ein Beispiel dafür, wie sich der Jugendstil ostasiatische Bauformen angeeignet hat. In der chinesischen Gartenarchitektur können Durchgänge und Tore die verschiedensten Formen haben: Neben rechteckigen Toren gibt es runde Mondtore, flaschen- und flammenförmige Öffnungen und viele andere Formen.[103] Um die Jahrhundertwende wurden sie von Architekten des Jugendstils in Europa aufgenommen und modifiziert. Als dann Jugendstilbauten von Ausländern in China errichtet wurden, kehrten diese ursprünglich chinesischen Bauelemente in gewandelter Form wieder in das Ursprungsland zurück. Vorbild für den Kreis um die Tür war das runde Mondtor. Hier wird er verwendet, um Treppenhausfenster und Eingangstür optisch zu verbinden.

The plan of this house is symmetrically divided into four apartments; the two entrances are at the sides of the building. The door leaves are decorated with wooden cat heads with extended tongues. Carved animals of this type are common in buildings by the architect Rothkegel.

The entrance to this apartment building is an example of how Jugendstil adopted elements of East Asian design. In Chinese garden architecture, passages and gates could have any number of forms: in addition to rectangular gates there are round moon gates, gates in the shapes of bottles and flames and many others.[103] Around the turn of the century these forms were adopted and modified by the Jugendstil architects in Europe. When Jugendstil buildings were then built by foreigners in China, these originally Chinese forms returned to their country of origin in a somewhat altered form. The circle around the door of the house is developed from the round moon gate. It is used here to create an optical link between the window of the staircase and the hall door.

Wohnhaus, Nordansicht, 1992
Eingang von Osten, 1992
Residence, view from the north, 1992
Entrance from the east, 1992

住宅

地址：天津徐州道二十九號；原特姆街，
　　　威廉街與大沽路之間
建築師：可能是羅克格
建造日期：一九零六年至一九零四年
現狀：樓體保存尚好，南面立面前的敞廊
　　　不同以前一九七六年地震後，立面
　　　安裝了圈樑。

這幢有四套寓所的住宅平面對稱工整。兩處入口位於樓房兩側。門扉上懸一只吐著舌頭的貓頭木雕。在羅格克的設計作品中，這種動物裝飾的雕刻屢見不鮮。由此推斷，這所宅院也是由他設計的。

公寓入口的優美造型是以說明，青年藝術派對東亞建築手法的借鑒。在中國的園林建築中，門廊的形式千姿百態，美不勝收：滿月式門，花瓶式門，葉片狀門等。〈103〉本世紀初，歐洲青年藝術派吸收並修改了這些手法。當外國人在中國建造具有青年派風格的建築時，這些起源於中國的建築手法經加工後也隨之返回發祥地。入口處上端的圓形裝飾線就是在滿月式圓門的基礎上演變而來的，這種裝飾手法在視覺上造成一種樓梯采光窗與主門渾然一體的效果。

住宅北立面，一九九二年。
東側入口，一九九二年。

TIANJIN

WOHNHAUS FAUST
THE FAUST HOUSE

Tai'erzhuang Lu/Xuzhou Dao
(Uferstraße/Mummstraße), Tianjin (Tientsin)

Entwurf. Design
unbekannter französischer Architekt
unknown French architect

Bauherr. Client
J. Faust, Hannover

Bauzeit. Construction time
um 1904
around 1904

Zustand. Condition
Das Gebäude existiert nicht mehr.
No longer exists.

Wohnhaus Faust. Nordostansicht
von der deutschen Uferstraße,
um 1905
Blick von Norden, um 1907
Faust Residence, view from
Ufer Strasse to the north-east,
around 1905
View from the north, around 1907

Die zweigeschossige Villa lag auf einem Grundstück an der deutschen Uferstraße, nahe der englischen Niederlassung. Die gut proportionierte Hauptfassade war nach Osten auf den Hai He-Fluß ausgerichtet. Balkone, Terrassen und ein gedeckter Sitzplatz waren dem warmen Klima Tianjins während des Sommers angepaßt. Der Haupteingang befand sich an der Nordecke und war durch einen dreigeschossigen Turm betont, der ein leichtes Ziergitter mit Jugendstilornamenten trug. Es war ein für die deutsche Niederlassung in Tianjin sehr untypisches Gebäude. Das Gebäude wurde von einem französischen Architekten im dekorativen französischen Jugendstil entworfen, der sich deutlich vom strengeren deutschen Jugendstil unterschied. Der Architekt verwendete bei der Gestaltung der beiden Giebelflächen die runde Form des chinesischen Mondtores. Häuser mit ähnlich schmückenden Jugendstildetails sind noch heute in den ehemaligen französischen und italienischen Niederlassungen Tianjins in gutem Zustand erhalten.

Der Kaufmann J. Faust war seit 1894 in China im Import-Export-Geschäft tätig. Zuerst in Shanghai, ab 1898 in Tianjin. Sein Geschäftshaus lag in der französischen Niederlassung in der Rue de l'Amirauté. Er war Mitglied des französischen Gemeinderates und Vorsitzender der deutschen Niederlassungs-Gemeinde. Faust war auch Herausgeber des deutschsprachigen *Tageblatt für Nordchina*, das seit dem 1. Oktober 1904 in Tianjin erschien.[104]

Im Jahre 1912, nach der Revolution und dem Sturz der Qing-Dynastie, verkaufte Faust sein Haus mit Grundstück an den Sohn des Prinzen Qing (Ch'ing), Prinz Zailun (Tsai-lun), mit einem Gewinn von 30 000 Taels, etwa 81 000 Goldmark. Das Auswärtige Amt, das Landverkäufe im Nordareal der deutschen Niederlassung an Chinesen genehmigen mußte, stimmte diesem Verkauf aus politischen Gründen zu. Prinz Zailun ließ noch im selben Jahr das Haus durch mehrere Anbauten erweitern.[105]

This two-storey villa was located on a site on the German Bund near the British concession. The well-proportioned main façade faced east to the Hai He river. Various elements provided for the warm summer climate of Tianjin, including balconies, terraces and a covered bench. The main entrance was on the northern corner of the house and was emphasised by a three-storey tower with a light decorative Jugendstil grating. This building was not at all typical for the German concession in Tianjin. The building was designed by a French architect in the decorative French Art Nouveau style, which was quite different to the more stark German version of Jugendstil. The architect used the round form of the Chinese moon gate in the design of the two gables. Houses with similar decorative details can still be found in the former French and Italian concessions in Tianjin and are generally well preserved.

J. Faust, a business man, was involved in the import-export market in China from 1894 – initially in Shanghai and later from 1898 in Tianjin. His business premises were in the French concession in Rue de l'Amirauté. He was a member of the French municipal council and president of the German concession authority. Faust was also editor of a German daily *Tageblatt für Nordchina* which was published in Tianjin from 1 October 1904.[104]

In 1912 after the revolution and the fall of the Qing dynasty, Faust sold his house and grounds to the son of Prince Qing (Ch'ing), Prince Zailun (Tsai-lun) and made a profit of 30 000 taels, approximately 81 000 gold marks. The Ministry of Foreign Affairs, which had to authorise sales of land in the north area of the German concession to Chinese buyers, approved the sale for political reasons. Prince Zailun had several extensions added to the house that same year.[105]

浮士德住宅

地址：台兒莊路（徐州道口）；原沿河大街／特姆大街
設計：法國建築師
業主：J‧浮士德‧漢諾威
建造日期：約一九零四年
現狀：已毀

這座兩層高的別墅位於沿江大道旁的德國租界裡，離英國租界不遠。主立面朝東，面向海河。陽台、平台以及設有遮陽頂蓬和躺椅供休憩納涼的場地都是為了適應天津炎夏而設置的。大門位於北面的轉角上，三層樓高的塔樓標示著這個主入口的處所。塔樓的頂端是一個以新藝術派手法裝飾起來的柵架。這是一座在天津德國租界裡並不典型的建築物。一位法國建築師採用重裝飾的法國新藝術派手法設計了這座住宅，法國新藝術派與嚴肅莊重的德國青年派風格截然不同。建築師採用中國的滿月式圓門圖案裝飾兩面的山牆。在當年的法國和意大利租界區建築物上類似的裝飾構件比比皆是。這些樓房至今保存完好。
一八九四年，J‧浮士德先後在上海、天津做進出口生意。他的商業事務所在法國租界區海軍路（音譯）。他既是法國僑民代表大會的代表，又是德國租界聯合會的主席。於一九零四年十月一日在天津創刊的德語報、北方日報也是由他主持發行的。[104]
一九一二年，清王朝垮台後，浮士德將這所房子連同地皮一起賣給了恭親王的兒子載倫，從中獲利三萬銀元，約合八十一萬金馬克。當時，向中國人出售德國租界北區的地皮必須得到外交部的許可。出於政治上的原因，外交部認可了這次交易。同年，載倫增建側樓，擴大了住宅的規模。[105]

浮士德住宅靠臨江大道上的東北角，約一九零五年。
北立面，約一九零七年。

HONGKONG

Hongkong war bereits vor der deutschen Gründung der Stadt Qingdao (Tsingtau) das Vorbild und der Maßstab für eine zukünftige deutsche Kolonie in Asien. Zu Beginn seiner Expedition entlang Chinas Küsten im Februar 1897 schreibt der Hafenbaudirektor Georg Franzius bei seinem Besuch Hongkongs: »Dabei male ich mir im Geiste aus, wie die zukünftige deutsche Kolonie nach dem Muster von Hongkong demnächst mit Wald und Teichen, mit Promenaden und natürlich auch mit einem Rennplatze geschmückt werden wird.«[106] Die Schönheit Hongkongs gab den deutschen Kolonisatoren ein Leitbild für ihre Arbeit.

1842 begannen die Briten mit dem Aufbau ihrer Kolonie Hongkong. Die Bedingungen waren zunächst denkbar ungünstig. 28 Prozent der hier stationierten 1500 britischen Soldaten starben in den ersten Jahren an Infektionskrankheiten.[107] Die chinesische Bevölkerungszahl stieg rasant an. War die Insel vor 1840 nahezu unbesiedelt, wohnten 1911 bereits rund 440 000 Chinesen hier. Die 13 000 ausländischen Zivilisten und 9 000 britischen Soldaten bildeten nur eine kleine Minderheit.[108] Die der chinesischen Bevölkerung zugewiesenen Stadtteile dehnten sich immer mehr aus und die Europäer wichen mit ihren Wohnhäusern immer höher auf die Hügel aus. Hongkong war um die Jahrhundertwende, nach 50 Jahren Entwicklung, dichter besiedelt als die englischen Industriestädte und bildete ein hohes Gesundheitsrisiko.[109] 70 000 chinesische Einwohner flüchteten im Frühjahr 1901 vor der Pest. Um die Stadt von der Seuche zu befreien, mußte die Verwaltung der Kolonie das Chinesenviertel erst für mehrere Millionen Dollar aufkaufen, um es dann abreißen zu können.[110]

Bei der Stadtplanung Qingdaos wurde ein späteres Wachstum bereits berücksichtigt, indem man getrennte Siedlungen für Europäer und Chinesen in weiträumigem Abstand zueinander anlegte. In Hongkong führte das

HONGKONG

Prior to the German foundation of the city of Qingdao (Tsingtao), Hongkong was the model for a future German colony in Asia. Setting out on an expedition along the Chinese coast in February 1897, the Naval Director of Dock Building, Georg Franzius, wrote on a visit to Hongkong: »I am drawing a mental image of how the future German colony will look modelled on Hongkong with forest and ponds, promenades and, of course a race course.«[106] The beauty of Hongkong was an inspiration to the German colonialists in their work.

In 1842 the British began building their colony in Hongkong. Initially, conditions in the colony were as unfavourable as it is possible to imagine. In the early years, 28 percent of the 1500 British soldiers stationed there died of infectious diseases.[107] The Chinese population increased rapidly. Prior to 1840, the island was unpopulated and by 1911 there were some 440 000 Chinese inhabitants. The 13 000 foreign civilians and 9 000 British soldiers represented a small minority.[108] The neighbourhoods allocated to the Chinese were expanding and the Europeans were forced to withdraw with their residences higher and higher into the hills. Around the turn of the century after 50 years of development, Hongkong was more densely populated than the infamous British industrial cities and was a vast health hazard.[109] In spring 1901, 70 000 Chinese inhabitants fled to escape the plague. To eradicate contamination from the city, the British were forced to buy up the Chinese neighbourhoods and demolish everything; this cost the administration several million dollars.[110]

The possibility of subsequent expansion was taken into account in the planning of Qingdao in that separate areas were allocated to the Europeans and Chinese which were located at considerable distances from each other. The system of auctions, short leases and land tax in Hongkong had led to a high degree of speculation which was generally con-

香港

在興建青島之前，香港是德國規劃未來殖民地建設圖景的範例。德國海軍樞密建築技術監督格奧爾格·佛朗求斯在去中國沿海地區的考察途中，於一八九七年二月參觀了香港。他寫道："在參觀香港時我就設想，未來的德國殖民地要按照香港的模式用樹林、池塘、林蔭道裝扮起來，當然還要修上一個賽馬場。"〈106〉香港的秀麗風景給德國殖民者以啟迪，他們為成建設自己的殖民地的楷模。

一八四二年，英國人開始興建殖民地香港，當初的條件極其惡劣。開始的幾年，百分之二十八的駐香港的英國士兵因傳染病喪生。〈107〉中國人口上升極快。這一在一八四零年以前幾乎無人居住的荒島，到一九一一年已有四十四萬中國人，一萬三千外國僑民和九千英軍士兵，其數量微不足道。〈108〉指定的中國人居住區的範圍日益擴大，歐洲人多擇山陵築舍以避開中國居民區。經過五十年的發展，至本世紀初，香港人口密度已打破了當時聲名狼藉的英國工業城的最高紀錄。在香港生活，健康得不到保障。〈109〉一九零一年春，七萬中國居民恐於染上瘟疫而逃離香港。為了消滅傳染病，英國殖民地當局被迫買下中國人的居住區，拆毀房屋。這次行動耗資幾百萬美金。〈110〉

在規劃青島的建設時，人們考慮到了將會出現的人口膨脹問題，因此將歐洲人和中國人的居住區遠遠地隔開。在香港，關於拍賣、有期限租賃及土地稅的管理體制不健全，導致投機倒把盛行。對此香港市民怨聲載道。鑒於香港的經驗教訓，人們在青島制定了土地管理法，以杜絕地產投機倒把活動。〈111〉

香港是不納入中國稅區的中國領土，因而清政府在其四周設立海關，這種做法在很大程度上束縛了貿易的發展。因此一九零六年德國的管轄區與中方締結了關稅同盟，因此只有從港口進到內地的貨物必須交納關稅。〈112〉

dort übliche System der Versteigerungen, der zeitlich begrenzten Pachtungen und der Grundsteuer zu einer starken Bodenspekulation, die allgemein beklagt wurde. Aufgrund dieser Erfahrungen führte man in Qingdao eine Landordnung ein, die Bodenspekulationen verhinderte.[111]

Hongkong war gegenüber China Zollausland und daher mit einem Ring von Zollämtern umgeben, was den Handel erheblich behinderte. Dagegen bildete das gesamte deutsche Schutzgebiet ab 1906 eine Zollunion mit China, lediglich der eng umgrenzte Hafen war Zollausland und Freihafen.[112]

demned. On the basis of this experience, land regulations were introduced in Qingdao which prevented land speculation.[111]

With respect to customs and excise, Hongkong was not part of China and was thus surrounded by a ring of customs offices, which represented a considerable obstacle to trade. In contrast, from 1906, the entire German protectorate formed a customs union with China, and only the area directly surrounding the harbour was outside the customs frontier and a free port.[112]

HONGKONG

CLUB GERMANIA

Kennedy Road (am Abhang des Peaks),
Hongkong
Kennedy Road (on the Peak incline),
Hongkong

Architekt. Architect
E. A. Ram

Baukosten. Building costs
etwa 315 000 Goldmark
approximately 315 000 gold marks

Ausführung. Contractors
Dennison, Ram & Gibbs

Bauherr. Client
Deutscher Club Germania in Hongkong
German Club Germania in Hongkong

Planungszeit. Planning phase
1899

Einweihung. Opening
31. Dezember 1902
31 December 1902

Zustand. Condition
Das Gebäude existiert nicht mehr.
No longer exists.

Club Germania, um 1907
Club Germania, around 1907

Der Deutsche Klub in Hongkong wurde 1859 gegründet und hatte im Jahr 1908 etwa 250 Mitglieder.[113] Der Neubau des Klubs glich mit seinen luftigen, schattenspendenden Veranden auf allen Stockwerken den damals in Hongkong üblichen Gebäuden. Die Briten selber hatten diesem undefinierbaren Stil ihrer subtropischen Bauten die Spottbezeichnung »Comprador Stil« gegeben.[114] Anders als später in Shanghai war es ein britischer Architekt, der den deutschen Klub in Hongkong plante. Es entstand ein unauffälliges Gebäude, das die nationale Identität seiner Mitglieder nicht widerspiegelte.[115]

Zur Eröffnung erschien im *Ostasiatischen Lloyd* eine detaillierte Beschreibung des Klubs: »Im Erdgeschoß befindet sich das große und geräumige Barzimmer, an das sich das Billardzimmer anschließt. Außerdem sind noch das Telephonzimmer und die Toilettenräume im Erdgeschoß gelegen. Im ersten Stock finden wir den Fest- und Speisesaal, außerdem ein durch ein paar Schiebetüren abgeschlossenes kleineres Gesellschaftszimmer, das eventuell als Bühne zu benutzen ist. Im zweiten Stockwerk befinden sich elf Bettzimmer und die nötigen Badezimmer usw., es sei hier gleich bemerkt, daß sämtliche Zimmer bereits vermietet sind. Unter dem Barzimmer befinden sich das Lesezimmer und die Räumlichkeiten für die Bibliothek sowie das Bureau des Sekretärs. Unter diesen Räumen hat die Doppelkegelbahn mit Bar und Ankleidezimmern Platz gefunden. Da das Gebäude am Abhange des Peaks liegt, ist das Flurgeschoß, von der Kennedy Road aus gesehen, von der entgegengesetzten Seite des Hauses betrachtet, das 2. Stockwerk, liegen das Lesezimmer im 1. Stockwerk und die Kegelbahn im Erdgeschoß. Vor dem Klubgebäude befindet sich noch ein etwa 3 500 m² großer, dem Klub gehörender Platz, der eventuell für Tennisplätze Verwendung finden wird.«[116]

The German club in Hongkong was founded in 1859 and by 1908, it had approximately 250 members.[113] With its airy, shady verandas on all floors, the style of the new building was similar to that common in Hongkong at the time. The British had given this undefinable style of their sub-tropical buildings the somewhat ironic title of the »comprador style«.[114] Unlike the German club which was later built in Shanghai, the German club, in Hongkong was designed by a British architect. The result was a modest building that did not reflect the nationality of its members.[115]

The *Ostasiatische Lloyd* published the following detailed description of the building on the occasion of the opening: »The ground floor has a large and roomy bar with a billiard room. There are also a telephone room and toilets. The first floor houses the party and dining rooms and a smaller function room which is closed off with sliding doors and could possibly be used as a stage. There are eleven bedrooms on the second floor with the necessary bathrooms etc. It should be noted that tenants have already been found for all of the rooms. On the floor beneath the bar there is the reading room and the rooms intended for the library and the secretary's office. On the floor below these rooms there is the double bowling lane with a bar and changing rooms. As the building is on the slope of the hill, what is the ground floor from the Kennedy Road, is the second floor on the opposite side of the building, thus from this perspective the reading room is on the first floor and the bowling alley is on the ground floor. In front of the club building there is an approximately 3 500 m² site belonging to the club which will possibly be used for tennis courts.«[116]

德國總會

地址：香港肯尼迪路（維多利亞山坡上）
建築師：E·A·拉姆
建築造價：約三十一萬五千金馬克
業主：香港德國總會
規劃期：一八九九年
落成典禮：一九零二年十二月三十一日
現狀：總會大樓已不存在

香港德國總會創辦於一八五九年。一九零八年總會有約二百五十名成員。⟨113⟩新建的總會與香港常見的樓房一樣，每屋都有通風遮蔭的拱券外廊。英國人把這種亞熱帶建築風格戲稱為"買辦建築式"。⟨114⟩與上海不同的是，香港總會是由英國建築師設計的。這座不起眼的樓房沒有反映出總會會員的國籍身份。⟨115⟩
《德文新報》對總會的開張作了詳盡的描述："一樓是寬敞的酒吧間，與此毗鄰的是彈子房。此外，電話間和廁所也設在一樓。二樓是兼作宴會廳的餐廳，還有一間可用多扇滑門隔成幾個小間的會客廳，必要時可當舞台使用。三樓有十一間臥室、浴室等。在這兒得聲明一下，所有的房間均已出租，酒吧間的下面是閱覽室，圖書館和文書辦公室。再往下一層是設有酒吧的雙軌九栓戲球場的更衣室。"樓房依山勢而建，故而從對面的肯尼迪大道看過去，實際上的二樓像是三樓，閱覽室的那層像二樓，九柱戲球場的樓房則如一樓。總會大樓前有一個面積為三千五百平米的廣場，也屬總會所有。人們偶爾也在廣場上打網球。⟨116⟩

德國總會，約一九零七年。

SHANGHAI

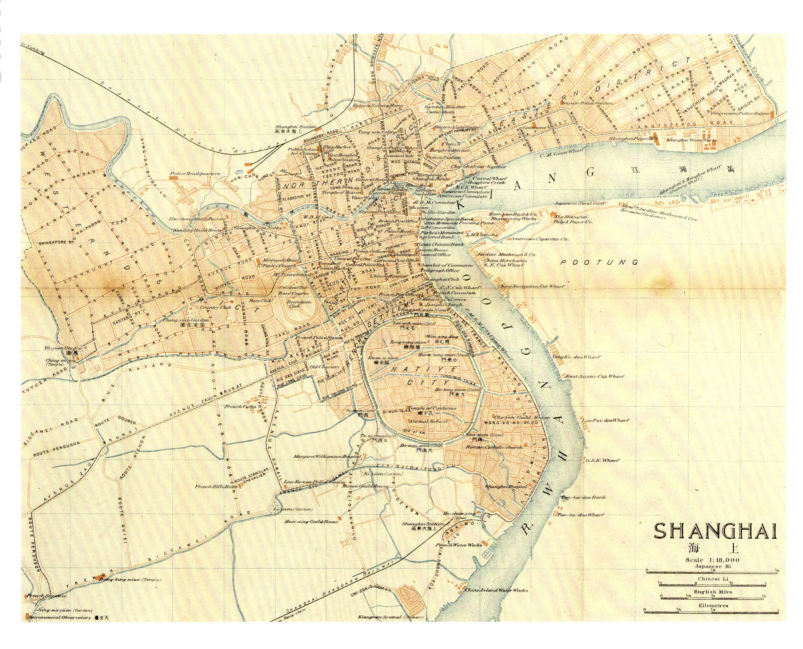

SHANGHAI (SCHANGHAI)

Ab 1843, seit der Eröffnung ausländischer Niederlassungen, entwickelte sich Shanghai zum größten Handelshafen Chinas, damals wirtschaftlich bedeutender als Hongkong oder Guangzhou (Kanton). Die Stadt liegt am Ufer des Huangpu-Flusses (Whangpoo), rund 10 km bevor er in den riesigen Yangzi-Strom mündet und dieser in das Meer.

Ausländer erhielten das Recht, innerhalb festgelegter Grenzen nördlich der chinesischen Stadt Grundstücke von den chinesischen Besitzern zu kaufen. Diese gingen dann aufgrund der Exterritorialitätsbestimmungen in die Rechtssphäre des Landes über, dessen Staatsangehörigkeit der Käufer besaß. Chinesen durften während der ersten Jahrzehnte offiziell keine solchen exterritorialen Grundstücke erwerben, jedoch konnten sie auf diesen Grundstücken wohnen und genossen dann den Schutz der Exterritorialität. Als die Taiping-Revolution 1860/64 die Umgebung Shanghais unsicher machte, und zehntausende Chinesen aus dem Umland den Schutz des Auslandes suchten, indem sie sich Wohnungen auf diesen exterritorialen Grundstücken mieteten, kam es zu einer gewaltigen Landspekulation. Chinesische Häuser bedeckten nahezu alle von Ausländern erworbenen Grundstücke und brachten hohe Mieten. Mit Hilfe von ausländischen Mittelsmännern beteiligten sich bereits damals chinesische Spekulanten an dem Geschäft und erwarben Grundstücke. Als nach Niederwerfung der Taiping-Revolution der größte Teil der chinesischen Bevölkerung wieder von Shanghai wegzog, bedeutete das den Bankrott für viele Spekulanten.[117]

Die erste Landordnung von 1845 drückte noch das Mißtrauen zwischen Ausländern und Chinesen aus. Die Europäer wollten sich durch Zusammenwohnen schützen, nur gemeinsam hätten sie gegen die Überzahl der einheimischen Bevölkerung Widerstand leisten können. Die Chinesen wollten dagegen die Europäer zwingen, sich auf einem be-

SHANGHAI

From 1843 and the founding of the foreign settlements, Shanghai developed into the biggest trading port in China, economically more important than Hongkong or Guangzhou (Canton). The city is on the banks of the river Huangpu (Whangpoo) some 10 km before it enters the great Yangtze river and the sea.

Foreigners were allowed to buy land from Chinese owners within defined boundaries to the north of the Chinese city. These sites were then transferred to the jurisdiction of the country of origin of the buyer in accordance with the extraterritorial regulations. During the first decades of this arrangement, the Chinese could not acquire any of these sites, but they could live on them and enjoy extraterritorial protection. When the Taiping Revolution of 1860/64 made the surroundings unsafe, tens of thousands of Chinese fled from the surrounding areas to seek the foreign protection by renting accommodation on these extraterritorial sites. This gave rise to widespread speculation. Chinese houses were built on nearly all of the sites acquired by foreigners, and the rents were high. Chinese speculators also became involved in the business and managed to acquire land with the help of foreign middlemen. After the defeat of the Taiping Revolution, when most of the Chinese population withdrew from Shanghai, many speculators faced bankruptcy.[117]

The first land allocation regulation of 1845 reflected the lack of trust between the foreigners and the Chinese. The Europeans wanted to protect themselves by living together, it was only as a united force that they could offer any resistance to the indigenous population who far outnumbered them. The Chinese, on the other hand, wanted to force the foreigners to settle in a certain area in order to keep them as far away as possible.[118] However, in subsequent years these positions changed and both sides came to recognise the advantages to be gained from co-opera-

上海

自一八四三年上海被闢為通商口岸以及外國租界的建立，上海很快發展成中國最大的貿易港口。較之香港、廣州，上海具有更強的經濟實力。上海地處黃浦江畔。在距上海十公里的地方，黃浦江與浩瀚的長江相聚，隨之匯入東海。

外國人有權在規定的地段內向中國人購買土地。根據治外法權的規定，這些被購買的土地隨之也納入買主國家權力管轄範圍。開始的幾十年內，中國人原則上不允許購買這種已換了國籍的土地，然而他們有權在那兒居住並享受治外法權的保護。一八六零年到一八六四年間太平天國革命也波及到上海地區，數以萬計的中國人千方百計要住進在屬於外國人的地皮上建造的房屋，以此得到外國法律的庇護。地產投機倒把也應運而生。借助於外國經濟法人的幫助，中國投機商買地建房，然後高價向中國人出租，大發橫財。而當太平天國革命失敗後，大部份中國人搬離上海時，許多投機商也因此傾家蕩產。[117]

從一八四五年制定的第一個土地法規還可以看出外國人和中國之間的隔閡頗深。歐洲人為了自衛，設法住在一起，他們認為只有聯合起來才能與數量上佔優勢的中國人抗衡。中國人則想讓外國人都住在指定的區域，而且離開得越遠越好。[118] 隨著時間的推移，人們漸漸地改變了原來的觀點，認識到合作能使雙方獲益。

外國人開始與中國商人和內地建立聯係。"力爭把盡可能多的中國人吸引到上海，以提高上海的經濟地位。"[119] 對中國人來說好處是治外法權："中國人馬上意識到財產放在外國人的租界上比官府的保護要保險得多。敲榨勒索在中國司空見慣，有錢的中國人也樂得避開中國官府的耳目。"[120]，一八九八年戊戌變法和辛亥革命之後，政治上受迫害者也在外國租界避難。一八六三年，上海成立了一個所謂多功能的法庭。該法庭授理住在外國租界內中國人之間，中國人與外國人之間的民事訴訟，負責懲辦發生在外國租界的犯罪行為。外國人必須服從本國的領事裁判權，住在租界外的中國人則要遵守中國的法律。[121] 盡管外國租界內房租昂貴，但

stimmten Gebiet niederzulassen, um sie sich dadurch so weit wie möglich vom Halse zu halten.[118] Doch in den folgenden Jahren veränderten sich diese Positionen, und man erkannte den beidseitigen Vorteil einer Zusammenarbeit. Die Ausländer suchten die Verbindung mit chinesischen Kaufleuten und zum Hinterland. »Maßgebend dafür war der Wunsch, eine möglichst große Zahl von Chinesen nach Shanghai zu ziehen, um dadurch die Bedeutung als Handelsplatz zu heben.«[119] Für die Einheimischen lag der Vorteil in der ausländischen Rechtssphäre: »Die Chinesen haben sehr bald eingesehen, daß der fremde Schutz für Eigentum viel weiter reicht, als der, den die chinesischen Behörden zu leisten vermögen. Angesichts der fortgesetzten in China üblichen Erpressung aber hatten sie andererseits geradezu ein Interesse daran, ihr Eigentum dem Machtbereich der heimischen Beamten zu entziehen.«[120] Ebenso suchten politisch Verfolgte nach dem Staatsstreich von 1898 und der Revolution von 1911 den Schutz der ausländischen Niederlassungen. Ab 1863 gab es in Shanghai einen sogenannten Gemischten Gerichtshof, der zuständig war für Prozesse von Chinesen untereinander, die in den ausländischen Niederlassungen wohnten, zwischen Ausländern und Chinesen sowie für Verbrechen, die in den Niederlassungen begangen wurden. Ausländer unterstanden der Gerichtsbarkeit ihrer Konsulate; Chinesen, die außerhalb der Niederlassungen wohnten, unterstanden der chinesischen Gerichtsbarkeit.[121] Aufgrund der größeren Sicherheit stieg trotz hoher Mieten die chinesische Einwohnerzahl in der Internationalen Niederlassung von etwa 75 000 Personen im Jahr 1870 auf eine halbe Million im Jahr 1905. Die chinesischen Familien wohnten größtenteils in sogenannten Lilong-Häusern – äußerst dicht bebauten, zwei- bis dreigeschossigen Reihen- und Hofhausgruppen. Obwohl der Anteil der Ausländer in den Niederlassungen kontinuierlich anstieg, betrug er nur rund 2 Prozent der Gesamtbevölkerung.[122] In Shanghai bewohnten die einzel-

tion. The foreigners were interested in contacts with Chinese businessmen and the hinterland. »This was characterised by the desire to attract as many Chinese as possible to Shanghai and thus raise the importance of Shanghai as a trade centre.«[119] The attraction for the natives lay in the foreign legal system: »The Chinese quickly realised that the foreign countries provided far greater protection for property than the Chinese system. Moreover, in view of the continued practice of blackmail common in China, they were also interested in removing their property from the power of the native officials.«[120] Similarly, political refugees pursued after the coup d'état of 1898 and the revolution of 1911 sought the protection of the foreign settlements. From 1863 there was a so-called »Mixed Court« in Shanghai which was responsible for legal action between Chinese parties resident in the foreign settlements, foreigners and Chinese and for crimes committed in the settlements. The foreigners were under the legal jurisdiction of their consulates. Chinese who did not live in the settlements were subject to Chinese jurisdiction.[121] Despite the higher rents, the number of Chinese inhabitants in the International Settlement rose from 75 000 in 1870 to half a million in 1905 due to the protection offered by the foreign legal systems. The Chinese families lived mainly in the so-called Li-long houses extremely densely built, two to three-storey terraced and courtyard buildings. Although the number of foreigners in the settlement rose continuously, they only represented 2 percent of the total population.[122] In Shanghai nationals from individual countries did not live in separate quarters as was the case for foreigners living in other Chinese ports, too.

Until 1912, Shanghai's Chinese quarter was surrounded by a circular city wall. The surrounding land was marsh with some farmsteads on higher sites. The foreign settlements were established to the north of the old Chinese city.[123] From 1843, the land was reclaimed, streets were laid in an irregular

為了安全起見，住在公共租界的中國人越來越多。一八七零年為七萬五千人。到一九零五年，已達到了五十萬人。大部份中國家庭住在密集、多層的成行或成矩陣的里弄樓房裡。租界裡的外國人人數也在不斷地增加，但只佔人口總數的百分之二。[122]在上海租界內，各國之間沒有劃分居住地段。其他的港口城市也是如此。

直到一九一二年，上海的城區為一堵圓形城牆所環繞。城外為沼澤地，地勢高處，散落著幾家農舍。老城區以北是外國租界。[123]一八四三年，人們開始治理沼澤地，在黃浦江畔修築防波堤，鋪設街道。建起了一個縱橫交錯的交通網。一八六五年，街道已由煤氣燈照明，一八八二年興建了一座發電廠。一八八三年，建起了第一個自來水廠。

城市發展日新月異。一八七四年，上海從第一輛人力車（黃包車）開始，至一九零二年已有汽車。電車軌道，也於一九零二年至一九零五年間鋪建完畢。本世紀初，上海已成了寸金之地，因此樓房也越建越高。一九零七年，商業區已有了七層樓高的商業辦公大廈。黃浦江邊康斜迪婭總會的地皮購於一九零四年，每平方米售價為三百二十金馬克，為當時最高價格。地皮價格與營造費用一樣高。[124]地皮價格飛漲，一八四三年至一八四四年中國初次向外國人出售土地時，每平方米售價零點一六金馬克，這個價格已比通敘價格要高出一倍。[125]

在租界裡，外國房地產主起著舉足輕重的作用。因為只有那些有地產的以及交納得起高稅額的人才有權選舉工部局議員或當選的議員。工部局，領事館和協約國的大使共同執政。因此也常常發生權力糾紛。工部局議員席位的分配並未體現各國的經濟實力，英國在工部局中勢力大，上海的德國僑民對此深感遺憾。

當時流行的建築形式也反映了英國的影響根深蒂固。直到本世紀初，那種屋頂坡度平緩，設有拱券外廊的典型英國殖民地建築物在上海還比比皆是。"上海像一座愴促建起的城市"。樓房都是清一色的紅磚或灰磚清水牆，屋頂都是千篇一律的鍍鋅鐵皮。我聽說，人們將這種單調的建築形式諷喻為上海式文藝復興風格。[126]一九

nen Nationen keine voneinander getrennten Stadtviertel, wie es unter den Ausländern in anderen chinesischen Hafenstädten ebenfalls üblich war.

Shanghais chinesischer Stadtteil war bis 1912 von einer ringförmig verlaufenden Stadtmauer umgeben. Das umliegende Land war ursprünglich Sumpfland. Nördlich dieser chinesischen Altstadt entstanden die ausländischen Niederlassungen.[123] Ab 1843 wurde das Land trockengelegt und aufgeschüttet, Straßen wurden in einem unregelmäßigen Raster parallel und rechtwinklig zum Fluß angelegt, das Ufer befestigt. Seit 1865 waren die Straßen mit Gas beleuchtet, 1882 wurde das erste Elekrizitätswerk gebaut, 1883 das erste Wasserwerk.

Die Stadt entwickelte sich sehr schnell. 1874 kam die erste Rikscha nach Shanghai, 1902 das erste Auto. Eine elektrische Straßenbahn wurde zwischen 1902 und 1905 erbaut. Shanghais Grundstückspreise waren bereits um die Jahrhundertwende so hoch, daß die Grundstücke immer dichter und höher bebaut werden mußten. So entstanden im Geschäftsviertel 1907 bereits siebengeschossige Gebäude. 320 Goldmark pro m² mußten 1904 für das Grundstück des Club Concordia am Bund bezahlt werden, der höchste bis dahin in Shanghai für Bauland bezahlte Preis. Das Grundstück kostete genausoviel wie der gesamte Neubau.[124] Gigantische Preissteigerungen hatten seit der Gründung der Niederlassung stattgefunden. 1843/44 waren die ersten Grundstücke für etwa 0,16 Goldmark pro m² von den chinesischen Grundbesitzern an Ausländer verkauft worden, das Doppelte des damals üblichen Preises.[125]

Die Regierung der Niederlassungen wurde durch die ausländischen Grundbesitzer bestimmt. Wahlberechtigt für den Stadtrat oder Mitglieder des Stadtrates selber waren nur Ausländer, die Grundbesitzer oder Mieter waren und deren Steuerzahlungen festgelegte hohe Werte überschritten. Der Stadtrat teilte sich die Macht mit dem Konsularkorps, den Konsuln der Vertragsmächte, was regelmäßig

grid parallel and at right angles to the river, the embankment was reinforced. From 1865 there were gaslights on the streets; in 1882 the first electricity station was built, in 1883 the first waterworks.

The city developed rapidly. In 1874 the first rickshaw came to Shanghai, in 1902 the first car, and an electric tram system was built between 1902 and 1905. The cost of land in Shanghai was so high at the turn of the century that the heights of the buildings began to increase dramatically. By 1907, there were seven-storey buildings in the commercial quarter. In 1904, 320 gold marks per square metre was paid for the site for the Club Concordia on the Bund, the embankment road, the highest price to be paid for a site in Shanghai at the time. The site cost as much as the new building.[124] The price of land had risen steeply since the foundation of the settlements. In 1843/44 the first sites had been sold by the Chinese to foreigners for approximately 0.16 gold marks per square metre which was double the standard price at the time.[125]

The settlement authority was elected by the foreign land owners. Only foreigners who owned or rented land and paid taxes in excess of the quotas could vote in elections for the city council or become members of the council. The city council shared power with the consular corps and the consuls of the treaty powers, an arrangement which resulted in frequent disagreements. To the regret of the German population of Shanghai, the individual nations were not represented on the city council in accordance with their economic power, the council was, in fact, dominated by the British.

The architecture also reflected this influence. The British colonial style with its verandas surrounding the building and low sloping roofs characterised the architecture of Shanghai up to the turn of the century. »Shanghai was a city that appeared to have been built in a hurry, the buildings being designed in a monotonous fashion with red and blue bricks,

零四至一九零七年，具有德國文藝復興式復古風格的德國總會大樓落成，這幢具有典型的德意志民族傳統形式的樓房與英國殖民地式的建築截然不同。在隨後的十年裡，黃浦江沿岸及幾條與其平行的商業街迅速發展。國際貿易大廈林立，上海成了世界矚目的城市。

一九一零年，約一萬五千外國人僑居上海，其中德國人一千左右。[127]第一次世界大戰前後上海都曾有過德國僑民文化娛樂中心。德國領事館一八八五年、基督教堂一九零一年和德國學堂均建在蘇州河與黃浦江的交匯處，構成了一個建築群體。從領事館可眺望黃浦江對岸的秀麗景色和沿岸停泊的船隻。在黃浦公園附近的綠色草坪上屹立著伊爾蒂斯青銅雕紀念碑一八九八年，其斜對面是當年外灘上最高的建築——德國總會康科迪婭。遠離市中心的商業區，在跑馬場以西的地段上，還有許多德國建築：德國花園總會一九零四年，醫學院一九零七年，威廉學堂一九一一年，德國工程學院——同濟大學一九一四年以及許多私人住宅。

一九一七年三月，中國向德國和奧匈帝國宣戰。兩年後，三千五百名德國人和奧地利人中的大部分人被驅逐出境。[128]一九二零年，德國商人重返中國。因為協約國施加壓力，中國政府才不得不把德國人遣送回國。但中德貿易關係並未受到影響。不少中國人出面保護德國合伙人的財產，把生意繼續做下去。德國在中國不再享受治外法權、領事司法權等特權，而作為平等的商業伙伴與中國通商。隨著時局的變化，德國僑民文化娛樂中心被遷移到遠離黃浦江和商業區的樹木茂盛環境幽靜的西部地區。在那兒，德國僑民文化娛樂中心、威廉學堂一九二九年，重新修復的伊利蒂斯紀念碑、新的基督教堂一九三二年，以及不遠處的德國總會約一九二五年形成了一個新的德國文化中心。

同濟大學的新校舍於一九二零年到一九二四年間在上海吳淞陸續竣工。吳淞區位於黃浦江和長江的交匯口不遠處。德國選擇這一地段作為同濟的校址是為了支持中國"大上海"城市發展規劃。[129]按照這一規劃，吳淞地區將興建一個與法國租界和公共租界鼎峙的中國人城區。一九三七

zu Unstimmigkeiten führte. Zum Bedauern der deutschen Bewohner Shanghais waren im Stadtrat die einzelnen Nationen nicht nach ihrer wirtschaftlichen Handelsstärke vertreten, vielmehr war der Stadtrat britisch dominiert.

Auch in der Architektur spiegelte sich dieser Einfluß wider. Der englische Kolonialstil mit seinen umlaufenden Veranden und den flach geneigten Dächern bestimmte das Bild Shanghais bis zur Jahrhundertwende. »Shanghai erschien wie eine in Eile erbaute Stadt, die Gebäude wurden auf monotone Art und Weise aus roten und blaugrauen Backsteinen errichtet und fast immer mit verzinkten Eisenblechen gedeckt. Ich habe gehört, wie dieser ›Stil‹ ironisch die ›Shanghai Renaissance‹ genannt wurde.«[126] Der deutsche Klub wurde 1904 bis 1907 in der Art der deutschen Neorenaissance errichtet; er war das erste Gebäude in einem typisch nationalen Baustil, das sich völlig von dem britischen Kolonialstil abhob. Im folgenden Jahrzehnt entstand am Bund – der Uferstraße – und den Parallelstraßen eine Reihe von internationalen Geschäftshäusern, die auch äußerlich die Internationalität Shanghais darstellten.

Im Jahre 1910 lebten etwa 1000 Deutsche in Shanghai, bei einer Gesamtzahl von damals etwas über 15000 Ausländern.[127] Vor und nach dem Ersten Weltkrieg gab es jeweils ein kleines kulturelles deutsches Zentrum in der Stadt: Das deutsche Generalkonsulat (1885 erbaut) mit der evangelischen Kirche (1901) und der deutschen Schule (1901) bildeten um die Jahrhundertwende eine Häusergruppe an der Einmündung des Suzhou-Creeks in den breiten Huangpu-Fluß. Vom Konsulat aus hatte man einen hervorragenden Blick über den Fluß und die gegenüberliegende Uferstraße, den Bund, an dem die Schiffe anlegten. In einer Parkfläche am Bund stand das bronzene Iltis-Denkmal (1898). Diesem schräg gegenüber lag der deutsche Club Concordia (1907), das bis in die 20er Jahre höchste Gebäude am Bund. Weit von diesem Zentrum entfernt, außerhalb der Geschäftsstadt und

and roofed almost invariably with galvanised iron sheets. I have heard the ›style‹ cynically named ›Shanghai Renaissance‹.«[126] The German club was built between 1904 and 1907 in German neo-Renaissance style; it was the first building to be built in a typical national style that was completely different to the British colonial style. During the subsequent decade, a series of buildings housing international companies sprang up on the Bund – embankment road – and the parallel streets which externally reflected Shanghai's cosmopolitan population.

In 1910 there were 1000 Germans living in Shanghai out of a total of over 15000 foreigners.[127] Before and after the First World War there was a small German cultural centre: around the turn of the century, the German consulate general (1885) with the Protestant church (1901) and the German school (1901) formed a small group of buildings where the Suzhou Creek entered the vast Huangpu river. There was an excellent view from the consulate across the river to the Bund, where the ships used to anchor. The bronze Iltis memorial (1898) was erected in the park area at the Bund. The German Club Concordia (1907) stood diagonally opposite this monument; the Club Concordia was the highest building in Shanghai until the 1920s. Quite a distance from this centre, outside the commercial centre and west of the race course, the German Garden Club (1904), the School of Medicine (1907), the Kaiser Wilhelm School (1911) and the German School of Engineering, Tongji University (1914), and several private residences had been built.

In March 1917, China declared war on Germany and Austria-Hungary, and two years later most of the 3500 Germans living in China were expelled.[128] The German traders began to return in 1920. As it was the Allies who had forced the Chinese government to repatriate the Germans, the relationship with Chinese business partners had not been affected, in many cases the latter had protected the foreign property and continued the business

年，當日軍佔領上海郊區時這一城區初具規模。

westlich der Pferderennbahn befanden sich der deutsche Gartenklub (1904), die Medizinschule (1907), die Kaiser-Wilhelm-Schule (1911) und die Deutsche Ingenieurschule – Tongji-Universität (1914) sowie mehrere private Wohnhäuser.

China erklärte Deutschland und Österreich-Ungarn im März 1917 den Krieg, zwei Jahre später wurden die meisten der in China lebenden 3 500 Deutschen und Österreicher ausgewiesen.[128] Ab 1920 kamen die deutschen Kaufleute zurück. Da es die Alliierten gewesen waren, die die chinesischen Behörden zur Repatriierung der Deutschen gedrängt hatten, war das Verhältnis zu den chinesischen Geschäftspartnern unbeeinflußt, oftmals hatten diese das fremde Eigentum geschützt und die Geschäfte fortgeführt. Die Rechte der Exterritorialität und die Konsulargerichtsbarkeit besaßen Deutsche in China jetzt nicht mehr. Deutschland war die erste der ehemaligen Kolonialmächte, die ohne koloniale Privilegien als gleichberechtigte Nation mit China Handel trieb. Unter diesen veränderten Bedingungen bildete sich ein neues deutsches Zentrum in Shanghai, jetzt weit vom Huangpu-Fluß und dem Geschäftsviertel entfernt, im grünen Westend der Stadt. Es bestand aus dem deutschen Gemeindehaus mit der Kaiser-Wilhelm-Schule (1929), dem dort wiedererrichteten Iltis-Denkmal (1929) und der neuen Deutsch-Evangelischen Kirche (1932); nicht weit entfernt lag der neue deutsche Gartenklub (um 1925).

Die Neubauten der Tongji-Universität wurden 1920/24 in Shanghais Vorort Wusong (Woosung), nahe der Mündung des Huangpu-Flusses in den Yangzi, fertiggestellt. Mit der Wahl dieses Standortes unterstützte Deutschland das chinesische Stadtentwicklungskonzept »Greater Shanghai«,[129] das ein neues chinesisches Stadtzentrum, eine Art chinesische Niederlassung neben den beiden ausländischen bilden sollte. Bis 1937 stellte man dieses Stadtviertel in großen Teilen fertig, dann wurden die Vororte Shanghais durch japanische Truppen besetzt.

links. Germans no longer enjoyed extraterritorial rights and consular jurisdiction in China. Germany was the first of the former colonial powers to engage in business with China on an equal basis without colonial privileges. It was under these new conditions that a new German cultural centre was established in Shanghai, this time far away from the Huangpu river and the commercial quarter in the leafy west end of the city. The new German centre consisted of the German Community Centre with the Kaiser Wilhelm School (1929) and the re-erected Iltis memorial (1929) and the new German Protestant Church (1932); the new German Garden Club was also nearby (around 1925).

The new buildings of the Tongji University were completed between 1920/24 in the suburb of Wusong (Woosung) which was near where the Huangpu entered the Yangtze. In selecting this location, Germany expressed its support for China's urban development concept for »Greater Shanghai«[129], which planned to establish a new Chinese urban centre, a kind of Chinese settlement beside the two foreign settlements. Large sections of this quarter were completed by 1937 when Shanghai's suburbs were occupied by Japanese troops.

SHANGHAI

CLUB CONCORDIA

Funktion ab 1923. Use after 1923
Bank of China
Zhongshan Dongyilu/Dianche Lu (The Bund 22/Jin Kee Road), Shanghai

Architekten. Architects
Heinrich Becker, A. Dörffel

Innenarchitekt. Interior architecture
Carl Baedecker

Baukosten. Building costs
etwa 388 800 Goldmark
approximately 388 800 gold marks

Innenausbau. Interior
etwa 224 100 Goldmark
approximately 224 100 gold marks

Ausführung. Contractors
Kang Yü-Ki

Bauherr. Client
Club Concordia, Shanghai

Bauzeit. Construction time
Oktober 1904 – Februar 1907
October 1904 – February 1907

Zustand. Condition
Das Gebäude wurde 1934 abgetragen für den Neubau der Bank of China.
Pulled down in 1934 and replaced by a new building for the Bank of China.

Club Concordia, Perspektivzeichnung. Blick von der Uferstraße, 1904
Ostansicht vom Bund, 1907
Club Concordia, perspective, view from the Bund, 1904
View from the east, from the Bund, 1907

Die deutschen Kaufleute hatten sich am Bund, der Uferstraße Shanghais, mit dem Club Concordia ein fast provozierend großes Gebäude errichtet. Am 22. Oktober 1904 wurde durch Prinz Adalbert von Preußen, Sohn des deutschen Kaisers Wilhelm II., der Grundstein gelegt. Der Architekt Heinrich Becker könnte die Idee zu diesem Entwurf durch Veröffentlichungen über das Deutsche Haus auf der Weltausstellung in Paris 1900 erhalten haben.[130] Aus klimatischen Gründen integrierte Becker allerdings die in Asien üblichen Veranden in die Fassade, so daß sie anstelle von Fenstern große offene Loggien besaß. Dies ergab eine gewisse Verfremdung der deutschen Neorenaissance.

Zur Einweihung des Klubs schrieben die *Shanghaier Nachrichten:* »In gut nationaler Überlieferung, d.h. in den besten Formen deutscher Renaissance, die trotz modernen und neudeutschem Stil auch heute noch ihren Platz zu behaupten weiß, ist der Bau entstanden. Der schlanke, kupfergedeckte Turm, der bis zu einer Höhe von 48 Metern aufstrebt, die breiten Giebel und die hohen pfannengedeckten Dächer sowie auch die weitausladenden Terrassen erinnern an die alten Zunft- und Gildenhäuser, wie sie in alten Städten aller deutschen Gauen zu finden sind, oder auch an die turmgeschmückten stolzen Kaufhäuser und Tuchhallen altflandrischer Orte. So mag der Turm am neuen Clubhaus als Wahrzeichen des stark erblühten deutschen Handels im Fernen Osten gelten, wenn es auch wohl in erster Reihe in der Absicht des Baumeisters lag, dem Bau dadurch mehr Silhouette zu geben und gleichzeitig das langgestreckte Panorama Shanghais zu beleben. Die hellen Verblendplättchen, die die Außenmauern bekleiden, geben dem Bau ein äußerst gefälliges, sauberes Aussehen, und wenn die dunklen Kupferdächer des Turmes und der Erker im Laufe der Zeiten durch Sonne und Regen erst eine hellgrüne Patina erhalten haben, wird der Eindruck des Ganzen noch gewinnen. Eine Sonnenuhr in unvergänglichem Glasmo-

With the Club Concordia, the German business community built themselves a large, almost audacious, building on the Bund, embankment road, in Shanghai. On 22 October 1904 the foundation stone was laid by Prince Adalbert of Prussia, the son of Kaiser Wilhelm II. The architect Heinrich Becker may have taken the inspiration for this German neo-Renaissance building from publications about the German building at the World Exposition in Paris in 1900.[130] For climatic reasons, however, Becker included in the façade some of the features common in Asian architecture at the time, such as the verandas, with the result that instead of glazed windows, the building had large open loggias. This alienated the German neo-Renaissance elements somewhat.

The *Shanghaier Nachrichten* had the following to say on the occasion of the opening of the club: »This building is an excellent product of the importation of national styles, i.e. the best features of the German Renaissance which, despite the emergence of a modern and new German style, can still hold its head up today. The slim, copper covered tower, which reaches a height of 48 metres, the wide gables and the high pantiled roofs, and also the wide protruding terraces are reminiscent of the guild houses which can be found in old towns in German areas, or also the proud commercial houses and textile halls with their decorative towers to be found in old Flemish towns. The tower of the new club house could be seen as a symbol of the great flourishing of German trade in the Far East, even if the Architect's primary motivation was to give the building a better silhouette and at the same time liven up Shanghai's long horizontal panorama. The bright surface panels covering the outer walls lend the building an extremely attractive, clean appearance and when the dark copper roofs of the tower and the oriels have acquired a bright green patina through the effects of the sun and rain, the appearance will still be impressive. A sun dial in exquisite glass mosaic decorates the

德國人委託建築師在上海外灘建了這幢氣勢雄偉的康科迪婭總會大廈。一九零四年十月二十二號普魯士王子阿達爾貝特（威廉二世之子）參加了奠基禮。建築師海因里希·貝克也許是參閱了一九零零年巴黎國際博覽會發表的關於德國館的資料，受啟發設計了這幢具有德國文藝復興式復古風格的大樓。〈130〉但考慮到氣候特點，貝克將在亞洲通行的敞廊取代立面上的玻璃窗。這一改動給德國文藝復興式風格增添了異彩。

《上海新聞》對總會大樓的落成作了描寫："德國總會承襲傳統的民族手法，再現了德國文藝復興風采並獲得了最佳效果。"盡管當前建築流派繁多，現代派和德國青年派異軍突起而文藝復興的古風仍久盛不衰。以青銅冠頂，高達四十八米的尖塔、寬寬的山牆，鋪著波形瓦高聳的樓頂以及開闊的平台令人想起德國行政區古城邑的行幫會建築，佛蘭德地區以塔裝飾的雄偉的商業大樓和布商行會堆棧倉庫。雖然建築師設計高塔的初衷只是要給康科迪婭總會的立體輪廓以更多的動感，同時使上海的全景更為錯落有致，然而總會的高塔本身卻又標誌著德國在遠東貿易的輝煌成就。鑲在外牆上淺色的裝飾板使總會大樓顯得舒適、潔淨。高塔及轉角挑樓的深色銅頂隨著歲月的流逝，經風吹日晒將變成淡綠色，從總體上就會更加壯觀。一只用彩色有機玻璃拼嵌的太陽鐘點綴著塔樓南牆。樓頂的平台上，立著一尊英武的衛士雕像。黃浦江邊的入口前鋪墊著有熟鐵護欄的寬闊花崗石台階。通向總會樓上的房間和十個單獨套房的入口設在錦江路。〈131〉

（音譯）英文月刊《上海社會》詳盡地描寫了總會大樓內的陳設："酒吧和入口都在一層樓，酒吧的內部裝飾別有風味，描繪柏林和不來梅風光的壁畫令人賞心悅目。華麗的枝形吊燈使酒吧大放光明……。天花板的裝飾也獨具匠心，在每一根頂樑上鐫刻著精選的名言警句。房間基調色是蘭色，間以淡黃和棕色。緊靠著酒吧是台球房和閱覽室。大廳粉刷成赤陶色，再以青銅色和乳白色作為喧染。大廳的交叉穹窿本身就是集華美與高雅於一身的藝術品。每個步入大廳目睹交叉穹窿的人都會體驗到一種藝術的升華。通向樓上

康科迪婭總會

用途：一九二三年後為中國銀行辦公樓
所在地：上海中山東一路（滇池路口）；
　　　　原外灘二十二號
建築師：海因里希·貝克
室內裝飾設計：卡爾·培迪克
建築造價：約三十八點八八萬金馬克，合
　　　　　銀元十四點四萬兩；室內：二
　　　　　十二點四一萬金馬克
施工：康裕科（音譯）
業主：上海康科迪婭總會
建造期：一九零四年十月至一九零七年二月
現狀：一九三四年被拆除，易建新的中國銀行大廈

外灘方向望康科迪婭總會透視圖，一九零四年。
臨外灘東面外觀，一九零七年。

saik schmückt die Südwand des Turms. Die breite granitene Eingangstreppe am Bund ziert ein schmiedeeisernes Geländer (…). An der oberen Terrasse hält ein stattlicher Landsknecht Wacht. Ein besonderer Eingang zu den oberen Clubräumlichkeiten und den 10 Privatzimmern befindet sich an der Jinkee Road.«[131]

In der englischen Monatsillustrierten *Social Shanghai* werden die Innenräume detailliert beschrieben: »Die Bar liegt auf gleicher Ebene mit der Eingangshalle und ist einzigartig, was ihre Ausstattung betrifft. Wunderschöne Wandmalereien stellen Berlin und Bremen dar, und eine Reihe eleganter Elektrolüster (…) dienen zur Beleuchtung. (…) Ungewöhnlich ist die Decke gestaltet, auf deren Balken mehrere gut ausgewählte bekannte Aussprüche in deutscher Sprache aufgemalt sind. Die Hauptfarbe dieses Raumes ist blau auf einem Hintergrund von cremefarben und zedernbraun. (…) Die Ausschmückung der Eingangshalle ist vollständig in Terrakottatönen gehalten, aufgelockert durch Kupfergrün und Elfenbein. Das hohe Kreuzgewölbe der Hallendecke ist in sich ein Kunstwerk, das den Eindruck von Würde und Pracht verstärkt, den man beim Betreten der Halle gewinnt. Und im ganzen Fernen Osten gibt es keinen grandioseren Treppenaufgang als diese weite Flucht aus weißen Stufen, die ins erste Obergeschoß führen. (…) Am Fuße dieser Treppe befindet sich ein wunderschöner Brunnen (…). Der Speisesaal befindet sich auf der ersten Etage und beeindruckt durch seine Weiträumigkeit und künstlerische Inneneinrichtung. Am Ende des Raumes befindet sich eine Bühne für die Musiker, und alle Möbel und Ausstattungsstücke beweisen ausgezeichneten Geschmack. Der Saal ist gut beleuchtet: zahlreiche fein bemalte, farbige Glasfenster tragen die Wappen fast aller Nationen. Ansichten von Berlin, Wien und München schmücken die Wände, und die Wandtäfelung ist ein richtiges Kunstwerk, wie überhaupt alle Holzschnitzarbeiten im ganzen Klub wundervoll sind und zu den wenigen

southern wall of the tower. The wide granite steps at the entrance at the Bund are decorated by a wrought iron hand rail (…). A sturdy rural knight guards the upper terrace. There is a separate entrance to the upper rooms of the club and the 10 private rooms on Jinkee Road.«[131]

The interior is described in detail in the British monthly magazine *Social Shanghai* as follows: »The bar-room is on the entrance floor, and it is quite unique as far as decorations are concerned. Beautiful mural paintings representing Berlin and Bremen decorate the walls, and a number of fine electroliers (…) are used for illuminating purposes. (…) A quaint idea is adopted in the decoration of the ceiling, on the rafters of which are painted several well-chosen quotations in German. The principle colour in this room is blue against a background of cream colour and cedar brown. The billiard and reading rooms both adjoin the bar. (…) The decorations of the hall are carried out entirely in a rich shade of terra cotta relieved with bronze green and ivory colour. The lofty groined ceiling is in itself a work of art that adds to the effect of dignity and grandeur which immediately impresses one on entering the hall, and there is no grander stairway in the Far East than the wide flight of white marble steps which leads to the first floor. (…) Near the foot of the stairway is a beautiful fountain (…). The dining-room is on the first floor and one is at once struck by its spacious dimensions and artistic fitments. There is a musician's gallery at one end and all the furniture and appointments display excellent taste and judgement. It is well lighted by means of innumerable fine-stained-glass windows bearing the coat of arms of nearly all the nations. Views of Berlin, Vienna and Munich decorate the walls and the panelling is quite a work of art, but indeed the carved wood-work throughout the Club is the most wonderful and is one of the few parts of the decoration that has not been imported from home, as it has been designed and made here in Shanghai (…).«[132]

Deutsches Haus auf der Weltausstellung in Paris, 1900
Der Bund in Shanghai. Blick von Süden nach Norden, vor 1914
German house, World Exhibition Paris, 1900
The Bund in Shanghai, south-north view, prior to 1914

外灘街景,從南望北,攝於一九一四年前。
巴黎世界博覽會德國館,一九零零年。

的白色階梯氣勢宏大,在整個遠東地區首屈一指……。在樓梯盡端是造型優美的噴泉。餐廳設在二樓,廳堂軒敞,陳設雅緻,令人難以忘懷。餐廳的一端設有樂台。家具等內部設施都體現了高雅的情趣。餐廳有眾多的彩色玻璃窗,窗上的精美圖案描繪出各國家的國徽。柏林、維也納和慕尼黑的風景畫裝點著牆壁。總會大樓裡的木雕裝飾品美不勝收,木製護牆鑲板也不例外,只有少數的內部裝修構件,如護牆鑲板不是從德國木土運來,而是在上海設計制作的"。〈132〉

一九零七年,德國總會約有五百四十名不同國籍的會員,其中的二百二十名並不住在上海。〈133〉竣工後的總會大樓比周圍的建築物要高出兩倍,成了外灘醒目的標誌。由於塔身高,直到二十年代總會大樓還是外灘上最高的建築物。大型海輪從東海駛進黃浦江,要正對著德國總會大廈航行幾公里,總會大樓成了"民族意識的豐碑,德國在遠東貿易蒸蒸日上的象徵。"〈134〉

建築師海因里希·貝克出生於什未林,在慕尼黑學習建築。〈135〉以後他在開羅工作了五年。埃及政府就他在那裡設計工作給予他很高的榮譽。一八九八年,貝克作為第一個德國建築師到上海,並成了德國各機構團體的建築師。德華銀行在中國的分行幾乎都由他設計。一九一一年四月,貝克結束了他在中國的工作,取道澳大利亞返回德國。貝克的同窗卡爾·培迪克曾是科隆城建部門的建築師。一九零五年,他到上海與貝克合作。一九一二年後培迪克先後設計了上海和武漢的德國工學院的校舍。〈136〉

Ausstattungsstücken gehören, die nicht aus der Heimat importiert, sondern hier in Shanghai entworfen und ausgeführt wurden. (…).«[132]

Der deutsche Klub hatte 1907 etwa 540 Mitglieder, von denen 220 nicht in Shanghai lebten. Er war ein kulturelles deutsches Zentrum mit internationaler Zusammensetzung seiner Mitglieder.[133] Das neue Klubhaus stellte ein markantes Zeichen dar, es überragte in den Jahren nach seiner Fertigstellung alle umliegenden Gebäude um das Doppelte. Durch seinen Turm war es bis in die Mitte der 20er Jahre das höchste Gebäude am Bund. Die großen Ozeandampfer fuhren vom Meer kommend den Huangpu-Fluß hinauf und dabei einige Kilometer direkt auf den Klub zu, bevor sie anlegten. Das »Denkmal nationaler Gesinnung« und »Wahrzeichen des emporgeblühten deutschen Handels im Fernen Osten«[134] wurde in britischen Veröffentlichungen als »wahrscheinlich das beeindruckendste Gebäude am Bund« [135] bezeichnet. Die englischen Kaufleute reagierten darauf mit einem Neubau ihres »Shanghai Club«, dessen Grundstein im Februar 1909 ebenfalls am Bund gelegt wurde.

Architekt Heinrich Becker wurde in Schwerin geboren und hatte in München studiert. Danach arbeitete er fünf Jahre in Kairo. Für seine Tätigkeit dort wurde ihm von der ägyptischen Regierung eine hohe Auszeichnung verliehen. 1898 kam Becker als erster deutscher Architekt nach Shanghai und wurde zum Architekten der deutschen Gemeinde. Er entwarf fast alle chinesischen Filialen der Deutsch-Asiatischen Bank. Am 4. März 1911 beendete Heinrich Becker seine Tätigkeit in China und kehrte über Australien nach Deutschland zurück.

Beckers Partner und Studienfreund Carl Baedecker war Architekt in der Stadtbauverwaltung von Köln, bevor er 1905 nach Shanghai kam. Baedecker baute ab 1912 die beiden deutschen Ingenieurschulen in Shanghai und Wuhan.[136]

Treppenhaus, 1907
Bar-Raum, 1907
Staircase, 1907
Bar, 1907

In 1907, the German Club had approximately 540 members, 220 of whom did not live in Shanghai. It was a German cultural centre with international members.[133] The new club house was a striking feature on the Bund and after completion it was twice the height of the surrounding buildings. Its tower made it the tallest building on the Bund until the mid 1920s. The great ocean liners coming from the sea approached from the Huangpu river and moved up towards the club for a few kilometres before they anchored. The »memorial to the national character« and »symbol of the blossoming of German trade in the Far East«[134] was described in British publications as »probably the most striking building on the Bund«.[135] The British traders reacted by rebuilding their »Shanghai Club«, the foundation stone of which was laid in February 1909, also on the Bund.

The architect Heinrich Becker was born in Schwerin and studied in Munich. He then worked in Cairo for five years and received an honour from the Egyptian government for his work there. In 1898 Becker was the first German architect to come to Shanghai and became the architect of the German community. He designed almost all of the Chinese branches of the German-Asian Bank. On 4 March 1911 he ended his work in China and returned to Germany via Australia.

Becker's partner and university friend Carl Baedecker was an architect in the municipal building department in Cologne before he came to Shanghai in 1905. From 1912 Baedecker built the two German engineering schools in Shanghai and Wuhan.[136]

樓道・一九零七年。
酒吧・一九零七年。

DEUTSCHER GARTENCLUB
GERMAN GARDEN CLUB

Huaihai Zhonglu/Maoming Nanlu
(Avenue Paul Brunat 474), Shanghai

Architekt. Architect

Heinrich Becker

Gartenarchitekt. Garden architecture

Th. Eckhardt

Bauherr. Client

Deutscher Gartenclub Shanghai
German Garden Club Shanghai

Bauzeit. Construction time

1904

Zustand. Condition

Das Gebäude wurde in den 20er Jahren abgetragen für den Neubau des Französischen Klubs, heute New Garden Hotel. Pulled down during the 1920s and replaced by the new building for the French Club, now the New Garden Hotel.

Deutscher Gartenclub, um 1907
German Garden Club, around 1907

Die Pläne für den Gartenklub wurden im November 1903 ausgestellt, ein Jahr vor dem Architektenwettbewerb für den Club Concordia. Der Architekt Becker wählte beim deutschen Gartenklub zum erstenmal in Shanghai einen typisch deutschen Heimatbaustil, in deutlicher Abgrenzung zum britischen Country Club. Als malerisch-altmodisch bezeichneten britische Journalisten dieses Gebäude. Die Innenräume werden in der Zeitschrift *Social Shanghai* detailliert beschrieben: »Der Salon ist mit einer malerisch gestalteten Einrichtung aus naturfarbenem Teakholz ausgestattet, die mit in Grüntönen gehaltenen, herkömmlich gemusterten Dekorationsstoffen bezogen ist. Der Teppich ist aus moosgrünem Velours, die Wände sind in sanftem Rosa gestrichen und durch einen zitronengelben Fries abgeschlossen.«[137]

Im Sommer nutzte man den Klub vor allem zum Tennisspielen: es gab 10 Doppeltennisplätze. 1910 wurde eine große Rollschuhbahn angelegt, ein damals in Shanghai sehr beliebter Sport. Zu festlichen Anlässen erleuchteten Lampions nachts den Park.

Mitglieder der deutschen Gemeinde Shanghais hatten den deutschen Gartenklub gegründet, weil der britische Country Club in der Bubbling Well Road nur eine begrenzte Anzahl britischer Mitglieder aufnahm. Man kaufte ein Grundstück in einer angemessenen Entfernung zum Geschäftsviertel der Internationalen Niederlassung und finanzierte den Bau über Anteilsscheine der zukünftigen Mitglieder.

The plans for the Garden Club were completed in November 1903, one year before the competition for the Club Concordia. The architect, Becker, initially chose a German architectural style for the German Garden Club, used here for the first time in Shanghai, which could be instantly recognisable and would immediately distinguish the building from the British Country Club. British critics described the building as quaintly old-fashioned. The interior is described in detail in the magazine *Social Shanghai*: »The drawing-room is entirely arranged with quaintly designed fitment furnishings, made of natural coloured teak, and upholstered with a tapestry of conventional design in shades of green. The carpet is moss velvet pile, and the walls are a soft pink, finished with a sulphur coloured freize.«[137]

The club was mainly used for tennis matches in summer: it had ten double tennis courts. In 1910 a big roller skating rink was built in the grounds; roller skating was a popular sport in Shanghai at the time. During festivities the park was lit at night using Chinese lanterns.

Members of Shanghai's German community had decided to found the German Garden Club because the British Country Club on Bubbling Well Road only accepted a limited number of members who had to be British nationals. A site was purchased at a suitable distance from the commercial quarter in the International Settlement and the building was financed through shares purchased by future members.

德國花園總會

所在地：上海淮海中路（茂名南路口）；
　　　　臣寶昌路四七四號
建築師：海因里蒂・貝克
園藝設計：Th・埃克哈德
業主：上海德國花園總會
現狀：在二十年代被拆除；新建法國俱樂
　　　部，現在為上海花園飯店

花園總會的設計圖完成於一九零三年十一月，比德國康科迪婭總會建築設計方案招標早一年。建築師貝克在設計花園總會時第一次在上海採用了風格與英國斜橋總會迥然不同的、具有濃厚德國鄉土氣息的建築形式。報社記者用古樸、典雅來評價這座花園建築。《上海社會》對花園總會的室內裝飾作了如下的描寫："交誼廳的陳設由本色的柚木製成，式樣精巧別緻。沙發、靠背椅的凳子等物均配有繪著美麗花紋的綠色裝飾罩。地毯由苔綠色的絲絨織成。牆壁刷成柔和悅目的粉紅色。黃色的裝飾線勾勒出牆壁的上沿"。〈137〉

夏天，總會基本上用作網球場，共有十個雙打的場地。一九一零年建造了一個大的旱冰場，溜旱冰是當時喜聞樂見的體育鍛煉形式。在晚間舉行慶祝活動時，花園裡燈籠高照，更加了喜慶的氣氛。位於泉涌路（意譯）的英國斜橋總會只接納數額有限的會員，而且只吸收英國人入會，所以僑居上海的德國人決定成立自己的花園總會。他們在遠離公共租界商業區的地段上購置了地皮，鼓勵未來的會員購買股票，以籌集建造資金。

德國花園俱樂部，約一九零七年。

SHANGHAI

ILTIS-DENKMAL
THE ILTIS MEMORIAL

Bis 1918. Location up to 1918
Zhongshan Dongyilu (The Bund), Shanghai
Ab 1929. Location from 1929
Yan'an Xilu/Huashanlu
(Great Western Road 1/Avenue Haig),
Shanghai

Entwurf. Design
Reinhold Begas, Bildhauer, Berlin;
Georg Alexander Müller, Korvettenkapitän
Reinhold Begas, sculptor; Lieutenant
Commander Georg Alexander Müller

Ausführung. Contractors
August Kraus, Bildhauer;
Gießerei Martin & Pillzing
August Kraus, sculptor,
Martin & Pillzing foundry

Einweihung. Unveiled on
21. November 1898
21 November 1898

Zustand. Condition
Das Denkmal wurde Ende 1950 abgetragen.
Pulled down at the end of 1950.

Iltis-Denkmal, um 1900
Iltis Memorial, around 1900

Das Iltis-Denkmal war das einzige deutsche Denkmal in Shanghai. Es stand innerhalb einer Grünanlage am nördlichen Teil der Uferstraße, doch noch außerhalb des »Public Gardens«. Seine Inschrift lautete: »Zur Erinnerung an den Heldentod der Besatzung SM Kanonenboot Iltis, gescheitert im Taifun an der Küste von Shantung am 23sten Juli 1896«.[138] Neun Jahre später wurde in 100 Meter Entfernung der deutsche Club Concordia eingeweiht.

Im einem Artikel der *Shanghaier Nachrichten* wurde das Denkmal beschrieben: »Ein sechs Meter hoher, zersplitterter Mast, von Lorbeerkranz, Flagge und Segeltuch umbauscht, ragt von einem granitenem Sockel auf. Die patinierte Bronze des Mastes macht durchaus den Eindruck von natürlichem verwittertem Holz. Die Flagge trägt ein eisernes Kreuz, die Flaggenbänder die Inschriften ›Die Deutschen Chinas‹ und ›Die Kaiserliche Marine‹. Der Sockel zeigt auf allen Seiten Gedenktafeln. Vorn ist ein Reliefbild der ›Iltis‹ unter vollen Segeln angebracht; hinten die Inschrift und die Namen der gefallenen Offiziere und Mannschaften. (…)«[139]

Prinz Heinrich von Preußen, der Bruder Kaiser Wilhelms II., enthüllte das Denkmal am 21. November 1898, nachdem er eine Woche zuvor in Qingdao (Tsingtau) das Denkmal »Diederichsstein« eingeweiht hatte. Am 2. Dezember 1918, nach dem Ende des Ersten Weltkrieges, wurde es durch eine Gruppe von Ausländern von seinem Platz am Bund gestürzt. Man stellte es am 22. Juni 1929 wieder auf dem Schulgrundstück der deutschen Gemeinde in Shanghai auf.

The Iltis Memorial was the only German monument in Shanghai. It initially stood in a park area at the northern end of the Bund but was outside the »Public Gardens«. It bore the following inscription: »To the memory of the heroic death of the crew of HM Gunboat Iltis, which sank in Taifun on the Shantung coast on 23 July 1896«.[138] Nine years later the German Club Concordia was opened on a site 100 metres away from the memorial.

An article in the *Shanghaier Nachrichten* describes the monument as follows: »A six-meter high shattered mast surrounded by laurel wreath, flag and sail projects out from a pedestal. The patinated bronze of the mast gives an authentic impression of naturally decayed wood. The flag bears an Iron Cross and the flag bands are inscribed with ›China's Germans‹ and ›The Imperial Navy‹. The pedestal has memorial plates on all sides. The front has a relief of the ›Iltis‹ in full sail; the plate at the back bears the inscription and names of the officers and crew killed in the accident. (…)«[139]

Prince Heinrich of Prussia, the brother of Kaiser Wilhelm II., unveiled the memorial on 21 November 1898 having unveiled the »Diederichsstein« memorial one week earlier in Qingdao. On 2 December 1918, after the end of the First World War it was pulled down from its place on the Bund by a group of foreigners. On 22 June 1929 it was remounted in the school grounds of the German Community Centre in Shanghai.

伊爾蒂斯－紀念碑

所在地：一九一八年前，上海中山東一路（外灘），一九二九年，延安西路（華山路口）：原大西路一號（海克路口）

設計：賴因霍爾德‧貝加斯，雕刻家：格奧爾木‧米勒，艦艇艇長

施工：奧古斯特‧克芬斯，雕刻家，馬丁‧皮爾率聯合鑄造廠

落成典禮：一八九八年十一月二十一日

現狀：五十年代末被拆除

伊爾蒂斯紀念碑是德國在上海唯一的紀念碑。紀念碑最初座落在外灘公園外側沿江大道的北端。碑文是："紀念一八九六年七月二十三日在中國黃海風暴中遇難的伊爾蒂斯號炮艦全體船員。"〈138〉九年後，在距紀念碑一百米的地方建造了德國康科迪婭總會。《上海新報》發表文章描寫這座紀念碑："高六米的斷桅愴然聳立在大理石的基座上，斑駁的銅鏽使斷桅看上去像一段飽經風雨滄桑而不向命運低頭的殘木。桅桿的下端圍放著花環，繪有十字架的軍旗和似乎仍被海風吹得微微鼓起的帆布。挽聯上的題詞為：'在中國的德國人和皇家海軍'。紀念碑基座的四面都是碑文和雕刻。基座的正面是一幅表現伊爾蒂斯號乘風破浪，揚帆前進的浮雕，後面是碑文和恂難官兵的名字……。"〈139〉

一八九八年十一月二十一日，普魯士亨利王子為紀念碑揭幕。在這前一周，他在青島參加紀念碑"狄特立克斯"的落成儀式。第一次世界大戰後，一九一八年十二月二日，紀念碑被一幫外國人推倒。一九二九年六月二十二號，紀念碑又重新移到在德國僑民文化娛樂中心的校園裡。

伊爾蒂斯紀念碑，約一九零零年。

KAISERLICH DEUTSCHES GENERALKONSULAT
IMPERIAL GERMAN CONSULATE GENERAL

Huangpu Lu (Whangpoo Road 9–10), Shanghai

Renovierung 1907. Restoration 1907
Becker & Baedecker[140]

Bauherr. Client
Auswärtiges Amt
The Ministry of Foreign Affairs

Bauzeit. Construction time
1884–1885

Zustand. Condition
Die Gebäude wurden 1937 abgetragen, heute steht dort das Seagull Hotel.
Pulled down in 1937; the Seagull Hotel now stands on the site.

Deutsches Generalkonsulat, Südansicht. Im Hintergrund die Deutsche Evangelische Kirche, um 1909
German Consulate General, south view with the German Protestant Church in the background, around 1909

Das Deutsche Generalkonsulat bestand aus zwei äußerlich sehr ähnlichen Bauten, einem Wohn- und einem Dienstgebäude. Beide standen nebeneinander am Flußufer und waren auf der Süd- und Westseite mit luftigen Veranden ausgestattet. »Die beiden großen, sehr prunkvollen, aber wenig zweckmäßigen dreistöckigen Häuser des Generalkonsulats lagen an bevorzugter Stelle an einer Biegung des Huangpu-Stromes, so daß man einen schönen Blick über den nur selten pausierenden Schiffsverkehr hatte.«[141] Um das Generalkonsulat herum bildete sich ein deutsches Zentrum. Bis 1898 befand sich in den Räumen des Konsulats das deutsche Postamt. Die Deutsche Evangelische Kirche wurde 1901 direkt dahinter erbaut, ebenso die erste deutsche Schule in Shanghai, die Kaiser-Wilhelm-Schule. Als diese 1911 in ein größeres Gebäude umzog, wurde das Mannschaftskasino für deutsche Seeleute in den alten Schulräumen eingerichtet.[142] Daneben lag die Schlachterei des Berliners Richard Neumann, zu der auch eine »altmodische deutsche Kneipe« und ein Frühstückszimmer gehörten.[143]

In der Huangpu Lu siedelten sich auch andere Konsulate an. Rechts neben dem deutschen wurde 1908 das amerikanische Konsulat eingerichtet; im Jahre 1911 entstand daneben der Neubau des japanischen Konsulats. Das Grundstück zwischen der 1906 erbauten »Garden Bridge« und dem deutschen Konsulat wurde bis zur Errichtung des russischen Konsulats 1914 als Park genutzt. Auf dem gegenüberliegenden Ufer des Suzhou Creeks lag das der Briten.

Im April 1937 zog das Deutsche Generalkonsulat in das »Green Line Building« Ecke Bund und Beijing Road um. Im Mai und Juni wurde der Altbau abgerissen, die Holzdecken waren morsch geworden. Ein Neubau auf dem Grundstück war bereits projektiert. Doch am 13. August 1937 besetzten japanische Truppen den nördlich des Suzhou Creeks gelegenen Teil der Internationalen Niederlassung. Der Neubau konnte nicht ausgeführt werden.

The German consulate general consisted of two externally very similar buildings, a residence and office building. The two buildings stood side by side on the river bank and had shady verandas on the south and west sides. »The two large, very majestic but impractical three-storey houses of the consulate general were situated on an attractive site on a bend in the Huangpu river giving an excellent view of the endless stream of passing ships.«[141] A German centre became established around the consulate. Up to 1898 the German post office was also located in the offices of the consulate. In 1901 the German Protestant church was built directly behind it and also the first German school in Shanghai, the Kaiser Wilhelm School. When the latter moved to a larger building in 1911, the building was used as a club for German sailors.[142] There was also a German butchers shop which belonged to Richard Neumann from Berlin and had an »old-fashioned German pub« and a breakfast room.[143]

Some of the other consulates also moved to locations on the Huangpu Lu. In 1908 the American consulate was built on the right of the German consulate and in 1911 the new building for the Japanese consulate was built beside the American consulate. The site between the »Garden Bridge« built in 1906 and the German consulate was used as a park until the Russian consulate was built on the site in 1914. The British consulate was on the opposite bank of Suzhou Creek.

In April 1937 the German consulate general moved to the »Green Line Building« on the corner of the Bund and Beijing Road. In May and June the old building was demolished; the wooden ceilings were rotten. Plans had already been drawn up for a new building on the site. However, on 13 August 1937 Japanese troops occupied the part of the International Settlement north of Suzhou Creek and work was not started on the new building.

德國總領事館

所在地：上海黃浦路；原黃浦路九至十號
建築師：貝克・培迪克〈140〉
業主：外交部
修繕期：一九零七年
建造期：一八八四年至一八八五年
現狀：一九三七年拆除；現在為海鷗飯店

德國總領事館由外表十分相似的住宅樓和辦公樓組成。這兩幢樓並排座落在黃浦江畔。在樓的西南兩面有通風遮蔭的券拱外廊。"總領事館這兩幢樓富麗堂皇但並不實用的三層樓房正好座落在黃浦江轉彎處，所以人們可以從那眺望到繁忙的船運偶爾間歇的情景"〈141〉。圍繞著總領事館形成了德國僑民聚會中心。

一八九八年前大德書信館（郵局）也設在領事館裡。一九零一年，在領事館的後面又落成了德國基督教堂和上海第一座德國學堂——威廉學堂。一九一一年，威廉學堂遷入更寬敞的樓房，舊的校舍改建成德國海員俱樂部〈142〉。貼鄰便是柏林人里夏德・諾伊曼經營的一家肉鋪，及一個按照德國古老風俗佈置的酒吧兼早餐部〈143〉。在黃浦路還有其它國家的領事館。德領事館的右邊緊鄰是一九零八年建造的美國領事館。在美國領事館旁邊，一九一一年又興建了日本領事館。德國領事館和一九零六年建造的外白渡橋之間是一座公園，一九一四年，在這個地段上建起俄國領事館。在蘇州河彼岸是英國領事館。

一九三七年四月，德國領事館遷到位於北京路與外灘交叉口的"怡泰大樓"辦公。六月到七月，舊樓被拆除，因為木製的天花板已腐爛。人們計劃在原址上重建領事館。一九三七年八月十三日，日本部隊佔領了公共租界蘇州河以北的區域。重建新領館的計劃也就此告吹。

德國總領事館南面外觀，其後立有德國基督教堂，約一九零九年

SHANGHAI

DEUTSCHE EVANGELISCHE KIRCHE UND DEUTSCHE SCHULE
GERMAN PROTESTANT CHURCH AND GERMAN SCHOOL

Ab 1911. Use from 1911
Deutsche Evangelische Kirche und
Deutsches Mannschaftskasino
The German Protestant Church
and German Marine Club
Huangpu Lu/Jinshan Lu (Whangpoo
Road/Astor Road 1A), Shanghai

Architekt. Architect
R.B. Moorhead

An- und Umbauten. Conversion and extensions
Heinrich Becker

Ausführung. Contractors
Dowdall & Moorhead

Bauherr. Client
Deutsche evangelische Gemeinde Shanghai
German Protestant Community Shanghai

Bauzeit. Construction time
Mai 1900 – September 1901
May 1900 – September 1901

Zustand. Condition
Das Gebäude wurde zwischen 1932 und 1934 abgetragen.
Pulled down between 1932 and 1934.

Gegenüber dem deutschen Konsulat wurde die »erste deutsche Gemeindekirche Chinas«[144] errichtet. Ihr Turm überragte deutlich das Generalkonsulat. Über die Vergabe des Auftrags wird zur Grundsteinlegung geschrieben: »Die Ausführung des Baues wurde, da ein deutscher Baumeister hierselbst nicht ansässig war, dem englischen Baumeister R.B. Moorhead übertragen.«[145]

Die wöchentlichen Gottesdienste besuchten im Jahr 1907 durchschnittlich 87 Personen, davon waren ein Drittel Angehörige der kaiserlichen Marine. Für die deutsche katholische Gemeinde Shanghais gab es keine eigene Kirche, sie nahmen an den Gottesdiensten der St. Joseph-Kirche in der französische Niederlassung teil. Zunächst waren der Kirche auch die Räume der Schule für die deutschen Kinder angegliedert. Die Schule hatte sie von der Kirchengemeinde gemietet.[146] Als Schulgarten wurde damals der Park neben dem Konsulat genutzt, auf dem später das Russische Konsulat erbaut wurde.

Als die Schule 1911 in einen größeren Neubau umzog, baute man die Räume zu einem Mannschaftskasino für die Unteroffiziere und Mannschaften der deutschen Kriegsschiffe um. In den ehemaligen Schulzimmern wurden auch eine Bibliothek und ein Billardzimmer eingerichtet.[147]

The »first church for the German community in China«[144] was built on a site opposite the German consulate. Its spire towered high above the consulate building. The following comment was recorded concerning the preparation of plans for the building when the foundation stone was laid: »As there was no German architect living here, the commission for the building was given to the British architect R.B. Moorhead.«[145]

In 1907, the weekly services were attended by an average of 87 people, one third of whom were members of the Imperial Navy. The German Catholic community in Shanghai did not have a church of its own; they attended services in St Joseph's Church in the French concession. Initially the rooms for the German school were attached to the church and the school rented the rooms from the church.[146] The park beside the consulate was used as a school yard; the Russian consulate was later built on this site.

When the school moved to a bigger new building in 1911, the school rooms were converted to a club for the non-commissioned officers and crews of the German warships. The former school rooms were then fitted as a library and billiards room.[147]

Deutsche Evangelische Kirche neben dem Deutschen Generalkonsulat, um 1912
Schulanbau, um 1906
German Protestant Church beside the German Consulate General around 1912
School extension, around 1906

新福音教堂和德國子弟學校

（一九一一年：德國基督教堂和德國水手之家）

所在地：黃浦路與金山路的交叉口（原黃浦路與查孔路1A）上海
建築師：R．B．莫赫德
增建與改建：海因里希．貝克
施工：上海道達洋行
業主：上海德國基督教僑民組織
建造期：一九零零年五月至一九零一年九月
現狀：一九三二年至一九三四年之間被拆除

建於德國領事館對面，此教堂為德國在中國的第一座僑民教堂⟨144⟩。教堂的塔頂比領事館高出許多。報界就該教堂奠基禮儀式報導了其設計施工任務交付安排的情況："因為找不到在這裡定居的德國教築師，教堂設計施工事宜已委託英國建築師莫赫德。"⟨145⟩

一九零七年，平均每周有八十七人做禮拜，其中三分之一是皇家海軍的家屬。上海的德國天主教徒還沒有自己的教堂，他們去法國租界的聖．約瑟夫教堂做禮拜。德國的子弟學校最初就設在教堂側廊的房間裡。⟨146⟩領館邊的公園也就成了該學校的植物園。後來這個公園割讓與俄國建造領事館。一九一一年該校遷入一幢較大的新樓。原來的教室被改建為德國戰艦士兵和下級軍官的會堂和娛樂中心在原來的校舍裡還造了一個圖書館和台球房。⟨147⟩

與德國總領事館并列的德國福音教堂，約一九一二年。
附設在教堂側廊裡的小學，約一九零六年。

SHANGHAI

KAISER-WILHELM-SCHULE
KAISER WILHELM SCHOOL

Weihai Lu (Weihaiwei Road 30), Shanghai

Architekt. Architect
Hans Emil Lieb

Baukosten. Building costs
etwa 95 000 Goldmark
approximately 95 000 gold marks

Bauherr. Client
Deutsche Gemeinde Shanghai
German community Shanghai

Bauzeit. Construction time
Frühjahr 1910 – April 1911
Spring 1910 – April 1911

ANBAU
EXTENSION

Architekt. Architect
Suhr & Woserau[148]

Bauzeit. Construction time
1925–1926

Zustand. Condition
Das Gebäude existiert nicht mehr.
No longer exists.

Kaiser-Wilhelm-Schule, Südansicht vom Garten, um 1912
Kaiser Wilhelm School, south view from the garden, around 1912

Das Gelände der Kaiser-Wilhelm-Schule lag im ruhigsten und vornehmsten Stadtteil im Westen Shanghais. Die Fenster der Klassenzimmer und der sich davor befindende große Spielplatz waren zum Garten orientiert. Die unscheinbare Nordfassade des Gebäudes zeigte dagegen zur Straße.

Das Schulgebäude hatte eine Länge von 40 Metern und eine Tiefe von 19 Metern, die Gesimshöhe betrug 12 Meter. Das Dach war mit roten Ziegeln gedeckt. Eine vier Meter breite Halle, deren flache Decke von gewölbten Bögen getragen wurde, erstreckte sich auf der Nordseite über die gesamte Länge des Gebäudes. An der Nordseite der Halle lag die Nebentreppe zu der vermieteten Privatwohnung, die Toilettenräume sowie die Haupttreppe zum oberen Stockwerk. Alle 8 Schulzimmer waren nach Süden ausgerichtet. Die beiden mittleren Klassenzimmer ließen sich durch Schiebewände zu einem Saal mit etwa 150 Sitzplätzen verbinden. Auf der Westseite des Gebäudes befand sich das Lehrerzimmer, das Zimmer des Schulleiters sowie im oberen Stockwerk die Bücherei. Da dem Gebäude keine Veranden vorgelagert waren, hatte man zur Kühlung alle Klassenzimmer mit Luftschächten versehen; an allen Fenstern gab es verstellbare Jalousien. Die Turnhalle lag in der Südostecke des Grundstücks, der eingeschossige Kindergarten in der Nordostecke.[149]

Im Jahre 1911 besuchten in Shanghai 2 255 nicht-chinesische Kinder 12 ausländische Schulen, von denen einige unter der Kontrolle des Shanghaier Stadtrats standen. Die Schülerzahl in den einzelnen Lehranstalten war sehr unterschiedlich. Sie lag zwischen 618 (St. Francis Xavier School) und 33 (Holy Trinity Cathedral School). Nach ihren Schülerzahlen war die Kaiser-Wilhelm-Schule 1911 die zweitkleinste ihrer Art in Shanghai. Im Unterrichtsjahr 1912/13 besuchten 133 Kinder die Schule, die Zahl stieg auf 180 bis 200 während des Ersten Weltkriegs.[150] Etwa ein Fünftel der Jungen und Mädchen waren europäische Ausländer.[151]

The site for the Kaiser Wilhelm School was in the quietest and most exclusive part of west Shanghai. The classroom windows and the large playground faced the garden. The rather plain north façade to the street gave a rather unfavourable impression of the school building.

The school building was 40 metres long and 19 metres wide, the eaves height was 12 metres. The roof had red tiles. Along the entire length of the north side of the building there was a four-metre wide corridor whose flat ceiling was supported by arches. To the north of the corridor there was a side stairs leading up to the rented private apartment, the toilets and the main stairway to the upper floor. All eight classrooms were south-facing. The two middle classrooms on the first floor could be converted into a hall with approximately 150 seats by opening the sliding partition. The staff room and headmaster's room were on the western side of the building and the library was on the upper floor. As there were no verandas on the building to aid ventilation, all of the classrooms had air vents; there were adjustable blinds on all of the windows. The wooden gymnasium was on the south east of the site and the single-storey kindergarten in the north eastern corner.[149]

In 1911, there were 2 255 non-Chinese children attending foreign schools in Shanghai. They were divided among 12 schools of which some were under more direct control of the Shanghai Municipal Council. The number of pupils in the individual schools varied considerably.

It ranged between 618 (St. Francis Xavier School) and 33 (Holy Trinity Cathedral School). On the basis of the number of pupils, the Kaiser Wilhelm School was the second smallest school in Shanghai in 1911. There were 133 children attending the school during the 1912/13 school year, the number rose to 180 to 200 during the First World War.[150] Approximately one fifth of the pupils were European foreigners.[151]

威廉學堂

所在地：上海威海路：原威海衛路三十號
建築師：漢斯·埃米爾·里勃
建築造價：約九點五萬金馬克，合銀元三
　　　　　點八萬兩
業主：上海德國僑民社團[148]
建造期：一九一零年春至一九一一年四月
建築師：蘇爾和瓦澤芬（只參加擴建工
　　　　程）
擴建期：一九二五年至一九二六年
現狀：建築已毀

威廉小學南面外觀，約一九一二年。

威廉學堂位於上海西部最幽靜高雅的城區內。學校佔地面積約七萬八千四百平方米。其中只有一條約三十米寬的地段與街道相連。教室的窗戶和前面的遊戲場面朝花園。教學樓裝飾簡練的北立面朝向街道。這多少影響到人們對學校的總印象。教學樓長四十米，深十九米，檐高十二米。紅瓦樓頂。在樓的北邊是一個與教學樓一樣長，四米寬的廊廳，圓頂拱柱托著平直的天花板。所有教室均朝南。正中的兩間教室面積為七米乘七米，兩邊的教室較小一些。廊廳的北邊是通向已出租了的私人套房的側梯，廁所以及通向樓上的主樓梯。兩間中間教室可通過滑動牆板合並成一個容一百五十個座位的廳堂。大樓的西邊是教師辦公室、校長辦公室。二樓是圖書館。因為教學樓前設有敞廊，教堂都裝設了降溫通風管道。所有的窗子均有活動的百葉窗，與廊廳北面的窗口相對，形成空氣對流。木製健身房在校園的東南角，幼兒園的平房在東北隅。[149]

一九一一年，二千二百五十五名外國兒童分別在上海的十二所外國學校學習。其中有幾位受到上海工部局的監護。其它的外國學校完全自主。各校學生人數相差懸殊，如：董家渡天主教堂學校有學生六百一十八人，大禮拜堂學校卻只有三十三名學生。從學生數量上看，威廉學堂在上海排在例數第二位。一九一二年至一九一三年，威廉在有學生一百三十三人。第一次世界大戰期間，學生人數從一百八十人增加到二百人。最多招收二百四十名學生。[150]約五分之一的學生來自歐洲，威廉學堂不招收父母不是同一國籍的兒童。[151]

SHANGHAI

KAISERLICH DEUTSCHE POST
IMPERIAL GERMAN POST OFFICE

Heutige Funktion. Current use
Geschäftshaus
Business premises
Fuzhou Lu/Sichuan Lu
(Foochow Road 6/Szechuan Road),
Shanghai

Architekt. Architect
Heinrich Becker

Ausführung. Contractors
W. Wutzler, Selberg & Schlüter,
Berlin, Tsingtau

Bauherr. Client
Kaiserlich Deutsche Post
Imperial German Post Office

Bauzeit. Construction time
Dezember 1902 – Mai 1905
December 1902 – May 1905

Zustand. Condition
Die Fassade ist stark verändert.
Façade considerably altered.

Kaiserlich Deutsche Post,
Südwestecke, um 1907
Imperial German Post Office,
view of the south-west corner,
around 1907

Die unruhige Fassade des Postgebäudes war mit Stilelementen der Neorenaissance und des Neobarock völlig überladen, ganz in der Art wie während des Historismus in Europa viele Geschäftshäuser gestaltet wurden. Für die Fassade verwendeten die Baumeister den »Ningpo Red Stone«. Im Erdgeschoß lag die etwa 100 Personen fassende Schalterhalle, hinter den Ausgabetischen waren der Annahme- und Ausgaberaum untergebracht sowie das Telegrafenzimmer und das Büro des Direktors. Die beiden großen Wohnungen des Postrats und des Direktors waren im ersten und zweiten Obergeschoß auf der Südseite des Gebäudes der Fuzhou Lu zugewandt. Die kleineren Wohnungen der Postbeamten befanden sich im ersten und zweiten Stock entlang der Sichuan Lu. Alle Wohnungen waren mit Bädern ausgestattet. Die Räume für die chinesischen Postbeamten und Privatdiener sowie die Küche lagen im Dachgeschoß. In allen Zimmern des Gebäudes gab es elektrisches Licht, während der heißen Jahreszeit kühlten elektrische Windfächer.[152]

Seit 1886 gab es eine deutsche Post in Shanghai, zunächst war sie in den Räumen des Generalkonsulats untergebracht. Ab 1905 dann in zentraler Lage im Geschäftsviertel Shanghais, nahe dem chinesischen Postamt und genau zwischen dem englischen und französischen Postamt. Shanghai war auch Sitz der deutschen Postdirektion, der übergeordneten Verwaltungsbehörde für alle deutschen Poststellen in China und im Schutzgebiet Kiautschou. Seit Januar 1901 bestand eine Telegraphenverbindung zwischen Shanghai und Qingdao. Die deutschen Postämter nahmen nur Post für chinesische Bestimmungsorte an, in denen sie eigene Postämter besaßen, somit war die Konkurrenz für die seit 1897 bestehende Kaiserlich Chinesische Post gering. Außer den bereits genannten Postämtern gab es in Shanghai je ein amerikanisches, japanisches und russisches.

Like many business premises during the period of historicism in Europe, the overwrought façade of the post office building was completely covered with neo-Renaissance and neo-Baroque details. »Ningpo red stone« was used for the façade. The ground floor housed the counter room which could hold approximately 100 persons; the rooms for sending and collecting items of mail were behind the counters as were the telegraph room and the director's office. There were apartments on the upper floors. The two large apartments for the postmaster and director were on the first and second floors on the south side of the building facing Fuzhou Lu. The smaller apartments for the post-office officials were in the first and second floor along the Sichuan Lu. All of the apartments were fitted with washing and bathing facilities. The kitchen and the accommodation for the Chinese post office clerks and private servants were in the attic. There was electric light in all of the rooms and during the hot season the building was cooled using electric fans.[152]

There had been a German post office in Shanghai since 1886 which was initially housed in the consulate offices. From 1905 it was in a central location in Shanghai's commercial centre near the Chinese post office, and exactly between the British and French post offices. Shanghai was also the seat of the German Regional Postal Directorate, the supervisory official body for all German post offices in China and the protectorate of Jiaozhou. Telegraph links had been established between Shanghai and Qingdao in January 1901. The German post offices only accepted post for places in China where they had their own post offices, thus there was little competition for the Imperial Chinese Post Office which was founded in 1897. In addition to the post offices listed above, Shanghai also had American, Japanese and Russian post offices.

德國郵政局（原德國書信館）

現用途：商業大廈
所在地：上海市福州路（四川路口）；原福州路六號（四川路口）
建築師：海因里希・貝克
施工：烏茨勒・西貝克和施旅特字，柏林，青島
業主：德國皇家郵政局
建造期：一九零二年十二月—一九零五年五月
現狀：立面有較大更改

像歐洲建築復古風盛行時所建的商業大樓一樣，郵局大樓的立面沿用文藝復興和巴洛克裝飾手法，然而雕琢過份，令人眼花繚亂。建築師選用寧波出產的紅石作立面材料。一樓是能容納一百人的，設有服務窗口的大廈。郵件包裹領取處後面是郵件收發室，電報間以及郵局主任辦公室。樓上是住房，郵局理事與主任的大套住房均朝南，分別設在二樓、三樓向著福州路的一面。郵局職員的幾套住房在二、三樓靠四川路的一側。所有的住房均配有盥洗的洗澡設備。中國職員和勤雜人員的用房及廚房設在頂樓。大樓的所有房間均有電燈在嚴熱的夏天用電風扇降溫。〈152〉

一八八六年，德國郵政局在上海的辦會地點最初設在領事館內。一九零五年，郵局遷到上海商業區中心，正好在英國和法國郵局的中間，離中國郵局很近。上海也是德國郵政管理局的所在地。郵政管理局統籌安排德國在中國以及殖民地膠州地區所有的分局和收發處的事務。一九零一年，在上海與青島之間建立了電報通訊網絡。德國郵政局只接收發送那些將投遞到其它也有德國郵局地區的郵件業務。因此，德國郵局與一八九七年成立的大清郵局沒有什麼競爭。除了德國郵政局，在上海還有美國郵局，日本郵局和俄國郵局。

大德帝國郵政局西南角，約一九零七年。

RUSSISCH-CHINESISCHE BANK
RUSSIAN-CHINESE BANK

Heutige Funktion. Current use
Devisenbörse
China Foreign Exchange Trade System
Zhongshan Dongyilu/Jiujiang Lu
(The Bund 15/Kiukiang Road), Shanghai

Architekten. Architects
Heinrich Becker, Richard Seel[153]

Bauherr. Client
Russisch-Chinesische Bank
Russian-Chinese Bank

Bauzeit. Construction time
1899 – Oktober 1902
1899 – October 1902

Zustand. Condition
Das Gebäude ist sehr gut erhalten.
Very well preserved.

Ehem. Russisch-Chinesische Bank,
Ostfassade zum Bund, 1991
The former Russian-Chinese Bank,
east façade, 1991

Der deutsche Architekt Heinrich Becker setzte mit diesem Gebäude neue Maßstäbe des Bauens in Asien. Es war das erste Haus in Shanghai, das dem Qualitätsstandard europäischer Bauten in Entwurf, Material und Ausführung entsprach. Die Fassade im Stil der italienischen Neorenaissance war ausgewogen proportioniert.[154]

Chinesische Betrachter hielten die zur Verzierungen des Gebäudes verwendeten Menschenskulpturen und Gesichtsmasken für Hausgeister der Ausländer.[155] Die Skulpturen wurden während der 50er Jahre entfernt.

Über den Fortgang der Bauarbeiten schrieb der *Ostasiatische Lloyd* rückblickend: »Manche der alten lang eingesessenen Bauleute schüttelten bedenklich die weisen Köpfe, als der Bau fortschritt, und es war nach ihrer ›maßgeblichen Meinung‹ ein ganz verkehrtes Unternehmen, von der ›guten alten‹ Art zu bauen abzuweichen und alle die Unannehmlichkeiten zu überwinden, die mit der Verwendung und Beschaffung von edlem Baumaterial hier in Shanghai verbunden ist, die jeder durchzukosten hat, der Naturbaustein beim Bauen verwenden will. Die Abscheulichkeit des damals und leider jetzt noch von Manchem verwendeten ›Paper Lime‹-Verputzes (einer Mischung von Papier, Kalk und Schwemmsand) war Beckers Empfinden durchaus zuwider, und das Vortäuschen einer, auf ganz anderen Materialien basierende Architektur durch diesen Verputz war ihm ganz und gar verhaßt. Becker aber ging noch weiter. Zum Entsetzen aller ›Experten‹ des Bauwesens in China wagte es der ›German Architect‹, ganz neue Gedanken, ›die nur für Europa paßten‹, auszuführen. Er konstruierte unter anderem große schwere Gitterträger und begann diese fertig montiert aufzuwinden, um dann an sie die schweren Granitblöcke anzuhängen, die jetzt so ›selbstverständlich‹ den oberen Abschluß am Dach der Veranda an der Wohnetage der Bank bilden. Die Bank, in ihrer Innen- und Außenarchitektur und Konstruktion, wurde ein durchschlagender Erfolg.«[156]

The German architect Heinrich Becker set new architectural standards in Asia with this building. It was the first building in Shanghai which completely corresponded to a building in Europe in terms of the quality of the design, material and execution. The Italian neo-Renaissance façade, the style preferred for prestigious bank buildings at the time, was well proportioned.[154]

Chinese observers at the time believed the sculptures of human figures and face masks used in the decoration of the building to be the foreigner's house gods (josses).[155] The sculptures were removed during the 1950s.

The *Ostasiatische Lloyd* had the following to say in retrospect about the progress of the building work: »Some of the older established building experts shook their wise heads pensively as the building progressed, and in their ›competent opinions‹ it was a completely perverse undertaking to deviate from the ›good old‹ style of building and try to overcome all of the problems involved in obtaining and using high quality building materials here in Shanghai that face anyone who wants to use natural stone. The atrocious ›paper lime‹ plaster widely used by then – and unfortunately in some cases still – was completely unacceptable as far as Becker was concerned, and it was entirely out of the question for him to pretend to produce an architecture based on quite different materials. But Becker went even further; to the horror of all the building ›experts‹ in China, the ›German Architect‹ dared to execute new ideas ›which were only workable in Europe‹. He constructed, among other things, a big heavy lattice frame and then proceeded to hoist it up already assembled and hang the heavy granite blocks on it, which now so ›self-evidently‹ create the upper termination of the roof of the veranda and the residential floor. The bank was a complete success in terms the interior and exterior architecture and the construction.«[156]

華俄道勝銀行

現用途：上海航運技術研究所
所在地：上海中山東一路（九江路口）；
　　　　原外灘十五號（九江路口）
建築師：海因里希‧貝克，里夏德‧賓午
〈153〉
業主：華俄道勝銀行
現狀：樓體保存完好

德國建築師海因里希‧貝克以設計建造這座銀行大廈向亞州的建築界提出了新的挑戰。這是上海第一幢從設計水平，材料到施工均能與歐洲建築物媲美的樓房。銀行的立面沿襲當時講究排場的銀行業崇尚的意大利文藝復興式復古建築風格。立面布局合理，對稱工整。〈154〉

中國人認為那些作為裝飾物件的人物雕像和頭像是外國人的神像。〈155〉五十年代期間，這些人物雕像被拆除。

《新德文報》回顧了銀行大廈的建造過程："當銀行大廈破土動工時，當地的建築界元老懷疑地搖著他們聰明的腦袋。依這些人的高見，不按著這套路建樓終究會碰壁。誰若想在上海用天然石料建房，只會自討苦吃。"貝克對那種沿至今的"用紙漿粉刷"（一種用紙，石灰和流沙攪拌成的灰漿）來假冒優質建築材料的施工手法深惡痛絕，故而反其道而行之。讓中國"建築行家"大為驚駭的是這個"德國建築師"竟然想把只適應歐洲的新思潮在中國付諸實踐，貝克自己構思設計重型網絡狀衍架，裝配好吊至屋檐下，以厚實沉重的大理石飾面。這座大樓《外觀造型到內部裝飾以及總體構思都達到了極高的水平。〈156〉

前華俄道勝銀行臨江的東立面，
一九九一年。

SHANGHAI

DEUTSCH-ASIATISCHE BANK
GERMAN-ASIAN BANK

Zhongshan Dongyilu/Hankou Lu
(The Bund 14/Hankow Road), Shanghai

Bauzeit. Construction time
um 1880
around 1880

ANBAU
EXTENSION

Architekt. Architect
Heinrich Becker

Bauherr. Client
Deutsch-Asiatische Bank, Berlin
German-Asian Bank, Berlin

Bauzeit. Construction time
1902

Zustand. Condition
Das Gebäude wurde in den
30er Jahre abgetragen.
The building was pulled down in the 1930s.

Ehem. Deutsch-Asiatische Bank,
Ostfassade zum Bund, um 1925
The former German-Asian Bank,
east façade, around 1925

Die Deutsch-Asiatische Bank lag an der Hauptgeschäftsstraße Shanghais, dem Bund. An dieser Uferstraße, die mit zwei Baumreihen bestanden war, hatten sich bereits in den 60er und 70er Jahren des 19. Jahrhunderts die großen Bankhäuser und Schiffahrtsgesellschaften niedergelassen. Ihre »Bauweise war englisch, aber beeinflußt vom tropischen Klima, was die Erbauer zu einer Hallen-Architektur der Schauseiten führte, die sich zum Teil an italienische Muster mit Glück anlehnen. Namentlich das Gebäude, welches gegenwärtig der Deutsch-Asiatischen Bank gehört, aber noch aus der ersten Zeit der Stadt stammt, zeichnet sich durch anmutige Verhältnisse seiner Hallen und Säulenstellungen aus.«[157]

In dem 1902 errichteten Erweiterungsbau orientierte sich der Architekt Heinrich Becker an dem bestehenden Bankgebäude. Er entwarf eine Fassade im Stil der italienischen Neorenaissance. Die Bank sollte als einheitlicher Bau erscheinen. Der Knick in der Fassade, durch den Straßenzug bedingt, wurde von einem Turm aufgenommen. In Erdgeschoß und erstem Stock des östlichen Bauteils waren die Schalterhalle und neue Geschäftsräume untergebracht; in den beiden unteren Stockwerken des westlichen Teils lagen Geschäftsräume, die vermietet wurden. Die zweite und dritte Etage des Anbaus war zu komfortablen Mietwohnungen ausgebaut.[158]

The German-Asian Bank was on Shanghai's main commercial street, the Bund. The large banking houses and shipping companies had established their offices as early as the 1860s and 70s on this embankment road which was lined with two rows of trees. The »architecture was British but the tropical climate which had led the architects to adopt ›an architecture of ostentatious halls‹ which in some cases were successfully derived from Italian models. The building in question is that currently belonging to the German-Asian Bank, but which originates from the early phase of the development of the settlement, its distinguishing features are the daring proportions of its halls and the positions of the columns.«[157]

In the extension built in 1902, the architect Heinrich Becker takes his direction from the existing bank building. He designed the façade in Italian neo-Renaissance style to give it a uniform appearance. The turn of the façade due to the street was marked by a tower. The counter room and new offices were located in the ground and first floors of the eastern part of the new building; there were additional rented offices in the western side of both of the lower floors. The second and third floors of the extension were fitted out as comfortable rented apartments.[158]

德華銀行

所在地：上海中山東一路（漢口路）；原
　　　　外灘十四號（漢口路口）
業主：德華銀行，柏林
建造期：約一八八零年增建
建築師：海因里希‧貝克
建造期：一九零二年
現狀：三十年代期間被拆除

德華銀行位於上海主要商業大街外灘上。
早在十九世紀六十至七十年代，一些大銀
行和航運公司就在這條林蔭大道上經營各
項業務。"這些樓房的建築風格學英國式
的，但因氣候的影響而帶有熱帶風味。"
該類建築多帶有敞廊及高闊的內廳，其中
不少則成功地借用了意大利建築手法。四
面層層開設敞廊使這類建築立面成格狀。
德華銀行大廈的敞廊拱券與廊柱在立面上
構成疏密有致的圖案。〈157〉
一九零二年，建築師海因里希‧貝克力圖
使擴建的部份也保持原來銀行大樓的風
格，他用意大利文藝復興式復古的手法設
計立面，使整個銀行成為統一的建築體，
由於街道彎曲不直，建築師隨之在立面曲
轉處增建了一個塔樓。在擴建新樓房東半
部的一樓和二樓是設有服務窗口的大廳和
業務接洽處；新樓西半部的一，二樓是供
出租的辦公室，新樓的三，四層是設備現
代化，布置舒適的公寓套房。〈158〉

前德華銀行臨江的東面外觀一九
二五年。

SHANGHAI

GESCHÄFTSHAUS CARLOWITZ & CO
CARLOWITZ & CO BUSINESS PREMISES

Heutige Funktion. Current use
Geschäftshaus
Business premises
Jiujiang Lu/Jiangxi Lu 255
(Kiukiang Road/Kiangsi Road),
Shanghai

Bauherr. Client
Firma Carlowitz
Carlowitz company

Bauzeit. Construction time
1899

Zustand. Condition
Das Gebäude ist gut erhalten.
Well preserved.

Geschäftshaus Carlowitz & Co.,
Südfassade zur Kathedrale,
um 1907
Südfassade, 1991
Carlowitz & Co. business premises,
south façade facing the Cathedral,
around 1907
South façade, 1991

Das Geschäftshaus wurde auf einem zentral gelegenen Grundstück der Geschäftsstadt errichtet, die Kathedrale »Trinity Cathedral« und ein Park lagen ihm gegenüber. Die umlaufenden Veranden waren als schattenspendende Hülle um das Gebäude gelegt. Durch diese Bauweise herrschten auch während des Sommers angenehme Temperaturen im Gebäude. Um den Innenraum zu erweitern, wurden die offenen Veranden nachträglich verglast.

In der *Deutschen Bauzeitung* wird der Bau 1904 beschrieben: »Auch etwas mehr im Inneren der Stadt befinden sich solche Gebäude, die den Charakter von Geschäfts- und Wohnhaus in recht glücklicher Weise vereinen. Ein besonders großes, indes erst neuerdings aufgeführtes Gebäude dieser Art ist dasjenige, in welcher die erste deutsche Firma Shanghai's, Carlowitz & Co., ihre Geschäftsräume hat; es ist in Ziegelfugenbau mit Werksteinen und auch mit Terrakotten ausgeführt, die zum Teil recht erhebliche Abmessungen zeigen. Bemerkenswert ist es, daß dieses Gebäude außer dem Erdgeschoß bereits drei Geschosse aufweist, (...)«.[159]

This business premises was on a very well located site within the commercial centre, it stood opposite the »Trinity Cathedral« and a park. Verandas surrounded the building, providing shade with the result that the interior temperature was always pleasant, even in summer. The open verandas were later glazed to increase the interior space.

The *Deutsche Bauzeitung* published the following description of the building in 1904: »There are more and more buildings in the city centre which successfully combine business premises and residential quarters. A particularly large and new building of this kind is that which houses the offices of the biggest German company in Shanghai, Carlowitz & Co.; the building is built in jointed brick with ashlar panels and also terracottas, some of which are extremely large. This building is remarkable in that it has three storeys in addition to the ground floor, (...)«.[159]

禮和商業大樓

現用途：商業大樓
所在地：上海九江路（江西路二百五十五號）；原九江路（江西路口）
業主：禮和公司
建造期：一八九九年
現狀：樓體保存良好

商業大樓座落在商業區內，對面是聖三一教堂。環繞大樓的敞廊如同散熱遮陰的涼蓬，因此，盡管夏日炎炎，大樓內的溫度依然舒適宜人，為了擴大使用空間，人們後來又給敞廊安裝了玻璃。一九零四年，《德國建築報》作了報導："在靠近市中心的地方，出現了越來越多的將商業辦公和屋住有機結合起來的樓房。這幢新近落成的，具有多種功能的上海第一家德國公司——禮和公司高聳的商業大廈就是一例，該樓以大塊天然石料和缸磚建造而成，值的一提是，這座商業大樓不算底層就已有三層樓了。"〈159〉

禮和商業大樓南立面面對大主教堂約一九零七年。
南立面，一九九一年。

SHANGHAI

GESCHÄFTSHAUS ARNHOLD, KARBERG & CO
ARNHOLD, KARBERG & CO BUSINESS PREMISES

Heutige Funktion. Current use
Geschäftshaus
Business premises
Sichuan Lu/Jiujiang Lu 320
(Szechuan Road/Kiukiang Road),
Shanghai

Entwurf. Design
Trussed Concrete Steel Co., Detroit

Bauleitung. Site architect
G.W. Phillips, Ingenieur
G.W. Phillips, engineer

Ausführung. Contractors
Trussed Concrete Steel Co., Detroit

Bauherr. Client
Arnhold, Karberg & Co.

Bauzeit. Construction time
Mai 1907 – Dezember 1908
May 1907 – December 1908

Zustand. Condition
Das Gebäude ist sehr gut erhalten.
Very well preserved.

Ehem. Geschäftshaus Arnhold, Karberg & Co., Südwestecke, 1992
Former business premises Arnhold, Karberg & Co., south-west corner, 1992

Nach dem ersten vollständig aus Stahlbeton erbauten Gebäude der Shanghai Mutual Telephone Company[160] war das Geschäftshaus von Arnhold, Karberg & Co. der erste Stahlbetonskelettbau in Shanghai. Dabei wurden aus Stahlbeton »nur eine Reihe von durch alle Stockwerke gehenden Stützsäulen, das Treppenhaus, der große Schornstein und an Stelle der sonst üblichen Balkenlage die Decken und Fußböden zwischen den Stockwerken hergestellt. Die Außenmauern und die einzelnen Zimmerabteilungen werden später dem rohen Gerippe aus anderem Material (Backstein und Holz sowie Glas) eingebaut. Die Vorteile dieser Bauart (…) sind ersichtlich. Das Gebäude hat vor allen Dingen durch das innige Zusammenfassen des Gerippes eine Stütze in sich, so daß die Fundamente weniger umfangreich ausfallen können, ein Umstand, der besonders in der aus Schwemmsand bestehenden näheren Umgebung des Huangpu sehr erwünscht ist.«[161]

Die ersten Stahlbetonbauten erregten damals noch großes Aufsehen. »War man anfänglich im Zweifel, ob die aus dem Erdboden emporstrebenden, gitterartigen Eisenstangen Unterkunft für wilde Tiere bilden sollten oder nicht, so sieht man jetzt, wo das Gebäude bis zum ersten Stockwerk gediehen ist, den Zweck jener Stangen schon deutlich.« Die moderne Industriearchitektur wurde damals zwar in der Handelsstadt Shanghai akzeptiert, trotzdem wünschte man sich aber aufwendiger gestaltete Fassaden. »Das Haus wird nach den vorliegenden Plänen einen nüchternen, aber praktischen Eindruck machen. Shanghai kann sich aber mit wenigen Ausnahmen überhaupt nicht künstlerisch angelegter Bauten rühmen; im allgemeinen ist die Nachfrage nach einfachen Häusern stärker als üppiger gebauten (…).«[162]

In Guangzhou (Kanton) ließ sich die Firma Arnhold, Karberg & Co. ebenfalls um 1907 ihr Geschäftshaus in Stahlbetonskelettbauweise errichten. Architekten waren die aus Australien und Amerika stammenden Arthur Purnell und Charles Paget.[163]

After the first building to be built in Shanghai using reinforced concrete throughout, the building of the Shanghai Mutual Telephone Company,[160] the business premises of Arnhold, Karberg & Co. was the first building to be built with a reinforced concrete frame. However, the only elements actually made of reinforced concrete were »a series of support columns which extended through all floors, the staircase, the big chimney and the floors which replaced the usual joists. This structure was later filled out and encloses other materials (brick, wood and glass). The advantages to this method of building are obvious.(…) As a result of the form of the structure the building has, above all, a support in itself and thus the foundations do not need to be as deep as usual and extensive. This is particularly useful considering that the land in the area near the Huangpu consists of alluvial sand.«[161]

The first reinforced concrete buildings still attracted a lot of attention at the time. »One may have been inclined to think that the cage-like iron rods protruding upright from the ground were intended to provide shelter for wild animals, but now that the building has reached the first floor it is possible to see the function of those rods quite clearly.« Modern industrial architecture was accepted in the trading city of Shanghai, but there was a wish for more elaborate façades. »On the basis of the presented plans the house will make a sober but practical impression. With few exceptions however, Shanghai cannot boast of more artistic buildings; in general there is now a greater demand for simple houses than for more elaborate ones.«[162]

Arnhold, Karberg & Co. also had a concrete and steel trussed building built for its premises in Guangzhou (Canton). The architects were Arthur Purnell from Australia and the American Charles Paget.[163]

瑞記商行

現用途：商業大樓
所在地：上海四州路（九江路口）；原四州路（九江路）
設計：美國底特律鋼筋混凝土建築公司工程指導：G‧W‧菲列普斯工程師
施工：美國底特律鋼筋混凝土建築公司
業主：瑞記商行
建造期：一九零七年五月至一九零八年十二月
現狀：樓體保存完好

瑞記商行是上海繼首座全鋼筋混凝土建築——上海電話局辦公樓後的第一座鋼筋混凝土框架結構建築。〈160〉使用這種方法的建築需要一定數量貫穿樓層的支柱，混凝土樓梯和取代橫樑的混凝土天花板及樓板。在這些粗糙的結構框架上再安裝其它材料制成的外牆（磚，木頭，玻璃）及室內裝飾。這種建築方法的優點是顯而易見的。樓體因鋼筋混凝土框架的內在連接而更加穩固，這樣地基就不必太深，太寬。這種建築方法非常適合黃浦江區域由流沙構成的地質。〈161〉

第一批鋼筋水泥建築在當時還引起很大的轟動，"人們當初還懷疑，這些拔地而起的鐵柵條是不是做野獸籠子用的，但當樓蓋至二層高時，那些鐵條的用途便已一目了然"。工業化了的現代建築手法在商業城上海雖然得到了認可，然而人們還是希望立面更美觀，裝飾材料質量更好。"從現有的建築圖紙看，這幢樓不尚奢華，注重實用，除了少數的例外，上海幾乎沒有什麼藝術價值高而值得炫耀的建築。總而言之，對實用，簡易建築的需求要遠遠超過對裝飾繁縟的建築的需求……"〈162〉

一九零七年，瑞記商行在廣州也同樣用鋼筋混凝土框架結構建造了一幢商業大廈。其建築師亞瑟‧普爾耐爾和查爾斯‧帕格忒分別來自澳大利亞和美國。〈163〉

瑞記商行西南角，一九九二年。

CHINA EXPORT, IMPORT, BANKING COMPANY

Heutige Funktion. Current use
Geschäftshaus
Business premises
Jiangxi Zhonglu 138 (Kiangsi Road 9–11), Shanghai

Architekten. Architects
Becker & Baedecker[164]

Bauherr. Client
China Export, Import, Banking Company, Hamburg

Bauzeit. Construction time
1907 – Januar 1908
1907 – January 1908

Zustand. Condition
Das Gebäude ist gut erhalten und um eine Etage aufgestockt.
Well preserved; an additional floor has been added.

Geschäftshaus der China Export, Import, Banking Company, Südwestansicht, 1908
Südwestansicht, 1992
Business premises of the China Export, Import, Banking Company, view from the south-west, 1908
View from the south-west, 1992

Die Architekten hatten gerade den Club Concordia fertiggestellt, als sie wenige 100 Meter entfernt dieses Wohn- und Geschäftshaus erbauten. Die Fassade wirkt unruhig und ist ungewöhnlich gegliedert. Rechteckige und bogenförmige Fenster und Loggien wurden zu Zweier- und Dreiergruppen zusammengefaßt, die unterschiedlich groß sind. Werksteinsäulen tragen die Rundbögen der Loggien; in den Laibungen der rechteckigen Öffnungen sitzen hölzerne Klappläden als Sonnenschutz. Ein zweigeschossiges Renaissanceportal betont den Eingang, wirkt aber fremd an diesem rechteckigen Baukörper.

Über die umliegenden Geschäftshäuser bemerkten die *Shanghaier Nachrichten*: »Nachdem die ursprüngliche Bauart des freistehenden Geschäftshauses mit breiten Veranden einer weniger Platz in Anspruch nehmenden hat weichen müssen, haben ausschließlich Nützlichkeitsgründe für den Bauherren wie für den Baumeister den Ausschlag gegeben. (…) Die furchtbaren roten und grauen hohen Backsteinbauten, die seine engen Straßen erdrückend einschließen, wirken (…) abstoßend. Daß dies nicht an dem Material liegt, (…) hat ein Neubau bewiesen, der diese Tage eingeweiht worden ist. (…) Wir können die Bauweise dieser deutschen Architekten nicht in allen Punkten unbedingt gutheißen; anerkennen aber müssen wir, daß sie (…) es verstanden haben, eine Revolution in das Straßenbild Shanghais zu bringen (…)«[165]

The architects had just completed the Club Concordia when they built this residential and business house just a few hundred metres away from the club grounds. The façade is overwrought with an unusual arrangement. Rectangular and arched windows and loggias were combined in groups of two and three openings with varying proportions. The arches of the loggias are supported by ashlar columns; the square-topped openings have wooden top-hung blinds to provide protection from the sun. A two-storey Renaissance portico emphasises the entrance but looks rather out of place on the rectangular building.

The *Shanghaier Nachrichten* had the following to say about the surrounding business premises: »When the original building style of the free-standing business premises with wide verandas had to be replaced by a style that was more economical in its use of space, the client and architect were ruled solely by functional considerations. (…) The dreadful red and grey brick buildings which close in repressively on its narrow streets are (…) repulsive. One new building recently opened proves that this is not caused by the building materials used. (…) We cannot approve of all aspects of the work of these German architects; however, we must acknowledge that they knew how to cause a revolution in the streets of Shanghai (…)«[165]

祥泰商行

現用途：商業大樓
所在地：上海江西中路一三八號；原江西
　　　　路九至十一號
建築師：貝克，培迪克⟨164⟩
業主：祥泰木行
建造期：一九零七年至一九零八年一月
現狀：樓體保存完好，增加了一個樓層

德國總會康科迪婭剛剛竣工，建築師們又在相距不到一百米的地段上著手建造這幢兼作住宅的商行的大樓。矩形窗，拱形窗以及敞廊拱券構成幾組面積不等的圖案，立面因而顯得散亂，缺乏韻律感，石廊柱支承著敞廊的穹窿，矩形窗裝配有折迭式百葉窗，以避免陽光直接照射，兩層樓高的文藝復興式的門廊標誌著正門入口，然而與長方形主體建築的風格卻不協調。

《上海新聞》對周圍的商業辦公樓作了評論："當初商業辦公樓建築往往獨佔一方土地，不與其它建築物毗鄰，因而可以附設寬闊的敞廊，而今這種佔地面積大的建築形式漸漸被淘汰，對業主和建築師來說，實用成了決定性的因素。在城裡，用青磚或紅磚砌築的高層建築鱗次櫛比地矗立在街道兩側，咄咄逼人地擠壓著本來就不寬闊的街面。這種情景令人望而生畏。一座剛剛慶祝過落成典禮的建築卻證明，這種感覺並不是材料引起的……我們雖不能完全贊同這些德國建築師的使用建築手法，然而我們必須承認，他們是懂得如何改變上海的面貌的。"⟨165⟩

祥泰木行西南隅，一九零八年。
西南角，一九九二年。

WOHNHAUS
RESIDENCE

Heutige Funktion. Current use
Bibliothek der Musikakademie
The library of the academy of music
Huaihai Zhonglu/Fenyang Lu
(Avenue Paul Brunat), Shanghai

Architekten. Architects
vermutlich Becker & Baedecker
probably Becker & Baedecker

Bauzeit. Construction time
etwa zwischen 1905 und 1911
approximately between 1905 and 1911

Zustand. Condition
Das Gebäude ist sehr gut erhalten.
Very well preserved.

Die deutschen Architekten Heinrich Becker und Carl Baedecker bauten nach ihrem großen Erfolg mit dem deutschen Club Concordia auch mehrere private Wohnhäuser im Stil der deutschen Neorenaissance. Die gemeinsamen Merkmale dieser Häuser waren die hohen, mit roten Ziegeln gedeckten Dächer und die reich verzierten Schmuckgiebel. Ecktürme, Dachreiter und Erker waren aus Fachwerk oder Stein gebaut, Loggien aus Holz. Oft wurden auch die Fenster farbig verglast.

Diese Villen lagen im grünen Westend Shanghais, den Erweiterungen der Niederlassungen.[166] Weitere Wohnhäuser, die diese Architekten entworfen hatten, standen in der Nanjing Xilu (Bubbling Well Road). Das ebenfalls nicht mehr existierende Wohnhaus mit dem Namen »Willfried« in der Yan'an Xilu (Great Western Road 10) gehörte dem deutschen Geschäftsmann Max Mittag.[167] Bereits vor 1904 hat Heinrich Becker für die Geschäftsleute Martin Krieg von der Firma Telge & Schroeter und R.H. Lundt von der Firma Buchheister & Co. je eine Villa in der Yan'an Xilu (Great Western Road 1) gebaut.[168]

After their success with the Club Concordia, the German architects Heinrich Becker and Carl Baedecker built several residences in German neo-Renaissance style. The common features of these houses were the high, red-tiled roofs and the richly decorated gables. Corner towers, ridge turrets and bay windows were made of stone or half-timbering, the loggias of wood. The windows were often glazed with coloured glass.

These villas were built in the extensions to the settlements in the leafy western side of Shanghai.[166] There were other houses designed by these architects in Nanjing Xilu (Bubbling Well Road), but they have all been pulled down. The house on Yan'an Xilu (Great Western Road 10), which was called »Willfried« and owned by the German business man Max Mittag, also no longer exists.[167] Prior to 1904, Heinrich Becker built villas on Yan'an Xilu (Great Western Road 1) for the businessmen Martin Krieg of Telge & Schroeter and R.H. Lundt of Buchheister & Co.[168]

Zentrale Halle und Treppe,
Blick nach Westen, 1992
Ehem. Wohnhaus, Westansicht, 1992
Jugendstil-Fensterglas im
Treppenhaus mit Schwalben und
Blättern, 1992
Entrance hall and main stairway,
view to the west, 1992
Former residence, west view, 1992
Coloured window pane in staircase
with swallows and leaves, 1992

住宅

現用途：音樂學院圖書館
所在地：上海准海中路（鳳陽路口）；原寶昌路
建築師：可能是貝克和培迪克
建造日期：約一九零五年至一九一一年
現狀：樓體保存完好

德國工程師海因里希·貝克和卡爾·培迪克建造德國總會康科迪婭大顯身手，獲得了巨大的成功，繼此之後他們又以德國文藝復興式復古風格設計了許多私人住宅。這些建築的共同特點是：高陡的紅瓦屋頂，裝飾華麗的山牆和木敞廊，角塔，屋脊小塔和挑樓用木構架或石牆承重結構。窗子往往用彩色玻璃裝飾，這些別墅座落在上海樹木茂盛的西部，即租界擴展區。〈166〉建築師所在南京西路設計的幾幢住房均已被拆除。如延安西路"維爾弗里德"住宅區內德國商人馬克斯·米塔爾的私宅現已不存在。〈167〉一九零四年，海因里希·貝克曾給來泰公司的商人馬丁·克里格以及生瑞公司的R·H·倫特在延安西路各設計一座別墅。〈168〉

前住宅西面俯瞰，一九九二年。
樓道內繪有燕子和葉片，具有青年藝術派風格的彩色玻璃窗。
入口大廳及主樓梯，一九九二年。

RUSSISCHES GENERALKONSULAT
RUSSIAN CONSULATE GENERAL

Huangpu Lu/Baidu Qiao
(Whangpoo Road 12/Gardenbridge),
Shanghai

Architekt. Architect
Hans Emil Lieb

Baukosten. Building costs
etwa 405 000 Goldmark
approximately 405 000 gold marks

Ausführung. Contractors
Chow Soey Kee, Contractor

Bauherr. Client
Russisches Reich
Russian Empire

Bauzeit. Construction time
Juni 1914 – Ende 1916
June 1914 – end of 1916

Zustand. Condition
Das Gebäude ist sehr gut erhalten.
Very well preserved.

Russisches Generalkonsulat,
Südansicht, Entwurfszeichnung,
1914
Blick von der ehem. Gardenbridge
auf das Russische Generalkonsulat,
1992
Russian Consulate General,
view from the south, 1914
View from the former Garden
bridge to the Russian Consulate
General, 1992

Von dem ehemaligen Konsulatsviertel Shanghais an der Mündung des Suzhou Creeks in den Huangpu-Fluß ist heute nur noch das russische Generalkonsulat erhalten. Es wurde neben dem damaligen deutschen Generalkonsulat auf der relativ kleinen Fläche des Astorhaus-Gartens errichtet und grenzt direkt an das Flußufer. Da auf diesem Grundstück keine Nebengebäude errichtet werden konnten, sind alle Funktionen des Konsulats in einem einzigen Gebäude zusammengefaßt. Entsprechend voluminös wurde es: drei volle Stockwerke, ein Souterrain und ein teilweise ausgebautes Dachgeschoß.

Die Fassaden des Gebäudes bestehen aus Betonsteinen, deren Oberfläche so bearbeitet wurde, daß sie wie Natursteine aussehen. Die tragende Konstruktion, Kellerdecke und feuersichere Treppen sind aus Stahlbeton. Die *Far Eastern Review* schreibt zu dem Haus: »Der Baustil des Gebäudes ist modern, die Ausstattung im Innern ist schlicht. Man legte Wert darauf, nur erstklassige Materialien wie Teakholz und Marmor zu verwenden.«[169]

Im Hochparterre befinden sich noch heute die Büro- und Diensträume sowie ein festlich gestalteter Versammlungssaal, im ersten Obergeschoß die Wohnungen und Repräsentationsräume des Generalkonsuls und mit einem getrennten Eingang die Wohnung des Vizekonsuls. Im zweiten Obergeschoß die Schlaf-, Bade- und Nebenräume der Wohnung des Generalkonsuls sowie eine Wohnung für einen zweiten Vizekonsul. Die Wohnung des Generalkonsuls in der Osthälfte des Gebäudes liegt dem Huangpu-Fluß zugewandt und bietet einen spektakulären Blick auf den Schiffsverkehr. Mehrere Küchen, dazugehörige Nebenräume, sowie die Wohnungen der Bediensteten und Kanzleiangestellten befinden sich im Souterrain und im Dachgeschoß.[170]

The Russian consulate general is the only building in the former diplomatic quarter of Shanghai where Suzhou Creek enters the Huangpu river that is still used today. The Russian consulate general was built next to the then German consulate general on the relatively small site of the Astorhaus garden and borders on the embankment. As it was not possible to build any ancillary buildings on this site, all of the consulate functions had to be accommodated in one single building. The size of the building reflects this necessity; three full storeys, a basement and a partly exploited attic.

The building façades consist of concrete blocks, the surface of which was treated to make them look like natural stone. The structure and stairs are made of fire-proof reinforced concrete. The *Far Eastern Review* wrote about the house: »The style of the building is modern, and the interior fittings are simple, and the effort has been made to employ only first class material, as teak and marble.«[169]

The office, service rooms and a festively designed assembly room were situated on the raised ground floor. The Consul's apartments and function rooms were on the first floor as was the Vice Consul's apartment which had a separate entrance. The second floor housed the bedrooms, bathrooms and ancillary rooms of the Consul's apartment as well as an apartment for a second Vice Consul. The Consul's apartment on the eastern side of the building faced the Huangpu river and had a spectacular view of the shipping traffic. The kitchens and ancillary rooms were on the basement and attic floors as were the apartments for the servants and consulate staff.[170]

俄國總領事館

所在地：上海黃浦路（白渡橋口）；原黃
　　　　浦路十二號（白渡橋）
建築師：漢斯・埃米爾・里勃
建築造價：約四十點五萬盒馬克，十五萬
　　　　　兩銀子
施工：周紹科（音譯），承包商
業主：沙俄帝國政府
建造期：一九一四年六月至一九一六年底
現狀：樓體保存完好新段在住於為州河與

黃浦江交匯處的上海領館區內只有俄國領事館尚存。該領館建在與當時德國領館毗鄰的禮查公園舊址上，緊臨黃浦江，因而也不可能再增建側樓。領事館的所有例行公務必須集中在一幢樓裡處理。領事館的規模也相應很大：三層樓面、一個半地下室層以及樓頂層的部份房間均被裝修，以投入使用。大樓的立面用仿天然石料質感的混凝土飾板裝飾，大樓的承重物架，地窖天花板和樓梯採用經防火處理的鋼筋混凝土。《遠東評論》寫道："大樓總體具有現代建築風格，內部陳設樸實無華，建築師注重建築材料的質量，採用了柚木，大理石等一流材料。"〈169〉

一樓是辦公室和一個佈置華麗的會議廳，二樓是領館的住房以及會客室。副領事的住房也在二樓並有單獨的入口，三樓是總領事的臥室，浴室。三樓的另一套住房是為第二副領事安排的，總領事在大樓東半部的住房面朝黃浦江，在那可以眺望到江上船運的繁忙景象。廚房，餐室，儲置室以及勤雜人員和文職人員的住房分別設在半地下的底層和頂層。〈170〉

俄國總領事館南立面設計圖，一
九一四年。
從白渡橋眺望俄國領事館，一九
九二年。

SHANGHAI

DEUTSCHE INGENIEURSCHULE
THE GERMAN SCHOOL OF ENGINEERING

Funktion ab 1918. Use after 1918
Institute Technique Franco-Chinoise

Heutige Funktion. Current use
Shanghai Machine School
Fuxing Zhonglu/Shanxi Nanlu
(Paulunstraße/Stone Road), Shanghai

Architekt. Architect
Carl Baedecker

Bauleitung. Site architect
Karsten Hermann Suhr

Baukosten. Building costs
etwa 370 000 Goldmark
approximately 370 000 gold marks

Bauherr. Client
Vereinigung zur Errichtung deutscher technischer Schulen in China
(Association for the establishment of German technological schools in China)

Eröffnung. Opening
1914

Bauzeit. Construction time
1908–1916

Zustand. Condition
Die Gebäude sind sehr gut erhalten. Einige Neubauten wurden auf dem Grundstück errichtet.
Very well preserved; some new buildings have been added.

Ehem. Deutsche Ingenieurschule. Lehrgebäude, heute Bibliothek, Ostansicht, 1992
Former classroom building of the German Engineering School, now library, view from the east, 1992

Nach der bereits 1909 in Qingdao gegründeten Deutsch-Chinesischen Hochschule war dies die zweite deutsche technische Hochschule in China. Auf demselben Grundstück lag die 1907 gegründete deutsche Medizinschule. Der Gebäudekomplex der Hochschule entstand in mehreren Abschnitten. Das Wohnheim I war bereits 1908 fertiggestellt worden, 1910 errichtete man das Gebäude des Vorklinikums und die Sprachschule, zwischen 1912 und 1914 entstanden das Maschinen-, das Lehr- und das Wirtschaftsgebäude, die Turnhalle und die Wohnheime II und III. Das Wohnheim IV kam 1916 hinzu.[171] Der Architekt Carl Baedecker baute 1913 bis 1915 als Folgeauftrag die deutsche Ingenieurschule in Wuhan (Hankou). Beide Hochschulen basierten auf Konzepten von Königlich Preußischen Maschinenbauschulen.[172]

Die *Shanghaier Nachrichten* veröffentlichten eine Beschreibung des Gebäudekomplexes: »Dem Eintretenden fällt vor allem das stattliche Lehrgebäude der Ingenieurschule auf. Diesem gegenüber liegt das Maschinengebäude mit den verschiedenen Laboratorien; der Kraftstation, der Lehrwerkstätte, der Gießerei, Schmiede und Tischlerei. An diese beiden den Eingang flankierenden Gebäude schließen sich die Sprachschule, die auch die Lehrerbibliothek enthält, und zwei Alumnatsgebäude aus der ersten Zeit der Medizinschule an. In der Mitte des ganzen Komplexes liegt ein schmuckes Haus, das auf der einen Seite die Bezeichnung: ›Physiologie‹, auf der anderen Seite die Aufschrift: ›Anatomie‹ trägt. Südlich begrenzen das ungefähr 30 000 Quadratmeter große Gelände das neue und größte aller Gebäude, das für 200 Schüler bestimmte Alumnat der Ingenieurschule, und die geräumige Turnhalle. (...) Die neueren Gebäude sind in sauberer Ziegelbauart ausgeführt, sind von frischgrünem Rasen umgeben (...).«[173]

Die Schüler der Ingenieurschule waren bei ihrer Aufnahme etwa 14 Jahre alt und mußten einen chinesischen Mittelschulabschluß ha-

This was the second German technical college in China, the first being the German-Chinese College which was founded in Qingdao in 1909. The German School of Medicine in Shanghai which was founded in 1907 was located on the same site. The buildings for the college were built in phases. Residence I was completed in 1908, the pre-clinical studies and language school building were built in 1910 and the machine, classroom and utilities/services building, the gymnasium and Residences II and III were built between 1912 and 1914. Residence IV was added in 1916.[171] The architect Carl Baedecker built the German School of Engineering in Wuhan (Hankow) as a follow-up commission from 1913 to 1915. The two school projects were based on the concepts for the Royal Prussian Schools of Machine Building.[172]

The *Shanghaier Nachrichten* published the following description of the complex: »The observer entering the complex is above all struck by the engineering school's majestic classroom building. Opposite this is the machine building with the different laboratories; the power station, the instruction workshops, the foundry, the forge and carpentry workshop. The language school, which also houses the teachers' library and two students, residences from the early phase of the medical school come after these two buildings which flank the entrance. There is a decorative house in the middle of the complex which bears the title »Physiology« on one side and »Anatomy« on the other. The south of the almost 30 000 m² site is bordered by the new and biggest of all the buildings, the students' residence for the engineering school, which can accommodate up to 200 students, and the spacious gymnasium. (...) The more recent buildings are built in clean brickwork and are surrounded by fresh green lawns (...).«[173]

The students at the engineering school entered the school around the age of 14; the entrance qualification was the Chinese intermediary school certificate. The course took eight years to complete starting with four

德國技術工程學院（同濟大學前身）

一九一八年後的用途：中法通惠工商學校
現用途：上海機械專科學校
所在地：上海復興中路（陝西南路口），
　　　　原寶隆路（石頭路口）
建築師：卡爾‧培迪先
工程指導：卡斯滕‧赫爾曼‧蘇爾
建築造價：約三十七萬金馬克，十三點七
　　　　萬兩銀子
業主：在中國設立德國工業技術學校籌備
　　　會
啟用期：一九一四年
建造期：一九零八年至一九一六年
現狀：樓體保存完好，另增建幾幢新樓

繼一九零九年在青島創辦的德華工業大學之後，這是德國在中國辦的第二所工業大學。一九零七年創辦的"同濟德文醫學堂"與技術工學院同在一所校園內，大學的校舍是陸陸續續建造起來的。一號宿舍樓修建於一九零八年，一九一零年，基礎理論課教學樓和語言學校教舍竣工。一九一二年到一九一四年，機電樓，後勤樓，教學大樓，健力房，以及第二、第三宿舍樓相繼建成。一九一六年四號宿舍樓也隨之完工。〈171〉一九一三年建築師卡爾‧培迪克又因此接受了設計武漢德國工程技術學校的委託。這兩所學校的構思，布局均以普魯士皇家機械學校的設計方案為藍本。〈172〉
《上海新聞》發表文章描述這一建築群體："步入校園，首先看到的是工程技術學院雄偉的教學大樓，在教學樓對面是機電樓，樓內設有各種實驗室，電機房，學徒實習車間，鑄造車間，鍛工場和木工房，走過位於校門兩側的教學樓與機電樓便是設有教師閱覽室的語言學校和兩座在同濟德文醫學堂創辦初期蓋的學生宿舍。在整個建築群的中間是一幢造形典雅的建築，其兩邊分別寫著"生理學"，〈173〉"解剖學"的字樣。在這約三萬平方米的校區南端，座落著寬敞的健身房和的在所有建築物中規模最大的新宿舍樓，這幢的宿舍樓可容納兩百名學生。新造的樓房均為磚塊砌築的清水牆面，其周圍是綠色的草坪。"
工程技術學院招收十四歲左右的初中畢業

當年前教學樓的主入口，一九九二年。

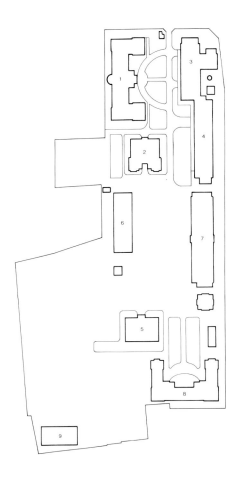

Lageplan der Deutschen Medizin- und Ingenieurschule für Chinesen in Shanghai, 1914
1. Lehrgebäude; 2. Sprachschule; 3. Maschinenlaboratorium; 4. Werkstätten; 5. Vorklinikum; 6. Wohnheim I; 7. Wohnheim II; 8. Wohnheim III; 9. Turnhalle
Haupteingang des ehem. Lehrgebäudes, 1992
Eingangshalle mit Deckengewölbe, 1992

Site plan of the German School of Medicine and Engineering for Chinese in Shanghai, 1914
1. Classroom building; 2. Language School; 3. Machine laboratory; 4. Workshops; 5. Pre-Clinical building; 6. Students' residence No. 1; 7. Residence No. 2; 8. Residence No. 3; 9. Gymnasium
Main entrance, 1992
Entrance hall with vaulted ceiling, 1992

ben. Die Studiendauer betrug 8 Jahre, nach vier Jahren Sprachschule folgte eine vierjährige Ausbildung an der Ingenieurschule. Im Sommersemester 1915 besuchten 122 Studenten die Sprach- und 78 die Ingenieurschule mit einer Bauingenieur- und Maschinenbauabteilung. Von den Medizinstudenten besuchten 162 die Sprachschule und 77 die medizinische Fakultät, Vorklinikum und Klinikum.[174] Außerdem gab es eine Lehrlingsschule mit 20 Plätzen und eine Werkmeisterschule mit vierjähriger Lehrzeit, um Schlosser und Monteure auszubilden.

Nur knapp drei Jahre konnte in dem im Juni 1914 eingeweihten Gebäude der Ingenieurschule unterrichtet werden. Im März 1917 schlossen französische Polizisten die auf dem Gebiet der französischen Niederlassung stehende Hochschule. Der Unterricht wurde in Ausweichquartieren fortgesetzt. 1924 wurde eine neue Schulanlage im etwa 15 km entfernten Stadtteil Wusong (Woosung) eingeweiht.

years at the language school followed by four years training at the engineering school. In summer term of 1915 there were 122 students attending the language school and 78 attending the engineering school which was divided into departments of construction and mechanical engineering. Of the medical students, 162 attended the language school and 77 attended the medical faculty, pre-clinical and clinical departments.[174] In addition there was a school for apprentices with 20 places and a school for foremen with 4-year courses for the training of fitters.

The engineering school which was officially opened in June 1914 was barely open for three years when in March 1917, the French police closed the college which was located in the French concession. In 1924 a new school complex was opened in Wusong (Woosung), a neighbourhood some 15 km away from the centre of Shanghai.

上海醫學和工程技術學院總平面圖，一九一四年。
一、教學樓；二、語言學校；三、機械實驗室；四、實習車間；五、醫學基礎知識教學樓；六、第一學生宿舍；七、第二學生宿舍；八、第三學生宿舍；九、體操房

生為學生。學制八年，前四年學德語，後四年在工程技術學院學習專業課程。一九一五年夏季學期，有一百二十二名學生在語言學校就讀，七十八名學生在工程技術學院土木工程學和機械與學習。醫科學生有中有一百六十二人在學語言，七十七人在醫學與學習基礎理論課或做臨床實習。〈174〉為培養鉗工和裝配工，學院還辦了一所可招收二十名學員的徒工學校。此外，還有一所培訓工段長和車間主任的學校，學制為四年。

在這座一九一四年六月落成的工程技術學院的教學樓只開了不到三年的課。一九一七年五月，法國警察查封了這所建在法國租界裡的高等學校，教學在備用的教學點繼續進行。一九二四年在距舊校址十五公里這所吳淞區該校又建起了新的校舍。

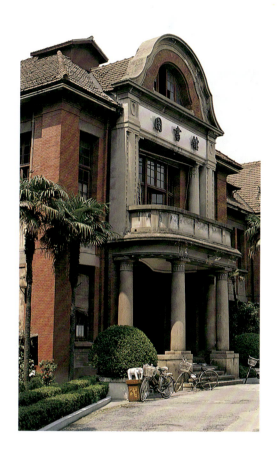

前德國工業技術學院教學樓，現為圖書館東立面，一九九二年。

有拱頂的門廳，一九九二年。

SHANGHAI

TUNG-CHI TECHNISCHE HOCHSCHULE
TUNG-CHI TECHNICAL UNIVERSITY

Tongji Lu; Vorort Wusong
(Tung-chi Road; Woosung), Shanghai
Tongji Lu; Wusong suburb
(Tung-chi Road; Woosung), Shanghai

Architekt. Architect
Erich Oberlein, Regierungsbaumeister a. D.[175]
Erich Oberlein, former government
architect [175]

Baukosten. Building costs
etwa 450 000 Goldmark
approximately 450 000 gold marks

Ausführung. Contractors
Mow Kee Baufirma
Mow Kee builders

Bauherr. Client
Verband für den Fernen Osten
(Far East Association)

Bauzeit. Construction time
Umbau der bestehenden Gebäude 1920/22,
Lehrgebäude, Laboratorien,
Werkstätten 1922/24
Conversion of existing buildings 1920/22,
Classroom building, laboratories,
workshops 1922/24

Zustand. Condition
Zerstört. 1958/59 Neubau der 5. Shanghaier
Stahlfabrik unter teilweiser Verwendung der
Fundamente der Hochschule.
The 5th Shanghai Steelworks was built in
1958–1959 using part of the foundations
of the college.

Lehrgebäude der Tongji-Universität
in Wusong, Südansicht, um 1928
Main classroom building of the
Tongji University in Wusong, view
from the south, around 1928

Der Vorort Wusong (Woosung) lag eine halbe Stunde Eisenbahnfahrt von der Shanghaier Innenstadt entfernt. Ausschlaggebend für die Entscheidung, die Neubauten außerhalb der Stadt zu errichten, waren nicht nur die viel günstigeren Grundstückspreise, sondern auch der geplante Ausbau Wusongs zu einer Hafen- und Industriestadt. Diese chinesische Planung eines »Greater Shanghai« zwischen der Internationalen Niederlassung und der Mündung des Huangpu in den Yangzi wurde von Deutschland ausdrücklich unterstützt. Als eine Art moderne chinesische Niederlassung sollte sie ein Gegengewicht zu den beiden ausländischen bilden.

Die Wiedereröffnung der Tung-chi Hochschule war von Anfang an ein deutsch-chinesisches Gemeinschaftsunternehmen. Das chinesische Unterrichtsministerium und die Provinzialregierung hatten auf Antrag des Tung-chi Komitees den Betrag von umgerechnet etwa 450 000 Goldmark zur Errichtung einer neuen Schulanlage bewilligt. 300 deutsche Firmen beteiligten sich durch Stiftungen an dem Aufbau. Die Hochschule wurde von einem chinesisch-deutschen Professorenkollegium gemeinsam geleitet. Am 26. Mai 1923 wurde ihr durch das chinesische Unterrichtsministerium der Rang einer Universität verliehen. Die sich 1927 in Nanjing konstituierende nationale Regierung erkannte sie ebenfalls als gleichberechtigt mit den übrigen chinesischen Staatsuniversitäten an.

Im Mai 1924 wurden das Lehrgebäude, die Laboratorien und Werkstätten eingeweiht. Der Mittelrisalit des Lehrgebäudes wirkt gedrungen, das Dach über dem aus zehn Säulen gebildeten monumentalen Eingangsportal hat zu wenig Volumen. Die dahinter liegenden Räume werden in der Denkschrift zur Einweihung beschrieben: »Das Lehrgebäude wird durch ein Vestibül betreten, aus dessen Hintergrund drei Glasgemälde hervorleuchten. (…) Die Pfeiler des Vestibüls sind mit brauner Holztäfelung umkleidet, die Wandfelder mit schönen bunten Industriebildern geschmückt. Rechts und links liegt je ein Aus-

The suburb of Wusong (Woosung) was half an hour by train from the centre of Shanghai. The reason for choosing this site outside the city was not just that the price of land was much lower there, but it was planned to develop Wusong into a harbour and industrial town. The Chinese plans for »Greater Shanghai« between the International Settlement and the entry of the Huangpu into the Yangtze was strongly supported by Germany. It was intended to provide a kind of Chinese settlement to balance the two foreign settlements.

From the outset, the reopening of the Tung-chi College was a combined Chinese-German project. The Chinese education ministry and the provincial administration had approved an application by the Tung-chi committee for approximately 450 000 gold marks to build the new college complex. 300 German companies contributed to the project through foundations. The college was run by a joint Chinese-German teaching body. On 26 May 1923 the college was conferred university status by the Chinese education ministry. The national government constituting in Nanjing in 1927 also recognised it as equal in status with the other Chinese state universities.

The newly-constructed classroom building, the laboratories and workshops were officially opened in May 1924. The central projection of the classroom building has a very forced appearance and the roof over the monumental entrance portico with its ten columns does not have sufficient volume. The rooms behind the entrance portal are described in the brochure published to mark the opening: »The classroom building is accessed through a vestibule with three glass paintings shining in the background. (…) The piers in the vestibule are covered in wood panelling and the walls are decorated with beautiful coloured industrial images. There is an exhibition hall both right and left of the hall both containing models of machines, machine parts, production samples and cycles from German industry. The built-in wall cupboards in the hall serve

吳淞同濟大學教學樓南立面，約一九二八年。

同濟工業大學

校址：上海吳淞區同濟路；原吳淞區同濟路
建築師：埃里希・奧伯業因，前政府工程師〈175〉
建築造價：約四十五萬金馬克
施工：茂記（音譯）建築公司
業主：遠東聯合會
建造期：一九二零年至一九二二年改建原有的樓房
一九二二年至一九二四年興建教學樓、試驗室、車間、舊房子
現狀：在舊校址上為上海第五鋼鐵廠，建廠時所用了部份地基。

從吳淞到上海市內要乘半小時的火車，把校址選在城外不僅是因為地皮價格要便宜得多，更主要的是為了實施把吳淞興建成商埠工業城的計劃，德國人大力支持這一由中國人制定的、把位於公共租界及黃浦江與長江交匯處之間的吳淞地區建成"大上海"的規劃。興建起來的吳淞在某種意義上是中國的一個經濟特區，它將與法租界和公共租界抗衡。

恢復同濟大學是中德雙方的共同願望，國民政府教育部的當地政府批准了同濟校委會關於重建學校的申請，並撥款四十五萬金馬克，三百家德國公司也捐款資助，學校由雙方教授共同領導。一九二三年五月二十六日國民政府教育部正式認可同濟大學。一九二七年南京國民臨時政府也將同濟大學和其它國立大學同時對待。

一九二四年五月，為新建的教學樓、試驗室和車間舉行了落成慶祝典禮。教學樓的正門廊的以十根廊柱裝飾，局部看來富麗堂皇，然而樓頂部份過低，使整個中間立面顯得毫無氣派。慶祝同濟大學重建吳淞的專輯這樣描寫教學樓內的設施："跨入教學大樓步入前廳，首先躍入眼簾的是三幅彩色玻璃畫……前廳的支柱鑲著粟色護板，牆上掛著色彩絢麗的工廠企業水彩畫，前廳左右各有一個展覽廳，廳裡陳列著機器、機器部件、工業樣品以及介紹德國工業成品和半成品工藝生產流程的模型。走廊上的壁廚裡也陳放著展品。前廳兩側的樓梯通向二樓的禮堂。禮堂佔了教

Maschinengebäude, Westansicht, um 1928
Lageplan, 1924
1. Lehrgebäude; 2. Maschinengebäude; 3. Wohnheim; 4. Küche und Speisesaal; 5. Lehrlingshaus; 6. Vorklinikum; 7. Dozentenhäuser
Machine building, view from the west, around 1928
Site plan, 1924
1. Classroom building; 2. Machine building; 3. Students' residence; 4. Kitchen and dining room; 5. Apprentice building; 6. Pre-clinical building; 7. Houses for teaching staff

stellungssaal, die beide mit Modellen von Maschinen und Fabrikationsproben der deutschen Industrie gefüllt sind. Dem gleichen Ausstellungs- und Anschauungszweck dienen in die Korridore eingelassene Wandschränke. Vom Vestibül aus führen beiderseitig Treppen zu der im Obergeschoß gelegenen, den ganzen Mittelbau einnehmenden Aula. Da dem Mittelbau aus Gründen der Kostenersparnis keine größere Geschoßhöhe gegeben werden konnte als den die Unterrichtsräume bergenden Seitenflügeln, so wurde durch möglichste Einbeziehung der Auladecke in den Dachraum erstrebt, den gedrückten Eindruck zu mildern, den die geringe Höhe bei der großen Flächenausdehnung von 350 m² hervorrufen mußte. (...) Die Seitenflügel beherbergen im Erdgeschoß die Verwaltungsräume, das Konferenzzimmer, die Bibliothek, das Lesezimmer, das Zeichenbüro, das Empfangszimmer, (...) im Obergeschoß die 10 Unterrichtsräume, in denen sowohl Vorlesungen als auch Zeichenübungen abgehalten werden. (...)«[176] Westlich des Lehrgebäudes lag das zweigeschossige Wohnheim mit 50 Zimmern für die Studenten, sowie 20 Zimmern für chinesische Lehrkräfte und Verwaltungsbeamte. Das Maschinengebäude, ein 110 Meter langer eingeschossiger Bau, begrenzt den Universitätscampus nach Westen. Alle Gebäude trugen mit roten Ziegeln gedeckte Walmdächer.

In einer zweiten Bauphase 1929 bis 1930 errichtete man das Gebäude für chemische Materialprüfung, das elektronische Laboratorium, das Lehrgebäude der Mittelschule und das Physiologische Institut. Im Februar und März 1932 wurde die Universität während des japanischen Angriffs auf Wusong stark beschädigt. Mit chinesischen Geldern wurden die Gebäude repariert; der Unterricht konnte im Herbst 1932 wieder aufgenommen werden. Im Mai 1937 wurde der 30. Jahrestag der Tung-chi Technischen Hochschule gefeiert. Im August 1937 besetzten japanische Soldaten die Vororte Shanghais und auch die Hochschule.[177]

the same exhibition purpose. There are stairs leading from both sides of the hall to the assembly room on the upper floor which takes up the entire central building. As for cost-saving reasons it was not possible to build the central building any higher than the side wings where the classrooms are located, the architect tried to reduce the impression created by the low height combined with the extensive 350 m² horizontal spread of the building by integrating the ceiling of the assembly hall as much as possible into the roof space. (...) The ground floor of the side wings house the administration, the conference room, the library, the reading room, the drawing studio, the reception room, (...) the ten classrooms are on the upper floor which will be used for both lectures and drawing practice. (...)[176]
To the west of the classroom building, there was a two-storey residence with 50 rooms for the students; a further 20 rooms in the building were intended for Chinese teachers and administrative officials. The machine building, a 110 metre-long single storey building, bordered the university campus to the west. All of the buildings had hipped roofs with red tiles.

The building for chemical material testing, the electronics laboratory, the classroom building for the intermediary school and the physiology institute were built during a second phase from 1929 to 1930. In February and March 1932 the university was badly damaged during the Japanese attack on Wusong. The repairs were financed by the Chinese and teaching was able to start again in autumn 1932. Tung-chi Technical University celebrated the 30th anniversary of its founding in May 1937. In August 1937, Japanese soldiers occupied the suburbs of Shanghai and, thus, the University also.[177]

學中間突出部分的整個樓面,為了節省資金,禮堂的層高實際上與側樓內教堂的高度一樣,天花板和屋頂之間的空間被盡量壓縮以增加地面與天花板之間的距離,以使禮堂顯得高些,多少消除一些由於層高與三百五十平方米的建築面積不協調而產生的壓抑感……在側樓的底層設有行政辦公室、會議室、圖書館、閱覽室、繪圖室、接待室……二樓共有十間教室,除了授課外,驗圖時上課在那裡進行……〈176〉教學樓的西邊是一座兩層宿舍樓,五十間房子用作學生宿舍,二十間供教師和行政人員住宿。在大學校園的西邊盡端,是一幢長一百一十米的平房,這是學校的電機房。同濟大學所有的樓房都是紅瓦四坡屋頂。在一九二九年到一九三零年的第二次擴建期先後建造了用於材料化學測試和電子儀器測試的測試樓,附中的教學樓和生理學研究所。一九三二年二、三月間日本轟炸吳淞時,同濟大學受到嚴重破壞,後來用中方的資金修復了損壞樓房,直到一九三二年秋教學才得以恢復。一九三七年五月同濟大學舉行三十年校慶。一九三七年八月日軍佔領上海郊區以及同濟大學。〈177〉

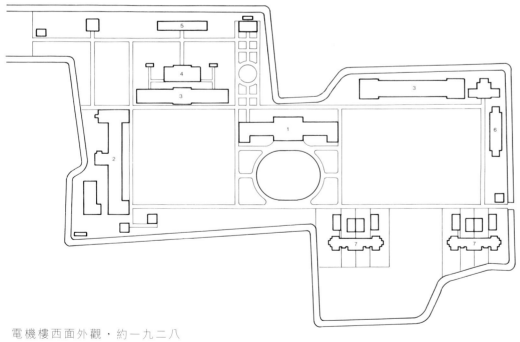

電機樓西面外觀,約一九二八年。
一九二四年的總平面圖
一、教學樓;二、電機樓;三、學生宿舍;四、廚房和餐廳;五、學徒工宿舍;六、醫學教學樓;七、助教宿舍

SHANGHAI

DEUTSCHES GEMEINDEHAUS UND KAISER-WILHELM-SCHULE
GERMAN COMMUNITY CENTRE AND THE KAISER WILHELM SCHOOL

Yan'an Xilu/Huashan Lu
(Great Western Road 1/Avenue Haig),
Shanghai

Architekt. Architect
E. Busch

Bauherr. Client
Deutsche Gemeinde Shanghai
German community Shanghai

Bauzeit. Construction time
14. Juni 1928 – 25. Mai 1929
14 June 1928 – 25 May 1929

Zustand. Condition
Das Gebäude wurde 1989 für den Neubau des International Equatorial Hotel abgetragen.
Pulled down in 1989 and replaced by the International Equatorial Hotel.

Deutsches Gemeindehaus, Nordansicht, um 1930
German Community Centre, view from the north, around 1930

Auf einem Eckgrundstück im grünen Westend der Stadt, weit entfernt vom Geschäftszentrum am Huangpu-Fluß, entstand 1929 ein neues deutsches Zentrum, »Deutsches Eck« genannt. Das Deutsche Gemeindehaus enthielt in den beiden unteren Stockwerken die Kaiser-Wilhelm-Schule, eine »anerkannte höhere deutsche Lehranstalt Oberrealschule für Knaben und Mädchen mit Vorschule und Kindergarten«. Im Park hinter dem Gemeindehaus wurde 1929 das Iltis-Denkmal wiedererrichtet, das 1918 vom Bund entfernt worden war, sowie 1932 die neue Deutsch-Evangelische Kirche eingeweiht. Lediglich das deutsche Generalkonsulat blieb an seinem alten Platz am Huangpu-Fluß.

Über 20 Jahre waren seit dem Bau des Club Concordia vergangen, der fast provozierend die Wirtschaftsmacht Deutschland in Shanghai darstellte. Der Erste Weltkrieg hatte große Veränderungen gebracht, mit ihnen änderte sich auch die Architektur. Der internationale Stil der neuen Architektur prägte die Bauten der deutschen Gemeinde in Shanghai.

1919 erhielt die Bank of China das Gebäude des Clubs Concordia am Bund als Teil der deutschen Reparationszahlungen. Nach ihrer Repatriierung kehrten 1920 die deutschen Kaufleute nach China zurück, ohne koloniale Privilegien wie Konsulargerichtsbarkeit oder eigene Niederlassungen, sondern als gleichberechtigte Partner. 1922 erfolgte die Rückgabe der Kaiser-Wilhelm-Schule an die deutsche Gemeinde. 1925 wurde diese durch einen Anbau erweitert, mußte jedoch im Frühjahr 1928 aufgegeben werden.[178] Um das Jahr 1925 wurde in einem unauffälligen Gebäude im Shanghaier Westend ein neuer deutscher Gartenklub eröffnet. Der erste Gartenklub war 1919 zum französischen Gartenklub geworden.

Der Architekt E. Busch war ab 1904 in Wuhan (Hankou) als Partner von Lothar Marcks tätig. Beide hatten zuvor in Qingdao gearbeitet. Lothar Marcks eröffnete nach dem Ersten Weltkrieg ein eigenes Architekturbüro in Shenyang (Mukden).[179]

A new German centre, the »German corner«, was established in 1929 on a corner site in the leafy west end of the city, far away from the commercial centre at the Huangpu river. The Kaiser Wilhelm School, a »recognised higher German teaching institute for boys and girls«, occupied the two lower floors of the community centre. The Iltis memorial was re-erected 1929 in the park behind the centre; it had been removed from the Bund in 1918. The new German Protestant Church was built here in 1932. The German consulate general was the only building to remain on the original site at the Huangpu river.

It was more than 20 years since the construction of the Club Concordia, the almost audacious embodiment of Germany as an economic power in Shanghai. The First World War had, however, brought about great political change and with it architecture also changed. The international style of modern architecture characterised the 1920s and, thus, the new buildings for the German community in Shanghai.

In 1919, the Bank of China was given the Club Concordia building on the Bund as part of German reparation payments. Following their repatriation, the German business community returned to China in 1920, this time without colonial privileges such as consular jurisdiction or their own settlements; they were now the equal partners of the Chinese. The Kaiser Wilhelm School was returned to the German community in 1922 and in 1925 an extension was built on to the school building which however had to be vacated in spring 1928.[178] Around 1925 a new German Garden Club was opened in a modest building in the west end of Shanghai. The first German Garden Club had been taken over by the French Garden Club in 1919.

From 1904, the architect E. Busch worked in Wuhan (Hankow) as a partner of Lothar Marcks. They had both previously worked in Qingdao. Lothar Marcks opened his own architectural practice in Shenyang (Mukden) after the First World War.[179]

上海德國僑民社區中心的北立面，約一九三零年。

上海德僑活動中心和威廉學堂

所在地：上海延安西路（華山路口）；原大西路一號
建築師：衛·布契
業主：上海德國僑民組織
建造期：一九二八年六月十四日至一九二九年五月二十五日
現狀：一九八九年被拆除，另建貴都大酒店。

一九二九年取名於"德意志之角"的上海德僑活動中心落成於草木茂盛且遠離黃浦江畔商業中心的城西一隅。這座文化娛樂中心大樓的一、二層樓面作為威廉學堂的校舍。威廉學堂是一所為德僑子女而辦的設有幼兒園和學前班的頗有名氣的理科中學。在活動中心後面的花園裡又重新豎起於一九一八年在外灘被人推倒的伊爾蒂紀念碑。一九三二年，在這個地段上還修建了一座德國基督教教堂，唯有德國領館仍留在外灘。

當時離那座雄偉的、充分顯示德國在上海經濟實力的康科迪婭總會的落成已二十多年。第一次世界大戰使政局發生了巨大的變化，建築手法也在隨之變化。德國文藝復興式復古風格已不再流行。國際現代派的建築藝術風格引導著二十年代的世界建築設計潮流。上海僑民機構活動中心的樓房自然也無例外地印上了這一新潮的烙印。
一九一九年，中國銀行遷入作為德國戰爭賠款一部份的德國總會康科迪婭。被遣送回國的德國商人於一九二零年又重返中國。他們已無權享受殖民者的優惠待遇（如領事裁判權等），失去了昔日的租界，成了與中國人平等的貿易伙伴。一九二二年威廉學堂退還給德國人。一九二五年學堂擴建，一九二八年春被迫關閉。⟨178⟩新德國花園總會於一九二五年前後落成。這座撲實無華、不起眼的建築位於上海西郊。第一個花園總會於一九一九被法國租界佔有。建築師E.布契自一九零四年起在武漢與洛塔爾·馬爾克斯合作，兩人都曾在青島工作過。第一次世界大戰後，洛塔爾·馬爾克斯在瀋陽開設了一家建築師事務所⟨179⟩

NEUE DEUTSCHE EVANGELISCHE KIRCHE
NEW GERMAN PROTESTANT CHURCH

Yan'an Xilu/Huashan Lu (Great Western Road 1/Avenue Haig), Shanghai

Architekt. Architect
Ladislaus Edward Hudec

Bauherr. Client
Deutsche evangelische Gemeinde Shanghai
German Protestant community Shanghai

Bauzeit. Construction time
Mai 1931 – Oktober 1932
May 1931 – October 1932

Zustand. Condition
Die Kirche wurde zwischen 1966 und 1976 abgetragen, Neubau des Hilton Hotels.
Pulled down between 1966 and 1976 and replaced by the Hilton Hotel.

Expressive Architektur mit Innenräumen voller Spannung, diese Formensprache beherrschte nur ein Architekt im Shanghai der 20er und 30er Jahre: L. E. Hudec.

Turm und Eingang der deutschen Kirche standen parallel zur Huashan Lu; das kurze aber hohe Kirchenschiff war um 45 Grad gedreht und zeigte in der Diagonale des Grundstücks auf die Straßenecke. Von hier aus betrachtet wirkte der Turm breiter, verstärkt durch sich verjüngende Mauerscheiben an seinen Kanten. Während die Fassade des benachbarten deutschen Gemeindehauses hell verputzt war, verwendete der Architekt bei der Kirche dunkelroten und schieferblauen Klinker. Dieses in Shanghai ortsübliche Baumaterial wurde von Hudec häufig eingesetzt. An der Westseite der Kirche schloß im gleichen Material ein schmales zweigeschossiges Gebäude mit Flachdach und Bandfenster an. Dort befanden sich weitere Räume der Kaiser-Wilhelm-Schule.[180] Der Innenraum der Kirche war hell verputzt.

Obgleich die Deutsch-Evangelische Kirche während der Kulturrevolution abgetragen wurde, kann man Hudecs ausdrucksreiche Kirchenbauten in Shanghai noch an zwei weiteren Beispielen erleben. 1929 erbaute er die Mo-en-tang (Moore Memorial Church) in der Xizhang Lu 31, Ecke Hankou Lu, gegenüber der ehemaligen Pferderennbahn. Um 1932 entwarf Hudec die katholische Kirche am Ausländerfriedhof in der Hami Lu (Rubicon Road) am Stadtrand. Heute als »Shanghai Animal Hospital« genutzt, ist sie in ihrem architektonischen Ausdruck das Schwestergebäude zur deutschen Kirche.

L. E. Hudec (1892–1958) wurde in der Slowakei als Kind einer Architektenfamilie geboren, er studierte in Budapest Architektur und kam als Flüchtling aus russischer Kriegsgefangenschaft 1918 nach Shanghai. Hudec arbeitete als Architekt für amerikanische, chinesische und deutsche Auftraggeber. Zwischen 1931 und 1934 baute er u. a. das Parkhotel, mit 22 Stockwerken und 87 Metern das damals höchste Gebäude Asiens.[181]

The formal language of Expressionism with its tense, vivacious interiors was mastered by only one of Shanghai's architects of the 1920s and 30s: L. E. Hudec.

The tower and entrance to the German church stood parallel to the Huashan Lu; the short but high nave was rotated at an angle of 45 degrees and was placed on the diagonal of the site from the street corner. The tower was made to look wider due to the emphasis created by the tapering masonry slabs at its corners. Whereas the façade of the neighbouring German Community Centre was covered in bright plaster, the architect used dark red and slate blue clinker brick for the church. Hudec used this common local material in many of his buildings. There was a narrow two-storey building with a flat roof and hinged windows built in the same material on the west side of the church. This building housed additional rooms belonging to the Kaiser Wilhelm School.[180] The church interior was rendered in a bright colour.

Although the »New German Protestant Church« was demolished during the Cultural Revolution, it is still possible to experience two examples of Hudec's strong expressionist churches can still to be found in Shanghai. In 1929 he built the Mo-en-tang (Moore Memorial Church) in Xizhang Lu 31, at the corner of Hankow Lu opposite the former race course. Around 1932 Hudec built the Catholic church at the foreign cemetery on Hami Lu (Rubicon Road) on the outskirts of the city. Now used as the »Shanghai Animal Hospital« it is the twin building of the German Church in terms of the architectural expression.

L. E. Hudec (1892–1958) was born in Slovakia, son of an architect family. He studied architecture in Budapest and fled as a Russian prisoner of war to Shanghai in 1918. Hudec worked as an architect for American, Chinese and German clients. Between 1931 and 1934 his commissions included the 22-storey Park Hotel which at 87 metres was then the highest building in Asia.[181]

德國新福音教堂

所在地：上海延安西路（華山路口），大西路一號（海洛路口）
建築師：鄔達克
業主：上海德國福音教派／基督教組織
建造期：一九三一年五月至一九三二年十月
現狀：文革期間被拆除，現為希爾頓賓館

二、三十年代的上海只有一位建築師掌握了表現派的真諦並能自如地運用其表現手法，設計引人入勝的作品，這位建築師就是鄔達克。

教堂的塔樓和入口處均朝著華山路方向；高大的教堂正廳而向交叉路口，位於矩形地段的對角線上，與塔樓，入口成四十五度角。由於塔四角的扶壁漸漸細上去，從路口看，塔樓顯得比實際要寬一些。毗鄰的上海德僑活動中心大樓淡色粉刷。鄔達克總就地取材，用紅磚間以青磚砌築教堂外牆。在教堂西側他又以同樣的建築材料設計了一座造型挺秀設有排窗的二層平頂樓房。樓內有兩間房子供威廉學堂使用。〈180〉教堂內壁粉刷成明快的淺色。盡管德國新福音教堂在文化大革命中被拆毀，人們還可以在上海欣賞到鄔達克設計的極有個性的其它兩座建築。一九二九年他在西芷路三十一號，即當年的跑馬場對面設計了沐恩堂，一九三二年前後他又在哈密路設計了一座天主教堂。這座位於西郊外僑公墓旁邊的教堂現為上海獸醫站。從外表上看，這座教堂可謂是新福音教堂的翻版。

鄔達克出身於斯洛伐克一個建築世家。他早年在布達佩斯攻讀建築學，一九一八年從沙俄戰俘營流亡到上海。他從美國，中國和德國承接建築設計業務。一九三一年至一九三四年間他設計了當時為亞洲最高建築——高八十七米，共二十二層的國際飯店。〈181〉

臨海洛路的教堂東面外觀，攝於一九三四年左右。
德國基督教堂，聖壇，約一九三四年。

SHANGHAI

PAULUN HOSPITAL

Heutige Funktion. Current use
Krankenhaus
Hospital
Fengyang Lu (Burkill Road), Shanghai

Architekt. Architect
Ladislaus Edward Hudec

Baukosten (Rohbau).
Building costs (structure)
200 000 Silberdollar
200 000 silver dollars

Ausführung (Rohbau).
Contractors (structure)
Voh Kee Construction Co.

Bauzeit. Construction time
März 1923 – 1927
March 1923 – 1927

Zustand. Condition
Umbau 1990/91, völlig veränderte Fassade.
Completely converted 1990/1991, façade completely altered.

Paulun Hospital, Blick von Westen, 1927
Paulun Hospital, view from the west, 1927

Im Jahre 1899 hatte die Deutsche Ärztevereinigung in Shanghai, damals bestehend aus den Ärzten Paulun und von Schab, das Tung-chi Hospital an der Burkill Road eingerichtet, ein kleines Hospital für arme Chinesen. Zunächst in zwei alten Wellblechbaracken untergebracht, erfreute es sich schon bald eines guten Rufes unter der chinesischen Bevölkerung. Mit chinesischen Spenden konnte nun ein zweistöckiger Backsteinbau errichtet werden. Im Erdgeschoß wurde eine Poliklinik eingerichtet, im Obergeschoß befanden sich 12 Krankenzimmer. Dieses Gebäude wurde um 1920 abgebrochen, an seiner Stelle errichtete man das neue Paulun Hospital.[182]

Die Fassaden des Paulun Hospitals bestanden aus zwei verschiedenen Materialien. Die unteren vier Stockwerke waren aus rötlichem Sichtmauerwerk, oberhalb eines umlaufenden Gesimsbandes war das letzte Stockwerk dann hell verputzt. Die beiden neoklassizistischen Giebel an der zur Straße gerichteten Nordfassade ähnelten den von Hudec beim Country Hospital verwendeten. Der U-förmige Grundriß der Stockwerke oberhalb des Erdgeschosses führte zu einer optimalen Belichtung aller Räume. Bedingt durch die Form des Grundstückes war der rechte, östliche Gebäudeflügel tiefer. Hier befand sich auch der große Vorlesungssaal, durch die hohen Fenster an der Fassade erkennbar. Dieser Baukörper bildete eine spitze 75-Grad-Ecke zur Straße.

Im Paulun Krankenhaus erfolgte die praktische Ausbildung der Medizinstudenten. Ihr Studiengang an der deutschen Medizinschule wurde in der Denkschrift beschrieben: »In Anlehnung an den Studiengang der Medizin an deutschen Universitäten haben die Studenten zunächst zwei Jahre dem vorklinischen Studium (Anatomie, Physiologie, medizinische Physik und Chemie) zu widmen; nach einer ungefähr dem tentamen physicum deutscher Universitäten entsprechenden Prüfung treten sie in das Klinikum über, das drei Studienjahre umfaßt und den Studenten Gelegenheit gibt, sich theoretische und prakti-

In 1899 the German Doctors' Association in Shanghai which at the time consisted of doctors Paulun and von Schab founded the Tung-chi Hospital on Burkill Road, a small hospital for poor Chinese. The hospital building initially consisted of two old corrugated iron huts. The hospital quickly earned itself a good reputation among the Chinese population. With donations from Chinese friends it then became possible to build a two-storey brick building. The ground floor contained an out-patient clinic and there were twelve wards on the upper floor. This building was pulled down around 1920 and replaced by the new Paulun Hospital.[182]

The façades of the Paulun Hospital consisted of two different materials. The lower four floors were clad with reddish fair-faced clay brickwork and with the upper floor rendered in bright plaster above a string course. The neo-classical gables on the northern façade facing the street were motifs which Hudec also used for the Country Hospital. The U-shaped plan of all floors above the ground floor provided optimal lighting for all rooms. The plan of the building was asymmetrical. The right, east wing was deeper. This also housed the large lecture theatre which could be seen through the high windows of the façade. This part of the building formed an acute 75 degree corner to the street.

Medical students received practical training at the Paulun Hospital. Their course of study at the German school of medicine was described in the memorial publication: »Based on the course of medical studies at German universities the students first follow two years of pre-clinical studies (anatomy, physiology, medical physics and chemistry); after an examination that roughly corresponds to the tentamen physicum at German universities they enter the clinical phase that lasts three years and gives the students an opportunity to acquire knowledge in the fields of pathology, inner medicine, surgery, skin and sexually-transmitted diseases and public health. Following completion of this five-year course

寶隆醫院（同濟醫院）

現用途：醫院
地址：上海鳳陽路（與南京路平行），臣白克路
建築師：鄔達克
建築造價：（不計室內外裝修費）二十萬洋元施工：（不包括室內外裝修）上海馥記營造廠
建造期：一九二三年三月至一九二七年
現狀：一九九零年至一九九一年徹底翻修改建，立面完全改觀

一八九九年，由寶隆和馮、沙伯兩位醫師創辦的德國醫生協會在白克路為中國窮人開設了一所醫院，即同濟醫院的前身。醫院最初辦在兩間瓦楞鐵皮棚屋裡。這所醫院很快就在社會上贏得了聲譽。由中國的熟人好友資助捐款又增蓋了一座兩層磚樓，一樓是門診部，二樓是設有十二張床位的住院處。一九二零年這幢樓房被拆除，在原址上建起了寶隆醫院。〈182〉

寶隆醫院的立面由兩種不同的材料裝飾。一至四樓的外牆的淡紅色的清水磚，腰線上的頂層立面則是淡色的粉牆。面朝馬路北面的山牆具有新古典主義的風格。鄔達克對華東醫院的立面也做了同樣的處理。二樓以上的樓層平面呈U型。這種格局使樓內房間的采光達到最佳效果。整座樓的平面並不對稱，右邊東側的樓翼朝北延伸要長些。立面上的大窗戶標示樓內設有大教室。整個大樓與街道城七十五度的銳角。醫學院的學生在室隆醫院做監床實習。同濟大學二十五年校慶專輯介紹了同濟醫學堂的學制安排情況："按照德國醫學院的學制，學生前兩年學習基礎理論課程（解剖學，生理學，醫用物理和醫用化學）。在通過與德國醫科大學水平相當的基礎考試後，進行如期三年的臨床實踐教學。這一階段學習病理學，內外科，皮膚科，婦科和衛生保健方面的理論和實踐知識。五年學習後學生要參加醫生開業執照考試。"〈183〉在學習醫學專業前要修德文四年。

除了寶隆醫院鄔達克在上海還設計了另外三所醫院：延安西路的華東醫院，當時有一百二十五張床位；九江路二百一十九號的同仁醫院，現為區政府所在地；位於當年中

寶隆醫院西北角，一九二七年。

Blick von Osten, 1927
Umgebautes Hospital,
Blick von Osten, 1992
View from the east, 1927
Hospital conversion,
view from the east, 1992

sche Kenntnisse in den Gebieten der Pathologie, der inneren Medizin, der Chirurgie, der Haut- und Geschlechtskrankheiten und der Hygiene zu erwerben. Nach Abschluß dieses fünfjährigen Studiums haben sich die Studenten der ärztlichen Approbationsprüfung zu unterziehen.«[183] Dem Studium vorangestellt war eine vierjährige Sprachschule.

Hudec baute außer dem Paulun Hospital noch drei weitere Krankenhäuser in Shanghai. Das Hua Dong Hospital (Country Hospital für Ausländer) mit 125 Betten in der Yan'an Xilu, das St. Luke's Hospital in der Jiujiang Lu 219, heute Stadtteilrathaus, und das Margaret Williamson Hospital in der Fangxie Lu 419 in der chinesischen Altstadt, heute Frauenklinik.

the students must take the examination to obtain a licence to practise medicine.«[183] The course of study was preceded by four years at a language school.

Hudec built three other hospitals in Shanghai, in addition to the Paulun Hospital. The Hua Dong Hospital (Country Hospital for Foreigners) with 125 beds on Yan'an Xilu, St. Luke's Hospital on Jiujiang Lu 219, today the local town hall, and the Margaret Williamson Hospital in Fangxie Lu 419 in the old Chinese city, now a women's clinic.

改建後的寶隆醫院東面一瞥，一
九九二年。
寶隆醫院的東面外觀，一九二七
年。

國人居位區的方斜路四百一十九號的西門
外婦孺醫院，現為上海市婦孺保健院。

VICTORIA-NURSES HOME

Heutige Funktion. Current use
Hua Dong Hospital
Yan'an Xilu (Great Western Road), Shanghai

Architekt. Architect
Dipl.-Ing. Hamburger, Beamter des Shanghai Municipal Council
Dipl.-Ing. Hamburger, civil servant at the Shanghai Municipal Council

Bauherr. Client
Shanghai Municipal Council

Eröffnung. Opening
April 1933

Zustand. Condition
Das Gebäude ist gut erhalten, mehrere Anbauten.
Well preserved; several extensions have been added.

Das Schwesternheim liegt im Westen der Stadt, nahe der Kaiser-Wilhelm-Schule. Das Gebäude ist acht Stockwerke hoch und etwa 60 Meter lang. Es bietet Unterkunft für 100 Krankenschwestern. Die gesamte Tragkonstruktion wird von Stahlbeton-Stockwerksrahmen gebildet. Da man befürchtete, daß

The nurses home is in the west of the city near the Kaiser Wilhelm School. The building is eight storeys high and approximately 60 metres long. It houses 100 nurses. The entire structure consisted of reinforced concrete floor frames. As it was feared that the building would, as a result, be very loud, slag

Südfassade, 1992
Victoria-Nurses Home, Südfassade (Gartenfassade), 1933
Eingangshalle, 1933
South façade, 1992
Victoria Nurses Home, south façade (garden façade), 1933
Entrance hall, 1933

das Gebäude sehr hellhörig sein könnte, verwendete man für den Innenausbau Schlackensteine und schalldämpfende Bodenbeläge. Das Heim hat eine 20 Meter tiefe Pfahlgründung.

In dem Gebäude kommt die klare Architektursprache des deutschen »Bauhaus« zum Ausdruck. Es ist einfach und sachlich und ausgesprochen horizontal gelagert. Die durchgehenden Balkonreihen an der Südfassade betonen diese Gliederung.[184]

stone and noise-insulating floor coverings were used. The home stands on 680 wooden piles.

This building is a manifest expression of the clearly-formulated architectural idiom of the German »Bauhaus« school. It is simple, stark and extremely horizontal. This is emphasised by the rows of continuous balconies on the south façade.[184]

維克多利亞護士宿舍

現用途：華東醫院
地址：上海延安西路；原大西路
建築師：哈姆布子格，工程師
業主：上海市政府
啟用日期：一九三三年四月
現狀：樓體保存完好，增建許多樓房

護士學校位於西市區威廉學堂附近。宿舍樓高八層，長約六十米，可供一百名護士住宿，為鋼筋混凝土樓層桓架承重結構。人們耽心房間會因此而不隔音，所以在內部裝修時採用爐渣石和隔音材料作地面鋪層。建宿舍樓用了六百八十根約二十米長的木樁作支柱。

護士宿舍樓顯然是採用了德國包豪斯流派的建築形式，立面樸實無華，用明快的水平線條稍加點綴，橫貫南立面的陽台連廊表現了這種橫向劃分的藝術手法。〈184〉

維多利亞護士宿舍南立面外觀，
（花園立面），一九三三年。
門廳，一九三三年。
南立面，一九九二年。

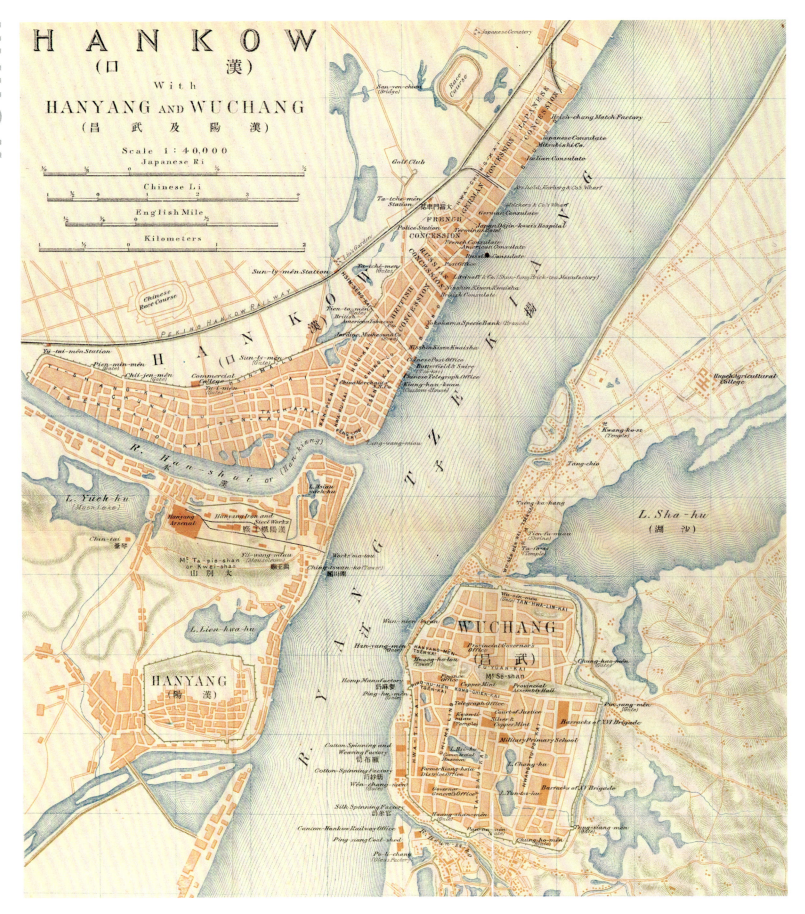

WUHAN (HANKOU, HANKAU)

Die Stadt Wuhan liegt am Yangzi-Strom, etwa 1 100 km von Shanghai und damit von seiner Mündung ins Meer entfernt. Drei Städte hatten sich hier gebildet: Hankou, Hanyang und Wuchang, voneinander getrennt durch den Yangzi und den Han-Fluß. Zusammen hatten diese Städte bereits im Jahr 1911 ca. 1 750 000 Einwohner,[185] die dreifache Anzahl der damaligen Einwohner Shanghais. Der Yangzi-Strom hat in Wuhan eine Breite von 1 500 Metern und ist so tief, daß er fast während des gesamten Jahres vom Meer aus mit bis zu 10 000 Tonnen großen Schiffen befahrbar ist. Die Stadt liegt also mitten in China und ist doch mit dem Meer verbunden.

1861 wurde hier die englische Niederlassung gegründet. Stromabwärts von Hankou, anschließend an die chinesische Stadt, erbauten die Ausländer ihre Niederlassungen. Das Land war damals als chinesisches Stadterweiterungsgebiet nicht nutzbar und somit wertlos, weil hier in der Außenkurve des Yangzi die Strömung so stark war, daß chinesische Dschunken nicht anlegen konnten. Sie ankerten vor der chinesischen Stadt Hankou in der Mündung des Han-Flusses. Die ausländischen Dampfer hingegen konnten hier festmachen. Der Wasserstand des Yangzi war starken Schwankungen unterworfen, rund 15 Meter lagen zwischen dem Winterniedrigwasser und dem Sommerhochwasser. Entsprechend veränderte sich der Anblick der Niederlassungen vom Schiff aus. Das Land, auf dem man die Niederlassungen errichtete, war Überschwemmungsland und mußte erst aufgeschüttet werden, die gesamte deutsche Niederlassung beispielsweise um über einen Meter. Trotzdem kam es in späteren Jahren zu Überschwemmungen. Die Stadt Hankou ist völlig flach, während es in Hanyang und Wuchang mehrere Hügel gibt.

Wie in Tianjin (Tientsin) hatte auch hier die englische Niederlassung einen wirtschaftlichen Entwicklungsvorsprung, der nicht mehr

WUHAN (HANKOW)

The city of Wuhan is on the Yangtze river, approximately 1 100 km from Shanghai and thus, from where the Yangtze enters the sea. Three cities were established here: Hankow, Hanyang and Wuchang which were divided from each other by the Yangtze and the Han rivers. In 1911 these three cities had a combined population of approximately 1 750 000 inhabitants,[185] three times the population of Shanghai at the time. The Yangtze river in Wuhan is 1 500 metres wide and so deep that it can be access all year round by ships of up to 10 000 tonnes. Thus, despite being in the middle of China, this city is linked with the sea.

The British concession in Wuhan was founded in 1861. Foreigners were able to acquire concessions downstream from Hankow, next to the Chinese city. The Chinese were not interested in using this land as an extension to their city area because the current was so strong in the outer curve of the Yangtze that they could not anchor their junks and the land was, thus, worthless to them. Instead they anchored their ships in the mouth of the Han river off the Chinese city Hankow. The foreign steamships, however, were also able to anchor in the strong current. The water level in the Yangtze was subject to considerable variations, there was a difference of some 15 metres between the low winter and high summer water levels. Those arriving by ship could therefore receive very different impressions of the foreign concessions. The land on which the concessions were built was flood land and first had to be reclaimed; for example over one metre had to be reclaimed across the entire German concession. Despite this in later years the area was still subject to flooding. The city of Hankow is completely flat whereas there are hills in Hanyang and Wuchang.

As in Tianjin (Tientsin), the British concession here enjoyed a lead in terms of economic development that could no longer be encroach-

武漢

武漢市位於長江畔，離上海以及長江和東海交匯處的一千一百公里。武漢由長江和漢水鼎立成三個地區。漢口，漢陽和武昌。一九一一年，武漢三鎮的人口為十七點五萬，[185]是當時上海人口的三倍。長江在武漢流域寬一千五百米，水位亦深。萬噸級運洋輪幾乎終年可以進出。武漢地理位置居中，同時又與江海毗鄰。

一八六一年建立了美國租界。外國人獲許在漢口下游中國人的居住區邊緣設立租界。當時那里是中國城的擴展區，沒有什麼使用價值。因為那裡是長江轉道的外沿，江水洶湧湍急，中國的帆船只能停靠在中國人城區前的漢江口。相反，外國的汽船可在租界區停泊。長江的水位起伏很大。冬季的水位與夏季的相差十五米。乘船遠道而來的人因此對外國租界的印象隨季節的不同而各異。租界區是一片易受洪水襲擊的窪地，必須填土加高地勢。例如，德國租界的地勢就加高了一米多。盡管如此，在以後的幾年仍屢屢遭受洪水的侵襲。漢口一馬平川，在漢陽和武昌倒還可見起伏的丘陵。

和在天津一樣，英租界在漢口的經濟也遙遙領先。其主要優勢是緊靠中國的商業區。在二十年代，英國人還給武漢起了個雅稱："東方芝加哥"。

一八五五年至一八九六年俄國、法國和德國在武漢分別設立了租界這三個國家在一八九四年至一八九五年的中日甲午戰爭中站在中國一邊，反對日本占領東北的重要軍事港口旅順，主張簽定求和的 "馬關條約"。[186]一九九八年，日本在武漢設立租界。外國租界沿江，延伸三千五百米。租界各行其政，有各自的財政，保安機構。租界之間沒有什麼界線，人們可以住在其國家的租界裡。一九一三年只有約一百個德國人住在本國的租界裡。這只佔在武漢德國僑民人數的三分之一。而住在法國租界的德國人甚至多於法國人本身。當時的武漢只有六十五名法國人。[187]

二十世紀初，武漢開始鋪設鐵路。大約在一八九七年，德國鐵路工程師海國里希，錫樂巴受中國政府的委托測量了武漢與北京之間一千五百公里長的路線，並制定了

141

aufgeholt werden konnte. Ihr Lagevorteil war die direkte Nähe zur chinesischen Geschäftsstadt. Die englische Niederlassung prägte auch Wuhans Namen in den 20er Jahren: »Chicago of the East«.[186] Um 1895/96 erhielten drei weitere Staaten je eine eigene Niederlassung in Wuhan: Rußland, Frankreich und Deutschland. Sie hatten sich nach dem japanisch-chinesischen Krieg 1894/95 auf Chinas Seite gestellt und Einspruch gegen die japanische Besetzung des wichtigen nordchinesischen Kriegshafens Lüshun (Port Arthur) erhoben sowie sich für den Frieden von Schimonoseki eingesetzt. 1898 kam die japanische Niederlassung hinzu. Die Uferlänge aller ausländischen Niederlassungen betrug zusammen rund 3 500 Meter. Jede Niederlassung hatte eine eigene Verwaltung, Steuerbehörde und Polizei. Für die Straßennamen wurde die jeweilige Landessprache verwendet. Räumlich waren sie dagegen nicht voneinander getrennt, und die Bevölkerung war international gemischt. Von den Deutschen wohnten 1913 beispielsweise nur etwa ein Drittel, rund 100 Personen, in der deutschen Niederlassung; in der französischen gab es sogar mehr deutsche als französische Bewohner – es lebten damals nur 65 Franzosen in Wuhan.[187]

Anfang des 20. Jahrhunderts erschloß man Wuhan mit der Bahn. Um 1897 hatte der deutsche Eisenbahningenieur Heinrich Hildebrand im Auftrag der chinesischen Regierung die 1500 km lange Bahntrasse zwischen Wuhan und Beijing vermessen und Pläne für die Streckenführung erarbeitet.[188] 1905 wurde die Bahnlinie eröffnet, und es kam zu einem starken Anstieg des Handels. Wuhan war jetzt über die Transsibirische Eisenbahn direkt mit Europa verbunden. Doch dies änderte nichts am Gefühl der Ausländer in den Niederlassungen, »sich zumindest im Unterbewußtsein wie ein Gefangener auf einer Insel zu fühlen.«[189] Selbst in den 20er Jahren gab es erst 40 km befestigte Straßen in Wuhan und Umgebung. Als »ein Einsprengsel der weißen Rasse« bezeichnet Alfons Paquet die

ed. Its main advantage lay in its direct proximity to the Chinese commercial centre. The British concession also gave Wuhan its name in the 1920s, the »Chicago of the East«.[186] Around 1895/96 three more states each acquired concessions in Wuhan: Russia, France and Germany. They had supported China after the Japanese-Chinese war of 1894/95 and had objected to the Japanese occupation of the important north Chinese naval port of Lüshun (Port Arthur) and had also supported the Treaty of Shimonoseki. The Japanese concession was established in 1898. Each of the foreign concessions were initially allocated approximately 3 500 metres of embankment. Each concession had its own administration, fiscal authorities and police and the street names were in the language of the relevant country. They were not, however, spatially divided from each other and the population was internationally mixed. In 1913, for example, of the Germans only around one third – 100 persons – actually lived in the German concession; there were actually more Germans living in the French concession than French – there were only 65 French living in Wuhan at the time.[187]

In the early 20th century Wuhan could be accessed by train. Around 1897 the German railway engineer Heinrich Hildebrand was commissioned by the Chinese government to survey the 1500 km railway track between Wuhan and Beijing and developed plans for the railway.[188] The line was opened in 1905 and led to a sharp increase in trade. Wuhan was now directly linked to Europe via the Transsiberian Railway. However, this did nothing to prevent the foreigners in the concessions »feeling like prisoners on an island, at least subconsciously.«[189] Even in the 1920s there were only 40 km of built roads in Wuhan and surroundings. Alfons Paquet described the few foreigners living in the concessions as »an embedded crystal of the white race«.[190] Only 1350 Europeans and Americans including the military lived in Wuhan in 1913 and 1550 Japanese. There were 27 700

火車軌道運行路線。[188]一九零五年，鐵路通車，貿易也隨之繁榮起來。武漢通過西利伯和亞大鐵路可直接與歐州通商。然而這一切並沒有改變租界中外國人的孤獨感：＂至少在潛意識中覺得象被禁錮在一個孤島上的犯人。＂[189]直到二十年代，在武漢和周圍的地區才修築了石板或石塊加固的街道。阿爾弗斯・派克書特用＂寥若晨星＂來說明租界裡外僑的稀少。[190]一九一三年在武漢加上軍隊也只有一千三百五十名歐州和美國人。此外一千五百五十名日本人。而在這五個租界裡住著的中國人就有二萬七千七百人。

武漢的夏天最難熬。濕熱的氣候，氣溫往往高達四十度。就是在夜裡也同樣是暑氣逼人。樓房設有寬敞的外廊以利於通風、散熱。位於樓房正中的樓梯間象像煙囪一樣起著排散熱氣的作用。

大部分外國人一到夏天就索性離開武漢去避暑區消夏。武漢周圍有兩處避暑地特別受到青睞。牯嶺別墅區位於武漢下游二百二十公里處高出江面一千米的廬山麓，是人們一致稱道的消夏避暑勝地。距牯嶺約一百八十公里處是七百五十米高的雞公山，自從廬山與北京通車後，雞公山成了第二個山地療養區。

一八九五年武漢就有了德國租界，租金也不貴，但是租界並沒有馬上就著手建設。一八九七年德國海軍樞密建築技術監督佛朗求斯參觀了武漢。他所著的《膠州，德國在東亞的領地》一書中有一張表現德國租界風光的插圖。[191]這幅素描繪出一幅充滿浪漫情調的長江漁家生活情景：停泊在江邊的魚舟，沙灘上的漁家茅舍，鋪晒著的魚網和幾棵稀疏的樹木。弗朗求斯批評了武漢和天津的德國租界無人問津的狀況：＂我不明白，為什麼我們的政府對這兩個租界長期以來漠不關心。在貼鄰的俄國漢口租界裡早就建起了碼頭，造了堆棧倉庫，一片蒸蒸日上的景象。更令我大惑不解的是：政府竟然同意把這些地盤無償轉讓給私人公司。英國人的慣例是把租界劃分成小塊出售，通過開發興建部分區域來提高所有地域的價格。這樣國家和租界雙方獲利。天津和漢口租界目前均在私人手裡，我只希望這些公司能協同制定統一的沿江交通線路，共同修築防洪堤壩。＂[192]

wenigen in den Niederlassungen lebenden Ausländer.[190] Nur 1350 Europäer und Amerikaner einschließlich des Militärs lebten im Jahr 1913 in Wuhan, außerdem 1550 Japaner. Allein in den fünf ausländischen Niederlassungen wohnten 27 700 Chinesen.

Äußerst unangenehm ist das sommerliche Klima in Wuhan, feuchte Hitze mit Temperaturen um 40 Grad Celsius, nachts kühlt es kaum ab. Die Gebäude mußten entsprechend luftig gebaut werden. Tiefe Veranden laufen um die Bauten, Treppenhäuser im Zentrum wirken als Kamine für die heiße Luft. Die meisten Ausländer verließen im Sommer die Stadt und fuhren in die Sommerfrische. In der weiteren Umgebung waren damals folgende Erholungsgebiete sehr beliebt: Der Berg Lushan mit der in 1000 Meter Höhe über dem Yangzi liegenden Siedlung Guling (Kuling), der auch heute noch ein wirklicher Geheimtip ist. Die Siedlung liegt etwa 220 km flußabwärts des Yangzi von Wuhan entfernt. Der zweite Höhenerholungsort, das 750 Meter hoch liegende Jigong Shan (Chi-kung-shan) in etwa 180 km Entfernung, wurde erst durch die Eisenbahnlinie Wuhan-Beijing erschlossen.

Die deutsche Niederlassung wurde 1895 erworben, man zahlte eine geringe Pachtgebühr, doch wurde sie zunächst nicht ausgebaut. Im Frühjahr 1897 besuchte Marine-Hafenbaudirektor Franzius die Stadt Wuhan und veröffentlichte in seinem Buch »Kiautschou – Deutschlands Erwerbung in Ostasien« eine Zeichnung der »Deutschen Niederlassung in Hankau«.[191] Eine romantisierende Uferszene zeigt den Lebensalltag der Flußfischer, am Ufer liegende Boote, strohgedeckte Hütten am Strand, trocknende Netze und ein paar Bäume. Franzius kritisiert den Zustand von Wuhan und Tianjin: »Es ist mir unverständlich, daß man in Deutschland diesen beiden Niederlassungen lange Zeit hindurch so wenig Interesse schenkte, während beispielsweise auf dem benachbarten russischen Gebiet in Hankau längst die nötigen Ufermauern, Magazine u. s. w. geschaffen

Chinese living in the five foreign concessions alone.

The summer climate in Wuhan is extremely unpleasant, humid heat with temperatures around 40° Celsius and little night cooling. Buildings thus need to be as well ventilated as possible. The buildings are surrounded by wide verandas and the stairways in the middle of the buildings function like chimneys for the hot air. However, most foreigners simply left the city in the summer and went to the summer resorts. There were two particularly popular venues at a distance from the city. The Lushan mountain with Guling (Kuling) estate at 1000 metres above the Yangtze is still a very well kept secret. The estate is approximately 220 km downstream on the Yangtze from Wuhan. The second mountain resort could only be reached by the train to Beijing: the 750 metre high Jigong Shan (Chi-kung-shan) approximately 180 km from Wuhan.

The German concession was acquired in 1895 and a minimal lease was paid for, but initially no work was done on its development. In spring 1897 the Naval Director of Dock Building Franzius visited Wuhan and published a drawing of the »German concession in Hankau« in his book »Kiautschou – Deutschlands Erwerbung in Ostasien«.[191] A romantic riverbank scene shows the day to day life of the fishermen, boots on the river bank, thatched huts on the strand, nets out to dry and a few trees. Franzius criticised the state of Wuhan and Tianjin »I cannot understand why Germany has shown so little interest in these two concessions for so long, whereas, for example, in the neighbouring Russian concession in Hankau the embankment wall, warehouses etc. have been built and it is a now a lively centre. I understand even less why the Government was prepared from the outset to cede the areas to private companies without seeking to make a profit, whereas, for example, the British usually sell such concessions plot by plot, raising the value by building on the first quarter and using

一八九八年，"德-漢租界公司"著手興建這個面積約半平方公里的租界地，人們將租界的窪地填平並用砂岩和水泥築起了江壩。租界平面呈矩形，長一千零七十五米，寬四百三十米。兩條與臨江大道平行的交通干道與六條南北走向的街道縱橫交錯把租界分成更小的矩陣塊。一九零三年，填土加高地勢的工程結束，街道的鋪設工作也基本完成。德國租界沒有和法國租界一起規劃城市道路的建設。法租界內街道的縱橫走向並不規則，昔日租界割據的遺跡至今尚清晰可見。人們在德國租界西面的中山大道一側以上海裡弄民居的建築手法建造了許多二層樓的住宅。這些排列擁擠的簡易民宅都裝著同一式樣的窗子，樓頂的坡度都一樣平緩，立面也都是清水磚牆。這一街景與街對面造型生動活潑的中國商行建築群形成鮮明的對比。民宅單一、呆板的造型與商行店舖的馬頭牆，線條優美的檐頂陽台以及門前的臨時堆棧有著天壤之別。日本某導遊手冊把這條德法邊界上的街道稱作"繁華的商業大街，素有'黃金街'的美名，沿街是中西建築風格結合的建築物"。[193] 一九零八年人們為如何在這條街上劃出一條確切的界線問題爭議紛繁。德國租界管理處要求對中國民宅進行衛生檢查並在一封給北京公使館的信中詳細地描寫了那兒的衛生狀況。[194] 一九一三年，曾有人建議放棄天津的擴展租界，以此交換從武漢的德國租界通向鐵道的路段。[195] 然而這項提議未被採納。

德國租界逐步沿發展。一九零五年人們在距長江江岸五百米處，沿著租界區的外緣鋪設了京-漢鐵路。三陽路上的聯軌線將德國租界和鐵路干線直接連接在一起。一九零七年德國租界正式通車。一九零六年武漢、天津租界同時成立了各自的租界管理機構，管理體制也大體一致。一九零九年工部局舉行落成典禮。一九一零年十月在工部局對面的花園裡落成基督教堂。[196] 一九一三年至一九一四年，一所德國子弟學校竣工。一九零八年專供華人子弟學習的華德學堂（上智中學）竣工。一九一五年德中技術工程學院開學。因為租界的地皮昂貴，學院建在中國城區內。[197]

sind und reges Leben herrscht. Ich begreife umsoweniger, als die Regierung von vornherein bereit war, die Gebiete an Privatgesellschaften abzutreten, ohne selbst dabei einen Gewinn zu machen, während es z.B. bei den Engländern Brauch ist, derartige Niederlassungen allmählich stückweise zu verkaufen und durch die Bebauung des ersten Viertels den Wert der übrigen zu steigern, so daß der schließliche Gewinn dem Staat oder der Niederlassung zugute kommt. Beide Gebiete sind übrigens jetzt an Privatgesellschaften übergegangen, und ich hoffe, daß sie die Uferlinien einheitlich festlegen und durch Uferwerke sichern.«[192]

Im Dezember 1898 begann die »Deutsche-Hankau-Niederlassung-Gesellschaft« mit dem Ausbau der etwa einen halben Quadratkilometer großen Niederlassung. Das Land wurde aufgeschüttet, eine Ufermauer aus Sandsteinen und Beton errichtet. Die Niederlassung nahm ein Rechteck von 430 Metern Tiefe und 1075 Metern Länge ein. Sie wurde durch zwei Parallelstraßen zur Uferstraße und sechs Querstraßen in rechteckige Blöcke aufgeteilt. Im Jahr 1903 waren die Auffüllarbeiten abgeschlossen und das Straßennetz nahezu fertiggestellt. Das Raster der Straßen war nicht mit der benachbarten französischen Niederlassung abgestimmt. Die ursprüngliche Verwaltungsgrenze kann man daher auch heute noch erkennen, denn die Straßen der französischen Niederlassung verlaufen in einem unregelmäßigen Raster. Im westlichen Teil der deutschen Niederlassung entlang der Zhongshan Dadao (Friedrichstraße) wurden zweigeschossige Wohnhäuser für Chinesen errichtet, in der sehr dichten Bauweise der Shanghaier Li-Long Häuser. Die Straße bildete die Westgrenze der deutschen Niederlassung, hier standen diese einfachen Miethäuser mit gleichen Fensteröffnungen, flach geneigten Dächern und schmucklosen Ziegelfassaden den lebendig gestalteten chinesischen Geschäftshäusern gegenüber. Ein exotisch wirkender Kontrast zu deren Treppengiebeln, geschwungenen Dächern, Bal-

the profits for the benefit of the state or the concession. Both areas are now in the hands of private companies and I can only hope that they will define the embankment line in a uniform manner and secure them through the construction of quays.«[192]

In December 1898 the »German-Hankow Settlement Society« began work on the development of the concession which was approximately 0.5 km^2 in size. The land was reclaimed and an embankment wall constructed from sandstone and concrete. The area allocated for the concession was rectangular, 430 metres wide and 1075 metres long. It was divided into rectangular blocks by two roads parallel to the Bund and six intersecting roads. The reclamation work was completed in 1903 and the road network almost completed. The road grid was not constructed to match that in the neighbouring French concession. The original administrative border can therefore still be recognised today because the roads in the French concession follow an irregular grid. Two-storey houses were built for the Chinese in the western part of the German concession along Zhongshan Dadao (Friedrich Strasse); they were built in the same dense style as the Shanghai Li-long houses. The road formed the western boundary of the German concession thus these simple houses with the same windows, low roofs and unembellished brick façades stood facing the Chinese business premises with their lively and decorative design and provided an exotic contrast to the stair gables, hipped roofs, balconies and storage spaces in front of the Chinese houses. A Japanese publication describes this border road as a »flourishing Chinese street called Hwa-ching-kai, which is lined with pretty houses built in semi-European style«.[193] Around 1908 a row started about the exact situation of the border on this street. Demands were made for hygiene checks to be made on the Chinese houses and the public health situation is described in detail in letters to the legation in Beijing.[194]

konen und Lagerplätzen vor den Häusern. In einer japanischen Publikation wird diese Grenzstraße als »blühend-geschäftige chinesische Straße namens Hwa-ching-kai, an der hübsche Häuser im halb-europäischen Stil stehen« beschrieben.[193] Um 1908 begann ein Streit über die genaue Grenzführung an dieser Straße. Die deutsche Verwaltung forderte eine sanitäre Kontrolle der angrenzenden chinesischen Häuser und schilderte in Briefen an die Gesandtschaft in Beijing ausführlich die hygienische Situation.[194] 1913 schlug man sogar den Tausch der »Erweiterten Niederlassung« in Tianjin gegen das westlich anschließende Land bis zum Bahndamm in Wuhan vor,[195] doch die alte Grenzführung blieb bestehen.

Die deutsche Niederlassung entwickelte sich kontinuierlich. Der Bahnhof der Wuhan-Beijing-Bahn befand sich seit 1905 direkt neben der Niederlassung. Die Bahntrasse verlief etwa 500 Meter vom Ufer entfernt, und es gab zusätzlich ein Anschlußgleis durch die Sanyang Lu (Luisenstraße) und somit eine direkte Verbindung zum deutschen Bund. Seit 1907 hatte die deutsche Niederlassung eine elektrische Stromversorgung. Bis 1906 wurde sie vom deutschen Konsulat verwaltet. Gleichzeitig mit der Niederlassung in Tianjin wurde auch in Wuhan eine deutsche Niederlassungsgemeinde gegründet, die Verwaltungsaufgaben übernahm; beide Gemeindeordnungen waren identisch. 1909 wurde das Rathaus eingeweiht, im Oktober 1910 die kleine evangelische Kirche im Park gegenüber,[196] 1913/14 entstand eine Schule für die deutschen Kinder. Bereits seit 1908 gab es eine Deutsch-Chinesische Schule für 30 bis 40 chinesische Schüler, 1915 wurde die Deutsch-Chinesische Ingenieurschule eröffnet. Ihr Grundstück lag außerhalb der deutschen Niederlassung auf chinesischem Territorium, da die Grundstückspreise viel zu hoch waren.[197]

In 1913 an exchange of the »Extended Concession« in Tianjin for the land up to the railway dam in Wuhan was proposed,[195] however, the old border was retained.

Once started, the development of the German concession continued steadily. The station for the Wuhan-Beijing railway was built right beside the concession in 1905. The railway track ran some 500 metres from the river bank and there was even a track through Sanyang Lu (Luisenstrasse) linking the railway directly to the German Bund. The German concession had electricity from 1907. Up to 1906 it was administered by the German consulate. At the same time as in Tianjin, a concession authority was also established in Wuhan which assumed the administration; the two local government laws were identical. In 1909 the town hall was opened, in October 1910 the small Protestant church in the park opposite the town hall,[196] in 1913/14 a school was built for German children. From 1908 there was a German-Chinese school with 30 to 40 pupils. In 1915, the German-Chinese College of Engineering was opened. Its grounds of the college were outside the German concession on Chinese territory as the land within the concession was far too expensive.[197]

KAISERLICH DEUTSCHES KONSULAT
IMPERIAL GERMAN CONSULATE

Heutige Funktion. Current use
Rathaus
Town Hall
Yanjiang Dadao/Yiyuan Lu
(Prinz-Heinrich-Ufer/Augustastraße),
Wuhan (Hankou. Hankow)

Architekt. Architect
W. Wutzler, Selberg & Schlüter, Berlin,
Tsingtau

Bauleitung. Site architect
G. L. Hempel

Baukosten. Building costs
160 000 Goldmark
160 000 gold marks

Ausführung. Contractors
Fechner & Kappler, Hankou

Bauherr. Client
Auswärtiges Amt
Ministry of Foreign Affairs

Bauzeit. Construction time
Februar 1904 – November 1905
February 1904 – November 1905

Zustand. Condition
Das Gebäude ist sehr gut erhalten,
das Dach verändert.
Very well preserved;
the roof has been altered.

Deutsches Konsulat. Südostansicht
von der Yangzi-Uferstraße, um 1906
Südostansicht mit Haupteingang,
1991
German Consulate, view from the
south-east from the Yangtze
embankment road, around 1906
View from south-east with
main entrance, 1991

Das Konsulat lag etwas zurückgesetzt auf dem ersten Grundstück der deutschen Niederlassung am Ufer des Yangzi, genau in der Achse der zweiten Straße der französischen Niederlassung, der Rue Dubail. Das Gebäude wurde von einem großer Garten umgeben, für dessen Anlage man Pflanzen und Baumaterial aus Japan und Shanghai kommen ließ. Im Erdgeschoß befanden sich die Personalräume, im Obergeschoß die Wohnung des Konsuls und seiner Familie. Die Eingänge der beiden Bereiche waren getrennt. Die Wohnung betrat man vom Bund aus; dort gab es auch eine Auffahrtsrampe für Kutschen. In die Diensträume ging man von der Seitenstraße, der Yiyuan Lu (Augustastraße). An dieser lag auch das Beamtenwohnhaus mit Räumlichkeiten für den Dolmetscher und den Sekretär. Das Wirtschaftsgebäude mit Küche und Personalräumen befand sich auf der Rückseite des Konsulats und war mit diesem durch einen überdachten Gang verbunden.[198]

Zeitgenössische Journalisten versuchten die ungewöhnliche Stilmischung des Konsulats aus Veranden und vier Ecktürmchen als einem »Barockstil nach deutschem Muster« zu bestimmen.[199] An der höchsten Stelle des Daches schwebte ein vergoldeter Reichsadler über einer Weltkugel – ob man im Land der Drachen diese Symbolsprache verstand? Das Klima Wuhans mit seinen extrem heißen und feuchten Sommermonaten ist berüchtigt und prägt die Architektur. Bewährt hatten sich umlaufende tiefe Veranden auf allen Seiten der Gebäude, die eine schattige Hülle bildeten. Weiträumige Treppenhäuser in der Mitte des Gebäudes wirkten wie ein Kamin, wobei die heiße Luft durch das Oberlicht im Dach abzog. Die Grundstücke der repräsentativen Häuser waren so groß, daß eigene Wohnhäuser für die Angestellten und auch gesonderte Wirtschaftsgebäude errichtet werden konnten. Weite Abstände zwischen den Gebäuden führten zu einer guten Belüftung. Nach diesen Erfahrungen waren die Wohnhäuser der Ausländer hier erbaut.

The consulate was built towards the back of the first site in the German concession on the banks of the Yangtze river, right in the axis of the second street of the French concession, the Rue Dubail. The building was surrounded by a large garden for which plants and material were imported from Japan and Shanghai. The service rooms were on the ground floor and the first floor housed the apartment for the consul and his family. There were separate entrances for the two areas. The entrance to the apartment was on the Bund and there was also a ramp for coaches. The offices were accessed from a side street, Yiyuan Lu (Augusta Strasse). The residence for the officials with rooms for the interpreter and secretary was also built on this side of the street. The building which housed the servants' quarters, the kitchen and utility rooms was at the back of the consulate and was linked to the consulate by a covered path.[198]

Contemporary journalists tried to describe the unusual stylistic mix of the consulate building with its verandas and four corner towers as »German-style Baroque«.[199] A gilded imperial eagle hovered over a globe on the highest point of the roof. It would be interesting to know how this symbol was interpreted in the land of the dragon.

Wuhan's climate with its extremely hot and humid summer months is still infamous today and this had a major influence on the architecture. Wide verandas running right around the building, which created a shady cover, had proven invaluable in counteracting the extreme heat. Roomy staircases in the centre of the building had the effect of chimneys with the hot air rising through the fanlight to the roof. As there was plenty of space on the sites at the time, it was possible to build separate buildings for employees residences and for the various utilities. Good distances between the buildings also made it possible to provide good ventilation. The houses for the foreigners were built on the basis of these proven principles.

德國領事館

現用途：市政府
地址：武漢沿江大道（一元路口）；原亨
　　　利王子大道（奧古斯塔街）
建築師：W・沃茨勒爾，薩爾貝克和施蘭
　　　特爾，柏林、青島
工程指導：G・L・亨姆普爾
建築造價：十六萬金馬克
施工：費希納和卡普勒
業主：外交部
建造日期：一九零四年二月至一九零五年
　　　　十一月
現狀：樓體保存完好，屋頂又改變

領事館座落在第一次劃分給德國租界的地段上。在建築紅線稍偏後一點的地方，正好對著法國租界的第二條街。領館的周圍是一座大花園，花園裡的花草樹木和庭園設施是從日本和上海運來的。辦公室在領館的一樓，二樓是領事及家眷的住宅。辦公處與住宅的入口也是分開的。領事住房的入口在臨江大道上，門前還有馬車的行車道。辦公室的入口在一元路上。領事館官員的住宅也在一元路上。住宅里還有幾間供翻譯和秘書使用的房間。沒有廚房和勤雜人員用房的后勤樓在領事館的背面。一條蓋著頂棚的長廊把這兩幢建築物連接在一起。〈198〉

當年的記者將這種集敞廊和角塔於一身的別具風格的建築稱作"德國式巴洛克風格"。〈199〉樓頂上有一隻鎦金的雄鷹在地球上盤旋的雕塑，龍的傳人能領悟這種像徵性的表達嗎？

武漢濕熱的酷夏是出了名的，這種氣候也影響了當地的建築形式。人們在樓房的四周建造寬敞的涼廊。這種為人稱道的外廊如同遮蔭隔熱的涼蓬。樓房中央一般有寬大的樓道。這種樓道像煙囪一樣使署氣通過六窗排散出去。因為當時租界有足夠的地皮，故而可建專門的領館官員建造住宅，後勤樓也可分開造。樓房之間足夠的開闊地保証了空氣的流通。武漢外國人的住宅均是根據建造領事館得來的這些經驗設計營造的。

德國領事館臨江東南面外觀，約
一九零六年。
設有主入口的南立面，一九九一
年。

WUHAN

DEUTSCH-ASIATISCHE BANK
GERMAN-ASIAN BANK

Yanjiang Dadao (Prinz-Heinrich-Ufer), Wuhan (Hankou. Hankow)

Architekten. Architects
Becker & Baedecker, Shanghai

Ausführung. Contractors
Lothar Marcks & Busch, Hankou

Bauherr. Client
Deutsch-Asiatische Bank, Berlin
German-Asian Bank, Berlin

Eröffnung. Opening
Juli 1908
July 1908

Zustand. Condition
Das Gebäude existiert nicht mehr.
No longer exists.

Deutsch-Asiatische Bank. Südostansicht von der Yangzi-Uferstraße, 1908
German-Asian Bank, south-east view from the Yangtze embankment road, 1908

Die Deutsch-Asiatische Bank lag als zweites Gebäude der deutschen Niederlassung an der Uferstraße rechts neben dem deutschen Konsulat. Wie dieses war das Bankgebäude etwas von der Straße zurückgesetzt. Ein schmiedeeisernes Gitter schloß das Grundstück zur Straße ab. Die Geschäftsräume waren weiträumig und hoch. Im Erdgeschoß befand sich außerdem noch der Salon und das Eßzimmer der Wohnung des Bankdirektors. Zu seiner Wohnung gehörten in der ersten Etage außerdem vier große und luftige Wohn- und Schlafzimmer mit Veranden. An der Südseite des Hauptgebäudes schloß sich ein Baukörper an, der im Erdgeschoß die Geschäftszimmer für den chinesischen Geschäftspartner, den sogenannten Komprador, enthielt. Auf der anderen Seite gab es einen Trakt mit Räumen für die chinesische Dienerschaft.[200]

Heinrich Becker hatte bereits in Shanghai die Russisch-Chinesische Bank in der Art der italienischen Neorenaissance gebaut. Die im folgenden zitierte Abschiedslaudatio scheint allerdings übertrieben: »Es ist von A bis Z eine ganze Meisterarbeit. Sie zeigt, welche wundervollen Formen ein Gebäude annehmen kann, wenn man einem guten Architekten freie Hand läßt, und der Leistung der Deutschen Bank gebührt großes Lob, daß dieser Bau, ›das schönste Gebäude östlich von Suez‹, wie sich ein hervorragender englischer Architekt ausdrückte, so entstehen durfte, wie es als schönstes Wahrzeichen Hankous vor uns steht, ebenso fein in der Architektur wie gediegen und schön von innen. Im ganzen genommen ist Beckers Arbeit in China eine hervorragende deutsche Kulturleistung.«[201]

The German-Asian Bank was the second building in the German concession on the Bund to the right of the German consulate. Like the consulate, the bank was also built towards the back of the site away from the street. The site was closed off from the street by a wrought iron grill. The offices were large and high. The ground floor also contained the drawing room and dining room of the bank director's apartment. There were four further large and equally airy living rooms and bedrooms on the first floor which were surrounded by verandas. There was a wing attached to the south side of the main building which housed offices for the Chinese business partner, the so-called comprador. On the other side of the building there was a wing with rooms for the Chinese employees.[200]

Heinrich Becker had already built the Russian-Chinese Bank in Shanghai in Italian neo-Renaissance style. The farewell eulogy to the architect quoted in the following would, however, appear rather strongly exaggerated. »A masterpiece from A to Z! It shows what wonderful form a building can take when a good architect is given a free hand, the German Bank deserves great praise for its part in allowing this building, ›the finest building east of Suez‹ according to an excellent British architect, to be built and stand as the most beautiful symbol of Hankow, as excellent in its architecture as it is noble and beautiful in its interior. Becker's work in China is in its entirety an outstanding German cultural service.«[201]

德華銀行

地址：武漢沿江大道，原享利王子路
建築師：貝克和培迪克·上海
施工：漢口寶的洋行
業主：柏林德華銀行
啟用期：一九零八年七月
現狀：樓房已不存在

德華銀行是德國租界內在臨江大道上建起的第二幢樓房，位於領館的右邊。與領館一樣銀行大樓建在房基線稍偏後一點的地方，朝街的一面圍著鐵柵欄。一樓寬敞高大的房間是營業部。客廳和銀行經理的餐室也在一樓。二樓是銀行經理的四大間通風良好的起居室和臥室。這些房間均有敞廊。南翼側樓的一盡是中國合伙人，即所謂買辦的辦公室；另一邊的側房供中國勤雜人員使用〈200〉

海因里希·貝克當時已在上海用意大利文藝復興式復古建築手法設計了華俄道勝銀行大廈。下面引摘在其告別答謝會上的一段贊詞多少有些言過其實："這是一個真正的大師的杰作。由此可見，若放手讓優秀的建築師自由發揮，他們能造出杰美絕倫的樓房。這座被一位美國建築師稱作為伊士以東最壯觀的建築也是漢口的驕傲。大樓典雅的造型，無以倫比的內部裝飾是對德華銀行的慷慨豁達最好的回報。總之，貝克通過在中國的建築設計活動對德國文化的傳播作出了杰出的貢獻。"〈201〉

德華銀行面對臨江大道的東南面外觀，一九零八年。

RATHAUS DER DEUTSCHEN NIEDERLASSUNG
GERMAN CONCESSION TOWN HALL

Heutige Funktion. Current use
Polizeistation
Police station
Shengli Lu/Eryue Lu (Wilhelmstraße, gegenüber dem alten Friedhof),
Wuhan (Hankou)
Shengli Lu/Eryue Lu (Wilhelm Strasse, opposite the old cemetery),
Wuhan (Hankow)

Architekt. Architect
Schaffrath, Mitarbeiter bei Lothar Marcks & Busch[202]

Ausführung. Contractors
Lothar Marcks & Busch

Bauherr. Client
Deutsche Niederlassungsgemeinde Hankau
German concession Authorities Hankow

Bauzeit. Construction time
März 1907 bis Januar 1909
March 1907 to January 1909

Zustand. Condition
Der Turmhelm und Teile des Turmes wurden abgetragen; mehrere Anbauten.
The tower has been reduced in height; several extensions have been added.

Im Zentrum der deutschen Niederlassung lagen das deutsche Rathaus und die Polizeistation. Ein Turm, wie er seit dem Mittelalter als Zeichen der Bürgerfreiheit an vielen Rathäusern in Deutschland errichtet wurde, wirkte hier mitten in China sehr ungewöhnlich. Doch die deutsche Gemeinde in Wuhan war »stolz auf diesen für die hiesigen Verhältnisse eigenartigen Bau, der wie ein Stück der Heimat nach China verpflanzt zu sein scheint.«[203]

Die Beschreibung des Rathauses aus dem Bericht über die Einweihungsfeier: »Das Rathaus ist ein schön proportionierter, zweistöckiger Bau mit schlankem Turm. Der Sitzungssaal liegt auf halber Höhe zwischen Ober- und Untergeschoß; (…) Der Sockel ist durchweg aus rohbehauenen Sandsteinquadern erbaut und reicht beim Turm und dem Sitzungssaalanbau bis an die Höhe des Fußbodens hinauf. (…) Der im spätgotischen Stil gehaltene Sitzungssaal ist in würdiger Einfachheit, aber doch solide und geschmackvoll ausgestaltet. Vier große Bogenfenster und eine Doppeltüre zu einem nach vorne hinausliegenden Altan geben reichliches Licht. Die Wände sind unten mit einem geschmackvollen, eine Eichentäfelung nachahmenden Lincrusta-Sockel versehen und oben pompejanisch-rot gestrichen. Die Decke ist einfach weiß mit dunkel gefirnißten Zierbalken. Die zu ebener Erde gelegenen Sekretariatsräume sind einfacher gehalten, ebenso die im anderen Flügel befindlichen Polizeiräume.«[204]

The German town hall and police station were in the centre of the German concession. A tower, similar to those in numerous town halls in Germany – a symbol of civic freedom since the Middle Ages – seemed rather out of place here in the middle of China. However, the German community in Wuhan was »proud of this building unusual in these surroundings and like a piece of home planted in China.«[203]

The town hall building is described as follows in the report published about the opening festivities: »The town hall is a well proportioned two-storey building with a slim tower. The assembly room is on mid-level between the upper and lower floor; (…) The base of the building is built entirely from rough-hewn sandstone and extends in the tower and the assembly hall annex to the level of the floor. (…) The late Gothic assembly hall is fitted out with appropriate simplicity but manages to be solid and tasteful. Four large arched windows and a double door to a front balcony provide sufficient light. The lower part of the walls are covered with a lincrusta imitation oak-panelling plinth and the upper part painted in pompeian red. The ceiling is simple in white with dark varnished decorative rafters. The offices on ground level are more modestly decorated as are the police rooms in the other wing.«[204]

Rathaus der Deutschen Niederlassung, Ostansicht, 1909
Ostansicht, 1991
German Concession Town Hall, view from the east, 1909
View from the east, 1991

德國租界工部局（行政署）

現用途：公安局
地址：武漢勝利路（二躍路口）：原老基
　　　地對面的威廉大街
建築師：沙天拉特、寶利建築事務所的建
　　　築師合伙人[202]
施工：寶利建築事務所
業主：漢口德國租界工部局
建造期：一九零七年三月至一九零九年一
　　　月
現狀：塔身短了一截，增建了許多樓房

德國工部局和警察署位於德國租界的中心地帶。中世紀以來德國許多市政廳的建築都附設塔樓用以表示自由精神至高無上。但在中國腹地建造塔樓似乎與當地的鄉俗不諧調。然而在武漢的德國人為這座在當地獨一無二的充滿德國鄉土氣息的建築物感到自豪。[203]

在關於工部局落成典禮的報導中有這麼一段描寫："工部局的兩層辦公樓有一座細長挺拔的塔樓，造型優美。會議廳在一樓和二樓之間。牆基用粗齒的砂石塊砌築而成，與塔樓和會議廳的地板齊高……會議廳採用晚期哥特式的手法，外觀簡潔而不失華貴，室內設施質量上乘，造型高雅。四只高大的拱窗以及通往陽台的雙開門使會議廳採光充足。牆的下端是美觀的仿橡木麻面塑料護牆板，上部漆成朱紅色。白色的天花板與深色的裝飾樑互相襯映。一樓的秘書處以及設在側樓的警察署都布置得樸實無華"。[204]

德國租界工部局東面外觀，一九
零九年。
東面外觀，一九九一年。

WUHAN

DEUTSCH-CHINESISCHE INGENIEURSCHULE
GERMAN-CHINESE SCHOOL OF ENGINEERING

Heutige Funktion. Current use
Technische Schule
nordwestlich der Jiefang Dadao
(Grundstück auf chinesischem Gebiet),
Wuhan (Hankou)
Technical college
north west of Jiefang Dadao
(site on Chinese territory),
Wuhan (Hankow)

Architekt. Architect
Carl Baedecker, Shanghai

Bauleitung. Site architect
Karsten Hermann Suhr, Shanghai, Hankou

Baukosten. Building costs
300 000 bis 400 000 Goldmark
300 000 to 400 000 gold marks

Bauherr. Client
Vereinigung zur Errichtung deutscher
technischer Schulen in China
Association for the construction of German
technological colleges in China

Bauzeit. Construction time
1913–1915

Zustand. Condition
Das Gebäude wurde 1992 abgetragen.
Pulled down in 1992

In Shanghai hatte Carl Baedecker kurz zuvor die Deutsche Ingenieurschule erbaut. Da in Wuhan ein vergleichbares Lehrgebäude entstehen sollte und man »Fehler nicht wiederholen wollte«, erhielt der Shanghaier Architekt den Auftrag, was unter den in Wuhan tätigen deutschen Architekten größten Protest hervorrief.[205] Beide Hochschulen zeigten deutlich, daß sie vom gleichen Architeken stammen, obwohl Baedecker seinen Entwurf weitgehend verändert hatte. In Wuhan flankierten zwei gleiche Treppenhäuser die Eingangshalle, sie lagen nicht in der Eingangsachse, wie beim Shanghaier Gebäude. Nach den Gesetzen der chinesischen Geomantik, des »fengshui«, werden Treppenanordnungen als »ungünstig« bezeichnet, wenn sie in der geraden Achse der Eingänge liegen.[206] Während das Gebäude in Shanghai äußerlich einem Schulbau in Deutschland entsprach, krönte in Wuhan ein chinesisch geformter Dachreiter die Schule. Seine technische Funktion war die Entlüftung der Flure und Treppenhäuser, zugleich war der Dachreiter als höchster Punkt eines Gebäudes nach den Regeln des »fengshui« der Ansatzpunkt der »Geister« und ihrer Kräfte.

Die Ansiedlung der Ingenieurschule außerhalb der deutschen Niederlassung bedeutete den Verlust des wichtigsten deutsch-chinesischen Kulturprojekts für die Niederlassung. Die relativ hohen Bodenpreise in der Niederlassung hatten den Erwerb eines Grundstücks verhindert.[207]

Shortly before he designed this building, Carl Baedecker had completed the German engineering school in Shanghai. As it was planned to build a comparable teaching institute in Wuhan and »there was no desire to repeat any mistakes«, the Shanghai architect was commissioned to design the building. This incited a major protest among the German architects working in Wuhan.[205] Although it is possible to see that both schools were designed by the same architect, Baedecker changed his design considerably. In Wuhan two identical staircases flanked the entrance hall and were not on the entrance axis as in the Shanghai building. According to the laws of Chinese geomancy »fengshui«, stairways that are on a direct axis with the entrance to a building are »unfavourable«.[206] Whereas the exterior of the building in Shanghai fully corresponded to the features of modern school architecture in Germany at the time, the school in Wuhan was crowned with a Chinese style ridge turret. The technical function of this roof was merely the ventilation of the halls and stairways, however, according to the rules of geomancy, the highest point of a building is also the point at which the »spirits« and their forces connect with the building.

The location of the engineering college outside the German concession meant the loss of the most important German-Chinese cultural project. The relatively high price of land in the concession had made it impossible for the college to purchase a site within the concession.[207]

德華技術工程學院

現用途：技校
地址：武漢解放大道西面（原中國城區內）
建築師：卡爾·培迪克，上海
工程指導：卡期騰，赫爾曼·蘇爾
建築造價：三十至四十萬金馬克
業主：中國建造德國技術學校促進會
建造期：一九一三年至一九一五年
現狀：一九九二年被拆除

卡爾·培迪克在完成上海德國工程技術學院的校舍的設計不久。就應邀在武漢設計一規模相當的教學樓。武漢該校方這一借口"以免除以往錯誤重演"，聘請上海的培迪克之舉在武漢的德籍建築師中掀起了一陣軒然大波。(205) 盡管不難看出這兩所學校的設計出自同一建築師之手，但其實培迪克在設計中已作了很大的改動。武漢技校兩個造型相同的樓梯位於前廳的兩側，而上海的教學樓的樓梯是正對著入口的。按照中國的風俗，如果樓梯與入口相對是"不吉利"的。(206) 上海教學樓的外觀與當時德國時興的校舍相似，而武漢工學院的教學樓則用中國式的屋頂造型。這種屋脊小塔與走廊和樓道構成一個通風散熱系統。按照"風水"之説，房子的最高處是容易招引鬼邪的致命點。

武漢工學院的校址在德國租界外。從中德文化交流的角度來看，這是一個損失。然而租界地價昂貴，所以也不可能兩全其美。

前德華技術工程學院南面及其主入口，一九九一年。
北立面上具有中國風格的屋脊，一九九一年。
門廳及樓梯，一九九一年。

SHANDONG

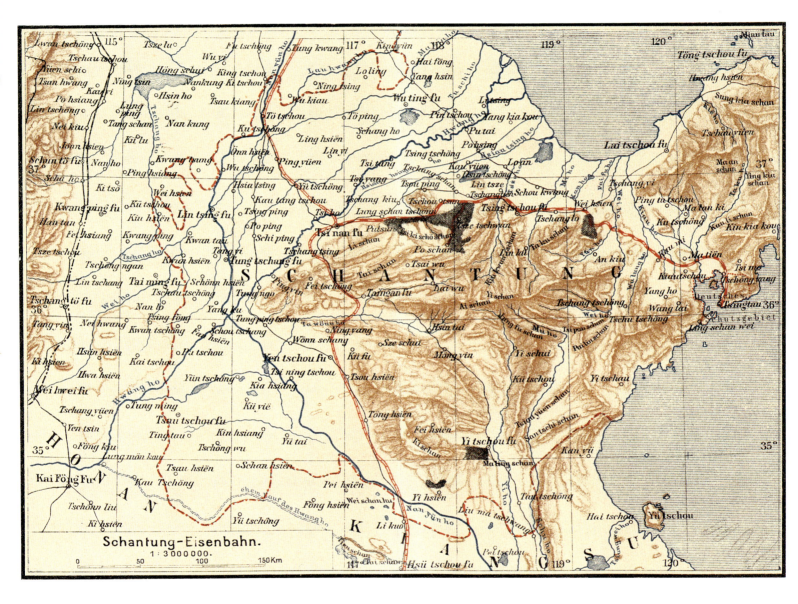

PROVINZ SHANDONG (SCHANTUNG)

Die Provinz Shandong wurde in mehrere Missionsgebiete aufgeteilt. Im Norden arbeiteten die Franziskaner, den Süden erhielt 1882 die katholische Steyler Missionsgesellschaft. Durch dieses Gebiet führte der Kaiserkanal.208 Innerhalb ihres Missionsgebietes lag der 1524 Meter hohe Berg Taishan, einer der fünf heiligen Berge Chinas. Er war Jahr für Jahr Pilgerziel von mehreren zehntausenden von Gläubigen. Am Fuß des Berges lag die Stadt Qufu (Küfu), der Geburtsort des Philosophen Konfuzius und Wohnort seiner Nachfahren sowie vieler Gelehrter.

In diesem religiösen Umfeld traf die katholische Mission auf größten Widerstand, dennoch gründete Bischof von Anzer die Missionszentrale und Bischofsresidenz in dem nur 16 km von Qufu entfernten Yanzhou (Yen-chou-fu). Ein weiteres großes Zentrum baute der Bischof in Jining (Tsining-tschou) am Kaiserkanal auf, einer Stadt mit damals mehr als 500 000 Einwohnern. Als am 1. November 1897 zwei Steyler Missionare nahe Juye (Küyeh) in Südshandong ermordet wurden, nahm das Kaiser Wilhelm II. zum Anlaß für die Besetzung der Jiaozhou-Bucht (Kiautschou-Bucht) am 14. November 1897. Als Wiedergutmachung mußte der chinesische Staat den Bau von drei »Sühnekirchen« in Südshandong mit je 66 000 Taels bezahlen, ein Tael entsprach damals etwa 3,10 Goldmark. Diese errichtete man bei den Städten Yanzhou (Yen-chou-fu, Jendschofu), Jining (Tsining) und Caozhou (Zaudschofu).209 Über den Kirchenportalen wurde das Schutzzeichen des chinesischen Kaisers angebracht: Zhejian Tianchu Tang (Tschi tzen Tien tau), »Diese katholische Kirche hat der Kaiser erbaut.« Während der Kulturrevolution (1966–1976) trug man die Sühnekirchen vollständig ab.

Die Kirchen der Steyler Missionsgesellschaft wurden mit Rücksicht auf die chinesische Geomantik ohne höhere Kirchtürme erbaut. Geister und Kraftströme der Erde werden

THE PROVINCE OF SHANDONG

The Province of Shandong was divided up into a number of mission areas. The Franciscans worked in the north, the Catholic Steyler Missionary Society was given the south in 1882. The most important north-south route of the time, the Imperial Canal, ran through this southern area.208 Within their missionary area was the 1524 metre-high Taishan Mountain, one of China's five holy mountains. Year in year out thousands of believers would make their pilgrimage to it. At the foot of the mountain was the town of Qufu (Küfu), the place where Confucius was born and many of his descendants and learned men lived.

In this religious environment the Catholic mission met with great resistance but, undaunted, Bishop von Anzer founded the headquarters of the mission and the Bishop's Residence in Yanzhou (Yen-chou-fu) which was only 16 kilometres away from Qufu. The Bishop also built up another large centre in Jining (Tsining-tschou), a town on the Imperial Canal, which at the time had over 500 000 inhabitants. When, on 1 November 1897, two Steyler missionaries were murdered near Juye (Küyeh) in Southern Shandong, Kaiser Wilhelm II seized the opportunity to occupy the Jiaozhou Bay (Kiaochow Bay) on 14 November 1897. As compensation the Chinese state had to pay for three »Churches of Atonement« to be built in southern Shandong at a cost of 66 000 taels each. A tael was equivalent to about 3.10 gold marks. These churches were built near the towns of Yanzhou (Yen-chou-fu, Jendschofu), Jining (Tsining) and Caozhou (Zaudschofu).209 The seal of approval of the Chinese Emperor was inscribed above the portals of the churches: Zhejian Tianchu Tang (Tschi tzen Tien tau), »This Catholic church was built by the Emperor.« During the Cultural Revolution (1966–1976) all three Churches of Atonement were torn down.

The churches of the Steyler Missionary Society were built without tall steeples, respect-

山東省

山東省被劃分為數個佈教區。方濟各會據北，天主教斯泰爾修會的聖言會於一八八二年領南。大運河——中國當時南北交通最重要的樞紐，穿經山東省南部。⟨208⟩海拔一千五百二十四米的泰山——中國宗教五岳之一，也座落在聖言會的佈教區內。年復一年，泰山始終是成千上萬名儒教信徒的朝聖地，臥於其趾的曲阜城更是思想家儒教始主孔夫子的誕生地及其諸多後裔和學者的故里。

天主教聖言會在這樣一種異教氛圍中自然是重重遇阻。盡管如此，安治泰主教仍在距曲阜城僅十六公里的兗州城創立了總傳教站，並於此築宅而居。此外，他還在大運河畔，當時人口逾五十萬的濟寧城建立了另一傳教中心。一八九七年十一月一日，兩名聖言會傳教士在山東省巨野縣附近遇害，德皇威廉二世乘機以此為由，於一八九七年十一月十四日侵佔膠州灣。清政府因此被迫在山東省南部即兗州、濟寧、曹州三城分別修建一座"賠償禮拜堂"，每座耗銀六萬六千兩。當時，一兩銀元約合三點一零金馬克。⟨209⟩每座禮拜堂大門上方橫幅均有清帝御筆："御敕天堂"。這三座禮拜堂均在文革期間一九六六至一九七六年被拆除。

聖言會的這三座禮拜堂，遵循中國風水之説而免築尖塔。據風水之原理，建築對神靈及地氣有至關重要的影響。而各種對自然之氣有害的影響均可通過避邪惡之氣，導平和之氣而得以糾正。（……）大多數建於較大區域內的寶塔的唯一功用便是：破邪風惡水之氣，導地文靈氣於一點如一座城池：一段河流：或一川平原。"⟨210⟩而風水先生則是唯一能夠觀氣擇址者，建築師必須納其所言，與其合作。⟨211⟩當時，鋪設鐵路，高築電線均被視為對地文靈氣的至命傷害。⟨212⟩

與此相反，在山東省北部佈教的方濟各會則建起了高塔聳立的哥特式復古風教堂。例如一九零八年在濟南城東兩公里處落成的一座教堂，其塔樓高達四十六米，為中國北方最高的教堂之一。該教堂位於方濟各會地產內，處身於在當時就已有數百年歷史的中國基督教團之鄉。盡管"風水

nach den Gesetzen des »fengshui« durch Bauwerke beeinflußt. »Schädlichen Einflüssen der Naturkräfte kann man entgegenwirken, wenn man die ungüstigen Strömungen ablenkt und die freundlichen, friedvollen herleitet. (...) Die meisten Pagoden in einem großen Distrikt haben den einzigen Zweck, entweder die zerstörenden Kräfte des schlimmen Feng-Shui zu vernichten oder die günstigen Ströme des Geisterflusses auf einen bestimmten Punkt – sei es nun eine Stadt, ein Fluß oder eine Ebene – hinzuleiten.«[210] Nur ein Geomant konnte den am besten geeigneten Standort für ein Gebäude feststellen; er arbeitete mit den Architekten zusammen.[211] Als fatale Störung der Kraftströme wurde damals die Errichtung von Telegrafenleitungen und Eisenbahnen gesehen.[212]

Dagegen bauten die in Nordshandong missionierenden Franziskaner neogotische Kirchen mit hohen Türmen. 1908 wurde in Jinan eine der höchsten Kirchen Nordchinas eingeweiht, mit einem Turm von 46 Meter Höhe. Trotz des starken Einflußes des »fengshui« war es den Franziskanern möglich gewesen, außerhalb einer ausländischen Niederlassung eine Kirche mit dieser ungewöhnlichen Turmhöhe zu errichten.

Die wirtschaftliche Erschließung der Provinz war nur durch den Bau von Eisenbahnen möglich; denn die Kanäle, Flüsse und das Straßennetz reichten für die modernen Bedürfnisse nicht aus. Die Hauptverkehrsader der Provinz Shandong vor dem Bau der Eisenbahn war der Kaiserkanal. Pater Stenz von der Steyler Missionsgesellschaft beschrieb 1903 den schlechten Zustand des Kanals und sprach sich für die Wiederherstellung der Wasserstraße aus. »Kostspielig würde diese Ausbesserung nicht, wenigstens nicht so teuer, wie der Bau einer Bahn.« Doch wäre solch ein Ausbau nicht zum Vorteil des deutschen Schutzgebietes gewesen. »Freilich die deutsche Kolonie Tsingtau hätte dadurch Schaden. Sollten aber andere nicht einmal auf den Gedanken kommen, den Kanal derartig zu benützen?«[213]

ing the Chinese theories of geomancy. According to the laws of »fengshui« the spirits and forces of the earth are affected by buildings. »Harmful influences on the forces of nature can be counteracted by diverting unfavourable currents and attracting friendly, peaceful ones. (...) Most pagodas in a large district have the sole purpose of either annihilating the destructive forces of the dreadful Feng-Shui or drawing the favourable currents in the flow of spirits to a particular point – either a city, a river or a plain.«[210] Only a geomancer could determine the most appropriate place for a building; he worked with the architects.[211] The building of railway tracks and erection of telegraph wires was seen at the time as a fatal destruction of the flow of forces.[212]

However, in Northern Shandong the Franciscan missionaries built neo-Gothic churches with tall towers. For example, in 1908 one of the tallest churches in North China was consecrated in Jinan; its tower was 46 metres high. It was on land which was part of the mission, some two kilometres to the east of the city walls of Jinan, in the midst of the Chinese Christian community which had existed there for centuries. Despite the strong influence of the »fengshui« the Franciscans managed to build a church outside a foreign settlement with an unusually high tower.

The economic development of the province was only possible through the building of railways: the canals, rivers and roads simply could not meet modern needs. The main transport artery in the Province of Shandong before the railways were built was the Imperial Canal. Father Stenz from the Steyler Missionary Society described the terrible condition of the canal in 1903. He advocated the restoration of the canal. »The improvements would not be expensive, or at least not as expensive as building a railway.« But improvements of this kind would not have been to the advantage of the German protectorate. »Admittedly it would be of detriment to the German colony of Tsingtao. But shouldn't others

經"在當時影響力極大，方濟各會的修道士們還是設法在外國租界范圍以外建造了這座塔樓高聳不同凡響的教堂。

山東省的經濟開發迫切需要修築鐵路，因為當時的運河、河流及公路網完全無法滿足現代化的需求。在鐵路建成之前，大運河是山東省的交通主動脈。一九零三年，聖言會的薛田資神甫對大運河年久失修的劣狀作有描述，並建議修復水路："修復大運河耗資微薄，較之修築鐵路更是微不足道。"然而此舉無益於德國保護地，"應該承認，德國的殖民地青島卻會因此受損。但是，其他人難道不應該想到改善大運河狀況而對其加以充分利用嗎？"〈213〉中國當時的道路窄陋不堪。"山東省內地的道路糟得無法形容，它們僅是人們踏踩出來的深溝，更無明溝排水，每遇雨天便成了天然排水道，交通完全阻斷。山東省從前並不是沒有良好的路段，有些路面甚至是由整塊的花崗石鋪成的。這些花崗石路主要是為皇帝及達官貴人某次外出所築。"〈214〉當時的交通工具有：車轅固定的雙輪馬車、抬轎、抬椅及獨輪手推車。手推車被視為窄陋道路上的理想交通工具，它可供六人乘坐，行李固定在中部大輪的兩側，順風時還可張帆乘風。介於安全之由，這些獨輪車常常是四十輪左右成隊而行，它們首尾相接，滿載貨物，浩蕩遠行。

早在一八六八年至一八七二年間，地質學家斐迪南·馮·里希特霍芬就受命於普魯士帝國，在中國做了旅行考察。他於一八六九年三月至五月間游歷山東省，研究其地質狀況並將所採集的煤及其它礦石標本寄到德國做分析。他還對當地簡陋卻歷史悠久的採煤方式有所報道。山東礦務公司便是根據希特霍芬的初級研究分別在距青島一百七十公里的濰坊附近及距青島三百四十五公里的博山內建立多處礦井。

由於博山鐵礦床的發現，山東礦務公司亦計劃於一九一五年在青島附近建造高爐和煉鋼廠。〈215〉。而山東鐵路溝通了採煤區與德國港口城市青島之間的聯繫。

一八九七年十一月，德國海軍佔領了膠州灣，並從清政府手中將其租借，租期九十九年。膠州保護地便得以持續發展為貿易殖民地。新建的青島大港逐漸形成經濟港

Die chinesischen Straßen waren schmal und in schlechtem Zustand: »Der Zustand der Landstraßen im Inneren Schantungs spottet jeder Beschreibung. Sie bilden eigentlich nur Pfade. Tief ausgefahren und ohne Gräben bilden sie den natürlichen Ablauf für die Niederschläge. Bei Regen wird daher jeder Verkehr eingestellt. In früheren Zeiten waren stellenweise gute Straßen, zum Teil sogar unter Verwendung von Granitquadern geschaffen worden. Diese Granitstraßen entstanden hauptsächlich bei Gelegenheit von Reisen der Kaiser oder der höchsten Beamten.«[214] Als Verkehrsmittel gab es von Ponys gezogene zweirädrige Reisekarren mit fester Deichsel, Tragesänften und Tragestühle sowie die von einer Person geschobene Einradkarre »wheelbarrow«, die als das ideale Verkehrsmittel für die schlechten Straßen beschrieben wurden. Bei diesen Schiebkarren wurde das Gepäck zu beiden Seiten des großen mittleren Rades befestigt, bis zu sechs Personen konnten damit befördert werden, bei günstigem Wind wurde ein Segel gesetzt. Aus Sicherheitsgründen schlossen sich Karrenschieber zusammen und transportierten ihre Güter in großen Kolonnen über die Landstraßen.

Bereits zwischen 1868 und 1872 hatte der Geograph Ferdinand von Richthofen im Auftrag Preußens Forschungsreisen durch China unternommen. Er bereiste die Provinz Shandong von März bis Mai 1869, führte geologische Untersuchungen durch und schickte die Kohle- und Erzproben zur Analyse nach Deutschland. Richthofen berichtete über Abbaugebiete, in denen bereits seit Jahrhunderten Kohle mit einfachen technischen Mitteln gefördert wurde. Aufgrund seiner Voruntersuchungen entstanden die großen Bergwerke der Schantung-Bergbau-Gesellschaft. Die Gruben lagen nahe der Stadt Weifang (Weihsien), 170 km von Qingdao entfernt, und im 345 km von Qingdao entfernten Boshan (Poshan) Gebirge. Da im Boshan-Gebirge auch Eisenerzlager festgestellt worden waren, plante die Schantung-Bergbaugesellschaft ab 1915 den Bau von Hochöfen und einem

have the idea of using the canal in that way?«[213]

The Chinese roads were narrow and in bad condition: »The state of the country roads in the interior of Shandong defies description. They are actually nothing more than footpaths. They are deep trenches without drainage ditches so that they are the natural course for rainwater. All forms of transport along them thus stop when it rains. In former times there were some good roads, some of them had even been built with granite slabs. These granite roads were usually built for one of the journeys undertaken by the Emperor or his highest ranking civil servants.«[214] The means of transport were two-wheeled carts with fixed shafts pulled by ponies, sedan chairs and wheelbarrows pushed by one person which were described as the ideal means of transport for the bad roads. The luggage was fastened to either side of the large, central wheel of these wheelbarrows; up to six people could be transported and if wind conditions were favourable a sail was put up. For reasons of safety wheelbarrow-pushers would often join forces and transport their goods in long convoys along the country roads.

Between 1868 and 1872 the geographer Ferdinand von Richthofen had undertaken expeditions for Prussia through China. He travelled in the Province of Shandong from March to May 1869, carried out geological analysis and sent samples of coal and ore for analysis in Germany. Richthofen reports of mining areas in which coal had been extracted for centuries with simple means. The large coal mines of the Shantung Mining Company were established as a result of his preliminary investigations. The pits were close to the city of Weifang, 170 kilometres from Qingdao, and in Boshan, 345 kilometres away. As iron ore deposits had also been found in the Boshan mountains, the Shantung Mining Company planned to start building furnaces and a steelworks near Qingdao in 1915.[215] The coal fields were linked to the German

灣，並在短短幾年內一躍而山東省最重要的貿易港口。其主要的出口商為草編和生絲。"山東中部的草編其精美價昂為國際市場所公認。"〈216〉一九零二至零六年間，一座現代化的巢絲廠在膠州保護地內滄口附近建成。與這一切相應，青島與內地之間的現代化交通網發展具有同等的重要性。

山東省境內的第一條鐵路於一八九九年至一九零四年間建成，從而溝通了青島與濟南的聯系。據中德於一八九八年簽訂的條約部份條款，德國不僅享有修築並營運這條長達四百一十二公里的鐵路線的特權，還可開採沿途煤礦。正如鐵路首次在歐洲出現時受挫一樣，當時由於中國人懼怕這一陌生的運輸形式會招引水災，築路之舉亦是百般阻撓〈217〉德國工程師不得不盡力周全。德國公司賠償所有搬遷費用：築路時繞開歷史文物所在地；將火車站台均設在居民點外幾公里處；其屋頂皆鋪以中國土磚瓦，其檐口及屋脊均砌築別緻的裝飾瓦。〈218〉這些努力很快使中國人對鋪設鐵路之舉棄疑而擁。一九零六年，乘坐三等車的旅客約八十一點七萬人次；二等車二點一萬人次；頭等車三千四百六十八人次其中三等車收入佔總客運收入的百分之八十六點五〈219〉

一九零八年至一九一二年間，清政府出資修築了津浦鐵路，其結構與技術之先進使山東省第一條鐵路望塵莫及。該鐵路的北段由天津延伸至山東南界，長六百二十五公里，為德國工程師承造；南段長三百七十五公里直抵南京，為英國工程師承造；該線走向大致與大運河平行。築路工程包括：輔設單軌鐵路及路基；架設橋樑；修建火車站，車站旅館，辦公樓以及鐵路員工宿舍。這期間於濟南以北几公里處修築的黃河鐵路橋，其跨度居當時中國橋樑之最，其工程成就亦是眾口皆碑。〈220〉

除鋪設鐵路以外，德國人還修築了許多公路以充分完善德國保護區腹地的交通基礎設施。至一九一二年，其所鋪設公路總長已達一百五十公里，且均可供汽車行駛。最初，因軍事需要，築路工程進展迅速。〈221〉至一九二五年，青島已有公路三百公里左右。該城為中國當時擁有最發達的公路網的城市之一。

Stahlwerk bei Qingdao.[215] Die Kohlereviere wurden durch die Schantung-Eisenbahn mit der deutschen Hafenstadt Qingdao (Tsingtau) verbunden.

Im November 1897 wurde die Bucht von Jiaozhou durch die deutsche Marine besetzt, im März 1898 das Gebiet für 99 Jahre von der chinesischen Regierung gepachtet. Das deutsche Schutzgebiet wurde kontinuierlich zu einer Handelskolonie ausgebaut. Der neu erbaute große Hafen von Qingdao bildete das wirtschaftliche Zentrum, bereits nach wenigen Jahren war Qingdao der bedeutendste Handelshafen der Provinz. Wichtige Ausfuhrgüter waren Strohgeflechte und Rohseide. »Die Strohgeflechte aus Mittelschantung gelten als die feinsten, höchst bezahlten Geflechte auf dem Weltmarkt.«[216] Noch innerhalb des deutschen Schutzgebietes, nahe dem Ort Cangkou (Tsangkou), 18 km von Qingdao entfernt, war zwischen 1902 und 1906 eine moderne Seidenspinnerei errichtet worden. Entsprechend wichtig war der Ausbau eines modernen Verkehrsnetzes zwischen Qingdao und dem Hinterland.

Die erste Eisenbahnlinie in Shandong wurde zwischen 1899 und 1904 gebaut und verband Qingdao mit der Provinzhauptstadt Jinan. Das Recht, diese 412 km lange Bahnlinie zu bauen und zu betreiben sowie dort liegende Kohlevorkommen auszubeuten, war Teil des 1898 mit China geschlossenen Pachtvertrages. Wie beim Bau der ersten Eisenbahnen in Europa wehrte sich auch die chinesische Bevölkerung gegen dieses unbekannte Transportmittel. Sie fürchtete Überschwemmungen, die durch den Bau der Bahndämme hervorgerufen würden.[217] Doch die deutschen Ingenieure bemühten sich um Rücksichtnahme. Für die Verlegung von Gräbern wurden der Bevölkerung Entschädigungen gezahlt, bei der Trassenführung berücksichtigte man die historischen Denkmäler und umfuhr sie. Die Bahnhöfe wurden in einigen Kilometern Entfernung von den Ortschaften angelegt. Bei diesen Landbahnhöfen deckte man die Dächer mit chinesischen Ziegeln, an

port town of Qingdao (Tsingtao) by the Shantung Railway.

In November 1897 the Bay of Jiaozhou was occupied by the German Navy and in March 1898 the area was leased from the Chinese government for 99 years. The German protectorate steadily developed into a trade colony. The newly-built large port at Qingdao formed the economic hub and after only a few years Qingdao had become the most important commercial port in the province. Important exports were straw basketwork and raw silk. »The basketwork from Central Shandong was considered to be the finest on the world market, commanding the highest prices.«[216] Still within the German protectorate, near the town of Cangkou (Tsangkou), 18 kilometres from Qingdao, a modern silk spinning mill was built between 1902 and 1906. The development of a modern transport network to link Qingdao with its hinterland was correspondingly important.

The first railway line in Shandong was built between 1899 and 1904 and linked Qingdao to the Jinan, the capital of the province. The right to build and operate this 412 kilometre long railway line and to work the coal reserves there was part of the treaty concluded with China in 1898. Similarly to when the first railway lines were built in Europe, the Chinese people initially resisted the construction of this unknown means of transport. They were afraid that the railway embankments would cause flooding.[217] Compensation was paid for any graves which had to be moved and the route took historic monuments into account and went around them. The stations were built several kilometres from the villages. The roofs of these rural stations were tiled with Chinese tiles and specially shaped ornamental tiles were used at the eaves and ridge.[218] Despite initial resistance the Chinese people rapidly accepted the Shantung Railways as a means of transport. In 1906 some 817 000 people travelled 3rd class, whilst 21 000 travelled 2nd class and 3 468 1st class. The 3rd class passengers accoun-

der Traufe und am First verwendete man besonders geformten Schmuckziegel.[218] Trotz des anfänglichen Widerstandes wurde die Schantung-Eisenbahn als Verkehrsmittel schnell von der chinesischen Bevölkerung angenommen. Rund 817 000 Personen fuhren 1906 in der III. Klasse, während etwa 21 000 Personen in der II. Klasse und 3 468 Personen in der I. Klasse reisten. Die Reisenden der III. Klassen machten mit 86,5 Prozent den Hauptteil der Einnahmen im Personenverkehr aus.[219]

Eine in Gestaltung und technischer Ausführung weitaus modernere Bahnlinie wurde in Shandong zwischen 1908 und 1912 gebaut; Auftraggeber der Tianjin-Nanjing-Bahn (Tientsin-Pukow-Bahn) war die chinesische Regierung. Deutsche Ingenieure planten und bauten den 625 km langen Nordteil von Tianjin bis zur Südgrenze Shandongs, britische Ingenieure konstruierten den 375 km langen Südteil bis Nanjing. Die Bahntrasse verlief meist in größerer Entfernung parallel zum Kaiserkanal. Zum Umfang der Arbeiten gehörte der Bau der einspurigen Gleisanlage, des Bahndamms, der Brücken, der Bahnhöfe, der Bahnhofshotels, der Verwaltungsgebäude und der Eisenbahnerwohnhäuser. Als eine vielbeachtete Ingenieurleistung galt der Bau der Eisenbahnbrücke über den Huang He, den Gelben Fluß, einige Kilometer nördlich von Jinan. Sie war damals in China die Brücke mit der größten Spannweite.[220]

Um das Hinterland des deutschen Schutzgebiets verkehrstechnisch optimal zu erschließen, wurden neben der Eisenbahn auch viele Straßen gebaut. Bis 1912 gab es bereits 150 km Straßen, die mit dem Auto befahren werden konnten. Ursprünglich waren es militärische Gründe, die den Straßenbau schnell vorangebracht hatten.[221] 1925 besaß die Umgebung von Qingdao bereits rund 300 km Straßen; es war damals eines der Gebiete in China, die straßentechnisch am besten erschlossen waren.

ted for 86.5 percent of the income from passenger fares.[219]

Between 1908 and 1912 a railway line was built in Shandong which was far more modern both in design and technology. The Tianjin-Nanjing Railway was commissioned by the Chinese government. German engineers planned and built the northern section from Tianjin to the southern border of Shandong which was 625 kilometres long and British engineers constructed the 375 kilometre-long southern section to Nanjing. The tracks ran for the most part parallel to the Imperial Canal. The works included building the single track line, the embankments, bridges, stations, station hotels, office buildings and houses for the railway men. A much-acclaimed feat of engineering was the railway bridge across the Huang He, the Yellow River, a few kilometres north of Jinan. It was the longest span bridge in China at the time.[220]

In order to develop the hinterland of the German protectorate with transport infrastructure a large number of roads were also built. By 1912 there were already 150 kilometres of roads suitable for cars. Originally the road building programme had been advanced rapidly for military reasons.[221] By 1925 there were already around 300 kilometres of road in the Qingdao area; it was one of the areas of China with the most advanced road network.

YANZHOU

BAHNHOF YEN-CHOU-FU
YEN-CHOU-FU RAILWAY STATION

Heutige Funktion. Current use
Bahnhofsverwaltung
Yanzhou (Yen-chou-fu, Yentschoufu),
507 km südlich von Tianjin
Railways Administration
Yanzhou (Yen-chou-fu),
507 km south of Tianjin

Entwurf. Design
Abteilungsbaumeister Jandl[223]
Jandl, company architect[223]

Ausführung. Contractors
Tientsin-Pukow Eisenbahngesellschaft
Tientsin-Pukow Railway Company

Bauherr. Client
Chinese Government Railways

Bauzeit. Construction time
um 1911
around 1911

Zustand. Condition
Das Gebäude ist gut erhalten,
die Nebengebäude wurden im Mai 1991
abgetragen. Der Bahnhofsneubau
ist fertiggestellt.
Ancillary buildings pulled down in May 1991;
new station building completed.

Der Bahnhof lag östlich außerhalb der Stadtmauern Yanzhous. Südlich der Stadt besaß die Steyler Missionsgesellschaft seit 1896 eine Missionsstation. Das markanteste Gebäude in der Stadt war eine etwa 59 Meter hohe Stufenpagode.

Als die Bahnlinie fertiggestellt war, berichtete der *Ostasiatische Lloyd* folgendes über den Bahnhof: »In kurzer Zeit sind schmucke Gebäude erstanden. Der runde Wasserturm erhebt sich schlank in die Lüfte. Seine romanische Form sticht vorteilhaft von dem altersgrauen Gemäuer des achteckigen Buddhaturms innerhalb der Stadtmauer ab. Jener Turm, der zwölf bis dreizehn Jahrhunderte an sich hat vorbeiziehen lassen, ist über 50 Meter hoch.«[224]

Die Stadt war ein wichtiges Handels- und Verwaltungszentrum und, begünstigt durch die Nähe der Konfuziusstadt Qufu (Küfu, Chufou), Wohnort zahlreicher Literaten. Sie liegt etwa 16 km westlich von Qufu und gehörte damit noch zum ›heiligen Lande‹, in dem Konfuzius gelehrt und gearbeitet hatte. Daher gab es Widerstände und Einsprüche gegen den Bau der Eisenbahn: »Als vor einigen Jahren die Eisenbahn gebaut wurde, erhob Herzog Kung, direkter Nachfahre von Konfuzius, Einwände gegen die Entweihung des heiligen Ortes durch ein derartig barbarisches Ding wie die ausländische Eisenbahn. So gelang es ihm, die Bahn aus der Stadt Chufou, wo er sehr einflußreich ist, fernzuhalten.«[225] Auch in Yanzhou gab es Widerstände: »(…) die Bevölkerung von Yen-chou-fu hat sich mit Rücksicht auf das Feng-shui lebhaft der Führung der Bahn durch ihre Grenzmarken widersetzt.«[226]

The station was to the east of Yanzhou, outside the city walls. The Steyler Missionary Society had had a Catholic missionary station to the south of the city since 1896. The most striking building in the city was a stepped pagoda which was some 59 metres high.

When the railway line was finished the *Ostasiatischer Lloyd* printed an exaggerated report about the station: »In a short time neat and tidy buildings have been put up. The slender, round water tower rises up to lofty heights. Its Romanesque form stands out advantageously against the walls of the octagonal Buddha tower inside the town walls, greying now with age. This tower which has seen the passage of twelve or thirteen centuries is over 50 metres high.«[224]

The city was an important centre for trade and administration and, due to the proximity of Confucius's city, Qufu (Küfu, Chufou), was the home of numerous literary men. It is 16 kilometres west of Qufu and thus belongs to the »Holy Land« where Confucius taught and worked. That is why there was resistance to and protests against the construction of the railway: »When the railway was being constructed a few years ago, the Duke of Kung, a lineal descendant of Confucius, objected to the defilement of the sacred place by such a barbarous thing as a foreign railway and so was able to keep it out of Chufou, where he is very influencial:«[225] In Yanzhou there were also protests: »(…) because of the feng-shui the people of Yen-chou-fu also very actively opposed the railway running within their boundaries.«[226]

Bahnhof Yanzhou, Westansicht,
1992
Detail der Gebäudeecke, 1992
Yanzhou Station,
view from the west, 1992
Detail of the corner of the building,
1992

兗州火車站

現用途：火車站辦公樓
所在地：兗州，天津以南五百零七公里
設計：楊德爾‧建築師⟨223⟩
施工：津浦鐵路公司
業主：中國鐵路局
建造期：約一九一一年
現狀：副樓於一九九一年五月拆除，新站正完工。

兗州火車站位於兗州東城外，城南是聖言會於一八九七年設立的天主教傳教站。當時城內最引人注目的建築是一座高五十九米的梯形寶塔。

津浦鐵路線峻工時，《德文新報》對兗州火車站作了大肆渲染："短短的時間之內，這裡便出現了幢幢漂亮的樓房。圓形水塔高聳入雲，其浪漫形式與城內灰舊的八角形磚石佛塔形成了鮮明對比。該塔年代久遠，已有一二零零至一三零零年的歷史，塔高五十餘米。"⟨224⟩

兗州城是一重要的商業中心，行政中心，並得益於近鄰曲阜城，那裡是許多文學家的故鄉。

孔夫子在曲阜傳道授業，兗州位於曲阜以西十六公里處，亦屬"聖地"。因此，在這裡修築鐵路時，自然會遇到阻力與責難。"幾年前修築鐵路時，孔子的一位直系後裔孔公爵強烈反對修建諸如外國鐵路一類的設施，稱之為對聖地的沾污。他成功地將鐵路擋在了孔教影響深入的曲阜城外。"⟨225⟩修築鐵路在兗州也遇到了阻力。"鑒於風水的影響，兗州紳民強烈反對鐵路通過縣邊界"。⟨226⟩

兗州火車站西面外觀，一九九二年。
東站大樓一角細部，一九九二年。

BAHNHOF TAI'AN
TAI'AN RAILWAY STATION

Heutige Funktion. Current use
Verwaltungsgebäude und Hotel
Lijaio Dao, Tai'an (Tai-an-fu),
423 km südlich von Tianjin
Administration Building and Hotel
Lijaio Dao, Tai'an (Tai-an-fu),
423 km south of Tianjin
Entwurf. Design
Bauinspektor Bach;
Bauassistent Hackbarth[227]
Bach, civil servant in the planning office of
the Administration; Hackbarth, assistant in
the same office[227]
Ausführung. Contractors
Tientsin-Pukow Eisenbahngesellschaft
Tientsin-Pukow Railway Company
Bauherr. Client
Chinese Government Railways
Bauzeit. Construction time
zwischen 1908 und 1912
between 1908 and 1912
Zustand. Condition
Das Gebäude ist gut erhalten.
Well preserved.

Der Bahnhof in Tai'an ist von den heute noch erhaltenen Stationen das schönste Bahnhofsgebäude der Eisenbahnlinie zwischen Tianjin und Nanjing. Als der Bahnhof gebaut wurde, hatte die Stadt etwa 100 000 Einwohner. Die Station liegt am Fuß des Taishan, der mit 1524 Metern der höchste der fünf heiligen Berge Chinas ist. Hierher pilgerten jedes Jahr zehntausende von Gläubigen. Aus diesem Grund war dem Bahnhof ein Hotel angeschlossen. Da die Bahnlinie eine wichtige Straße kreuzte, wurde eine Unterführung gebaut. Der Turm des Bahnhofs macht diesen Kreuzungspunkt bereits von weitem sichtbar. Die Baumeister ließen sich von der chinesischen Architektur der Provinz Shandong inspirieren: Die Giebelform des Turmdachs findet man bei den Bauernhäusern dieser Region.[228] Die Traufe bildet eine Reihung von Konsolenkapitellen in einer stark abstrahierten Form. Dies ist eigentlich ein Detail des Holzbaus, man findet es aber auch an chinesischen Bauten in einer einfachen Ziegelversion, bei einigen Gebäuden sind sie kunstvoll aus Terrakotta geformt.[229] Bis auf wenige verputzte Flächen am Turm ist das gesamte Gebäude mit Granitstein verkleidet.

Tai'an is the finest of all the stations still in existence on the railway line between Tianjin and Nanjing. When the station was built the city had some 100 000 inhabitants. The station is at the foot of Mount Taishan, which, at 1524 metres, is the most imposing of China's five holy mountains. Tens of thousands of believers came here on pilgrimage every year. For this reason the station had its own hotel. As the railway line crossed an important street a tunnel was built underneath the railway tracks. The tower of the station marks this crossing point, making it visible for miles. The architect took his inspiration from the Chinese architecture in the Province of Shandong. The gable shape of the tower roof can be found in the farmhouses of this region.[228] The eaves are formed by a row of console capitals in a very abstract form. They are actually a detail from wooden buildings but an abstract tile version is also found in Chinese buildings, and on some buildings they are artistically formed in terra-cotta.[229] Apart from a few rendered areas on the tower the whole building is clad with granite.

Typen von Backsteingiebeln in der Provinz Shandong, um 1910
Various types of brick gable in the Province of Shandong, around 1910

Bahnhof Tai'an, Ostansicht, 1992
Detail der Natursteinfassade, 1992
Tai'an Station, view from the east, 1992
Detail of the stone façade, 1992

泰安火車站

現用途：辦公樓，賓館
所在地：泰安立交道口，天津以南四百二十三公里
設計：巴赫
建築總監：哈克巴爾特，建築助理〈227〉
施工：津浦鐵路公司
業主：中國鐵路局
建造期：一九零八年至一九一二年
現狀：建築體保存良好。

泰安火車站是津浦線現今尚存車站中最美觀的建築。車站動工時，該城人口約十萬左右。泰安火車站座落在泰山腳下。泰山海拔一千五百二十四米，巍然屹立，為中國五岳之首。每年，數以萬計的信徒來此朝聖。鑒於這一原因，車站旁又增建了一座賓館。由於鐵路線與一條重要馬路交叉，鐵軌下方鑿了一條通道，旁邊的塔樓使人遠遠看到交叉的位置。
山東省的中式建築賦予建築師創作靈感。〈228〉車站塔樓的山牆形式取樣於當地的農舍，檐口為一排形式非常抽象的斗拱。這實際上是木結構的一個細部，但在中國建築中也做成抽象的磚石結構，有些建築則使用琉璃瓦，充滿藝術情趣。〈229〉除塔樓的幾處粉牆外，整個建築的牆面用花崗石砌成。

泰安火車站東面外觀，一九九二年。
花崗石立面細部，一九九二年。
山東省磚砌山牆的各種類型，約一九一零年。

SHANDONG

LANDBAHNHÖFE DER TIENTSIN-PUKOW BAHN
RURAL STATIONS ON THE TIENTSIN-PUKOW RAILWAY

Cangzhou (Tsang-chou),
121 km südlich von Tianjin
Nanxiakou (Nan-hsia-kou),
160 km südlich von Tianjin
Dezhou (Te-chou, Tetschow),
225 km südlich von Tianjin
Pingyuan (Ping-yuan-hsien),
268 km südlich von Tianjin
Cangzhou (Tsang-chou),
121 km south of Tianjin
Nanxiakou (Nan-hsia-kou),
160 km south of Tianjin
Dezhou (Te-chou),
225 km south of Tianjin
Pingyuan (Ping-yuan-hsien),
268 km south of Tianjin

Entwurf. Design
Deutsche Ingenieure
German engineers

Ausführung. Contractors
Tientsin-Pukow Eisenbahngesellschaft
Tientsin-Pukow Railway Company

Bauherr. Client
Chinese Government Railways

Bauzeit. Construction time
zwischen 1908 und 1912
between 1908 and 1912

Zustand. Condition
Die Gebäude existieren nicht mehr.
No longer exists.

Bahnhof Cangzhou, um 1912
Bahnhof Dezhou, um 1912
Bahnhof Pingyuan, um 1912
Bahnhof Nanxiakou, um 1911
Cangzhou Station, around 1912
Dezhou Station, around 1912
Pingyuan Station, around 1912
Nanxiakou Station, around 1911

Bei Gestaltung und Entwurf der Landbahnhöfe hatten sich die Ingenieure an die chinesische Bauweise angepaßt. Die Gebäude waren aus Ziegeln und Natursteinen errichtet und trugen rote Ziegeldächer. Sie müssen damals aufsehenerregend gewesen sein, denn es wurde viel darüber geschrieben. So beispielsweise der *Ostasiatische Lloyd*: »Sehr stattlich sieht das Bahnhofsgebäude in Te-chou aus. Es ist im modernen deutschen Stil, aber mit einem Einschlag ins Chinesierende gebaut. (…) Man muß es den Erbauern dieser Bahn lassen, daß sie in ästhetischer Hinsicht wirklich recht viel geleistet haben. Kein Stationsgebäude ist wie das andere gebaut. Jedes hat seine kleinen Besonderheiten im Stil und ist der Umgebung angepaßt.«[230]

Auch britische Autoren erkannten die architektonische Qualität der Landbahnhöfe an, hielten diese sorgfältige Gestaltung jedoch für zu aufwendig: »Die deutschen Bahnhöfe sind in vielerlei Hinsicht recht stattlich anzusehen und der Entwurf schließt sogar die Nebengebäude, die Wassertürme und sogar die Häuschen der Stellenwärter mit ein. Die Dächer sind mit roten Ziegeln gedeckt, und doch ist fast jedes Bahnhofsgebäude unterschiedlich gestaltet. Im wesentlichen sind aber chinesische Stilelemente verwendet und mit europäischen vermischt worden, was in den meisten Fällen zu harmonischen Ergebnissen führte. Die graziös geschwungenen chinesischen Giebel sind bei der Mehrzahl der größeren Bahnhöfe verwendet worden und bilden einen ausdrucksreichen Abschluß. Insgesamt sind aber alle Bahnhöfe für den Zweck, dem sie dienen sollen, viel zu teuer gebaut worden.«[231]

Während die beiden Bahnhöfe in den Städten Tianjin und Jinan in Maßstab und Qualität des Entwurf städtischen Bahnhöfen in Deutschland glichen, versuchte man, die Landbahnhöfe an die chinesische Architektur anzupassen. Vielleicht sollte auch dadurch die am Anfang sehr skeptische Bevölkerung von dem neuen Verkehrsmittel überzeugt werden.

When designing the rural stations, the planners adapted their work to Chinese architecture. The buildings were of brick and stone and had red tiled roofs. They must have caused quite a stir since a lot was written about them. The *Ostasiatischer Lloyd* wrote for instance: »The station building in Te-chou looks really magnificent. It is built in the modern German style but with a touch of Chinese influence. Simple means have been employed to achieve truly great effects and the atmosphere created is balm to the European eye. It must be handed to those who built this railway that they have achieved an enormous amount in aesthetic terms. No station is exactly like the next. Each has its own stylistic features and is adapted to fit in with its surroundings.«[230]

British authors also recognised the architectural quality of the rural stations, although they considered the care taken with the design to be too costly: »The German stations are in many respects certainly handsome to behold, and the design is carried down to the out-buildings, the water towers, and even the pointsmen's huts. The roofs are of red tiles, and the design differs with almost every station, but in the main Chinese ideas have been utilised to leaven European notions, and the result is harmonious in most cases. The graceful curved gables of China have been adopted in most of the first class stations and give an effective finish. But all are infinitely too expensively built for the purpose they are destined to serve.«[231]

Whilst the two stations in the cities of Tianjin and Jinan were both in terms of quality and scale comparable to railway stations in cities in Germany, an attempt was made to adapt the rural stations to Chinese architecture. Perhaps the intention was to try and convince the initially very sceptical population of the new means of transport. Chinese architectural forms had also been used for the rural stations on the Shantung Railway built between 1900 and 1904.

津浦鐵路沿線中小火車站

所在地：滄州，天津以南一百二十一公里
　　　　南霞口，天津以南一百六十公里
　　　　德州，天津以南二百二十五公里
　　　　平原，天津以南二百六十八公里
設計：德國工程師
施工：津浦鐵路公司
業主：中國鐵路局
建造期：一九零八至一九一二年
現狀：建築物已不存在。

設計師在設計這些車站時注意適應中國的建築形式。所有這些建築均為磚石結構，覆以紅色瓦頂，令人刮目相看。一時間，各種評論紛紛見諸報端。如《德文新報》中有過這樣一段描述"德州火車站氣勢雄偉，具現代德國風格，又不失中國建築的特點。用料質樸，卻頗具效果，非常符合歐洲人的情趣。從美學角度來說，必須承認，建築師的確成績斐然。這些車站建築各具特點，風格迥異，與周圍環境渾然一體。"〈230〉

英國作者雖然對這些車站的建築質量予以首肯，卻認為如此精細的設計未免過於奢糜："就很多方面而言，德國人的火車站的確非常氣派，大多甚至設有副樓，水塔，乃至護站工的站房。車站皆覆紅色瓦頂，然外觀又各不相同。建築形式以中國風格為主，同時採用歐洲建築的處理手法，令人賞心悅目。較大的火車站使用中國式曲線優美的山牆形式，屋頂處理得極富效果。但是，就其用途用而言，這些火車站的造價未免過高。"〈231〉

如果説天津、濟南兩座火車站在設計的規模、質量上都類同於德國的都市火車站，那麼，滄州等地的車站則試圖與中國建築相適應。這一作法意在取得民眾對鐵路這一新興運輸形式的信任感。起初，中國人對鐵路不是不無疑慮的。德國工程師在一九零零年至一九零四年修築山東鐵路時，就已注意使車站的建築式樣與中國的建築形式相適應。

滄州火車站，約一九一二年。
德州火車站，約一九一二年。
平原火車站，約一九一二年。
南霞口火車站，約一九一一年。

LUOKOU

HUANG HE EISENBAHNBRÜCKE
HWANG HO RAILWAY BRIDGE

Luokou (Lokou), nahe Jinan (Tsinanfu), etwa 345 km südlich von Tianjin
Luokou (Lokou), near Jinan (Tsinanfu), approx. 345 km south of Tianjin

Entwurf. Design
M.A.N. Augsburg-Nürnberger AG, Werk Gustavsburg
M.A.N. Augsburg-Nürnberger AG, Gustavsburg works

Bauleitung. Site architect
Julius Dorpmüller; Borkowetz

Baukosten. Building costs
13 000 000 Goldmark
13 000 000 gold marks

Bauherr. Client
Chinese Government Railways

Ausführung. Contractor
M.A.N. Augsburg-Nürnberger AG, Werk Gustavsburg
M.A.N. Augsburg-Nürnberger AG, Gustavsburg works

Bauzeit. Construction time
März 1909 – November 1912
March 1909 – November 1912

Zustand. Condition
Das Bauwerk ist gut erhalten, westlich der alten Brücke wurde eine neue Bahnbrücke gebaut.
Structure well preserved, to the west of the old bridge a new bridge was built which is now used by the railway.

Perspektivzeichnung, um 1909
Eisenbahnbrücke, 1912
Perspective drawing, around 1909
Railway Bridge, 1912

Der Huang He (Hoangho), der Gelbe Fluß, war der Wasserlauf Chinas, der die schlimmsten Überschwemmungen verursachte. Seine mitgeführten Schlammassen waren zwar fruchtbar, doch lagerten sie sich im Flußbett ab und ließen ihn über die Dämme treten. Zuletzt hat der etwa 5 500 km lange Strom im Jahre 1852 seinen Verlauf weitläufig geändert.[232] Er mündet jetzt nördlich der Shandong-Halbinsel ins Bohai-Meer, zuvor lag seine Mündung 400 km weit entfernt, in der Provinz Jiangsu. Im Laufe der Jahre hatte er Namen wie »Chinas Kummer« oder »der Unregierbare« erhalten.

Das Wissen um die Unberechenbarkeit des Stroms ließ die chinesischen Auftraggeber keine Kosten bei der Planung und dem Bau der Brücke sparen. So mußte der erste Entwurf, der mehr Pfeiler im Flußbett vorsah, völlig überarbeitet werden. Dafür nahm man eine Verzögerung der Bauzeit um ein Jahr in Kauf, weil man befürchtete, die vielen Brückenpfeiler würden den Stromquerschnitt zu sehr verengen und zu Überschwemmungen führen. Bei dem neuen Entwurf hatten die einzelnen Bögen größere Spannweiten, benötigten dadurch weniger Pfeiler im Flußbett. Die Strombrücke bestand aus zwei Bögen von je 128 Metern Stützweite und einer Mittelöffnung von 165 Metern Stützweite. Neun Flutbrücken mit je 91 Metern Stützweite gaben der Brücke eine Gesamtlänge von 1255 Metern. Die Flutbrücken waren als Parallelträger ausgebildet, die Strombrücke war als Auslegerträger ausgebildet, und das eingehängte Mittelfeld hatte eine Stützweite von 110 Metern. Die Brücke war einspurig, aber bereits vorbereitet für einen zweispurigen Ausbau. Die bestehende Tragkonstruktion mußte nur durch Ergänzung eines weiteren Trägers an jeweils den Außenseiten verstärkt werden; der Zugverkehr wäre durch diese Umbauarbeiten nicht behindert worden.

Die Huang He Brücke war damals die Brücke mit der größten Spannweite in Asien, man verglich sie mit der »Forth Bridge« in Schottland.[233]

The Huang He, the Yellow River, was the river which had caused the worst floods in China. The muds carried by it were fertile but they were deposited on the river bed and caused it to burst its damns. The Province of Shandong experienced terrible flood disasters. The 5 500 km long river had last changed its course significantly in 1852.[232] It now runs into the Bohai Sea to the north of the Shandong Peninsula, previously its estuary was 400 kilometres to the south, in the neighbouring Province of Jiangsu. Over the years it had been called names such as »China's Sorrow« or »the Ungovernable.«

The knowledge about the unpredictable nature of the river meant that the Chinese client spared no costs in the planning and construction of the bridge. For example, the first scheme, which had more piers in the riverbed, had to be completely revised. This meant accepting a delay in construction time of one year. They were afraid that the large number of piers would reduce the width of the current too much and cause flooding. In the new scheme the individual arches had wider spans, so that fewer piers in the river bed were required. The bridge spanning the river consisted of two arches, each with an effective span of 128 metres, and a central opening 165 metres wide. Nine side arches, each 91 metres wide, meant that the bridge was 1 255 metres long in total. The side arches took the form of parallel girders, the bridge spanning the river was a cantilever girder and the suspended central section had a width of 110 metres. The bridge was single track, but the distance between the girders and the foundations of the piers were designed in a way that it would be possible to add a second track. The existing girders would only have to be strengthened by the addition of another girder on either side; the trains could thus continue to run unhindered during these works.

The Huang He Bridge was designated the bridge with the longest span in Asia, it was compared to the Forth Bridge in Scotland.[233]

黃河鐵路大橋透視圖，約一九零九年。
黃河鐵路大橋，一九一二年。

黃河鐵路大橋

所在地：洛口，濟南附近，天津以南三百四十五公里
設計：奧格斯堡—紐倫堡Ｍ・Ａ・Ｎ・有限公司・古斯塔夫堡工廠
工程指導：尤利烏斯・多普未勒，博庫維茨
建築造價：一千三百萬金馬克
業主：中國鐵路局
施工：奧格斯堡紐倫堡Ｍ・Ａ・Ｎ・有限公司・Ｍ・古斯塔夫堡工廠
建造期：一九零三年三月至一九一二年十一月
現狀：大橋狀況良好。老橋以西架起一座新橋，供火車行駛。

黃河是中國的一條大河，它所裹攜的大量泥漿雖土質肥沃，但累積於河床之上，長年累月，淤泥高出河堤從而導致洪災。山東省歷遭大型洪災劫難。這條長約五千五百公里的大河於一八五二年最後一次大大地改變了河道，[232]現在山東半島的北部匯入渤海。改道前，其入海口位於山東省的南鄰江蘇省，河道北移了四百公里。歷史上黃河素有"中國之憂患"、"不可治理之河"的別稱。

該大橋的業主中國鐵路局雖然了解黃河反復無常的習性，但這並未能為其節約造橋的設計費和施工費。最初的方案由於在河床中設計了過多的橋墩而必須予以修改，開工時間因此而滯後一年。人們擔心橋墩多會縮小河流橫截面，導致洪災。新方案加寬了各橋拱的跨距以減少河床中橋墩數量。河水橋由一寬一百六十五米的主跨及兩個跨距各為一百二十八米的橋拱組成。九座洪水橋跨度各為九十一米。全橋總長一千二百五十五米。洪水橋成平行樑結構；河水橋成縣臂樑結構，中間的懸浮跨度為一百一十米。大橋是單軌的，但可擴建成二十二軌，因各樑之間及橋墩基礎之間的距離正是為此目的而設計的。這只須在現有樑結構外側再各加一根樑，以加固原樑。橋樑擴軌並不影響火車的運行。黃河大橋是當時亞洲跨度最大的橋樑，可與蘇格蘭的"福斯灣大橋"相媲美。[233]

SHANDONG

LANDBAHNHÖFE DER
SCHANTUNG-EISENBAHN
RURAL STATIONS ON THE
SHANTUNG RAILWAY

Gaomi (Kaumi),
107 km westlich von Qingdao
Zhoucun (Tschoutsun),
320 km westlich von Qingdao
Pinglingcheng (Lungschan),
378 km westlich von Qingdao
Guodian (Kotien),
389 km westlich von Qingdao
Ostbahnhof in Jinan (Tsinanfu),
406 km westlich von Qingdao
Gaomi (Kaumi),
107 km west of Qingdao
Zhoucun (Tschoutsun),
320 km west of Qingdao
Pinglingcheng (Lungschan),
378 km west of Qingdao
Guodian (Kotien),
389 km west of Qingdao
Jinan East Station (Tsinanfu),
406 km west of Qingdao
Entwurf. Design
Deutsche Ingenieure
German engineers
Bauherr. Client
Schantung-Eisenbahn-Gesellschaft
Shantung Railway Company
Bauzeit. Construction time
zwischen 1899 und 1904
between 1899 and 1904
Zustand. Condition
Die Gebäude existieren nicht mehr.
No longer exist.

Eisenbahnbrücke über den Jiao he, 1901
Bahnhof Gaomi, 1901
Bahnhof Zhoucun, um 1905
Bahnhof Guodian, um 1905
Bahnhof Jinan-Ost, um 1905
Railway Bridge over the Jiao he
(Kiao ho), 1901
Gaomi Station, 1901
Zhoucun Station, around 1905
Guodian Station, around 1905
Jinan East Station, around 1905

Die Eisenbahn von Qingdao nach Jinan hatte auf ihrer 412 km langen Strecke 64 Haltestellen. Alle Gebäude der Bahnlinie waren aus Backsteinen hergestellt. In den Gegenden, in denen Naturstein kostengünstig war, ließ man die Sockel aus Bruchsteinen, die Ecken, Fensterbänke und Gesimse in Werkstein aus-

führen. In den eingeschossigen Gebäuden blieben die Dachsparren sichtbar. Die Dächer sollten denen chinesischer Tempel gleichen. So wurden die Dachtraufen mit besonders geformten chinesischen Traufziegeln verziert, die beispielsweise Blumenmuster oder das chinesiche Glückszeichen trugen. Die Dachfirste wurden ebenfalls denen der Tempel nachgebildet und endeten wie die Giebelgesimse in Drachenköpfen und Drachengestalten.
Die meisten Empfangsgebäude hatten einen Warteraum, ein Dienstzimmer und eine Wohnung für den chinesischen Stationsbeamten, die zumeist nur aus einem Zimmer und der Küche bestand. In größeren Bahnhöfen gab es außerdem einen Gepäckraum und zusätzliche Warteräume. Einige der Bahnhofsgebäude waren auch zweistöckig, damit mehrere Beamte dort wohnen konnten.[236]

There were 64 stops on the 412 kilometre-long railway from Qingdao to Jinan. All the buildings along the railway line were in brick. In the areas where natural stone was abundant the bases of the buildings were made of rough stone and the quoins, window sills and cornices of ashlar. Virtually all the buildings were single storey and without ceilings so that the rafters were visible from below. The roofs were intended to look like those of a Chinese temple. The eaves were therefore decorated with specially shaped tiles which had flower patterns or the Chinese symbol for luck. The ridges were also often modelled on temple roofs and, like the cornices on the gables, terminated in dragons or dragons' heads.
Most of the terminal buildings contained a waiting room, an office and a flat for the Chinese stationmaster which usually consisted of one room and a kitchen. In larger stations there was also a luggage room and additional waiting rooms. Some of the station buildings were also two-storeys high so that all the railway officials could be accommodated.[236]

膠濟鐵路沿線中小火車站

所在地：高密，青島以西一百零七公里
　　　　周村，青島以西三百二十公里
　　　　平陵城，青島以西三百七十八公里
　　　　郭店，青島以西三百八十九公里
　　　　濟南東站，青島以西四百零六公里
設計：德國工程師
業主：山東鐵路公司
建造期：一八九九年至一九零四年
現狀：建築體已不存在。

膠濟長四百一十二公里，沿途有六十四個停靠站，所有建築都是磚砌牆身。在天然石料便宜的地區，牆基多用碎石砌成，拐角、窗台和裝飾線則用粗石砌成。這些小站幾乎都是平房，房內不做天花板，屋椽清晰可見。屋頂類似於中國的廟宇建築，檐口飾造型別致的中式檐瓦，上有花卉圖案或中國吉祥物。屋脊也多模仿廟宇建築，兩端象山牆裝飾線一樣，飾以龍頭或龍形圖案。
大多數車站內設候車室，辦公室和中國護站員工住房各一間。較大的火車站內還有一間行李房和附加候車室。也有幾座兩層樓的車站，附設可容納車站全體員工的宿舍。〈236〉

高密火車站，一九零一年。
周村火車站，約一九零五年。
郭店火車站，約一九零五年。
濟南火車站，約一九零五年。
膠河鐵路橋，一九零一年。

YANZHOU

BISCHOFSRESIDENZ UND KATHEDRALE
BISHOP'S RESIDENCE AND CATHEDRAL

Heutige Funktion. Current use
Chinesische katholische Kirche
Chinese Catholic Church
Libaisi Jie/Xiqiaonan
(Moslemstraße/Glockenturmstraße),
Yanzhou (Jenchoufu, Yen-chou-fu)

Architekt. Architect
Pater Heinrich Erlemann SVD
Father Heinrich Erlemann,
Societas Verbi Divini

Bauherr. Client
Steyler Missionsgesellschaft,
Bischof J. B. von Anzer
Steyler Missionary Society,
Bishop J. B. von Anzer

Bauzeit. Construction time
Kathedrale 1898–1904,
Bischofsresidenz 1901
Cathedral 1898–1904,
Bishop's Residence 1901

Zustand. Condition
Die Bischofsresidenz und das Priesterseminargebäude sind gut erhalten; die Kathedrale wurde während der Kulturrevolution (1966–1976) abgetragen.
Bishop's Residence and priests' seminary well preserved; cathedral torn down during the cultural revolution (1966–1976)

Bischofsresidenz in Yanzhou, Südansicht, um 1902
Kathedrale in Yanzhou, Ostansicht, um 1905
Bishop's Residence in Yanzhou, view from the south, around 1902
Cathedral in Yanzhou, view from the east, around 1905

Bischof von Anzer leitete die katholische Mission in Südshandong seit 1882. Um nahe der Stadt Qufu (Kü-fu) zu sein, dem Geburtsort des Philosophen Konfuzius und Wohnsitz seiner Nachfahren und vieler Gelehrter, wollte von Anzer eine Missionsstation in der benachbarten Stadt Yanzhou eröffnen. Dies wurde lange durch die chinesischen Beamten verhindert. Erst Ende 1896 konnte die Mission hier ein Grundstück erwerben. Yanzhou wurde zur Missionszentrale der Steyler Missionsgesellschaft.

Nach der Ermordung der beiden Missionare am 1. November 1897 wurde zwei Wochen später die Bucht von Jiaozhou (Kiautschou) durch die deutsche Marine besetzt. Auch die katholische Mission stellte Wiedergutmachungsforderungen. Von der chinesischen Regierung verlangte Bischof von Anzer unter anderem etwa 200 000 Goldmark zum Bau einer Sühnekirche in Yanzhou.

Im *Ostasiatischen Lloyd* wurde die Kathedrale während der Bauzeit beschrieben: »Die Kirche ist eine dreischiffige, gotische Kreuzkirche, 53 Meter lang und 18 Meter breit. (…) Man kann sich denken, daß es keine kleine Arbeit war, im Innern Chinas, wohin niemals vorher europäische Kultur gedrungen ist, einen solchen Bau auszuführen. Die Chinesen kennen z. B. den Gewölbebau nicht.[245] Und doch hat Pater Erlemann es fertig gebracht, ein untadliges Gewölbe zu bauen. Die Kirche ist bis zum Schlußstein der Gewölbe 14 Meter hoch. Die 20 Säulen (fünf Meter hoch) sind Monolithen, die Kapitelle (1,80 m) sind mit Blumenwerk verziert. Säulen, Fenster, Treppen, Gewölberippen sind aus Stein, während der ganze übrige Bau aus Ziegeln besteht. Es gelang dem Pater, mit Hilfe eines Laienbruders auch bunte glasierte Ziegel selbst herzustellen und damit Gesimse und Pfeilerrippen etc. mit grünen, roten und gelben Farben zu zieren. Das Dach hat rote, glasierte Pfannen, die Wasserspeier (in Drachengestalt) sind ebenfalls aus glasiertem Ton gebrannt. Unter dem Altarpodium ist eine recht geräumige, gewölbte Krypta angelegt.

Bishop von Anzer had been the head of the Catholic Mission in South Shandong since 1882. In order to be near the city of Qufu (Kü-fu), the birthplace of Confucius, still inhabited by his descendants and many learned men, Bishop von Anzer wanted to open a missionary station in the neighbouring city of Yanzhou. For a long time this was prevented by Chinese officials. Not until the end of 1896 was the mission able to acquire a plot of land here. Yanzhou became the headquarters of the Steyler Missionary Society.

Two weeks after the murder of two missionaries on 1 November 1897 the German Navy occupied the Bay of Jiaozhou (Kiaochow). The Catholic Mission also demanded compensation. One of the things Bishop von Anzer asked for from the Chinese government was approximately 200 000 gold marks to build a church of atonement in Yanzhou.

Ostasiatischer Lloyd describes the cathedral during construction: »The church is a triple-naved, Gothic cruciform church, 53 metres long and 18 metres wide. (…) You can imagine that it was no small feat to build such a building in the interior of China in a place so far untouched by European culture. The Chinese, for example, are completely unfamiliar with vaulted buildings.[245] And yet, Father Erlemann has managed to build an impeccable vault. The church is 14 metres high to the keystone. The 20 columns (five metres high) are monoliths, the capitals (1.80 metres) are decorated with floral work. Columns, windows, stairs, vault ribs are in stone, whilst the rest of the building is in brick. The father managed with the help of a lay brother to manufacture coloured glazed bricks himself which he used to decorate the cornices and ribs of the piers in green, red and yellow. The roof has red glazed pantiles, the gargoyles (dragon figures) are also in glazed clay. Under the altar steps is a spacious, vaulted crypt. Due to Chinese superstition it was unfortunately not possible to build the seven towers very high, because the Chinese believes that fortune sits tight on the highest building.«[246]

兗州主教府邸南立面，約一九零二年。
兗州大教堂東立面，約一九零五年。

主教府邸、大教堂

現用途：中國天主教堂
所在地：兗州第六中學附近，原回回巷（鐘樓街口）
建築師：恩博仁、神甫
業主：聖言會J‧B‧安治泰主教
建造期：教堂：一八九八年至一九零四年
主教府邸：一九零一年
現狀：主教府邸和教士神學院大樓保存完好，大教堂於文革期間一九六六至一九七六年被拆除。

自一八八二年起，安治泰主教主持山東南部的基督教傳教站。為了靠近曲阜——思想家孔夫子的誕生地及其后裔和許多文人墨客的家鄉，安治泰想在曲阜的鄰城兗州設立一座傳教站。由於清朝政府的長期阻礙，一八九六年底，傳教會才在兗州得到一片地產。兗州從此便成了聖言會的傳教中心。

一八九七年十一月一日，兩位傳教士遇害。兩星期後，德國海軍占領膠州灣。基督教傳教會也提出了賠償要求。安治泰主教要求清政府出資約二十萬金馬克（合銀元六千六百兩），在兗州建造一座賠償禮拜堂。

施工期間，《德文新報》載文描述了這座大教堂："該堂為哥特式十字形三廊堂，長五十三米寬十八米。……可以想象，在從未接觸過西洋文化的中國內地建造這樣一座教堂，絕非易事。例如，中國人不了解拱形建築。"(245) 然而，恩博仁神甫造出的穹窿卻使人無可非議。教堂拱頂高十四米。二十根五米之高的楹柱用整塊石料做成，柱頭高一點八米，上刻花卉圖案。楹柱，窗戶，樓梯，拱肋用石砌成，其他部分則為磚體。在一位教友的幫助下，恩博仁神甫成功地做出了五顏六色的琉璃瓦，並用綠、紅、黃三色裝飾檐板、楹柱的筋條等處。屋頂覆紅色波形琉璃瓦，（龍形）滴水嘴也是用釉土燒制而成的。祭台下設一寬敞的拱形地下室。由於中國人迷信，七座塔樓不能做得很高。中國人認為，幸運附著於最高的建築上。"(246)

教堂舉行落成典禮之前，又有如下文字描述了教堂內部的情況："祭壇室的大窗及

YANZHOU

Säulenkapitell der zerstörten Kathedrale, 1992
Säulenkapitell an der ehem. Bischofsresidenz, 1992
Südansicht der ehem. Bischofsresidenz, 1992
Veranda auf der Südseite der ehem. Bischofsresidenz, 1992
Capital on column of the destroyed cathedral, 1992
Capital on column in the former Bishop's Residence, 1992
Former Bishop's Residence, view from the south, 1992
Veranda on the south façade, 1992

Die sieben Türme konnten leider des chinesischen Aberglaubens halber nicht sehr hoch gebaut werden, weil der Chinese glaubt, das Glück setze sich auf den höchsten Gebäuden fest.«²⁴⁶

Kurz vor der Einweihung wurde der Innenraum erneut beschrieben: »Die großen Fenster des Chores sind mit prächtigen Glasmalereien ausgeschmückt, ebenso auch die unteren Seitenfenster; die oberen Seitenfenster weisen nur Teppichmuster auf. Auch die Dekoration des Gewölbes und der Innenwände, (…) ist recht hübsch, zumal am sternenbesäten Gewölbe. An den Seitenwänden wurde vielleicht dem chinesischen Geschmacke – nämlich recht bunt – etwas viel Rechnung getragen.«²⁴⁷

Shortly before it was consecrated the cathedral was described once more: »The large windows of the choir are decorated with splendid stained glass, as are the lower side windows; the upper side windows have only a pattern like a carpet. The decoration of the vaults and the interior walls (…) is also very pretty, particularly the star-spangled vault. On the side walls a little too much account was perhaps taken of the Chinese taste – namely for very bright colours.«²⁴⁷

被毀的大教堂所采用的柱頭，一九九二年。
原主教府邸柱頭細部一九九二年。

原主教府邸南立面，一九九二年。
原主教府邸南西敞廊，一九九二年。

下部的側窗都飾有華麗的玻璃畫，上部側窗的圖案則為象地毯一樣的花樣。拱頂和內牆的裝飾非常華美。尤其是綴滿繁星的拱頂簡直美不勝收。側牆則五彩斑斕，以符合中國人的欣賞可習慣。"（247）

JINING

**KIRCHE UND SCHULE
»FRANZ-XAVER-KOLLEG«
CHURCH AND SCHOOL
»FRANZ XAVER COLLEGE«**

Taibailou Zhonglu/Nanbaizhaojia Jie,
Jining (Tsing-tschou)

Entwurf. Design
Pater Heinrich Erlemann SVD
Father Heinrich Erlemann,
Societas Verbi Divini (SVD)

Bauleitung. Site Architect
Pater Heinrich Erlemann SVD
Father Heinrich Erlemann SVD

Bauherr. Client
Steyler Missionsgesellschaft,
Bischof J. B. von Anzer
Steyler Missionary Society,
Bishop J. B. von Anzer

Bauzeit. Construction time
Kirche 1895–1898, Schule 1914
Church 1895–1898, school 1914

Zustand. Condition
Die gesamte Anlage existiert nicht mehr.
The entire complex no longer exists.

Franz-Xaver-Kolleg,
Westansicht, um 1915
Kirche in Jining,
Westansicht, um 1905
Innenraum der Kirche, 1900
Franz Xaver College,
view from the west, around 1915
Church in Jining, view from the
west, around 1905
Interior, 1900

Jining war damals ein wichtiges Handelszentrum am Kaiserkanal mit über 500 000 Einwohnern. Im Gegensatz zu Yanzhou, entwickelte sich zwischen der Mission und den Gelehrten und reichen Kaufleuten der Stadt bald ein freundschaftliches Verhältnis. Der damalige Mandarin, der höchste chinesiche Beamte, ermöglichte sogar den Kauf eines Grundstücks innerhalb der Stadt.[248] 1891 wurde das große Missionsgrundstück gekauft. Es lag in der Akademiestraße nahe der Stadtmauer, gleich neben einer großen Tempelanlage. Außer der Kirche wurden hier die Residenz des Bischofs und Wohnungen für die Missionare errichtet. Die Mission blieb von dem Ansturm während des Boxeraufstands im Jahre 1899 verschont. Einflußreiche Bürger Jinings waren der Mission freundlich gesonnen und hatten gegenüber den Boxern vermittelnd gewirkt.

Im Zentrum der Missionsstation befand sich die neogotische Kirche. »Die Kirche hatte einen ganz eigenen Stil. Um nicht gegen die Landessitte zu verstoßen, wurde sie sehr niedergedrückt und hatte dabei doch gotische Formen, mit chinesischen Zutaten gleichsam einen gotisch-chinesischen Stil.« An den großen Kapitellen der 14 monolithischen Säulen waren Blumenmuster eingemeißelt.[249]

1902 wurde das »Franz-Xaver-Kolleg«, die damals größte deutsche katholische Missionsschule Chinas eröffnet. 1913 erhielt die Schule die staatliche Anerkennung und war den chinesischen Staatsschulen gleichgestellt. Im Frühjahr 1914 hatte die Schule 190 Schüler, die aus mehr als 30 Landkreisen stammten. Die meisten kamen aus der Provinz Shandong, der Rest aus Hebei und Henan. In den oberen Klassen wurde auch die deutsche Sprache gelehrt. Im gleichen Jahr baute man ein neues dreigeschossiges Schulgebäude, das eine Grundfläche von 35 Metern mal 16 Meter hatte. Damit konnten 300 bis 400 Schüler aufgenommen werden.[250]

At the time Jining was an important trade centre on the Imperial Canal with over 500 000 inhabitants. Unlike in Yanzhou, a friendly relationship soon developed here between the mission and the learned men and rich merchants of the city. The mandarin of the time, the highest Chinese official, even made it possible for the mission to acquire a piece of land within the city limits.[248] In 1891 the large plot for the mission was purchased. It was on Akademie Strasse, near the city walls, next to a large temple complex. Apart from the church the Bishop's Residence and living quarters for the missionaries were also built here. The mission was not stormed during the Boxers' Uprising in 1899. Influential citizens of Jining were kindly disposed to the mission and had mediated with the Boxers.

The neo-Gothic church was in the centre of the mission station. »The church had a quite individual style. In order to avoid offending the customs of the land it was built very low and yet still retained Gothic forms with additional Chinese elements so that a sort of Sino-Gothic style was created.« Floral patterns were cut into the large capitals on the 14 monolithic columns.[249]

In 1902 the »Franz Xaver College«, the largest German Catholic missionary school in China, was opened. In 1913 the school gained official state recognition and enjoyed the same status as the Chinese state schools. In 1914 the school had 190 pupils, who came from over 30 districts of China. Most came from the Province of Shandong, the rest from Hebei and Henan. In the higher classes German was also taught. A new three-storey school building was built which had a surface area of 35 × 16 metres. This meant that there was room for between 300 and 400 pupils.[250]

教堂、聖方濟各沙勾略修院

所在地：濟寧太白樓（南北晁家街街口）
設計：恩博仁，神甫
工程指導：恩博仁，神甫
業主：聖言會J‧B‧安治泰，主教
建造期：教堂：一八九五年至一八九八年
修院：一九一四年
現狀：整個建築群已不存在

濟寧是大運河畔的一座重要商業中心，人口逾五十萬。與兗州的情況相反，傳教站與當地的文人、富商之間很快便形式了一種友好的關係。清朝的一位高官甚至幫助傳教站在城內購進一片地產。〈248〉這一大片產業置於一八九一年。座落在學院街上，緊鄰一座龐大的廟宇離城牆很近。這里建起了一座教堂，一所主教宅邸和幾套傳教士住房。一八九九年，義和團運動爆發，傳教站卻免受沖擊。這是因為當地有影響的市民對傳教站懷有善意，從中幹旋的結果。

這座教堂屬哥特式復古風格，位於傳教站中心。"教堂風格獨特。為了尊重當地習俗，教堂高度壓低，但仍保持哥特風格，並揉以中國建築式樣，呈現出中國式的哥特風格。"十四根楹柱用整塊石料做成，粗大的柱頭上鑿有花卉圖案。〈249〉

一九零二年，當時德國在中國最大天主教傳教學校—聖方濟各沙勾略修院開學。一九一三年，該校獲官方承認，與中國的國立學校享有同等權利。一九一四年，該校在校學生一百九十人。他們分別來自三十多個地區，其中大多數為山東人，也有河北人、河南人，高年級設德語課。後又建有一座三層樓的校舍，平面長三十五米，寬十六米。學校可招收學生三至四百名。〈250〉

聖方濟各沙勿略院西面外觀，約一九一五年。
濟寧教堂西面外貌，約一九零五年。
教堂內部，一九零零年。

MISSIONSSTATION TAIKIA
TAIKIA MISSION STATION

Heutige Funktion. Current use
Jining Medical Hospital and Mental College;
Teaching Center for Mental Health
Daijia Zhuang, drei Kilometer nördlich von
Jining (Stadtteil Taikia, Ta-chia,
Dä-tja, Taikaichwang)
Daijia Zhuang, three kilometres north of
Jining (Taikia, Ta-chia, Dä-tja, Taikaichwang).

Entwurf. Design
Pater Heinrich Erlemann SVD
Father Heinrich Erlemann SVD

Bauherr. Client
Steyler Missionsgesellschaft
Steyler Missionary Society

Bauzeit. Construction time
Kirche 1911–1912, Exerzitienhaus 1914
Church 1911–1912, retreat centre 1914

Zustand. Condition
Die gesamte Anlage ist sehr gut erhalten.
Entire complex very well preserved.

Die Steyler Missionsgesellschaft konnte 1897 einen großen Park von einer verarmten Beamtenfamilie kaufen.[251] Daijia war fast einen Quadratkilometer groß und wurde Sitz des Provinzoberen der Steyler Missionsgesellschaft. Während des Sommers fanden hier die Exerzitien für die europäischen und chinesischen Brüder und Priester statt.

In den Jahren 1911/12 wurde eine dreischiffige Kirche mit über 400 Sitzplätzen nach den Plänen von Pater Erlemann, 1914 ein großes Exerzitienhaus erbaut. In diesem Gebäude befanden sich eine Privatkapelle, ein Speisesaal, zwei Rekreationssäle, zwei Rekreationshallen für den Sommer, 30 Zimmer sowie Nebenräume. Man plante das Gebäude so, daß für eine eventuell notwendige Erweiterung ein gleichgroßer Bau angefügt werden konnte.[252]

Beim Kauf des Geländes war der einstmals überaus prächtige Park, angelegt nach dem Vorbild der kaiserlichen Gärten in Beijing, verwildert und seine Häuser befanden sich in schlechtem Zustand. Doch bereits nach kurzer Zeit wurde der Garten zum schönsten Ort in der Mission. Im Park gab es einen Teich mit einer Insel, darauf ein Pavillon, viele seltene Pflanzen, weitläufige Hofhausanlagen mit reichen Schnitzereien. Ausführlich wird dieser riesige chinesische Garten von einem Pater beschrieben: »Wir gehen durch eine große, reichgeschnitzte Türe weiter und stehen in einem ganz von Gitterwänden umschlossenen kleinen Raum, einem chinesischen Teepavillon. Schaut man von hier aus nach Westen, so hat man den schönsten Teil des Gartens vor sich, die Felsenpartie, von hohen, seltenen Bäumen bestanden, und auf der Spitze eines Felsens sehen wir einen schönen Bergpavillon.«[253] Am 17. November 1897 wurden hier die beiden ermordeten Missionare Nies und Henle beigesetzt.

In 1897 the Steyler Missionary Society was able to purchase a large park from a Chinese official and his family who had fallen on hard times.[251] Daijia was almost one square kilometre and became the centre for the head of the Steyler Missionary Society in the province. During the summer the European and Chinese brothers and priests came here for spiritual exercises.

In 1911/1912 a triple-naved church to seat over 400 was built to plans by Father Erlemann and in 1914 a large retreat centre was built. This building housed a private chapel, dining room, two recreation rooms, two recreation halls for the summer, 30 rooms and ancillary rooms and a tower. The building was planned in a way that would make it possible to add another building of the same size should the need arise.[252]

When the land was bought the park, which had once been magnificent, modelled on the Imperial Gardens in Beijing, was overgrown and its buildings were in a bad state. However, after only a short time the garden became the most beautiful place in the mission. It had a pond which had an island with a pavilion on it, many rare plants, rambling courtyard houses with lavish wood carvings. This immense Chinese garden was extensively described by a father: »We walk through a large, wonderfully carved door and stand in a small room completely surrounded by railings, a Chinese tea house. Looking to the west you see the most beautiful part of the garden before you, the crags with their tall, rare trees and on the top of one of the crags is a lovely mountain pavilion.«[253] On 17 November 1897 the two missionaries who were murdered, Nies and Henle, were buried here.

Exerzitienhaus in Daijia, Südansicht, 1914
Kirche in Daijia, Nordansicht, 1912
Spiritual retreat centre in Daijia, view from the south, 1914
Church in Daijia, view from the north, 1912

戴家庄傳教站

現用途：濟寧醫院學附屬醫院，濟寧精神
　　　　病學院，濟寧精神康復康教育中
　　　　心
所在地：戴家庄，濟寧以北三公里
設計：恩博仁，神甫
業主：聖言會
建造期：教堂：一九一一年至一九一二
　　　　年；祈禱樓：一九一四年
現狀：整個建築群保存完好。

一八九七年，聖言會從一破落的官宦文家買進一座大花園。〈251〉戴家花園占地約一平方公里，它成了聖言會山東傳教長的駐地。夏天，歐洲和中國的教友及教士在這裡進行祈禱練習。

一九一一年至一九一二年間，聖言會在所置地產上建起了一座有四百多個座席的三廊教堂，設計者為恩博仁神甫。一九一四年又增建一幢祈禱大樓，內設一私人小教堂，一處餐廳，兩間活動室，兩所夏季用活動大廳，三十間正房和附屬房間，一座保護塔。根據恩博仁的設計，樓房在必要情況下可成信擴建。〈252〉

當時買下的這座花園原是按照北京皇家花園的模式設計的，曾一度華麗無比。花園易主時，這裡卻是一片荒蕪，房屋破舊失修。然而，時隔不久，這裡便成了傳教站最美的地方。園內的一池碧水擁著一片島嶼，上有一方翠亭。園內栽種了很多稀有植物。四合院寬敞宜人，門窗上雕有大量圖案。恩博仁神甫曾對這座中國式大花園作了詳盡描述："我們穿過一扇雕花大門，步入一座花格牆圍就的中國菜館。由此西望，可見園內最美的景致：假山上稀有樹木昂首向天，山頂聳立著一座漂亮的翠亭。"〈253〉一八九七年十一月十七日，兩名遇害的傳教士能方濟和韓理葬於此地。

戴家庄傳教站祈禱樓南面外觀，
一九一四年。
戴家庄教堂北立面，一九一二
年。

JINAN

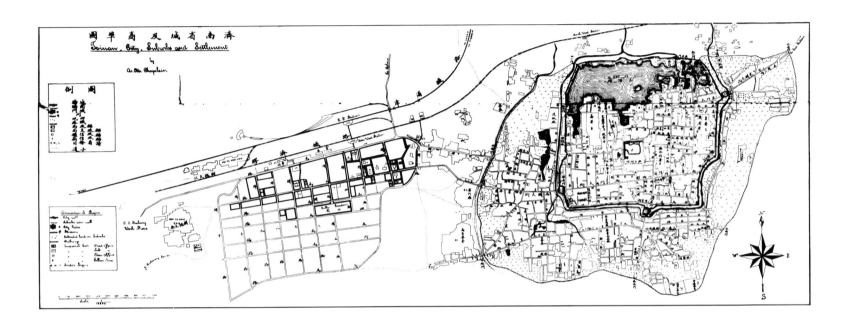

JINAN (TSINANFU)

Jinan ist die Hauptstadt der Provinz Shandong und Sitz der Provinzregierung. Die Einwohnerzahl betrug 1914 etwa 300 000. Die chinesische Stadt war von einer Stadtmauer umgeben, die erst nach 1949 abgetragen wurde. Östlich, außerhalb der Stadt, lag die katholische Mission der Franziskaner, der Endbahnhof der Schantung-Eisenbahn befand sich auf der Westseite. Dieser 1904 erbaute Bahnhof wurde zum Zentrum der ausländischen Handelsniederlassung, die 1906 entstand. Das Deutsche Reich hatte dort bereits 1903 ein Grundstück für sein Konsulat erworben. Das Straßennetz der knapp einen Quadratkilometer großen Handelsniederlassung bildete eine Baublockgröße, die mit dem Qingdaoer Händlerviertel Dabaodao (Tapautau) vergleichbar war. Obwohl die chinesischen Bauvorschriften für die Niederlassung flexibler als im deutschen Schutzgebiet formuliert waren, entstanden die gleichen zweigeschossigen Gebäude wie im Qingdaoer Händlerviertel.222 Nahe dem Westbahnhof der Schantung-Eisenbahn wurde 1912 auch der Zentralbahnhof der Tientsin-Pukow-Eisenbahngesellschaft gebaut sowie deren großes Verwaltungsgebäude.

Die Handelsniederlassung für Ausländer in Jinan wurde von der chinesischen Provinzialregierung 1906 eingerichtet und auch von ihr verwaltet, sie war die erste ihrer Art in China. Durch die wirtschaftliche Konkurrenz anderer Handelsnationen sollte der deutsche Einfluß in Shandong zurückgedrängt werden. Zur gleichen Zeit wurden entlang der Schantung-Eisenbahn zwei weitere Niederlassungsgebiete für Ausländer eröffnet, in den Städten Zhoucun (Chou-tsun) und Weifang (Wei-hsien), 92 km und 216 km von Jinan entfernt. Diese Einrichtungen wurden allerdings nur sehr zögernd durch ausländische Kaufleute angenommen und entwickelten sich langsam.

JINAN (TSINANFU)

Jinan is the capital of the Province of Shandong and the seat of the Provincial Government. In 1914 the number of inhabitants totalled approximately 300 000. The Chinese city was surrounded by town walls which were not demolished until after 1949. To the east, outside the city, was the Catholic Franciscan Mission and on the western side of the city was the terminal of the Shantung Railway. This station, built in 1904, became the centre of the foreign trade settlement which grew up in 1906. The German Reich had already acquired the land for a consulate in 1903. The street network in the trade settlement which barely covered a square kilometre created a size of block which was comparable to that in Dabaodao (Tapautau), the Chinese trader's district of Qingdao. Although the Chinese building regulations for the settlement were more flexible in wording, the same two-storey buildings as in the trader's district of Qingdao grew up.222 The central station for the Tianjin-Nanjing Railway and its largest office building were built in 1912 near to the western station of the Shantung Railway.

The trade settlement for foreigners in Jinan was set up by the Chinese Provincial Government in 1906 and run by it; it was the first of its kind in China. It was intended to push back the German influence in Shandong by allowing other trading nations to build up economic competition. At the same time two more settlement areas for foreigners were opened along the Shantung Railway, in the cities of Zhoucun (Chou-tsun) and Weifang (Wei-hsien), 92 and 216 kilometres from Jinan. Foreign businessmen were very hesitant in accepting these settlements and accordingly they developed quite slowly.

濟南

濟南是山東省省會既省政府所在地。一九一四年，其人口約為三十萬。其城池四周的城牆於一九四年後才被拆除。東郊城外是方濟各會的天主教傳教站。城西是山東鐵路終點站，該站建於一九零四年，後成為於一九零六年形成的外國商埠的中心。早在一九零三年，德意志帝國就在這一帶獲得一片地產以供營建領事館之用。外國商埠區方圓不足一公里，其面積與大鮑島即青島商埠區相當。盡管中國政府所制定的濟南商埠區的較之青島德國保護區內商埠建築條例措詞靈活，這一帶的建築卻仍像青島商埠區一樣，兩層樓房整齊劃一。〈222〉一九一二年，山東鐵路濟南西站附近又增建了津浦鐵路濟南火車站及其最大的車站辦公樓。

濟南的外國商埠區是由中國當時地方省政府於一九零六年設立並為其所管。這在當時中國尚屬首例。此舉意在發展各國之間的商業競爭以限制德國在山東的經濟影響力。與此同時，山東鐵路沿線的周村和濰坊亦開闢了外國商埠區。周村、濰坊分別距濟南九十二公里和二百一六公里。然而，外國商人對此卻遲疑不決，致使這兩處商埠區的發展極為緩慢。

JINAN

ZENTRALBAHNHOF
CENTRAL STATION

Heutige Funktion. Current use
Hauptbahnhof Jinan
Chezhan Jie, Jinan (Tsinanfu),
352 km südlich von Tianjin
Jinan Central Station
Chezhan Jie, Jinan (Tsinanfu),
352 km south of Tianjin

Architekt. Architect
Hermann Fischer[234]

Ausführung. Contractors
Tientsin-Pukow Eisenbahngesellschaft
Tientsin-Pukow Railway Company

Bauherr. Client
Chinese Government Railways

Bauzeit. Construction time
zwischen 1908 und 1912
between 1908 and 1912

Zustand. Condition
Beide Gebäude wurden trotz guten Zustands im Juli 1992 abgetragen.
Despite its good condition, the building was pulled down in July 1992.

Bahnhof der Tianjin-Nanjing-Bahn, Südansicht, 1992
Ehem. Frachtverkehrsgebäude, Blick von Südosten, 1992
Central Station of the Tianjin-Nanjing Railway in Jinan, view from the south, 1992
Former storage and administration building, view from the south-east, 1992

In Jinan, der Hauptstadt der Provinz Shandong, wurde der größte und am aufwendigsten gestaltete Bahnhof der früheren Tientsin-Pukow-Bahn, heute Tianjin-Nanjing-Bahn, errichtet. Nördlich der chinesischen Stadt, die damals noch von einer Mauer umgeben war, verlief die 1904 fertiggestellte Bahnlinie von Qingdao nach Jinan. Sie endete nordwestlich der Stadt. Parallel, in etwa 60 Meter Abstand, wurde zwischen 1908 und 1912 die Tianjin-Nanjing-Bahn erbaut. Die beiden Bahnhöfe lagen sich gegenüber und bildeten die Nordgrenze der erst 1906 eröffneten ausländischen Handelsniederlassung. Die Nähe dieser schnell expandierenden Niederlassung und die dort errichteten europäischen Gebäude waren die passende Umgebung für diesen großen Stadtbahnhof.

Der Zentralbahnhof in Jinan bestand aus zwei Gebäuden. Es gab ein großes Empfangsgebäude mit Schalterhalle, Warteräumen und Büros; in das Gebäude integriert war ein großer Uhrturm, verziert mit Jugendstilornamenten und gedeckt mit grünglasierten Ziegeln. In etwa 70 Meter Entfernung zum Empfangsgebäude lag das große Lager- und Verwaltungsgebäude für den Frachtverkehr. Seine Giebelformen entsprachen denen des Bahnhofs. Zwischen den beiden Bauwerken befanden sich die Kartenkontrolle und der Zugang zu den Gleisen. Die Anlage war der schönste Jugendstilbahnhof Chinas. Die Qualität des Entwurfs konnte jedem Vergleich mit europäischen Bahnhöfen standhalten. Der Architekt, Hermann Fischer, hatte sich mit seinem Entwurf an einem der damals berühmtesten Bahnhöfe Europas orientiert, dem von dem finnischen Architekten Eliel Saarinen gebauten Hauptbahnhof in Helsinki. Saarinens Bahnhof war zwar erst 1911 bis 1913 gebaut worden, doch sein Wettbewerbsentwurf stammte bereits aus dem Jahr 1904 und wurde damals häufig publiziert.

The largest and most elaborately designed station of the former Tientsin-Pukow Railway, now the Tianjin-Nanjing Railway, was built in Jinan, the capital of the Province of Shandong. The railway line from Qingdao to Jinan, completed in 1904, ran to the north of the Chinese city which at that time was still surrounded by walls. Between 1908 and 1912, the Tianjin-Nanjing Railway was built parallel to it, at a distance of about 60 metres. Their stations were opposite each other and formed the northern boundary of the foreign trade settlement which had been opened in 1906. The proximity of this rapidly expanding settlement and the European buildings built there provided the right setting for this large city station.

The central station in Jinan consisted of two buildings: a large terminal building with ticket hall, waiting rooms and offices. Integrated into the building was a tall clock tower decorated with Jugendstil ornaments and a roof of green glazed tiles. About 70 metres from the terminal building was the large storage building and freight offices. The ticket barriers and access to the platforms were between the two buildings. The building was the finest Jugendstil station in China. The quality of the design bears comparison with any European station. The architect, Hermann Fischer, had modelled his design on one of the most famous stations in Europe, Helsinki central station, designed by the Finish architect, Eliel Saarinen. This station was not actually built until between 1911 and 1913, but Saarinen's competition entry dated from 1904 and had been widely published.

濟南火車站

現用途：濟南火車站
所在地：濟南車站街，天津以南三百五十二公里
建築師：赫爾曼・菲舍爾〈234〉
施工：津浦鐵路公司
業主：中國鐵路局
建造期：一九零八年至一九一二年
現狀：盡管車站大樓狀況良好，仍於一九九二年七月拆除。

濟南是山東省省會。濟南火車站是原津浦線上規模最大、外觀最為奢華的車站。當時，濟南城四周築有城牆。一九零四年完工的膠濟鐵路通向城北，止於城的西北端。距膠濟鐵路六十開外，津浦鐵與其沿平行方向延伸。津浦鐵路建築於一九零八年至一九一二年，其濟南車站正對膠濟鐵路濟南車站，構成一九零六年開闢的外國商埠區的北界。高大的車站緊靠迅速膨脹的商埠區和區內的西洋建築，整體環境協調一致。

津浦鐵路濟南東站由兩幢樓房組成。一幢是候車大樓，內有售票廳，候車室和辦公室。與候車大樓相接的是一座高大的鐘樓，樓頂覆綠色琉璃瓦，外部裝飾為德國青年派手法。距車站七十米開外的另一幢大樓內設貨運倉庫和辦公室。貨運及辦公大樓的山牆形式與車站的相仿。兩樓之間是檢票處和月台通道。濟南車站大樓是德國青年風格派在中國的最好實例。其設計質量完全可與歐洲火車站相媲美。建築師赫爾曼・菲舍爾在設計過程中參照了芬蘭設計師伊力爾・薩里寧所建造的赫爾辛基火車站，這是歐洲當時最著名的火車站之一，建於一九一一年至一九一三年間。薩里寧的參賽設計早在一九零四年便已完成，並經常發表於各種出版物中。

津浦鐵路濟南中心火車站南立面，一九九二年。
原貨運大樓東南面外觀，一九九二年。

JINAN

VERWALTUNGSGEBÄUDE DER TIENTSIN-PUKOW-BAHN
ADMINISTRATION BUILDING FOR THE TIENTSIN-PUKOW RAILWAY

Heutige Funktion. Current use
Verwaltungsgebäude
Administration building
Wei Yilu/Jing Yilu (Wei-i-lu/I-ma-lu),
Jinan (Tsinanfu)

Entwurf. Design
Deutsche Ingenieure
German engineers

Ausführung. Contractors
Tientsin-Pukow Eisenbahngesellschaft
Tientsin-Pukow Railway Company

Bauherr. Client
Chinese Government Railways

Bauzeit. Construction time
zwischen 1908 und 1912
between 1908 and 1912

Zustand. Condition
Das Gebäude ist sehr gut erhalten.
Very well preserved.

Das Verwaltungsgebäude der Tientsin-Pukow-Bahn befand sich in der ausländischen Handelsniederlassung Jinans. Es lag an ihrem Ostrand, in etwa 250 Meter Entfernung zur Stadtmauer. Die von der chinesischen Stadt zu den Bahnhöfen führende Straße lief direkt auf diesen Bau zu. Auf der südlichen Hälfte des Grundstücks standen außerdem das Wohnhaus des stellvertretenden deutschen Chefingenieurs Linow sowie ein Wohnhaus für die leitenden chinesischen Bahnbeamten.

Das Verwaltungsgebäude war, wie auch der Zentralbahnhof, ein sehr moderner Bau. Großzügig dimensioniert, gab es damals bereits einen baulichen Maßstab für die ausländische Handelsniederlassung vor, der erst nach jahrzehntelangem Wachstum erreicht werden sollte. Die Architekten entwarfen das Gebäude in einem klassizierenden Jugendstil, Anpassungen an die chinesische Bautradition wie bei den Landbahnhöfen gab es nicht. Große Eichenblätter wurden in die Fensterleibung der obersten Fensterreihe modelliert. Waren die Blätter des heiligen Baumes der Germanen ein Ausdruck des Heimwehs der deutschen Ingenieure, oder sollten die Blätter zu einem die Herkunft der Baumeister verratenden Erkennungszeichen werden?

The administration building of the Tientsin-Pukow Railway was in Jinan's foreign trade settlement. It was on its eastern edge, about 250 metres from the city walls. The road leading from the Chinese town to the stations ran straight towards this building. On the southern half of the plot was the house of the German deputy chief engineer Linow and a house for the leading Chinese railway officials.

The administration building, like the central station, was a very modern building. It had generous dimensions and set the scale in advance for the foreign trade settlement which would not however be attained until after many decades of growth. The architects designed the building in a simplified form of Jugendstil. No adaptation to Chinese architecture was made as had been the case in the rural stations. Large oak leaves were modelled into the soffits of the upper row of windows. Were the leaves of the sacred tree of the Teutons an expression of the homesickness of German engineers or were the leaves to become a leitmotif, revealing the origins of the architect?

Fensterdetail mit Eichenblättern, 1992
Verwaltungsgebäude, Ostansicht, 1913
Ostansicht, 1992
Detail of window with oak leaves, 1992
Administration building, view from the east, 1913
View from the east, 1992

津浦鐵路辦公樓

現用途：辦公樓
所在地：濟南市緯一路（經一路口），原緯一路（一馬路口）
設計：德國工程師
施工：津浦鐵路公司
業主：中國鐵路局
建造期：一九零八年至一九一二年
現狀：建築物保存完好

津浦鐵路辦公樓位於濟南市外國商埠區的東端，距城牆約二百五十米。連接華人城區和火車站的馬路直通這座辦公樓。這片地產的南半邊是德國副總工程師里諾的宅邸及高級華人鐵路官員的住房。同津浦鐵路濟南車站一樣，車站辦公樓也是一座現代式的建築。

龐大的樓體在當時企圖預示外國商埠區經數十年發展之後所應達到的建築規模。

該樓的設計采用了簡化的青年風格派手法，摒棄其他車站兼顧中國建築傳統的做法。大樓頂排窗的窗楣飾以一片片碩大的橡樹葉。這些日耳曼人的聖樹之葉是德國工程師思鄉之情的表達，還是透露建築師故鄉的暗符？

辦公樓東立面，一九一三年。
東立面，一九九二年。
飾有橡樹葉的窗楣細部，一九九二年。

NEUER SCHANTUNG-BAHNHOF MIT HOTEL
NEW SHANTUNG STATION WITH HOTEL

Heutige Funktion. Current use
Chinesische Eisenbahnverwaltung
Jing Yilu (I-ma-lu, gegenüber Wei Sanlu),
Jinan (Tsinanfu), 412 km westlich
von Qingdao
Administration of the Chinese Railways
Jing Yilu (I-ma-lu, opposite Wei Sanlu),
Jinan (Tsinanfu), 412 km west of Qingdao

Entwurf. Design
Deutsche Ingenieure
German engineers

Bauherr. Client
Schantung-Eisenbahn-Gesellschaft
Shantung Railway Company

Bauzeit. Construction time
1914–1915

Zustand. Condition
Das Gebäude ist gut erhalten.
Die Innenräume wurden umgebaut,
die Bahngleise entfernt.
Well preserved; interiors re-modelled;
railway tracks removed.

Südfassade des ehem.
Schantung-Bahnhofs, links das
Bahnhofshotel, 1992
South façade of the former
Shantung Station and Station
Hotel, 1992

1904 wurde die Bahnlinie von Qingdao nach Jinan fertiggestellt, 1906 wurde ihr Endbahnhof zum Zentrum der neugegründeten Handelsniederlassung. Als 1912 die Bahnlinie von Tianjin nach Nanjing mit ihrem modernen Zentralbahnhof eröffnet wurde, wirkte der nur 8 Jahre zuvor erbaute Endbahnhof der Schantung-Eisenbahn nicht mehr repräsentativ genug. Die Entwicklung des Eisenbahnverkehrs und auch die Eröffnung einer ausländischen Handelsniederlassung durch die chinesische Regierung waren bei seiner Fertigstellung 1904 nicht absehbar gewesen. Die Konkurrenz mit der chinesischen Bahngesellschaft brachte die deutsche Schantung-Eisenbahn-Gesellschaft dazu, zwei Jahre nach Fertigstellung des Zentralbahnhofs einen neuen, größeren Endbahnhof für ihre Linie zu bauen.[235] Dieser lag dem Zentralbahnhof genau gegenüber. Ihm war ein Bahnhofshotel angeschlossen.

Die deutsche Eisenbahngesellschaft wollte in der Provinzhauptstadt ein Bahnhofsgebäude, das mit dem der chinesischen Gesellschaft an Größe konkurrieren konnte. Das zu massive Eingangsportal scheint Ausdruck dieses Repräsentationsbedürfnisses zu sein. Es wirkt wie nachträglich vor die Bahnhofshalle gestellt. Der Maßstab des Gebäudes wurde mit der zusätzlichen Funktion eines Bahnhofshotels vergrößert. Der Schantung-Bahnhof hatte den Vorteil, direkt an die ausländische Handelsniederlassung anzuschließen. Auf seiner Südseite gab es einen gut proportionierten Bahnhofsvorplatz, der von einer zweigeschossigen Blockbebauung umgeben war.

In 1904 the railway line from Qingdao to Jinan was completed and in 1906 its terminal became the centre of the newly founded foreign settlement. When the railway line from Tianjin to Nanjing was opened in 1912 with a modern central station, the terminal of the Shantung Railways, which had only been built 8 years previously, did not seem prestigious enough. The development of rail transport and also the opening of a foreign trade settlement by the Chinese Government could not have been foreseen on its completion in 1904. The competition with the Chinese railway company motivated the German Shantung Railway Company to build a new, larger terminal for the line only two years after the completion of the central station.[235] This was directly opposite the central station. Linked to it was a station hotel.

The German Railways Company wanted to own a station building in the capital of the province which could compete in size with the station belonging to the Chinese company. The inharmonious proportions of the entrance portal would seem to be an expression of this overriding need for prestige. It looks as if it was added onto the station concourse as an after-thought, as if the intention had been to improve it with a bit of glamour. The scale of the building was also increased by the addition of a station hotel. In the area of the foreign trade settlement the Shantung railway station did, however, have the advantage of proximity. On its southern side there was a well-proportioned station square, which was surrounded by a continuous two-storey development.

膠濟鐵路濟南新站、車站旅館

現用途：膠濟鐵路辦公樓
所在地：濟南市經一路，原一馬路（緯三路對面），青島以西四百一十二公里
設計：德國工程師
業主：山東鐵路公司
建造期：一九一四年至一九一五年
現狀：建築體保存完好；內部空間有所改建；鐵軌已拆除。

膠濟鐵路於一九零四年峻工。一九零六年，其終點站——濟南火車站成了新闢商埠區的發展中心。一九一二年，現代式的津浦鐵路濟南火車站落成之後，山東鐵路公司八年前建造的膠濟鐵路南站便相形見絀。一九零四年該站峻工時，人們尚無法預見鐵路交通的發展及外國商埠區的形式。與華人津浦鐵路公司的競爭促使德人膠濟鐵路公司重建一座規模較大的車站，該站在津浦鐵路濟南站運行兩年之後破土動工。〈235〉新站正對津浦線濟南站。車站旁還加建了一座旅館。

德國人的鐵路公司想在省會擁有一座在規模上可與華人鐵路公司相匹敵的車站大樓。比例欠佳的大門似乎是建業主追求排場的一種表達形式。它猶如添加之作，企圖增加東站大廳的豪華感。車站建築規模增大的另一原因在於內設旅館這一附屬功能。山東鐵路濟南站緊鄰外國商埠區，處地甚佳。其南面是比例均衡的站前廣場，周圍是二層樓房。

原山東鐵路火車站南面外觀，其左側是東站旅館，一九九二年。

JINAN

WOHNHAUS DES DEUTSCHEN KONSULS
KAISERLICH DEUTSCHES KONSULAT
RESIDENCE FOR THE GERMAN CONSUL
IMPERIAL GERMAN CONSULATE

Heutige Funktion. Current use
Stadtregierung
City Government
Jing Erlu (Erh-ma-lu/Wei-erh-lu), Jinan (Tsinanfu)

Architekt. Architect
Paul Friedrich Richter, Tsingtau[237]

Baukosten. Building costs
200 000 Goldmark
200 000 gold marks

Bauherr. Client
Auswärtiges Amt
Ministry of Foreign Affairs

Bauzeit. Construction time
Juli 1906 – März 1908
July 1906 – March 1908

Zustand. Condition
Das Gebäude ist sehr gut erhalten; Neubau des Rathaushochhauses auf dem Grundstück.
Very well preserved; new high-rise building on the site of the City Hall.

Ehem. Wohnhaus des deutschen Konsuls, 1992
Former Residence of the German Consul, 1992

Nach der Pachtung des deutschen Schutzgebietes und Gründung der Stadt Qingdao durch das Reichsmarineamt, kam es verstärkt zu Kontakten mit der chinesischen Provinzregierung in Jinan. Das deutsche Gouvernement des Schutzgebietes, als Vertreter des Reichsmarineamtes, durfte allerdings nicht direkt mit der chinesischen Regierung verhandeln, dies lag im Aufgabenbereich des Auswärtigen Amtes, das 1902 ein Konsulat eröffnete. So durften Reisepässe immer nur über das Konsulat beim chinesischen Gouverneur beantragt werden.[238] Mit der Eröffnung der Handelsniederlassung für Ausländer 1906 wurde das Konsulat durch die chinesische Regierung offiziell anerkannt.

In den ersten Jahren hatte das deutsche Konsulat einen Häuserkomplex der amerikanischen Mission in Jinan gemietet. Als man 1903 ausziehen mußte und es kein anderes europäisches Gebäude in Jinan zu mieten gab, zog Konsul Lange in ein chinesisches Hofhaus. Vom Chefingenieur der Schantung-Eisenbahn, Heinrich Hildebrand, ließ er sich Pläne für ein Konsulat zeichnen. In weiteren Schreiben an das Auswärtige Amt schildert er die Notwendigkeit einer repräsentativen Wohnung, geeignet zum Empfang hoher chinesischer Würdenträger, beschreibt Details der chinesischen Höflichkeitsformen und erinnert an die Notwendigkeit eines großen Gartens: »Bei den hiesigen Verhältnissen, die dem deutschen Beamten Erholung außer Hause kaum bieten, namentlich nicht im heißen Sommer, bitte ich gehorsamst, auch die Anlage eines größeren Gartens berücksichtigen zu wollen.«[239]

Auf dem Grundstück wurden zwei Gebäude errichtet, ein Wohnhaus für den deutschen Konsul mit den erforderlichen Repräsentationsräumen und ein Dienstgebäude mit Wohnungen für den Sekretär und den Dolmetscher sowie ihren Amtszimmern.

Following the establishment of the German protectorate and the founding of the city of Qingdao by the German Admiralty (Reichsmarineamt) there was increased contact with the Chinese Provincial Government in Jinan. The German Administration of the protectorate, as representative of the Admiralty, was, however, not allowed to negotiate directly with the Chinese government, this was the jurisdiction of the Ministry of Foreign Affairs which for this reason opened a consulate in 1902. Application for passports, for example, could be made to the Chinese Governor via the consulate only.[238] When the trade settlement for foreigners was opened in 1906 the consulate was officially recognised by the Chinese government.

In the first years the German consulate rented a complex of buildings from the American Mission in Jinan. When they had to move out in 1903 and there were no other European buildings available for rent in Jinan, Consul Lange moved into a Chinese courtyard house. He had plans for a consulate drawn up by the chief engineer of the Shantung Railways, Heinrich Hildebrand. In a letter to the Ministry of Foreign Affairs he sets out the necessity for a prestigious house, suitable for receiving holders of high Chinese honours, describes details of Chinese forms of courtesy and recalls the necessity for a large garden: »In the local conditions, which offer little opportunity for the German civil servant to relax, particularly not in the heat of summer, I request most humbly that the creation of a larger garden might also be considered.«[239]

Two separate buildings were built on the site, a house for the German consul with all the necessary official reception rooms and a building with flats and offices for the secretary and interpreter.

德國領事住宅

德國領事館
現用途：市政府
地址：濟南經二路（原二馬路，緯二路口）
建築師：保爾·弗里德里希·里希特，青島〈237〉
建築造價：二十萬金馬克
業主：帝國外交部
建造期：一九零六年七月至一九零八年
現狀：樓體保存良好。市政府地產上另建一幢市政府大樓。

德意志帝國海軍部租借膠州保護地、建立青島城後，加強了與山東省府濟南之間的聯系。然而膠州保護地的德國總督作為帝國海軍部的代理人不能直接與清朝山東省府對話，這屬外交部的事務范圍。因此，外交部於一九零二年在濟南設立了德國領事館。於是，護照可以通過德國領事館在山東巡撫那里申請。〈238〉隨著一九零六年外國商埠區的開設，德國領事館得到了清政府的官方承認。

領事館成立的頭兩年，租用了美國傳教會在濟南的一套房舍。一九零三年，領事館必須遷出此處，又因租不到洋房。朗格領事便搬進了一處中國四合院。朗格請山東鐵路公司總工程師海因里希·錫樂巴為其繪制領事館的設計圖。他在給外交部的信函中提出修建一套體面的住房，供接待中國的顯貴之用的要求。朗格詳細描述了中國的禮儀，並陳述了建造花園的必要性："在這里，尤其是在盛夏，宅邸幾乎是唯一可供德國官員休息的地方。為此，謹請考慮修建一座大型花園。"〈239〉

德國領事館的地產上建起了兩幢樓房。一幢是德國領事的住宅，內有體面的接待室。另一幢是辦公樓，樓內還設有秘書和口譯人員的辦公室及住房。

原德國領事住宅，一九九二年。

JINAN

DEUTSCH-ASIATISCHE BANK
GERMAN-ASIAN BANK

Heutige Funktion. Current use
Bank of China
Jing Erlu 191 (Erh-ma-Lu/Wei-erh-lu),
Jinan (Tsinanfu)

Architekten. Architects
Becker & Baedecker, Shanghai

Ausführung. Contractors
F. H. Schmidt, Altona, Hamburg, Tsingtau

Bauherr. Client
Deutsch-Asiatische Bank, Berlin
German-Asian Bank, Berlin

Bauzeit. Construction time
Mai 1907–1908
May 1907–1908

Zustand. Condition
Das Gebäude ist gut erhalten,
die Fassadenoberfläche wurde verändert.
Well preserved, façade surface changed.

Deutsch-Asiatische Bank,
Südwestansicht, 1908
Südansicht, 1992
German-Asian Bank in Jinan,
view from the south-west, 1908
View from the south, 1992

Die Deutsch-Asiatische Bank lag neben dem Deutschen Konsulat in der Hauptgeschäftsstraße der ausländischen Handelsniederlassung. Das Gebäude mit vielen Anklängen an die deutsche Neorenaissance wirkt mit seinen Giebeln und dem kleinen Eckturm romantischer und weniger monumental als der Club Concordia in Shanghai oder die Deutsch-Asiatische Bank in Beijing, die von denselben Architekten entworfen wurden.[240] Für die Deutschen in Jinan, die hier vor den Stadtmauern in der gerade erst gegründeten ausländischen Handelsniederlassung lebten, muß dieses Gebäude in einem gewohnten heimatlichen Baustil wie ein herbeigeflogenes Objekt aus dem fernen Deutschland gewirkt haben. Doch es war auch ein Symbol für den politischen und wirtschaftlichen Einfluß der Deutschen, der von Qingdao aus in der ganzen Provinz Shandong wirksam war. Vielleicht hatte man auch aus diesem Grund nicht den damals bei Banken üblichen Baustil der italienischen Renaissance gewählt.

Der *Ostasiatische Lloyd* beschrieb 1913 die ausländische Handelsniederlassung in Jinan: Nach wenigen Jahren »(…) ist ein fast ganz deutsches Viertel entstanden. Dort stehen die imposanten Gebäude der Deutsch-Asiatischen Bank, des Konsulats, des deutschen Krankenhauses und eine Reihe deutscher Firmen. Deutsche Architektur verraten auch die Bahnhofsdirektions- und Wohngebäude der Tientsin-Pukouer Bahn, denen sich demnächst ein neues stattliches Empfangsgebäude der Shantungbahn und wahrscheinlich auch ein deutscher Gasthof zugesellen werden.«[241]

Heinrich Becker und Carl Baedecker aus Shanghai waren in China die Hausarchitekten der Deutsch-Asiatischen Bank, die fast alle ihre Filialen gebaut hatten.

The German-Asian Bank was next to the German consulate on the main commercial street in the foreign trade settlement. The building was in the style of the German neo-Renaissance and with its many gables and its small corner tower made a less monumental impression than the Concordia Club in Shanghai, for instance, or the German Asian Bank in Beijing, which had both been built by Becker and Baedecker.[240] For the Germans in Jinan, who lived here outside the city walls in the foreign trade settlement which had only just been established, this building in an architectural style familiar from home must have seemed like an object flown in from the far-away climes of Germany. But it was also a symbol of the political and economic influence of the Germans, which was felt not only in Qingdao but in the whole Province of Shandong. Perhaps this also accounts for why the Italian Renaissance style usually used for banks was not chosen here.

In 1913 the *Ostasiatischer Lloyd* says of the foreign trade settlement in Jinan: After only a few years »(…) an almost entirely German district has sprung up. There are the impressive buildings of the German-Asian Bank, the Consulate, the German hospital and a number of German firms. The Business Premises and living quarters of the Tientsin-Pukow Railway Company also have a veil of German architecture and they will soon be joined by a magnificent terminal building for the Shantung Railway and probably also a German hotel.«[241]

Heinrich Becker and Carl Baedecker from Shanghai were the permanent architects to the German-Asian Bank; they built virtually all their branch offices.

德華銀行

現用途：中國銀行
所在地：濟南經二路一百九十一號，原二馬路(緯二路口)
建築師：貝克．培迪克　上海
施工：漢堡　阿爾托納爾區F·H·施密特公司
業主：伯林德華銀行
建造期：一九零七年五月至一九零八年
現狀：建築體保存良好，立面表面有變化。

德華銀行位於外國商埠區的主要商業街上，緊鄰德國領事館。這幢建築是貝克和培迪克的作品，屬德國文藝復興式復古風格。它那面面山牆和小小的角樓透露著一種浪漫情調，不同於上海的德國總會和北京的德華銀行。盡管二者也同樣出自貝克．培迪克之手。但它們更多地給人以雄偉之感。〈240〉在濟南的德國人住在城牆內剛剛開通的外國商埠區內。他們所熟悉的家鄉建築風格再現於這幢銀行大樓，於其而言，這一定象是一棟從遙遠德國飛來的建築。這幢樓房也是德國人以青島為中心，進而在政治，經濟上影嚮整個山東省的一種象徵。或許正是出於這一原因，建築師才沒有選用當時銀行建築中常見的意大利文藝復興風格。

一九一三年，《德文新報》報道了濟南外國商埠區的情況："几年之後……這里幾乎完全德國化了：德華銀行、德國領事館、德國醫院和一系列德國公司的建築雄偉莊嚴。津浦鐵路公司的車站辦公樓和住宅樓也是德國風格的建築，將與之為伍的是山東鐵路公司雄偉的新候車大樓，或許還有一家德國餐館。"〈241〉海因里希·貝克和卡爾·培迪克是德華銀行在中國上海的建築師，二人幾乎建造了該行的所有分行。

德華銀行西南面外觀，一九零八年。
南立面，一九九二年。

JINAN

KATHOLISCHE KATHEDRALE
CATHOLIC CATHEDRAL

Heutige Funktion. Current use
Chinesische katholische Kirche
Chinese Catholic Church
Hongjia Lou (Hung kia lu), Jinan (Tsinanfu)

Entwurf. Design
Pater Corbinarius
Father Corbinarius

Bauherr. Client
Franziskanermission Nord-Schantung
North Shantung Franciscan Mission

Eröffnung. Consecration
Ende Mai 1908
Late May 1908

Zustand. Condition
Das Bauwerk ist sehr gut erhalten,
auch der ältere Kirchenbau.
Very well preserved,
also the older church building.

Kathedrale in Jinan,
Westansicht, 1992
Cathedral in Jinan,
view from the west, 1992

Die Missionsstation wurde im Jahre 1866 gegründet. Sie lag etwa zwei Kilometer östlich außerhalb der Stadtmauern Jinans.[242] 1906 wurde auf der gegenüberliegenden Seite im Westen der Stadt die ausländische Handelsniederlassung angelegt. Entsprechend überrascht ist noch heute jeder Besucher, so weit vom Stadtzentrum und den anderen europäischen Gebäuden entfernt, in einem Vorort, diese große katholische Kirche zu finden.

Die chinesischen Handwerker haben dieser neogotischen Kirche durch ihre Interpretation von Details zu einer besonderen Exotik verholfen. So ähneln die an den Kanten gotischer Bauteile verwendeten blattförmigen Verzierungen – »Krabben« genannt – bei dieser Kirche eher kleinen Wolken. Man findet sie über dem Eingangsportal, am Giebel des Daches und an den Turmdächern. Das Dach der Kirche wurde mit chinesischen Mönch- und Nonnenziegeln gedeckt und bei den Traufziegeln wurden die in China üblichen Blütenmuster verwendet. Die Fassade besteht aus Sichtmauerwerk, Werksteinen und kleinen Putzflächen.

Zur Eröffnung erschien im *Ostasiatischen Lloyd* folgende Beschreibung: »Die Kirche ist ein majestätischer Bau im gotischen Stil. Sie ist über 60 Meter lang und 28 Meter breit. Das Mittelschiff ist 25 Meter hoch, eine breite Freitreppe führt von dem Vorplatz zu den drei Kirchenportalen empor. Besonders eindrucksvoll wirkt die wuchtige Fassade mit dem Radfenster und den beiden 46 Meter hohen Türmen. Zwei kleinere Türme mit reicher Steinhauerarbeit befinden sich zu beiden Seiten des Chors. Im Innern ziehen namentlich der monumentale Hochaltar, ein Kunstwerk ersten Ranges, und die schöne Kommunionsbank aus Lei-chou-fuer-Marmor die Blicke auf sich. Rings um die Apsis des Chors schließen sich fünf Kapellen. Rechts und links vom Hochaltar sind zwei geräumige Emporen eingebaut. (...) Die Chorfenster, die eine bekannte Düsseldorfer Firma hergestellt hat, bilden einen bedeutenden künstlerischen Schmuck des Gotteshauses. Die übrigen Kir-

The missionary station was founded in 1866. It was about two kilometres east of Jinan, outside the city walls.[242] In 1906 the foreign trade settlement was founded on the opposite side of the city, in the west. Correspondingly the European visitor is still surprised to find this large Catholic church in a suburb so far from the city centre and the other European buildings. From 1907 onwards the mission station was under the protection of the German Consulate. At time 17 German fathers and 9 other Europeans worked there.

The way the Chinese craftsmen interpreted the details of this neo-Gothic church have lent it a certain exotic look. For instance, in this church the decorative leaf-shapes used on the edges of Gothic elements – known as crockets – look more like little clouds. They can be found above the entrance portal, on the gable of the roof and on the roofs of the towers. The roof of the church was in mission tiling and at the eaves the blossom patterns customary in China were used. The façade is of fair-faced brickwork, ashlar and small rendered areas.

When the church was consecrated the following article appeared in Ostasiatischer Lloyd: »The church is a majestic building in the Gothic style. It is over 60 metres long and 28 metres wide. The nave is 25 metres high, a broad flight of steps leads up from the forecourt to the three portals of the church. The powerful façade is particularly impressive with its rose window and the two 46 metre-high towers. There are two smaller towers with prolific dressed stone work on either side of the choir. Inside the church the monumental high altar, a first-class work of art, and the beautiful communion bench of Lei-chou-fuer marble attract the greatest attention. Around the apse of the choir there are five chapels. To the right and left of the high altar there are two spacious galleries. The paintwork is also of excellent quality and adapted to the overall style. The choir windows, made by a famous Düsseldorf firm, provide this house of God with important artistic orna-

天主大教堂

現用途：天主教堂
所在地：濟南洪泉樓
設計：科比那利烏期・神甫
業主：山東北部方濟各會傳教會
啟用期：一九零八年五月底
現狀：建築群保存完好。

方濟各會傳教站建於一八六六年，位於濟南東城外兩公里處。[242] 一九零六年，外國商埠區在城西開通。至今仍令每一位歐洲游客惊奇的是，能在遠離市中心和其他西洋建築群的郊區找到這樣一座龐大的天主教堂。自一九零七年起，傳教站受德國領事館的保護。當時，有十七位德國神甫九名其他歐洲國家的神甫在傳教站供職。中國工匠按照他們對建築細部的理解，把這座哥特式復興風格的教堂建造得富有異國情調。例如，教堂的哥特式建築構件的邊棱上所用的葉形裝飾恰似朵朵游雲。教堂大門上方、山牆和塔頂上也綴以葉形裝飾。屋頂覆中國陰陽瓦，檐磚上雕有中國常見的花卉圖案。立面由清磚、粗石和小塊粉牆組成。

教堂落成時，《德文新報》上載有如下報道："天主大教堂是一座雄偉的哥特式建築，長六十餘米，寬二十八米，中堂高二十五米。寬闊的露天台階由廣場通向教堂大門。開有輪形窗的凝重立面和兩座四十六米的高大塔樓給人以深刻印象。祭壇室兩側兩座塔樓略小一些，上面飾以大量的石刻。教堂內最引人注目的是庄嚴雄偉的大祭台，堪稱一流的藝術品。精美的主餐長凳用雷州大理石做成，同樣倍受垂青。五座小教堂環繞祭壇室圓形後殿的四周。大祭台左右兩側是寬敞的廊台。教堂內的繪畫肅穆莊嚴，與整座教堂的風格協調一致。祭壇室的窗戶系杜塞爾多夫一家名公司制做，是堂內重要的藝術飾品。其他的教堂窗雖然形式簡潔，但卻使寬敞的廳堂充滿明亮、和煦的陽光。濟南天主大教堂是中國最美麗、最高大的教堂。科比那利烏斯神甫雖然遇到了很多困難但卻創造了無與倫比的作品。天主堂離濟南東門只有十分鐘的路，周圍是許多基督教村莊，有些已有幾百年的歷史。[243]

濟南大教堂西立面，一九九二年。

JINAN

Eingangsportal in der
Westfassade, 1992
Detail des Daches neben dem
Querschiff, Nordfassade, 1992
Blick nach Osten durch das
Mittelschiff, 1992
Deckengewölbe über dem
Querschiff, 1992
Entrance portal in the west façade,
1992
Detail of the roof near the transept,
north façade, 1992
View eastwards from the nave to
the choir and apse, 1992
Ceiling vaults over the transept,
1992

chenfenster sind einfacher gehalten, gestatten indessen, daß die weiten Hallen stets von hellem, freundlichen Lichte durchflutet sind. Die Kathedrale, in der Pater Corbinarius trotz vieler entgegenstehender Hindernisse, die in den Verhältnissen selbst begründet liegen, ein vollendetes Werk geschaffen hat, ist eine der schönsten und größten Kirchen in ganz China. Sie liegt nur etwa zehn Minuten vom Osttor der Stadt Tsi-nan-fu entfernt, mitten zwischen zahlreichen Christendörfern, die teilweise noch aus vergangenen Jahrhunderten stammen.«[243]

Während der Kulturrevolution (1966–1976) und bis zu ihrer Wiedereröffnung in den frühen 80er Jahren wurde die Kirche als Sandpapierfabrik genutzt und dadurch vor Verfall und Abriß geschützt.[244] Die neue Bemalung der Gewölbe könnte mit dem Originalzustand übereinstimmen. Entsprechend der chinesischen Tradition wurden auch die Innenräume von Kirchen schon immer recht bunt gestaltet.

ments. The other windows are simpler, allowing the wide halls to be constantly flooded with bright, friendly light. The cathedral, which Father Corbinarius has managed to accomplish as a finished work, despite numerous hindrances which were due to the nature of the task itself, is one of the largest and finest churches in the whole of China. It is only ten minutes from the eastern gate to the city of Tsi-nan-fu, in the midst of numerous Christian villages, some of which date from past centuries.«[243]

During the Cultural Revolution (1966–1976) and until it was re-opened in the early eighties, the church was used as a sandpaper factory and thus protected from decay or demolition.[244] The painting of the vaults, as it exists today, could be true to the original condition. Following Chinese taste the interiors of churches in China were often very brightly coloured.

教堂在文革一九六六至一九七六年至八十年代初期成了一家砂紙廠的廠房,而免遭坍塌和拆除之運。八十年代初,教堂被重新啟用。〈244〉拱頂的顏色或許與原先的一樣。中國教堂內部的著色都非常鮮艷,以符合中國人的欣賞習慣。

東望中廊堂,一九九二年。
十字形耳堂的拱頂,一九九二年。
西面入口,一九九二年。
十字形耳堂北面屋頂細部,一九九二年。

濟南

193

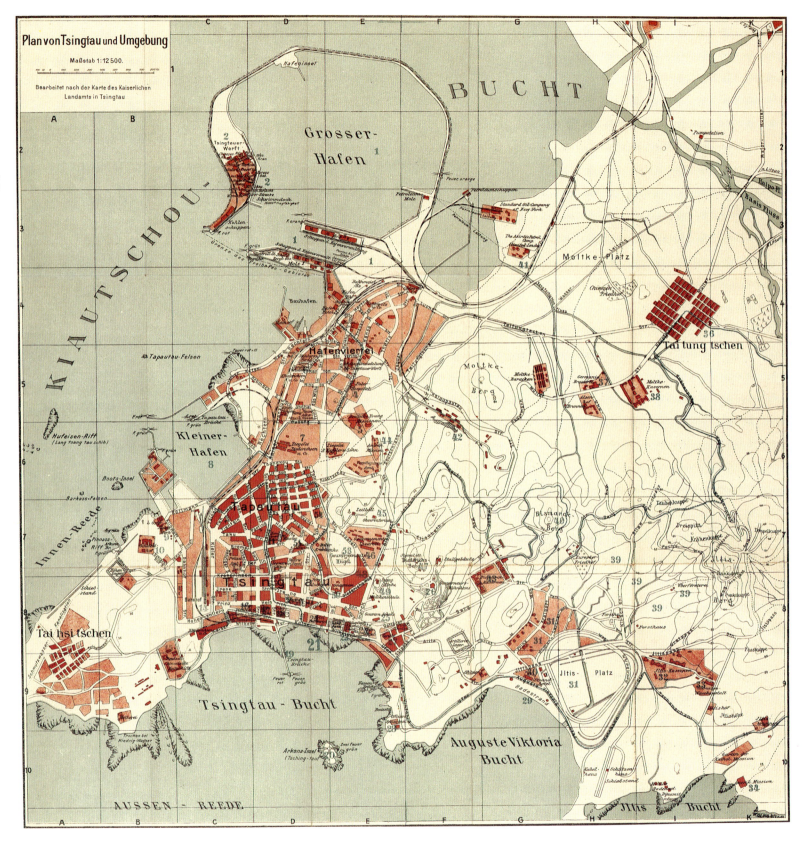

QINGDAO (TSINGTAU)

Qingdao in der Provinz Shandong (Schantung) ist eine auf Hügeln erbaute Stadt, ganz im Gegensatz zu den meisten anderen chinesischen Hafenstädten, die auf aufgeschüttetem Sumpfland errichtet wurden. Mehrere Hügel, 60 bis 130 Meter hoch, prägen die Stadt und unterteilen den Stadtraum; die Kuppen sind fast immer unbebaut geblieben. Die Straßen passen sich der Geländeform dieser Hügellandschaft an, bilden durch Richtungswechsel interessante Perspektiven. Die Stadtplanung hatte sich an der Topographie orientiert.

Das europäische Stadtviertel lag am Südhang der Hügelkette und grenzte an das Meer. Dort wurde eine Uferpromenade angelegt, die zum Spazieren einlädt. Anders als an den Uferstraßen in Shanghai, Wuhan oder Tianjin legten hier keine Schiffe an, wurde hier keine Fracht zwischengelagert. Der Hafen Qingdaos befand sich nördlich, in drei Kilometer Entfernung. In der *Hongkong Daily Press* wurde Qingdao 1913 beschrieben: »Wenn man (Qingdao, d. Verfasser) von der See aus erblickt, in seiner herrlichen Lage, entzückt es das Auge mit seinen reinlich gebauten schmucken Häusern, die mit ihren roten Ziegeldächern aus dem frischen Grün des Hintergrundes hervorleuchten. Es ist ein Stück Deutschland, das aus der Heimat dahin verpflanzt ist und bei diesem Umzug noch gewonnen hat.«[254] Da alle noch vor der Besetzung bestehenden chinesischen Dörfer durch das deutsche Gouvernement aufgekauft und abgetragen worden waren, fehlt in Qingdao die chinesische Architektur. Nur der Tempel und das Yamen – die Residenz des chinesischen Generals – blieben erhalten. Es wurde lediglich unter Berücksichtigung der Landschaft eine vollkommen neue Stadt erbaut.

Im Jahre 1897 hatte die deutsche Marine unter Leitung des Marine-Hafenbaudirektors Georg Franzius eine Expedition entlang Chinas Küste durchgeführt. Man untersuchte meh-

QINGDAO (TSINGTAO)

Qingdao, in the province of Shandong (Shantung), is a hilly city quite unlike most other Chinese harbour towns which were built on filled-in marshland and are therefore completely flat. A number of hills, 60 to 130 metres high, give the city its character and divide it up; the hilltops are virtually always free of buildings. The roads adapt to the contours of this hilly landscape and their changes of direction offer interesting perspectives. Urban planning here followed the natural topography.

The European quarter of the city was next to the sea, on the southern slopes of the chain of hills. A seashore promenade was built, providing a pleasant place for people to walk. Unlike the roads along the sea-front in Shanghai, Wuhan or Tianjin no ships anchored here and no cargoes were stored for further transportation. Qingdao's docks were to the north, some three kilometres away. In 1913, Qingdao was described as follows in the *Hong Kong Daily Press*: »Looking at (Qingdao – the author) from the sea, in its wonderful setting, it delights the eye with its neatly built, tidy houses, their red tiled roofs glistening against the fresh green background. It is a little piece of Germany which has been transplanted from the homeland and has even improved in the move.«[254] Since the German Administration (Gouvernement) had bought up and demolished all Chinese villages during the first years of the occupation, there was no Chinese architecture left in Qingdao. Only the temple and the Yamen – the residence of the Chinese general – remained. A new city was built influenced only by the landscape.

In 1897 the German navy, under the command of the Naval Director of Dock Building, Georg Franzius, had undertaken an expedition along the coast of China. They surveyed a number of China's bays and islands to determine their suitability for building a German naval base. In May 1897 the bay of Jiaozhou

青島

青島位於山東省境內。與中國大多數建於沖積平原上而地勢平坦的港口城市不同，青島境內山陵起伏。幾座高六十米至一百三十米的山岳不僅將城市分為數個區域，而且予城市以個性。青島市規劃充分考慮其地形特點，建築一般避開山頂，街道順山勢蜿蜓，換向處構成有趣視野。

歐洲城區建在丘陵帶的南坡上，面向大海。其沿岸林蔭道是散步的好去處。與上海、武漢和天津不同，青島市內沿岸既無船隻停泊，也無貨物中轉。其港口座落在歐洲城區以北三公里處。一九一三年的《香港每日新聞》對青島有如下報道："從海上眺望青島城，只見其座落在一片旖旎風光之中。其建築整齊美觀。重重紅色屋頂躍動於層層翠綠之中，令人心曠神怡。這景色簡直像是德國的一個小小剪影，這剪影在移植過程中變得愈加完美。"〈254〉德國總督府買下了青島所有建於德軍佔領前的漁村，並將其絕大部分拆除，僅留下天后宮和總兵衙門（俗稱"老衙門"）兩座中國傳統式建築。青島新城因而完全不受原有建築影響，城內中國建築了了無幾。

一八九七年，德國海軍在其軍港建設總管喬治‧佛朗求斯的帶領下，沿中國海岸進行了考察旅行並測量了幾處海灣和島嶼以研究其作為德國海軍基地的可能性。一八九七年五月對膠州灣的測量結果表明，此處海灣最宜於建港。〈255〉一八九七年十一月一日，由馮‧安治泰主教主持的天主教傳教治的兩名傳教士在山東南部被害。十一月六日，德皇威廉二世在聞訊的當日便下令德國海軍艦隊佔領膠州灣。當時，德國政府對在華建軍港基地早有蓄謀，"原野教案"便成為實施其預謀的最好借口。德國巡洋艦在水師提督馮‧狄特立克斯的率領下由上海起程，直取山東，艦隊停泊於膠州灣的戰略重點，並於一八九七年十一月十四日登陸。由於膠州灣連年常有外國艦隊造訪，駐扎當地的近兩千名清兵對此未起一絲疑心。清軍守將章高元誤以為德軍登陸是一次軍事演習。因此，當他接到德軍限其三小時之內撤離軍營、撤銷駐防的最後通牒時，驚恐莫名。章高元屈服

QINGDAO

rere Buchten und Inseln Chinas auf ihre Eignung zur Anlage einer deutschen Marinestation. Im Mai 1897 vermaß die Expedition die Bucht von Jiaozhou (Kiautschou), die als am besten geeignet für einen Hafen erschien.255 Als am 1. November 1897 zwei deutsche Missionare der von Bischof von Anzer geleiteten katholischen Mission in Südwestshandong ermordet wurden, gab Kaiser Wilhelm II. noch am gleichen Tag, an dem er die Nachricht erhalten hatte – am 6. November -, den Befehl zur Besetzung dieser Bucht durch die deutsche Flotte. Der Missionarsmord war der geeignete Anlaß zur Durchführung eines lange vorbereiteten Plans zur Anlage eines deutschen Marinestützpunktes an der chinesischen Küste.

Die Schiffe der Kreuzerdivision unter Admiral von Diederichs liefen von Shanghai nach Shandong aus, ankerten an den strategisch wichtigen Punkten in der Bucht und brachten am 14. November 1897 Truppen an Land. Von den dort stationierten fast 2 000 chinesischen Soldaten wurde kein Verdacht geschöpft, da die Bucht in den letzten Jahren wiederholt von ausländischen Flottenverbänden besucht worden war. Der chinesische General Zhang (Tschang) hielt die Truppenlandung für ein Manöver und war völlig überrascht von dem Ultimatum, das ihn innerhalb von drei Stunden zur Räumung des Lagers und zum Rückzug seiner Soldaten aufforderte. Er beugte sich der Übermacht der deutschen Schiffskanonen und übergab die Lager widerstandslos. Qingdao wurde ohne Kampf und Blutvergießen besetzt.256

Am 6. März 1898 wurde mit der chinesischen Regierung der sehr diplomatisch formulierte »Kiautschou-Vertrag« abgeschlossen. Für 99 Jahre pachtete das Deutsche Reich von China ein Gebiet, das 553 km² Land- und 560 km² Wasserfläche umfaßte. Gleichzeitig erhielt die deutsche Regierung das Recht, Eisenbahnlinien in Shandong zu bauen und Bodenschätze entlang der Bahnlinie auszubeuten.257

Bereits zu Beginn des Ersten Weltkrieges in

(Kiaochow) had been surveyed and considered to be the most suitable.255 On 1 November 1897, two German missionaries from the Catholic mission in Southern Shandong under Bishop von Anzer were murdered. When Kaiser Wilhelm II heard the news on 6 November, he immediately issued the order for the German fleet to occupy the bay. The murder of the missionaries provided the perfect excuse to put into action the long prepared plan to build a German naval base on the coast of China.

The ships of the cruiser division under Admiral von Diederichs set sail from Shanghai to Shandong, anchored at strategically important points in the bay and landed their troops on 14 November 1897. The almost 2 000 Chinese soldiers stationed there suspected nothing, since in the preceding years the bay had frequently been visited by foreign fleets. The Chinese General Zhang (Tschang) thought the landing was a manoeuvre and was completely surprised by the ultimatum he received, requiring the camp to be cleared and all soldiers withdrawn within three hours. He bowed to the supremacy of the German ships' canons and surrendered the camp without resistance. Qingdao was occupied without fight or bloodshed.256

On 6 March 1898 the very diplomatically worded »Kiaochow Treaty« was concluded with the Chinese government. The German Empire would have a 99-year lease on an area which comprised 553 km² of land and 560 km² of water. At the same time the German government was granted the right to build railway lines in Shandong and excavate natural resources along the railway lines.257

Right at the beginning of the First World War the first rumours circulated in Europe that Japan was going to attack the German protectorates in China. On 23 August 1914 Japan declared war on Germany. The siege of Qingdao began and on 7 November 1914 the city was taken. As early as 1904/1905, during the war between Japan and Russia, Japan had conquered the Russian concession and new

於德軍艦隊的優勢，交出了軍營。德軍未損一兵，不廢一彈便佔領了青島。〈256〉

一八九八年三月六日，清政府簽訂了措詞極為圓滑的《膠州租借條約》。德意志帝國向清政府租地九十九年，其中陸地五百五十三平方公里，水域五百六十平方公里。同時，德國政府得到了在山東修築鐵路的特許權以及採礦權。〈257〉

當第一次世界大戰在歐洲硝煙初起時，在歐洲就有日本要侵佔德國在中國的保護地的傳聞。一九一四年八月二十三日，日本對德宣戰，並包圍了青島。一九一四年十一月七日，日軍攻克青島。早在一九零四年至一九零五年的日俄戰爭中，日本就已佔領了距青島五百公里的俄國租界—新建城市大連和軍港旅順。這兩座城市由日本人統轄至一九四五年。青島則於一九二二年十二月十日歸還中國。當日軍在一九三八年一月十日再度佔領青島時，它已是亞洲最受人喜愛的海濱渡假勝地之一。

青島在一八九七年德國佔領之前只是一片村舍零落的半島，村民們以捕魚為生。一八九一年起，清政府在此設置軍事基地，其中有五所土牆高築的軍營，一所電報站、總兵衙門，以及泊船而建的"棧橋"。與大多數設有外國商埠的中國沿海城市不同，青島既無傳統的商業基礎，也非傳統的河運交通樞紐之濱。〈258〉青島只有以提供就業機會為手段吸引工人和商人遷進新城。德國人在青島建城時，不僅重建了整個城市設施，而且為溝通青島與內地的各項聯系；為疏通海運而大興土木。一座大港從而在青島落成，三道防洪堤中的第一道於一九零四年三月竣工。一八九九年九月，青島和山東省府濟南之間的膠濟線開工並於一九零四年六月一日竣工。但是，一直到一九零八年至一九一二年間修建的津浦鐵路線正式通車時，青島才第一次與國際鐵路網連接起來。由青島至柏林的西伯利亞聯運鐵路長一點二萬公里，行期四十天。〈259〉

青島建城初期，衛生狀況極差。一八九九年至一九零零年之間流行的傷寒使大量的德國士兵喪命。德國總督葉世克也於一九零一年一月二十七日染疾身亡。其結果加速了青島擴建的步伐，並使之一躍而為亞洲環境衛生水准最高的城市。為此，青島

Europa entstanden die ersten Gerüchte, daß Japan das deutsche Schutzgebiet in China angreifen würde. Am 23. August 1914 erklärte Japan Deutschland den Krieg; die Belagerung von Qingdao begann, und am 7. November 1914 wurde die Stadt erobert. Bereits 1904/05 hatte Japan im russisch-japanischen Krieg die von Qingdao nur 500 km entfernte russische Pachtung und Stadtneugründung Dalian (Dalny, Dairen) und den Kriegshafen Lüshun (Port Arthur) erobert. Aber während diese Städte bis 1945 japanisch blieben, wurde Qingdao am 10. Dezember 1922 an China zurückgegeben. Bis zu seiner erneuten Besetzung durch japanische Truppen am 10. Januar 1938 entwickelte sich Qingdao zu einem der beliebtesten Seebäder Asiens.

Vor der deutschen Besetzung 1897 war Qingdao nur eine mit wenigen Dörfern besiedelte Halbinsel gewesen. Die Bevölkerung hatte vom Fischfang gelebt; 1891 wurde hier ein chinesischer Militärstützpunkt eingerichtet. Dieser bestand aus fünf mit hohen Lehmmauern umgebenen Lagern, einer Telegrafenstation sowie dem Yamen. Außerdem hatte man als Anlegeplatz für Schiffe die »Tsingtau-Brücke« erbaut.

In Qingdao gab es keine chinesische Stadt mit traditionellen Handelsbeziehungen wie in den anderen Küstenstädten, in denen ausländische Niederlassungen eingerichtet waren. Diese Städte lagen an traditionellen Verkehrswegen wie Flüssen oder Kanälen.[258] In Qingdao mußten chinesische Arbeiter und Händler erst durch attraktive Arbeitsangebote in die neue Stadt geholt werden. Bei der deutschen Neugründung war nicht nur die Stadtanlage völlig neu zu erbauen, sondern es mußte auch erst eine Verbindung mit dem Hinterland und dem Meer geschaffen werden. Ein riesiger Hafen wurde in Qingdao gebaut; die erste von drei Molen weihte man im März 1904 ein. Im September 1899 wurde mit dem Bau der Schantung-Eisenbahn begonnen, die Qingdao mit der Provinzhauptstadt Jinan verbinden sollte. Am 1. Juni 1904 war

city of Dalian (Dairen) and the war harbour of Lüshun (Port Arthur), only 500 kilometres away from Qingdao. But whilst these cities remained Japanese until 1945, Qingdao was returned to China on 10 December 1922. Qingdao developed into one of Asia's most popular seaside resorts, until it was conquered once more by Japanese troops on 10 January 1938.

Before the German occupation in 1897 Qingdao had been a peninsular with only a few scattered villages. The population had made their living from fishing; since 1891 there had been a Chinese military base. This consisted of five camps surrounded by high clay walls, a telegraph station and the Yamen. The »Tsingtao Bridge« had also been built as a landing stage for ships.

In Qingdao there was no Chinese city with traditional trade links such as existed in other coastal towns where foreign concessions had been set up. These towns were situated on traditional transport routes such as rivers or canals.[258] In Qingdao it was first of all necessary to provide work to attract Chinese workers and traders into the new city. When the German new town was founded not only did the whole town have to be re-built, but links to the hinterland and to the sea had to be established. A huge port was built in Qingdao; the first of three moles was inaugurated in March 1904. In September 1899 work began to build the Shantung Railway, which would link Qingdao with the provincial capital of Jinan. This was completed on 1 June 1904 but it was not until the Tianjin-Nanjing railway line (Tientsin-Pukow), built between 1908 and 1912, was opened, that Qingdao was connected to the international railway network. It was 12 000 kilometres on the Transsiberian Railway from Qingdao to Berlin, a journey which took 14 days.[259]

The hygienic conditions in Qingdao were initially highly unsatisfactory. Numerous German soldiers were victims of the typhus epidemics of 1899 and 1900. The German Governor Paul Jaeschke also died of this infection on

不僅將飲用水水源設於遠離市區的水井，而且分別建成了為排除雨水、污水以及除理過的糞便的地下水道系統；多所現代化的醫院以及寬敞明朗的軍營，並實施了以洋人和華人健康居住環境為宗旨的城市規劃。一九零四年，一所療養院在嶗山落成，取名"梅克倫堡之家"。嶗山距離青島約三十三公里，群山中某些山峰高達海拔一千一百米。

德國政府在青島實行的地產政策是在德皇帝國史上前無先例的。其方法由德國總督府出面，以金額相當於土地所有者每年應向清政府上交的地稅稅額為補償費與土地所有者換取對其土地的購買權。在獲得面積為二十平公里的規劃區內所有土地的購買權後，德國政府便著手購買建設新城及其基礎設施所需的土地，並以德佔之前清政府所定地價為准。規劃區內預定拆除的原建築物均得到付加補償費，從而使購地費用相應增加。

德國總督府在土地測量、道路堪定、建築及城市規劃等工作完成後，於一八九八年十月三日舉行首次土地公開拍賣，並獲得第一筆財政收入。〈260〉按規定，購地者必須在三年之內實施建築規劃方案，否則，每逾期三年，必增繳地稅，其稅率以百分之三累進最高可達百分之二十四。為杜絕人們以爭購而放荒土地為手段來抬高地價的陋行，德國政府向所有土地購得者按年徵稅，其稅率為百分之六，為當地一般清政府稅率相當。〈261〉此外，轉售土地者亦須上交稅額為其售購差價的三分之一的增值稅。徵收此稅的目的，是為使德國政府也能受惠於因其建設基礎設施引導的土地增值。這種對不勞而獲的土地增值加以徵稅的政策，在當時世界仍為創舉。〈262〉它也是德國政府總結中國其他沿海通商城市的經驗教訓的結果。例如，一八四二年至一九一零年間，上海外國租界地價的增值幅度為其原值的五百至一千倍，而其增值利潤卻全部落入了投機商的腰包。

青島市由數座城區所構成：歐洲區、別墅區、華人經濟貿易商業區以及兩處勞工區。一九一四年止，港區以及增中外商行的方案僅部分得以實施。一八九八年十月十一日即首次土地公開拍賣之後，《臨時工務巡捕章程》生效。一八九九年四月二十日，

sie fertiggestellt, doch erst durch die Tianjin-Nanjing-Eisenbahnlinie (Tientsin-Pukow), zwischen 1908 und 1912 gebaut, wurde Qingdao an das internationale Eisenbahnnetz angeschlossen. Mit der Transsibirischen Eisenbahn waren es etwa 12 000 Kilometer von Qingdao nach Berlin, 14 Tage dauerte diese Reise.[259]

Die hygienischen Verhältnisse in Qingdao waren zunächst höchst unzureichend. Den Typhusepidemien der Jahre 1899 und 1900 fielen zahlreiche deutsche Soldaten zum Opfer, auch der deutsche Gouverneur Paul Jaeschke starb am 27. Januar 1901 an dieser Infektionskrankheit. Daraufhin beschleunigte man den konsequenten Ausbau Qingdaos und machte sie zur Stadt mit dem höchsten hygienischen Standard in Asien. Das Trinkwasser kam aus weit vom Ort entfernten Brunnen; Fäkalienbeseitigung, Regen- und Schmutzwasserkanalisation, moderne Krankenhäuser, großzügige Unterkünfte für die Truppen und eine auf gesundes Wohnen ausgerichtete Stadtplanung für Europäer und Chinesen schufen dafür die Voraussetzungen. 1904 wurde 33 km von Qingdao entfernt im bis zu 1 100 Meter hohem Laoshan-Gebirge (Laushan) das Erholungsheim »Mecklenburghaus« eröffnet.

In Qingdao führte man eine im Deutschen Reich einzigartige Bodenpolitik durch. Das deutsche Gouvernement erwarb von den chinesischen Grundeigentümern zu einem der jährlichen chinesischen Grundsteuer entsprechenden Betrag das Vorkaufsrecht für alles Land innerhalb des geplanten Stadtgebiets, einer Fläche von etwa 20 km². Grundstücke, die für den Bau der neuen Stadt und ihrer Infrastruktur benötigt wurden, kaufte man von den chinesischen Grundeigentümern für den Preis, der auch bereits vor der deutschen Besetzung durch die chinesische Regierung dafür gezahlt worden war. Auf den Grundstücken stehende Gebäude wurden zusätzlich vergütet, was besonders den Kauf der zum Abriß bestimmten Ortschaften relativ teuer machte.[260] Nachdem das Land ver-

27 January 1901. As a result of this the expansion of Qingdao was pushed forward and it became the city with the highest standards of hygiene in the whole of Asia. Various factors created the conditions necessary for this: the drinking water came from wells a good distance outside the town, a system for disposal of excrement was installed along with pipes to take away rainwater and sewage, modern hospitals, salubrious accommodation for troops and town planning based on providing healthy living accommodation for Europeans and Chinese. In 1904, 33 kilometres away from Qingdao, a convalescent home, the »Mecklenburghaus«, was opened in the Laoshan (Laushan) mountains, some of which were as high as 1 100 metres.

A land policy was implemented in Qingdao which was unique throughout the whole German Empire. For a sum which corresponded to the annual Chinese ground tax, the German Administration acquired from Chinese landowners the right to purchase all the land within the planned city limits, an area covering some 20 km². Plots of land which were required to build the new city and its infrastructure were purchased from the Chinese landowners for the price which the Chinese Government had already paid before the German occupation. An additional fee was paid for buildings on the land which made the purchase of villages destined for demolition relatively expensive.[260] After the land had been surveyed, the development plan drawn up and location of roads decided, the first plots were put up for public auction: the very first revenue for the German Administration. The first auction took place on 3 October 1898. Land purchased had to be built on as prescribed by the development plan within three years, otherwise there would be a progressive increase in ground tax by three percent every three years up to a ceiling of 24 percent.[261] The normal annual ground tax was six percent of the capital value of the land which was relatively high but corresponded to the local interest rate. The aim of this

《青島城市規劃圖》出版。〈263〉"歐洲城區"位於半島南坡面向大海，此處設有德國殖民行政辦公機構，以及歐籍商行、賓館、學校和住宅等。別墅區則建於俾斯麥克山西南、濱臨江泉灣（即奧古斯特・維多利亞・博特灣）。一脈山巒將其與市中心分隔開來。區內的建築有：原總督官宅、總督副屬官宅、以及青島海關總監恩斯特・奧爾瑪住宅和中國事務特派員威廉・席阿密爾的住宅。中國人除為外國人所僱傭者外均不得在"歐洲區"內居住；直至一九一一年秋的辛亥革命之後，中國人才取得在歐洲區內購地建房並留居的權利。中國政府極力主張在所有通商城市內劃分出洋人區和華人區。〈264〉華裔商業區一大鮑島建於青島岳巒的西部和北部，南臨歐洲區，北界免稅港區，並與華人的棧橋碼頭直接相連。建城初期，華人與洋人確曾相互合作，樂業於此。該區建築多為二層，傳統的四合院佈局。院內一側設木製外廊和樓梯。當時的營建章程已對建築密度及房間最小尺度均有明確規定。

一八九八年至一九零五年間，位於市區內的九座中國村落的土地被全部征購，原房主可用所得賠償金在台東鎮建新居。〈265〉當時的新聞媒介僅對新勞工居住區的建設予以贊揚，對民眾的抗議卻隻字未提。二十年代末一位美國人對此予以譴責："德國人拆除青島漁村以在其原址建立一現代德國城市的行徑深為中國村民所義忿。誠然，台東鎮新建居民區比原漁村要優越得多，但那些熱衷於 '開化' 世界上 '落後' 民族的人士應認識到：他們的 '成就' 並非廣為贊賞，因為任何人都不喜歡強制性的 '文明'。"〈266〉

距歐洲區二至五公里處，辟有兩處居住區：台東鎮和台西鎮，供中國港口和鐵路的建築工人居住。在此之前，來自山東省各地的工人栖集於極簡陋，不啻為疫源地的席棚區。一八九九年台東鎮建成，次年，台西鎮完工。華人區成矩形網格狀，每個方格長五十米、寬二十五米，路寬十米。建築區內的單層四合院呈中國傳統建築式樣。建築僅遵守基本的衛生章程，如建築密度及房屋大小等。由於中國北方城鎮多有狹窄碗胡同，新建華人勞工居住區內的街道較其而言，便顯得寬闊無比。中

messen war, die Straßenführung und der Bebauungsplan feststanden, wurden die ersten Grundstücke öffentlich versteigert: die ersten Einnahmen des Gouvernements. Die erste Versteigerung fand am 3. Oktober 1898 statt. Erworbene Grundstücke mußten dann entsprechend dem Baubauungsplan innerhalb von drei Jahren bebaut werden, ansonsten drohte eine progressive Erhöhung der Grundsteuer um drei Prozent alle drei Jahre bis auf 24 Prozent.[261] Die reguläre jährliche Grundsteuer betrug relativ hohe sechs Prozent des Kapitalwerts des Grundstücks, was dem ortsüblichen Zinssatz entsprach. Preistreibende Spekulation durch Kaufen und Brachliegenlassen des Landes sollte so verhindert werden. Bei einem späteren Eigentümerwechsel des Grundstücks mußte außerdem ein Drittel des Gewinns abzüglich der eigenen Investitionen an das Gouvernement als Wertzuwachssteuer abgeführt werden. Ziel dieser Steuer war es, das deutsche Gouvernement an der Steigerung des Bodenwerts der Grundstücke zu beteiligen, da die Wertzunahme besonders auf die vom Gouvernement geschaffenen Infrastrukturen zurückzuführen sind. Die Besteuerung des zukünftigen unverdienten Bodenwertzuwachses wurde damit zum ersten Mal in der Welt eingeführt.[262] Dem lagen Erfahrungen aus anderen chinesischen Küstenstädten zugrunde; so hatten sich zum Beispiel in den ausländischen Niederlassungen Shanghais die Grundstückspreise zwischen 1842 und 1910 um das 500 bis 1000fache erhöht – Gewinne, die ausschließlich den Spekulanten und Grundbesitzern zugute kamen.

Qingdao bestand aus mehreren Stadtteilen: einem Europäerviertel, einem Villenviertel, einer chinesischen Händler- und Geschäftsstadt sowie zwei Arbeitervierteln. Der Ausbau des Hafenviertels mit weiteren europäischen und chinesischen Geschäftshäusern war bis 1914 erst teilweise vollzogen. Am 11. Oktober 1898 traten nach der ersten Landversteigerung die »Vorläufigen baupolizeilichen Vorschriften« in Kraft; am 20. April 1899 wurde

was to prevent people from buying land and leaving it unused in order to force up prices. If the property subsequently changed hands, a third of the profit after deduction of the original investment also had to be passed on to the German Administration in the form of capital gains tax. The aim of the capital gains tax was to give the German Administration a share in the increase in land values, since the main cause of this was the infrastructure which the German Administration had provided. Thus taxing of unearned increase in land values was introduced for the first time in the world.[262] This was based on experience in other Chinese coastal towns; for instance, between 1842 and 1910 in the foreign settlements in Shanghai land prices had increased 500 to 1000-fold. These profits benefitted no-one but speculators and landowners.

Qingdao consisted of several different town quarters: a European quarter, a villa quarter, a Chinese trade and commerce quarter and two districts for workers. The expansion of the harbour district and the addition of more buildings for European and Chinese firms was only partially completed by 1914. On 11th October 1898, following the first public land auction, the »Preliminary regulations of the building inspectorate« came into force and on 20th April 1899 the »Town development plan for Tsintao« was published.[263] The »European town« was built on a hillside with a view of the sea in the south of the peninsular. Here the first buildings for the German government were built along with European office buildings, hotels, schools and housing. The villa district was laid out on the edges of the Bismarck Mountain, on the Huiquan Bay (Auguste-Viktoria-Bucht). The hill separated this quarter of the town from the town centre. It was here that the first Governor's Residence, the Residence of his adjutant, of the Maritime Customs and Excise Director, Ernst Ohlmer, and the house of the Commissioner for Chinese Affairs, Wilhelm Schrameier, were built. Chinese were allowed to buy land and build

國城鎮的街道擇南北向或東西向，而青島勞工區內的馬路則設在四十五度的軸線上，以順主風向，而避免陰濕的北立面。青島勞工區成了東亞最衛生的工人住宅區，它集歐式寬敞街道和中式四合院住宅於一體。前者滿足了衛生要求："光線＋空氣＝健康"，後者則為居民提供了其所習慣的生活方式。一九一零年，青島市區內的華人人口為三點四萬，一九一三年已達五點三萬，其中婦女僅佔百分之十六。青島在文學作品中被描述為貿易殖民地。實際上，從人口組成看，它卻具有駐防城的特徵。一九一三年七月，青島德國駐軍人數達二千四百名，歐洲居民二千零六十九人，其中婦女八百八十六人，一八九九年至一九零九年間，三座兵營在青島城外建成，第一座兵營是伊爾蒂斯兵營。營前寬大的練兵場和濱臨江泉灣的跑馬道。俾斯麥兵營於一九零二年至一九零九年間在原清軍東營址上建成。莫爾特克兵營為第三座兵營，遠離大海，近距台東鎮勞工區。一九零六年，駐防於高密城的騎兵部隊曾在此宿營。〈267〉

青島作為亞洲唯一的貿易及駐防城，符合現代衛生標准，得以不斷發展，成了受人喜愛的海濱浴場及夏季避暑勝地，城市污水道避開浴場海灣，僅雨水排水管道通向南灣。匯泉灣一帶由於興建跑馬道和海濱浴場而發展成一業餘娛樂和體育活動場所。海灘邊挺立著一間間木結構小浴室，其中有一百一十三間建於一九零四年。音樂涼亭常有第三海軍營小樂隊演奏。距海岸僅百米處是一座三層樓的海灘旅館。其後是跑馬場。早在一九零三年夏，就有一百二十六名療養者光臨青島城。其後，每年總有五百名左右的療養者從中國其他城市湧向青島，其中也有很多英國人。旅館客房逢夏緊缺的現象愈年激化。英文版的文化雜誌《上海社會》定期報道中國的海濱浴場和避暑勝地，其中有關於青島的詳細報道，並附以大量照片。〈268〉

一九一一年秋的辛亥革命推翻了清朝一六四六至一九一一年統治，宣告了中華民國的成立。下台官員攜室帶產，或投向天津、上海的外國租界，或逃往香港、青島、大連，以尋求外國領事館的庇護，國民政府對其及其財產無法採取行動。外國

der »Stadtbauplan von Tsintau« veröffentlicht.²⁶³ Im Süden der Halbinsel entstand in Hanglage mit Blick auf das Meer die »Europäerstadt«; hier errichtete man die deutschen Regierungsbauten, europäischen Geschäftshäuser, Hotels, Schulen und die Wohnhäuser. Das Villenviertel wurde an den Ausläufern des Bismarckberges, an der Huiquan-Bucht (Auguste-Viktoria-Bucht) angelegt. Der Höhenzug trennte diesen Stadtteil vom Stadtzentrum. Hier standen unter anderem das erste Gouverneurswohnhaus, das Wohnhaus des Adjutanten, das Wohnhaus des Seezolldirektors Ernst Ohlmer und das Haus des Chinesenkommissars Wilhelm Schrameier. Chinesen, das Personal ausgenommen, durften in diesen »Europävierteln« zwar Grundstücke erwerben und bauen, doch bis zur chinesischen Revolution im Herbst 1911 nicht hier wohnen. Diese Aufteilung der chinesischen Städte in Viertel für Ausländer und Einheimische war seit der Öffnung Chinas in allen für den ausländischen Handel geöffneten Städten von der chinesischen Regierung ebenfalls gewollt worden.²⁶⁴

Die chinesische Händler- und Geschäftsstadt Dabaodao (Tapautau) wurde an den West- und Nordhängen der Hügel Qingdaos angelegt. Sie lag zwischen der Europäerstadt und dem im Norden gelegenen zollfreien Hafenbezirk und schloß direkt an den chinesischen Dschunkenhafen an. Hier wohnten und arbeiteten Europäer und Chinesen in den ersten Jahren gemeinsam. Eine zweigeschossige Bebauung aus Ziegelsteinen mit hölzernen Laubengängen und Treppen auf der Hofseite entwickelte sich hier. Die Bebauungsdichte war durch die Bauordnung auf 70 Prozent festgelegt worden, ebenso gewisse Mindestgrößen für Räume.

Die im Stadtgebiet gelegenen 9 chinesischen Dörfer waren zwischen 1898 und 1905 alle von dem deutschen Gouvernement gekauft worden. Man hatte die chinesischen Hausbesitzer entschädigt, so daß sie sich neue Häuser in Taidong Zhen bauen konnten.²⁶⁵ Während der Bau von neuen Arbeitersiedlun-

property in these »European Quarters«, but until the Chinese revolution in autumn 1911 they were not allowed to live there unless they worked for Europeans. This division of the Chinese towns into neighbourhoods for foreigners and natives had been desired by the Chinese government in all the towns which were open to foreign trade.²⁶⁴

The Chinese trade and commerce district, Dabaodao (Tapautau), was built in the western and northern part of the Qingdao hills. It was situated between the European quarter and the custom-free harbour district to the north and was next to the Chinese junk harbour. In the early years the Europeans and Chinese lived and worked together. Two-storey buildings with wooden galleries and staircases on the courtyard side sprang up here. The building regulations had fixed the density of buildings at a maximum of 70 percent and specified a certain minimum size for rooms.

The nine Chinese villages within the city limits had all been bought up between 1898 and 1905. The Chinese property owners had received compensation to enable them to build new houses in Taidong Zhen.²⁶⁵ Whilst the building of new housing estates for workers was praised in the press of the time and protests by the public ignored, this approach was criticised by an American at the end of the 1920s for being authoritarian: »The demolishing of the village of Tsingtao so that a modern German city might be erected on the site was accompanied by wailings of protest by villagers. Of course they were given better dwellings in a better village, Taitungchen, built by the German authorities, but it has been the experience of those who would ›civilise‹ the ›backward‹ people of the earth that they are not fully appreciated. No one likes to have ›civilisation‹ imposed upon him.«²⁶⁶

Two villages, Taixi Zhen (Taihsichen) and Taidong Zhen (Taitungchen), for Chinese construction workers building the port and railways were erected at a distance of two and five kilometres respectively from the European district. Previously the workers brought

領事館之所以對下台官實行保護政策，是因為他們對辛亥革命的成敗持懷疑態度。而向可靠的談判伙伴和老朋友提供保護，一旦其復辟得成，各國均受惠於此。因此，各國競相大肆招徠失勢官員。營造青島土地法規的單維廉博士曾對此種變化予以抨擊。"膠州督府一時性起，竟於一九一二年放手已有的利益，放棄歐洲區。"〈269〉單維廉的批評是以中國以往的革命經驗為依據的。每逢革命之時，許多中國家庭便逃往外國租界尋求保護。這雖使地價陡漲，但也排擠了外國人。例如，至一九一零年，上海外國租界內的外國人口佔總人口的比例，總是徘徊在百分之二。

下台官員舉家遷居青島大大振興了該地的建築業。一九零七至一九一一年間，僅有三十九處地產為華人所購，而一九一二年一年，華人購地八十處；華人取得建築許可的數字也在上升。但新建房屋必須遵照建築章程，如：房屋外觀成西洋建築式樣，別墅區內建築密度不得超過百分之四十，房屋與地界之距離亦有規定。住慣了中式寬敞四合院的中國人很難接受這種文化變異。因此，有幾處新建房屋在平面佈置上仍採用四合院結構。例如，衛禮賢曾對恭親王的遷居做過如此描述："恭親王由景山腳下久負盛名的華麗宮殿遷出，他放棄了北京西山弁台寺內莊嚴秀美夏日行宮，離開了他的珍寶和所鍾愛的書籍，遷入了青島一德國上尉的夏季別墅，在這幢輕型結構的建築內，親王及其家眷寒酸地安頓下來。至今我仍清晰地記得他怎樣興致勃勃地帶我看新挖的金魚塘，池塘內有一噴泉。他那興奮的神態令人感動。我也記得他如何企圖將蹩腳的小園改造成一座花園。"〈270〉

gen in der zeitgenössischen Presse nur gelobt wurde und von Protesten der Bevölkerung nichts berichtet wurde, kritisierte am Ende der 20er Jahre ein Amerikaner diese Vorgehensweise als autoritär: »Die Zerstörung des Dorfes Tsingtau – und der Bau einer modernen deutschen Stadt an gleicher Stelle – wurde von den Dorfbewohnern mit Klagen und Protesten begleitet. Natürlich bekamen sie bessere Häuser in einem schöneren Dorf, Taitungchen, das von den deutschen Behörden errichtet wurde. Aber diejenigen, die ›rückständige‹ Völker der Welt ›zivilisieren‹wollten, haben die Erfahrung gemacht, daß dies nicht voll gewürdigt wurde. Niemand hat es gern, wenn ihm ›Zivilisation‹ aufgezwungen wird.«[266]

In zwei bzw. fünf Kilometern Entfernung von der Europäerstadt wurden zwei Siedlungen für chinesische Hafen- und Eisenbahnbauarbeiter angelegt: Taixi Zhen (Tai hsi tschen) und Taidong Zhen (Tai tung tschen). Zuvor hatten die aus der ganzen Provinz herangezogenen Arbeiter in äußerst primitiven Mattenunterkünften gewohnt, einem Brutherd für Seuchen. 1899 wurde Taidong Zhen gegründet, ein Jahr später Taixi Zhen. Die chinesischen Viertel waren in ein rechteckiges Blockraster von je 25 Metern mal 50 Meter aufgeteilt, die Straßenbreite betrug 10 Meter. Diese Baublöcke wurden in traditioneller chinesischer Bauweise bebaut, mit eingeschossigen Hofhäusern. Lediglich die minimalen hygienischen Vorschriften zur Bebauungsdichte und Größe der Zimmer mußten eingehalten werden. Die Straßenbreite dieser beiden Siedlungen war für chinesische Dörfer und Städte sehr großzügig; in den Dörfern und Städten Nordchinas gab es sonst nur sehr enge und verwinkelte Gassen. Auch die Orientierung der Straßen war gegenüber dem traditionellen chinesischen Städtebau verändert. Während chinesische Städte und Dörfer immer in Nord-Süd- sowie Ost-West-Richtung verlaufende Straßen haben, wurde dieses Raster bei den Qingdaoer Arbeitersiedlungen um 45° gedreht. Dadurch bildeten

in from all over the province had lived in extremely primitive dwellings with mats, a breeding ground for epidemics. Taidong Zhen was founded in 1899 and Taixi Zhen a year later. The Chinese quarters were divided up on a rectangular grid with blocks of 25 × 50 metres; the streets were 10 metres wide. These blocks were developed with traditional Chinese architecture, with one-storey courtyard houses. Only a minimum of hygienic regulations such as density of buildings and size of rooms had to be adhered to. The streets were very wide by Chinese standards; in the villages and towns of Northern China there were only very narrow alleys full of nooks and crannies. The direction of the streets was also different from traditional Chinese towns. Streets in Chinese towns and villages always run north-south and east-west, whereas this pattern was rotated by 45 degrees in the workers' villages in Qingdao. This meant there were no shady, damp, north-facing façades and the streets ran in the direction of the prevailing wind. This combination of streets of European widths, which corresponded to all the hygiene demands »light + air = health« and houses which enabled the inhabitants to live their accustomed lifestyles produced the most hygienic and healthy workers village in East Asia. In 1910, 34 000 Chinese lived in Qingdao; in 1913 there were over 53 000, only 16 percent of these were women.

Although Qingdao is always mentioned in literature as a trade colony, the composition of its population must have given it the character of a garrison town. In July 1913, 2 400 German soldiers were stationed in Qingdao, the European civilian population numbered 2 069 people of whom 886 were women. Three large barracks were built between 1899 and 1909. They were all outside the town. The first to be built were the Iltis Barracks and in front of it were the vast parade ground and the racecourse on the Huiquan Bay. The Bismarck Barracks were built on the site of the Chinese Eastern Camp between 1902 and 1909. The third complex to be built was

sich keine schattigen und feuchten Nordfassaden, und die Straßen lagen zugleich in den Hauptwindrichtungen. Mit dieser Kombination von europäisch breiten Straßen, die allen Anforderungen der Hygiene: »Licht + Luft = Gesundheit« entsprachen sowie mit Häusern, die die gewohnte Lebensweise für die Bewohner ermöglichten, wurde die hygienischste und gesündeste Arbeitersiedlung in Ostasien erbaut. 1910 wohnten 34 000 Chinesen im Stadtgebiet von Qingdao, 1913 waren es bereits mehr als 53 000, davon allerdings nur 16 Prozent Frauen.

Obwohl in der Literatur immer von Qingdao als einer Handelskolonie gesprochen wurde, muß die Stadt von der Bevölkerungszusammensetzung den Charakter einer Garnisonsstadt gehabt haben. Im Juli 1913 waren 2 400 deutsche Soldaten in Qingdao stationiert, die europäische Zivilbevölkerung zählte 2 069 Personen, davon waren 886 Frauen. Drei große Kasernenkomplexe wurden zwischen 1899 und 1909 geschaffen. Sie lagen alle außerhalb der Stadt. Als erste entstand die Iltis-Kaserne, ihr war die weite Fläche des Exerzierplatzes und der Pferderennbahn an der Huiquan-Bucht vorgelagert. Die Bismarck-Kaserne wurde an Stelle des chinesischen Ostlagers in den Jahren 1902 bis 1909 errichtet. Als dritte Anlage folgte die Moltke-Kaserne. Diese lag am weitesten vom Meer entfernt, nahe der Arbeitersiedlung Taidong Zhen. Hier wurden die bis 1906 in der Stadt Gaomi (Kaumi) stationierten Reitertruppen untergebracht.[267]

Als einzige Handels- und Garnisonsstadt Asiens wurde Qingdao konsequent zu einer Sommerfrische ausgebaut, die allen Anforderungen der modernen Hygiene entsprach, so daß sich die Stadt zu einem beliebten Seebad entwickelte. Bei der Anlage der Schmutzwasserkanalisation achtete man darauf, daß die Abwässer nicht in die Badebuchten abgeführt wurden, lediglich die Regenwasserkanalisation mündete in die südliche Bucht. Das Gelände an der Huiquan-Bucht wurde durch die Anlage der Pferderennbahn

the Moltke Barracks. This was the furthest from the sea, close to the workers village, Taidong Zhen. Here the cavalry troops were accommodated who, until 1906, had been stationed in the town of Gaomi (Kaumi).[267]

As the only trade and garrison town in Asia, Qingdao was consequently developed into a healthy seaside resort and summer resort. When the sewage system was built care was taken to ensure that the effluent was not discharged into bays reserved for bathing, only the rainwater drainage system ran into the southern bay. Due to the building of the racecourse and the bathing beach the Huiquan Bay became a sport and recreation area. Small wooden bathing cabins were put up on the sandy beach; by 1904 there were already 113 of them. The band of the III Sea Battalion gave concerts from a bandstand. Only 100 metres from the shore a three-storey beach hotel was built. Behind it was the grandstand of the racecourse. By the summer of 1903 there were already 126 holiday-makers in Qingdao. In the years which followed there were always some 500 holiday-makers from other Chinese towns, including a large number of British. The lack of hotel rooms in the summer season was bemoaned repeatedly. The English language cultural magazine *Social Shanghai* ran regular articles about bathing resorts and summer resorts in China, including extensive descriptions and photographs of Qingdao.[268]

The revolution of autumn 1911 led to the downfall of the Qing Dynasty (1644–1911) and the establishment of the Republic of China. The politically disenfranchised families fled with their wealth to the foreign concessions of Tianjin and Shanghai, to Hongkong, Qingdao and Dalian. Here they were under the protection of the foreign consulates, they and their property could not be touched by the Chinese authorities. The political decision to offer protection to the formerly powerful families was based on doubts about the success of the revolution and its benefit to the outside world. If a nation offered protection to familiar

und des Badestrandes zum Freizeit- und Sportareal. Auf dem Sandstrand errichtete man kleine hölzerne Badehäuschen, von denen es 1904 bereits 113 gab. In einem Musikpavillon fanden Konzerte der Kapelle des III. See-Bataillons statt. Nur 100 Meter vom Ufer entfernt wurde das dreigeschossige Strandhotel erbaut. Dahinter befand sich die Tribüne des Rennplatzes. Im Sommer 1903 gab es in Qingdao bereits 126 Badegäste. In den folgenden Jahren wurden immer um die 500 ausländische Badegäste aus anderen Städten Chinas gezählt, darunter auch viele Engländer. Der Mangel an Hotelzimmern wurde immer wieder betont. Im englischsprachigen Kulturmagazin *Social Shanghai* erschienen regelmäßig Artikel über Badeorte und Sommerfrischen in China, in denen ausführlich mit Fotografien über Qingdao berichtet wurde.[268]

Die Revolution im Herbst 1911 führte zum Sturz der Qing-Dynastie (1644–1911) und zur Errichtung der Republik China. Die politisch entmachteten Familien flüchteten mit ihrem Vermögen in die ausländischen Niederlassungen Tianjins und Shanghais, nach Hongkong, Qingdao und Dalian. Hier standen sie unter dem Schutz der ausländischen Konsulate, sie und ihr Eigentum waren vor dem Zugriff durch chinesische Behörden geschützt. Die politische Entscheidung, den ehemals mächtigen Familien Schutz zu bieten, war begründet in dem Zweifel am Erfolg der Revolution und an ihrem Nutzen für das Ausland. Bot man den vertrauten Verhandlungspartnern und alten Freunden Schutz, hatte die jeweilige Nation bei einer eventuellen Rückkehr zur Macht mit großen Vorteilen zu rechnen. So fand damals unter den Ausländern ein regelrechtes Werben um diese Familien statt. Kritisiert wird diese Veränderung durch Wilhelm Schrameier, der die Landordnung für Qingdao geschaffen hatte: »Aus einer Augenblicksstimmung heraus hat das Gouvernement von Kiautschou die Vorteile, die es besaß, im Jahre 1912 aus der Hand gegeben und auf ein Europäerviertel in Tsingtau ver-

negotiating partners and old friends it could expect great advantages if they ever returned to power. And so the different foreign countries positively vied with each other for these families. This change of tack was criticised by Wilhelm Schrameier who had created the land regulations for Qingdao: »In 1912, on the whim of a moment, the German Administration of Kiaochow forfeited the advantages it possessed and gave up the European quarter in Tsingtao.«[269] His criticism was based on the experience of previous revolutions in China when numerous Chinese families had sought protection in the foreign concessions. This had led to an enormous rise in land prices, but had also driven away the foreigners. Up to 1910 the percentage of foreigners in the foreign settlements of Shanghai, for instance, was only ever around two percent of the population.

The arrival of Chinese families led to a strong revival of the building trade in Qingdao. Whilst between 1907 and 1911 only 39 plots of land had been sold to Chinese, this number had risen to 80 by 1912. The number of planning applications granted rose correspondingly. The new buildings were, however, required to comply with the building regulations, i. e. look European, not exceed the building density of 40 percent in districts with »country house development« and adhere to the plot boundaries. Families who were accustomed to living in spacious Chinese houses built around courtyards found it very difficult to make this cultural adjustment, and the planning of some of their new buildings was based on the structures of the courtyard houses. Richard Wilhelm describes how things had changed for Prince Gong (Kung), the elder brother of the last Emperor, as follows: »He had moved out of his magnificent palace on the foot of the Coal Hill, one of the most famous cultural monuments of ancient times. He had abandoned his summer residence in the magnificent temple Tsiä T'ai Si (Jietai Si, the author) in the western hills near Peking. He had torn himself away from most of his

zichtet.«[269] Seine Kritik gründete in der Erfahrung früherer Revolutionen in China, als jeweils viele chinesische Familien in den ausländischen Niederlassungen Schutz suchten, was zwar zu einem ungeheuren Anstieg der Grundstückspreise führte, andererseits die Ausländer verdrängte. So betrug der Anteil der Ausländer in den ausländischen Niederlassungen Shanghais bis 1910 immer nur rund zwei Prozent der Bevölkerung.

Der Zuzug der chinesischen Familien führte zu einer starken Belebung des Baugeschäfts in Qingdao. Während zwischen 1907 und 1911 insgesamt nur 39 Grundstücke an Chinesen verkauft wurden, waren es allein 1912 bereits 80. Ebenso stieg die Anzahl der Baugenehmigungen. Die Neubauten mußten sich allerdings nach der Bauordnung richten, d.h. ein europäisches Aussehen haben, die Bebauungsdichte von 40 Prozent in Stadtvierteln mit »landhausmäßiger« Bebauung sowie die Abstände zu den Grundstücksgrenzen einhalten. Familien, die es gewohnt waren, in weitläufigen chinesischen Hofhäusern zu wohnen, fiel diese kulturelle Umstellung sehr schwer, einige ihrer Neubauten enthalten im Grundriß die Strukturen der Hofhäuser. So beschreibt Richard Wilhelm die Veränderung für Prinz Gong (Kung), den älteren Bruder des letzten Kaisers: »Er war aus seinem herrlichen Palast am Fuß des Kohlenhügels, der zu den berühmtesten Denkmälern alter Zeit gehörte, ausgezogen. Er hatte seine Sommerwohnung in dem herrlichen Tempel Tsiä T'ai Si (Jietai Si, d. Verfasser) in den Westbergen bei Peking aufgegeben. Er hatte sich von seinen Schätzen und seinen geliebten Büchern getrennt. Er war in Tsingtau in die leichtgebaute Sommervilla eines deutschen Hauptmanns gezogen, in der er mit seiner Familie nur aufs Dürftigste unterkam. Ich erinnere mich noch der rührenden Freude, mit der er mir seinen neu angelegten Goldfischteich mit Springbrunnen zeigte, und der Versuche, das kümmerliche Gärtchen zu einem Park umzuwandeln.«[270]

treasures and beloved books. He had moved into the lightly built summer villa of a German captain in which he had only the most meagre accommodation for himself and his family. I remember the touching joy with which he showed me his new goldfish pond and his attempts to turn the pathetic little garden into a park.«[270]

GOUVERNEURSWOHNHAUS
GOVERNOR'S RESIDENCE

Heutige Funktion. Current use
Gästehaus, Hotel Longshan Lu
(Südhang des Signal- oder Diederichsberges),
Qingdao (Tsingtau)
Guest house, hotel
Longshan Lu (southern slope of Signalberg
or Diederichsberg), Qingdao (Tsingtao)

Architekt. Architect
Hochbaudirektor Strasser
Vorentwurf: Regierungsbaumeister Mahlke
Strasser, director of public works
Preliminary design: Mahlke, government architect

Baukosten. Building costs
über 450 000 Goldmark
over 450 000 gold marks

Bauherr. Client
Deutsches Gouvernement Kiautschou
German Administration of Kiaochow

Bauzeit. Construction time
Oktober 1905 – Oktober 1907
October 1905 – October 1907

Zustand. Condition
Das Gebäude ist sehr gut erhalten.
Very well preserved.

Südansicht, im Hintergrund
der Signalberg, 1907
Ehem. Wohnhaus des deutschen
Gouverneurs, Westfassade mit
Haupteingang, 1992
View from the south, Signal Hill in
the background, 1907
Former Residence of the
German Governor, west façade
with main entrance, 1992

Das Gouverneurswohnhaus war mit Abstand das spektakulärste Gebäude in Qingdao.[271] Es lag am Hang des Signalberges, genau zwischen der Bismarck-Kaserne und dem mit Villen bebauten europäischen Teil der Stadt. Umgeben war das Gebäude von einem großen Park, dem Gouvernementspark. Es ist vom Stadtzentrum aus nicht sichtbar.

Das dreigeschossige Wohnhaus wirkt sehr wuchtig: Teile der Fassade sind mit massivem rustikal behauenem Granitstein verblendet. Aus grünlichem und grauem Granit sind die Strahlen der Sonne im Giebel über dem Haupteingang. Eine von einem Steinpflock aus gespannte »Ankerkette« legt sich darum. Aus Stein gemeißelte Seemannsknoten bilden die Ecken des Giebels. Auf der mit einem Wellenmuster dekorierten Granittraufe sitzt ein Drachenkopf – kein chinesischer Drache, sondern ein Wikingerdrache mit gefletschten Zähnen. Die für die wilhelminische Ära typische Verbindung dieser Formen und Materialien mit Elementen des Jugendstils zeigt sich in der Fassadengliederung rechts neben dem Haupteingang, der Form einiger Giebel und in der häufigen Verwendung von quadratischen Mustern im Innenraum sowie den zweifarbig verlegten Granitsteinen an den Fassaden.

Im Zentrum des Hauses liegt eine zweigeschossige Halle. Von hier ging es in die Amtsräume und in den Speisesaal. Im ersten Obergeschoß waren die Privatzimmer der Gouverneursfamilie, die Gästezimmer und Dienerzimmer im zweiten Obergeschoß. Die Küche befand sich im Tiefparterre des Hauses. Chinesische Diener wohnten in einem getrennten Gebäude.

Gerüchte, daß die Baukosten eine Million Goldmark betragen hätten, wurden bereits 1922 in japanischen Reiseführern veröffentlicht.[272] Die zur Verfügung stehende Summe von 450 000 Goldmark war überschritten worden. Baudirektor Strasser mußte sich deswegen vor dem Rechnungshof rechtfertigen.[273]

Der deutsche Gouverneur von Qingdao, Oskar Truppel, wohnte hier bis zu seiner

The Governor's Residence was by far the most spectacular building in Qingdao.[271] It was on the slope of Signal Hill, directly between the Bismarck Barracks and the European district of Qingdao with its villas. The building was surrounded by a large park, the Gouvernement Park. It has its back to the city centre and is not visible from there.

The three-storey house makes a very heavy impression: parts of the façade are clad in solid granite cut to give an air of rusticality. The rays of the sun on the gable above the main entrance are carved from greenish and grey granite. An »anchor chain« stretching from a stone post winds around it. Sailor's knots carved in stone form the corners of the gable. On top of the granite eaves decorated with a wavy pattern sits a dragon's head – not a Chinese dragon but a Viking dragon with its teeth bared. The architect combined these forms and materials, which were typical of the Wilhelminian era, with Jugendstil elements such as the articulation of the façade to the right of the main entrance, the form of some of the gables and the frequent use of a square pattern in the interiors and in the two-tone granite panels on the façades.

In the centre of the house is a two-storey hall which gives access to the official rooms and the dining room. On the first floor were the private rooms for the Governor's family and the guest rooms and servants quarters were on the second floor. The kitchen was in the basement. Chinese servants lived in a separate building.

Rumours that the building costs had totalled a million gold marks were published as early as 1922 in Japanese travel guides.[272] The allocated sum of 450 000 gold marks was exceeded. Strasser, the director of public works, had to account for this to the Public Auditors in Germany.[273]

The German Governor of Qingdao, Oskar Truppel, lived here until his return to Germany in May 1911. His successor was Alfred Meyer-Waldeck, who was taken prisoner of war by the Japanese in autumn 1914. After the Ger-

總督私邸

現用途：賓館
所在地：青島龍山路，原信號山（狄特立克斯山）南麓
建築師：施特拉塞爾，房建總監
馬爾克（草圖設計者），政府建築師
建築造價：逾四十五萬金馬克
業主：德國膠州總督府
建造期：一九零五年十月至一九零七年十月
現狀：樓體保存完好。

總督私邸堪稱青島建築的一枝奇葩。[271] 它位於信號山南村麓，其左右分別為俾斯麥兵營和歐洲區內的別墅。這座公館座落在巨大的總督公園內，背向市中心，由市區難以望見。

這座三層樓的建築氣勢雄偉。部分牆面飾以一塊塊巨大的花崗石料，石面加工粗樸。淡綠和灰色的花崗石在正門的山牆上組成光芒四射的太陽形像。牆角伸出一根粗大石柱，由之引出的"錨鏈"環繫於太陽的四周。山牆角以石料鑿成的帆結作裝飾。在波浪形的檐口上飾有一只龍頭，可它不是中國式的龍，而是呲牙咧嘴的諾曼龍。建築師把威廉時代的典型建築式樣和建築材料與青年風格派的手法結合起來，如正門右側的立面分割、幾處山牆的建築式樣、樓內的大量方形裝飾、外牆面上的雙色花崗岩砌體。

樓內正中是一間雙層大廳，通向辦公室和餐廳。二樓是總督家眷的私房，客房和家僕住房均設在第三層，廚房設在底層。中國傭工住在與此隔開的另一幢房舍裡。

曾有言傳該建築耗資達百萬金馬克。[272] 一九二二年，這一說法還被載入日本的導遊手冊中。至少，營建費超出可供使用的四十五萬金馬克是確有實據的。為此，房建總監施特拉塞爾不得不在總會計署申辯原由。[273]

德國駐青島總督都沛祿文在一九一一年五月回國前一直在此居住。其後任為邁爾‧瓦爾德克。一九一四年秋，瓦爾德克落為日本戰俘。繼德國總督之後住進此處的先是若干日軍將領，其後則有幾位青島的華人市長。它也一度成為毛澤東的下榻處。

南面外觀，背景為信號山，一九零七年。
原德國總督臨時住宅西立面，正門，一九九二年。

QINGDAO

Detail der Westfassade:
Kopf eines Wickingerdrachen, 1992
Großes Empfangszimmer, 1908
Speisesaal, 1908
Halle, 1908
Zentrale Halle,
Blick zum Haupteingang, 1992
Detail of the west façade; head of a
Viking dragon, 1992
Large reception room, 1908
Dining room, 1908
Hall, 1908
Central hall,
view of main entrance, 1992

Rückkehr nach Deutschland im Mai 1911. Sein Nachfolger war Alfred Meyer-Waldeck, der im Herbst 1914 in japanische Kriegsgefangenschaft geriet. Nach den deutschen Gouverneuren wohnten hier die japanischen Generäle, dann die chinesischen Bürgermeister von Qingdao, später auch Mao Zedong. Während der Kulturrevolution wurde die Villa nicht von den Roten Garden »gesäubert«. So findet man noch fast alle originalen deutschen elektrischen Leuchten. Die hölzernen Wandtäfelungen und Fliesenarbeiten sind komplett erhalten. Im Wintergarten funktioniert die mechanische Belüftungsanlage noch immer. Auch einige der Möbel, wie ein großer Billardtisch, werden noch heute genutzt.

man Governors the house was occupied by Japanese generals, then by the Chinese mayors of Qingdao and later even by Mao Zedong. During the Cultural Revolution the villa was spared being »purged« by the Red Guards. As a result virtually all the original German electric light fittings are still in place. The wooden wall panelling and tiling are intact. In the conservatory the mechanical ventilation system still works. Some of the furniture, including a large billiard table, is still in use today.

西立面細部:諾曼龍龍頭,一九九二年。

文革期間,這一別墅幸免紅衛兵的"洗劫"。因而,樓內幾乎所有的電燈仍為德製的原裝貨。瓷磚牆和木製壁板亦完好無損。暖房中的機械通風設備運轉如常。某些室內設施,如一張大臺球桌,至今還在使用之中。

大型接待室,一九零八年。
餐廳,一九零八年。
大廳,一九零八年。
中央大廳,正門內側,一九九二年。

QINGDAO

GOUVERNEMENTS-DIENSTGEBÄUDE
HEADQUARTERS OF THE GERMAN ADMINISTRATION

Heutige Funktion. Current use
Rathaus
Yishui Lu/Shifu Gongyuan (Gouvernementsplatz), Qingdao (Tsingtau)
City Government and Town Hall
Yishui Lu/Shifu Gongyuan (Gouvernements Platz), Qingdao (Tsingtao)

Architekt. Architect
Mahlke, Regierungsbaumeister[274]
Mahlke, Government Architect[274]

Baukosten. Building costs
850 000 Goldmark
850 000 gold marks

Ausführung. Contractors
F. H. Schmidt, Altona, Hamburg

Bauherr. Client
Deutsches Gouvernement Kiautschou
German Administration of Kiaochow

Bauzeit. Construction time
April 1904 – April 1906

Zustand. Condition
Das Gebäude ist sehr gut erhalten; 1989 Erweiterung durch spiegelsymmetrischen Neubau auf der Nordseite.
Very well preserved; building extended to twice its size in 1989.

Luftbildaufnahme, um 1930
Rathaus von Qingdao,
Südansicht, 1991
Aerial photograph, around 1930
Qingdao Town Hall,
view from the south, 1991

Das Regierungsgebäude liegt am Südhang eines gleichmäßig geformten Hügels mit Blick über die Meeresbucht. Hier treffen sich der elegant geschwungene Hohenloheweg und die Wilhelmstraße, die Sichtachse zum Meer. Der Grundriß des Baues ist bereits im »Stadtbauplan von Tsintau« von 1899 eingetragen.[275] Vor dem massiv wirkenden Granitbau – im Volksmund »Tintenfaß« genannt – lag der Gouvernementsplatz.

Die Fassaden des Gebäudes wurden mit Granitquadern verblendet, einem Baustoff, der im ganzen Schutzgebiet zu finden war. Er galt als das einzige Baumaterial, mit dem sich in Qingdao dauerhafte und präzise Fassaden herstellen ließen. Bis zu 240 Steinhauer waren mit der Bearbeitung des Granits beschäftigt. Für den Einbau der teilweise sehr schweren Quader wurde ein Gerüst aus amerikanischem Kiefernholz errichtet, das eine auf Schienen laufende Hebevorrichtung trug. Für die Tischlerarbeiten in den Innenräumen wurde Teakholz verwendet, da sich dieses unter dem Wechsel der Witterung am wenigsten verzog.

An die chinesischen Handwerker wurden hohe Anforderungen gestellt, und Architekt Mahlke lobte ausdrücklich deren Geschicklichkeit. In den offenen Hallen und Flurgängen des ersten Obergeschosses mauerten und verputzten sie die ihnen bis dahin unbekannten Tonnengewölbe mit Stichkappen. Bei vielen der deutschen Gebäude wurden diese oder Kreuzgewölbe zur Gestaltung von räumlich wichtigen Deckenbereichen verwendet.[276] Am Gouvernements-Dienstgebäude sind sie sogar ein wichtiger Teil der Hauptfassade, da sie durch die offenen Bögen der Veranda deutlich vom Gouvernementsplatz aus zu sehen waren.

1989 wurde das ehemals deutsche Rathaus verdoppelt. Der Altbau war als Gebäude für die heutige Stadtregierung zu klein geworden. Grundlegende Idee für den Entwurf des Neubaus war: »Was die Deutschen damals konnten, können wir auch.« Der U-förmige Altbau wurde auf seiner Nordseite »gespie-

The government building is on the southern slope of an evenly-shaped hill overlooking the bay. At this point the elegantly curving Hohenlohe Weg meets Wilhelmstrasse, the visual axis to the sea. The plan of the building, which is symmetrical about the centre, appears in the »Town development plan for Tsintao« published in 1899.[275] In front of the granite building, which has a very solid appearance and is known locally as the »ink pot«, was the square »Gouvernements Platz«. The façades of the building were clad with granite slabs, a material which was available throughout the protectorate. It was considered to be the only material which could be used to produce façades with a neat finish. Up to 240 stonemasons were involved in processing the granite. To put the slabs, some of them very heavy, into place, scaffolding of American pine with a lifting device on a track system was erected. Teak was chosen for the carpentry work in the interiors, since it was the wood which warped the least under changing climatic conditions.

High demands were placed on the Chinese craftsmen and the architect, Mahlke, specifically praised their skill. In the open halls and corridors of the first storey they built brickwork and plastered barrel vaults with lunettes, elements with which they were totally unfamiliar. These barrel vaults and cross vaults were used in many of the German buildings for the spatially important parts of the ceilings.[276] On the headquarters of the German Administration they are even an important part of the main façade as they can be clearly seen from Gouvernements Platz through the open arches of the veranda.

In 1989 the former German town hall was doubled in size. The old building had become too small for today's city government. The basic idea underlying the new building was: »What the Germans could do then, we can do too.« A mirror image of the U-shaped original building was built to the north. The details of the granite façade and the mansard roof were copied exactly. The overall propor-

總督官署

現用途：青島市人民政府
所在地：青島沂水路（市府公園旁），原
　　　　總督府廣場
建築師：馬爾克，政府建築師⟨274⟩
建築造價：八十五萬金馬克
業主：德國膠州總督府
施工：漢堡阿爾托納區F·H·施密特公司
建造期：一九零四年五月至一九零六年四
　　　　月
現狀：樓體保存完好。一九八九年老樓北
　　　側新建一座格局完全相同的新樓

德國總督府座落在地勢平緩的觀海山南麓，面向青島灣。成漂亮弧形的霍恩洛厄路與威廉大街交匯於此，後者構成通向大海的視線軸。總督官署的平面成中軸對稱狀，早在一八九九年就被列入《青島城市規劃圖》中。⟨275⟩民間俗稱這座氣勢宏偉的花崗石建築為"墨水瓶"，其前方為總督府廣場。

這幢建築物的立面用花崗岩細方石砌成。這種建築材料在整個保護區內隨處可見，被公認為青島城內唯一可砌出乾淨牆面的建築材料。當時從事石材加工業的石匠有二百四十人。要將某些沉重的細方石砌入牆體，須搭建美國松木製成的腳手架，其上設有導軌，供起重裝置運行。總督府內的門、窗等木工皆用柚木做成，此種木材在氣候變化的情況下很少變形。

這項建築任務向中國工匠提出了很高的要求。建築師馬爾克對心靈手巧的中國匠人倍加贊賞，他們建成了其平生未見的兩層敞開式大廳和券廊內的凸出圓拱頂。許多德國建築在重要空間的頂部都採用這種圓拱或十字拱。⟨276⟩總督府大樓的凸出圓拱甚至是正立面的一個重要組成部分，可由總督府廣場通過敞開式外廊的拱券望及。一八八九年，原德國督府辦公樓被作了一次"拷貝"。老樓作為現青島市人民政府辦公樓顯得過小。新樓設計的主旨是："德國人當時能夠做到的，我們也能做到。"於是老樓在其北側又有了翻版。花崗石立面及孟莎頂這些細部都仿造得極其精確。由於樓高有所降低，建築的整體比例有細微變動。鋁合金製成的新樓窗呈煙

青島鳥瞰，攝於約一九三零年。
青島市政府南立面，一九九一年。

211

QINGDAO

Westansicht des Rathauses
(1906 erbaut, rechts) und des
Neubaus (1989, links), 1991.
Eingang in den Neubau
(1989 erbaut), Nordansicht, 1991
View from the west of Town Hall
(building on the right constructed
in 1906) and of the new building
(left, 1989)
Entrance to the new building
(constructed in 1989),
view from the north, 1991

gelt«. Die Details der Granitfassade und des Mansarddaches sind exakt kopiert. Die Gesamtproportion wurde jedoch leicht verändert, da man die Stockwerkshöhe verringerte. Die Fenster aus Aluminium haben Rauchglasscheiben. Der neue Haupteingang wurde zu einer Übersteigerung des »typisch Deutschen«: man betritt das neue Regierungsgebäude über eine Brücke wie eine Burg.

tions of the building were however changed slightly because the storey heights were made smaller. The new aluminium windows have smoked glass panes. The new main entrance turned out to be an exaggeration of a »typical German building«. The entrance to the new government building is via a bridge; it is like entering a castle.

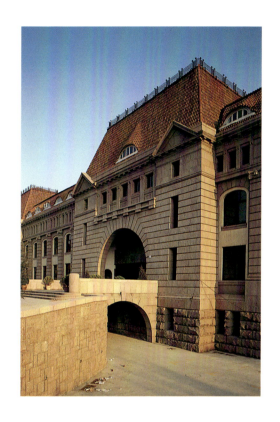

新樓(建於一九八九年)入口,北面外觀,一九九一年。
市政府西面外觀,(右側大樓建於一九零六年,左側新樓建於一九八九年),一九九一年。

青色。主入口高高的台基較典型的德國建築有過之而不無及。一座小橋通向猶如城堡的市政府大樓。

QINGDAO

KAISERLICHES GERICHT
IMPERIAL COURT

Heutige Funktion. Current use
Qingdaoer städtisches Volksgericht der mittleren Instanz Dexian Lu/Hunan Lu (Gouvernementsplatz), Qingdao (Tsingtau)
Qingdao Municipal People's Court Dexian Lu/Hunan Lu (Gouvernements Platz), Qingdao (Tsingtao)

Architekt. Architect
Hans Fittkau[277]

Ausführung. Contractors
F.H. Schmidt, Altona, Hamburg

Bauherr. Client
Deutsches Gouvernement Kiautschou
German Administration of Kiaochow

Bauzeit. Construction time
Frühjahr 1912 – April 1914
Spring 1912 – April 1914

Zustand. Condition
Das Gebäude ist sehr gut erhalten.
Very well preserved.

Gericht, Blick vom Rathaus auf die Nordwestecke, 1992
Courthouse, view from Town Hall of north-west corner, 1992

Das Gerichtsgebäude bildete den westlichen Abschluß des Gouvernementsplatzes. Mit einer Komposition zusammenhängender Baukörper versuchte der Architekt Hans Fittkau, auf die komplizierte städtebauliche Situation einzugehen: im Norden die landhausartige Bebauung des Hohenlohewegs, im Süden die geschlossene zwei- bis dreigeschossige Bebauung der Irenenstraße. Zum Platz sollte das Gericht eine gewisse Monumentalität zeigen, gleichzeitig aber nicht in Konkurrenz zu dem Gouvernements-Dienstgebäude treten. So entwickelte sich ein Entwurf mit sehr unterschiedlichen Fassaden und Traufhöhen. Der Haupteingang am Gouvernementsplatz liegt in der Schnittstelle des voluminösen Saalbaukörpers und des kleineren Büroflügels. Plastizität erhält die Fassade durch etwa 50 cm tiefe Fenstergewände, die Fenster sind gegliedert durch senkrechte und einige waagerechte Balken aus Granit, die einen guten Sonnenschutz bilden.

Ausländer in China unterstanden seit 1842 der Gerichtsbarkeit ihrer Konsulate. In den Verträgen von Nanjing war festgelegt worden, daß chinesische Gesetze auf sie nicht angewendet werden durften und es auch keine Prozesse vor chinesischen Gerichten gab. Selbst Prozesse zwischen Chinesen und Ausländern wurden vor den Konsulatsgerichten geführt. Für deutsche Staatsbürger endete dieses koloniale Privileg 1917.

Im deutschen Schutzgebiet Jiaozhou war die rechtliche Situation folgendermaßen geregelt: Alle Bewohner waren »einander in der Jurisdiktion gleichgestellt. Sie unterstehen (…) dem deutschen Rechte nach den Normen der vorbezeichneten Gesetze und Verordnungen. Die Gerichtsbarkeit wird ausgeübt teils von dem Kaiserlichen Richter als Einzelrichter, teils von dem Kaiserlichen Gerichte, welches aus dem Richter und zwei bzw. vier Beisitzern besteht. Der Richter ist vom Kaiser als solcher ernannt und mit allen Garantien der richterlichen Unabhängigkeit ausgestattet. Die Beisitzer werden vom Richter mit Genehmigung des Gouverneurs ernannt, sie sind

The court building forms the western side of Gouvernements Platz. The architect Hans Fittkau used a composition of different buildings linked to each other to deal with a complicated urban design situation: to the north is the country-house style development of Hohenlohe Weg, to the south the continuous two- to three-storey buildings on Irenenstrasse. The court was intended to have a certain degree of monumentality as seen from the square, yet, at the same time, it was not meant to compete with the headquarters of the German Administration. As a result a scheme with very different façades and building heights evolved. The main entrance on Gouvernements Platz is on the intersection of the voluminous building housing the main hall and the smaller office wing. The windows, which are set back by about half a metre, give the façade a certain plasticity. They are articulated by vertical and sometimes horizontal bars of granite which provide good sun-shading.

From 1842 onwards foreigners in China were subject to the jurisdiction of their consulates. In the Treaty of Nanjing it had been laid down that Chinese laws could not be applied to them and there were no trials in Chinese courts. Even court cases between Chinese and foreigners were presided over by courts of the consulates. This colonial privilege ended for German nationals in 1917.

In the German protectorate of Jiaozhou the legal situation was as follows: all inhabitants were »equal to each other before the law. They are subject to (…) German law in accordance with the standards of the aforementioned laws and ordinances. The jurisdiction is exercised in part by the Imperial judges acting alone and in part by the Imperial courts which consisted of a judge and two or four assessors. The judge is appointed to his position by the Kaiser and invested with all the guarantees of impartiality befitting a judge. The assessors are appointed by the judge with the approval of the Governor; they are select-

膠州法院

現用途：青島市中級人民法院

所在地：青島德縣路（湖南路口），原總
　　　　督府廣場
建築師：漢斯‧費特考爾〈277〉
施　工：漢堡阿爾托納區F‧H‧施密特公司
業　主：德國膠州總督府
建造期：一九一二年春至一九一四年四月
現　狀：樓體保存完好。

膠州法院位於總督府廣場西側，其北是霍恩洛厄路的別墅建築，南側的伊雷妮大街佈滿二至三層的樓房。為適應這一複雜的城市建設佈局，建築師漢斯‧費特考爾用幾組建築體藝術地組合成法院大樓。膠州法院朝向廣場的一側庭展示出某種紀念意義，同時又不能與總督府競相爭妍。因此，設計者對建築物的立面和高度都採用了極其不同的處理。主入口朝向廣場，並在龐大的廳堂建築體與相對見小的側翼辦公樓的交匯點上。立面的窗體深入牆體五十公分左右，並用花崗石做縱向，間或亦做橫向分割，構成良好的遮陽設施。這種處理手法賦予整個立面以立體感和生動性。

自一八四二年以來，在華的外國人在法律上受其領事館管轄。根據《南京條約》的規定，外國人不受中國法律制約，中國法庭不受理對外國人的訴訟。即使中國人與外國人之間的訴訟也由領事館法庭審理。至一九一七年，德國公民一直享受這種殖民特權。

德國膠州保護區對法事有如下規定：租界內所有居民"在法律上一律平等，均受德國法律條文、規定的制約。訴訟由皇家法官一人或皇家法庭審理。後者由一名皇家法官和兩至四名陪審法官組成。皇家法官由皇帝任命，具有絕對的獨立性。陪審法官選自當地德高望重的商人或民官，由法官任命。"〈278〉

在德國租界內居住的華人服從德國法律。青島、李村兩地設有地方法庭，由通曉華語的德國審判官受理華人訴訟。民事訴訟以中國當地法律為准繩。由於歐洲人視中國法律過於嚴厲，刑事訴訟則按德國法

由市政府望法院西北角，一九九二年。

QINGDAO

Blick vom Villenviertel auf die
Nordostecke, 1992
Südostecke, 1992
View from villa district of north-east
corner, 1992
South-east corner, 1992

aus der Zahl der ansässigen angesehenen Kaufleute und Zivilbeamte genommen.«[278]

Im deutschen Schutzgebiet Jiaozhou lebende Chinesen unterstanden ebenfalls der deutschen Gerichtsbarkeit. Ihre Rechtsstreitigkeiten wurden in den beiden Bezirksämtern Qingdao und Licun (Litsun) von Chinesisch sprechenden deutschen Beamten verhandelt. Bei bürgerlichen Rechtsstreitigkeiten legte man das lokale chinesische Recht zugrunde. Anstelle des chinesischen Strafrechts, das nach europäischen Begriffen zu harte Strafen enthält, bezog man sich auf die wichtigsten strafbaren Tatbestände des deutschen Rechts, aber unter weitgehender Berücksichtigung der Rechtsanschauungen der Chinesen. So wurde die Prügelstrafe für Männer beibehalten. Die grausamen Strafen des chinesischen Rechts und verschärften Formen der Todesstrafe wurden dagegen abgeschafft.

ed from the resident merchants and civil servants of repute.«[278]

Chinese who lived in the German protectorate of Jiaozhou were also subject to German jurisdiction. Their legal disputes were dealt with in the two district town halls of Qingdao and Licun (Litsun) by Chinese-speaking German civil servants. In the case of civil disputes the local Chinese law was applied. Instead of the Chinese criminal law which prescribed punishments too harsh by European standards reference was made to the major criminal acts punishable under German law, but incorporating, as far as possible, the legal attitude of the Chinese. An example of this was the retention of punishment by whipping for men. The gruesome punishments prescribed under Chinese law and the worst forms of the death penalty were however abolished.

律,同時盡量兼顧華人的法律觀念。於是,對男人施以體罰的懲罰方式得以保留,而對中國法律中的殘忍懲罰方式及死刑則予以廢除。

法院東南角,一九九二年。
由別墅區望法院東北角,一九九二年。

QINGDAO

KAISERLICH CHINESISCHES SEEZOLLAMT
IMPERIAL CHINESE MARITIME CUSTOMS AND EXCISE OFFICE

Heutige Funktion. Current use
Zollamt
Customs and Excise Office
Xinjiang Lu (Am großen Hafen),
Qingdao (Tsingtau. Tsingtao)

Architekten. Architects
Hochbaudirektor Strasser; Hans Fittkau [279]
Strasser, director of public works;
Hans Fittkau [279]

Baukosten. Building costs
etwa 180 000 Goldmark
approximately 180 000 gold marks

Ausführung. Contractors
F. H. Schmidt, Altona, Hamburg

Bauherr. Client
Ernst Ohlmer, chinesischer Seezolldirektor
Ernst Ohlmer, director of Chinese Maritime Customs and Excise

Bauzeit. Construction time
August 1913 – April 1914

Zustand. Condition
Das Gebäude ist sehr gut erhalten.
Very well preserved.

Zollamt, Ostansicht, 1992
Customs and Excise Office, view from the east, 1992

Die ersten Gebäude des Seezollamtes lagen noch an der alten Schiffsanlegestelle, der Tsingtau-Brücke. 1911 verlegte man das Zollamt zum großen Hafen; 1914 wurde dort dieses Gebäude bezogen. Mit seinem hohen Walmdach, den beiden Jugendstilgiebeln an den Längsseiten und dem von einfachen zylindrischen Säulen getragenen Eingangsportal an der Schmalseite war das Gebäude des Seezollamtes das modernste Verwaltungsgebäude in Qingdao. Granitstein wurde bei diesem Bau nur noch sehr sparsam verwendet. Eine chinesische Seezollbehörde gab es seit 1860; sie wurde nach europäischem Muster organisiert und stand unter britischer Verwaltung. Die Zolldirektoren in den Hafenstädten waren europäische Beamte. 1898 wurde das gesamte deutsche Schutzgebiet zum Freihafen erklärt. Die ein- und ausgeführten Güter waren zollfrei; Zoll war nur zu entrichten, wenn sie in das chinesische Hinterland gingen oder von dort zur Ausfuhr über See in das Schutzgebiet kamen. Die politische Landgrenze des Schutzgebietes bildete zugleich die Zollgrenze.

Der Bau des Hafens und der Eisenbahn nach Jinan führte 1906 zu einem neuen Zollabkommen, dem »Tsingtauer System«.[280] Das deutsche Schutzgebiet gehörte nun zollrechtlich zu China; der Verkehr zwischen der Provinz Shandong und dem Schutzgebiet verlief ohne jegliche Verzollung an der Grenze. So konnten Rohstoffe aus China im deutschen Schutzgebiet verarbeitet werden und die Erzeugnisse danach ohne Kontrolle des Seezollamtes in China verkauft werden. Das war eine wichtige Voraussetzung dafür, daß Industrie in dem Schutzgebiet entstehen konnte. Nur das Hafengebiet bildete einen begrenzten Zollfreibezirk, in dem über See eingeführte Waren zollfrei lagern konnten. Das war ein wesentlicher Vorteil gegenüber den anderen chinesischen Hafenstädten, in denen ausländische Niederlassungen bestanden.

The first buildings of the Maritime Customs and Excise Office were at the Tsingtao Bridge, the old landing stage. In 1911 the Customs and Excise Office was moved to the main docks and in 1914 this building was put into service. With its high hipped roof, the two Jugendstil gables on the long sides and the entrance portal on simple cylindrical columns on the short side, the building for the Maritime Customs and Excise Office was the most modern administrative building in Qingdao. Granite was used very sparingly in this building.

There had been a Chinese Maritime Customs and Excise authority since 1860; it had been modelled on the European system and was under British administration. The directors of customs and excise in the port towns were European civil servants. In 1898 the entire German protectorate had been declared a free port. The goods imported and exported were tax-free. Customs duty had to be levied only if the goods were destined for the Chinese hinterland or came from there into the protectorate for export through the port. The political border of the protectorate was thus simultaneously a customs border.

The building of the port and the railway to Jinan led to a new customs agreement being reached in 1906, the »Tsingtao System.«[280] The German protectorate now belonged for the purposes of customs and excise to China. Trade between the province of Shandong and the protectorate was not, however, subject to any kind of customs levy at the border. This meant, for instance, that raw materials from China could be processed in the German protectorate and the finished goods could be sold in China without being checked in any way by the Maritime Customs Authority. This was an important prerequisite for the growth of industry in the protectorate. Only the port area formed a limited tax-free area in which the goods imported from overseas could be stored tax free. That was an advantage enjoyed by the Chinese port towns which had foreign settlements.

大清國膠海關

現用途：海關
所在地：青島新疆路，原大港一帶
建築師：施特拉塞爾，房建總監：漢斯・弗特考爾〈279〉
建築造價：約十八萬金馬克
施工：漢堡阿爾托納區Ｆ・Ｈ・施密特公司
業主：大清國海關稅務司恩斯特・阿里文
建造期：一九一三年八月至一九一四年四月
現狀：樓體保存完好。

海關大樓最初建在棧橋老碼頭。一九一一年，海關移至大港，並於一九一四年遷入那裡新落成的海關大樓。這是當時青島現代化程度最高的辦公大樓。它有高高的斜屋頂，橫向的兩處山牆為德國青年風格派手法，主入口開在縱側面，由造型簡單的圓形壁柱承重。

中國海關的歷史可上溯至一八六零年。海關按歐洲模式組織，屬英帝國管轄。港口城市的稅務司皆由歐洲官員充任。一八九八年，整個膠州原護區宣佈成為自由港。所有由海路運進或運出青島口岸的貨物均不徵稅。若貨物運進中國內地，或由中國內地運進膠州保護地，再由海路運往他處，則須照章完稅。關境以保護地的勢力範圍為界。為了簡化關界的徵稅過程，德國總督府同意在青島設立一處中國海關。大港的落成和膠濟鐵路的通車釀成了一九零六年的新關稅協定—青島關稅體系。〈280〉自此，德國膠州保護地的海關主權歸中國所有。海關對山東省與保護地之間的來往貨物均不徵稅。這樣，便可在膠州保護區內加工中國原料，其產品勿須海關查驗，便可直接運往中國各地銷售。這為膠州保護區工業的興起創造了先決條件。由海路運進保護區的貨物可在港口一帶劃定的免稅區內免稅存放。與其他設有外國租界的中國港口城市相比，這是膠州保護區的一大優勢。

海關東面外觀，一九九二年。

QINGDAO

POLIZEIDIENSTGEBÄUDE UND BEZIRKSAMT
POLICE HEADQUARTERS AND DISTRICT TOWN HALL

Heutige Funktion. Current use
Qingdaoer Polizei
Qingdao police
Hubei Lu/Mongyin Lu
(Kronprinzenstraße/Münchener Straße),
Qingdao (Tsingtau. Tsingtao)

Entwurf. Design
Regierungsbaumeister Wentrup
Wentrup, Government Architect

Baukosten. Building costs
über 75 000 Goldmark
over 75 000 gold marks

Bauherr. Client
Deutsches Gouvernement Kiautschou
German Administration of Kiaochow

Bauzeit. Construction time
1904–1905

Zustand. Condition
Das Gebäude ist sehr gut erhalten.
Very well preserved.

Polizei, Südansicht, 1992
Schmuckgiebel und Turm, Südostecke, 1992
Police station, view from the south, 1992
Gable element and tower, south-east corner, 1992

Das Polizeigebäude lag an der stadträumlichen Schnittstelle zwischen der Europäerstadt und dem chinesischen Händlerviertel Dabaodao (Tapautau), nicht weit vom Bahnhof entfernt auf einem markanten achteckigen Grundstück. Ging man auf den Bahnhof zu, bot sich dem Auge der überraschende Anblick des sechsgeschossigen Turms der Polizeistation in der Seitenstraße. Er markierte den Haupteingang und lag genau in der Achse der Münchener Straße. Die Polizeistation überragte bei weitem die umliegende, früher nur zweigeschossige Bebauung. In den Formen der deutschen Neorenaissance gebaut, hat das Gebäude ein sehr hohes, steiles Dach. Die großen Schmuckgiebel sind durch Werkstein- und Ziegelsteinstreifen vertikal und horizontal gegliedert; diese Linien setzen sich in kleinen obeliskartigen Spitzen über dem Giebel fort. Alfons Paquet konnte schreiben: »Das in neu-nürnberger Art mit stolzem Turm und Giebel hingesetzte Gebäude, die Behausung des Gerichts, der Polizeistation, des Gefängnisses und des Rikschadepots, erinnert an ein Rathaus daheim.«[281]

Auf dem großen Grundstück befand sich außerdem je ein Wohngebäude für die europäische und chinesische Polizei sowie das Gefängnis für Chinesen.[282] Östlich neben der Polizeistation wurde 1908/09 ein zentrales Rikschadepot eingerichtet. Es war vom Gouvernement subventioniert und umfaßte Werkstätten zur Herstellung und Ausbesserung von Rikschas, eine Waschanstalt, Badezimmer, Schlaf- und Speiseräume. 600 bis 800 Kulis, die sich das Fahrzeug jeweils von einem der chinesischen Rikschaeigentümer mieteten, lebten hier unter besseren Bedingungen als zuvor in den Herbergen Dabaodaos.

The police headquarters was at the intersection of the two separate parts of the town, the European district and the Chinese tradesmen quarter Dabaodao (Tapautau). It was not far from the railway station on a site which was octagonal and made a striking image on the plan of the town. Approaching the station the eye was met by the surprising sight of the six-storey tower of the police station. It marked the main entrance and was exactly on the axis to Münchener Strasse. The police station was far higher than the surrounding buildings which were only two storeys high. In the style of the German neo-Renaissance the building has a very high, steep roof. The large decorative gables are horizontally and vertically articulated by strips of stone and brick. These lines are continued into small obelisk-like points above the gables. Alfons Paquet wrote: »The building in neo-Nürnberg style with proud towers and gables, which houses the court, the police station, the gaol and the rickshaw depot, looks like a town hall back home.«[281]

On the large site there were also two residential buildings, one for the European and one for the Chinese police and a gaol for Chinese.[282] In 1908/09 a central rickshaw depot was built to the east, next to the police station. It was subsidized by the German Administration and comprised workshops for making and repairing rickshaws, a wash house, bathrooms, dormitories and dining rooms. 600 to 800 coolies, who rented their vehicles from one of the Chinese rickshaw owners, lived here under better conditions than previously in the hostels of Dabaodao.

警察公署和地方法庭

現用途：青島市公安局
所在地：青島湖北路（蒙沂路口），原太子路（慕尼黑路口）
設計：建築管理局
建築造價：逾七點五萬金馬克
業主：德國膠州總督府
建造期：一九零四年至一九零五年
現狀：樓體保存完好。

從城市平面圖上看，警察公署座落在一片引人注目的八邊形土地上，位於城內歐洲區和華人貿易商業區的交界處，距火車站很近。如迎車站而行，首先映入眼簾的便是警察公署高達六層的塔樓。它位於一條側馬路上，正居於慕尼黑路的軸線上，顯著地標誌出主入口的位置。警察公署大樓猶如異峰突起，遠遠高出周圍的二層建築。這是一幢德國文藝復興式復古風格的建築。上覆高大陡直的尖頂，花崗石與紅磚縱橫相間，砌出巨大山牆的"半木構"圖案，砌體高出山牆，呈方尖塔狀。阿爾豐斯·派克韋特曾這樣寫道："警察公署大樓屬新紐倫堡派風格，其塔樓與山牆氣勢宏偉。樓內設青島地方法庭、警察公署和一所監獄。它與東洋停車場所構成的畫面，使人聯想起家鄉的市政廳。"〈281〉

警察公署所在的八邊形地產上還有一所華人監獄及歐洲警察和華人警察住宅樓各一幢。〈282〉其東端是於一九零八年至一九零九年間建的東洋車中心停車場。它由總督府資助，包括東洋車修理間、製造間、清洗間及浴室、臥室和餐廳。六至八百名的拉車工在此生活。以前他們住在大鮑島條件較差的小客棧裡。拉車工們分別向華人車主租借所用車輛。

公安局南立面，一九九二年。
東南角山牆裝飾及塔樓，一九九二年。

QINGDAO

TSINGTAU HAUPTBAHNHOF
TSINGTAO CENTRAL RAILWAY STATION

Heutige Funktion. Current use
Qingdaos Bahnhof
Qingdao's railway station
Tai'an Lu/Guangxi Lu
(Kieler Straße/Prinz-Heinrich-Straße),
Qingdao (Tsingtau. Tsingtao)

Entwurf. Design
Luis Weiler, Heinrich Hildebrand,
Alfred Gaedertz

Ausführung. Contractors
Schantung-Eisenbahn-Gesellschaft
Shantung Railway Company

Bauherr. Client
Schantung-Eisenbahn-Gesellschaft
Shantung Railway Company

Bauzeit. Construction time
Januar 1900 – Herbst/Winter 1901
January 1900 – Autumn/Winter 1901

Zustand. Condition
Das Gebäude wurde 1991 abgetragen; beim 1993 fertiggestellten Neubau wurde die historische Fassade kopiert.
Pulled down in 1991; the historical façade was copied on the new building which was completed in 1993.

Während die Landbahnhöfe der Schantung-Eisenbahn in einem europäisch-chinesischen Mischstil gebaut wurden, entwarf man den Stadtbahnhof in Qingdao in der Art der deutschen Neorenaissance. Der zur Stadt orientierte Haupteingang wurde durch einen hohen Schmuckgiebel betont. Ein kräftiger Uhrturm bildete die südliche Ecke und war bereits von weitem sichtbar, da er genau in den Straßenachsen der Guangxi Lu (Prinz-Heinrich-Straße) und der Lanshan Lu (Hohenzollernstraße) lag. Der Sockel des Turms, Fenster- und Türeinfassungen sowie die Verzierungen der Giebel und der Turmspitze wurden mit Granitstein verblendet.

Die Bahnlinie nach Jinan stellte die wirtschaftliche Verbindung zwischen der deutschen Stadtneugründung und der Provinz Shandong her. Die Strecke wurde ab 1901 stückweise eröffnet und war 1904 durchgängig befahrbar. Vom Bahnhof führten Gleise zur Landungsbrücke (Tsingtau-Brücke), durch die man die Grundstücke der Handelshäuser erschloß, denn die erste Mole des großen Hafens wurde erst 1904 fertiggestellt. Im ersten Bebauungsplan war vorgesehen, den Bahnhof an der Landungsbrücke zu errichten, doch wären bogenförmig anzulegende Bahnhofsanlagen technisch zu aufwendig gewesen. Der Bahnhof wurde nach Westen verschoben und lag nun an gerade geführten Gleisen am westlichen Stadtrand.

Der neue Qingdaoer Großbahnhof wurde 1993 fertiggestellt. Eine Kopie der Ostfassade des historischen Bahnhofsgebäudes markiert den Haupteingang. Dieses Fassadenrelief wurde aus Stahlbeton hergestellt und gegenüber dem Vorgängerbau um 10 Meter nach Westen verschoben. Den Uhrturm erhöhte man um drei Meter, um dadurch bessere Proportionen zu der Glasfassade des Neubaus zu erhalten.

Whilst the rural stations of the Shantung Railways were built in a mixture of European and Chinese styles, the station in the city of Qingdao was built in the style of the German neo-Renaissance. The main entrance facing the city was emphasised by a high ornamental gable. A powerful clock tower marked the southern corner and could be seen from afar as it was exactly on the axes of two streets, Guangxi Lu (Prinz-Heinrich-Strasse) and Lanshan Lu (Hohenzollernstrasse). The base of the tower, the door and window frames and the decoration of the gable and the steeple were clad in granite.

The railway line to Jinan was the economic lifeline between the new German city and the province of Shandong. The line was opened in sections from 1901 onwards and was in full operation by 1904. Tracks went from the station to the landing stage (Tsingtao Bridge) and there was access from them to the trading companies' property because the first mole of the large docks was not completed until 1904. In the first development plan for the city the station was at the landing stage but the arch-shaped railway tracks would have proved technically too complicated. The station was shifted westwards, was now on straight tracks and formed the western edge of the city.

The new central station in Qingdao was completed in 1993. The main entrance is marked by an exact copy of the eastern façade of the station building. The relief on the façade was made in reinforced concrete and moved 10 metres to the west of where the original façade had been. The clock tower was extended by three metres to improve the proportions with the glass façade.

青島火車站

現用途：青島火車站
所在地：青島泰安路（廣西路口），原基
　　　　爾路（亨利王子路口）
設計：路易斯・魏爾勒，海因里希・錫樂
　　　巴阿爾弗雷德・格德爾茨
施工：山東鐵路公司
業主：山東鐵路公司
建造期：一九零零年一月到一九零一年秋
　　　　（冬）
現狀：原車站大樓於一九九一年拆除。新
　　　樓於一九九三年完工。其正立面為
　　　舊樓的歷史再現。

如果説膠濟線沿途中小火車站是中西建築風格聯姻的產物，那末，青島火車站則為純粹的德國文藝復興風格作品。高大的裝飾山牆突出了面向市區的主入口。大樓南角聳起一座厚實的鐘塔，正居於廣西路（原亨利王子路）和蘭山路（原霍恩措倫路）的軸線上。鐘塔的基座、窗邊、門邊以及山牆和塔頂的裝飾都用花崗石砌成。通往濟南的鐵路溝通了膠州保護區青島與山東省之間的聯繫。自一九零一年起，線路部分開通，一九零四年全線通車。由於大港的第一座防波堤直到一九零四年才告完工，由火車站通向棧橋的鐵路便成了各商行開發地產的必要條件。最初的城市規劃方案將火車站設立棧橋一帶，但弧狀的軌道對當時的技術而言顯然要求過高。於是，車站西移至筆直的軌道旁，構成城市的西端。
青島火車站新站於一九九三年峻工。其向西擴建十米的東立面完全是舊樓的重現，顯著地標誌出主入口的位置。該建築為鋼筋混凝土結構，極富立體感。新鐘塔增高三米，與新樓延長的東立面比例協調。

由東站廣場望火車站東面外觀，
一九九零年十二月。
新火車站，一九九三年五月。
火車站南面外觀，一九零七年。

QINGDAO

GOUVERNEMENTS-SCHLACHTHOF
ABATTOIR OF THE GERMAN ADMINISTRATION

Heutige Funktion. Current use
Fabrik
Factory
Guancheng Lu 65 (Schlachthofstraße),
Qingdao (Tsingtau. Tsingtao)

Architekt. Architect
Regierungsbaumeister Stoessel[283]
Stoessel, Government Architect[283]
Anlagenplanung. Technical Planning
Gouvernements-Tierarzt Eggebrecht
Eggebrecht, Government Veterinarian

Baukosten. Building costs
750 000 Goldmark

Bauherr. Client
Deutsches Gouvernement Kiautschou
German Administration of Kiaochow

Bauzeit. Construction time
1903 – Juni 1906
1903 – June 1906

Zustand. Condition
Das Gebäude ist sehr gut erhalten;
mehrere Neubauten.
Very well preserved;
several new buildings added.

Gouvernements-Schlachthof,
Gesamtansicht von Südosten, 1906
Ehem. Schlachthof-Verwaltungs-
gebäude, Südostansicht, 1992
Abattoir of the German
Administration, view of the entire
complex from the south-east, 1906
Former administration building of
abattoir, view from the south-east,
1992

Der Schlachthof war Teil der umfassenden Gesundheitsvorsorgemaßnahmen für Qingdao. Der Anlage wurden die neuesten hygienischen Standards Deutschlands zugrunde gelegt. Da es hier um die Gesundheit der Truppen und der Bevölkerung ging, bewilligte der Reichstag relativ hohe Geldbeträge. Als Standort wurde ein Grundstück westlich des Bahnhofs gewählt, wo in der weiteren Entwicklung keine Wohnviertel angelegt werden sollten. Damit war die Möglichkeit gegeben, den Schlachthof an das Gleisnetz der Schantungbahn anzuschließen. Außerdem konnte die Anlage problemlos erweitert werden und die »unschädliche Ableitung aller üblen Ausdünstungen ohne Belästigung der Nachbarn, bequeme Abführung aller Abwässer in das nahe Meer« war möglich.[284]

Im Verwaltungsgebäude befanden sich die Diensträume der Schlachthofverwaltung, ein großes, mit den modernsten Einrichtungen versehenes Laboratorium und die Wohnungen für die Schlachthofbeamten. Hinter dem Verwaltungsgebäude gab es einen Pferdestall mit Wagenraum. Dem Eingang gegenüber, durch einen großen Hof getrennt, befanden sich drei geräumige Schlachthallen. Gleich dahinter war das Hauptgebäude mit Kühlhaus, Wasserturm, Maschinenhaus, usw. Die Schlachthäuser bestanden aus je einer Großvieh-, Kleinvieh- und Schweineschlachthalle. Die Wände der Schlachthallen waren weiß gefliest. Die Kühlhalle war in Zellen von verschiedener Größe aufgeteilt; diese wurden an die Schlächter vermietet.[285]

Die Verordnung über »Schlachtzwang und Fleischbeschau« sah vor, daß im Stadtgebiet von Qingdao das Schlachten, Häuten oder Ausnehmen von Tieren verboten war und nur noch in dem öffentlichen Schlachthof vorgenommen werden durfte. Chinesische und deutsche Schlächter brachten ihr eigenes Vieh, dessen Gesundheitszustand vom Tierarzt kontrolliert wurde; in den Hallen mußten sie selbst schlachten. Der Vorstand des Schlachthofs überprüfte den Zustand des Fleisches, bevor es die Halle verließ.

The abattoir was part of the comprehensive measures implemented to ensure better health in Qingdao. The complex was built to the latest standards of hygiene in force in Germany. Since the health of the troops and the population were at stake, the Reichstag approved relatively high funding for its construction. A site to the west of the station was chosen and specifications enforced preventing residential areas from being built anywhere near it. This made it possible to link the abattoir directly to the network of the Shantung Railways. It also meant that the complex could be easily extended whenever necessary and that »all noxious smells could be released without causing annoyance to people living nearby and all effluent could be conveniently discharged into the nearby sea.«[284]

The administration building housed all the offices for the abattoir, a large laboratory equipped with the latest apparatus and living quarters for the officials of the abattoir. Behind this building there were stables and a coachhouse. Opposite the entrance, separated by a large yard, were three spacious slaughterhouses. Immediately behind them was the main building with cold storage depot, water tower, plant room, etc. The slaughterhouses each had a section for large animals, small animals and pigs. The walls were tiled in white. The cold storage hall was divided into cells of different sizes which were let to the slaughtermen.[285]

The ordinance on »Compulsory slaughtering and meat inspection« stipulated that within the city limits of Qingdao, the slaughter, skinning or gutting of animals was forbidden anywhere except at the public abattoir. Chinese and German butchers brought their own animals to the abattoir where the health of the animals was checked by the vet. They would slaughter the animals themselves in the slaughterhouses, but the process was strictly controlled by the supervisors. The head of the abattoir checked the meat before it was allowed to leave the slaughterhouse.

總督府屠宰場

現用途：工廠
所在地：青島觀城路六十五號，原屠宰場
　　　　路
建築師：斯蒂塞爾，政府建築師〈283〉
平面設計：埃格布雷希特，政府獸醫
建築造價：七十五萬金馬克
業主：德國膠州總督府
建造期：一九零三年至一九零六年六月
現狀：原建築保存良好，另建數棟新樓。

膠州屠宰場的興建是當時在青島城全面實施的衛生預防措施之一。青島正是得益於這些措施而成為當時中國最新健康的港口城市。屠宰場按德國最新衛生標準設立。由於這關系到部隊和居民的健康，德意志帝國議會同意撥給這項工程較高的費用。屠宰場選址於火車站西側，其四周禁止建造民宅，它緊靠山東鐵路的鐵路網，且易於日後擴建。更重要的是："所有濁氣可無害排除，對當地居民不會產任何影響。其廢水也可方便地排入近海。"〈284〉
屠宰場管理樓內設有各部門的辦公室，一座配有當時極現代化的設施的大型實驗室及該場官員的住房。樓後建有馬廄及供屠夫停放畜力車的車庫。三間寬敞的屠宰大廳與大門正相對應，中間隔一大院。穿過屠宰廳便是設有冷庫、水塔、機房等設施的主樓。屠宰廳包括大畜、小畜及肉豬宰殺幾個部分，其四壁砌有白色瓷磚。冷藏大廳分為大小不一的小間，供屠夫租用。〈285〉
《宰殺章程》規定：嚴禁在市區，包括台西鎮、台東鎮內對牛、小牛、豬、綿羊、山羊、馬、騾、驢進行宰殺、剝皮、剖腹，此等事項僅可在公共屠宰場辦理。德、華屠戶須先將其所要屠宰的牲畜牽入屠宰場供獸區檢查，附合健康標准者方可由各屠戶本人在嚴格的監視下屠宰。所有肉類離廳之前，須經屠宰場場長查驗。肉類可存於租用的大小不一的冷室內。

德國總督府屠宰場東南面全景，
一九零六年。
原屠宰場辦公樓東南面外觀，一
九九二年。

QINGDAO

GERMANIA BRAUEREI
GERMANIA BREWERY

Heutige Funktion. Current use
Tsingtao Beer Brewery
Dengzhou Lu (Hauptmann-Müller-Straße),
Qingdao (Tsingtau. Tsingtao)

Entwurf. Design
Maschinenfabrik Germania, Chemnitz

Ausführung. Contractors
F.H. Schmidt, Altona, Hamburg

Bauherr. Client
Anglo-German Brewery Company

Fertigstellung. Date of completion
Herbst 1904
Autumn 1904

Zustand. Condition
Die Anlage ist teilweise erhalten.
Parts of the building have been preserved.

Germania-Brauerei, Südansicht,
um 1905
»Tsingtao Beer«-Brauerei, 1992
Germania Brewery,
view from the south, around 1905
»Tsingtao Beer« Brewery, 1992

Eine deutsch-englische Gesellschaft, die in Shanghai bereits die Victoria Brauerei besaß, entschloß sich zum Bau der Brauerei in Qingdao; bei damals über 2400 deutschen Soldaten in der Stadt bedeutete das ein sicheres Geschäft.

Die Gebäude dieser privaten Brauerei sind viel einfacher ausgeführt als der fast gleichzeitig erbaute Schlachthof des Gouvernements. Die Maschinenfabrik Germania plante die Gebäude und lieferte die gesamte Maschinenanlage, wie Sudwerk, Dampf- und Kühlmaschinen, Dampfkessel, Pumpen und Rohrleitungen.[286] Vier Brunnen konnten die Brauerei auch in regenarmen Monaten mit genügend Wasser versorgen. Das Waschen, Korken, Drahten und Ettikettieren der Flaschen erfolgte maschinell.

»Das Bier, das die Germania-Brauerei herstellen wird, soll nur aus bestem mährischen Malz und böhmischen und bayerischen Hopfen ohne jede Zutat, wie z.B. Reis (der bekanntlich in Japan vielfach verwandt wird) gebraut werden. Die Brauerei wird sich in dieser Beziehung streng unter das deutsche Gesetz stellen. Es wird helles Bier nach Pilsener und dunkeles nach Münchener Art gebraut werden.«[287] Auf der Münchener Brauereiausstellung erhielt die Brauerei im Sommer 1906 die höchste Auszeichnung: eine goldene Medaille.[288]

Das »Tsingtao Beer« ist heute das in Europa bekannteste Exportprodukt Qingdaos und gehört zu den besten Bieren Asiens. Außerdem gibt es Qingdao noch eine Mineralwasserfabrik aus der deutschen Zeit, »Iltisbrunnen«; sie produziert heute Mineralwasser unter dem Warenzeichen »Laoshan«-Wasser.

An Anglo-German company which already owned the Victoria Brewery in Shanghai decided to build a brewery in Qingdao; a surefire enterprise, given the fact that there were over 2400 German soldiers in the city.

The buildings of this private brewery were of a much simpler design than those of the abattoir built by the German Administration at almost exactly the same time. The Germania engineering company planned the building and supplied all the plant, machines such as the brewing apparatus, steam generators, refrigerating machines, boilers, pumps and piping.[286] Four wells could provide the brewery with sufficient water even in the dry months. All washing, corking, and labelling of the bottles was done by machines.

»The beer which the Germania Brewery will produce will be brewed from the best Moravian malt and Bohemian and Bavarian hops without any additional ingredient, such as rice (which, as is well-known, is often used in Japan). In this respect the brewery will strictly observe the German law. A pale beer will be brewed in the Pilsner tradition and a dark one in the Munich tradition.«[287] In the summer of 1906 the brewery was awarded the highest honour at the Munich Breweries Exhibition: a gold medal.[288]

Today »Tsingtao Beer« is Qingdao's most famous export to Europe and is one of Asia's best beers. There is also a mineral water factory, the »Iltisbrunnen« in Qingdao, dating from the German period. It now produces mineral water which sells under the brand name »Laoshan« water.

德國啤酒廠

現用途：青島啤酒廠
所在地：青島登州路，原米勒上尉路
設計：克姆尼茨市德國機械廠
施工：漢堡阿爾托訥區F‧H‧施米特公司
業主：英德釀業公司
峻工期：一九零四年秋
現狀：建築群部分保存。

已在上海建有維多利亞啤酒廠的一家英德聯營公司決定在青島開辦啤酒廠。青島當時駐有德國士兵二千四百餘名，啤酒的銷路顯示毫無問題。

與幾乎是同期建造的膠州屠宰場相比，這家私營啤酒廠的大樓施工要簡單得多。德國機械廠除設計廠房外，還提供了全套機械設備，如熬汁機、氣壓機、冷凝機、汽鍋、水泵及管道等。〈286〉四座水井即使在旱季也可向啤酒廠提供充足的水源。酒瓶的清洗、裝塞、纏繞金屬絲及加貼商標這些工序全部實行機械化。"德國啤酒廠的啤酒只應選用優質麥里斯麥芬，波希米亞和巴伐利亞啤酒花釀成，不許加稻類等其他任向附加配加料（眾所周知，許多日本啤酒用稻類作配料）。在配料方面，德國啤酒廠嚴格遵守德國啤酒純度法。淡啤酒絕對按照比爾森的傳統釀制；黑啤酒則源於慕尼黑的方式釀制。"〈287〉一九零六年夏，青島德國啤酒廠在慕尼黑啤酒博覽會上獲最高榮譽金獎。

如今，"青島啤酒"是青島在歐洲最負盛名的出口產品，屬亞州名啤之一。〈288〉除原德國啤酒廠外，青島還有一家德國殖民地時期的礦泉小廠——"伊爾蒂斯文井"礦泉水廠。如今，這家工廠的產品使用"嶗山礦泉水"的商標。

德國啤酒廠南面外觀，約一九零五年。
青島啤酒廠，一九九二年。

OBSERVATORIUM
OBSERVATORY

Heutige Funktion. Current use
Meteorologisches Observatorium
Guanxiang Shan (Wasserberg),
Qingdao (Tsingtau)
Meteorological Observation Station
Guanxiang Shan (Wasserberg),
Qingdao (Tsingtao)

Architekt. Architect
Paul Friedrich Richter[289]

Baukosten. Building costs
175 000 Goldmark
175 000 gold marks

Bauherr. Client
Deutsches Gouvernement Kiautschou
German Administration of Kiaochow

Bauzeit. Construction time
Juni 1910 – Januar 1912
June 1910 – January 1912

Zustand. Condition
Das Gebäude ist sehr gut erhalten.
Very well preserved

*Deutsche fern vom Heimatland,
haben hier am fremden Strand
diesen Bau geschichtet.
Schiffen soll er in der Not,
künden, wenn das Wetter droht,
wann der Sturm sich schlichtet;
So als Helfer aufgestellt,
sei der Gruß er, den der Welt,
deutsches Volk entrichtet.*[292]

*Germans far from native soil
Here have given us their toil
This building to provide.
To ships in danger on the seas
News as gales arise and cease
It sends to oceans wide.
And so, as helper here installed,
Be it hailed, given to the world
With sincere German pride.*[292]

Das Observatorium war außer der Signalstation das einzige Gebäude Qingdaos, das auf einem der hohen Hügel stand. Wie eine Burgfestung war es vollständig mit Granitquadern verkleidet.

In der Denkschrift des Reichmarineamts wird die Anlage beschrieben: »Das fertiggestellte Vorprojekt umfaßt ein Hauptdienstgebäude, das außer den Geschäftszimmern ein geräumiges Laboratorium, die Bibliothek, ein der Öffentlichkeit zugängliches Lesezimmer, einen gegen rasche Temperaturänderungen geschützten Uhrenkeller, einen leicht heizbaren Raum zur Bestimmung von Temperaturkoeffizienten von Instrumenten, eine mechanische Werkstatt und Nebenräume enthalten wird. Ferner sind Räume für erdmagnetische Beobachtungen projektiert.«[290] Die Aufgaben des Observatoriums bestanden in Sturmwarndienst, der Wettervorhersage und Beobachtungen zum Erdmagnetismus. Es besaß außerdem eine Normaluhr-Anlage mit einer Einrichtung zum selbständigen Fallenlassen des Zeitballes.

In Ostasien gab es zu Beginn dieses Jahrhunderts nur an wenigen Orten meteorologische Observatorien: Xujiahui (Sikawei) nahe Shanghai, Inch'ön (Chemulpo) in Südkorea, Manila auf den Philippinen und Hongkong. Wetterbeobachtungen waren aber wegen drohender Taifune für die Seefahrt äußerst wichtig. So hatte die deutsche Marine ihr Kanonenboot »Iltis« am 23. Juli 1896 in einem Taifun vor der Küste Shandongs verloren. Das Geld zur Errichtung des Qingdaoer Observatoriums war eine Spende des Verbandes Deutscher Flottenvereine.[291]

Im Observatorium befindet sich noch heute in der Eingangshalle eine steinerne Schrifttafel mit dem nebenstehenden Text.

Apart from the signals station the observatory was the only building in Qingdao on the top of the hill. It was completely clad in slabs of rough-textured granite, giving it the appearance of a hill fortress.

The building is described in the memorandum written by the German Admiralty (Reichsmarineamt) as follows: »The preliminary project comprises a main building which apart from the offices also houses a spacious laboratory, the library with a public reading room, a basement for the clocks which is protected from sudden changes of temperature, a room which can be heated easily to determine the temperature coefficients of instruments, a mechanical workshop and ancillary rooms. Rooms for geomagnetic observations are also planned.«[290] The duties of the observatory included provision of a storm warning service, weather forecasting and observations of the earth's magnetism. It also had a synchronised clock with a device which allowed automatic dropping of the time ball.

There were only a few places with meteorological observatories in East Asia at the beginning of this century: Xujiahui (Sikawei) near Shanghai, Inch'ön (Chemulpo) in South Korea, Manila in the Philippines and Hongkong. Weather forecasts were, however, extremely important for shipping, due to the risk of typhoons. The German Navy, for instance, had lost its gunboat »Iltis« on 23 July 1896 in a typhoon off the coast of Shandong. The money for setting up the Qingdao Observatory was a donation from the Federation of German Fleet Associations.[291]

There was a stone memorial plaque in the foyer of the observatory which is still there today and bears the German inscription, given in the margin.

觀象台

現用途：氣象台
所在地：青島觀象山，原水山
建築師：保爾・弗里德里希・里希特⟨289⟩
建築造價：十七點五萬金馬克
業主：德國膠州總督府
建造期：一九一零年六月至一九一二年一月
現狀：建築體保存完好。

除信號站外，觀象台是當時青島市唯一座落在山頂上的建築，通體由粗面石塊砌成，猶如一座堅固的城堡。

帝國海軍部的備忘錄對觀象台有如下記載："所完成的預設計包括一座主辦公樓。內設辦公室、寬敞的實驗室、圖書館、公共閱覽室、存放時鐘的恆溫地下室、裝有取暖設備的儀器溫度系數測定室、金工車間及其他附屬房間。除此之外，地磁觀察室也在規劃之內。"⟨290⟩觀象台的任務是，預報風暴和天氣情況，觀測地磁。觀象台內還有一帶有時球自動下落裝置的標准鐘。

東亞一帶在本世紀初只有少數地區設有觀象台，如上海附近的徐家匯，南朝鮮的仁川，菲律賓島的馬尼拉及香港。由於台風的危險性，氣象觀察對於航海尤為重要。如一八九六年七月二十三日，德國海軍的一艘炮艇"伊爾蒂斯"號在山東黃海上突遇風暴沉沒。後來，德國海軍協會聯合會捐款修建了青島觀象台。⟨291⟩

觀象台門廳內立有一塊石匾，匾文這樣寫道：
"遠離家鄉的德國人，
在這陌生的海邊
築起了觀象台。
它向船只預告：
老天何時變臉，
風暴何時止息。
它是船家的助手，
更是德國人民
向世界發出的問候。"⟨292⟩

觀象台南面外觀，一九九二年。

QINGDAO

DIEDERICHSSTEIN
DIEDERICHS STONE

Xinhaoshan Gongyuan (Diederichsberg oder Signalberg), Qingdao (Tsingtau)
Xinhaoshan Gongyuan (Diederichsberg or Signalberg), Qingdao (Tsingtao)

Entwurf. Design
Pionierhauptmann Müller[293]
Müller, captain of the pioneers[293]

Einweihung. Inaugurated
14. November 1898
14 November 1898

Zustand. Condition
Das Denkmal wurde 1922 entfernt und nach Tokio gebracht.
The memorial was removed and taken to Tokyo in 1922

Diederichsstein, um 1900
Diederichs' Memorial, around 1900

Der Diederichsstein wurde von Prinz Heinrich von Preußen eingeweiht, genau ein Jahr nach der Besetzung der Jiaozhou-Bucht. Das Denkmal lag etwa auf halber Höhe des Diederichsberges. Die beiden übereinanderliegenden Schrifttafeln waren zusammen etwa fünf Meter hoch.

Der Jahrestag der Besetzung war ein Feiertag in Qingdao. »Am 14. November 1897 ergriff der Admiral von Diederichs Besitz vom Kiautschou-Gebiet, und die Stelle, wo der feierliche Vorgang sich abspielte, eine vorspringende Felswand des Signalberges, wurde mit unbehauenen Felsstücken zu einer mächtigen Felsenkanzel ausgebaut. In die senkrechte Rückwand wurde ein gewaltiger Reichsadler eingemeißelt, und darunter stehen als unauslöschliches Merkmal tief eingegraben in doppeltem Bogen die Worte: ›Der hier für Kaiser warb und Reich ringsher das Land nach ihm sei dieser Felsen Diederichsstein genannt.‹«[294]

Als die japanische Armee Qingdao besetzte, überschrieben sie das Denkmal mit 9 Schriftzeichen, die an das Datum der japanischen Besetzung, den 7. November 1914, erinnerten. Das Denkmal wurde vor der Rückgabe Qingdaos an China, am 10. Dezember 1922, von der japanischen Armee abgetragen und nach Tokio in das Militärmuseum gebracht.

Diederichs Stone was inaugurated by Prince Heinrich of Prussia exactly one year after the occupation of Jiaozhou Bay. The memorial stone was about half way up the Diederichs Hill. The two plaques, which were arranged one on top of the other, were approximately five metres high.

The anniversary of the occupation was a public holiday in Qingdao. »On 14 November 1897 Admiral von Diederichs took the area of Kiaochow and the spot where the memorable event took place, a protruding part of the cliff face on Signal Hill, was made into a colossal pulpit of stone by the addition of unhewn boulders. A huge Imperial eagle was carved into the vertical wall behind and under it, the words are inscribed to form two arches as an indelible memorial »He who valiantly fought for Emperor and Empire here in this land, after him shall be named this cliff, the Diederichs Stone.«[294]

When the Japanese army occupied Qingdao they wrote a new inscription on the memorial over the old one to commemorate 7th November 1914, the date of the Japanese occupation. Before Qingdao was returned to China on 10 December 1922 the Japanese army removed the memorial and took it to the military museum in Tokyo.

狄特立克斯石

所在地：青島信號山公園，原狄特立克斯山（也稱信號山）
設計：米勒，工兵卜尉⁽²⁹³⁾
落成典禮：一八九八年十一月十四日
現狀：狄特立克斯石手一九九二年運往東京。

德國佔領膠州整整一年之後，普魯士的亨利王子主持了狄特立克斯石的落成典禮。這座紀念碑矗立在狄特立克斯山的半山腰上。碑上兩行上下重 的碑文總高約五米左右。

德國佔領膠州灣日當時被定為青島的公眾節日。"一八九七年十一月十四日，海軍上將馮‧狄特立克斯率軍佔領膠州地區，並在信號山一塊突出的懸崖上插上了贏戰旗。後來，這裡用天然岩石砌起一方巨大的岩台。岩台背面的垂直方向上鑿有一個龐大的帝國鷹徽，下方碑文雕刻成雙弧線狀，刀法遒勁，碑文雋永："他為皇帝、為帝國贏得了這片土地，這塊岩石以他的名字命名為'狄特立克斯石'。"⁽²⁹⁴⁾

日軍佔領青島後改寫了碑文，以紀念其佔領日——九一四年十一月七日。在青島歸還中國之前，日軍於一九二二年十二月十日拆除了紀念碑，並將其運往東京的軍事博物館。

狄特立克斯石，約一九零零年。

ILTIS-KASERNE
ILTIS BARRACKS

Heutige Funktion. Current use
Chinesische Marine-Kaserne
Wendeng Lu (Iltispaßstraße, Auguste-Viktoria-Bucht), Qingdao (Tsingtau)
Barracks for the Chinese Navy
Wendeng Lu (Iltispass Strasse, Auguste-Viktoria-Bucht), Qingdao (Tsingtau)

Entwurf. Design
Hauptmann Müller, Ingenieuroffizier[295]
Müller, captain, engineer[295]

Bauleiter. Site architect
Regierungsbaumeister a. D. Raffelt
Raffelt, former Government Architect

Ausführung. Contractors
Industriesyndikat
Industrial syndicate

Bauherr. Client
Deutsches Gouvernement Kiautschou
German Administration of Kiaochow

Bauzeit. Construction time
Oktober 1899 – April 1901
October 1899 – April 1901

Zustand. Condition
Die gesamte Anlage ist sehr gut erhalten.
Very well preserved.

Iltis-Kaserne, Mannschaftsgebäude.
Blick von Süden, um 1902
Südansicht, 1992
Iltis Barracks, barrack rooms,
view from the south, around 1902
View from the south, 1992

1899 waren einer Typhusepidemie 29 Soldaten, damals immerhin zwei Prozent der deutschen Truppe, zum Opfer gefallen. Daher beschleunigte man die Errichtung hygienischer Unterkünfte für die Soldaten, die bisher nur provisorisch untergebracht waren. Es wurde ein Grundstück außerhalb der zukünftigen Stadt gewählt, wo die Kasernen dem frischen Meereswind ausgesetzt waren.

In der Denkschrift des Reichsmarineamtes wird der Ort beschrieben: »Der Bauplatz mit einem schönen Ausblick auf die See befindet sich an der Klarabucht (Auguste-Viktoria-Bucht, d. Verfasser). Die Kasernen selbst, je für die Aufnahme eines Offiziers, der Unteroffiziere und Mannschaften einer kriegsstarken Kompanie bestimmt, erstrecken sich mit Front nach See in einer Länge von 110 Metern. Bei Bemessung des Luftraumes für die Bewohner war von der Voraussetzung ausgegangen worden, daß derselbe gegen die heimischen Gebührnisse etwa die Hälfte mehr erhalten soll. Die einzelnen Räume führen auf der Süd- (See-) Seite auf breite offene Veranden, während gegen Norden, der winterlichen Sandstürme wegen, die Korridore angelegt sind. Die Gebäude enthalten außer dem Kellergeschosse das bewohnte Erd- und Obergeschoß. Im Äußeren sind die Gebäude unter Verwendung von Granitwerkstein zur Hervorhebung einzelner Partien glattgeputzt. Außer diesen Mannschaftskasernen sind 2 Wirtschaftsgebäude angeordnet, welche die Speisesäle, Mannschafts- und Unteroffiziersküchen sowie sonst erforderliche Wirtschaftsräume enthalten.«[296]

Mit ihren flachen Walmdächern und dem weiten Dachüberstand wirken die Kasernengebäude sehr südeuropäisch. Lediglich der jeweils mittlere Baukörper trägt einen Schmuckgiebel. Markant sind die Türme mit den spitzen Kegeldächern auf der Nordseite der Seitenflügel. Die Geländerbrüstungen des Wirtschaftsgebäudes bestehen aus Dachziegeln, die in typisch chinesischer Weise in verschiedenen geometrischen Mustern verlegt wurden.

In 1899 29 soldiers, at that time two percent of the German troops, had died during a typhoid epidemic. As a result, the construction of salubrious living quarters for the soldiers, who had been living in temporary accommodation, was accelerated. A site outside the future town was chosen, where the barracks would be exposed to fresh sea winds.

The place is described in a memorandum of the German Admiralty: »The site, which has a fine view of the sea, is on Klara Bay (Auguste-Viktoria-Bucht). The barracks rooms themselves, each intended to house an officer, the non-commissioned officers and men of a company at wartime strength, have a frontage 110 metres long facing the sea. When calculating the cubic footage per occupant it was assumed that the quota should be half as much again as the domestic allowance stipulated. The rooms on the south (sea-facing) side opened onto verandas, whilst the corridors were put on the northern side owing to the winter sand storms. As well as a basement the buildings all had a ground floor and first floor with living accommodation. The outside of the buildings are all smooth render with some parts clad in granite to make them stand out. Apart from these barracks there are two service buildings, housing the officers mess, messes for non-commissioned officers and men and other rooms required for catering.«[296]

With their shallow, hipped roofs and deep overhang the barracks look very southern European. Only the central part of each has an ornamental gable. Outstanding features are the towers on the northern side of the side wings with their pointed conical spires. They presumably house the stairwells. The parapets of the service buildings are made of roof tiles laid in different geometric patterns in typical Chinese style. These elements of Chinese architecture were never used again on any of the buildings subsequently built in Qingdao.

伊爾蒂斯兵營

現用途：中國海軍兵營
所在地：青島文登路，原伊爾蒂斯關路奧古斯塔、維克多利亞灣畔
設計：米勒，上尉，軍官工程師[295]
建築總管：拉菲爾特，退職政府工程師
業主：總國膠州總督府
建造期：一八九九年十月至一九零一年四月
現狀：建築體保存完好。

一八九九年，宿於歸時營地佔總人數百分之二的德國士兵（二十九人）成了傷寒症的犧牲品。為此，建設健康兵營的進程加快了。營址造在城外，淋浴於清新的海風之中。

德意志帝國海軍部的備忘錄裏對營地有如下描述："工地位於克拉拉灣畔（即奧古斯特·維多利亞灣——作者），可遠眺大海的美景。營房面向大海，總共一百一十米。每所營房可容納一名尉官、若干名士官及一個戰鬥連的全體士兵。分配居住空間時，居住者所得面積約比國內的大二分之一。住房均安排在有敞廊的南面。由於冬季砂暴的關係，北面設走廊。兵營大樓包括地窖和一、二樓的住房。樓體用花崗石砌成，清水勾縫粉飾，以突出各個局部。除營房外，還有兩幢附屬建築，內設餐廳，士兵廚房，士官廚房以及其他必要的後勤事務房屋。"[296]

營房覆坡度平後的斜屋頂，屋頂大大伸出牆體，具典型的南歐建築風格。裝飾性山牆僅設在中部的建築體上。側翼的北面塔樓聳立，塔頂呈尖錐形，格外引人注目。塔樓內可能設有樓梯間。附屬建築的敞廊欄杆用中國瓦，以典型的中國建築方式砌成不同的幾何形狀和花卉圖案。在此之後的青島建築已不再採用這一形式。

原伊爾蒂斯兵營士兵營房南面外觀，約一九零二。
南面外觀，一九九二年。

QINGDAO

**BISMARCK-KASERNE
MANNSCHAFTSGEBÄUDE DES
III. SEE-BATAILLONS
BISMARCK BARRACKS
BARRACK ROOMS FOR THE
III MARINE BATTALION**

Heutige Funktion. Current use
Qingdaos Ozeanographische Hochschule
Daxue Lu (zwischen Ostpaßstraße und
Bergstraße), Qingdao (Tsingtau)
Qingdao College of Oceanography
Daxue Lu (between Ostpass Strasse and
Berg Strasse), Qingdao (Tsingtao)

Entwurf. Design
Bauverwaltung
Planning office of the administration

Bauleitung. Site architect
Lothar Marcks

Ausführung. Contractors
F.H. Schmidt, Altona, Hamburg

Bauherr. Client
Deutsches Gouvernement Kiautschou
German Administration of Kiaochow

Bauzeit. Construction time
1. und 2. Mannschaftsgebäude 1903–1905,
3. und 4. Mannschaftsgebäude bis 1909
1st and 2nd barrack room 1903–1905,
3rd and 4th barrack room up to 1909

Zustand. Condition
Die Anlage ist gut erhalten,
das Wirtschaftsgebäude wurde abgetragen.
Well preserved.
Service Building was pulled down.

Die vier Mannschaftsgebäude sind jeweils in einem H-förmigen Grundriß angelegt und umschließen den Exerzierplatz. Die Stufengiebel und neogotischen Verzierungen wurden damals auch häufig bei Militärkasernen in Deutschland verwendet. Während Giebel, Sockel und Verandabrüstungen bei den ersten beiden Mannschaftsgebäuden aus Granitwerkstein gefertigt wurden, verzichtete man bei den nachfolgend erbauten auf diese aufwendige Gestaltung.

Auch hier hatte man auf moderne hygienische Standards Wert gelegt, wie Waschräume, die getrennt von den Schlafsälen lagen und Toiletten mit Wasserspülung.

Nach der Iltis-Kaserne war dies die zweite der drei deutschen Militärkasernen in Qingdao. Die Bismarck-Kaserne lag am nächsten zur Stadt, war aber durch die umliegenden Hügel räumlich abgetrennt. Der Gouverneur hatte von seinem 1907 fertiggestellten Wohnhaus einen guten Überblick über die Kaserne und den Exerzierplatz.

The four barrack rooms are H-shaped on plan and are built around the parade ground. Their stepped gables and neo-Gothic ornament were often used in military barracks in Germany. The gables, bases and parapets of the verandas of the first two barrack rooms were in granite but this expensive design was abandoned in the later buildings.

Here too great store was set by modern standards of hygiene which included washrooms which were separate from the dormitories and flush toilets.

This was the second of the three German barracks in Qingdao, the first being the Iltis Barracks. The Bismarck Barracks were closest to the city but separated from it by the surrounding hills. The Governor had a good view of the barracks and the parade ground from his residence, which was completed in 1907.

Bismarck-Kaserne, Mannschaftsgebäude. Blick von Süden, um 1907
Ehem. Mannschaftsgebäude 1 und 2, 1991
Bismarck Barracks, barrack rooms, view from the south, around 1907
Former barrack rooms nos. 1 and 2, 1991

俾斯麥兵營（第三海軍營營房）

現用途：青島海洋大學
所在地：青島大學路，原東關路與山路之間
設計：建築管理局行政規劃處
工程指導：洛塔爾·馬爾克斯
施工：漢堡阿爾托納區F·H·施密特公司
業主：德國膠州總督府
建造期：一九零三年至一九零五年（第一、二營房）
約一九零六年至一九零九年（第三、四營房）
現狀：建築體保存良好，附屬建築已拆除。

這四座營房的平面分別呈"H"型，圍成一練兵場。營房的階梯式山牆及新哥特式的裝飾為當時德國兵營建築的通例。先期完工的兩座營房的山牆、牆基和外廊護欄均用花崗粗石砌成，後來建造的另外兩座營房則摒棄了這一奢靡的外形結構。營房的南面築敞廊。盡管如此，整個建築仍具明顯的德國建築風格。這些營房也同樣符合當時新的衛生標準。其中建有同宿舍和廁所分開的盥洗間。

青島共有三座德國兵營，俾斯麥兵營是繼伊爾蒂斯兵營之後的第二座。它離市區最近，卻為周圍的丘陵所隔。德國總督可由他一九零七年建成的私邸一覽兵營和練兵場上的情景。

原俾斯麥兵營士兵房南面俯視，約一九零七年。
原第一、第二士兵營房，一九九一年。

QINGDAO

GOUVERNEMENTS-LAZARETT
MILITARY HOSPITAL OF THE GERMAN ADMINISTRATION

Heutige Funktion. Current use
Qingdaos Medizinisches Hochschul-Krankenhaus
Hospital of the Qingdao Medical School
Jiangsu Lu/Pingyuan Lu (Bismarckstraße/Lazarettweg), Qingdao (Tsingtau. Tsingtao)

Entwurf. Design
Bauverwaltung
Planning office

Bauherr. Client
Deutsches Gouvernement Kiautschou
German Administration of Kiaochow

Bauzeit. Construction time
1899–1905

Zustand. Condition
Einige Krankenpavillons sind gut erhalten; das Verwaltungsgebäude wurde abgetragen.
Some of the hospital wards are well preserved; administration building was pulled down.

Gouvernements-Lazarett. Blick vom Gouvernementshügel, im Hintergrund der Signalberg, um 1906
Krankenpavillon, 1992
Military hospital of the German Administration, view from Gouvernement Hill, in the background Signal Hill, around 1906
Ward pavilion, 1992

In den ersten Monaten nach der Besitznahme Jiaozhous wurden Kranke in einfachen Baracken versorgt; sehr bald wurde ein Lazarettneubau erforderlich. Mit Rücksicht darauf, daß auch Zivilisten Aufnahme finden sollten, wurde er von Anfang an größer geplant als für die Garnison notwendig. Schon 1899 waren der erste Krankenpavillon, zwei Ökonomiegebäude, die Apotheke und zwei Wohnhäuser für das Pflegepersonal bezugsfertig. Im Jahre 1904 war der Bau abgeschlossen. Das Lazarett umfaßte jetzt fünf größere und einen kleineren Pavillon, darunter eine Abteilung für Frauen und Kinder, eine Isolierstation, Ökonomiebauten, Apotheke, bakteriologisches Laboratorium nebst Tollwutstation, Leichenhaus mit Sektionsraum, Eiskeller, ein kleines Pförtnerhaus und einige Nebengebäude. Die chirurgische sowie die Frauen- und Kinderabteilung verfügten über je einen Operationsraum. Auch ein Röntgenlaboratorium war vorhanden. Das Lazarett hatte eine Kapazität von etwa 250 Betten.[297]

Die Hospitalanlage bildete mit ihren 10 bis 15 im Pavillonstil erbauten Häusern einen kleinen Stadtteil für sich. Rechts der Bismarckstraße lag das zweigeschossige Verwaltungsgebäude, links lag auf dem terrassenförmig ansteigenden Gelände das eigentliche Hospital. Die Anlage war durch die umliegenden Hügel gegen die rauhen Nordwinde geschützt.

Typhus, Darmkatarrh und Geschlechtskrankheiten waren bis etwa 1902 die häufigsten Krankheiten in Qingdao. Durch umfangreiche Vorsorge- und Hygienemaßnahmen entwickelte sich Qingdao in den folgenden Jahren zu der gesündesten Hafenstadt Chinas. Die in Qingdao lebenden Deutschen waren stolz auf diese Leistung: »Während die südlichen Häfen Chinas von schweren Pest- und Choleraepidemien heimgesucht wurden, gelang es durch verständige, Handel und Verkehr kaum belästigende Quarantänemaßregeln, unsere Kolonie vor Einschleppung derselben zu bewahren.«[298]

In the first few months after Jiaozhou was taken the sick were cared for in simple huts; very soon a new military hospital was needed. Since it was intended to admit civilians as well as soldiers, it was from the outset of the planning larger than the size of the garrison would have warranted. By 1899 a ward pavilion, two service buildings, chemist's shop and two hostels for the nursing staff were already completed. In 1904 the entire building works were finished. The hospital now comprised five large ward pavilions and one small pavilion, including a ward for women and children, a quarantine ward, service buildings, chemist's shop, bacteriological laboratory as well as a rabies ward, mortuary with autopsy room, ice cellar, small porter's lodge and some ancillary buildings. The surgical ward and the ward for women and children each had an operating theatre. There was also an X-ray laboratory. The hospital had a total of 250 beds.[297]

The hospital complex with its 10 to 15 separate pavilion-style buildings formed a small town of its own. To the right of Bismarck Strasse was the two-storey administration building and to the left on a piece of land which stepped up in terraces was the hospital itself. The pavilions were sheltered from the fierce north winds by the surrounding hills.

Until around 1902 typhus, enteritis and venereal diseases were the most common illnesses in Qingdao. Due to comprehensive preventive action and hygienic measures Qingdao developed over the years to follow into the healthiest harbour town in China. The Germans who lived in Qingdao were proud of this achievement: »Whilst the southern ports of China are prey to plague and cholera epidemics we have managed to introduce quarantine regulations which were comprehensible and have hardly disrupted trade and commerce and have thus prevented our colony from being contaminated.«[298]

總督府野戰醫院

現用途：青島醫學院附屬醫院
所在地：青島江蘇路（平原路口），原俾斯麥路（野戰醫院路口）
設計：建築管理局規劃處
業主：德國膠州總督府
建造期：一八九九至一八零五年
現狀：幾所病房保存良好辦公樓已拆除。

德國佔領膠州灣初期，病員只被安置在簡易的臨時木板房裡，建造新野戰醫院已勢在必行。考慮到市民的就診問題，醫院設計得大於駐防部隊的實際需要。早在一八九九年，一所病房、兩座醫院附屬建築及藥房和兩處護理人員住房便可供遷入使用。一九零四年，整個工程全部完工。醫院當時有五所大病房，一所小病房，其中包括婦科病房和兒科病房。除此之外，還有隔離病房、後勤事務房、藥房、配有狂犬病病房的細菌實驗室、配有解剖室停屍房、冰窖、看門房及幾幢副樓。外科、婦科和兒科各有一間手術室。供醫院使用的還有一間X光室及二百五十張病床。⁽²⁹⁷⁾
醫院自成一片小城區，散布著十多座樓房。院部辦公樓高兩層，設在俾斯麥路的右側，門診大樓位於馬路左側的梯形坡地上。病房周圍的山丘成了凜冽北風的天然屏障。
一九零二年前，傷寒、腸炎和性病是青島的常見病。幾年之後，青島通過制訂並實施內容詳廣的預防措施和衛生條例一躍而為中國最健康的港口城市。生活在青島的德國人對這一成就引以為榮。"中國南方的港口城市深受鼠疫、霍亂之害而我們的殖民地卻通過採取理智的檢疫措施，將瘟疫有效地拒之港外。檢疫卻幾乎沒有為來往貿易、交通增添麻煩。"⁽²⁹⁸⁾

由總督府山麓望總督府野戰醫院，其後為信號山，約一九零六年。
病房樓，一九九二年。

QINGDAO

GOUVERNEMENTSSCHULE FÜR JUNGEN
GERMAN SCHOOL FOR BOYS

Heutige Funktion. Current use
Grundschule
Primary school
Jiangsu Lu (Bismarckstraße),
Qingdao (Tsingtau. Tsingtao)

Architekt. Architect
Bernatz, leitender Regierungsbaumeister
Bernatz, government architect

Ausführung. Contractors
Picolo, chinesischer Unternehmer
Picolo, Chinese contractor

Bauherr. Client
Deutsches Gouvernement Kiautschou
German Administration of Kiaochow

Bauzeit. Construction time
Dezember 1900 – August 1901
December 1900 – August 1901

Zustand. Condition
Das Gebäude ist sehr gut erhalten.
Very well preserved.

Südansicht der zweiten Gouvernementsschule (1907 fertiggestellt)
Gouvernementsschule für Jungen,
Einweihung 1901
Westansicht, 1992
View from the south of the second German Administration School (finished in 1907)
German School for Boys,
inauguration 1901
View from the west, 1992

Die Schule folgt in ihrer Anlage den traditionellen chinesischen Bauregeln. So entspricht ihr Standort den Gesetzen des »fengshui«: am Hang erbaut, schützt ein Hügel vor den Nordwinden; auf seiner Südseite befindet sich die Meeresbucht. Das Gebäude ist symmetrisch, sein Haupteingang liegt in der Mitte, der mittlere, zurückgesetzte Baukörper ist höher als die beiden seitlichen. Die südliche Fassade des Hauptgebäudes ist offen, aufgelöst in steinernen Säulenarkaden im Erdgeschoß und hölzernen Veranden mit chinesischen Schnitzarbeiten im ersten Obergeschoß. Alle Wandflächen sind aus verputztem Mauerwerk, die Ost- und Westfassaden wirken trotz der Fensteröffnungen relativ geschlossen.

Die *Deutsch-Asiatische Warte* veröffentlichte eine Beschreibung der Schule: »Beim Entwurf haben die hiesigen klimatischen Verhältnisse die eingehendste Berücksichtigung gefunden. (…) Einen Reiz verleiht dem Gebäude die säulengezierte Vorhalle, die zwischen den beiden vorstehenden Nebengebäuden zu der Aula führt. (…) Das Haus enthält vier Schulzimmer von je 60 m² Bodenfläche bei 250 Kubikmetern Luftraum und ist somit nach den vom Preußischen Kultusministerium für höhere städtische Schulen getroffenen Bestimmungen zur Aufnahme von je 40 größeren Kindern geeignet.«[299] Die Dienstwohnung des Lehrers befand sich im ersten Stock.

In dieser Schule wurden bis 1907 die deutschen Jungen unterrichtet, die Mädchen gingen ins Heilig-Geist-Kloster, danach war eine größere Gouvernementsschule fertiggestellt worden, in der dann Jungen und Mädchen gemeinsam unterrichtet wurden. Angehörige fremder Rassen und Mischlinge waren von der Aufnahme grundsätzlich ausgeschlossen. Die Schülerzahlen stiegen kontinuierlich an. Von 15 im Jahre 1902, 78 im Jahre 1907, 146 im Jahre 1910 auf 162 im Jahre 1911. Für die auswärtigen Schüler war ein Wohnheim eingerichtet worden.[300]

The school building follows the traditional Chinese rules of architecture. For example, the site was chosen according to the laws of »fengshui« – the school is built on a slope with a hill to protect it from the north winds and the bay is to the south. The building is symmetrical, its main entrance is in the middle of the building and the central, receding part of the building is higher than the two flanking it. The southern façade of the main building is open in character with colonnaded arcades at ground floor level and wooden verandas with Chinese carvings on the first floor. All the walls are built of rendered brick; the east and west façades make a closed impression despite the fenestration.

The *Deutsch-Asiatische Warte* published a description of the school: »The design of this building takes local climatic conditions into careful consideration. (…) The portico decorated with columns, which runs from the projecting side buildings to the main hall in the centre, gives the building great charm. (…) Inside the building there are four classrooms, each measuring 60 m², with a cubage of 250 cubic metres, which according to the regulations governing municipal senior schools, issued by the Prussian Ministry for Education, can each accommodate 40 older children.«[299] The teacher's living quarters were on the first floor.

Until 1907 the German boys attended this school, the girls went to the Convent of the Holy Ghost. After that a larger school was built by the German Administration, in which boys and girls were taught together. Children of foreign races and mixed race pupils were not admitted to the school. The number of pupils rose continually: from 15 in 1902 to 78 in 1907 to 146 in 1910 and to 162 in 1911. A boarding house was built for pupils who did not live locally.[300]

· 總督府童子學堂 ·

現用途：小學
所在地：青島，江蘇路，原俾斯麥路
建築師：貝爾納茨，政府總建築師
施工：中方企業皮科羅公司
建造期：一九零零年十二月至一九零一年
　　　　八月
現狀：樓體保存完好

該校舍建築格局體現了傳統的中國式建房規範。其選址符合"風水"的理想要求，即背山面水。它依坡而建，以山丘遮擋住北風，而南面則與海灣遙遙相對。樓體造形對稱，大門設在中央，內凹的中段建築體高於兩側配樓。主樓南牆呈開放式，其底層以數根直立石柱構成拱門，頂層是配有中式雕飾的木制陽台。樓房的所有立面均以粗灰泥塗飾外表；東西兩側面牆盡管開有窗孔，仍顯示出一種較為封閉的體式。

在《德屬膠州官報》周刊上登載的一篇文章曾對該校舍作有如下描寫："樓房的設計充分考慮到當地的氣候條件。（……）通向禮堂的前廳配有粗石立柱，兩座突向前方的配樓簇擁左右，給這一建築帶來了一種特別魅力。（……）該校舍包括四間面積為六十平方米，空間達二百五十立方米的教室，符合普魯士文化部對城區中等學校做出的容納四十名中學生的教室規定。⁽²⁹⁹⁾教師的公用房間設在二層。"

到一九零七年止，該校一直用作德籍男學生的教學場所。女學生則在聖心修道院讀書。此後，又建有一座更大的總督府學校供男女共同授課。學校原則上不招收異族以及混血兒學生。這裏的學生數量持續增長。從一九零二年的十五名、一九零七年的七十八名、一九一零年的一百四十六名，增至一九一一年的一百六十二名。對於遠途的學生，還建有專門宿舍。

總督府童子學堂，一九零一年落成典禮。
西面外觀，一九九二年。
總督府第二學堂南面外觀。（一九零七年竣工）。

QINGDAO

DEUTSCH-CHINESISCHE HOCHSCHULE
GERMAN-CHINESE COLLEGE

Heutige Funktion. Current use
Chinesische Eisenbahn-Verwaltung
Guizhou Lu/Chaocheng Lu
(Kaiser-Wilhelm-Ufer), Qingdao (Tsingtau)
Headquarters of the Chinese Railway
Guizhou Lu/Chaocheng Lu
(Kaiser-Wilhelm-Ufer), Qingdao (Tsingtao)

Entwurf. Design
Bauverwaltung
Planning office of the administration

Baukosten. Building costs
640 000 Goldmark
640 000 gold marks

Bauherr. Client
Deutsches Gouvernement Kiautschou
German Administration of Kiaochow

Bauzeit. Construction time
1910–1912

Zustand. Condition
Die Anlage ist gut erhalten;
ein Internatsgebäude wurde abgetragen.
Well preserved; one of the students
residences was pulled down.

Ehem. Deutsch-Chinesische
Hochschule. Lehrgebäude, rechts
Aula und Bibliothek.
Ostansicht, um 1924
Ehem. Lehrgebäude der
Deutsch-Chinesischen Hochschule.
Haupteingang auf der Südseite,
1992
Former German-Chinese College,
classroom building with hall and
library to the right, around 1924
Former classroom building of the
German-Chinese College, main
entrance on the south side, 1992

Das Grundstück der Hochschule befindet sich südwestlich des Bahnhofs und grenzt direkt ans Meer. Bis zur Fertigstellung aller Bauten wurde die ehemalige Feld-Artillerie-Kaserne genutzt, zwei dieser Gebäude standen auch später der Hochschule zur Verfügung. Das etwa 80 Meter lange zweigeschossige Lehrgebäude mit den Unterrichtsräumen lag auf der südlichen Hälfte des Grundstücks. Sockel und Fensterbänke waren in rustikalem Granitstein ausgeführt. Das Dach war als Walmdach, über dem höheren mittleren Baukörper als Mansarddach ausgebildet. Die große Aula und die Bibliothek schlossen sich auf der Rückseite des Lehrgebäudes an seiner östlichen Ecke an. Die in der Art des Jugendstils abgerundeten Giebel der Aula sind die markantesten Merkmale des Baus; sie erinnern an die kurz zuvor in Qingdao fertiggestellte Christuskirche. Granitsteine an den außenliegenden Mauerpfeilern erhöhen den plastischen Ausdruck des Gebäudes. Auf der Nordhälfte des Grundstücks wurden zwei Internate für je 125 Studenten erbaut. Die Internate waren zweigeschossige Gebäude die jeweils einen Innenhof bildeten. Außerdem gab es auf dem Campus ein Wirtschaftsgebäude und ein Wohngebäude für drei deutsche Lehrer.[301]

Im Herbst 1914 besuchten bereits über 300 Schüler die Hochschule. Die Organisation der Deutsch-Chinesischen Hochschule wurde stark durch Forderungen des chinesischen Unterrichtsministeriums bestimmt. Die Hochschule war in zwei Teile gegliedert: eine Unterstufe, in der allgemeine Vorbildung vermittelt wurde, und eine Oberstufe, die in die höheren Spezialwissenschaften einführte. Neben dem abendländischen lief in beiden Stufen parallel der chinesische Bildungsgang. In der sechsjährigen Unterstufe wurden die folgenden Fächer gelehrt: Deutsch, Geschichte, Geographie, Mathematik (Rechnen, Algebra, Geometrie), Logik, Naturkunde (Botanik und Zoologie), Physik, Chemie und Zeichnen. Dazu der chinesische Unterricht: Klassiker, Geschichte, Geographie, Ethik und

The site of the college is to the south-west of the station, directly beside the sea. Until all the buildings were completed the former field artillery barracks were used and two of these buildings continued to be used by the college. The two-storey teaching building, 80 metres long, which housed the classrooms was on the southern part of the site. The base of the building and window sills were in rough-textured granite. The roof was a hipped roof becoming a mansard hipped roof above the higher central section. The main hall and the library adjoined the eastern corner on the rear side of the classroom wing. The rounded Jugendstil-like gables of the hall are the most striking features of this wing; they recall the Christ Church which had been completed shortly before. Granite slabs on the exterior buttresses increase the plastic appearance. On the northern part of the site two boarding houses for 125 students each were built. They were two-storey buildings each built around a courtyard. On the campus there was also a service building and a house for the three German teachers.[301]

In autumn 1914, 300 students were already attending the college. The organisation of the German-Chinese college was strongly influenced by the demands of the Chinese Ministry of Education. The college was divided into two sections, a lower school which provided a general education and a higher school which gave an introduction to more specialised subjects. The Chinese system of education ran in parallel the western system. The following subjects were taught in the lower school where the students spent six years: German, history, geography, mathematics (arithmetic, algebra and geometry), logic, natural history (botany and zoology), physics, chemistry and drawing. In addition to this there were the Chinese subjects: classics, history, geography, ethics and literature. The upper school was divided into four sections: political science, medicine, technology, forestry and agriculture. The students specialised at this stage. German and Chinese lessons con-

德華高等學堂

現用途：鐵路局辦公樓
所在地：青島貴州路（朝城路口），原威
　　　　廉皇帝岸
設計：建築管理局規劃處
建築造價：六十四萬金馬克
業主：德國膠州總督府
建造期：一九一零年至一九一二年
現狀：樓體保存良好；一座奇宿校舍已被
　　　拆除

原德華高等學堂教學樓東面外
觀，其右側為大禮堂和圖書館，
約一九二四年。
原德華高等學堂教學樓，南立面
主入口，一九九二年。

該校地處火車站西南，其校園一直延展至海邊。在所有建築竣工之前，學校曾借用前野戰炮兵部隊的兵營；其中有兩座樓直到後來仍被用作學生活動場所。教學樓位於校園南部，高二層，長約八十米。樓頂為四坡斜頂，而較高的中部樓體則蓋有複折式屋頂。大禮堂和圖書館建立教學樓後側，並與其東翼相接。建築特點最為突出的是禮堂前的圓頂山牆，其青年藝術派風格與建造期略早的青島福音堂十分近似。外牆扶壁的花崗岩攫腳增強了樓體的塑性感。校園北區建有兩棟學生宿舍，可分別容納一百二十五名學生。它們均有二層建築，而且各有一內院。此外，校園裡還有一座服務樓及一座住宅，供三名德籍教師使用。〈301〉

一九一四年秋季，已有高三百多名學生在此就讀。德華高等學堂的體制在較大程度上受控於中國政府禮部的政策。它基本分為兩大部分，即傳授基礎知識的初級部和修習專門學科的高級部。在這兩個階段中，除引入西方課程外，還並行教授中國傳統課程。初級階段為時六年，所教課程為德語、歷史、地理、數學（分為算術、代數、幾何）邏輯學、生物學（分為植物學和動物學）、物理學、化學和繪畫課。同時教授的中國課程是古籍、歷史、地理、倫理和文學。高級階段由幾類學科構成：國政學、醫學、科技學和農林學。此外，學生開始為時三年或四年的定向專業學習，但各系仍開設德文和中文課，年齡在十三到十五歲的學生由當時的清政府地方教育機構選拔至該校深造，均住校學習。畢業考試通過者有資格進入京城的國子監，在那裡實現取得文學學銜的願望。

Literatur. Die Oberstufe bestand aus den vier Fachbereichen: Staatswissenschaft, Medizin, Technik, Forst- und Landwirtschaft. Hier spezialisierten sich die Studenten. Je nach Bereich dauerte die Oberstufe drei oder vier Jahre, begleitet durch Unterricht im Deutschen und Chinesischen. Die Schüler wurden durch die chinesische Unterrichtsbehörde von Shandong der Schule zugewiesen und waren zwischen 13 und 15 Jahre alt; sie sollten innerhalb der Anstalt wohnen. Die Schüler, die die Abschlußprüfung bestanden hatten, konnten auf ihren Wunsch in die Kaiserliche Chinesische Universität in Beijing eintreten und dort die literarischen Grade erwerben. An der Abschlußprüfung war ein Kommissar des chinesischen Unterrichtsministeriums beteiligt. Den gesamten Unterrichtsbetrieb beaufsichtigte ein unabhängiger chinesischer Beamter. Religiöse Propaganda durfte in der Anstalt nicht stattfinden.[302]

Anfang dieses Jahrhunderts war zusammen mit den politischen Reformen auch das chinesische Schulsystem modernisiert worden. Zur gleichen Zeit wurden ausländische Mittel- und Hochschulen in China vor allem durch anglo-amerikanische Missionsgesellschaften gegründet. Bis auf wenige Ausnahmen wurde diesen Schulen die Anerkennung vom chinesischen Unterrichtsministerium versagt. Die Deutsch-Chinesische Hochschule in Qingdao war 1909 die erste deutsche Hochschule in China, die durch dieses Ministerium anerkannt und den chinesischen Hochschulen gleichgestellt worden war. Die chinesische Regierung übernahm einen Teil der Unterrichtskosten.[303]

tinued in all four sections. The students remained here for three or four years depending on the section. The students, aged between 13 and 15, were assigned to the school by the Chinese education authority of Shandong. They were meant to live on the premises. The students who passed their final examinations could go to the Imperial Chinese University in Beijing, if they wished to, and attain literary degrees. A commissioner from the Chinese Ministry of Education took part in the final examination. All the teaching was supervised by independent Chinese officials. Religious propaganda was not permitted in the school.[302]

At the beginning of this century the political reforms were accompanied by reforms in the Chinese school system. At the same time, foreign secondary schools and colleges were founded in China by Japan and by Anglo-American missionary societies. Apart from a few exceptions these schools were refused recognition by the Chinese Ministry of Education. In 1909 the German-Chinese College in Qingdao was the first German college in China to be recognised by this ministry and given equal status with Chinese colleges. The Chinese government also assumed part of the teaching costs.[303]

Ehem. Studentenwohnheim, Südansicht, 1992
Former students' residence, view from the south, 1992

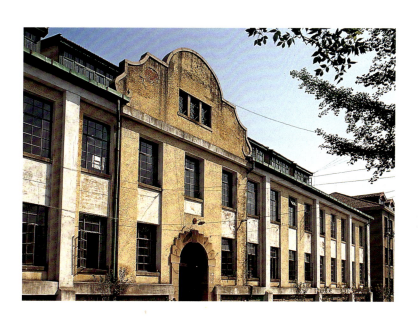

原學生宿舍南面外觀，一九九二年。

所有的教學活動均處在一位專門的中方官員的監管之下。校內禁止宗教宣傳。⟨302⟩
本世紀初，在政治維新的影響下，中國的教育體制亦開始改良。同時，主要來自英美的傳教機構相繼在中國開辦了中學和大學。不過，除少數例外，這些學校大部份未能得到中國當局的承認。一九零九年開辦的德中高等學堂是德國第一所設立在中國並得到清政府的承認的德國大學；它和中國的其它高等學府受到一視同仁的待遇。中國政府還承擔了其中的部分教學經費。⟨303⟩

QINGDAO

CHRISTUSKIRCHE, GOUVERNEMENTSKIRCHE
CHRIST CHURCH, GERMAN ADMINISTRATION CHURCH

Heutige Funktion. Current use
Evangelische Kirche
Protestant Church
Yishui Lu/Jiangsu Lu
(Diederichsweg/Bismarckstraße),
Qingdao (Tsingtau. Tsingtao)

Architekt. Architect
Curt Rothkegel, Tientsin

Baukosten. Building costs
236 000 Goldmark
236 000 gold marks

Ausführung. Contractors
F. H. Schmidt, Altona, Hamburg

Bauherr. Client
Deutscher Evangelischer
Kirchenausschuß, Berlin
German Protestant Church
Committee, Berlin

Bauzeit. Construction time
April 1908 – Oktober 1910
April 1908 – October 1910

Zustand. Condition
Das Gebäude ist sehr gut erhalten.
Very well preserved.

Blick von Nordosten auf die Kirche,
um 1912
Evangelische Kirche,
Südansicht, 1991
View of the church from the
north-east, around 1912
Protestant church,
view from the south, 1991

Die Kirche wurde auf einem kleinen Hügel am Ostrand des mit Villen bebauten Europäerviertels errichtet. Schon im ersten Bebauungsplan war dieser Platz für eine Kirche ausgewählt worden. Sie lag, wie auch die zweite Gouverneursvilla, zwischen der Stadt und der Bismarck-Kaserne. Die 1899 errichtete Gouvernementskapelle und die Gouvernementsschule befanden sich etwas weiter südlich. In historischen Beschreibungen wird der Blick von dem hochgelegenen Kirchplatz über die Meeresbucht als einer der schönsten Asiens bezeichnet.

Der Architekt Rothkegel beteiligte sich mit einem Entwurf an dem Wettbewerb, der bauliche Anforderungen und topographische Bedingungen miteinander verband: »Die Unterbringung sämtlicher Plätze im Erdgeschoß verlangt eine Breitenentwicklung. Die Höhenausdehnung tritt dementsprechend nicht hervor. Hierdurch hat der Verfasser das erreicht, was die hochgelegene Baustelle verlangt. Der Turm ist ca. 27 Meter hoch und beeinträchtigt deshalb nicht die umliegenden Höhen.«[304] Die Wettbewerbsarbeit zeigt einen Kirchturm, der bei der Ausführung deutlich verändert wurde. Der ausgeführte Turm hat eine Höhe von 36 Metern, die ausgeführte Turmhaube erscheint traditioneller als in Rothkegels Projekt. Folgende Baumaterialien wählte Rothkegel: »Sämtliche Mauersteine aus dem an Ort und Stelle leicht erhältlichen Granit, die Ansichtsflächen unbearbeitet, so wie sie aus dem Bruch kommen. Ebenso die Gesimse, einfach als rauhe Wülste. Der Putz ganz rauh und nicht getönt. Das Dach mit Mönch und Nonne gedeckt, das Fachwerk mit Ochsenblut gestrichen.«[305] Wie auch bei der zweiten Gouverneursvilla wurden bei diesem Gebäude Formen des Jugendstils mit Historisierendem kombiniert.

Die Christuskirche war die Kirche der evangelischen Gemeinde und der deutschen Garnison in Qingdao. Sie wurde nicht als Missionskirche für chinesische Christen genutzt. Am 23. Oktober 1910 fand die Eröffnungsfeier der Kirche statt, ein Gedenkstein im Eingang

The church was built on a small hill on the eastern edge of the European villa district. This site had been earmarked for a church in the very first development plan. Like the second Governor's villa it was situated between the city and the Bismarck Barracks. The German Administration Chapel built in 1899 and the German School for boys were a little further south. Historical descriptions of the Christ Church describe the view over the bay from the square in front of the church high up on the hill as one of the most beautiful in Asia.

The scheme which the architect Rothkegel submitted for the competition combined the architectural requirements with topographical conditions: »Accommodating all seating on the ground floor means that the church will cover a fairly large area and will therefore not be very high. In this the architect has achieved what this hill-top site demands. The tower is approximately 27 metres high and thus does not detract from the surrounding hills.[304] The elevations submitted for the competition show a tower which was clearly different from the one which was built. The built tower is 36 metres high and its roof is more traditional in style than Rothkegel's modern competition design. Rothkegel specified the materials: »All the walls should be built in the granite which is so easily available locally; the exposed areas should be unfinished, as they come from the quarry. The same applies to the cornice – a simple crude roll. The render should be rough and uncoloured. The roof is tiled in mission tiles, the timber frame painted in ox-blood.«[305] Like the second Governor's villa, this building combines elements of Jugendstil and neo-Romanesque.

The Christ Church was the church of the Protestant community and the German garrison in Qingdao. It was not used as a mission church for Chinese Christians. On 23 October 1910 the church was consecrated and a stone slab in the entrance near the tower still commemorates the event today.

Today the view of the church from the sea is

青島福音堂（總督教堂）

現用途：基督教堂
所在地：青島沂水路（江蘇路口），原迪
　　　　特里希路（俾斯麥路口）
建築師：天津羅克格
施工：漢堡阿爾托那區F・H・施密特
業主：柏林德意志福音教會
建造期：一九零八年四月至一九一零年十
　　　　月
現狀：整體結構保存完好

該教堂建立一座小山丘上，西面與別墅林立的歐洲人住區相毗臨。早在建房規劃的第一方案中，這塊地皮便已辟為教堂所用。同總督第二別墅一樣，它的位置恰處於內城和俾斯麥兵營的中間。一八九九年落成的總督小教堂和總督學校位於該址的南側。據史書記載，從福音堂高地瞭望海灣，當屬亞洲最佳景觀之一。

在招標競賽中，建築師羅克格提出的設計方案將建築要求與地形條件成功地結合起來："鑒於各種設施均設在建築底層，教堂需要較寬大的基座。與此相應，其縱向空間延展並不顯得過份引人注目。這一設計十分吻合高地建築的要求，塔樓的設計高度為二十七米，從而不至於導致與周圍山地高下懸殊的效果。"〈304〉不過，塔樓的設計理想與實際施工方案有一定差異。建成的塔樓實高三十六米，塔蓋的風格也比羅克格的現代風格的招標設計方案更為保守。羅克格對建築材料的要求是："所有外牆用石均採用當地易取的花崗岩，其外露面無需任何加工，保持開採後的自然形態。同樣，檐口（裝飾線）也僅僅是粗糙的隆起。牆面抹以原色粗灰泥。房頂用陰陽瓦交錯鋪蓋，桁架用牛血著色"〈305〉同一九零七年所建的第二幢總督別墅一樣，這一建築的造型屬於青年藝術派和新羅馬風的結合。"

福音堂是青島福音教教區和德國衛戍部隊共用的教堂，它沒有作為針對華人基督徒的傳教機構使用。一九一零年十月二十三日，這裡舉辦了教堂的落成典禮；為了紀念這一日期，塔樓一側的入口處還設有一塊石碑。

八十年代初，教堂南側建起了高大的樓

教堂東北面俯視，約一九一二年。
福音堂南面外觀，一九九一年。

neben dem Turm erinnert noch heute daran. Heute ist der Blick vom Meer aus auf die Kirche durch hohe Wohnhäuser versperrt, die Anfang der 80er Jahre südlich von ihr errichtet worden sind. Der Kirchplatz hat dadurch auch seinen ursprünglichen Charakter einer riesigen Aussichtsterrasse verloren. Die Kirche selbst ist gut gepflegt; mehrmals in der Woche finden dort evangelische Gottesdienste statt.

blocked by high-rise blocks of flats which were built to the south of the church in the early 1980s. The square in front of the church has thus lost its original character as a vast viewing terrace. The church itself is well looked after and Protestant services are held there several times a week.

Säulendetail im Innenraum, 1991
Innenraum, Blick zum Altar, 1991
Perspektivzeichnung von Westen, 1907
Columns in the interior, 1991
Interior, view of altar, 1991
Perspective drawing from the west, 1907

教堂內廊柱細部,一九九一年。
教堂內部,大祭壇一瞥,一九九一年。
教堂西面全景透視圖,一九零七年。

群。今天,人們已經無法從海邊望到這座古教堂了,教堂高地自然失去了它原有的觀景點意義。教堂建築本身至今維護甚好;這裡每週仍要舉辦若干次福音教禮拜儀式。

ST. MICHAELS KATHEDRALE
ST MICHAEL'S CATHEDRAL

Heutige Funktion. Current use
Qingdaos katholische Kirche
Catholic Church of Qingdao
Feicheng Lu/Zhejiang Lu
(Bremer Straße/Luitpoldstraße),
Qingdao (Tsingtau. Tsingtao)

Architekt. Architect
Alfred Fräbel SVD

Bauleitung. Site Architect
Arthur Bialucha

Bauherr. Client
Bischof Georg Weig

Bauzeit. Construction time
Mai 1931 – Oktober 1934
May 1931 – October 1934

Zustand. Condition
Das Gebäude ist sehr gut erhalten.
Very well preserved.

Die Kathedrale liegt auf einer Hügelkuppe in der Mitte der Stadt. Ihre Gesamtlänge beträgt 65 Meter, die Länge des Querschiffes 34 Meter, die Höhe des Daches 18 Meter und die der Türme 54 Meter.[306] Das rund 12 Meter hohe Kirchenschiff und das Querschiff werden von einer Kassettendecke abgeschlossen. Durch die nicht vorhandenen Deckengewölbe fehlt dem Innenraum die nach oben strebende Raumwirkung. Die beiden Seitenschiffe sind überwölbt, doch sind sie im Verhältnis zum hohen Hauptschiff schmal und niedrig, so daß sie nur wie ein Umgang wirken.

Beim Bau der neoromanischen Kathedrale wurde der ursprüngliche Entwurf abgeändert: Die Turmdächer sind auf den veröffentlichten Zeichnungen des Entwurfs als glockenförmig dargestellt und wirken weicher, sie haben nicht die geometrische Strenge der ausgeführten Turmdächer.

Es dauerte fast 30 Jahre, bis der Plan, eine katholische Kirche in Qingdao zu bauen, verwirklicht wurde: »Schon der Missionsbaumeister Pater Erlemann hatte im Auftrag von Bischof Hennighaus (...), einen Plan für eine dreischiffige gotische Kirche entworfen. Pater Bartels begann bereits mit dem Kauf von Baustoffen. Die Eroberung Tsingtaus durch die Japaner im Spätjahr 1914 machte alle Pläne zunichte. (...) Der ursprünglich gotische Plan ward fallen gelassen, da er zu dem neuzeitlichen Stadtbild von Tsingtau weniger zu passen schien (...). Pater Alfred Fräbel entwarf einen romanisch gehaltenen Plan.«[307]

Die Kathedrale überragt die Stadt Qingdao. Vielleicht sollte der evangelischen Kirche ein mächtiger Bau gegenübergestellt werden, nachdem diese für 24 Jahre der größte Sakralbau Qingdaos gewesen war – vielleicht sollten aber auch die 46 Meter hohen Türme der Franziskanerkirche in Jinan übertroffen werden. Die Türme der Kathedrale in Qingdao waren höher als die aller anderen Kirchen in den nordchinesischen Großstädten Tianjin, Beijing, Dalian oder auch Jinan.

The cathedral stands on top of a hill in the centre of the city. It is 65 metres long in total, the length of the transept is 34 metres, the roof is 18 metres high and the tower 54 metres high.[306] Above the 12 metre high nave and the transept is a coffered ceiling. The fact that the ceiling is not vaulted means that the interior does not convey a feeling of striving upwards. There are vaults above the two aisles, but they are so narrow and low in comparison to the high nave that they are more like an ambulatory.

The original design of the neo-Romanesque cathedral was altered during construction: on the published drawings the roofs of the towers are bell-shaped and make a softer impression, they do not have the geometrical severity of the towers which were built.

It was almost 30 years before the plan to build a Catholic church in Qingdao was finally implemented: »The mission architect, Father Erlemann, had been commissioned by Bishop Hennighaus, (...), to design a church and had produced a scheme for a three-aisled Gothic church. Father Bartels began buying building materials. The conquering of Tsingtao by the Japanese in 1914 put an end to all the plans. (...) The original Gothic plan was abandoned because it no longer seemed appropriate for the modern townscape of Tsingtao (...). Father Alfred Fräbel came up with a Romanesque design.«[307]

The cathedral is far too large for the scale of Qingdao. Its position on top of a hill makes this even more evident. Perhaps the idea was to produce a powerful building to hold its own with the Protestant Church, which for 24 years had been the largest religious building in Qingdao, or perhaps the intention was to outstrip the 46 metre-high towers of the Franciscan church in Jinan. The towers of the cathedral in Qingdao were higher than all the other churches in the major cities of Northern China – Tianjin, Beijing, Dalian or Jinan. They dominate the silhouette of Qingdao; they are particularly impressive from a ship entering the harbour.

聖彌愛爾大教堂

現用途：青島天主教堂
所在地：青島肥城路，（浙江路口，原布萊梅路盧伊特波爾德路口）
建築師：阿爾弗雷德·弗萊波爾
工程指導：阿圖爾·畢亞盧恰
業主：魏嘉祿主教
建造期：一九三一年五月至一九三四年十月
現狀：樓體保存完好

主教座堂坐落在市中心的一個半球狀丘頂它的總長度為六十五米，十字形耳堂長三十四米，檐高十八米，塔樓高五十四米。〈306〉高約十二米的中殿和耳堂以鋼筋混凝土結構的方格天花板為頂，故而沒有拱形頂那種拔向天穹的空間效果。左右兩個側廳盡管修有拱頂，但與中殿相比則過於低矮狹長，因而只能顯示一種過道的效果。

這座新羅馬風式的教堂的施工方案對原設計做有若干改動：在曾經發表過的設計圖案上，塔樓頂有座鐘形，造型感比較柔和，而建成的塔頂側表現了較為冷峻的幾何形式。

在青島修建一座天主教堂的計劃花了近三十年的時間才得以實現："事情發端於安治泰的繼任者朝寧鎬主教。他曾委托傳教使團的建築師恩博仁神甫籌建一座三廳規格的哥特體教堂。而後，白明德神甫開始著手採購建築材料。然而日本人一九一四年侵佔青島後，一切計劃都付諸東流。（……）原為的哥特體設計方案被束之高閣，因為它與後期的青島市容已經不甚相稱。（……）阿·弗萊波爾神甫則提出一項羅馬風式的方案。"〈307〉

與青島市區的規模相比，這座主教座堂顯得過於龐大。在山丘頂部修建該教堂進一步強化了這種效果。也許，在青島福音堂存在二十四年之後，設計者認為有必要修一座雄偉的建築來與當地最大的宗教殿堂平分秋色；也許，濟南方濟會教堂那四十六米高的塔樓曾被視為競爭對象。總之，青島愛彌爾大教堂的塔樓高度超過北京、天津、大連以及濟南等中國北方大城市的所有其它教堂。它曾經屬於青島市景之焦點：乘船駛出港口再回首望之，這一印象則會更強烈。"

聖彌愛爾大教堂西面外觀，一九九二年。
由有平頂格子藻井的中廊堂，望大祭壇，一九九二年。
十字形耳堂內的壁畫，一九九一年。

RESIDENZ DER STEYLER MISSIONSGESELLSCHAFT
RESIDENCE OF THE STEYLER MISSIONARY SOCIETY

Heutige Funktion. Current use
Verwaltung, Hotel und Polizei
Administration, hotel and police station
Qufu Lu/Zhejiang Lu (Berliner Straße/Luitpoldstraße), Qingdao (Tsingtau. Tsingtao)

Architekt. Architect
Bernatz, München
Bernatz, Munich

Bauleitung. Site Architect
Pater Franz Bartels SVD
Father Franz Bartels SVD

Bauherr. Client
Bischof J.B. von Anzer
Bishop J.B. von Anzer

Bauzeit. Construction time
1899–1902

Zustand. Condition
Das Gebäude ist sehr gut erhalten.
Very well preserved.

Residenz der Steyler Missionsgesellschaft, Westansicht vom Kirchplatz, 1902
Detail der Westfassade, 1991
Residence of the Steyler Missionary Society SVD, view from the west from the square in front of the church, 1902
View of west façade, 1991

Die katholische Mission lag im Zentrum von Qingdao. Der große Platz zwischen der Residenz und dem Heilig-Geist-Kloster blieb 35 Jahre lang unbebaut, bis dort die St. Michaels Kathedrale errichtet wurde. Die zum Kirchplatz gerichtete Fassade der Residenz schmückt noch heute ein Renaissance-Erker. Ein schmaler Vorgartenstreifen umgibt das Gebäude, das eine Kapelle, eine Druckerei und die Verwaltungsräume der Mission beherbergte. Ein Blumengarten befand sich im Innenhof. Im Südflügel, an der Qufu Lu, lag der Eingang zur Kapelle, einer einfachen Basilika mit offenem Dachwerk, die etwa 300–400 Personen aufnehmen konnte.

1910 waren von den 1621 Europäern in Qingdao nur 241 katholisch; der Raum für die sonntäglichen Gottesdienste der Europäer war also reichlich bemessen. Gleichzeitig diente diese Kapelle auch den chinesischen Christen, deren Predigt, wie man damals begründete, der Sprache wegen getrennt gehalten wurde.

Noch im ersten Bebauungsplan aus dem Jahre 1898/99 lagen sich die evangelische und katholische Kirche an den Endpunkten der Guangxi Lu (Prinz-Heinrich-Straße) gegenüber.[308] Wahrscheinlich war dieses Grundstück dem Bischof zu weit von der chinesischen Händlerstadt entfernt und lag außerdem nicht wie das der evangelischen Kirche auf einem Hügel. Die katholische Mission erhielt darauf weiter nördlich ein 30 000 m² großes Grundstück. Wie alle Missionsgrundstücke wurde es vom deutschen Gouvernement kostenlos zur Verfügung gestellt. Es lag an der Schnittstelle zwischen dem europäischen Stadtviertel und dem chinesischen Händlerviertel Dabaodao.

The Catholic mission was on a hill in the centre of Qingdao. The large square between the Residence and the Holy Ghost Convent was without buildings for 35 years until St. Michael's Cathedral was built. The façade facing the square was decorated with a Renaissance oriel. A narrow strip of garden surrounded the building, which housed a chapel, a printing shop and the offices of the mission. In the courtyard of the Residence there was a flower garden. The entrance to the chapel was in the southern wing on Qufu Lu. It was a simple basilica with a visible roof framework and could hold between 300 and 400 people.

In 1910 only 241 of the 1621 Europeans in Qingdao were Catholic; there was thus ample space for the Sunday services. This chapel was used at the same time by Chinese Christians, whose sermon was preached separately for language reasons.

In the first development plan for the city, dating from 1898/1899, the Protestant and Catholic churches were at opposite ends of Guangxi Lu (Prinz-Heinrich-Strasse).[308] The bishop probably thought that this site was too far away from the Chinese trader's part of the city and apart from that was not on a hill like the Protestant church. The German Administration then gave the Catholic Mission a present of a 30 000 m² site a little further to the north. It was on the boundary between the European district of town and the Chinese trader's district, Dabaodao.

斯泰爾修會聖言會會館

現用途：地方機關、旅店、派出所
所在地：青島曲阜路（浙江路口），原柏林路（盧伊特波爾路口）
建築師：聖言會天主教團神甫（弗蘭茨·）白昭德
業主：安治泰主教
建造期：一八九九年至一九零二年
現狀：建築保存完好

由教堂前的廣場望斯泰勒修會會館西立面，一九零二年。
西立面細部，一九九一年。

這一天主教傳教機構設立青島市中心的一座小山上。聖言會和聖心修道院之間的大片空地曾被閒置了三十五年之久，直到聖彌爾大教堂的建成。會館朝向大教堂的一面外牆飾有文藝復興風格的八角窗。條狀的樓前花園環繞著這座建築，樓內設有一個小教堂，一個印刷廠和修會的若干辦公室。內院是一片花圃。毗臨曲阜路的會館南翼是小教堂的入口處。這一設計樸素、屋架裸露的教堂可以容納三百至四百人。一九一零年，在一千六百二十一名旅居青島的歐洲人當中，只有二百四十一人信奉天主教，可見，祈禱室用於歐洲人做禮拜是綽綽有餘。小教堂也供華人基督徒使用，鑒於語言不同，其布道儀式與歐洲人分開進行。

在一八九八年到一八九九年間制定的城市規劃第一方案中，福音教堂和天主教堂被分別安排在廣西路的（原享利王子路）兩個遙相對應的端點。(308)在主教看來，這一位置似乎離華人的商業區過遠。此外，這里也不如福音堂所佔的高地位置那樣理想。聖言會後曾按照所有傳教機構的慣例從總督府無償地得到一塊相當靠北的地皮，其面積達三萬平米。它位於歐洲區和華人商業區大鮑島的臨接處。

QINGDAO

**HEILIG-GEIST-KLOSTER
FRANZISKANERINNEN
MISSIONARINNEN MARIENS
HOLY GHOST CONVENT FRANCISCAN
MISSIONARIES OF MARY**

Heutige Funktion. Current use
Verwaltungsgebäude
Administration building
Feicheng Lu/Zhejiang Lu (Bremer Straße/
Fischerstraße), Qingdao (Tsingtau. Tsingtao)

Architekt. Architect
Bernatz, München
Bernatz, Munich

Bauleitung. Site Architect
Pater Franz Bartels SVD
Father Franz Bartels SVD

Bauherr. Client
Bischof J.B. von Anzer
Bishop J.B. von Anzer

Bauzeit. Construction time
1901–1902

Zustand. Condition
Das Gebäude ist gut erhalten,
das Dach verändert.
Well preserved; roof altered.

Das Kloster betrieb eine Schule für ausländische Mädchen, mit der ein Pensionat und ein Kindergarten verbunden waren. Am 1. April 1902 wurden diese Einrichtungen eröffnet. Das Kloster, die Waisenabteilung wie auch die Kapelle wurden in den folgenden Jahren ausgebaut. Anfang 1904 hatte die Schule 48 Schülerinnen, darunter befanden sich 12 auswärtige aus Tianjin, Shanghai und Japan. Ende 1906 besuchten 70 Mädchen die Schule.

Der Münchner Baumeister hatte mit diesem Kloster ein in seinem Ausdruck typisch süddeutsches Gebäude in Qingdao errichtet, inklusive des charakteristischen Innenhofs. Der ursprünglich nur zweigeschossige Bau wurde in den 20er Jahren um ein Stockwerk erhöht. Dabei wurden auch die neobarocken Turmhelme der Ecktürme am Kirchplatz entfernt.

Bischof von Anzer hatte die Franziskanerinnen nach Qingdao eingeladen, da Missionsschwestern mit den Muttersprachen Deutsch, Englisch und Französisch gebraucht wurden. Über ihre Ankunft im Jahre 1902 in Qingdao berichtet eine Franziskanerin: »Wir hatten uns ein echt chinesisches Quartier vorgestellt – statt dessen fanden wir ein schönes, europäisches Haus. Alles ist sehr gut eingerichtet: Zellen, Säle, Refektorium, Küche, im ersten Stock ein breiter Gang von 20 Fenstern erhellt. Es fehlt uns also weder an Luft, noch Licht. Gute Öfen verbreiten überall Wärme. (...) Unsere Wohnung liegt hoch. Wir haben die Stadt zu unseren Füßen und einen herrlichen Blick über das Meer. (...)«[309]

The convent ran a school for foreign girls which also had a boarding school and a kindergarten attached to it. These facilities were opened on 1 April 1902. The convent, the orphanage and the chapel were all extended over the years to come. At the beginning of 1904 the school had 48 pupils, 12 of those boarders from Tianjin, Shanghai and Japan. At the end of 1906 there were 70 girls of school age.

With this convent the Munich architect designed a building for Qingdao which was typically south German right down to the courtyard. The building originally only had two storeys, but an extra floor was added in the twenties. In the process the neo-Baroque roofs were removed from the corner towers on the square in front of the church.

Bishop von Anzer had invited the Sisters of the Franciscan Mission to Qingdao because Sisters who spoke German, English and French as their native tongue were needed. One of the Franciscan Sisters wrote of her arrival in Qingdao in 1902: »We had imagined a genuine Chinese quarter – instead we find a lovely, European building. Everything is very well equipped: the cells, halls, refectory, kitchen, on the first floor a broad corridor is lit by 20 windows. There is no lack of light or fresh air. Good stoves radiate warmth everywhere. (...). Our living quarters are high up. We have the city at our feet and a wonderful view of the sea. (...)«[309]

Heilig-Geist-Kloster, Ostansicht,
1902
Innenhof des ehem. Klosters, 1992
Holy Ghost Convent, F.M.M.,
view from the east, 1902
Courtyard of the former convent,
1992

聖心修道院（聖母方濟傳教女修會）

現用途：辦公樓
所在地：青島肥城路（浙江路口），原不
　　　　來梅路（菲舍爾路口）
建築師：墨尼黑建築工程師貝爾納茨
工程指導：聖言會天主教團神甫白明德
業主：安治泰主教
建造期：一九零一年至一九零二年
現狀：樓體保存良好；頂蓋已改建

該修道院辦有一所供外國女孩就讀和寄宿的學校，此外還兼辦一所幼兒園。建校日為一九零二年四月一日。此後，修道院進一步擴建，增設了孤兒部和一個小教堂。至一九零四年初，學生數達到四十八人，其中包括來自天津、上海以及日本的十二個女生。一九零六年底，這裡學齡少女增至七十人。

來自慕尼黑的建築師在青島所建的這座修道院表現了典型的德國南部建築風格，造型別致的內院並不例外。到了本世紀二十年代，在原有的二層建築基礎上又增建了一層頂樓。教堂廣場一側的新巴羅克式角樓屋頂被拆除。

主教安治泰特地把方濟會的修女請到青島，因為這裡很需要以德語、英語和法語為母語的修女。一九零二年，一位駐青島的方濟傳教女修會成員曾經這樣介紹她們的住所："當初，我們想像中的住處完全是中國式的。與此相反，我們看到的卻是很漂亮的一座地道的歐式樓房。所有的設施都十分完美：修道室、大小廳堂、餐廳、廚房，還有二層樓那條開有二十扇窗戶的走廊，既寬敞又明亮。這裡毫無缺少空間和光線的感覺。優質的壁爐將溫暖送向每個角落。（……）樓上是我們的住房，而城市在我們的腳下。從這裡，可以望到一幅秀麗的海景（……）。"〈309〉

聖心修道院東立面，一九零二年。
原修道院內院，一九九二年。

QINGDAO

BERLINER MISSION, MISSIONARSWOHNHAUS
HOUSE FOR MISSIONARIES OF THE BERLIN MISSION

Heutige Funktion. Current use
Qingdaos Hospital für chinesische Medizin
Chengyang Lu 5 (nahe Shanghaistraße),
Qingdao (Tsingtau)
Qingdao's hospital for Chinese Medicine
Chengyang Lu 5 (near Shanghai Strasse),
Qingdao (Tsingtau)

Entwurf. Design
Kunze, Missionar
Kunze, missionary

Bauherr. Client
Berliner Mission
Berlin Mission

Bauzeit. Construction time
1899–1900

Zustand. Condition
Das Gebäude ist sehr gut erhalten.
Very well preserved.

Das Wohnhaus für die Berliner Mission wurde von Kunze, einem ihrer Missionare entworfen.[310] Das Gebäude besteht aus dem nach Süden ausgerichteten Mittelbau und zwei Seitenflügeln, die mit zwei schlichten Giebeln die Südfassade einfassen. Trotz der großen Veranden an der Südfassade wirkt das Gebäude nicht wie ein englischer Kolonialbau. Der einzige Schmuck des Wohnhauses war ein kleiner, auf das Dach aufgesetzter Ziergiebel mit einem Kreuz.

Das deutsche Gouvernement hatte den beiden in Qingdao tätigen evangelischen Missionsgesellschaften, der Berliner und der Weimarer Mission, nebeneinander liegende Grundstücke überlassen, die relativ weit entfernt waren vom europäischen und chinesischen Geschäftsviertel.[311] Die Berliner Mission hatte sich die Sammlung einer Christengemeinde im deutschen Schutzgebiet und den angrenzenden Kreisen zur Hauptaufgabe gemacht. Diesem Zwecke dienten Kapellen in Dabaodao, Taidong Zhen und Licun (Li tsun). Mit der Mission war eine deutsch-chinesische Schule verbunden, in der deutsche Sprache, Rechnen, Geographie, chinesische Klassiker, biblische Geschichte und der Katechismus unterrichtet wurden.[312]

Ab etwa 1930 war das Missionarswohnhaus ein Krankenhaus der American Lutheran Mission.

The house for the Berlin Mission was designed by Kunze, one of their own missionaries.[310] The building consists of a central section facing south, with verandas in front of it, and two side wings whose two simple gables flank the southern façade. Despite the large verandas, the building does not look like an English colonial house. The only decoration was a small Renaissance gable with a cross which was simply set on the roof, not actually part of it.

The German Administration had given the two Protestant Missionary Societies working in Qingdao, the Berlin and the Weimar Mission society, adjacent pieces of land which were quite a distance from the European and the Chinese business quarters.[311] The Berlin Mission had made it its main task to gather together a Christian community in the German protectorate and the adjacent towns. Chapels in Dabaodao, Taidong Zhen and Licun (Li tsun) served this purpose. A German-Chinese school was attached to the mission which taught arithmetic, geography, Chinese classics, bible history and the Catechism in German.[312]

From about 1930 onwards the missionaries' house was used as a hospital by the American Lutheran Mission.

Wohnhaus der Berliner Mission,
Südansicht, um 1903
Südansicht, 1992
House of the Berlin Mission,
view from the south, around 1903
View from the south, 1992

柏林傳敎會（信義會）住宅

現用途：青島市中醫院
所在地：青島城陽路五號（上海路附近）
設計：路切維茨，傳教士
業主：柏林傳敎會（福音敎）
建造期：一八九九年至一九零零年
現狀：樓體保存完好

柏林傳敎會的這一住宅樓是由該會的傳教士路切維茨設計的。⑶¹⁰⁾樓體的主部南面設有游廊式陽台，其兩端各建有側翼。設計樸素的翼樓山牆構成南立面的的外圍。盡管該樓南立面前側的陽台大而突出，可它並不落英式殖民建築的巢臼。住宅樓的唯一裝飾是在樓頂上添修的一堵小型山牆。它具有文藝復興式風格，用作十字架的托座。

德國駐青島行政當局劃給柏林傳敎會和魏瑪傳敎會的地域緊緊相臨，並使這兩個在青島地區活動的福音教傳教機構遠離歐洲區及華人商業區。⑶¹¹⁾柏林傳敎會的主要任務是在德租界和臨近的幾個縣建立一個基督教區。設在大鮑島、台東鎮和李村的幾個小教堂均隸屬這一教區。此外，傳教會兼辦一所德華學校，開設德語、算術、地理、古漢語、聖經史、教義學等課程。⑶¹²⁾

一九三零年前後，這座傳敎會住宅樓被美國路德傳敎會的一所醫院移用。

柏林傳敎會住宅南面外觀，約一九零三年。
南面外觀，一九九二年。

QINGDAO

WEIMARER MISSION – RICHARD WILHELM

Heutige Funktion. Current use
Qingdaos Stadt-Oberschule Nummer 9
Municipal College no. 9 of Qingdao
Shanghai Lu/Chengyang Lu (Shanghaistraße), Qingdao (Tsingtau. Tsingtao)

Architekt. Architect
Franz Xaver Mauerer (Wohnhaus)

Bauherr. Client
Weimarer Mission/Allgemeiner Evangelisch-Protestantischer Missionsverein
Weimar Mission/General Evangelical-Protestant Missionary Association

Bauzeit. Construction time
1899–1900

Zustand. Condition
Das Gebäude ist gut erhalten; das Schulgebäude wurde abgetragen.
Well preserved; school was pulled down.

Wohnhaus von Richard Wilhelm, Westansicht, um 1903
Ehem. Wohnhaus von Richard Wilhelm, Ostansicht, 1992
Residence of Richard Wilhelm, view from the west, around 1903
Former residence of Richard Wilhelm, view from the east, 1992

Die Anlage der Weimarer Mission bestand aus dem Wohnhaus der Missionare, dem Faber-Hospital für chinesische Patienten und der Schule, dem deutsch-chinesischen Seminar, mit angeschlossenem Internat. Bereits 1899–1900 war das Wohnhaus in europäischer Bauweise errichtet worden. Das Hospital und die 1902 fertiggestellte Schule wurden in chinesischer Bauweise als Komplex aus Hofhäusern geplant. Der Missionar Richard Wilhelm beschrieb das deutsch-chinesische Seminar als »eine chinesische Schule, auch in der baulichen Anlage. Es besteht aus eingeschossigen Gebäuden, die sich nach der bekannten chinesischen Bauweise um einzelne Höfe gruppieren. (…) Tritt man zum Haupteingang herein, so kommt man auf einen viereckigen Hof, der durch die Unterrichtsräume gebildet wird. (…) Östlich daran schließt sich ein großer Hof mit Schülerwohnungen. Die vorgerückten Schüler haben einen Wohnhof für sich, südlich davon. Ein besonderer Hof im Westen wird durch die Wohnräume der Unterstufe gebildet. Am Eingang jedes der Wohnhöfe befindet sich ein Zimmer eines chinesischen Lehrers, der die Schüler des betreffenden Hofes beaufsichtigt. Der große Schülerhof ist ein fast quadratischer Platz, eingeschlossen von niedrigen Hausreihen, die nur durch den ungefähr fünf Meter breiten Zugang, der vom Eingangshof herführt, unterbrochen wird. Man sieht hier Tür an Tür und dazwischen je ein Fenster, (…). Dieser Platz, wo ungefähr sechzig junge Leute wohnen, dient zugleich als Spiel- und Tummelplatz.«[313]

Im Jahre 1903 wurden zusätzlich ein kaufmännisch-technischer Kurs, mit dem Hauptgewicht auf deutscher Umgangssprache, und ein wissenschaftlicher Kurs für künftige chinesische Beamte und Lehrer eingerichtet. Später wurde das Seminar in drei Stufen gegliedert: eine Elementarschule mit 30 Schülern, eine Mittelstufe mit 97 Schülern, in der man die Zugangsberechtigung zur Deutsch-Chinesischen Hochschule erwerben konnte, und ein Lehrerseminar mit sechs Schülern.

The complex for the Weimar Mission consisted of a house for the missionaries, the Faber Hospital for Chinese patients and the school, the German-Chinese Seminar with a boarding school attached. The house had already been built in 1899/1900 in western style. But the hospital and the school, which was completed in 1902, were built in the Chinese fashion around a courtyard. The missionary, Richard Wilhelm, described the German-Chinese Seminar as »a Chinese school, also in the way it is built. It consists of one-storey buildings which are grouped around different courtyards in the famous Chinese style. (…) When you come in through the main entrance, you enter a rectangular courtyard surrounded by the classrooms. (…) To the east is a large yard with living quarters for the pupils. The older pupils have a quadrangle to themselves to the south of this. A special yard to the west is surrounded by the living quarters for the lower school. At the entrance to each of these quadrangles is a room for the Chinese teacher who supervises the pupils who live there. The large schoolyard is almost square and is surrounded by rows of low buildings which are interrupted by a passageway only five metres wide from the entrance courtyard. You see here pair after pair of doors each with a window between them, (…). This square, where some sixty young people live, is also used as a place to play and romp.«[313]

In 1903 an additional course in commerce and technical subjects with emphasis on colloquial German and a scientific course intended for future Chinese civil servants and teachers were set up. Later the seminar was divided into three levels: an elementary school with 30 pupils, a secondary school with 97 pupils where they could prepare for the entrance exam to the German-Chinese College and a teacher training college with six students. In 1906 the pupils came from 30 Chinese provinces and were for the most part sons of Chinese civil servants.

The mission also ran two girls' schools which

魏瑪傳教會（同善會）── 兼談衛禮賢牧師

現用途：青島市第九中學
所在地：青島上海路（城陽路口），原上海路
建築：聖方濟各沙勿修會毛利公司（住宅部分）
業主：同善會魏瑪傳教會
建造期：一八九九年至一九零零年
現狀：樓體保存完好；校舍樓已被拆除

魏瑪傳教會建區由傳教士住宅樓、華之安華人病院以及德華書院——一所寄宿學校——組成。早在一八九九年到一九零零年間，具有西方建築風格的住宅樓已經落成。醫院和一九零二年竣工的學校則按中國建築傳統建成群落式四合院。傳教士衛禮賢曾如此描寫德華書院："這是一所中國式的學校，包括它的建築佈局。學校的房屋各自封閉，並以著名的中國建房風格結為單獨的院落。（……）踏入正門，可以看到一個正方形的院子，四周被教室包圍起來。（……）與此相連的東院面積較大，裡面設有學生宿舍。高年級學生擁有獨立的宿舍內院，位於校南。西校區則建有一座專供低年級學生住宿的四合院。每個四合院的入口處均設有一間中國教師專用的門房，以便與他掌握院內學生的情況。寬大的中心校院是一片幾乎正方的場地，四周圍有低矮的排房；一條約五米寬的過道從中穿過，並由此通向前院。很引人注目的是，這裡一道道門緊密相接，其間僅隔一窗，（……）。這個大約住著六十個名學生的院落同時也作為游戲和運動場地使用。"〈313〉

一九零三年，書院增設了商務技術課，以德語口語作為授課重點。此外，還為培養中國官員和教師開設了一門科學技術課。其後，書院調整為三部制：初級部收三十名學生；中級部九十七名，他們學成後可報考德華高等學堂；另有一教師部收有六名學員。一九零六年，學校接收的學生來自中國三十個不同省份，其中大部分是中國官僚子弟。在青島的歐洲區，傳教會還開辦了兩個女子學校。其中，美懿書院是一個強調基督教傳統的女子學校，它對學生進行家政教育並從中培養女教師。學生

禮賢住宅西面外觀，約一九零三年。
原禮賢住宅東面外觀，一九九二年。

1906 kamen die Schüler aus 30 chinesischen Provinzen und waren zum größeren Teil Söhne chinesischer Beamter.

Die Mission unterhielt zudem zwei Mädchenschulen, die im europäischen Stadtteil Qingdaos lagen. Die Me-I-Schule war eine Mädchendorfschule auf christlicher Grundlage mit einer Ausbildung als Lehrerin und für das Hauswesen; sie hatte 43 Schülerinnen. Im Herbst 1911 eröffnete die Schu-Fan-Schule; sie war eine weiterführende Mädchenschule und hatte das Ziel der »Verbreitung deutscher Kultur und Sprache unter den Töchtern höherer Stände in China unter ausdrücklichem Verzicht auf religiöse Propaganda.«[314] Die Schu-Fan-Schule war im europäischen Stil gebaut.

Die Weimarer Mission hatte sich neben der Missionsarbeit die Förderung der wissenschaftlichen Sinologie zur Aufgabe gemacht. Missionare wie Ernst Faber (1839–1899) und Richard Wilhelm (1873–1930) waren für die Mission in Qingdao tätig.[315] Man sah die Aufgabe der Mission nicht in der Gründung von christlichen Gemeinden und taufte auch nicht, sondern unterhielt weiterführende Schulen und förderte das Hospitalwesen; die Mission wollte durch Unterricht aufklären. Der Weimarer Mission unterstand ursprünglich auch die evangelische Seelsorge der deutschen Kolonie, später gab es dann einen Gouvernementspfarrer.

Nach der Revolution im Herbst 1911 flüchteten viele ehemalige hohe Beamte der Qing-Regierung nach Qingdao. Mit ihnen zusammen gründete Richard Wilhelm die Konfuziusvereinigung, »der eine große Anzahl der in Tsingtau befindlichen chinesischen Beamten angehörte. Gelder kamen zusammen. Man baute eine Bibliothek. Man brachte eine größere Anzahl wertvoller chinesischer Werke zusammen. Ein Versammlungsraum und eine Arbeitsstätte wurden damit verbunden. Der Gedanke war, dazu beizutragen, daß die Schätze der chinesischen Kultur (...) auf die Zukunft gerettet würden.«[316]

were in the European quarter of Qingdao. The Me I School was a village school for girls run on Christian principles and trained girls in housekeeping or teaching. It had 43 pupils. In autumn 1911 the Schu-Fan School opened; it was a higher school for girls and its aim was to »spread the German culture and language to the daughters of the higher classes in China whilst explicitly avoiding religious propaganda.«[314] The aim of the teaching was designed in such a way as to not tear the girls out of their social structures. The Schu-Fan School was built in European style.

Apart from missionary work the aim of the Weimar Mission (General Evangelical-Protestant Missionary Association) was to promote academic sinology. Missionaries such as Ernst Faber (1839–1899) and Richard Wilhelm (1873–1930) worked for the mission in Qingdao.[315] The mission did not consider it its duty to found Christian communities and did not carry out baptisms, but ran higher schools and helped hospitals. Its aim was to bring enlightenment through education. The Weimar Mission was originally also responsible for Protestant spiritual counselling for the German colony, but later there was a pastor to the German Administration.

After the revolution in autumn 1911 many former senior civil servants of the Qing government fled to Qingdao. Richard Wilhelm founded with them the Confucius Association, »to which a great number of the Chinese civil servants in Tsingtao belonged. Money came in. We built a library. We gathered together a large number of valuable Chinese books. A meeting room and a workshop were attached to it. The idea was to help rescue the treasures of Chinese culture (...) for future generations.«[316]

Deutsch-Chinesisches Seminar.
Speise- und Küchengebäude der Knabenschule, um 1912
Zugang zum Schulgrundstück, um 1912
German-Chinese Seminar. Building with dining room and kitchen of the boys' school, around 1912
Entrance to school premises, around 1912

德華書院。男子學校食堂,約一九一二年。
校院入口,約一九一二年。

總數為四十三人。一九一一年秋開辦的淑苑女學則是一所中等學校,辦學宗旨在於"向中國的名門閨秀普及德意志語言文化,同時廢止一切宗教宣傳。"(314)該校的教學方針致力於避免學生脫離其自身的社會基礎。淑苑女學的校舍為歐式建築。除傳教活動之外,魏瑪傳教會(同善會)還大力推動系統漢學的發展。著名傳教士華之安一八三九至一八九九年和衛禮賢一八七三至一九三零曾作為該教會代表在青島極活躍。(315)他們並不把建立教區和從事洗禮看成傳教會的使命,而是著眼於發展教育和推進醫療衛生事業;他們試圖通過有益的教學活動進行啟蒙。魏瑪傳教會的原定任務還包括德國殖民地範圍內的福音教宣教對話活動。後來,這裡專設了一位德管區神甫。

在一九一一年秋的辛亥革命之後,原清政府的許多上層官員逃往青島。衛禮賢與他們共同建立了青島尊孔文社,"當時留駐青島的一大批中國官僚皆加入其中。他們共同集資,建起禮賢書院,收集了大量珍貴的文物典籍。書院分設藏書樓和修研館。建社的主導思想在於拯救中華文薈(⋯⋯),以開拓未來。"(316)

QINGDAO

SEEMANNSHAUS
SEAMAN'S CLUB

Heutige Funktion. Current use
Bürogebäude
Office building
Zhongshan Lu/Hubei Lu
(Friedrichstraße/Kronprinzenstraße),
Qingdao (Tsingtau. Tsingtao)

Bauherr. Client
Seemannshaus für Unteroffiziere und
Mannschaften der Kaiserlichen Marine,
gemeinnützige Gesellschaft.
Seaman's Club for non-commissioned
officers and ordinary seamen of the
Imperial Navy, charitable organisation

Bauzeit. Construction time
1901 – Mai 1902
1901 – May 1902

Zustand. Condition
Das Gebäude ist sehr gut erhalten,
das Turmdach wurde verändert.
Very well preserved;
roof of the tower altered.

Das Semanshaus lag in der Mitte des europäischen Geschäftsviertels von Qingdao, nahe der Landungsbrücke.[317] In historisierender Weise wurde der Bau mit typischen Elementen gestaltet: einem hohen Eckturm, einem von einem Giebel überhöhten mittleren Baukörper und einer hölzernen Veranda. Am Turm und den Verandabrüstungen wurden noch die in China mißverständlichen Fachwerkkreuze als Dekoration verwendet, auf die bei späteren Bauten völlig verzichtet wurde.

Zweck des Seemannshauses war es, »den Mannschaften (…) ein Heim für ihre Erholungszeit zu bieten, damit sie sich den demoralisierenden Einflüssen ziellosen Straßenlebens, schlechter Wirtschaften und des Schnapsgenusses entziehen können. Außerdem soll das Seemannshaus in Tsingtau auch als Erholungsheim für Genesende der in Ostasien stationierten Marine- und Truppenteile Verwendung finden.«[318] Es sollte »für edle Erholung und zum Anhören belehrender und bildender Vorträge Gelegenheit schaffen, kurz es ist Alles zu fördern, was dem geistigen und leiblichen Wohle des Besuchers förderlich sein kann. (…) Dienstliche und konfessionelle Beeinflussungen sind dagegen ausgeschlossen.«[319]

Das Seemannshaus war das erste Gebäude in Qingdao mit einem großen Festsaal, hier fanden regelmäßig Theaterspiele statt. Der Saal ist etwa 14 Meter breit und 20 Meter tief und hat eine dreiseitig umlaufende Galerie; er bietet Platz für etwa 200 Personen. Der Saal wird durch ein gläsernes Oberlicht sowie Nordfenster belichtet. Seine Holzkonstruktion ist noch heute in sehr gutem Zustand.

Das Gebäude stand in einem relativ großen Abstand von der Straße. Entlang der Zhongshan Lu wurde diese Fläche in den 20er Jahren für einen eleganten Anbau durch japanische Architekten genutzt. Seit 1915 war hier der japanische Klub untergebracht.

The Seaman's Club was in the centre of the European business district of Qingdao, near the landing stage.[317] The building had the typical elements of the German neo-Renaissance style: a high corner tower, a gabled building marking the entrance and a wooden veranda. The timber crosses, which could be misinterpreted in China, were used as decoration. Their use was subsequently abandoned completely.

The purpose of the Seaman's Club was »to give the crews (…) a home for their recreational time so that they could escape the demoralising influence of aimless street life, sleazy bars and the influence of alcohol. The Seaman's Club in Tsingtao was also intended to be used as a convalescence home for the soldiers and sailors stationed in East Asia.«[318] It was meant to »create the opportunity for refined recreation and for listening to instructive and educational lectures, in short, to promote everything which can be of value to the mental and physical well-being of the visitor. (…) Any professional or religious influence is out of the question.«[319]

The Seaman's Club was the first building in Qingdao to have a large hall for functions, where theatrical performances were regularly given. The hall is some 14 metres wide and 20 metres long and has a gallery on three sides. It seats approximately 200 people. The hall is lit by a top-light and a northern window. Its wooden structure is still in good condition.

The building is set quite far back from the streets. This space along Zhongshan Lu was used in the twenties by Japanese architects who added an elegant extension. Since 1915 the Japanese club has been housed here.

水師飯店

現用途：辦公樓
所在地：青島中山路（湖北路口），原佛里德里希路（太子路口）
業主：皇家海戰軍水師飯店、公益社團
建造期：一九零一年五月至一九零二年
現狀：樓體保存完好；塔樓頂經過改建

水師飯店位於青島棧橋附近的歐洲商業區中心。〈317〉這座建築具有德國中古時期新文藝復興風格的典型結構：高聳的角樓、橫跨正門的前立面山牆、木製的外廊。塔樓之下和外廊扶欄處的交錯桁架被用作裝飾體；這種常常引起中國人誤解的構架在以後的建築上被完全放棄。
建水師飯店的意圖是"為士官和水兵（……）提供休養栖留場所，以免他們游蕩街頭、出入下等餐館和酗酒，並由此引致道德倫落。此外，水師飯店又作為德國駐東亞海陸部隊傷病員的療養所使用。"〈318〉此處"既有一流的療養條件，又能提供各種開蒙心智、陶冶情操的講演報告。總之，來訪者應該在這裡得到各種有益身心健康的機會。（……）反之，一切公務負擔和宗教影響均屬避忌之列。"〈319〉
在青島，水師飯店是第一座設有大型禮堂的建築。這裡定期上演各類劇目。禮堂寬約十四米，縱深二十米，廳內的三面牆設計為迴廊式，能容納坐席約二百個。禮堂以玻璃罩頂燈和一排北窗為照明手段。它的木製結構直到今天仍保持著原狀。
這座樓與街道的距離較遠。在二十年代，日本建築師沿中山路兩側修建了十分優雅的街旁裝飾物。自一九一五年始，此處移用為日本俱樂部。

原德國水師飯店(自一九一五年為日本人居留民會)西南面外觀，約一九二零年。
禮堂，一九九二年。

TSINGTAU-KLUB
TSINGTAO CLUB

Heutige Funktion. Current use
Gesellschaft für Technik und Wissenschaft
Society for Science and Technology
Zhongshan Lu 1/Taiping Lu
(Friedrichstraße/Kaiser-Wilhelm-Ufer),
Qingdao (Tsingtau. Tsingtao)

Architekt. Architect
Curt Rothkegel

Bauleitung und Innenraumentwurf.
Site Architect and Interior Design
Werner Lazarowicz

Ausführung. Contractors
Paul Friedrich Richter

Bauzeit. Construction time
Mai 1910 – Oktober 1911
May 1910 – October 1911

Zustand. Condition
Das Gebäude ist sehr gut erhalten.
Very well preserved.

Tsingtau-Klub, Südansicht vom Kaiser-Wilhelm-Ufer, 1912
Halle mit blauem Kamin. Blick nach Osten zum Eingang, 1992
Tsingtao Club, view from the south from Kaiser-Wilhelm-Ufer, 1912
Hall with blue fireplace, view of the entrance to the east, 1992

Bereits 1904 wurde eines der am besten gelegenen Grundstücke Qingdaos, wo die Landungsbrücke an die Uferpromenade trifft, als Standort für ein zukünftiges Klubgebäude ausgewählt. Der Architekt Rothkegel entwarf 1910 für dieses Grundstück ein modernes Gebäude in strengem Jugendstil.[320] Granitsteine wurden nur noch für die Fensterbänke und an der Traufe verwendet. Der Eingang im kleinen Anbau an der Westseite führt den Besucher ganz der chinesischen Bautradition entsprechend über Eck, wie um eine »Geistermauer«, in die großzügige lange Halle, an deren Ende sich erst die Treppe befindet.

Im Erdgeschoß des Tsingtau-Klubs befanden sich das Spielzimmer, ein Billardsaal, ein Lesezimmer mit »Sofa-Platz«, eine Bar mit einem gedeckten Sitzplatz zum Garten, die Büroräume und eine Garderobe in der Vorhalle des großen Treppenhauses. Der blaue Kamin in der Halle wird noch heute durch einen Reichsadler in Blattgold verziert. Im ersten Obergeschoß lag der große Speisesaal mit je einer vorgelagerten Terrasse nach Süden und Osten, das Vorstandszimmer sowie die Wohnung des Sekretärs. Im Keller befand sich eine rustikal gestaltete Weinstube, die Küche mit einer Anrichte, eine Wäschekammer, Vorratsräume, Haustechnik und mehrere Dienstbotenzimmer.[321]

Über die Rolle, die der Klub im Qingdaoer Gesellschaftsleben spielte, schreiben die *Tsingtauer Neuesten Nachrichten*: »Sechs Jahre hat die Kolonie bestanden, ohne daß man an die Gründung eines Klubs, wie ihn hier draußen doch beinahe jeder Europäern geöffnete Platz hat, gedacht hätte (…). Der Klub ist eine englische Erfindung, und in Tsingtau leben fast ausschließlich Deutsche, die im Früh- und Abendschoppen am Stammtisch einen Ersatz für den Klub zu haben meinen. (…) Als Treffpunkt der Vertreter der Kaufmannschaft wie aller Beamtenkreise, der Offiziere der Garnison und des Kreuzergeschwaders spielt der Klub eine bedeutsame (…) Rolle im öffentlichen Leben der Kolonie.«[322]

In 1904, one of the best situated plots of land in Qingdao, beside the sea where the landing stage joins the shore promenade, was chosen as the site for a future club house. The architect Rothkegel designed a modern building in strict Jugendstil style.[320] Rough-textured granite was used only for the window seats and the eaves. The entrance in the small lean-to on the western side leads the visitor, exactly as in traditional Chinese architecture, around a corner as if around a »ghost wall« into the long spacious hall with the staircase right at the end.

On the ground floor of the Tsingtao Club there were the games room, a billiards room, a reading room with »sofa seats«, a bar with a covered seating area opening onto the garden, offices and a cloakroom in the foyer in front of the main staircase. The blue fireplace in the hall is still adorned with an Imperial eagle in gold leaf. On the first floor was the large dining room with a terrace on the south and east side, a board room and a flat for the secretary of the club. In the cellar there were a rustic wine bar, the kitchen with serving hatch pantry, a scullery, larders, plant room and several servant's bedrooms.[321]

The *Tsingtauer Neueste Nachrichten* writes of the role the club played in Qingdao society: »The colony had existed for six years before anyone thought of founding a club like those out here where every European has a place (…). The club is an British invention and Tsingtao is inhabited almost exclusively by Germans who believe that their morning and evening drink with the other regulars at their local bar is a substitute for the club. (…) The club plays an important (…) role in the civic life of the colony, providing a meeting place for sales representatives, for groups of civil servants at all levels, for officers from the garrison and the cruiser squadron. It provides on a day-to-day basis and in an informal manner the opportunity for people to exchange ideas and get to know all social groups in the colony (…).«[322]

青島俱樂部

現用途：青島市科技協會辦公樓
所在地：中山路一號太平路口（原菲特烈
　　　　大街威廉皇帝岸路）
建築師：庫爾特・羅克格
工程指導和內部設計：W・拉察羅維茨
施工：保爾・弗里德里希・里希特
建造期：一九一零年五月至一九一一年十
　　　　月
現狀：樓體保存完好

青島沿海最好的地皮之一是棧橋與岸邊林蔭道相交之處。早在一九零四年，該處便被選定為修建俱樂部的地址。一九一零年建築師羅克格嚴格地按照德國青年派風格為該址設計了一座現代式的俱樂部樓。〈320〉粗樸的花崗岩石料僅用於窗台和檐口。來訪者從樓西側的邊房入門後，要先順斜對角方向繞進寬敞的長廳，再由長廳盡頭處走上樓梯；這一設計與中國建築傳統中的"照壁"如出一轍。

在俱樂部的底層有一間游戲室、一個台球廳、一間帶"沙發座"的閱覽室、一個帶有遮蓬座席的園前酒吧、若干辦公室，在大型樓梯間的前廳裡還有一個存衣處。廳內那座籃色的壁爐上有鑲金鉑的德意志帝國鷹徽至今尤存。二層設有一個很大的餐廳，其東南兩面各露台出挑；此外，經理室和秘書住房也設在這裡。在地下室裡設有一個造型粗樸的酒窖、一個帶配菜室的廚房、一個洗衣間、樓內設備及工具間、幾個儲藏室以及若干僕人用房。〈321〉

關於俱樂部在青島社交生活中的作用和影響，《青島時報》曾做有如下報導："在（德國）殖民地建立之後的六年中，竟沒有人想到修一個俱樂部——一個幾乎在每一片歐洲人開闢的新土地上大約都不會缺少的俱樂部（……）。俱樂部是英國人的發明，而住在青島的這些德國人多數認為同老酒友湊在一起泡一個上午或晚上已經足以代替俱樂部的作用。（……）俱樂部作為商人、政客、衛戍部隊和巡洋艦隊軍官的聚會中心在殖民地的社會生活中起到重要作用。它以無拘無束和愜意的形式促進了殖民地各界人士之間的日常交流和相互了解（……）。"〈322〉

自一九二二年始，這座樓房被國際俱樂部挪用。

由威廉皇帝岸望青島俱樂部南面
外觀，一九一二年。
砌有藍色壁爐的大廳，東入口內
側，一九九二年。

QINGDAO

BAHNHOFSHOTEL
STATION HOTEL

Heutige Funktion. Current use
Wohnhaus
Residential
Yancheng Lu/Lanshan Lu
(Wilhelmshavener Straße/Hohenzollernstraße), Qingdao (Tsingtau. Tsingtao)
Bauherr. Client
R. Martwig
Bauzeit. Construction time
um 1913
around 1913
Zustand. Condition
Das Gebäude ist gut erhalten.
Well preserved.

Ehem. Bahnhofshotel,
Nordostecke, 1992
Detail der Balkonbrüstung, 1992
Former Bahnhofshotel,
north-east corner, 1992
Detail of balcony railing, 1992

Das Bahnhofshotel lag am Bahnhofsplatz; dieser war damals lediglich mit einer Grünfläche gestaltet. Den Platz umgaben einige freistehende Landhäuser, das Bahnhofshotel hatte dagegen den Charakter einer Blockrandbebauung.

Das Hotel erinnert an süddeutsche Gebäude. Es hat einen achteckigen Eckturm, neobarocke Giebel und Dachgauben; die Balkonbrüstung ist mit einer ursprünglich spätgotischen Maßwerkform, Fischblase genannt, verziert, die später während der deutschen Neorenaissance häufig als Dekoration verwendet wurde. In der chinesischen Symbolsprache gibt es dieses Zeichen ebenfalls: Das Yin-Yang-Zeichen aus zwei Kürbisflaschen. Der »Hulu« (Flaschenkürbis) war das traditionelle Gefäß zum Aufbewahren von Alkohol. »Unterhaltung, Schnaps trinken und Feiern« wird die Assoziation eines chinesischen Betrachters beim Anblick dieser Zeichen gewesen sein.[323] Für das Bahnhofshotel wären es sicherlich die richtigen chinesischen Schriftzeichen gewesen.

The Bahnhofshotel was on the square in front of the station. The only design feature of the square was a lawn. There were a few scattered country houses around the square, but the Bahnhofshotel was the first element in the block perimeter development.

The hotel looks like a typical south German building. It has an octagonal corner tower and neo-Baroque gables and roof dormers; the decoration on the balcony parapet is something called a vesica piscis which was originally a late Gothic tracery form and was later frequently used as a decorative element during the German neo-Renaissance. This sign is also a Chinese pictogram: the Yin-Yang symbol consisting of two gourds. The »Hulu« (marrow) was the traditional vessel for storing alcohol. »Conversation, drinking alcohol and having a good time« would have been what a Chinese observer would think of when he saw this symbol.[323] No doubt this was the correct Chinese character for the Bahnhofshotel.

車站飯店

現用途：住宅
所在地：青島鄭城路（蘭山路口），原威
　　　　廉港路（霍恩指倫路口）
業主：R·瑪特維希
建造期：約一九一三年
現狀：樓體保存良好

車站飯店位於原車站廣場，當時這個廣場只是一片綠地。廣場四周零散地蓋有若干平房。車站飯店是這裡唯獨的一座方整的沿街建築。

這一飯店看上去像是典型的南德地區樓房。它有一頂八角樓，山牆為新巴洛克式，房頂有老虎窗。陽台欄杆上的幾何形花格屬於晚期哥特體形式，素有魚鰾紋的雅稱，它在後來的德國新文藝復興體建築中也常常用作裝飾圖案。在中國的象徵性圖形中可見到同樣的圖案：葫蘆體陰陽圖。在中國傳統中，葫蘆是用來盛酒的。中國人看這一圖形，很可能會聯想到"吃喝玩樂"。〈323〉對於車站飯店來講，這一形容無疑是再恰當不過的了。

原東站飯店東北角，一九九二年。
護欄細部，一九九二年。

QINGDAO

STRANDHOTEL
BEACH HOTEL

Heutige Funktion. Current use
Huiquan Restaurant und Hotel
Huiquan restaurant and hotel
Nanhai Lu/Wendeng Lu (Auguste-Viktoria-Ufer), Qingdao (Tsingtau. Tsingtao)

Bauherr. Client
Tsingtauer Hotel Aktiengesellschaft
Tsingtao Hotel Joint Stock Company

Bauzeit. Construction time
1903–1904

Zustand. Condition
Das Gebäude ist gut erhalten.
Well preserved.

Das Strandhotel lag an dem größten Badestrand Qingdaos. Es hatte drei Stockwerke mit 31 Doppelzimmern, eine große Halle, Badezimmer, Salon-, Lese- und Restaurationszimmer und einen Tanzsaal. Von seiner breiten Terrasse aus gab es einen schönen Ausblick auf das Meer und das Leben an dem Strande. Auf der Rückseite des Hotels befand sich die große Pferderennbahn mit einer Besuchertribüne.[324] Das Hotel gleicht den Hotels in den großen Seebädern der deutschen Ostseeküste, die zu derselben Zeit erbaut wurden. Ungewöhnlich ist allerdings die große Loggia über dem Haupteingang.

Ein englischer Kaufmann berichtet über seinen Aufenthalt im Sommer 1910 in Qingdao: »Der Strand beim Strandhotel ist ideal zum Baden. Er liegt geschützt in einer sandigen Bucht und ist frei von Steinen und Muscheln. Auf der ganzen Ausdehnung stehen Gartenbänke zum Ausruhen. Die beliebteste Zeit zum Baden ist zwischen vier und sieben Uhr abends. Parallel mit der Bucht laufen zwei oder drei Reihen Privatbadebuden in der Ausdehnung von etwa einer Meile. Sie machen mit ihrem bunten Flaggenschmuck und in ihren oft drolligen Farben einen malerischen Eindruck. Hydranten mit frischem Wasser sind zwischen den Badebuden verteilt. Für die kühneren Schwimmer ist ein Baumfloß im Wasser verankert.«[325]

The Strandhotel was on one of the longest bathing beaches in Qingdao. It had three floors with 31 double rooms, a large hall, bathrooms, lounges, reading rooms and refreshment rooms and a dance hall. Its spacious terrace afforded a lovely view of the sea and life on the beach. Behind the hotel was the large racecourse with a spectators' grandstand.[324] The hotel looks like the hotels in the major seaside resorts on the German Baltic coast which were built at the same time. The large loggia over the main entrance is, however, rather unusual.

A British businessman reports of his stay in Qingdao in the summer of 1910: »The beach in front of the Strandhotel is ideal for bathing. It is in a sheltered spot in a sandy bay and has no stones or shells. There are garden benches to rest on along the whole length of it. The most popular time for bathing is between four and seven o'clock in the evening. Parallel to the bay there are two or three rows of private bathing cabins over a length of about a mile. They look very picturesque with their brightly coloured flags and often quite quirky colours. Fresh water drinking fountains are distributed amongst the bathing cabins. A raft is anchored in the water for the more daring swimmers.«[325]

Strandhotel, Südansicht vom Meer, um 1906
Auguste-Viktoria-Bucht. Badehäuser und Strandhotel, im Hintergrund die Iltis-Kaserne, Sommer 1904
Südansicht, 1992
Strandhotel, view from the south from the beach, around 1906
Auguste-Viktoria Bay, bathing cabins and Strandhotel, in the background the Iltis Barracks, summer 1904
View from the south, 1992

海濱旅館

現用途：匯泉酒家
所在地：青島南海路（文登路口），原奧古斯特－維多利亞岸）
業主：青島旅店業股份公司
建造期：一九零三年至一九零四年
現狀：樓體保存良好

海濱旅館的建築位置臨近青島市最大的海濱浴場。這是一座三層建築，內含三十一間雙人客房、一個大門廳、若干浴室、餐廳、閱覽室、沙龍客廳以及一個舞廳。以旅館前寬大的晒台上可以望到美麗的海景和海灘上的人群。旅館背面是一個設有看台的大型跑馬場。〈324〉在總體上，它與那些同期在德國東海岸各大型浴場修建的旅館並無區別。不過，其正門頂上的大柱廊卻使之頗具特色。

一九一零年夏，有一位英國商人客居青島並記有如下印象："海濱旅館前的那片海灘是露天浴的佳地，由於受到沙底海灣的保護，這裡全然沒有石塊和貝殼。海灘延展之處，均設有可供休憩的長凳。下午四點到七點之間，是最為誘人的海浴時光。海灣的延線上有兩三排浴斗，延綿一里之遠。浴斗上五顏六色的彩旗組成了一幅有趣的畫面。在浴斗之間還裝有汲水龍頭，供人們取用新鮮的自來水。有一付木筏繫於岸邊，以便膽大的戲水者用來逗海。"〈325〉

奧古斯特·維多利亞灣，洛皇及海濱旅館，背景為伊爾蒂斯兵營，一九零四年夏。
南面外觀，一九九二年。
由海灘望海濱旅館南立面，約一九零六年。

PRINZ-HEINRICH-HOTEL

Heutige Funktion. Current use
Büro des Qingdaoer Volkskomitees
der Konsultativkonferenz
Office of the Qingdao People's Committee
of the Consultative Conference
Taiping Lu/Qingdao Lu (Kaiser-
Wilhelm-Ufer/Wilhelmstraße),
Qingdao (Tsingtau. Tsingtao)

Bauzeit. Construction time
Januar – September 1899
January – September 1899

Zustand. Condition
Das Gebäude ist gut erhalten;
die Fassade wurde verändert.
Well preserved; façade changed.

Prinz-Heinrich-Hotel, Blick von
Südosten, um 1900
Prinz-Heinrich-Hotel, view from the
south-east, around 1900

Das Prinz-Heinrich-Hotel bot von den Zimmern mit Südveranda einen schönen Blick auf die Uferpromenade, die Bucht und die Inseln. Die hohe Eingangshalle war mit bequemen grünen Ledersofas ausgestattet; unmittelbar daran schloß sich das Treppenhaus an. Zu beiden Seiten der Halle befanden sich breite Veranden. Links vom Eingang lagen das Restaurant, ein Billard- und ein Lesezimmer. Den Abschluß bildete der Speisesaal, der 80 Gästen Platz bot. Seine Ausstattung, rote, goldgepreßte Lederstühle und ein geschnitztes Büffet, erinnerte an die großen europäischen Hotels. Rechts der Eingangshalle lagen Gästezimmer und Clubräume. Im ersten Stockwerk waren die übrigen Gästezimmer; die Mitte nahm nach der Seeseite hin ein Damensalon ein. Die etwa 40 Hotelzimmer waren alle mit eigenen Badezimmern ausgestattet. An der Ostfassade des Hotels zur Qingdao Lu war das Ziegelmauerwerk mit dem chinesischen Schriftzeichen »shou« mit der Bedeutung »Langes Leben« verziert.

Das Prinz-Heinrich-Hotel war das erste Hotel in der Stadt und ist somit eines der ältesten Gebäude. Viele der europäischen Kaufleute, die zuerst wegen des herrschenden Wohnungsmangels in chinesischen Mietshäusern in Dabaodao gewohnt hatten, zogen nach seiner Fertigstellung in dieses Hotel. »Schon dem von der Wasserseite sich Tsintau Nähernden bietet der prächtige, langgestreckte, nachts mit hellem elektrischen Licht erleuchtete Bau einen hübschen Anblick.«[326]

The Prinz-Heinrich-Hotel was in a central position in the city and the rooms with south-facing verandas offered a fine view of the seashore promenade, the bay and the islands. The high entrance hall was furnished with comfortable green leather sofas; immediately behind it was the staircase. There was a broad veranda on either side of the hall. To the left of the entrance was a restaurant, with a billiards room behind it and a reading room behind that. The sequence of rooms was concluded by the dining room which could seat 80 guests. Its furnishings – red leather chairs with gold embossing and a carved sideboard – called to mind the large European hotels. To the right of the entrance hall were guest bedrooms and club rooms. The remaining guest bedrooms were on the first floor, in the centre of which, on the side facing the sea, was a ladies lounge. The 40 hotel rooms each had their own bathroom. The brick masonry on the eastern façade of the hotel on Qingdao Lu was decorated with the Chinese character »Shou« meaning »long life.«

The Prinz-Heinrich-Hotel was the first guest house in Qingdao and one of the oldest buildings in the city. Many of the European businessmen who had at first lived in Chinese houses in Dabaodao due to the shortage of accommodation moved into this hotel as soon as it was finished. »The magnificent, long building, lit up at night with bright electric lights, is a pretty sight to the traveller approaching Tsingtao from the seaside.«[326]

亨利王子飯店

現用途：青島人民政治協商委員會辦公樓
所在地：青島太平路（青島路口），原威廉皇帝岸（威廉路口）
建造期：一八九九年一月至九月
現狀：樓體保存良好；立面經過改裝

從亨利王子飯店裝有南向陽台的房間裡，可以望到一條景色秀麗的岸邊林蔭道以及遠處的海灣和海島。在高大開闊的門廳裡擺設著綠色的皮沙發，廳後部是樓梯間。廳的兩側則修成寬大的游廊。入口處左側依次為餐館、台球室和閱覽室，最後方有一間可容八十個客席的大餐廳。其中的裝璜擺設，尤其那些紅底燙金的皮椅和那精雕細刻的食品櫃，會使人聯想起歐洲本土的大賓館。正門右側是幾間客房和活動室，其餘客房均在二層。在朝海的樓中段還設有一間女士專用沙龍。所有的四十間客房都配有獨立的浴間。在正對著青島路的東山牆上刻有一個中文"壽"字作為裝飾。

亨利王子飯店是青島市最早竣工的旅館，也是該市最古老的樓房建築之一。許多當初由於住房匱乏而臨時住在大鮑島中國工人住宅裡的歐洲商賈在這座飯店完工後立即都搬遷於此。"當人們從海岸駛近青島城時，這座輝弘而舒闊、在夜間配有炫目的照明燈的歐式建築群呈現出一幅十分壯麗的景象。"〈326〉

亨利王子飯店東南面外觀，約一九零零年。

QINGDAO

KONZERTSAAL PRINZ-HEINRICH-HOTEL
CONCERT HALL OF THE PRINZ-HEINRICH-HOTEL

Heutige Funktion. Current use
Saal des Qingdao Volkskomitees der Konsultativkonferenz
Hall of the Qingdao People's Committee of the Consultative Conference
Qingdao Lu/Guangxi Lu (Wilhelmstraße/Prinz-Heinrich-Straße), Qingdao (Tsingtau. Tsingtao)

Architekt. Architect
Curt Rothkegel

Ausführung. Contractors
F. H. Schmidt, Altona, Hamburg

Bauherr. Client
Prinz-Heinrich-Hotel

Bauzeit. Construction time
1905

Zustand. Condition
Das Gebäude ist sehr gut erhalten; die Bühneneinfassung wurde verändert.
Very well preserved; stage surround changed.

Konzertsaal des Prinz-Heinrich-Hotels, Blick von Nordosten, 1905
Konzertsaal, 1905
Innenraum. Blick zur Bühne nach Norden, 1992
Concert hall of the Prinz-Heinrich-Hotel, view from the north-east, 1905
Concert hall, 1905
Interior, view to the north of the stage, 1992

Der Konzertsaal wurde nördlich an die Rückseite des Prinz-Heinrich-Hotels angebaut. Da er in der Mittelachse des Hotels lag, konnten Eingang, Halle und die Treppe als Foyer mitgenutzt werden. Der Jugendstilsaal wurde nur durch Fenster auf der Ostseite belichtet. Auf dieser Seite war dem Raum ein Garten an der Qingdao Lu vorgelagert, der heute teilweise bebaut ist. Der Saal verfügte über 400 bis 500 Sitzplätze im Parkett und zusätzliche Plätze auf einer Galerie. Damit war der Konzertsaal etwa doppelt so groß wie der Saal im Seemannshaus.

Der Architekt Rothkegel (1876–1946) begann mit dem Entwurf für dieses Gebäude seine berufliche Selbständigkeit in China. Davor war er seit Herbst 1903 Bautechniker in der Bauabteilung III b (Hochbau) der Qingdaoer Bauverwaltung.[327]

The concert hall was added to the back of the Prinz-Heinrich-Hotel. As it was exactly on the central axis of the hotel, the hotel entrance, hotel hall and the staircase were used as its foyer. The Jugendstil hall had daylight from windows on the east side only. There was a garden on Qingdao Lu in front of this side of the building, today part of it has been developed. The hall could seat between 400 and 500 people in the stalls and had a gallery with additional seats. The hall was thus roughly twice the size of the hall in the Seaman's Club.

The design for this building was the beginning of the architect Rothkegel's (1876–1946) free-lance career in China. Before that he had been working as a site engineer in section III b (public works) of the Qingdao planning office, where he had started in autumn 1903.[327]

亨利王子飯店音樂廳

現用途：青島市人民政治協商委員會禮堂
所在地：青島青島路（廣西路口），原俾斯麥路（野戰醫院路）
建築師：庫爾特‧羅克格
施工：漢堡阿爾托納區F‧H‧施米特公司
業主：亨利王子飯店
建造期：一九零五年
現狀：建築體保存完好。舞台飾邊有變化。

音樂廳加建於亨利王子飯店的後側。由於它正居於飯店的中軸線上，飯店的門廳、大廳及樓梯都用作其休息廳。音樂廳具德國青年派風格，僅靠東側窗採光。東側樓前青島路旁的空地上建有花園。部分園地現已用來造房。大廳的前排座位部分可容納四百至五百人，在後面的畫廊裡還另加有座位。亨利王子飯店的音樂廳差不多要比水師飯店的演出廳大一倍。
建築師羅克格一八七六至一九四六年以此樓的設計開始了他在中國的職業自立生涯。在此之前，他從一九零三年秋起一直擔任建築管理局建築處（房建）的建築工程師。〈327〉

音樂廳，一九零五年。
音樂廳內部，北面舞台一瞥，一九九二年。
亨利王子飯店音樂廳東北面外觀，一九零五年。

QINGDAO

PRINZ-HEINRICH-HOTEL, LOGIERHAUS
PRINZ-HEINRICH-HOTEL, LODGING HOUSE

Heutige Funktion. Current use
Zhanqiao Hotel
Taiping Lu (Kaiser-Wilhelm-Ufer),
Qingdao (Tsingtau. Tsingtao)

Architekt. Architect
Paul Friedrich Richter[328]

Bauherr. Client
Firma Sietas Plambeck

Eröffnung. Opening
Juni 1912
June 1912

Zustand. Condition
Das Gebäude ist gut erhalten, die Fassade wurde verändert; Anbau auf der Nordseite.
Well preserved; façade changed, building added on the northern side.

Qingdao entwickelte sich seit 1903 zu einem in Asien sehr beliebten Seebad, in dem während des Sommers die Unterkünfte knapp waren. Daher entschloß sich die Direktion des Prinz-Heinrich-Hotels zur Erweiterung.
Der Architekt Richter entwarf die Fassade in einem klassizierenden Jugendstil. Die Dekorationen im Giebelfeld sind noch gut erhalten. Der dreigeschossige Hotelneubau wurde westlich neben dem 1899 eröffneten Prinz-Heinrich-Hotel errichtet und war mit diesem verbunden.

From 1903 onwards Qingdao developed into one of Asia's most popular seaside resorts so that summer accommodation was in short supply. The management of the Prinz-Heinrich-Hotel therefore decided to expand.
The architect Richter designed the façade in strict Jugendstil style. The decorations on the gable are still in good condition. The new three-storey building for the hotel was built to the west next to the Prinz-Heinrich-Hotel which had opened in 1899 and was connected to it.

Prinz-Heinrich-Hotel und Logierhaus, um 1919
Südansicht des Hotels, 1992
Prinz-Heinrich-Hotel and Lodging House, around 1919
View of the hotel from the south, 1992

亨利王子飯店旅館部

現用途：棧橋賓館
所在地：青島太平路，原威廉皇帝岸
建築師：保爾‧弗里德里希‧里希特⟨328⟩
業主：西塔斯‧普拉姆拜克公司
落成期：一九一二年六月
現狀：原建築保存良好，立面有變化，北側加建新樓。

一九零三年後，青島發展成了亞洲最受人喜愛的海濱浴場。逢夏時節，旅館床位便格外緊缺。鑒於此種情況，亨利王子飯店的管理部門決定對飯店予以擴建。
建築師里希特對立面採用了嚴格的青年風格派處理手法。山牆上的裝飾仍保存良好。新擴建的賓館樓共三層，位於一八九九年開業的亨利王子飯店的西側，並與其相通。

飯店南立面，一九九二年。
亨利王子飯店旅館部及迎賓樓，約一九一九年。

PENSION LUTHER

Heutige Funktion. Current use
Gesundheits- und Hygieneamt, Rotes Kreuz
Health and public hygiene office of the Red Cross
Hubei Lu/Dexian Lu 4
(Kronprinzenstraße/Hohenloheweg),
Qingdao (Tsingtau. Tsingtao)

Architekt. Architect
Curt Rothkegel[329]

Ausführung. Contractors
H. Bernick & Pötter

Bauherr. Client
Helene Luther

Bauzeit. Construction time
November 1905–1907

Zustand. Condition
Das Gebäude ist sehr gut erhalten.
Very well preserved.

Ehem. Pension Luther, Ostansicht, 1992
Former Pension Luther, view from the east, 1992

Der Hohenloheweg war eine der schönsten Straßen in Qingdao; hier war eine landhausartige Bebauung vorgeschrieben. Die Pension lag in der Mitte eines 2 700 m² großen Grundstücks mit dem Haupteingang nach Osten zum Hohenloheweg. Im Erdgeschoß der Pension befanden sich vier Gastzimmer, jedem war eine Veranda vorgelagert. Auf der Nordseite des Erdgeschosses waren Aufenthaltsraum und Speisesaal untergebracht, darunter im Kellergeschoß die Küche. Eine großzügige Treppe führte in das erste Obergeschoß hinauf zu zwei Apartments und fünf einzelnen Gastzimmern, die mit einer Ausnahme alle ohne eigene Bäder und Toiletten waren. Im Süden des Grundstücks befand sich der Tennisplatz, an der westlichen Grundstücksgrenze die Garage.

Der Chef eines der größten britischen Handelshäuser Tianjins berichtete über seinen Aufenthalt im Sommer 1910 in Qingdao: »… vom Hafen aus bestellten wir uns Zimmer in einer Pension und erhielten solche auch glücklicherweise in der Pension Luther. Dort wohnten wir sehr behaglich während unserer ganzen Anwesenheit. Dieses sehr geräumige, im deutschen Stil erbaute Haus hat allen Komfort der Neuzeit und ist wirklich erstklassig. Die Pensionsinhaberinnen sind sehr nett und aufmerksam gegen die britischen Gäste. Die Preise sind mäßig.«[330]

Hohenlohe Weg was one of the most attractive streets in Qingdao; country house style development had been specifically stipulated here. The guest house was in the middle of a plot of land comprising some 2 700 m² and the main entrance was on the eastern side of Hohenlohe Weg. On the ground floor there were four guest bedrooms, each with a veranda in front of it. On the northern side of the ground floor were the lounge and dining room and under them in the basement was the kitchen. A large main staircase led to the first floor where there were two apartments and five single rooms which with one exception, did not have their own bathroom or toilet. On the south side of the site was a tennis court and on the western border of the plot a garage.

The head of one of Tianjin's largest British trading companies wrote of his stay in Qingdao in the summer of 1910: »… at the port we reserved rooms in a guest house and fortunately were allocated places in the Pension Luther. There we lodged very comfortably throughout our entire stay. This very spacious house, built in the German style, has all the modern comforts and is really first class. The ladies who own the pension are terribly nice and attentive to the British guests. The prices are moderate.«[330]

路德公寓

現用途：青島市衛生局，青島市紅十字會
所在地：青島市湖北路（德縣路四號），
　　　　原太子路（霍恩洛厄路口）
建築師：庫爾特·羅克格〈329〉
業主：海倫·路德
建造期：一九零五年十一月至一九零七年
現狀：建築體保存完好。

霍恩洛厄路是青島最美麗的街道之一，此處規定只准建花園住宅。路德公寓座落在一片面積達二千七百平方米的土地上。主入口開於東側，在霍恩洛厄路上。公寓的一樓有四間帶敞廊的客房，北面是客廳和餐廳，其下方的地窖裡設有廚房。寬敞的主樓梯通向二樓，上設兩間套房和五個單人間。除了一間單人房外，其餘單人間內均無浴室和廁所。公寓的南面有一座網球場，西邊則設有車房。

天津一家英國大公司的老板記敘了他一九一零年的青島之行："我們在港口向一家公寓訂了房間。幸運的是我們在路德公寓拿到了房間。我們在那兒度過了非常愉快的時光。這座德國風格的寬敞公寓堪稱一流，具有舒適的現代化設備，價格也很適中。公寓女主人和藹可親，對待英國客人殷勤周到。"〈330〉

原路德公寓東立面，一九九二年。

QINGDAO

DEUTSCH-ASIATISCHE BANK
GERMAN-ASIAN BANK

Heutige Funktion. Current use
Wohnhaus
Residential
Taiping Lu/Qingdao Lu
(Kaiser-Wilhelm-Ufer/Wilhelmstraße),
Qingdao (Tsingtau. Tsingtao)

Entwurf. Design
Heinrich Hildebrand; Luis Weiler[331]

Baukosten. Building costs
etwa 81 000 Goldmark
approximately 81 000 gold marks

Bauherr. Client
Deutsch-Asiatische Bank, Berlin
German-Asian Bank, Berlin

Bauzeit. Construction time
1899–1901

Zustand. Condition
Das Gebäude ist gut erhalten;
Umbauten im Inneren.
Well preserved;
modifications to the interiors.

Hildebrand hatte ein Gebäude entworfen, das aus klimatischen Gründen auf der Süd- und Westseite von luftigen Veranden umgeben war, wie die britischen Kolonialbauten Hongkongs. Die Stockwerkhöhe betrug etwa vier Meter. Die beiden asymmetrisch liegenden Eingänge wurden durch eine breitere Fensterachse und Traufbalustraden betont. Die Säulen und Rundbögen, der Sockel, die Traufe, die Gesimsbänder und die Quader an den Gebäudeecken waren aus Granitwerkstein. Im Zentrum der Bank befand sich eine Halle. Auf seiner Nordseite lag ein kleines Gebäude mit den Nebenräumen.

Ein italienischer Renaissancepalast könnte dem Architekten Anregungen für Proportion und Fassadendetails gegeben haben. Das steile Mansarddach war ungewöhnlich für ein deutsches Gebäude in Qingdao. Eine ähnliche Fassade hat Hildebrand 1903 für das Deutsche Konsulat in Jinan entworfen.[332] Alle anderen Filialen der Deutsch-Asiatischen Bank in China wurden durch die Shanghaier Architekten Becker & Baedecker errichtet.

Gleich bei der ersten Landversteigerung im Oktober 1898 hatte die Deutsch-Asiatische Bank dieses Grundstück an der Uferstraße erworben. Bankgebäude und Prinz-Heinrich-Hotel bildeten den Rahmen der langen Blickachse vom Ufer und dem 1904 dort errichteten Denkmal für den verstorbenen Gouverneur Paul Jaeschke hinauf zum 1906 fertiggestellten Gouvernements-Dienstgebäude, dem Regierungssitz.

Ab 1923 befand sich das japanische Konsulat in dem Gebäude.

Hildebrand designed a building which, because of the climate, was surrounded by airy verandas on the south and west side, like the British colonial buildings in Hongkong. The floor height was about four metres. The two asymmetrical entrances were emphasised by short panels of eaves balustrades on the roof. The columns and rounded arches, the base, eaves, cornices and stones on the quoins of the building were in granite. There was a hall in the centre of the bank. On its northern side there was a small building housing ancillary rooms.

An Italian Renaissance palace may have given the architect inspiration for the proportion and façade details. The steep mansard roof was equally unusual on a German building in Qingdao. Hildebrand designed a similar façade subsequently in 1903 for the German Consulate in Jinan.[332] All the other branches of the German-Asian Bank in China were built by the Shanghai architects Becker & Baedecker.

The German-Asian Bank had taken the opportunity to acquire this piece of land on the embankment road at the very first land auction in October 1898. The bank and the Prinz-Heinrich-Hotel framed the long visual axis from the shore and memorial erected there in 1904 in memory of Governor Paul Jaeschke up to the Headquarters of the German Administration, the seat of government completed in 1906.

Since 1923 the building was used as the Japanese Consulate.

Haupteingang auf der Südseite,
1992
Deutsch-Asiatische Bank, Blick von
Südwesten, 1901
Blick von Südwesten, 1992
Main entrance on the south side,
1992
German-Asian Bank, view from the
south-west, 1901
View from the south-west, 1992

德華銀行

現用途：住宅
所在地：青島太平路（青島路口），原威廉皇帝岸（威廉路口）
設計：海因里希・錫樂巴、路易斯・魏爾勒⟨331⟩
建築造價：約八點一萬金馬克
業主：柏林德華銀行
建造期：一八九九年至一九零一年
現狀：建築體保存良好，內部有所改建。

錫樂巴所設計的德華銀行類似於香港的英國殖民地式建築。出於對氣候的考慮，西面和南面設兩層通風的券柱式外廊，層高約四米。兩面的入口呈不對稱狀，其屋頂邊緣檐口欄杆的短分格更加突出了這種非對稱性。大樓的支柱、券拱、牆基、屋檐、裝飾線及頂部的細方石皆用花崗石砌成。銀行的中央是一間大廳，北側是一幢設有附屬建築的小樓。
建築師或許是從某座意大利文藝復興式官殿那裡獲得了關於建築比例和立面細部的靈感。其大坡度的蒙莎頂在青島的德國建築中堪稱獨樹一幟。錫樂巴於一九零三年設計濟南德國領事館時對其立面也採用了類似的處理手法。⟨332⟩除青島分行外，德華銀行在中國的其他分行均由上海建築師貝克和培迪克設計。
德華銀行在一八九八年十月青島的第一次土地拍賣活動中就置下了岸邊的這塊地產。由岸邊和已故總督葉世克紀念碑向總督官署眺望，只見德華銀行大廈和亨利王子飯店構成一長長視線軸的邊框（葉世克紀念碑建於一九零四年，總督官署於一九零六年竣工）。
自一九二三年起，日本領事館設於德華銀行大樓內。

德華銀行西南面外觀，一九零一年。
西南面外觀，一九九二年。
南面主入口，一九九二年。

QINGDAO

DIREKTIONSGEBÄUDE DER SCHANTUNG-BERGBAU-GESELLSCHAFT
SHANTUNG MINING COMPANY BUSINESS PREMISES

Heutige Funktion. Current use
Wohnhaus
Residential
Taiping Lu/Jiangsu Lu
(Kaiser-Wilhelm-Ufer/Bismarckstraße),
Qingdao (Tsingtau. Tsingtao)

Bauherr. Client
Schantung-Bergbau-Gesellschaft
Shantung Mining Company

Bauzeit. Construction time
um 1902
around 1902

Zustand. Condition
Das Gebäude ist gut erhalten;
spätere Erweiterung.
Well preserved; extension added.

Schantung-Bergbau-Gesellschaft,
Direktionsgebäude,
Südansicht, um 1907
Südansicht, 1992
Shantung Mining Company,
business premises,
view from the south, around 1907
View from the south, 1992

Das Direktionsgebäude der Schantung-Bergbau-Gesellschaft lag neben den Häusern der Schantung-Eisenbahn-Gesellschaft und der Deutsch-Asiatischen Bank an der Uferstraße. In seinem Giebelfeld befand sich früher eine Steinplatte mit dem Zunftzeichen der Bergleute: Schlägel und Eisen. Die Fassadenflächen sind zu etwa gleichen Teilen verputzt und mit Granitstein verkleidet, bei einigen hochliegenden Wandflächen findet man Fachwerk. Ein Erker aus Granit verleiht der relativ geschlossenen Ostfassade Plastizität. Die zum Meer gerichtete Südfassade wirkt durch ihre sehr unterschiedlichen Veranda- und Fensteröffnungen unruhig. Erst durch die spätere Erweiterung erhält sie eine gewisse Harmonie.

Als Teil des 1898 abgeschlossenen 99jährigen Pachtvertrages mit China erhielt Deutschland die Bergwerksrechte in einer Zone von je 15 Kilometern beidseitig der in der Provinz Shandong zu bauenden Eisenbahnlinien. Diese Rechte wurden auf die Schantung-Bergbau-Gesellschaft übertragen, die die Kohlenreviere erschloß.

Als erste Kohlengrube wurde 1902 das »Fangtse-Revier« eröffnet und die Kohle mit der Bahn nach Qingdao gebracht. Dieses Bergwerk liegt etwa 170 Eisenbahnkilometer von Qingdao entfernt südöstlich der Stadt Weifang (Wei-hsien). Hier waren Förderschächte von 177, 252 und 387 Meter Tiefe angelegt. Doch die Qualität der Kohle entsprach nicht den Erwartungen, deshalb wurde das Revier 1914 geschlossen.

Kohle von besserer Qualität wurde ab 1907 im »Hungshan-Revier« bei Boshan (Po-shan) im Gebirge gefördert, das durch eine 43 km lange Zweigbahn erschlossen wurde und 345 Bahnkilometer von Qingdao entfernt lag. Mit dem Bau des ersten Schachtes hatte man 1904 begonnen, 1906 konnte die erste Kohle gefördert werden. 1913 lag die Jahresproduktion bereits bei 410 000 Tonnen. Hauptabnehmer waren die Dampferlinien und das Kreuzergeschwader. Die Schantung-Bergbau-Gesellschaft beschäftigte etwa 90 deutsche Beamte und rund 8 000 chinesische Arbeiter.[333]

The headquarters of the Shantung Mining Company were next to the buildings housing the Shantung Railway Company and the German-Asian Bank on the embankment road. On its pediment was a panel of stone with the symbol of the miners' guild: two crossed hammers. The façades are half plastered and half clad with granite blocks; some areas at the top of the walls are half-timbered. An oriel of granite adds an element of plasticity to the relatively closed eastern façade. The southern façade which faces the sea looks somewhat restless due to the very different proportions of the veranda openings and windows. The extension added later improved its proportions.

As part of a 99 year lease signed in 1898 by China and Germany, Germany was granted mining rights in a zone 15 kilometres to either side of the railway lines to be built in the province of Shandong. These rights were transferred to the Shantung Mining Company who developed coal fields.

The first mine was the »Fangtse Pit« opened in 1902 which brought the first coal by rail to Qingdao. This mine is about 170 kilometres from Qingdao south-east of the town of Weifang (Wei-hsien). Here shafts 177, 252 and 387 metres deep were dug. But the quality of the coal did not come up to expectations and the field was closed down in 1914.

Better quality coal was excavated from 1907 onwards in the »Hungshan Pit« near Boshan (Po-shan) in the mountains which were reached by a 43 kilometre-long branch railway line and which was 345 kilometres by railway from Qingdao. Work to dig the first shaft had begun in 1904 and the first coal was extracted in 1906. By 1913 annual production figures had already reached 410 000 tonnes. The main buyers of the coal were the large steamship companies and the German cruiser squadron. The Shantung Mining Company employed some 90 German civil servants and 8 000 Chinese workers.[333]

山東礦務公司總部大樓

現用途：住宅
所在地：青島太平路（江蘇路口），原威
　　　　廉皇帝岸（俾斯麥路口）
業主：山東礦務公司
建造期：約一九零二年
現狀：建築體保存良好並有所擴建。

山東礦務公司總部大樓座落在岸邊的一條馬路上，與山東鐵路公司和德華銀行相鄰。該樓的山牆上原砌有一塊石板，上飾礦工的行業標誌──兩把交叉的鐵錘。建築立面半是清水粉牆，半為花崗石砌體。幾處高牆則呈桁架建築式樣。東立面上突起一座花崗石挑樓，使相對封閉的立面富有立體感。朝海的南立面上設有大小不一的敞廊和窗洞，給人一種不協調的感覺。該樓經擴建後，這一立面的比例才處理得較為協調。

根據德中一八九八年簽訂的為期九十九年的租借條約的部分條款，德國有在山東所築鐵路線兩側十五公里區域內採礦的特權。這一特權為開發煤炭的山東礦務公司所享用。一九零四年完工的膠濟線上有兩處大煤礦，當時已由中國的礦山企業開採。一九零二年，第一座煤礦礦場"坊子煤礦"開始採掘，不久便將其第一批煤炭運入青島。該礦位於濰坊市的東南面，距青島約一百七十公里。首批煤由鐵路運往青島。煤礦的礦井深度分別為一百七十七米、二百五十二米和三百八十七米。十二年內共出煤一百八十萬噸。由於煤質不如預期的好，煤礦於一九一四年關閉。

自一九零七年起，山東礦務公司開採博山附近的福山煤礦。此處的煤質較好。福山煤礦距青島的鐵路三百四十五公里。一條長四十三公里的鐵路支線伸向礦區。一九零四年，福山煤礦豎起了第一座礦場，一九零六年採出首批煤。一九一三年的年產量已達四十一萬噸。煤礦的主要客戶為大輪船公司和中型巡洋艦隊。山東礦務公司約有九十名德國職員、八千名中國礦工。礦區內建有別墅式的職員住房和牢固的工人住房，供煤礦職員和礦工骨幹居住。〈333〉

山東礦務公司總部大樓南面外
觀，約一九零七年。
南面外觀，一九九二年。

QINGDAO

KAISERLICH DEUTSCHES POSTAMT
IMPERIAL GERMAN POST OFFICE

Heutige Funktion. Current use
Qingdaos Postamts Verwaltung
Headquarters of Qingdao's Post Office
Guangxi Lu/Anhui Lu
(Prinz-Heinrich-Straße/Albertstraße),
Qingdao (Tsingtau. Tsingtao)

Ausführung. Contractors
F. H. Schmidt, Altona, Hamburg

Bauherr. Client
Firma von Tippelskirch & Co.

Bauzeit. Construction time
1900 – Mai 1901
1900 – May 1901

Zustand. Condition
Das Gebäude ist gut erhalten;
die Fassade ist heute verputzt.
Well preserved; façade now rendered.

Kaiserlich Deutsches Postamt,
Südansicht, um 1907
Postamt, Südansicht, 1992
Imperial German Post Office,
view from the south, around 1907
Qingdao Post Office,
view from the south, 1992

Die Fassade des privaten Geschäftshauses bestand ursprünglich aus rotem Sichtmauerwerk. Die Wandflächen im Bereich der Brüstungen und Bögen waren hell verputzt. Zwei Türme betonen die beiden Straßenecken, zwei Giebel den seitlichen Gebäudeabschluß. Das Dach ist nur zur Straße mit roten Ziegeln gedeckt, auf der Rückseite ist es flach und mit Blech gedeckt. In den beiden oberen Stockwerken des dreigeschossigen Gebäudes befanden sich Wohnungen, im Erdgeschoß das Postamt und im linken Flügel die Apotheke.

Bereits 1898, im ersten Jahr der Besetzung, wurde innerhalb der Stadt und als Verbindung zum Marktflecken Licun (Lit'sun) ein Telefonnetz errichtet. Im Oktober 1901 gab es schon 56 private Telefonanschlüsse und 38 Telefonanschlüsse des Gouvernements. Anfangs war die Post in Qingdao nur provisorisch untergebracht worden. Lange war es strittig, ob ein neues Postgebäude durch die Post selbst oder vom Gouvernement errichtet werden sollte, oder ob es nicht zweckmäßiger wäre, Räume anzumieten. Schließlich mietete das Gouvernement für das Postamt das Erdgeschoß dieses Gebäudes.[334]

Schon vor der deutschen Besetzung im November 1897 hatte es eine chinesische Telegraphenlinie von der chinesischen Militärgarnison in Qingdao nach Jinan gegeben. Sie war dort an die Telegraphenlinie von Beijing nach Shanghai angeschlossen. Die deutsche Postverwaltung in China und im Schutzgebiet Jiaozhou wurde von der deutschen Postdirektion geleitet, die in Shanghai eingerichtet worden war. Um von der unzuverlässigen Landverbindung unabhängig zu sein, verlegte man ein Seekabel von Qingdao nach Shanghai; es wurde am 1. Januar 1901 in Betrieb genommen.

The façade of the private office building was originally red fair-faced brick. The areas of wall near the parapets and arches were in pale coloured render. Two towers emphasise the two street corners, two gable elements the sides of the building. The roof has red tiles on the slope facing the street only, the other side is flat and covered with sheet metal. There were flats on both upper floors of the three- storey building; the Post Office was on the ground floor and there was a chemist's in the left wing.

As early as 1898, the first year of occupation, a telephone network was set up for communications within the city and to the small market town Licun (Lit'sun). By October 1901 there were already 56 private and 38 government telephones. Initially the post office in Qingdao was in temporary accommodation. For a long time there was dispute over whether a new building should be built by the Post Office itself or by the German Administration and whether it would not be more sensible to rent premises. Finally the German Administration rented the ground floor of this building for the Post Office.[334]

Even before the German occupation in November 1897 there had been a Chinese telegraph line from the Chinese military garrison in Qingdao to Jinan. There it was connected to the telegraph line from Beijing to Shanghai. The German postal services in China and in the protectorate of Jiaozhou was run by the Regional Postal Directorate which had been set up in Shanghai. In order to be independent of the unreliable land connection, a cable was laid on the sea-bed from Qingdao to Shanghai; the new telegraph line went into operation on 1 January 1901.

德國膠州郵政局

現用途：青島郵電局機關樓
所在地：青島廣西路（安徽路口），原亨
　　　　利王子路（阿爾貝特路口）
施工：漢堡阿爾托納區F・A・施密特公司
業主：馮・提帕斯基希公司
建造期：一九零零年至一九零一年五月
現狀：建築體保存完好，立面重予裝修。

這家私人商業大樓的立面原為紅磚牆體，護牆和拱券則做成淺色清水粉牆。角部高起塔樓，突出了面向街口的轉角。兩處山牆體強調了建築的側面。臨街的屋頂覆以紅磚，背面的平屋頂則用鐵皮鋪成。這座三層樓的建築一樓闢為郵局，其左翼設醫藥商店，二、三樓用作宿舍。

早在一八九八年德國佔領膠州的第一年，青島市內就架設了一直通到李村的電話網。至一九零一年十月，已接通私人電話五十六部，總督府公用電話三十八部。起初，青島的郵政局只是臨時性的。很長一段時間，對於營建新郵政大樓應由郵政局還是總督府出資，以及為郵政局租房是否更為實用這些問題一直爭議不斷。最後，還是由總督府為郵政局租下了這幢商業大樓的底層。〈334〉

在德國一八五七年十一月佔領膠州之前，駐防青島的清軍已有一條通往濟南的電報線，它接在由北京通往上海的線路上。德國在中國及膠州保護地的郵政業務由其在上海設立的郵政管理處管理。為了擺脫不可靠的陸路聯繫，由青島至上海鋪設了一條海底電纜，並於一九零一年一月一日啟用。

膠州郵政局南面外觀，約一九零七年。
郵政局南面外觀，一九九二年。

WOHN- UND GESCHÄFTSHAUS
COMMERCIAL AND RESIDENTIAL BUILDING

Heutige Funktion. Current use
Wohnhaus
Residential
Guangxi Lu/Juxian Lu
(Prinz-Heinrich-Straße/Tirpitzstraße),
Qingdao (Tsingtau. Tsingtao)

Bauzeit. Construction time
1903–1904

Zustand. Condition
Das Gebäude ist sehr gut erhalten.
Very well preserved.

Wohn- und Geschäftshaus,
Blick von Südwesten, 1904
Südansicht, 1992
Commercial and residential
building, view from the south-west,
1904
View from the south, 1992

Dieses Wohn- und Geschäftshaus erinnert an Bauten in norddeutschen Küstenstädten. Ähnliche Giebelformen und der Materialwechsel zwischen Ziegelsteinflächen und Natursteinstreifen waren entlang der Nord- und Ostseeküste von den Niederlanden bis nach Danzig verbreitet.

In der Denkschrift des Reichsmarineamtes wird das Gebäude als »Geschäftshaus für Europäer« bezeichnet. Durch die geschickte Photoaufnahme entsteht der Eindruck, als läge das Haus in einem in weiten Teilen bereits bebauten Stadtviertel, was zu jenem Zeitpunkt jedoch noch nicht zutraf.[335] Die Prinz-Heinrich-Straße war als »europäische Geschäftsstraße« konzipiert. Sie verlief als erste Parallelstraße zur Uferstraße. Die Bauordnung von 1898 erlaubte hier eine dreigeschossige Bebauung mit einer Traufhöhe von 18 Metern. Die Fassaden mußten parallel zur Straße liegen, 60 Prozent der Grundfläche eines Grundstücks durften bebaut werden, bei Eckgrundstücken waren es 70 Prozent.[336] Aus Brandschutzgründen mußten benachbarte Gebäude einen Abstand von sechs Metern zueinander haben, was der Geschäftsstraße einen lichten und offenen Eindruck gab. Diese Art der Bebauung findet man nur im Westteil der Europäerstadt, obwohl der symmetrische Stadtplan eine Gleichbehandlung beider Viertel westlich und östlich des Regierungsgebäudes erwarten läßt. Im Ostteil wurden die Grundstücke in einer lockeren, »landhausmäßigen« Art nur mit freistehenden Wohnhäusern bebaut.

This commercial and residential building looks like a typical building in any North German seaside town. Similar gable shapes and the change of material between large areas of brick, and bands of natural stone could be found all along the coast of the North Sea and Baltic from the Netherlands to Danzig.

In a memorandum of the German Admiralty the building is described as a »commercial building for Europeans«. Clever photography creates the impression that the building was in a district of the city which was already extensively developed, which was not the case at all.[335] Prinz-Heinrich-Strasse was designed to be a »European commercial street«. It was the first street to be built parallel to the embankment road. The building regulations of 1898 permitted here a continuous three-storey development, 18 metres high to the eaves. The façades had to run parallel to the street and 60 percent of the plot could be built on, 70 percent in the case of corner plots.[336] For reasons of fire safety, the buildings had to be six metres apart which meant that, despite the continuous development, there was a light and open feel to the street. This continuous style of development is found only in the western part of the European district although from the symmetrical town plan it would have been natural to expect equal treatment of both districts to the west and to the east of the government building. The buildings on the plots in the eastern part are all »country-house style« detached houses.

住宅兼商業樓

現用途：住宅
所在地：青島廣西路（莒縣路口），原亨
　　　　利王子路（蒂爾皮茨路口）
建造期：一九零三年至一九零四年
現狀：建築體保存完好。

這幢住宅兼商業大樓使人聯想到德國北方沿海城市的建築。類似於此的山牆形式、紅磚與花崗石交相砌築的牆面在從荷蘭到但澤一帶的沿岸上隨處可見。

帝國海軍部的備忘錄稱這幢建築為"歐洲人商業大樓"。拍攝巧妙的照片會給人一種錯覺，以為這幢大樓座落在建築繁多的市區裡。其實並不然。(335)亨利王子路被規劃為"歐洲商業街"，它與海岸平行，並離之最近。一八九八年的建築條例規定，此處只准建封閉式的三層樓房。檐高以十八公尺為限。臨街立面必須與街道平行。建築面積應為宅地面積的百分之六十，拐角處建築面積可達百分之七十。(336)出於防火考慮，兩樓之間必須保持六公尺的距離。這條馬路上的建築雖呈封閉式，但整條商業街仍給人以寬敞明亮之感。青島城市規劃方案對歐洲區總督官署東西兩側的區域原決定做對稱處理，但這種封閉式建築卻僅為歐洲區的西部所獨有。東部小區內僅建鄉村別墅式花園住宅。

住宅樓，商業樓西南面外觀，一
九零四年。
南面外觀，一九九二年。

QINGDAO

GESCHÄFTSHAUS DER HAMBURG-AMERIKA-LINIE
HAMBURG-AMERICA LINE BUSINESS PREMISES

Heutige Funktion. Current use
Qingdaos Lebensmittel Laden
Qingdao's Grocery Store
Zhongshan Lu/Feicheng Lu
(Friedrichstraße/Bremer Straße),
Qingdao (Tsingtau. Tsingtao)

Bauherr. Client
Henn

Bauzeit. Construction time
vor 1904
before 1904

Zustand. Condition
Das Gebäude ist gut erhalten.
Well preserved.

Die Ecken des Gebäudes bilden drei Giebelbauten mit Erkern. Gestaltet in der Art der deutschen Neorenaissance, sind ihre Kanten durch Natursteinquader betont. Vor den Wohnungen im ersten und zweiten Obergeschoß lagen schattige Loggien. Die Fenster im Erdgeschoß wurden durch Bambusvorhänge vor Sonneneinstrahlung geschützt. Der asymmetrisch plazierte Erker über dem Haupteingang war als »malerisches« Motiv in der deutschen Architektur dieser Zeit durchaus üblich. 1904 befand sich in dem Haus außer der Hamburg-Amerika-Linie auch das Büro des Kaiserlichen Bezirksamts.[337]

Die Friedrichstraße verband das europäische Geschäftsviertel mit dem chinesischen Händlerviertel Dabaodao. Das Geschäftshaus lag an dieser wichtigsten Verkehrsstraße Qingdaos auf einem Eckgrundstück mit Südlage. Schräg gegenüber befand sich der rund 6 000 m² große Stadtpark, für den man einen ganzen Block unbebaut gelassen hatte. Erst in den Jahren 1932/34 wurden dort Bank- und Geschäftsgebäude errichtet.

The corners of the building are formed by three gable elements with oriels. Designed in the style of the German neo-Renaissance, their quoins are emphasised by blocks of natural stone. There were shady loggias in front of the flats on the first and second floor. The windows on the ground floor had bamboo curtains for sun-shading. The asymmetrical oriel over the main entrance was, as a »picturesque« motif, quite innovative for German architecture at the time. In 1904 it housed not only the Hamburg-America Line but also the office of the district town hall.[337]

Friedrich Strasse linked the European business district to the Chinese traders' quarter of Dabaodao. This office building was on one of the busiest streets in Qingdao, occupying a south-facing corner plot. Diagonally opposite was the 6 000 m² municipal park for which a whole block had been left undeveloped. Not until 1932/34 were banks and office buildings built there.

Hamburg-Amerika-Linie,
Westansicht vom Stadtpark,
um 1907
Westansicht, 1992
Hamburg-America Line,
view from the west from the
Municipal Park, around 1907
View from the west, 1992

亨寶商業大樓

現用途：青島食品商店
所在地：青島中山路（肥城路口），原弗里德里希路（不來梅路口）
業主：亨內舍
建造期：一九零四年前
現狀：建築體保存良好。

亨寶商業大樓角部的山牆體上分別伸出三座挑樓，其棱邊用天然細方石砌成，具德國文藝復興式復古風格。二、三樓的住房前築遮蔭券式敞廊，一樓的窗前懸掛遮陽竹簾。大樓中部拐角上的挑樓位於主入口的側上方，呈不對稱狀，突出了整幢建築的不協調感。這是一幢非常典型的德國建築。一九零四年，該樓內除亨寶海運公司外，膠州地方法庭的辦公室亦設於此。〈337〉
弗里德里希路溝通了歐洲商業區與華人商業區大鮑島之間的聯係。亨寶商業大樓座落在這條青島市最重要的交通幹道上，位於一塊朝南的拐角地上。大樓斜對面是佔地約六千平方米的青島市公園。公園街區內原來未建任何房屋。一九三二年至一九三四期間，這裡矗立起了幢幢銀行大廈和商業大樓。

由青島市公園望亨寶商業大樓西面外觀，約一九零七年。
西面外觀，一九九二年。

QINGDAO

GESCHÄFTSHAUS CARLOWITZ & CO.
CARLOWITZ & CO. BUSINESS PREMISES

Heutige Funktion. Current use
Grundschule
Primary school
Taiping Lu 41 (Kaiser-Wilhelm-Ufer),
Qingdao (Tsingtau. Tsingtao)

Bauherr. Client
Carlowitz & Co.

Bauzeit. Construction time
um 1902
around 1902

Zustand. Condition
Das Gebäude ist sehr gut erhalten.
Very well preserved.

Bereits um 1904 war dieser Baublock am Kaiser-Wilhelm-Ufer vollständig bebaut. Die in Qingdao vertretenen Handelsgesellschaften hatten hier Wohn- und Geschäftsgebäude errichten lassen. Ein Bahngleis führte über die Geschäftsgrundstücke vom Bahnhof zur Landungsbrücke, so daß sie einen direkten Anschluß an die Schantung-Eisenbahn hatten. Doch verlor der Standort der Geschäftshäuser nahe der Brücke mit der Eröffnung des großen Hafens 1904 schnell an Bedeutung, da keine Frachtschiffe mehr hier anlegten. Der Gleisanschluß wurde nicht mehr benötigt und in den 20er Jahren entfernt. Im etwa vier Kilometer entfernten »Großen Hafen« standen größere Lagerhallen, ein Lastkran und natürlich auch ein Eisenbahnanschluß zur Verfügung. Das Seezollamt zog von hier zum großen Hafen, und auch die Handelshäuser errichteten im neuen Hafenviertel ebenfalls größere Gebäude.

Carlowitz & Co. war eine der größten deutschen Handelsfirmen in China. Sie eröffnete Geschäftshäuser in Hongkong (1866), Shanghai (1877), Tianjin (1886) und vielen anderen Städten.[338] In der noch sehr jungen Handelsstadt Qingdao wurde nur ein kleines Geschäftshaus erbaut, vergleicht man es mit den Häusern in den Handelsmetropolen Shanghai oder Hongkong.

By 1904 this entire block on Kaiser-Wilhelm-Ufer was already fully developed. The trading companies established in Qingdao had built their residential and office buildings here. A railway line passed over all these commercial plots, linking the station to the landing stage so that all the companies had a direct link to the Shantung Railway. But when the large port was opened in 1904, it became less important for businesses to be close to the landing stage as no cargo ships docked there any more. The railway line was no longer needed and was taken up in the 1920s. In the docks, which were some four kilometres away, there were large warehouses, a crane, and of course a railway line. The Maritime Customs and Excise Office moved from here down to the docks, and the trading companies also built larger buildings in the new dock area.

Carlowitz & Co. was one of the largest German trading companies in China. It opened offices in Hongkong (1866), Shanghai (1877), Tianjin (1886) and many other cities.[338] Since Qingdao was a very young trading city, the branch office it built here was small compared to those in the major trading centres of Shanghai or Hongkong.

Geschäftshaus Carlowitz & Co.,
Blick vom Kaiser-Wilhelm-Ufer,
um 1907
Blick von Südosten, 1992
Business premises of Carlowitz & Co., view from Kaiser-Wilhelm Ufer,
around 1907
View from the south-east, 1992

禮和商業大樓

現用途：小學
所在地：青島市太平路四十一號，原威廉皇帝岸
業主：禮和公司
建造期：約一九零二年
現狀：建築體保存完好。

一九零四年前後，沿威廉皇帝岸街區的建築全部完工。駐青島的各貿易分公司紛紛蓋起了住宅樓和商廈。由車站伸向棧橋碼頭的鐵軌近在咫尺，直接與山東鐵路相連。一九零四年，隨著大港的建成，貨船不再停泊於棧橋碼頭，棧橋附近的商廈很快便失去了其重要性。閒置不用的鐵軌於二十年代被拆除。新建的"大港"與棧橋碼頭相距四公里，擁有較大的倉庫和起重機，以及鐵路。原位於棧橋碼頭的海關亦遷往大港，各商號也在新港區建起了較大規模的樓房。

禮和公司是德國在中國最大的一家貿易公司，分別在香港一八六六年、上海一八七七年、天津一八六二年和其他許多城市設有分公司。〈338〉與上海或香港這些商業都市相比，青島只是一座年輕的貿易城。"禮和"在此只有一家小規模的分公司。

由威廉皇帝岸望禮和商業大樓，
約一九零七年。
東南面外觀，一九九二年。

QINGDAO

APOTHEKE
CHEMIST'S SHOP

Heutige Funktion. Current use
Restaurant Rotes Haus
Red House Restaurant
Guangxi Lu 33 (Prinz-Heinrich-Straße),
Qingdao (Tsingtau. Tsingtao)

Architekt. Architect
vermutlich Curt Rothkegel
probably Curt Rothkegel

Bauherr. Client
Apotheker Larz
Larz, the chemist

Bauzeit. Construction time
1905

Zustand. Condition
Das Gebäude ist sehr gut erhalten.
Very well preserved.

Die ehemalige Apotheke Qingdaos besitzt die schönste Jugendstilfassade der Stadt. Rotes Ziegelmauerwerk, helle Putzflächen und quadratische Muster aus farbigen Wandfliesen schmücken die Fassade. Charakteristisch für den Jugendstil sind die geschwungenen durchgehenden Linien, die die beiden oberen Geschosse der Südfassade zusammenfassen, aber auch die Ausbildung der Kaminaufsätze. Der Architekt verwendete Granit an der Traufe und den Wasserspeiern sowie im Erdgeschoß bei den kurzen gedrungenen Säulen. Einige der dunkelroten Wandfliesen tragen Eichenblätterreliefs. Im Wappenfeld oberhalb der großen Dachgaube ist das Symbol der Heilkunst, der Äskulapstab, eingeschnitzt. Der Architekt nutzte das Grundstück so effektiv wie möglich. Eine Traufhöhe von 18 Metern war zulässig, das erhöhte Mansarddach bot Raum für eine zusätzliche vierte Ebene, die durch eine große Gaube und eine Reihe kleiner Fenster im vertikalen Teil des Daches belichtet wurde.

Es liegen zwar keine schriftlichen Unterlagen vor, daß Rothkegel der Architekt des Gebäudes ist, doch trägt die Fassade Schmuckformen, die sich bei vielen seiner Bauten finden. Der Giebel ähnelt dem der Pension Luther, das abgesetzte Mansarddach dem des Club Concordia in Tianjin. Die geschwungenen Linien finden sich im Konzertsaal des Prinz-Heinrich-Hotels. Die breiten Säulen aus Granit im Erdgeschoß findet man auch beim östlichen Nebeneingang der Christuskirche.

Neben der ehemaligen Apotheke gab es eine relativ breite Baulücke. Hier wurde 1985 ein spektakulärer Neubau errichtet: das erste chinesische Gebäude Qingdaos, das sich in seiner Gestaltung am Stil der historischen deutschen Bauwerke der Stadt orientierte. Die chinesischen Architekten verwendeten Bogenfenster und übernahmen die Fassadengestaltung aus in Quadratmustern verlegten, farbigen Wandfliesen. Die wirkliche Höhe des fünfgeschossigen Gebäudes wurde optisch reduziert, indem man das obere Stockwerk als Mansarddach ausbildete.

Qingdao's former Chemist's Shop has the finest Jugendstil façade in the city. Red brick masonry, pale coloured rendered areas and square patterns of coloured wall tiles form the façade. The arches and curves which draw together the two upper storeys of the southern façade and the two fireplaces are characteristic of the Jugendstil. The architect used granite for the eaves and gargoyles and in the short, stout columns on the ground floor. Some of the dark red wall tiles have embossed oak leaves. Carved into the coat of arms above the large roof dormer is the physicians' symbol, the Staff of Aesculapius. The architect made the best possible use of the plot. Buildings could be 18 metres high to the eaves, but the higher mansard roof offered the possibility of a fourth level which was lit by a large dormer and a row of smaller windows in the vertical part of the roof.

Although there are no written documents to prove that Curt Rothkegel was the architect of this building, the façade has stylistic elements which are found in many of his buildings. The gable is similar to that of the Pension Luther, the mansard roof is like the Concordia Club in Tianjin. The sweeping lines can be seen in the concert hall of the Prinz-Heinrich Hotel. The broad columns of granite on the ground floor can also be found at the side entrance on the east side of the Christ Church.

Next to the building there was quite a wide empty plot. In 1985 a spectacular new building was built here: the first Chinese building in Qingdao which recalled the architectural style of the historical German buildings in the city. Arched windows were used and the façade design incorporated coloured tiles laid in a square pattern. The true height of the five-storey building was optically reduced by disguising the top floor in a mansard roof.

醫藥商店

現用途：紅房子餐廳
所在地：青島廣西路三十三號，原亨利王子路
建築師：庫爾特‧羅克格
業主：拉爾茨，藥劑師
建造期：一九零五年
現狀：建築體保存完好。

青島市原醫藥商店是該城最漂亮的青年風格派建築。立面為紅色牆體，間以清水粉牆和彩色方形牆磚。上部兩個樓層及兩座煙囪所採用的拱形與曲線，具有青年風格派的典型特徵。上面兩個樓層因此而給人以珠聯璧合之感。建築師用花崗石裝飾檐口、滴水嘴以及底部粗短的承重柱。幾塊暗紅色的牆磚上壓八橡樹葉的圖案。巨大的老虎窗上方的紋章上鑿有醫生的標誌——一根蛇體纏繞的圓杖。建築師充分利用寸土之地。檐高恰為規定的十八公尺，但高起的蒙莎頂卻為這幢樓房另外開闢了第四層空間。它靠巨大的老虎窗和屋頂的一排豎窗採光。

這幢樓房的建築師是否為羅克格，對此雖無文字記載，但在他設計的許多建築物中都可見到類似於該樓立面的處理風格。例如：此處的山牆與路德公寓的有異曲同工之妙；對蒙莎頂的處理手法又類似於天津的康科迪亞德國總會；曲線的運用亦見於亨利王子飯店音樂廳；而藥店底層的粗大花崗石柱則可在基督堂的東邊門上覓到其縱影。

藥店的旁邊曾是一大塊建築空地。一九八五年，這兒豎起了一座轟動一時的新樓，它是青島市第一座由中國人設計、但造型完全遵循該城德國歷史建築建造風格的樓房。中國建築師將拱形窗砌入牆體，在立面上使用彩色方形牆磚。這座五層樓的建築頂層採用蒙莎頂，從而使人對樓房的實際層數產生一種視覺錯覺。

醫葯商店南面外觀，一九零五年。
南面外觀，一九九二年(其左側的新樓建於一九八五年)
南立面細部，一九九二年。

WARENHAUS MAX GRILL
MAX GRILL DEPARTMENT STORE

Heutige Funktion. Current use
Wohn- und Geschäftshaus
Residential and commercial building
Guangxi Lu 26/Anhui Lu
(Prinz-Heinrich-Straße/Albert-Straße),
Qingdao (Tsingtau. Tsingtao)

Architekt. Architect
Paul Friedrich Richter[339]

Bauherr. Client
Max Grill

Bauzeit. Construction time
1911 – April 1912

Zustand. Condition
Das Gebäude ist sehr gut erhalten.
Very well preserved.

Die Warenhäuser europäischer Großstädte dienten als Vorbild für die äußere Form dieses Geschäftshauses.

Der Anzeigenzeigentext dieses Warenhauses lautete: »Größtes Specialgeschäft für Manufaktur- und Modewaren. Herren-, Damen- und Kinderkonfektion, sowie Wäsche. Kurz-, Galanterie- und Bijouteriewaren. Parfümerie- und Toiletten-Artikel. Glas- und Porzellanwaren. Weine, Liköre, Cigaretten, Tabacke. Engros und Detail. Abteilung Kunst- und Handelsgärtnerei. Blumen-, Samen- und Pflanzenhandlung. Anfertigung von Blumenarrangements, Tafeldekorationen, Buketts und Kränze, Import von holländischen Blumenzwiebeln. Export von japanischen und chinesischen Blumenzwiebeln.«[340]

The architect modelled this department store on the outer form of the department stores of European cities in which the sales area occupied several floors of a building.

The advertisement for this department store read: »Largest specialist for textiles and fashion goods. Gentlemen's, ladies' and children's clothing and underwear. Haberdashery, fashion accessories and jewellery. Perfumes and toiletries. Glass and porcelain. Wines, liqueurs, cigarettes, tobaccos. Wholesale and retail. Horticulture and market gardening department. Flowers, seeds and plants. Flower arrangements, table decorations, bouquets and wreaths, bulbs imported from Holland. Japanese and Chinese bulbs exported.«[340]

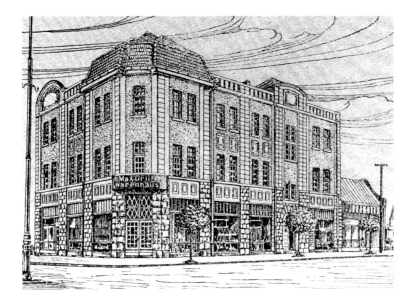

Warenhaus Max Grill, Perspektivzeichnung von der Prinz-Heinrich-Straße, 1912
Blick von Nordwesten, 1992
Max Grill Department Store from Prinz-Heinrich-Strasse, perspective drawing, 1912
View from the north-west, 1992

吉利百貨公司

現用途：住宅、商店
所在地：青島廣西路二十六號，原亨利王
　　　　子路（貝特路口）
建築師：保爾・弗里德里希・里希特[339]
業主：馬克斯・吉利
建造期：一九一一年至一九一二年四月
現狀：建築體保存完好。

建築師在設計這家商店時，採取歐洲大城市百貨商店的外部建築形式，售貨區分佔幾個樓層。這種類型的建築產生於十九世紀末。

吉利百貨公司的廣告詞宣稱它是青島 "最大的專業商店。經營範圍包括：手工製品、流行商品。男女時裝、童裝、內衣、床上用品、新潮服飾用品、珠寶飾品、香水、化妝品、玻璃器皿、瓷器。葡萄酒、甜燒酒、香煙、煙葉。公司兼營批發與零售業務。另外還設有觀賞園藝部和商業園藝部，並有花卉、種子和植物供應部。配置花束、花環、花籃及宴席裝飾品。進口荷蘭花莖，出口日本、中國花莖。"[340]

西北面外觀，一九九二年。
由亨利王子路望吉利百貨公司透視圖，一九一二年。

QINGDAO

GOUVERNEURSWOHNHAUS
GOVERNOR'S RESIDENCE

Bis Herbst 1907. Until autumn 1907
Fushanzhi Lu (Auguste-Viktoria-Bucht),
Qingdao (Tsingtau. Tsingtao)

Ausführung. Contractors
F. H. Schmidt, Altona, Hamburg

Bauherr. Client
Deutsches Gouvernement Kiautschou
German Administration of Kiaochow

Bauzeit. Construction time
1899

Zustand. Condition
Das Gebäude existiert nicht mehr.
No longer exists.

Erstes Gouverneurswohnhaus,
Blick von Südosten, 1902
Speisesaal, 1901
First Governor's Residence,
view from the south-east, 1902
Dining room, 1901

Das Gouverneurswohnhaus lag am Westhang des heutigen Xiaoyu Shan über der Auguste-Viktoria-Bucht. In direkter Nachbarschaft befanden sich das Wohnhaus des Adjutanten, das des Kommissars für chinesische Angelegenheiten sowie etwas höher am Hang das Wohnhaus des Seezolldirektors. Dieser Teil Qingdaos war für die Anlage eines Villenviertels vorgesehen.

Mehrere hölzerne Fertighäuser, sogenannte »Exporthäuser«, wurden durch die Firma F.H. Schmidt nach Qingdao gebracht. Für das Gouverneurswohnhaus kombinierte man zwei Fertighäuser über Eck und errichtete einen gemauerten Turm.

Bis zur Fertigstellung des größeren Gouverneurswohnhauses am Signalberg im Jahr 1907 wohnten hier die deutschen Gouverneure mit ihren Familien. Bereits 1902 projektierte man einen Neubau, »da der Gouverneur bis jetzt immer noch in einem – sogenannten schwedischen – Holzhaus wohnt.«[341] Dieses »Schwedenhaus« konnte in den ostasiatischen Handelsplätzen dem damals üblichen Repräsentationsstandard bei weitem nicht genügen. Die Villen großer Kaufleute, besonders in Shanghai, waren äußerst großzügig dimensioniert und luxuriös ausgestattet.[342]

Die aussteifenden Holzkreuze am Dach des Hauses und am umlaufenden Balkon konnten leicht zu Mißverständnissen führen, da das chinesisches Schriftzeichen »X« die Bedeutung von »falsch« hat. Sehr groß geschriebene Schriftzeichen findet man häufig in China an Hausfassaden, Säulen und besonders über Eingängen. Ihre Bedeutung ist meist »Glück« oder »Wohlstand«. Die chinesischen Besucher der Gouverneursvilla, wie der Gouverneur der Provinz Shandong Chou-fu im Dezember 1902, mußten bei diesen »Unglück zeigenden« Zeichen über dem Eingang äußerst irritiert gewesen sein. Bei später errichteten Gebäuden in Qingdao wurde auf diese Kreuze im Fachwerk verzichtet.

The Governor's Residence was on the western slope of the Xiaoyu Shan above the Auguste-Viktoria Bay. Its direct neighbours were the residence of his adjutant, that of the Commissioner for Chinese Affairs and a little further up the hill the residence of the Director of Maritime Customs and Excise. This part of Qingdao was earmarked for development as a villa district.

Several wooden prefabricated houses, known as »export houses«, were brought to Qingdao by the firm F.H. Schmidt. For the Governor's Residence two of these prefabricated houses were joined together and a stone tower was added.

Until the larger residence for the Governor on the Signalberg hill was completed in 1907 the German Governors lived here with their families. As early as 1902 a new building was planned »because the Governor is still living in a – so-called Swedish – wooden house.«[341] This »Swedish House« was far from meeting the standards of prestige required in East Asian trading cities at the time. The villas of important businessmen, particularly in Shanghai, were very large and luxuriously furnished.[342]

The wooden crosses which provided bracing for the roof of the building and on the continuous balcony around the building were apt to cause misunderstandings because the Chinese character »X« means »wrong«. Large pictograms are often found in China on the façades of buildings, on columns and especially above entrances. They usually mean »Happiness«, »Good Fortune« or »Prosperity«. The Chinese visitors to the Governor's Residence, such as the Governor of the Province of Shandong Chou-fu in December 1902, must have been extremely perturbed by this symbol »showing bad luck« above the entrance. These timberwork crosses were no longer used in the buildings constructed later in Qingdao.

總督臨時私邸（至一九零七年秋）

所在地：青島福山路（原奧古斯特・維多利亞海灣）
施工：漢堡阿爾托納區F・H・施密特公司
業主：膠州德國總督府
建造期：一八九九年
現狀：該建築不存在。

總督臨時私邸位於現小魚山西坡，面向奧古斯特・維多利亞海灣。與總督副官和駐中國特派員的住宅為鄰。沿坡上行，可見海關稅務司的宅邸。當時，青島的這一帶區域曾預定為別墅區。

F・A・施密特公司將所謂的"出口房"——幾所木結構的預製房運到了青島。總督私邸由兩所預製房縱橫交錯拼裝而成，另建有一磚砌塔樓。交誼室和餐廳旁的"花房"對當時無樹木綠化，灰塵四揚的青島來說猶如一片沙漠綠洲。

在一九零七年信號山坡上的總督新宅完工前，德國總督及其家眷一直住在這幢臨時府邸裡。早在一九零二年，新的總督官邸就已在規劃之中了，因為"總督及其家眷不能還住在這所謂的瑞典木屋裡。"〈341〉在東南亞的商業區裡，這種"瑞典木屋"甚至達不到一般的禮儀水准。當時的殷商，特別是上海的富賈，其別墅都設計得非常寬綽，陳設豪華。〈342〉

用於支撐屋頂和環屋露台的木十字架易於引起誤解，因為中文"x"表示錯誤的意思。中國人習慣於在房屋立面上，樑柱上，尤其是正門上裝飾以巨大的象形字符，用來祈願"壽貴喜"。這個在總督官邸入口上方的"不吉"符號肯定使到過那兒的中國人，如一九零二年十二月到訪的山東巡撫周福（音譯），感到極為不安。這些木製的十字架就再也沒有在以後的青島建築物中使用了。

總督臨時私邸東面外觀，一九零二年。
餐廳，一九零一年。

QINGDAO

ADJUTANTENHAUS
ADJUTANT'S RESIDENCE

Heutige Funktion. Current use
Kang-You-wei-Museum
Fushanzhi Lu (Auguste-Viktoria-Ufer),
Qingdao (Tsingtau. Tsingtao)

Bauherr. Client
Deutsches Gouvernement Kiautschou
German Administration of Kiaochow

Bauzeit. Construction time
1899–1900

Zustand. Condition
Das Gebäude ist gut erhalten,
die Fassade verändert.
Well preserved; façade changed.

Adjutantenhaus, 1901
Blick von Süden, 1992
Adjutant's Residence, 1901
View from the south, 1992

Das Adjutantenhaus befand sich in unmittelbarer Nähe zum ersten Gouverneurswohnhaus, mit Blick über die Meeresbucht, den Strand mit den Badehäuschen und die Pferderennbahn.[343] Das Wohnhaus ähnelt mit seinem chinesisch gedeckten Dach und der umlaufenden Veranda vielen der Sommerhäuser, die sich die ausländischen Kaufleute damals im Seebad Beidaihe (Peitaiho) errichteten. Das vorgestellte Portal des Haupteingangs und die hinaufführende dreiläufige Freitreppe sollten dem Gebäude wohl einen repräsentativen Charakter geben. Die Küche und andere Nebenräume befanden sich auf der Rückseite in einem angebauten Hofhaus. In Qingdao machen viele der Gebäude der ersten Generation einen provisorischen Eindruck, sehen unbeholfen aus. Man sieht diesen Bauten an, daß ihr Entwurf nicht von professionellen Architekten stammte und es an städtebaulichen Vorgaben fehlte. Wahrscheinlich mangelte es am Anfang auch an qualifizierten deutschen Baumeistern und Architekten. Außerdem hatte man wenig Erfahrung mit den klimatischen Bedingungen des Ortes.

The adjutant's residence was in the immediate vicinity of the first Governor's Residence with a view over the bay, the beach with the bathing cabins and the racecourse.[343] The house, with its Chinese tiled roof and the continuous veranda around the building, looks like many of the summer houses which the foreign businessmen built for themselves at the time in the seaside resort of Beidaihe (Peitaiho). The portal in front of the main entrance and the triple-flight stairs leading up to it were intended to give the building a grand character, but in fact they make it look like a collage. The kitchen and other ancillary rooms were at the rear in a building around a courtyard which was added on to the main house.

Many of the buildings of the first generation in Qingdao have an air of the provisional, they often look as if the inhabitants built them themselves. These buildings demonstrate the fact that they were designed without any architectural model or town planning criteria. Probably there was also a lack of qualified German architects and master builders at the beginning. Furthermore no-one had any experience of the local climatic conditions.

總督副官住宅

現用途：康有為紀念館
所在地：青島福山支路，原奧古斯特‧維
　　　　多利亞岸
業主：膠州，德國總督府
建造期：一八九九年至一九零零年
現狀：建築體保存良好；立面有變化。

總督副官住宅與原總督私邸為鄰。身處其中可將海灣、沙灘、沙灘上的小浴室及跑馬道這些景致盡收眼底。〈343〉這幢住宅在風格上類似於當時許多外國商人在北戴河海濱浴場的夏季別墅：屋頂鋪中國瓦，四周圍以敞廊。其主入口處凸出的大門和三進式露天台階意在體現這幢建築的非凡氣派，但看上去卻像一幅拼貼畫。廚房和附屬房間設在加建於住宅後側的四合院裡。青島的許多第一代建築給人一種臨時應急的印象，看上去像是房主自行設計建造的。細看這些建築，不難發現其設計對建築範例及城市建設的總體規劃的缺乏。也許初期階段缺乏高水平的德國建築師和工匠。除此之外，建築師不了解當地的氣候條件也可能是其原因之一。

總督副官住宅，一九零一年。
南面外觀，一九九二年。

WOHNHAUS OHLMER
OHLMER RESIDENCE

Heutige Funktion. Current use
Wohnhaus
Residential
Yüshan Lu 1 (Atilastraße),
Qingdao (Tsingtau. Tsingtao)

Entwurf. Design
Ernst Ohlmer

Bauherr. Client
Chinesischer Seezoll
Chinese Maritime Customs and Excise

Bauzeit. Construction time
1899–1900

Zustand. Condition
Das Gebäude ist sehr gut erhalten.
Very well preserved.

Im Sommer des 25. Jahres des Kaisers Guang Xu errichtet.
Hohe Hügel, steile Hänge, am Süd-Meer,
hier baute man ein Haus,
in dem man glücklich und harmonisch leben kann.
Qingdaos Hafenzolldirektor Ohlmer.[344]

Built in the summer of the 25th year of Emperor Guang Xu.
High hill, steep slopes, on the southern sea,
here a house has been built,
in which it is possible to live happily and in harmony.
Qingdao's Director of the Maritime Customs and Excise office, Ohlmer.[344]

Der Zolldirektor Ohlmer wählte eines der besten Grundstücke im Villen- und Badeviertel Qingdaos. Noch höher als das erste Gouverneurswohnhaus oder das Wohnhaus von dessen Adjutanten über der Auguste-Viktoria-Bucht, war es über eine Paßstraße von der Stadt aus leicht zu erreichen. Man hatte einen weiten Blick über die Bucht, den Strand und die Rennbahn. Mit der Lage am Hang, einem schützenden Berg im Rücken und einer großen Wasserfläche auf der Südostseite, entsprach dieses Gebäude allen Fengshui-Regeln, was auch im nebenstehenden Text des chinesischen Grundsteines ausgedrückt wird.

Neben seiner Tätigkeit im Zolldienst interessierte sich Ohlmer besonders für das Bauwesen. Alle europäischen Zollgebäude Beijings, die vor dem Boxeraufstand errichtet wurden, stammten von ihm, wurden jedoch 1900 zerstört. Er baute dort auch die deutsche, russische und italienische Gesandtschaft. Als ein Mitbegründer des Peking Clubs und des Peking Race Clubs legte er nacheinander zwei Rennbahnen an. Auch die Qingdaoer Rennbahn war im wesentlichen sein Entwurf.[345] Symmetrische, klare Bauvolumen mit flach geneigten Dächern zeichneten Ohlmers Entwürfe für Qingdao aus. Ohlmer baute das 1901 eröffnete Seezollamtsgebäude an der Landungsbrücke und die daneben liegenden Wohnhäuser. An der Einfahrt zu seinem Wohnhaus hat Ohlmer eine Besonderheit im damaligen Qingdao errichten lassen: ein Torwächterhäuschen mit einem typisch chinesischen Dach.

Ernst Ohlmer lebte seit 1868 in China und arbeitete für den Seezoll. 1887 wurde er zum Seezolldirektor ernannt. Seit September 1898 war er in Qingdao tätig. Im Mai 1914, kurz vor der japanischen Eroberung Qingdaos, kehrte Ohlmer 67jährig zurück nach Deutschland. Seine umfangreiche Sammlung chinesischen Porzellans befindet sich heute im Museum in seiner Geburtsstadt Hildesheim.

The director of Maritime Customs and Excise office, Ohlmer, chose one of the best plots in the Qingdao's villa and seaside district. Even higher above the Auguste-Viktoria bay than the first Governor's Residence and the Adjutant's Residence it was easy to get to and from the city via a pass. There was a magnificent view over the bay, the beach and the racecourse. With its position on the hillside, a sheltering mountain behind and a large stretch of water to the south-east, this building fulfilled all the Fengshui rules which is also testified to in the Chinese text of the foundation stone.

Apart from his work in the Maritime Customs and Excise authority, Ohlmer was also very interested in architecture. All the European customs buildings in Beijing which had been built before the Boxers' Uprising were designed by him. They were, however, destroyed in 1900. He also built the German, Russian and Italian legations there. As one of the co-founders of the Peking Club and Peking Race Club he built two racecourses in quick succession. The Qingdao racecourse was also mainly his work.[345] Symmetrical, simple building volumes with shallow-pitched roofs, these were Ohlmer's designs for Qingdao. Ohlmer built the Maritime Customs and Excise Building at the landing stage, which opened in 1901, and the apartment buildings next to it. At the drive to his own house Ohlmer had a feature built which was unusual in Qingdao at that time: a gatekeeper's lodge with a typical Chinese roof.

Ernst Ohlmer lived in China from 1868 onwards and worked for the Maritime Customs and Excise authority. In 1887 he was appointed its director. From September 1898 he worked in Qingdao. In May 1914, just before Qingdao was conquered by the Japanese, Ohlmer, then 67 years old, returned to Germany. His extensive collection of Chinese porcelain is still in the museum of his home town of Hildesheim.

阿里文住宅

現用途：住宅
所在地：青島魚山路一號，原炮兵部隊路
設計：恩斯特·阿里文
業主：中國海關
建造期：一八九九年至一九零零年
現狀：建築體保存完好。

膠州海關稅務司阿里文選擇了青島別墅區和海濱浴場區的最佳地段之一建宅。它瀕臨奧古斯特·維多利亞海灣，高居於原督府邸和總督副官住宅之上。由市區順一山路而行很快便可抵達。從這所住宅可遠眺海灣、沙灘和跑馬道。它背靠山之屏障，東南方則面向大海，符合所有的風水原則。住宅基石上的一段中文碑文也表達了這一點：
"光緒貳拾伍年陽月造
陡坡高崗，
瀕臨南海。
築室於此，
宜其遐福。
膠海關稅務司阿里文誌"〈344〉
阿里文除卻海關公務外，對建築業有著濃厚的興趣。北京所有在義和團起義之前建造的歐洲海關大樓皆出自阿里文之手。一九零零年這些建築遭破壞。阿里文還在北京建造了德國、俄國和意大利公使館。作為北京俱樂部和北京賽馬俱樂部的創建者之一，他還先後修築了兩條跑馬道。青島的跑馬道也由他擔任主設計。〈345〉
棧橋附近一九零一年啟用的海關大樓及旁邊的住宅也為其所建。他為青島設計的建築取對稱外形，手法簡潔。屋頂略作傾斜處理。在他的作品中看不到德國文藝復興式復古風格的非對稱挑樓和小巧的塔樓。阿里文在其住宅的入口處設置一間覆典型中國屋頂的門房，這在當時的青島可謂獨樹一幟。
恩斯特·阿里文自一八六八年起在中國生活，並為海關工作。一八八七年被任命為海關稅務司。一八九八年九月就職於青島。一九一四年五月，日本佔領青島前夕，時年六十七歲的阿里文返回德國。他所收集的大量中國瓷器現收藏於他的家鄉希爾德斯海姆博物館內。

稅務司恩斯特·阿里文住宅西南面外觀，前部為門衛室，約一九零五年。
南面外觀，一九九二年。

WOHNHAUS BERNICK
BERNICK RESIDENCE

Heutige Funktion. Current use
Wohnhaus
Residential
Qixia Lu/Fushan Lu
(Prinz-Adalbert-Straße/Christweg),
Qingdao (Tsingtau. Tsingtao)

Entwurf. Design
Ingenieur Pötter[346]
Pötter, engineer[346]

Ausführung. Contractors
Bernick & Pötter

Bauherr. Client
Hermann Bernick

Bauzeit. Construction time
1905

Zustand. Condition
Das Gebäude ist sehr gut erhalten.
Very well preserved.

Diese Villa ist eines der schönsten Wohnhäuser in Qingdao. Es könnte ebenso im Villenviertel einer deutschen Stadt stehen. Besser als die meisten anderen Gebäude in Qingdao reagiert der Entwurf auf die Hanglage des Grundstücks. Das etwa 55 Grad steile Dach ist auf der Bergseite bis zum Erdgeschoß herabgezogen, so daß die große Dachfläche fast in den Hang hineinläuft. Die dreigeschossige Südwestfassade ist eine Komposition aus Formen und Elementen der deutschen Neorenaissance: Erker, Balkon, Terrasse, hölzerne Loggia, Werksteinverkleidung, Fachwerk und verputzte Wandflächen. Von der Villa aus blickt man auf die Meeresbucht mit dem weißen Strand.

This villa is one of finest houses in Qingdao. It would not look at all out of place in a German city. The design is more sensitive to the hillside site than most other buildings in Qingdao. On the hill side of the house the roof, which has a 55 degree pitch, has been drawn down to the ground floor so that the large roof almost merges into the hillside. The three-storey south-west façade is a composition of forms and elements taken from the German neo-Renaissance: corner-tower like oriels, balconies, terraces, wooden loggias, stone cladding, half-timbering and rendered areas of walls. The villa commands a splendid view of the blue bay and white beach.

Wohnhaus Bernick, Ostansicht.
Im Vordergrund Wohnhaus
Schrameier, 1906
Südansicht, 1992
Bernick Residence, view from the east. In the foreground the Schrameier Residence, 1906
View from the south, 1992

伯恩尼克住宅

現用途：住宅
所在地：青島栖霞路（福山路口），原阿達爾貝特王子路（克里斯特路口）
設計：波特爾，工程師⁽³⁴⁶⁾
施工：伯恩尼克&波特爾公司
業主：海爾曼・伯恩尼克
建造期：一九零五年
現狀：建築體保存完好。

伯恩尼克住宅是青島市最精致的別墅之一，堪與任何一座德國城市的別墅相媲美。其設計完全依地形山勢，因而較青島的大多數建築棋高一招。其依山一面的大坡度屋頂傾斜約五十五度，巨大的屋頂一直伸向底層，幾乎插入山坡。西南立面共有三層，是德國新文藝復興風格形式與該建築內容的完美結合：如角形塔狀挑樓、陽台、平台、木製敞廊、粗石飾面、桁架結構和清水粉牆。由別墅可遠眺尉藍的海灣和潔白的沙灘。

南立面局部，一九九二年。
伯恩尼克住宅東面俯視，其前方為單威廉住宅，一九零六年。

DIENSTWOHNGEBÄUDE XI, BATAILLONSHAUS
OFFICIAL LIVING QUARTERS XI, BATTALION HOUSE

Heutige Funktion. Current use
Eisenbahn-Gästehaus
Guest house of the railways
Yishui Lu 9/Shifu Gongyuan (Diederichsweg),
Qingdao (Tsingtau. Tsingtao)

Entwurf. Design
Bauverwaltung
Planning office of the administration

Bauherr. Client
Deutsches Gouvernement Kiautschou
German Administration of Kiaochow

Bauzeit. Construction time
1899

Zustand. Condition
Das Gebäude ist sehr gut erhalten.
Very well preserved.

Bataillonshaus, Westansicht,
um 1905
Südansicht, 1992
Battalion House,
view from the west, around 1905
View from the south, 1992

Der Grundriß entspricht dem einer deutschen Villa: ein großzügiger Treppenflur im Zentrum des Gebäudes, im Erdgeschoß auf der Südseite das Herrenzimmer, der Salon und das Wohnzimmer. Auf der Westseite lagen das Speisezimmer, daneben nach Norden gerichtet Küche und Anrichte. Hinter dem Haupteingang im Osten befand sich in einem turmartigen Anbau die Dienstbotentreppe. Im ersten Obergeschoß gab es drei Schlafzimmer, eine große Garderobe, ein Ankleidezimmer und das Bad. Die Zimmer für das Personal lagen im Dachgeschoß.

Das »Bataillonshaus« wurde gleichzeitig mit dem ersten Gouverneurswohnhaus errichtet und ist somit eines der ältesten deutschen Gebäude in Qingdao. In den Plänen wird es als »Dienstwohngebäude XI« bezeichnet.[347] Während die deutschen Soldaten damals noch in den chinesischen Lagern wohnten, wurde mit dem Bau der Iltis-Kaserne begonnen. Die Offiziere wohnten dagegen bereits in »Dienstwohngebäuden« im europäischen Stadtviertel Qingdaos. Auf dem Nachbargrundstück wurde 1906 das Gouvernements-Dienstgebäude fertiggestellt. Im Jahre 1912 bezeichnete man es als »Stabshaus«.

On plan this building is modelled on a German villa: a spacious hallway with staircase leading off it in the centre of the building and on the south side of the ground floor the study for the gentleman of the house, the drawing room and the living room. On the western side of the house was the dining room and next to it to the north the kitchen with pantry. Behind the main entrance in the east was the servants' staircase in a tower-like structure. On the first floor there were three bedrooms, a large cloakroom, dressing room and the bathroom. The staff quarters were in the attic.

The »Battalion House« was built at the same time as the first Governor's Residence and is thus one of the oldest German buildings in Qingdao. On the maps of the city it is marked »Official living quarters XI«.[347] Whilst the German soldiers at the time were still living in Chinese camps, building work began on the Iltis Barracks. The officers, however, were already living in »staff quarters« in the European district of Qingdao. The headquarters of the German Administration was completed in 1906 on the neighbouring plot. In 1912 this building became known as a »staff house.«

十一號官邸（第二海軍營營部大樓）

現用途：鐵路局招待所
所在地：青島沂水路九號（市府公園附近），原狄特立克斯路
設計：建築管理局
業主：膠州德國總督府
建造期：一八九九年
現狀：建築體保存完好。

這幢樓房的平面設計得像一座德國別墅，樓房正中是寬敞的樓梯廳堂。男主人的書房、交誼室和客廳設在一樓南側，西面是餐廳。旁邊靠北是廚房和餐具室。主入口設在東面，其後的塔形附屬建築內是供僕人使用的樓梯。二樓有三間臥室、一間寬大的衣帽間及更衣室和浴室各一間。雜役人員住在閣樓上。

"營部大樓"與原總督私邸同期建造，屬青島年代最久的建築之一。設計圖上將其稱為"十一號官邸"。〈347〉伊爾蒂斯兵營動工之前，德國士兵駐扎在原清軍的營房裡，而軍官們卻住在市內歐洲區的"官邸"裡。一九零六年，十一號官邸旁邊的總督官邸竣工。一九一二年，這幢建築改稱"營部大樓"。

營部大樓西面外觀，約一九零五年。
南立面局部，一九九二年。

QINGDAO

DIENSTWOHNUNG DES GOUVERNEMENTSPFARRERS
HOUSE FOR THE PASTOR TO THE GERMAN ADMINISTRATION

Heutige Funktion. Current use
Wohnhaus
Dexian Lu, gegenüber Hubei Lu (Hohenloheweg, gegenüber Kronprinzenstraße), Qingdao (Tsingtau)
Residential
Dexian Lu, opposite Hubei Lu (Hohenlohe Weg, opposite Kronprinzen Strasse), Qingdao (Tsingtao)

Bauzeit. Construction time
1901–1902

Zustand. Condition
Das Gebäude ist sehr gut erhalten.
Very well preserved.

Wohnhäuser am Hohenloheweg,
Südansicht, 1902
Südansicht, 1992
Houses on Hohenlohe Weg,
view from the south, 1902
View from the south, 1992

Bei dem kleinen Wohnhaus sind reichlich Formen der deutschen Neorenaissance verwendet worden. Der schöne Schmuckgiebel und reich verzierte Dachgauben zeichnen dieses Haus aus. Das Gebäude könnte vom gleichen unbekannten Architekten stammen, der auch das Geschäftshaus der Hamburg-Amerika-Linie entworfen hat.
Der Gouvernementspfarrer wohnte hier wahrscheinlich nur vorübergehend.[348]

An abundance of forms of the German neo-Renaissance were used for this small house. For instance, the over-sized roof dormers and the verandas on the ground floor and first floor compete with the well designed ornamental gable. The house could be the work of the same unknown architect who designed the building for the Hamburg-America Line.
The house was probably only temporarily occupied by the pastor to the German Administration.[348]

總督牧師官邸

現用途：住宅
所在地：青島德縣路（湖北路對面），原霍恩洛厄路（太子路對面）
建造期：一九零一年至一九零二年
現狀：建築體保存完好。

這棟小小的樓房運用了大量德國文藝復興復古風格的建築形式。一樓巨大的老虎窗和敞廊與二樓造型別緻的裝飾山牆競相爭琦。這幢樓房或許由設計亨寶商業大樓的同一位無名建築師設計。
總督牧師在此的居住時間有可能極為短暫。[348]

霍恩洛厄路住宅南面外觀，一九零二年。
南面外觀，一九九二年。

DANKSAGUNG

Dem Deutschen Akademischen Austauschdienst (DAAD) danke ich verbindlichst für die Finanzierung meines zweijährigen Aufenthalts in China, ohne die diese Untersuchung nicht zustande gekommen wäre. Mein herzlichster Dank gilt allen Freunden und Kollegen in China, die meine Arbeit unterstützt haben. Ohne ihre Hilfe wäre diese Studie nicht möglich gewesen. Besonders bedanken möchte ich mich bei Frau Professor LUO Xiaowei, die meine Studie an der Tongji-Universität in Shanghai während der zwei Jahre betreut hat, bei Herrn QIAN Zonghao, Historiker im Shanghaier Museum, mit dem ich alle wichtigen Gebäude Shanghais erkundet habe, und bei Herrn Generalkonsul Dr. Helmut Arndt, ohne dessen Initiative dieses Buch nicht zustande gekommen wäre. In Qingdao waren es Frau SHAN Lanyu und Herr LI Houji, die mir die Arbeit ermöglicht haben. In Tianjin unterstützten mich der Architekt MEI Danyu und der Historiker CHEN Ke. Ihnen bin ich sehr zu Dank verpflichtet. Besonderer Dank gehört Herrn Professor Dr. Wilhelm Matzat für seine wertvollen Anregungen. Der Kulturabteilung des Auswärtigen Amtes danke ich sehr für die Ermöglichung der Veröffentlichung dieses Bildbandes. Herrn Professor Dr. Dittmar Machule verdanke ich die Einrichtung eines von der Deutschen Forschungsgemeinschaft geförderten Forschungsvorhabens an der Technischen Universität Hamburg-Harburg, in dessen Rahmen ich mit weiteren Untersuchungen betraut wurde.

Den nachstehend genannten Persönlichkeiten und Institutionen möchte ich an dieser Stelle meinen verbindlichen Dank aussprechen:

Beijing
Dr. LAI Delin, Architekturfakultät, Qinghua University
Prof. Dr. ZHANG Fuhe, Architekturfakultät, Qinghua Universität
ZHANG Ling, Dolmetscher
ZHANG Naixing, Architekt
National Library of China

Qingdao
LI Houji, Qingdao Museum
LIU Shan Zhang, Verein Deutsch-Chinesische Beziehungen
SHAN Lanyu, Vice-Director of Qingdao Municipal Planning Bureau
SUN Xiaotong, Dolmetscher
XU Feipeng, Qingdao Institute of Architecture
ZHOU Quan, Kang you wei-Museum
ZHUANG Lijuan, Dolmetscher
Qingdao Museum Library
Qingdao Urban Construction Archive

Shanghai
Dr. Helmut Arndt, Deutscher Generalkonsul
Prof. CHEN Congzhou, Architekturfakultät, Tongji Universität
Tess Johnston, Amerikanisches Generalkonsulat
Prof. CHEN Longfei, Bauingenieurfakultät, Tongji Universität
Dieter Langbein, Kulturattaché, Deutsches Generalkonsulat
Prof. LUO Xiaowei, Architekturfakultät, Tongji Universität
PEI Meirong, Tongji Universität
QIAN Zonghao, Shanghai Local History Museum
Prof. WANG Zhaosen, Germanistikfakultät, Tongji Universität
Prof. ZHENG Shiling, Architekturfakultät, Tongji Universität
Shanghai Local History Museum Library

ACKNOWLEDGEMENTS

I would like to express my sincerest thanks to the Deutscher Akademischer Austauschdienst (DAAD) for financing my two-year stay in China; this book could not have been written without this help. I would also like to thank all of my friends and colleagues in China whose help was invaluable. I would particularly like to thank Professor LUO Xiaowei who supervised my work at Tongji University in Shanghai over the two years, Mr QIAN Zonghao, historian at the Shanghai Museum who helped me trace all of the important buildings in Shanghai and the German Consul General Dr. Helmut Arndt whose initiative was central to this project. Ms SHAN Lanyu and Mr LI Houji made my work possible in Qingdao. In Tianjin my work was supported by Mr MEI Danyu and the historian Mr CHEN Ke. I am indebted for their help. I would like to express my particular thanks to Professor Dr. Wilhelm Matzat for his helpful comments. I would like to express my gratitude to the cultural division of the Department for Foreign Affairs for its cooperation in the publication of this volume. I would like to thank Professor Dr. Dittmar Machule for the organisation of the research project financed by the Deutsche Forschungsgemeinschaft at the Technical University Hamburg where my continuing research is being supervised.

I would like to express my sincerest thanks to the following persons and institutions:

Beijing
Dr. LAI Delin, Faculty of Architecture, Qinghua University
Professor Dr. ZHANG Fuhe, Faculty of Architecture, Qinghua University
ZHANG Ling, interpreter
ZHANG Naixing, architect
National Library of China

Qingdao
LI Houji, Qingdao Museum
LIU Shan Zhang, Organisation of German-Chinese Relations
SHAN Lanyu, Vice-Director of Qingdao Municipal Planning Bureau
SUN Xiaotong, interpreter
XU Feipeng, Qingdao Institute of Architecture
ZHOU Quan, Kang you wei Museum
ZHUANG Lijuan, interpreter
Qingdao Museum Library
Qingdao Urban Construction Archive

Shanghai
Dr. Helmut Arndt, German Consul General
Professor CHEN Congzhou, Faculty of Architecture, Tongji University
Tess Johnston, American Consulate
Professor CHEN Longfei, Faculty of Construction Engineering, Tongji University
Dieter Langbein, Cultural attaché, German Consulate General
Professor LUO Xiaowei, Faculty of Architecture, Tongji University
PEI Meirong, Tongji University
QIAN Zonghao, Shanghai Local History Museum
Professor WANG Zhaosen, Faculty of German, Tongji University
Professor ZHENG Shiling, Faculty of Architecture, Tongji University
Shanghai Local History Museum Library

鳴 謝

我對德國對外學術交流中心為我的中國之行所提供的兩年資助致以最誠摯的謝意。此資助是這項研究的經濟前提。並且衷心地感謝所有支持此項工作的中國朋友和同仁。沒有他們幫助，這項研究便如無本之木。特別感謝上海同濟大學教授羅小未女士、上海博物館的歷史學家錢宗灝先生及前德國駐滬總領事赫爾穆特．安德博士先生。羅女士在兩年的時光裡指導了我在同濟大學的工作；錢先生與我共同查明了上海所有的重要建築；安德先生的創見為此書的形成提供了靈感；我在青島的工作得以進行主要歸功於單蘭玉女士和李厚基先生。天津的建築師摩丹宇和歷史學家陳克給我以支持，對此深表謝意。予以特別感謝的還有威廉．馬察特教授及其富有見地的建議。感謝德國外交部文化處為此項研究成果的發表鋪平了道路。感謝迪特馬爾．馬手勒教授在漢堡—漢堡工業大學設立一項由德國研究聯合會資助的研究課題，使我在此領域內的研究得以繼續。此外，還要對以下人士及單位表示誠摯的謝意：

北 京
賴德林，清華大學建築學院博士
張復合，清華大學建築學院教授、博士
張玲，翻譯
張乃昕，建築師
北京圖書館

青 島
劉善章，中德關係研究會
孫曉彤，翻譯
徐飛鵬，青島建築工程學院建工系
周 荃，康有為故居博物館
莊麗娟，翻譯
青島市博物館圖書館
青島市城市建設檔案館

上 海
赫爾穆特．安德，前德意志聯邦共和國駐滬領事館總領事
陳從周，同濟大學建築城規學院教授
江似虹，美國駐滬領事館
陳龍飛，同濟大學建工系教授
迪特爾．朗拜恩，前德意志聯邦共和國駐滬領事館文化專員
裴美蓉，同濟大學
王趙森，同濟大學留學預備部教授
鄭時齡，同濟大學建築城規學院教授
上海市歷史博物館圖書館

Tianjin

CHEN Ke, Tianjin Historical Museum
LAN Guowei, Real Estate Büro
LIU Haiyan, Tianjin Academy of Social Science
MEI Danyu, Architekturfakultät, Tianjin Univesity
Prof. ZHOU Zushi, Architekturfakultät, Tianjin University
Tianjiner Stadtbibliothek (Altbau)
Tianjin Social Science Institute

Wuhan

MIN Wei, Dolmetscher
SUI Luming, Stadtplanungsamt
XI Shaowen, Architekt
PANG Xueqing, Historiker

Deutschland

Prof. Max Bächer, Darmstadt
Dr. Ruth Cremerius, Hamburg
Johnny Erling, Hannover
Prof. Dr. Per Fischer, Botschafter a.D., Bonn
Lydia Gerber, Hamburg
Prof. Emil Hädler, Wiesbaden
Prof. Dr. Rudolf Hoberg, Darmstadt
Michael Hundrup, Telgte
Prof. Dr. Georg Friedrich Koch, Darmstadt
Prof. Dr. Dittmar Machule, Hamburg
Pater Dr. Roman Malek SVD, Sankt Augustin
Prof. Dr. Wilhelm Matzat, Bonn
Georg Müller, Darmstadt
Annemarie Rothkegel-Engler, Berlin
Prof. Dr. Mohamed Scharabi, Darmstadt
SHI Yanzhi, Übersetzer, Darmstadt
WANG Fang, Übersetzerin, Darmstadt
WANG Weiwei, Übersetzerin, Darmstadt
Prof. Dr. Alfred Warner, Darmstadt
Dr. Heinrich Wolf, Frankfurt
Bayerische Staatsbibliothek München
Bundesarchiv Koblenz
Bundesarchiv – Militärarchiv Freiburg
Bundesarchiv Potsdam
Deutsche Bibliothek, Frankfurt
Hessische Landesbibliothek, Darmstadt
Monumenta Serica Institut, Steyler Mission, St. Augustin
Sinicum, Institut für Chinesische Sprache, Bochum
Stadt- und Universitätsbibliothek, Frankfurt am Main
Technische Hochschule Darmstadt:
Bibliothek der Kunst- und Baugeschichtsinstitute

Sonstiges Ausland

Prof. Dr. Friedrich Achleitner, Hochschule für Angewandte Kunst, Wien
Heiner Fürst, Hochschule für Angewandte Kunst, Wien
Prof. Wilhelm Holzbauer, Hochschule für Angewandte Kunst, Wien
HU Bolin, Hochschule für Angewandte Kunst, Wien
Lynn Min, Boca Raton, USA
Dr. Mara Reissberger, Hochschule für Angewandte Kunst, Wien
Helmuth Rothkegel, Republik Südafrika
Beat Schwarzenbach, Frauenfeld, Schweiz
Archiv der Steyler Missionare SVD, Rom
Bibliothek der Hochschule für Angewandte Kunst, Wien

Tianjin

CHEN Ke, Tianjin Historical Museum
LAN Guowei, Real Estate Bureau
LIU Haiyan, Tianjin Academy of Social Science
MEI Danyu, Faculty of Architecture, Tianjin University
Professor ZHOU Zushi, Faculty of Architecture, Tianjin University
Tianjin Municipal Library (old building)
Tianjin Social Science Institute

Wuhan

MIN Wei, interpreter
SUI Luming, Municipal Planning Office
XI Shaowen, architect
PANG Xueqing, historian

Germany

Professor Max Bächer, Darmstadt
Dr. Ruth Cremerius, Hamburg
Johnny Erling, Hannover
Professor Dr. Per Fischer, ambassador (retired), Bonn
Lydia Gerber, Hamburg
Professor Emil Hädler, Wiesbaden
Professor Dr. Rudolf Hoberg, Darmstadt
Michael Hundrup, Telgte
Professor Dr. Georg Friedrich Koch, Darmstadt
Professor Dr. Dittmar Machule, Hamburg
Father Dr. Roman Malek SVD, Sankt Augustin
Professor Dr. Wilhelm Matzat, Bonn
Georg Müller, Darmstadt
Annemarie Rothkegel-Engler, Berlin
Professor Dr. Mohamed Scharabi, Darmstadt
SHI Yanzhi, translator, Darmstadt
WANG Fang, translator, Darmstadt
WANG Weiwei, translator, Darmstadt
Professor Dr. Alfred Warner, Darmstadt
Dr. Heinrich Wolf, Frankfurt
Bayerische Staatsbibliothek Munich
Bundesarchiv Koblenz (National archives)
Bundesarchiv – Militärarchiv Freiburg
Bundesarchiv Potsdam
Deutsche Bibliothek Frankfurt
Hessische Landesbibliothek, Darmstadt
Monumenta Serica Institute, Steyler Mission, St. Augustin
Sinicum, Institute for the Chinese Language, Bochum
Municipal and University Library, Frankfurt am Main
Technische Hochschule Darmstadt: Art and Architectural History Library

Others

Professor Dr. Friedrich Achleitner, Heiner Fürst, Professor Wilhelm Holzbauer, HU Bolin and Dr. Mara Reissberger, Hochschule für Angewandte Kunst (University of Applied Art), Vienna
Lynn Min, Boca Raton, USA
Helmuth Rothkegel, Republic of South Africa
Beat Schwarzenbach, Frauenfeld, Switzerland
Archive of the Steyler Mission SVD, Rome
Library of the Hochschule für Angewandte Kunst, Vienna

天 津

藍國偉．天津市房地產管理局
劉海岩．天津市社會科學院
周祖爽．天津大學建築系教授
天津市圖書館（舊館）
天津社會科學院

武 漢

閔 偉．翻譯
眭錄明．武漢市城市規劃土地管理局
席紹雯．建築師．總工程師
彭雪晴．歷史學家
閔寶寶．建築師．總工程師

德 國

馬克斯．拜歇爾．教授．達姆施塔特
露特．克萊梅里烏斯．博士．漢堡
約翰尼．厄林．漢諾威
斐培誼．教授．博士．前德意志聯邦共和國前駐華大使．波恩
呂迪亞．格貝爾．漢堡
埃米爾．海德勒．教授．博士．威斯巴登
魯道夫．霍貝克．教授．博士．達姆施塔特
米夏埃爾．洪德魯普．特爾格特
格奧爾格．弗里德里希．科赫．教授．博士．達姆施塔特
羅曼．馬雷克．神甫．博士．聖奧古斯汀
格奧爾格．米勒．達姆施塔特
安內瑪麗．羅特格．恩格勒．柏林
默哈邁德．沙拉畢．教授．博士．達姆施塔特
石燕致．本書中文譯者（青島篇部分章節）．達姆施塔特
王 芳．本書中文譯者（北京篇至武漢篇）．達姆施塔特
汪薇薇．本書中文譯者（山東篇）．達姆施塔特
阿爾弗雷德．華納．教授．博士．達姆施塔特
海因里希．沃爾夫．博士．法蘭克福
慕尼黑巴伐利亞國家圖書館
科布倫茨聯邦檔案館
弗賴堡聯邦檔案軍事檔案館
波茨坦聯邦檔案館
法蘭克福德文圖書館
達姆施塔特黑森州立圖書館
聖奧古斯汀斯泰勒修會中華資訊中心
波鴻漢語研究所
法蘭克福（萊茵河畔）市立兼大學圖書館
達姆施塔特工業技術大學藝術史和建築史研究所圖書館

其他國家

弗里德里希．阿赫萊特納．教授．博士．維也納應用藝術大學
海納爾．菲爾斯特．維也納應用藝術大學
威廉．霍斯包目．教授．維也納應用藝術大學
胡寶林．維也納應用藝術大學
閔東紅．建築師．本書中版主編．美國
瑪拉．賴斯貝格爾．博士．維也納應用藝術大學
赫爾穆特．羅特克格爾．南非共和國
貝阿特．施瓦真巴赫．瑞士弗勞恩菲爾德
羅馬斯泰爾修會檔案館
維也納應用藝術大學圖書館

ANMERKUNGEN

1. Wilhelm, Richard, *Die Seele Chinas*, Berlin 1926, S. 266. Richard Wilhelm lebte von 1899–1920 in Qingdao (Tsingtau) und gründete 1925 in Frankfurt das China-Institut.
2. Hildebrand, Heinrich, *Der Tempel Ta-chüeh-sy (Tempel des großen Erkennens) bei Peking*, Berlin 1897, Nachdruck Peking 1943.
3. Boerschmann, Ernst, *Chinesische Architektur*, Berlin 1925 und ders., *Chinesische Pagoden*, Berlin und Leipzig 1931.
4. Segalen, Victor, *René Leys*, Frankfurt 1982, S. 43. Das Buch wurde 1913/14 in Beijing geschrieben, 1922 erschien es erstmals in Buchform.
5. Fischer, Martin, *Szetschuan. Diplomatie und Reisen in China während der letzten drei Jahre der Kaiserzeit*, München und Wien 1968, S. 53.
6. »Um die Jahrhundertwende begannen sich in den chinesischen Küstenstädten europäische und amerikanische Einflüsse im Hauptstrom der chinesischen Architekturtradition bemerkbar zu machen. Seit dieser Zeit zählen auch Gebäude im westlichen Baustil, entworfen und gebaut von ausländischen, zum Teil deutschen Architekten, zur modernen Architektur Chinas. Architekturhistoriker in China sehen diese Gebäude als Teil der modernen chinesischen Architekturgeschichte.« Prof. LUO Xiao-wei, Architekturfakultät der Tongji-Universität, Shanghai, 5. April 1992.
7. Muthesius, Hermann in: *Centralblatt der Bauverwaltung*, Berlin, 8. September 1900, S. 429.
8. *Ostasiatischer Lloyd*, Shanghai, 13. September 1912, S. 232.
9. Vgl. *Tsingtauer Neueste Nachrichten*, Tsingtau, 16. Dezember 1913, S. 2.
10. Paquet, Alfons, *Li oder Im neuen Osten*, Frankfurt 1913, S. 297. Paquet war ab 1910 im Vorstand des Deutschen Werkbundes.
11. Kaiser Wilhelm II. interessierte sich für Architektur, versuchte die Architektur im Deutschen Reich zu beeinflussen. Vgl. Seidel, Paul: *Der Kaiser und die Kunst*, Berlin 1907, S. 36.
12. Vgl. z. B. Lauber, Wolfgang, *Deutsche Architektur in Togo. 1884–1914*, Stuttgart 1993.
13. Vgl. Rohrbach, Paul, *Die deutschen Kolonien*, Dachau 1914.
14. *Ostasiatischer Lloyd*, Shanghai, 13. Januar 1905, S. 82 und 8. September 1905, S. 459f.
15. Rothkegel, Curt, *Tätigkeit des Architekten Curt Rothkegel in China*, Liechtenstein 1940, unveröffentlichtes Manuskript.
16. Segalen, Victor, *René Leys*, Frankfurt 1982, S. 9.
17. Die große Stadtmauer Beijings wurde seit dem Jahre 1958 abgetragen und an ihrer Stelle eine Ringstraße angelegt. Hinter dem heutigen Hauptbahnhof befindet sich noch ein verfallenes Reststück der Mauer. Nur wenige Stadttore sind erhalten geblieben.
18. *Ostasiatischer Lloyd*, Shanghai, 15. September 1911, S. 222.
19. Wilhelm, Richard, *Die Seele Chinas*, Berlin 1926, S. 25.
20. Wilhelmy, Emil, *China. Land und Leute*, Berlin 1904. S. 548.
21. *Potsdamer Schlösser in Geschichte und Kunst*, Leipzig 1984, S. 152.
22. *Ostasiatischer Lloyd*, Shanghai, 29. Mai 1903, S. 874.
23. »Wer längere Zeit als Ausländer in der Hauptstadt des Chinesischen Reiches gelebt hat, wird ohne weiteres zugeben, daß die Angehörigen der fremden Nationen in Peking, abgesehen von den etwas faden, sich stets gleichbleibenden Gesellschaften und Empfängen, doch sehr wenig zu ihrem Vergnügen und ihrer Unterhaltung haben.« *Ostasiatischer Lloyd*, Shanghai, 20. Dezember 1912, S. 560.
24. Hildebrand, Heinrich, *Der Tempel Ta-chüeh-sy bei Peking*, Berlin 1897.
25. Bundesarchiv Potsdam, Gesandtschaft China, Akte 1588, S. 44, 74.
26. *Social Shanghai*. A Magazine for Men and Women, Shanghai, July 1906.
27. Die rund 1500 km lange Bahntrasse von Beijing nach Wuhan war im Auftrag des obersten Beamten für Eisenbahnwesen und Fabrikanten Taotai Tseng in den Jahren 1896/97 durch den deutschen Regierungsbaumeister Heinrich Hildebrand geplant und vermessen worden. Hildebrand leitete 1899–1904 auch den Bau der deutschen Schantung-Eisenbahn von Qingdao nach Jinan (...). Vgl. Franzius, Georg, *Kiautschou. Deutschlands Erwerbung in Ostasien*, Berlin 1898, S. 68f.
28. *Ostasiatischer Lloyd*, Shanghai, 13. Februar und 5. Juni 1914.
29. *The East of Asia Magazine*. A non-political illustrated quarterly, Shanghai 1902, S. 5.
30. *The Far Eastern Review*, Manila, Shanghai, Yokohama, July 1915, S. 44f.
31. Sirén, Osvald, *The walls and gates of Peking*, London 1924, S. 171.
32. Fünf Zwischenpodeste, die alle 16 Stufen angeordnet sind, machen das Hinaufsteigen angenehm. Die Stufen haben ein Steigungsverhältnis 15/34 cm.
33. Höhe des Gesimses 43 cm, Tiefe etwa 30 cm.
34. Sirén, Osvald, a. a. O., S. 173. Der Umbau wurde generell bedauert: »Was hilft es, daß man das trotzige äußere Tor schönt, den Fenstern schwierige Verdachungen gibt und es mit einer vorkragenden Galerie umgibt, zu der man kostspielige Freitreppen hinaufbaut, die doch niemand besteigt, das schönste und monumentalste Tor Pekings ist doch für ewig verloren.« *Ostasiatischer Lloyd*, Shanghai, 17. September 1915.
35. *Ostasiatischer Lloyd*, Shanghai, 7. Juli 1911, S. 17.
36. Vgl. Curt Rothkegel, a. a. O.
37. Rothkegel, Curt, a. a. O.
38. *Centralblatt der Bauverwaltung*, Berlin 1894, S. 443.
39. Rothkegel schreibt später: »Der Präsident des provisorischen Parlaments bezeichnete die mir vom Bauamt vorgeschriebene Abgeordnetenzahl für das Unterhaus von 450 als zu gering (...) und auf etwa 600 Sitzplätze erhöht wissen wollte.« Bundesarchiv Potsdam, Gesandschaft China, Akte 853, S. 13. Es erfolgte die Umplanung durch den Architekten.
40. *Ostasiatischer Lloyd*, Shanghai, 9. Dezember 1910, S. 565f.
41. Vgl. Woodhead, H. G. W., *The Truth About The Chinese Republic*, London, 1925. S. 13–26 und Weggel, Oskar, *Geschichte Chinas im 20. Jahrhundert*, Stuttgart 1989, S. 28.
42. Bundesarchiv Potsdam, Gesandtschaft China, Akte 853, Blatt 105.
43. *Ostasiatischer Lloyd*, Shanghai, 11. November 1910, S. 463.
44. *The Far Eastern Review*, Manila, Shanghai, Yokohama, September 1913, S. 121f.
45. Bundesarchiv Potsdam, Gesandtschaft China, Akte 853, Blatt 92–93.
46. Curt Rothkegel, a. a. O.
47. *Ostasiatischer Lloyd*, Shanghai, 18. April 1913, S. 375.
48. *Ostasiatischer Lloyd*, Shanghai, 29. Mai 1914, S. 485.
49. von Salzmann, Erich, »Die deutsche Gesandtschaft in Peking«, in: *Die Woche*, Berlin, 1. Januar–31. März 1914, S. 24–29.
50. FEI-SHI (Fischer, Emil), *Guide to Peking and its Environs*, Tientsin 1909, S. 19.
51. *Ostasiatischer Lloyd*, Shanghai, 17. Februar 1911, S. 178.
52. Eine vergleichbare Proportion besitzt das erste Ehrentor vor den Ming-Gräbern bei Beijing. Es ist mit fünf Durchgängen jedoch breiter.
53. FEI-SHI, a. a. O., S. 66. Der lateinische Text wurde im *Ostasiatischen Lloyd* am 28. November 1902, S. 983, veröffentlicht.
54. *Ostasiatischer Lloyd*, Shanghai, 28. November 1902.
55. Wilhelm, Richard, a. a. O., S. 30, 263.
56. Bundesarchiv Potsdam, Gesandtschaft China, Akte 1048, Blatt 221.
57. Vgl. Bundesarchiv Potsdam, Gesandtschaft China, Akte 266, Blatt 272.
58. *Ostasiatischer Lloyd*, Shanghai, 20. Mai 1904, S. 872.
59. Loesch, Karl C., *Deutsche Züge im Antlitz der Erde*, München o. J., S. 171.
60. Wright, Arnold und Cartwright, H. A., *Twentieth Century Impressions of Hongkong, Shanghai, and other Treaty Ports of China*, London 1908, S. 604.
61. Vgl. dazu Bundesarchiv Potsdam, Gesandtschaft China, Akte 266, Blatt 272.
62. *Ostasiatischer Lloyd*, Shanghai, 20. Dezember 1912, S. 560.
63. Bundesarchiv Potsdam, Gesandtschaft China, Akte 697, Blatt 116.
64. Vgl. Bundesarchiv Potsdam, Gesandtschaft China, Akte 1588, Blatt 133 (Karte aus dem Jahr 1915).
65. *Ostasiatischer Lloyd*, Shanghai, 26. Juni 1908, S. 1215.
66. *Social Shanghai*, Shanghai 1906, S. 125.
67. *Hai-Ho Conservancy Board 1898–1919*, Tientsin, 1919, S. 37. Während der Wintermonate fror der Hai He zu, der die Verbindung Tianjins mit dem Meer bildete, dann kam der Handelsverkehr zum Erliegen.
68. 1894 führte die Bahn bis Shanhaiguan (Schanhaikwan), die Stelle, an der die Große Mauer das Meer erreicht, 1899 bis zur Stadt Jinzhou (Chin Chow). Vgl. Rasmussen, O. D., *Tientsin. An Illustrated Outline History*, Tientsin, 1925, S. 95f.
69. Die »Chinese Gouvernement Railways« waren der Auftraggeber. Die Bahnlinie läuft östlich parallel mit dem Kaiserkanal bis Dezhou, überquert nahe Jinan (Tsinanfu) den Huang He (Gelben Fluß) und führt weiter nach Süden bis an den Yangzi-Fluß. Die nördlichen 625 km dieser Linie wurden von deutschen Ingenieuren erbaut.
70. Rasmussen, O. D., a. a. O., S. 27.
71. Die amerikanische Niederlassung ging 1902 in die englische über. Vgl. Bundesarchiv Potsdam, Gesandtschaft China, Akte 1015, Blatt 314.
72. 1772 Japaner, 1530 Briten, 753 Deutsche, 542 Amerikaner, 294 Franzosen, 154 Russen, 93 Italiener, 85 Schweizer, 74 Dänen, 54 Österreich-Ungarn und andere. Vgl. Imperial Japanese Government Railways: An official Guide to Eastern Asia, Vol. 4 China. Tokio 1915, S. 25.
73. So lebten im Jahre 1902 in der englischen Niederlassung 255 Briten, 145 Japaner, 104 Deutsche, 46 Amerikaner, 25 Russen, 19 Dänen, 11 Österreicher, 26 andere Europäer. Von den etwa 4300 dort wohnenden Chinesen waren etwa 1900 Personen bei Ausländern angestellt. Vgl. *Ostasiatischer Lloyd*, Shanghai, 28. November 1902, S. 977.
74. Vgl. Navarra, Bruno, *China und die Chinesen*, Bremen und Shanghai 1901, S. 1073, und Wilhelmy, Emil, *China. Land und Leute*, Berlin 1904, S. 692ff.
75. Die Anzahl der in Nordchina stationierten Offiziere und Mannschaften wurde im Jahr 1902 wie folgt angegeben: 1920 Franzosen, 1900 Engländer, 1600 Deutsche, 1280 Japaner, 980 Russen, 880 Italiener, 150 Amerikaner; zusammen etwa 8700 Mann.
76. Sie bestanden aus 1720 Engländern, 1200 Franzosen, 420 Japanern, 220 Italienern, 170 Amerikanern, 120 Russen und 100 Deutschen.

77 *Ostasiatischer Lloyd*, Shanghai, 20. Dezember 1912, S. 556.
78 China hatte den japanisch-chinesischen Krieg 1894/95 verloren. Japan erhielt die Insel Taiwan (Formosa), mußte aber auf seine in Nordchina eroberten Gebiete verzichten, sowie auf den ebenfalls in ihre Hände gefallenen wichtigsten nordchinesischen Kriegshafen Lüshun (Port Arthur). Vgl. Wilhelmy, Emil, a.a.O., S. 516ff.
79 Rasmussen, O.D., a.a.O., S. 95.
80 Vgl. Bundesarchiv Potsdam, Gesandtschaft China, Akte 1051, Blatt 55
81 Die Höhe der jährlichen Gemeindeabgaben bestimmte die Anzahl der Stimmen pro Mitglied in der Gemeindeversammlung, wobei die maximale Stimmenzahl pro Mitglied auf 12 festgelegt war. So gehörten nahezu die Hälfte der Stimmen 1911 der Tientsin Baugesellschaft und der zur Deutsch-Asiatischen-Bank gehörenden Deutschen-Niederlassungs-Gesellschaft. Vgl. Bundesarchiv Potsdam, Gesandtschaft China, Akte 1050, Blatt 11 und Akte 1048, Blatt 99 und 110.
82 Eine Volkszählung wurde 1913 in der deutschen Niederlassung durchgeführt: 1205 Chinesen, 284 europäische, amerikanische und japanische Zivilisten – davon 117 Deutsche sowie zusätzlich 304 deutsche Soldaten. Damals lebten etwa 750 deutsche Zivilisten in Tianjin. Vgl. *Ostasiatischer Lloyd*, Shanghai, 30. Mai 1913 und *The Imperial Japanese Governement Railways*, a.a.O., S. 25.
83 Bundesarchiv Potsdam, Gesandtschaft China, Akte 1050, Blatt 184f und 310.
84 Bundesarchiv Potsdam, Gesandtschaft China, Akte 1050, Blatt 216 (Schreiben vom 7. Mai 1912).
85 ebd.
86 Bundesarchiv Potsdam, Gesandtschaft China, Akte 1050, Blatt 454 (Erlaß vom 15. August 1912).
87 Unter anderen ließen sich ein ehemaliger chinesischer Seezolldirektor, die Söhne des Prinzen Qing (Ch'ing), Zailun (Tsai-lun), Zaixun (Tsai-hsün) und Zaifu (Tsai-fu) und General Zhang Xun (Chang Hsün), »der neben Yuan Shi-kai und außerhalb Pekings zur Zeit wohl mächtigste Mann in China« in der deutschen Niederlassung nieder und kauften sich Grundstücke und Häuser. Vgl. Bundesarchiv Potsdam, Gesandtschaft China, Akte 1050, Blatt 190f und 274.
88 *Tianjin jindai jianzhu*, Tianjin 1990, S. 174.
89 Wright, Arnold, a.a.O., S. 730.
90 Bundesarchiv Potsdam. Gesandtschaft China, Akte 1015, Blatt 198.
91 Bundesarchiv Potsdam, Gesandtschaft China, Akte 1015, Blatt 193 (*Tageblatt für Nordchina*, Tientsin, 1. August 1907).
92 *China Times*, 1. August 1907: »Einigkeit läßt die kleinsten Geschäfte wachsen; Uneinigkeit die größten Unternehmen zerbrechen.« Bundesarchiv Potsdam, Gesandtschaft China, Akte 1015, Blatt 195.
93 *Ostasiatischer Lloyd*, Shanghai, 3. April 1908, S. 639.
94 *Ostasiatischer Lloyd*, Shanghai, 15. Juni 1913, S. 61.
95 Koberstein, F., *Tientsin und Umgebung*, Tientsin 1906, S. 38.
96 Solche Rolandsäulen waren zwischen dem 14. und 18. Jahrhundert in norddeutschen Städten als Symbol ihrer städtischen Rechte und Freiheiten errichtet worden. Vgl. Wright, Arnold, a.a.O., S. 726.
97 *Ostasiatischer Lloyd*, Shanghai, 6. November 1903, S. 727; bei dem erwähnten Buch handelt es sich um Franzius, Georg, *Kiautschou, Deutschlands Erwerbung in Ostasien*, Berlin 1898.
98 Wright, Arnold, a.a.O., S. 604.
99 Bundesarchiv Potsdam, Gesandtschaft China, Akte 1051, Blatt 50.
100 *Ostasiatischer Lloyd*, Shanghai, 8. April 1910.

101 Vgl. *Huazhong Architecture*, No. 2, Wucang und Hubei 1987; Irrtümlich wird das Gebäude in dem »Symposium of conference« als Deutsches Konsulat bezeichnet.
102 Bundesarchiv Potsdam, Gesandtschaft China, Akte 1049, Blatt 76.
103 Vgl. Boerschmann, Ernst, *Chinesische Architektur*, Bd. 1, Berlin 1925, S. 15.
104 Vgl. Wright, Arnold, a.a.O., S. 746, und Koberstein, F., a.a.O., S. 40.
105 Bundesarchiv Potsdam, Gesandtschaft China, Akte 1051, Blatt 141.
106 Franzius, Georg, *Kiautschou*, Berlin 1898, S. 17.
107 Wright, Arnold, a.a.O., S. 59.
108 Arnold, *Picturesque Hong Kong*, Hongkong 1911, S. 15.
109 So schrieb der *Ostasiatische Lloyd* am 27. September 1901: »In London kommen auf einen Acre bebaute Fläche 60 Einwohner, in Glasgow 61 und in Hongkong 66. Diese Überbevölkerung fördert natürlich auch in hohem Maße das endemische Vorkommen der Pest, wohl auch der Malaria und ähnlicher Seuchen.« Die Bevölkerungsdichte entsprach also in London 14 826 E/km², in Glasgow 15 074 und war am höchsten in Hongkong mit 16 309 E/km².
110 Schrameier, Wilhelm, *Aus Kiautschous Verwaltung*, Jena 1914, S. 28.
111 ebd., S. 18f, S. 43f und Wright, Arnold, a.a.O., S. 59.
112 *Ostasiatischer Lloyd*, Shanghai, 29. Mai 1914, S. 485.
113 Wright, Arnold, a.a.O., S. 171.
114 *Tsingtauer Neueste Nachrichten*, Tsingtau, 16. Dezember 1913, S. 2.
115 Nur fünf Jahre später entstand in Shanghai der deutsche Club Concordia. Er war in der Art der Neorenaissance entworfen und als typisch deutsches Gebäude erkennbar.
116 *Ostasiatischer Lloyd*, Shanghai, 23. Januar 1903, S. 158.
117 Pott, F.L.H., *A Short History of Shanghai*, Shanghai 1928, S. 51, 79.
118 *Ostasiatischer Lloyd*, Shanghai, 7. September 1906, S. 460.
119 *Ostasiatischer Lloyd*, Shanghai, 21. September 1906, S. 555.
120 *Ostasiatischer Lloyd*, Shanghai, 7. September 1906, S. 461.
121 *Ostasiatischer Lloyd*, Shanghai, 14. September 1906, S. 508.
122 *Ostasiatischer Lloyd*, Shanghai, 31. August 1906, S. 415–416.
123 1843 wurde als erstes die englische Niederlassung eingerichtet; 1862/63 wurde sie mit der amerikanischen zusammengelegt zur Internationalen Niederlassung. Direkt zwischen der chinesischen Stadt und der Internationalen Niederlassung entstand 1848 die französische Niederlassung, die immer unabhängig von der internationalen verwaltet wurde. Die Internationale Niederlassung wurde 1899 von 7,15 km² auf 22,6 km² erweitert, die französische Niederlassung folgte mit einer Erweiterung 1914.
124 *Ostasiatischer Lloyd*, Shanghai, 8. Januar 1904, S. 40.
125 Um die Steigerung zu verdeutlichen: im Jahr 1843 0,30 Goldmark pro m², im Jahr 1903 44,50 Goldmark pro m²; vgl. Woas, Franz, »Ostasiatische Architektur der neueren Zeit«, in: *Deutsche Bauzeitung*, Berlin, 7. September 1904, S. 451.
126 Luff, Reginald, »Buildings in Shanghai«, in *Social Shanghai*, Shanghai, July 1908, S. 26.
127 *Ostasiatischer Lloyd*, Shanghai, 16. Dezember 1910, S. 403.
128 Pott, F.L.H., a.a.O., S. 233.

129 *Far East Magazine*, Shanghai und Tientsin, December 1934.
130 Vgl. *Centralblatt der Bauverwaltung*, Berlin, 1899, S. 515.
131 *Shanghaier Nachrichten*, Beilage zum *Ostasiatischen Lloyd*, Shanghai, 18. Januar 1907. S. 10f.
132 *Social Shanghai*, Shanghai, January–June 1907, S. 289 bis 295.
133 Finanziert wurde der Neubau durch 20 000 Taels aus dem eigenen Vermögen des Clubs; 100 000 Taels als von Mitgliedern gezeichnete 7,5 Prozent Anteilsscheine und 280 000 Taels als Hypothek der Deutsch-Asiatischen Bank zu 7 Prozent Zinsen. 1 Tael waren etwa 2,70 Goldmark.
134 *Shanghaier Nachrichten*, 8. Februar 1908, S. 27.
135 Wright, Arnold, a.a.O., S. 373.
136 Vgl. zu den beiden Architekten: *Shanghaier Nachrichten*, Shanghai, 10. März 1911, 8. Februar 1907 (Abbildungen der Architekten) und *Social Shanghai*, Shanghai 1907. S. 294.
137 *Social Shanghai*, Shanghai, January–June 1906, S. 17–20.
138 Die 71 Opfer hatte man auf dem »Iltisfriedhof« an der Küste Shantungs bestattet, das Denkmal wurde alljährlich am 23. Juli mit Kränzen geschmückt. Vgl. *Ostasiatischer Lloyd*, Shanghai, 31. Juli 1903, S. 168.
139 *Shanghaier Nachrichten*, 11. September 1908, S. 197.
140 Bundesarchiv Potsdam, Gesandtschaft China, Akte 918, Blatt 289–295.
141 Franke, Otto, *Erinnerungen aus zwei Welten*, Berlin 1954, S. 61.
142 *Der Auslandsdeutsche*, Stuttgart, 1. Jg., Nr. 6, Juni 1912, S. 3.
143 Vgl. *Ostasiatischer Lloyd*, Shanghai, 4. Dezember 1903, S. 897, und Wright, Arnold, a.a.O., S. 656.
144 *Ostasiatischer Lloyd*, Shanghai, 5. April 1901, S. 283.
145 *Ostasiatischer Lloyd*, Shanghai, 11. Mai 1900, S. 340f.
146 Der *Ostasiatischer Lloyd* schreibt über die Schule: »Im Erdgeschoß liegen zwei Klassenzimmer, die für je 30 Kinder Platz bieten. Im oberen Stockwerk liegen ebenfalls zwei Klassenzimmer, die durch verschiebbare Türen voneinander getrennt sind, durch deren Öffnung eine geräumige Aula geschaffen werden kann.« *Ostasiatischer Lloyd*, Shanghai, 13. September 1901, S. 790f.; die Aula faßt mehr als 100 Personen.
147 Vgl. *Der Auslandsdeutsche*, Stuttgart, 1. Jahrgang, Juni 1912.
148 Nellist, George F., *Men of Shanghai and North China*, Shanghai 1933, S. 375.
149 *Shanghaier Nachrichten*, Shanghai, 28. April 1911.
150 Vgl. *Shanghaier Nachrichten*, Shanghai, 7. Juli 1911, »Bericht des Schulausschusses der Internationalen Niederlassung.«
151 Informationen zur Kaiser-Wilhelm-Schule in: Weber, Dietrich (Hrsg.), *Kaiser-Wilhelm-Schule zu Schanghai*, Shanghai 1935, S. 17.
152 Vgl. *Ostasiatischer Lloyd*, Shanghai, 12. Mai 1905, S. 865.
153 Vgl. Meid, Michiko, *Europäische und Nordamerikanische Architekten in Japan*, Dissertation, Köln 1977, S. 264f.
154 Ausführliche Beschreibung des Gebäudes und der Innenräume in: *Ostasiatischer Lloyd*, Shanghai, 24. Oktober 1902, S. 869–871.
155 Vgl. Darwent, C.E., *Shanghai: A Handbook for Travellers and Residents*, Shanghai, 1920. S. 7: »Die neue Russisch-Chinesische Bank (...) ist im italienischen Stil erbaut, mit symbolhaften Figuren über den Türen. Die Chinesen haben diese Figuren mißverstanden und sie für die Hausgötter der Ausländer gehalten.«

156 Vgl. *Ostasiatischer Lloyd*, Shanghai, 10. März 1911, S. 71f.
157 Vgl. *Deutsche Bauzeitung*, Berlin, 7. September 1904, S. 450–452.
158 Vgl. *Ostasiatischer Lloyd*, Shanghai, 1. August 1902, S. 616–617.
159 Woas, Franz, »Ostasiatische Architektur der neueren Zeit«, in: *Deutsche Bauzeitung*, Berlin, 7. September 1904, S. 450–452.
160 Das fünfgeschossige Gebäude Ecke Hankou Road und Kiangsi Road wurde vom Architekten Davis & Thomas geplant, ausgeführt von Jardine, Matheson & Co. Vgl. *Shanghaier Nachrichten*, 22. März 1907.
161 *Shanghaier Nachrichten*, 22. März 1907, S. 64.
162 *Shanghaier Nachrichten*, 3. Januar 1908, S. 3–4.
163 Wright, Arnold, a.a.O., S. 794.
164 Wright, Arnold, a.a.O., S. 604.
165 *Shanghaier Nachrichten*, 31. Januar 1908, S. 33.
166 Franz Woas beschrieb diese Villengegenden 1904: »Die Folge dieser hohen Grundstückspreise im Inneren der Stadt ist auch für Shanghai die gewesen, daß die eigentlichen Wohnhäuser immer mehr und mehr auf das noch offene Land hinausgedrängt werden. Es hat sich geradezu ein ›Shanghai-West‹ entwickelt, wo jetzt die Europäer mit Vorliebe wohnen; aber auch reiche Chinesen haben ihren Wohnsitz hier aufgeschlagen. Die neueren hier errichteten Villen zeigen keine besondere Eigenart, sondern ahmen allzuviel englische oder amerikanische Vorbilder nach. Von der alten Art, in der anfangs hier Wohnhäuser für Europäer errichtet wurden, findet sich manch' Beispiel, das in seiner Einfachheit anmutig wirkt. Im übrigen wiegt jetzt hier der Ziegelfugenbau vor.« Woas, Franz, »Ostasiatische Architektur der neueren Zeit«, in: *Deutsche Bauzeitung*, Berlin, 7. September 1904, S. 451.
167 Wright, Arnold, a.a.O., S. 604. Eine Abbildung des Hauses »Willfried«, S. 656.
168 Vgl. *Social Shanghai*, Shanghai, January–June 1907, S. 294.
169 »Building Activities of Shanghai«, in: *The Far Eastern Review*, Manila, Shanghai, Yokohama, September, Oktober 1916. S. 144 und S. 181f.
170 Vgl. *Shanghaier Nachrichten*, Shanghai, 12. Juni 1914, S. 194–195.
171 Vgl. *Festschrift anläßlich des 25jährigen Bestehens der Staatlichen Tung-Chi Universität zu Woosung, China*, Woosung 1932, S. 4.
172 Vgl. Berrens, B., »Die Entwicklung der deutschen Medizin- und Ingenieurschule Schanghai«, in: *Schülerverzeichnis 1916*, Shanghai 1916, S. 27f.
173 *Shanghaier Nachrichten*, Shanghai, 5. Juni 1914, S. 181f.
174 Vgl. *Bericht über die Deutsche Ingenieurschule für Chinesen in Schanghai für das dritte Schuljahr (1914/15)*, Shanghai 1915, S. 16.
175 *Berliner Illustrierte Zeitung*, Berlin, 8. April 1923, S. 264
176 *Denkschrift aus Anlaß der Feierlichen Einweihung der Tungchi Technischen Hochschule in Schanghai-Woosung*, Woosung 1924, S. 27.
177 Zur Geschichte der Technischen Hochschule vgl. *Denkschrift aus Anlaß der Feierlichen Einweihung der Tungchi Technischen Hochschule in Schanghai-Woosung*, Woosung 1924, und *Festschrift anläßlich des 25jährigen Bestehens der Staatlichen Tung-Chi Universität zu Woosung, China*, Woosung 1932.
178 Weber, Dietrich (Hrsg.), a.a.O., S. 24.
179 Vgl. *The Directory & Chronicle of China, Japan, Korea, Indo-China,* Hongkong 1937, S. E83.
180 Weber, Dietrich (Hrsg.), a.a.O., S. 26.
181 Nähere Angaben zu Hudec vgl. *Slovensky Biograficky Slovnik, (833–1990)*, Martin 1987 und Nellist, George F., a.a.O., S. 182, 187.
182 Vgl. von Schab, »Geschichte der Deutschen Medizin- und Ingenieurschule 1907–1919«, in: *Festschrift anläßlich des 25jährigen Bestehens der Staatlichen Tung-Chi Universität zu Woosung, China*, Woosung 1932, S. 1.
183 *Festschrift anläßlich des 25jährigen Bestehens der Staatlichen Tung-Chi Universität zu Woosung, China*, Woosung 1932, S. 2–3.
184 Vgl. Stumpf, Richard, »Neuzeitliches Hochbauen in Shanghai im Jahre 1932/33«, in: *Festschrift anläßlich des 25jährigen Bestehens der Staatlichen Tung-Chi Universität zu Woosung, China*, Woosung 1932. S. 166f.
185 Hankou hatte 850 000, Hanyang 400 000 und Wuchang 500 000 Einwohner.
186 Kawata, T., *Glimpses of China and Japan Trade Records*, Osaka 1919, S. 173.
187 Vgl. *Ostasiatischer Lloyd*, Shanghai, 30. Mai 1913, S. 522.
188 Franzius, Georg, *Kiautschou. Deutschlands Erwerbung in Ostasien*. Berlin 1898, S. 69.
189 Macmillan, Allister, *Seaports of the Far East*, 2. Auflage, London 1925, S. 169.
190 Paquet, Alfons, *Li oder Im neuen Osten*, Frankfurt 1913, S. 232.
191 Franzius, Georg, *Kiautschou. Deutschlands Erwerbung in Ostasien*, Berlin 1899, S. 70f.
192 ebd., S. 70.
193 Kawata, T., a.a.O., S. 176.
194 Bundesarchiv Potsdam, Gesandtschaft China, Akte 1033 und 1034.
195 Bundesarchiv Potsdam, Gesandtschaft China, Akte 1050, Blatt 300.
196 *Ostasiatischer Lloyd*, Shanghai, 21. Oktober 1910, S. 402.
197 1905 kostete der Quadratmeter an der Uferstraße 18 Goldmark und im rückwärtigen Teil 11 Goldmark, 1912 betrugen die Grundstückspreise an der Uferstraße 43 Goldmark/m^2 und im rückwärtigen Teil dagegen nur 17 bis 21 Goldmark/m^2. Chinesisches Land in der Nähe der Niederlassungen kostete 8,50 bis 15 Goldmark/m^2, das etwas weiter entfernte Grundstück der Ingenieurschule nur 0,90 Goldmark/m^2. Vgl. Bundesarchiv Potsdam, Gesandtschaft China, Akte 640, Blatt 416f und 425, und Akte 1032, Blatt 267.
198 Vgl. *Ostasiatischer Lloyd*, Shanghai, 5. Mai 1905, S. 816.
199 *Ostasiatischer Lloyd*, Shanghai, 1. Dezember 1905, S. 1009.
200 Vgl. *Ostasiatischer Lloyd*, Shanghai, 10. Juli 1908, S. 88f.
201 *Shanghaier Nachrichten*, Shanghai, 10. März 1911, S. 71f.
202 *Ostasiatischer Lloyd*, Shanghai, 29. März 1907, S. 547f.
203 *Ostasiatischer Lloyd*, Shanghai, 19. Februar 1909, S. 373.
204 ebd.
205 Ihre aufwendig gezeichneten Alternativentwürfe sandten sie an die deutsche Gesandtschaft in Beijing, doch ohne Erfolg. Vgl. Bundesarchiv Potsdam, Gesandtschaft China, Akte 640, Blatt 404–571.
206 Vgl. zur Theorie der Geomantik Walters, Derek, *Feng Shui. Perfect Placing of your happiness and prosperity*, London, Singapore 1988.
207 In Qingdao dagegen, das nicht von einer privaten Gesellschaft erschlossen wurde, waren die Grundstücke für Schulen und Missionen kostenlos vom Gouvernement abgegeben worden.
208 Eine detaillierte Beschreibung in Stenz, Georg Maria, »Der Kaiserkanal« in *Beiträge zur Kolonialpolitik und Kolonialwirtschaft*, Berlin 1903/04.
209 Wilhelmy, Emil, a.a.O., S. 385.
210 Dukes, E.J. und Fielde, A., *Alltagsleben in China*, Basel 1892, S. 149.
211 Vgl. Walters, Derek, a.a.O., und Navarra, Bruno, *China und die Chinesen,* Bremen, Shanghai 1901, S. 491ff.
212 »Die Errichtung von Kirchtürmen und Fabrikschornsteinen wäre ein unverzeihliches Verbrechen, denn dadurch würde ja die gute Laune der Geisterwelt zerstört.« Dukes, E.J. und Fielde, A., a.a.O., S. 146–154.
213 Stenz, Georg Maria, »Der Kaiserkanal« in: *Beiträge zur Kolonialpolitik und Kolonialwirtschaft*. Berlin 1903/04, S. 130.
214 Bökemann, »Über Wirtschaft und Verkehr in der Provinz Schantung«, in: *Koloniale Monatsblätter*, Berlin 1913, S. 132.
215 *Ostasiatischer Lloyd*, Shanghai, 1. November 1912, S. 397.
216 Bökemann, a.a.O., S. 96.
217 Vgl. *Ostasiatischer Lloyd*, Shanghai, 25. September 1903, S. 476.
218 Vgl. Bach, Kurt, »Vom Bau der Schantung-Eisenbahn«, in: *Zentralblatt der Bauverwaltung*, Berlin, 16. September 1905, S. 467, 493.
219 Vgl. Dost, Paul, *Deutsch-China und die Schantungbahn*, Krefeld 1981, S. 131f.
220 Der Huang He spielte als Wasserstraße keine wichtige Rolle. Durch seine mitgeführten Schlammassen war er im Unterlauf kaum schiffbar. Zuletzt hatte er nach riesigen Überschwemmungen 1852 seinen Lauf geändert und floß danach 400 km weiter nördlich ins Meer.
221 »Für die Sicherheit der Kolonie (…) ist eine leichte Beweglichkeit der Besatzungstruppen eine Hauptbedingung.« Gerstenberg, Hans, »Die Wegebauten in Tsintau«, in: Deutsche Kolonialgesellschaft (Hrsg.), *Beiträge zur Kolonialpolitik und Kolonialwirtschaft*, 1. Jahrgang, Berlin 1899/1900, S. 128.
222 Vgl. zu den Bestimmungen Betz, Heinrich, *Die wirtschaftliche Entwicklung der Provinz Schantung*, Tsingtau 1911, S. 60 ff.
223 *Adressbuch des Deutschen Kiautschou-Gebiets für 1911–1912*, Tsingtau 1911, S.75.
224 *Ostasiatischer Lloyd*, Shanghai, 20. September 1912, S. 262.
225 Crow, Carl, *Handbook for China*, Shanghai 1921, S. 277.
226 *Ostasiatischer Lloyd*, Shanghai, 28. Mai 1909, S. 1073.
227 *Adress-Buch*, 1911–1912, a.a.O., S. 75f.
228 Boerschmann, Ernst, *Chinesische Architektur, Band 1*, a.a.O., Tafel 33 (Backsteingiebel) und Tafel 37 (Ziegelarchitektur).
229 Boerschmann, Ernst, *Baukunst und Landschaft in China*, Berlin 1926, S. 78.
230 *Ostasiatischer Lloyd*, Shanghai, 4. November 1910, S. 440.
231 *The Far Eastern Review*, Manila, Shanghai, Yokohama, January 1913, S. 341.
232 Franzius, Georg, *Kiautschou*, a.a.O, S. 92f.
233 *Ostasiatischer Lloyd*, Shanghai, Oktober, November 1912.
234 Bayerische Staatsbibliothek München, Signatur Ana 517.
235 Für diesen Wettbewerb spricht die Tatsache, daß der Bahnhof am anderen Ende der Schantung-Bahn, der Stadtbahnhof in Qingdao, nicht erweitert wurde, obwohl auch er eher die Maße eines Kleinstadtbahnhofs hatte.
236 Vgl. Bach, Kurt, »Vom Bau der Schantung-Eisenbahn«, a.a.O., S. 492f.
237 Bundesarchiv Potsdam, Gesandtschaft China, Akte 985, Blatt 152.
238 Bundesarchiv Potsdam, Gesandtschaft China, Akte 984, Blatt 196, 226.

239 Bundesarchiv Potsdam, Gesandtschaft China Akte 984, Blatt 33.
240 Wright, Arnold, a.a.O., S. 604.
241 *Ostasiatischer Lloyd*, Shanghai, 15. Juni 1913, S. 67.
242 Forsyth, Robert Coventry, *Shantung. The Sacred Province of China*, Shanghai 1912, S. 165.
243 *Ostasiatischer Lloyd*, Shanghai, 26. Juni 1908.
244 Samagalski, Alan und Buckley, Michael, *China. A Travel Survival Kit*, Victoria, Australia 1984, S. 479.
245 Kreuzgewölbe gibt es in der chinesischen Architektur äußerst selten, Tonnengewölbe sind dagegen bei Gräbern und Torbauten sehr verbreitet.
246 *Ostasiatischer Lloyd*, Shanghai 6. Juli 1900, S. 509.
247 *Ostasiatischer Lloyd*, Shanghai, 28. Oktober 1904, S. 741.
248 Stenz, Georg Maria, *In der Heimat des Konfuzius*, Steyl 1902, S. 135.
249 Vgl. Hartwich, Richard, *Steyler Missionare in China*, Bd. 1, »Missionarische Erschließung Südshantungs 1879–1903«, St. Augustin 1983, S. 198f, 319, 384.
250 Vgl. *Ostasiatischer Lloyd*, Shanghai, 13. März 1914, S. 232f.
251 Vgl. Hartwich, Richard, a.a.O., Bd. 1, Lageplan S. 526f.
252 Vgl. ebd., Bd. 3, »Republik China und der Erste Weltkrieg 1911–1919, S. 126, 291.
253 Ebd., Bd. 1, S. 500f.
254 Übersetzung aus der *Hongkong Daily Press* erschienen in: *Tsingtauer Neueste Nachrichten*, Tsingtau, 5. September 1913.
255 Vgl. Franzius, Georg, *Kiautschou*, a.a.O., S. 98f.
256 Vgl. Huguenin, C., *Geschichte des III. See-Bataillons*, Tsingtau 1912, S. 3–8.
257 Dieser Vertragstext wurde zum Vorbild für Großbritanniens 99jährige Pachtung der »New Territories« bei Hongkong. Das Ablaufen der Pachtzeit 1997 und die Diskussionen um der Rückgabe der englischen Kronkolonie erinnern an die Parallele mit dem ehemaligen deutschen Schutzgebiet Qingdao. Vgl. Mohr, F.W. *Handbuch für das Schutzgebiet Kiautschou*, Tsingtau 1911.
258 So liegt Tianjin (Tientsin) am Kaiserkanal und am Hai He-Fluß (Paiho), Shanghai am Huangpu-Fluß (Whangpoo), kurz bevor er in den Yangzi (Yangtze) und dieser in das Meer mündet, Wuhan (Hankou) 1100 km flußaufwärts am Yangzi (Yangtze) und Guangzhou (Kanton) am Zhujiang (Perlfluß). Die britische Kolonie Hongkong und die portugiesische Kolonie Macao liegen im Mündungsbereich des Perlflusses. Als einzige vergleichbare europäische Stadtneugründung in China wurde ab 1898 die Stadt Dalian durch russische Ingenieure angelegt. Auf der Liaodong-Halbinsel (Liautung-Halbinsel, Kwantung-Halbinsel) bestand damals vor der russischen Besetzung ebenfalls keine Infrastruktur. Erst der Bau der Transsibirischen Eisenbahn zwischen Moskau, Wladiwostok, Harbin und Dalian – 1891 begonnen und am 3. November 1901 vollendet – machte diese äußerst großzügige Stadtanlage und den eisfreien Seehafen am südöstlichen Endpunkt der Transsibirischen Eisenbahn möglich.
259 Wagner, Rudolf und Buchmann, E., *Eine Reise durch die Deutschen Kolonien*. Bd. 6, »Kiautschou«, Berlin 1913.
260 Vgl. Reichsmarineamt (Hrsg.), *Denkschrift betreffend die Entwicklung des Kiautschou-Gebiets in der Zeit vom Oktober 1904 bis Oktober 1905*, Berlin 1906, S. 7.
261 Vgl. Schrameier, Wilhelm, *Aus Kiautschous Verwaltung*, Jena 1914, S. 52.
262 Matzat, Wilhelm, *Die Tsingtauer Landordnung des Chinesenkommissars Wilhelm Schrameier*, Bonn 1985, S. 27f.
263 *Deutsch-Asiatische Warte*, Tsintau, 20. April 1899.
264 Ab 1842 wurden die ersten ausländischen Niederlassungen von Großbritannien gegründet. Nur in festgelegten Gebieten, die sich an bestehende chinesische Hafenstädte anschlossen, durften Ausländer Land erwerben. Ebenso war in Beijing nur das Gesandtschaftsviertel für Ausländer zum Wohnen freigegeben. Lediglich Missionare bildeten die Ausnahme.
265 Weicker, Hans, *Kiautschou. Das deutsche Schutzgebiet in Ostasien*, Berlin 1908, S. 67.
266 Godshall, Wilson Leon, *Tsingtau under Three Flags*, Shanghai 1929, S. 130.
267 Vgl. zur Entwicklung Qingdaos die Denkschriften 1897 bis 1909 des Reichsmarineamts (Hrsg.)
268 *Social Shanghai*, Shanghai, 1906–1912.
269 Schrameier, Wilhelm, *Aus Kiautschous Verwaltung*, Jena 1914, S. 32.
270 Wilhelm, Richard, a.a.O., S. 188.
271 So schrieb Alfons Paquet: »Auf der Anhöhe liegt der Gouverneurspalast, der in seiner herausfordernden Wucht an das Posener Kaiserschloß erinnert.« Paquet, Alfons, a.a.O., S. 297.
272 Vgl. Hobow, Junichi, *Tsingtao. The Riviera of the Far East*, Tsingtao 1922.
273 Er hält den »unzulässigen Termindruck, der einen Kostenvoranschlag nicht möglich machte,« für die Verteuerung verantwortlich. »Die entstandenen Mehrkosten haben nicht die Fassade zur Ursache«, die Verblendung in Granitsteinmauerwerk kostete in Qingdao damals nur ein Fünftel des in Berlin üblichen. Vgl. Bundesarchiv Freiburg, Kiautschou-Akte RM 3/v. 6995, Blatt 17f.
Eine Geschichte dieser Villa läßt sich an dieser Stelle aufklären: Der deutsche Gouverneur von Qingdao, Oskar Truppel, wurde nicht vom Kaiser Wihelm II. persönlich abgesetzt, weil er sich einen Palast hat bauen lassen. Truppel hielt sich während des Baues zu einem 22-monatigen Heimaturlaub in Deutschland auf und kam erst im September 1906 wieder zurück.
274 Mahlke, »Das neue Gouvernements-Dienstgebäude in Tsingtau (Kiautschou)« in: *Zentralblatt der Bauverwaltung*, Berlin, 17. August 1907, S. 444–447.
275 *Deutsch-Asiatische Warte. Amtlicher Anzeiger des Kiautschou-Gebietes*, Tsintau, 20. April 1899. 1. Jg. S. 1.
276 Kreuzgewölbe waren Ausdruck der europäischen Baukultur und Bautechnik, die hier im Wettstreit mit der chinesischen Kultur stand. Einfache Tonnengewölbe wurden in der chinesischen Architektur regelmäßig bei Torgebäuden verwendet, dagegen waren Kreuzgewölbe oder Überschneidungen von zwei Tonnengewölben in China nahezu unbekannt.
277 Nellist, George F., a.a.O., S. 135f.
278 Reichsmarineamt, a.a.O. *Denkschrift 1897–1898*, Berlin 1899, S. 12.
279 Nellist, George F., a.a.O., S. 135f.
280 *Ostasiatischer Lloyd*, Shanghai, 29. Mai 1914, S. 485.
281 Paquet, Alfons, a.a.O., S. 297.
282 Häftlinge, die länger als sechs Monate einsitzen mußten, wurden ins Chinesengefängnis in dem 15 km entfernten Dorf Licun (Litsun) gebracht. Die Tafel mit der Aufschrift »Chinesengefängnis« befindet sich heute im Qingdaoer Stadtmuseum. Das Gefängnis für Europäer lag im Ostteil der Europerstadt und war bereits 1900 fertiggestellt worden. Es lag neben dem früheren chinesischen Yamen, in dem in den ersten Jahren die gesamte deutsche Verwaltung untergebracht war.
283 Behme, Fr. und Krieger, M., *Führer durch Tsingtau und Umgebung*. 3. Auflage, Wolfenbüttel 1906, S. 99.
284 Reichsmarineamt, a.a.O. *Denkschrift 1902–1903*, Berlin 1904, S. 44.
285 *Ostasiatischer Lloyd*, Shanghai, 9. August 1907.
286 »Die Maschinenfabrik Germania, das erste Spezialwerk des Kontinents für den Bau von Brauereien und Mälzereien, hat eine große Zahl überseeischer gut prosperierender Brauereien nach modernem deutschen System eingerichtet, so sind unter anderem fast sämtliche japanische Großbrauereien nach ihren Plänen gebaut und mit ihren Maschinen eingerichtet worden.« *Ostasiatischer Lloyd*, Shanghai, 16. Dezember 1904.
287 *Ostasiatischer Lloyd*, Shanghai, 2. September 1904, S. 402.
288 Vgl. *Ostasiatischer Lloyd*, Shanghai, 1. März 1907, S. 367.
289 Wang Tan; Fujimori, Terunobu; Xü Feipeng, *The architectural heritage of modern China: Qingdao*, Beijing 1992, S. 59.
290 Reichsmarineamt, a.a.O., *Denkschrift 1908–1909*, Berlin 1910, S. 54.
291 *Ostasiatischer Lloyd*, Shanghai, 19. Januar 1912, S. 56.
292 Ebd. Es handelt sich um ein Gedicht von Ernst von Wildenbruch (1845–1909).
293 *Deutsch-Asiatische Warte*, Tsintau, 20. April 1899.
294 *Deutsch-Asiatische Warte*, Tsingtau, 20. November 1901.
295 Huguenin, C., *Geschichte des III. See-Bataillons*, Tsingtau 1912, S. 128.
296 Reichsmarineamt, a.a.O., *Denkschrift 1899–1900*, Berlin 1901, S. 37.
297 Vgl. Kronecker, Franz, *Fünfzehn Jahre Kiautschou. Eine kolonialmedizinische Studie*, Berlin 1913, S. 15.
298 ebd. S. 20f.
299 *Deutsch-Asiatische Warte*, Tsingtau, 4. September 1901.
300 Vgl. Mohr, F.W., *Handbuch für das Schutzgebiet Kiautschou*, Tsingtau 1911, S. 392: »Schulordnung für die Kaiserliche Gouvernements-Schule in Tsingtau« vom 24.7.1909.
301 Vgl. *Ostasiatischer Lloyd*, Shanghai, 12. Februar 1909, S. 323.
302 Vgl. ebd., 11. Dezember 1914, S. 553.
303 Am 29. September 1912 besuchte der Reformpolitiker Sun Yixian (Sun Yat-sen) die Hochschule und hielt eine Rede vor den Studenten, in: *Ostasiatischer Lloyd*, Shanghai, 11. Oktober 1912, S. 331.
304 Rothkegel, Curt, »Evangelische Kirche für Tsingtau-Kiautschou«, in: *Zentralblatt für das Deutsche Baugewerbe*, Berlin, 26. März 1909.
305 ebd.
306 Vgl. *Tsingtauer Missions Korrespondenz*, Tsingtau, 3. Jg., 1. Juni 1933, H. 2, S. 31f.
307 *Steyler Missionsbote*, 1934. S. 146, »Kirchweih in Tsingtau«.
308 Vgl. *Deutsch-Asiatische Warte*, Tsintau, 20. April 1899.
309 Hartwich, Richard, a.a.O., Bd. 1, S. 472.
310 Lutschewitz plante die 1908 eingeweihte Christus-Kirche in der 45 km von Qingdao entfernten Kreisstadt Jimo (Tsimo). Vgl. *Ostasiatischer Lloyd*, Shanghai, 12. Juni 1908, S. 1121.
311 Inhaltlich unterschieden sich die beiden Missionen stark voneinander: »Die evangelische Berliner Mission treibt Mission in der Art, wie seit alters Mission getrieben wird. Die Missionare suchen durch persönlichen Verkehr und durch Liebestätigkeit, namentlich durch Schulen und Hospitäler, an das Herz der Leute heranzukommen. (…) Heiden, die Christen werden wollen, werden dann als Taufbewerber in einem meistens ein Jahr dauernden Taufunterricht über die Hauptstücke des Katechismus belehrt und nach einer Prüfung (…) getauft.« Weicker, Hans, *Kiautschou, das deutsche Schutzgebiet in Ostasien*, Berlin 1908, S. 188.

312 Vgl. Behme, Fr. und Krieger, M., a.a.O., S. 71f.
313 Wilhelm, Richard und Blumhardt, Hanna, *Unsere Schulen in Tsingtau*, Berlin o.J., S. 3f.
314 Vgl. Mohr, F. W., a.a.O., S. 451.
315 Richard Wilhelm lebte bis 1920 in Qingdao und gründete 1925 in Frankfurt/Main das China-Institut.
316 Wilhelm, Richard, a.a.O., S. 171f.
317 Man hatte den Standort so gewählt, daß er bequem von den Schiffen aus erreicht werden konnte. Allerdings verlagerte sich nach Eröffnung des großen Hafens im März 1904 der gesamte Schiffsverkehr weg vom Geschäftszentrum ins etwa 3 Kilometer entfernte Hafenviertel.
318 Reichsmarineamt, a.a.O., *Denkschrift 1901–1902*, Berlin 1903, S. 25.
319 *Nachrichten aus Kiautschou*, Shanghai, 28. Oktober 1899.
320 Architekt Rothkegel hatte bereits den deutschen Klub Concordia in Tianjin erbaut, ein Jahr später stellte er das Gebäude des Pekingklubs fertig.
321 Archiv T. Warner, Darmstadt.
322 *Tsingtauer Neueste Nachrichten*, Tsingtau, 2. November 1913, S. 2.
323 Vgl. Granet, Marcel, *Das chinesische Denken, Inhalt, Form, Charakter*, Frankfurt 1985.
324 Während seines zweitägigen Besuches in Qingdao ab dem 28. September 1912 wohnte der chinesische Reformpolitiker Dr. Sun Yixian (Sun Yat-sen, Sun Zhongshan; 1866–1925) im Strandhotel. Mit seiner Familie und den Begleitern hatte er dort 16 Zimmer belegt. Vgl. *Ostasiatischer Lloyd*, Shanghai, 11. Oktober 1912.
325 *Ostasiatischer Lloyd*, Shanghai, 18. November 1910, S. 498.
326 *Nachrichten aus Kiautschou*, Beiblatt zum *Ostasiatischen Lloyd*, Shanghai, 30. September 1899.
327 Vgl. *Adress-Buch des Deutschen Kiautschou-Gebietes für 1905*, Tsingtau, S. 21.
328 Archiv T. Warner, Darmstadt
329 Archiv T. Warner, Darmstadt
330 *Ostasiatischer Lloyd*, Shanghai, 18. November 1910, S. 498.
331 Falkenberg, Rainer, *Luis Weilers Briefe aus China.* in Kuo Heng-yü und Leutner, Mechthild, *Beiträge zu den deutsch-chinesischen Beziehungen*, München 1986, S. 123.
332 Bundesarchiv Potsdam, Gesandtschaft China, Akte 984, Blatt 54f.
333 Weicker, Hans, a.a.O., S. 145.
334 Maercker, *Die Entwicklung des Kiautschougebiets. Zweiter Teil.* Berlin 1903, S. 62f.
335 Reichsmarineamt, a.a.O., *Denkschrift 1903–1904*, Berlin 1905, Abbildung 6a.
336 Mohr, F. W., a.a.O., S. 206.
337 Vgl. Behme, Fr. und Krieger, M., a.a.O., S. 42.
338 Vgl. Wright, Arnold, a.a.O., S. 614.
339 Wang Tan; Fujimori, Terunobu; Xü Feipeng, a.a.O., S. 42.
340 *Adressbuch des Deutschen Kiautschou-Gebietes für 1913–1914*, Tsingtau 1913.
341 Reichsmarineamt, a.a.O, *Denkschrift 1901–1902*, Berlin 1903, S. 36.
342 In der in Shanghai monatlich erscheinenden Illustrierten *Social Shanghai* wurden regelmäßig diese »Beautiful homes in Shanghai« vorgestellt.
343 Der erste Bewohner dieses Hauses, Hauptmann Freiherr von Liliencron, war von 1899 bis 1902 Adjutant des Gouverneurs, kehrte nach Deutschland zurück und war von 1912 bis 1913 wieder in Qingdao, diesmal als Kommandeur des III. See-Bataillons. Vgl. Huguenin, C., a.a.O., S. 58.
344 Im Sockelgeschoß des Gebäudes.
345 Vgl. *Ostasiatischer Lloyd*, Shanghai, 29. Mai 1914.
346 Archiv Prof. Dr. Matzat, Bonn.
347 Archiv T. Warner, Darmstadt.
348 Im Führer durch Tsingtau von 1904 wird ein Rundgang durch die Stadt beschrieben: »Am Gouvernementsplatz wendet man sich nach Nord-Westen und schlägt den Hohenloheweg ein nach der Mission zu. Auf dem Wege kommt man an mehreren hübschen Villen vorbei, in deren zweiter sich die Dienstwohnung des Gouvernementspfarrers befindet, und genießt eine hübsche Aussicht auf die Stadt und den Hafen.« Schon in der folgenden Auflage des Reiseführers wurde das Wohnhaus nicht mehr erwähnt. Vgl. Behme, F. und Krieger, M., a.a.O. S. 44. und dies., *Führer durch Tsingtau und Umgebung*, 3. Auflage, Wolfenbüttel 1906, S. 67.

NOTES

1 Wilhelm, Richard, *Die Seele Chinas*, Berlin 1926, p. 266.
Richard Wilhelm lived in Qingdao (Tsingtao) from 1899 to 1920 and founded the Chinese Institute in Frankfurt in 1925.
2 Hildebrand, Heinrich, *Der Tempel Ta-chüeh-sy (Tempel des grossen Erkennens) bei Peking*, Berlin 1897, Reprint Peking 1943.
3 Boerschmann, Ernst, *Chinesische Architektur*, Berlin 1925, and *Chinesische Pagoden*, Berlin and Leipzig 1931.
4 Segalen, Victor, René Leys, Frankfurt 1982, p. 43. The book was written in Beijing in 1913/14 and was published in 1922.
5 Fischer, Martin, *Szetschuan. Diplomatie und Reisen in China während der letzten drei Jahre der Kaiserzeit,* Munich and Vienna 1968, p. 53.
6 »At the turn of the 20th century, in the coastal cities of China, there was an advent of European and American influences entering the mainstream of Chinese architectural tradition. From then on examples of modern architecture in China include Western style buildings designed by foreign architects and part of them were by German. Architectural historians in China consider these buildings a part of the history of Chinese modern architecture.« Prof. LUO Xiao-wei, Faculty of Architecture Tongji University, Shanghai, 5 April 1992.
7 Muthesius, Hermann in *Centralblatt der Bauverwaltung,* Berlin, 8 September 1900, p. 429.
8 *Ostasiatischer Lloyd*, Shanghai, 13. September 1912, p. 232.
9 Cf. *Tsingtauer Neueste Nachrichten*, Tsingtao, 16 December 1913, p. 2.
10 Paquet, Alfons, *Li oder Im neuen Osten,* Frankfurt 1913, p. 297. Paquet was the secretary of the Deutscher Werkbund from 1910.
11 Kaiser Wilhelm II was interested in architecture. He was able to draw and thus influenced architecture during the German Empire. Cf. Seidel, Paul: *Der Kaiser und die Kunst*, Berlin 1907, p. 36.
12 Cf., for example, Lauber, Wolfgang, *Deutsche Architektur in Togo. 1884–1914*, Stuttgart 1993.
13 Cf. Rohrbach, Paul, *Die deutschen Kolonien*, Dachau 1914.
14 *Ostasiatischer Lloyd*, Shanghai, 13 January 1905, p. 82 and 8. September 1905, p. 459f.
15 Rothkegel, Curt, *Tätigkeit des Architekten Curt Rothkegel in China*, Liechtenstein 1940, unpublished manuscript.
16 Segalen, Victor, *René Leys*, Frankfurt 1982, p. 9.
17 Beijing's great city wall was demolished in 1958 and replaced by a ring road. A remainder of the wall can be found behind todays central station. Only few of the city gates still stand.
18 *Ostasiatischer Lloyd*, Shanghai, 15 September 1911, p. 222.
19 Wilhelm, Richard, *Die Seele Chinas*, Berlin 1926, p. 25.
20 Wilhelmy, Emil, *China. Land und Leute.* Berlin 1904. p. 548.
21 *Potsdamer Schlösser in Geschichte und Kunst*, Leipzig 1984, p. 152.
22 *Ostasiatischer Lloyd*, Shanghai, 29 May 1903, p. 874.
23 »Anyone who has lived for a longer period of time in the capital of the Chinese empire will be willing to admit that representatives of foreign nations in Peking have little for their pleasure and amusement apart from the rather dull, ever unchanging societies and receptions.« *Ostasiatischer Lloyd*, Shanghai, 20 December 1912, p. 560.
24 Hildebrand, Heinrich, *Der Tempel Ta-chüeh-sy bei Peking*, Berlin 1897.
25 Bundesarchiv Potsdam, Gesandtschaft China, File 1588, p. 44, 74.
26 *Social Shanghai.* A Magazine for Men and Women, Shanghai, July 1906.
27 The survey and planning of the 1,500 km long railway track from Beijing to Wuhan had been commissioned by the German Government Architect, Heinrich Hildebrand, who in turn, was under commission from the Executive Official for Railways and Manufacturers, Taotai Tseng in 1896/97. Hildebrand directed the construction of the German Shantung Railway from Qingdao to Jinan (...). Cf. Franzius, Georg, *Kiautschou. Deutschlands Erwerbung in Ostasien*, Berlin 1898, p. 68f.
28 *Ostasiatischer Lloyd*, Shangai, 13 February and 5 June 1914.
29 *The East of Asia Magazine*. A non-political illustrated quarterly, Shanghai 1902, p. 5.
30 *The Far Eastern Review*, Manila, Shanghai, Yokohama, July 1915, p. 64f.
31 Sirén, Osvald, *The walls and gates of Peking*, London 1924, p. 171.
32 Intermediate landings every sixteen steps make climbing the stairs pleasant and easy. The steps are 15/34 cm in proportion.
33 Eaves height 43 cm, depth approximately 30 cm.
34 Sirén Osvald, loc cit., p. 173. The conversion was unpopular in general »What use is it to preserve the defiant outer gate, to give the windows elaborate covers and to surround it with a gallery accessed by an expensive open staircase that no one actually climbs, Peking's most beautiful and monumental gate is lost forever.« *Ostasiatischer Lloyd*, Shangai, 17 September 1915.
35 *Ostasiatischer Lloyd*, Shanghai, 7 July 1911. p. 17.
36 See Curt Rothkegel, loc cit.
37 Rothkegel, Curt, loc cit.
38 *Centralblatt der Bauverwaltung*, Berlin 1894, p. 443.
39 Rothkegel later wrote: »The president of the provisional parliament said that the number of deputies, prescribed to me by the building authority, for the lower house at 450 as too low (...) and wanted to have it raised to approximately 600.« Bundesarchiv, Potsdam, Gesandtschaft China, File 853, p. 13. The plan was revised by the architect.
40 *Ostasiatischer Lloyd*, Shanghai, 9 December 1910. p. 565f.
41 See Woodhead, H.G.W., *The Truth about the Chinese Republic*, London, 1925, p. 13–26 and Weggel, Oskar, *Geschichte Chinas im 20. Jahrhundert*, Stuttgart 1989. p. 28.
42 Bundesarchiv Potsdam, Gesandtschaft China, File 853, Sheet 105.
43 *Ostasiatischer Lloyd*, Shanghai, 11 November 1910, p. 463.
44 *The Far Eastern Review*, Manila, Shanghai, Yokohama, September 1913, p. 121f.

45 Bundesarchiv Potsdam, Gesandtschaft China, File 853, Sheet 92–93.
46 Curt Rothkegel, loc cit.
47 *Ostasiatischer Lloyd*, Shanghai, 18 April 1913, p. 375.
48 *Ostasiatischer Lloyd*, Shanghai, 29 May 1914, p. 485.
49 von Salzmann, Erich, »Die Deutsche Gesandtschaft in Peking«, in *Die Woche*, Berlin, 1 January–31 March 1914, p. 24–29.
50 FEI-SHI (Fischer, Emil), *Guide to Peking and its Environs*, Tientsin 1909, p. 19.
51 *Ostasiatischer Lloyd*, Shanghai, 17 February 1911, p. 178.
52 The first of the honorary arches in front of the Ming tombs near Beijing is of similar proportions. It is, however, wider due to its five passageways.
53 FEI-SHI, loc cit., p. 66. The Latin text was published in the *Ostasiatischer Lloyd* on 28 November 1902, p. 983.
54 *Ostasiatischer Lloyd*, Shanghai, 28 November 1902.
55 Wilhelm, Richard, loc cit. p. 30, 263.
56 Bundesarchiv Potsdam, Gesandtschaft China, File 1048, Sheet 221.
57 Cf. Bundesarchiv Potsdam, Gesandtschaft China, File 266, Sheet 272.
58 *Ostasiatischer Lloyd*, Shanghai, 20 May 1904, p. 872.
59 Loesch, Karl C., *Deutsche Züge im Antlitz der Erde*, München (year not specified), p. 171.
60 Wright, Arnold, and Cartwright, H. A., *Twentieth Century Impressions of Hongkong, Shanghai and other Treaty Ports of China*, London 1908, p. 604.
61 Cf. Bundesarchiv Potsdam, Gesandtschaft China, File 266, Sheet 272.
62 *Ostasiatischer Lloyd*, Shanghai, 20 December 1912, p. 560.
63 Bundesarchiv Potsdam, Gesandtschaft China, File 697, Sheet 116.
64 Cf. Bundesarchiv Potsdam, Gesandtschaft China, File 1588, Sheet 133 (map from 1915).
65 *Ostasiatischer Lloyd*, Shanghai, 26 June 1908, p. 1215.
66 *Social Shanghai*, Shanghai 1906, p. 125.
67 *Hai-Ho Conservancy Board 1898–1919*, Tientsin, 1919, p. 37. During the winter months, the Hai He, which was Tianjin's link with the sea, froze and trading came to a standstill.
68 In 1894 the railway reached Shanhaiguan (Schanhaikwan), the point at which the Great Wall meets the sea, in 1899 it reached the city of Jinzhou (Chin Chow). See Rasmussen, O.D., *Tientsin. An Illustrated Outline History*, Tientsin, 1925, p. 95f.
69 The client was the »Chinese Government Railways«. The railway line runs parallel to the east bank of the Imperial Canal to Dezhou, crosses the Huang He (Yellow River) near Jinan (Tsinanfu) and goes further south to the Yangtze River. The north 625 km of this line were built by German engineers.
70 Rasmussen, O.D., loc cit. p. 27.
71 The American settlement was transferred to the English settlement in 1902. See Bundesarchiv Potsdam, Gesandtschaft China, File 1015, Sheet 314.
72 1772 Japanese, 1530 British, 753 Germans, 542 Americans, 294 French, 154 Russians, 93 Italians, 85 Swiss, 74 Danes, 54 Austro-Hungarians and others. See Imperial Japanese Government Railways: *An official guide to Eastern Asia*, Vol. 4 China. Tokyo 1915, p. 25.
73 Thus, in 1902 there were 255 British, 145 Japanese, 104 Germans, 46 Americans, 25 Russians, 19 Danes, 11 Austrians and 26 other Europeans resident in the English settlement. Of the 4300 Chinese residents approximately 1900 were employed by foreigners. See *Ostasiatischer Lloyd*, Shanghai, 28 November 1902, p. 977.
74 See Navarra, Bruno, *China und die Chinesen*, Bremen und Shanghai 1901, p. 1073, and Wilhelmy, Emil, *China. Land und Leute*, Berlin 1904, p. 692ff.
75 The number of officers and troops stationed in north China in 1902 was given as follows: 1920 French, 1900 English, 1600 Germans, 1280 Japanese, 980 Russians, 880 Italians, 150 Americans; a total of approximately 8700 men.
76 They consisted of 1720 British, 1200 French, 420 Japanese, 220 Italians, 170 Americans, 120 Russians and 100 Germans.
77 *Ostasiatischer Lloyd*, Shanghai, 20 December 1912, p. 556.
78 China lost the Japanese-Chinese War of 1894/95. Japan won the Island of Taiwan (Formosa) but had to relinquish its claim to the areas conquered in north China and Lüshun (Port Arthur), the most important north Chinese navy port which had also fallen into their hands. See Wilhelmy, Emil, loc cit. p. 516ff.
79 Rasmussen, O.D., loc cit., p.95.
80 See Bundesarchiv Potsdam, Gesandtschaft China, File 1051, Sheet 55.
81 The level of annual contributions determined the number of votes per member in the local authority assembly, whereby the maximum number of votes per member was fixed at 12. Thus, in 1911 almost half of the votes belonged to the Tientsin Construction Company and the Deutsche Niederlassungs Gesellschaft (German Settlement Company) which belonged to the German-Asian Bank. See Bundesarchiv Potsdam, Gesandtschaft China, File 1050, Sheet 11 and File 1048, Sheet 99 and 110.
82 A census was taken in the German settlement in 1913. The results of the census were: 1205 Chinese, 284 Europeans, Americans and Japanese civilians which included 117 German civilians and 304 German soldiers. At the time, however, there were a total of 750 German civilians living in Tianjin. See *Ostasiatischer Lloyd*, Shanghai, 30 May 1913 and *The Imperial Japanese Government Railways*, loc cit., p. 25.
83 Bundesarchiv Potsdam, Gesandtschaft China, File 1050, Sheet 184f and 310.
84 Bundesarchiv Potsdam, Gesandtschaft China, File 1050, Sheet 216 (Letter of 7 May 1912).
85 ibid.
86 Bundesarchiv Potsdam, Gesandtschaft China, File 1050, Sheet 454 (Decree of 15 August 1912).
87 Those who settled in the German settlement and bought sites and houses included a former Chinese sea customs director, the sons of Princes Qing (Ch'ing), Zailun (Tsai-lun), Zaixun (Tsai-hsün) and Zaifu (Tsai-fu) and General Zhang Xun (Chang Hsün), »who next to Yuan Shi-kai is the most important man in China at present outside Peking«. See Bundesarchiv Potsdam, Gesandtschaft China, File 1050, Sheet 190f and 274.
88 *Tianjin jindai jianzhu*, Tianjin 1990, p. 174.
89 Wright, Arnold, loc cit., p. 730.
90 Bundesarchiv Potsdam, Gesandtschaft China, File 1015, Sheet 198.
91 Bundesarchiv Potsdam, Gesandtschaft China, File 1015, Sheet 193 (*Tageblatt für Nordchina*, Tientsin, 1 August 1907).
92 *China Times*, 1 August 1907: »With concord small affairs grow; with discord the greatest concerns fall to pieces.« Bundesarchiv Potsdam, Gesandtschaft China, File 1015, Sheet 195.
93 *Ostasiatischer Lloyd*, Shanghai, 3 April 1908, p. 639.
94 *Ostasiatischer Lloyd*, Shanghai, 15 June 1913, p. 61.
95 Koberstein, F., *Tientsin und Umgebung*, Tientsin 1906, p. 38.
96 These Roland columns (statues of bare-headed, sword-bearing knights in armour) were erected in north German towns between the 14th and 18th centuries as a symbol of their municipal rights and freedom. See Wright, Arnold. loc. cit., p. 726.
97 *Ostasiatischer Lloyd*, Shanghai, 6 November 1903, p. 727; the book in question is Franzius, Georg, *Kiautschou, Deutschlands Erwerbung in Ostasien*, Berlin 1898.
98 Wright, Arnold, loc cit., p. 604.
99 Bundesarchiv Potsdam, Gesandtschaft China, File 1051, Sheet 50.
100 *Ostasiatischer Lloyd*, Shanghai, 8 April 1910.
101 See *Huazhong Architecture*, No. 2, Wucang and Hubei 1987; the building in the »Symposium of conference« is mistakingly identified as the German Consulate.
102 Bundesarchiv Potsdam, Gesandtschaft China, File 1049, Sheet 76.
103 See Boerschmann, Ernst, *Chinesische Architektur*, Vol. 1, Berlin 1925, p. 15.
104 See Wright, Arnold, loc cit., p. 746 and Koberstein, F., loc cit., p. 40.
105 Bundesarchiv Potsdam, Gesandtschaft China, File 1051, Sheet 141.
106 Franzius, Georg, *Kiautschou*, Berlin 1898, p. 17.
107 Wright, Arnold, loc cit., p. 59.
108 Arnold, *Picturesque Hongkong*, Hongkong 1911, p. 15.
109 The *Ostasiatischer Lloyd* wrote on 27 September 1901: »In London there are 60 inhabitants for every acre of built area, in Glasgow it is 61 and in Hongkong 66. This overpopulation of course fosters the endemic incidence of plague, and probably also malaria and similar diseases.« The population density was therefore 14,826 inhabitants/km^2 in London, 15,074 in Glasgow and was highest in Hongkong at 16,309 inhabitants per km^2.
110 Schrameier, Wilhelm, *Aus Kiautschous Verwaltung*, Jena 1914, p. 28.
111 ibid. p. 18f, p. 43f and Wright, Arnold, loc cit., p. 59.
112 *Ostasiatischer Lloyd*, Shanghai, 29 May 1914, p. 485.
113 Wright, Arnold, loc cit., p. 171.
114 *Tsingtauer Neueste Nachrichten*, Tsingtao, 16 December 1913, p. 2.
115 The German Club Concordia in Shanghai was built only five years later. It was in neo-Renaissance style and instantly identifiable as a typical German building.
116 *Ostasiatischer Lloyd*, Shanghai, 23 January 1903, p. 158.
117 Pott, F. L. H., *A Short History of Shanghai*, Shanghai 1928, p. 51, 79.
118 *Ostasiatischer Lloyd*, Shanghai, 7 September 1906, p. 460.
119 *Ostasiatischer Lloyd*, Shanghai, 21 September 1906, p. 555.
120 *Ostasiatischer Lloyd*, Shanghai, 7 September 1906, p. 461.
121 *Ostasiatischer Lloyd*, Shanghai, 14 September 1906, p. 508.
122 *Ostasiatischer Lloyd*, Shanghai, 31 August 1906, p. 415–416.
123 The first settlement to be established in 1843 was the English settlement; in 1862/63 it was joined by the American settlement and became the International Settlement. The French concession was established in 1848 and was located between the International Settlement and the Chinese city; the French concession was administered independently of the International Settlement. In 1899 the International Settlement was expanded from 7.15 km^2 to 22.6 km^2 in, the French concession was expanded in 1914.
124 *Ostasiatischer Lloyd*, Shanghai, 8 January 1904, p. 40.

125 To clarify the increases: in 1843 the price was 0.30 gold marks per m^2, in 1903, 44.50 gold marks per m^2; cf. Woas, Franz, »Ostasiatische Architektur der neueren Zeit«, in *Deutsche Bauzeitung*, Berlin, 7 September 1904, p. 451.
126 Luff, Reginald, »Buildings in Shanghai«, in *Social Shanghai*, Shanghai, July 1908, p. 26.
127 *Ostasiatischer Lloyd*, Shanghai, 16 December 1910, p. 403.
128 Pott, F. L. H., loc cit., p. 233.
129 *Far East Magazine*, Shanghai and Tientsin, December 1934.
130 Cf. *Zentralblatt der Bauverwaltung*, Berlin 1899, p. 515.
131 *Shanghaier Nachrichten*, supplement to the *Ostasiatischer Lloyd*, Shanghai, 18 January 1907. p. 10f.
132 *Social Shanghai*, Shanghai, January–June 1907, p. 289 bis 295.
133 The new building was financed by 20,000 taels from the Club's own resources; 100,000 taels from members specified as 7.5 percent shares and 280,000 taels mortgage from the German-Asian Bank at 7 percent interest. 1 tael was equivalent to approximately 2.7 gold marks.
134 *Shanghaier Nachrichten*, 8 February 1908, p. 27.
135 Wright, Arnold, loc cit., p. 373.
136 Cf. on both architects: *Shanghaier Nachrichten*, Shanghai, 10 March 1911, 8 February 1907 (pictures of the architects) and *Social Shanghai*, Shanghai 1907, p. 294.
137 *Social Shanghai*, Shanghai, January – June 1907. p. 17–20.
138 The 71 victims were buried in the »Iltis Cemetary« on the coast of Shandong, the memorial was decorated with wreaths each year on 23 July. Cf. *Ostasiatischer Lloyd*, Shanghai, 31 July 1903, p. 168.
139 *Shanghaier Nachrichten*, 11 September 1908, p. 197.
140 Bundesarchiv Potsdam, Gesandtschaft China, File 918, Sheet 289–295.
141 Franke, Otto, *Erinnerungen aus zwei Welten*, Berlin 1954, p. 61.
142 *Der Auslandsdeutsche*, Stuttgart, Vol. 1, No. 6, June 1912, p. 3.
143 Cf. *Ostasiatischer Lloyd*, Shanghai, 4 December 1903, p. 897 and Wright, Arnold, loc cit., p. 656.
144 *Ostasiatischer Lloyd*, Shanghai, 5 April 1901, p. 283.
145 *Ostasiatischer Lloyd*, Shanghai, 11 May 1900, p. 340f.
146 The *Ostasiatischer Lloyd* writes about the school: »There are two classrooms on the ground floor, each of which can accommodate 30 children. There are two more classrooms on the upper floor which are separated by sliding doors. A spacious assembly hall can be created by opening the doors.« *Ostasiatischer Lloyd*, Shanghai, 13 September 1901, p. 790f.; the assembly hall could accommodate more than 100 persons.
147 Cf. *Der Auslandsdeutsche*, Stuttgart, Vol. 1, June 1912.
148 Nellist, George F., *Men of Shanghai and North China*, Shanghai 1933, p. 375.
149 *Shanghaier Nachrichten*, Shanghai, 28 April 1911.
150 Cf. *Shanghaier Nachrichten*, Shanghai, 7 July 1911, »Bericht des Schulausschusses der Internationalen Niederlassung.« (Report of the School Committee of the International Settlement)
151 Information on the Kaiser Wilhelm School in: Weber, Dietrich (ed.), *Kaiser Wilhelm Schule zu Schanghai*, Shanghai 1935, p. 17.
152 Cf. *Ostasiatischer Lloyd*, Shanghai, 12 May 1905, p. 865.
153 Cf. Meid, Michiko, *Europäische und Nordamerikanische Architekten in Japan*, Dissertation, Cologne 1977, p. 264f.
154 Detailed description of the building and the interior in *Ostasiatischer Lloyd*, Shanghai, 24 October 1902, p.869–871.
155 Cf. Darwent, C.E., *Shanghai: A Handbook for Travellers and Residents*, Shanghai, 1920, p. 7: »The new Russian-Chinese Bank (…) is in the Italian Style with emblematic figures over the doors. The Chinese have misunderstood these figures, taking them for the foreign man's josses.«
156 Cf. *Ostasiatischer Lloyd*, Shanghai, 10 March 1911, p. 71f.
157 Cf. *Deutsche Bauzeitung*, Berlin, 7 September 1904, p. 450–452.
158 Cf. *Ostasiatischer Lloyd*, Shanghai, 1 August 1902, p. 616–617.
159 Woas, Franz, »Ostasiatische Architektur der neueren Zeit«, in *Deutsche Bauzeitung*, Berlin, 7 September 1904, p. 450–452.
160 The five-storey building on the corner of Hankou Road and Kiangsi Road was designed by the architects Davis & Thomas, built by Jardine, Matheson & Co. Cf. *Shanghaier Nachrichten*, 22 March 1907.
161 *Shanghaier Nachrichten*, 22 March 1907, p. 64.
162 *Shanghaier Nachrichten*, 3 January 1908, p. 3–4.
163 Wright, Arnold, loc cit., p. 794.
164 Wright, Arnold, loc cit., p. 604.
165 *Shanghaier Nachrichten*, 31 January 1908, p. 33.
166 Franz Woas described these villa neighbourhoods in 1904: »In Shanghai, the high price of land in the city centre has also resulted in houses being built further and further out in the open countryside. A ›Shanghai West‹ quarter has emerged which is particularly favoured by the Europeans, although rich Chinese have also taken up residence here. The new villas built here are not particularly distinctive and are all too similar to the British and American models. There are some examples of the old style in which houses here were initially built for the Europeans which are touching in their simplicity. Otherwise brick masonry dominates.« Woas, Franz, »Ostasiatische Architektur der neueren Zeit«, in *Deutsche Bauzeitung*, Berlin, 7 September 1904, p. 451.
167 Wright, Arnold, loc cit., p. 604. A picture of the house »Willfried«, p. 656.
168 Cf. *Social Shanghai*, Shanghai, January–June 1907, p. 294.
169 »Building Activities of Shanghai«, in *The Far Eastern Review*, Manila, Shanghai, Yokohama, September, October 1916. p. 144 and 181f.
170 Cf. *Shanghaier Nachrichten*, Shanghai, 12 June 1914, p. 194–195.
171 Cf. *Festschrift anläßlich des 25jährigen Bestehens der Staatlichen Tung-Chi Universität zu Woosung, China*, (Publication to mark the 25th jubilee of Tung-Chi State University in Woosung, China), Woosung 1932, p. 4.
172 Cf. Berrens, B., »Die Entwicklung der deutschen Medizin- und Ingenieurschule Schanghai«, in *Schülerverzeichnis 1916*, Shanghai 1916, p. 27f.
173 *Shanghaier Nachrichten*, Shanghai, 5 June 1914, p. 181f.
174 Cf. *Bericht über die Deutsche Ingenieurschule für Chinesen in Schanghai für das dritte Schuljahr (1914/15)*, Shanghai 1915, p. 16.
175 *Berliner Illustrierte Zeitung*, Berlin, 8 April 1923, p. 264.
176 *Denkschrift aus Anlaß der Feierlichen Einweihung der Tungchi Technischen Hochschule in Schanghai-Woosung*, (Publication to mark the opening of the Tung-Chi Technical Collage in Shanghai Woosung), Woosung 1924, p. 27.
177 On the history of the technical college cf. *Denkschrift aus Anlaß der Feierlichen Einweihung der Tungchi Technischen Hochschule in Schanghai-Woosung 1924*, and *Festschrift anläßlich des 25jährigen Bestehens der Staatlichen Tung-Chi Universität zu Woosung, China* Woosung 1932.
178 Weber, Dietrich (ed.), loc cit., p. 24.
179 Cf. *The Directory & Chronicle of China, Japan, Korea, Indo-China*, Hongkong 1937, p. E83.
180 Weber, Dietrich (ed.), loc cit., p. 26.
181 For more detailed information on Hudec, cf. *Slovensky Biograficky Slovnik, (833–1990)*, Martin 1987 and Nellist, George F., loc cit., p. 182, 187.
182 Cf. von Schab, »Geschichte der Deutschen Medizin- und Ingenieurschule 1907–1919«, in *Festschrift anläßlich des 25jährigen Bestehens der Staatlichen Tung-Chi Universität zu Woosung, China*, Woosung 1932, p. 1.
183 *Festschrift anläßlich des 25jährigen Bestehens der Staatlichen Tung-Chi Universität zu Woosung, China*, Woosung 1932, p. 2–3.
184 Cf. Stumpf, Richard, »Neuzeitliche Hochbauen in Shanghai im Jahre 1932/33«, in *Festschrift anläßlich des 25jährigen Bestehens der Staatlichen Tung-Chi Universität zu Woosung, China*, Woosung 1932, p. 166f.
185 Hankow had 850,000 inhabitants, Hanyang 400,000 and Wuchang 500,000.
186 Kawata, T., *Glimpses of China and Japan Trade Records*, Osaka 1919, p. 173.
187 Cf. *Ostasiatischer Lloyd*, Shanghai, 30 May 1913, p. 522.
188 Franzius, Georg, *Kiautschou. Deutschlands Erwerbung in Ostasien*. Berlin 1898, p. 69.
189 Macmillan, Allister, *Seaports of the Far East*, 2nd edition, London 1925, p. 169.
190 Paquet, Alfons, *Li oder Im neuen Osten*, Frankfurt 1913, p. 232.
191 Franzius, Georg, *Kiautschou. Deutschlands Erwerbung in Ostasien*. Berlin 1898, p. 70f.
192 ibid., p. 70.
193 Kawata, T., loc cit., p. 176.
194 Bundesarchiv Potsdam, Gesandtschaft China, File 1033 and 1034.
195 Bundesarchiv Potsdam, Gesandtschaft China, File 1050, Sheet 300.
196 *Ostasiatischer Lloyd*, Shanghai, 21 October 1910, p. 402.
197 In 1905 a m^2 on the embankment road cost 18 gold marks and at the back end 11 gold marks, in 1912 sites on the embankment road cost 43 gold marks/m^2 but only 17 to 21 goldmarks/m^2 at the back end. Chinese land in the vicinity of the concessions cost 8.50 to 15 gold marks/m^2 and the more remote site for the engineering school only 0.9 gold marks/m^2 Cf. Bundesarchiv Potsdam, Gesandtschaft China, File 640, Sheet 416f and 425, and File 1032, Sheet 267.
198 Cf. *Ostasiatischer Lloyd*, Shanghai, 5 May 1905, p. 816.
199 *Ostasiatischer Lloyd*, Shanghai, 1 December 1905, p. 1009.
200 Cf. *Ostasiatischer Lloyd*, Shanghai, 10 July 1908, p. 88f.
201 *Shanghaier Nachrichten*, Shanghai, 10 March 1911, p. 71f.
202 *Ostasiatischer Lloyd*, Shanghai, 29 March 1907, p. 547f.
203 *Ostasiatischer Lloyd*, Shanghai, 19 February 1909, p. 373.
204 ibid.
205 They sent detailed alternative designs to the German legation in Beijing, but with no success. Cf. Bundesarchiv Potsdam, Gesandtschaft China, File 640, Sheet 404–571.

206 Cf. on the theory of geomancy, Walters, Derek, *Feng Shui. Perfect placing of your hapiness and prosperity*, London, Singapore 1988.
207 In Qingdao, on the other hand, which was not developed by a private company, sites for schools and missions were provided free of charge by the German administration.
208 A detailed description can be found in Stenz, Georg Maria, »Der Kaiserkanal« in *Beiträge zur Kolonialpolitik und Kolonialwirtschaft*, Berlin 1903/04.
209 Wilhelmy, Emil: loc cit., p. 385.
210 Dukes, E.J.; Fielde, A., *Alltagsleben in China*, Basel 1892, p. 149.
211 Cf. Walters, Derek, loc cit., and Navarra, Bruno, loc cit., p. 491ff.
212 »It was believed that building church towers and factory chimneys was an unpardonable crime, because it disturbed the good mood of the spirit world.« Dukes, E.J. and Fielde, A., loc cit., p. 146–154.
213 Stenz, Georg Maria, »Der Kaiserkanal« in *Beiträge zur Kolonialpolitik und Kolonialwirtschaft*, Berlin 1903/04, p. 130.
214 Bökemann, »Über Wirtschaft und Verkehr in der Provinz Schantung« in *Koloniale Monatsblätter*, Berlin 1913, p. 132.
215 *Ostasiatischer Lloyd*, Shanghai, 1 November 1912, p. 397.
216 Bökemann, loc cit., p. 96.
217 Cf. *Ostasiatischer Lloyd*, Shanghai, 25 September 1903, p. 476.
218 Cf. Bach, Kurt, »Vom Bau der Schantung-Eisenbahn«, in *Zentralblatt der Bauverwaltung*, Berlin, 16 September 1905, p.467, 493.
219 Cf. Dost, Paul, *Deutsch-China und die Schantungbahn*, Krefeld 1981, p. 131f.
220 The Huang He was not important for transport. Due to the mud it carried along shipping could barely use it in its lower reaches. It had last changed its course after massive floods in 1852 and from then on flowed into the sea 400 kilometres further to the north.
221 »Easy movement of the troops of occupation is one of the prime criteria for the security of the colony (...)« Gerstenberg, Hans, »Die Wegebauten in Tsintau«, in Deutsche Kolonialgesellschaft (publisher), *Beiträge zur Kolonialpolitik und Kolonialwirtschaft*, vol. 1, Berlin 1899/1900, p. 128.
222 Cf. on the regulations: Betz, Heinrich, *Die wirtschaftliche Entwicklung der Provinz Schantung*, Tsingtao 1911, p. 60ff.
223 *Adressbuch des Deutschen Kiautschou-Gebiets für 1911–1912*, Tsingtao 1911, p. 75.
224 *Ostasiatischer Lloyd*, Shanghai, 20 September 1912, p. 262.
225 Crow, Carl, *Handbook for China*, Shanghai, 1921, p. 277.
226 *Ostasiatischer Lloyd*, Shanghai, 28 May 1909, p. 1073.
227 *Adress-Buch*, 1911–1912, loc cit., p. 75f.
228 Boerschmann, Ernst, *Chinesische Architektur*, Band 1, loc cit., plate 33 (brick gable) and plate 37 (brick architecture).
229 Boerschmann, Ernst, *Baukunst und Landschaft in China*, Berlin 1926, p. 78.
230 *Ostasiatischer Lloyd*, Shanghai, 4 November 1910, p. 440.
231 *The Far Eastern Review*, Manila, Shanghai, Yokohama, January 1913, p. 341.
232 Franzius, Georg, *Kiautschou*, loc cit., p. 92f.
233 *Ostasiatischer Lloyd*, Shanghai, October, November 1912.
234 Bayerische Staatsbibliothek, Munich, ref. Ana 517.
235 It is to the credit of this competition that the station at the other end of the Schantung Railway, the city station in Qingdao, was not extended, although it too was more in the scale of a small-town station.
236 Cf. Bach, Kurt, »Vom Bau der Schantung-Eisenbahn«, loc cit., p. 492f.
237 Bundesarchiv Potsdam, Gesandtschaft China, File 985, Sheet 152.
238 Bundesarchiv Potsdam, Gesandtschaft China, File 984, Sheet 196, 226.
239 Bundesarchiv Potsdam, Gesandtschaft China, File 984, Sheet 33.
240 Wright, Arnold, loc cit., p. 604.
241 *Ostasiatischer Lloyd*, Shanghai, 15 June 1913, p. 67.
242 Forsyth, Robert Coventry, *Shantung. The Sacred Province of China*, Shanghai 1912, p. 165.
243 *Ostasiatischer Lloyd*, Shanghai, 26 June 1908.
244 Samagalski, Alan and Buckley, Michael, *China. A Travel Survival Kit*, Victoria, Australia 1984, p. 479.
245 Cross vaults are extremely rare in Chinese architecture, whereas barrel vaults are very common in tombs and gate buildings.
246 *Ostasiatischer Lloyd*, Shanghai, 6 July 1900, p. 509.
247 *Ostasiatischer Lloyd*, Shanghai, 28 October 1904, p. 741.
248 Stenz, Georg Maria, *In der Heimat des Konfuzius*, Steyl 1902, p. 135.
249 Cf. Hartwich, Richard, *Steyler Missionare in China*, vol. 1, »Missionarische Erschließung Südshantungs 1879–1903«, St. Augustin 1983, p. 198f, 319, 384.
250 Cf. *Ostasiatischer Lloyd*, Shanghai, 13 March 1914, p. 232f.
251 Cf. Hartwich, Richard, loc cit., vol. 1, site plan p. 526f.
252 Cf. ibid., vol. 3, »Republik China und der Erste Weltkrieg 1911–1919,« p. 126, 291.
253 Ibid., vol. 1, p. 500f.
254 Translation from the *Hongkong Daily Press*, appeared in *Tsingtauer Neueste Nachrichten*, Tsingtao, 5 September 1913.
255 Cf. Franzius, Georg, *Kiautschou*, loc cit., p. 98f.
256 Cf. Huguenin, C., *Geschichte des III. See-Bataillons*, Tsingtao 1912, p. 3–8.
257 The text of this treaty was used as the model for Great Britain's 99 year lease on the »New Territories« near Hongkong. The end of the lease in 1997 and the discussions about the return of the British Crown Colony are reminiscent of parallels with the former German protectorate of Qingdao. Cf. Mohr, F.W., *Handbuch für das Schutzgebiet Kiautschou*, Tsingtao 1911.
258 Tianjin (Tientsin) is on the Imperial Canal and the Hai He River (Haiho), Shanghai is on the Huangpu River (Whangpoo) just before it flows into the Yangzi (Yangtze) and the Yangzi into the sea, Wuhan (Hankow) is 1,100 kilometres up the Yangzi (Yangtze) and Guangzhou (Canton) is on the Zhujiang (Pearl River). The British colony of Hongkong and the Portugese colony of Macao are on the estuary of the Pearl River. The only comparable new city in China after 1898 was the city of Dalian (Dairen) founded by Russian engineers. There was likewise no infrastructure on the Liaodong Peninsula (Liautung Peninsula, Kwantung Peninsula) before the Russian occupation. It was the building of the Transsiberian Railway between Moscow, Vladivostock, Harbin and Dalian – begun in 1891 and completed on 3 November 1901 – which made it possible to build this extremely spacious town and ice-free sea port on the most southeasterly point of the Transsiberian Railway.
259 Wagner, Rudolf and Buchmann, E., *Eine Reise durch die Deutschen Kolonien*. Vol. 6, »Kiautschou«, Berlin 1913.
260 Cf. Reichsmarineamt (publ.), *Denkschrift betreffend die Entwicklung des Kiautschou-Gebiets in der Zeit vom Oktober 1904 bis Oktober 1905*, Berlin 1906, p. 7.
261 Cf. Schrameier, Wilhelm, *Aus Kiautschous Verwaltung*, Jena 1914, p. 52.
262 Matzat, Wilhelm, *Die Tsingtauer Landordnung des Chinesenkommissars Wilhelm Schrameier*, Bonn 1985, p. 27f.
263 *Deutsch-Asiatische Warte*, Tsingtao, 20 April 1899.
264 From 1842 onwards the first foreign settlements were founded by Britain. Foreigners were allowed to buy land only in specified areas which were next to existing Chinese harbour towns. Similarly in Beijing foreigners were allowed to live only in the diplomatic district. Missionaries were the only exception.
265 Weicker, Hans, *Kiautschou. Das deutsche Schutzgebiet in Ostasien*, Berlin 1908, p. 67.
266 Godshall, Wilson Leon, *Tsingtao under Three Flags*, Shanghai 1929, p. 130.
267 Cf. on the development of Qingdao the memoranda (Denkschrift) of 1897 to 1909 published by the German Admiralty (Reichsmarineamt).
268 *Social Shanghai*, Shanghai, 1906–1912.
269 Schrameier, Wilhelm, *Aus Kiautschous Verwaltung*, Jena 1914, p. 32.
270 Wilhelm, Richard, loc cit., p. 188.
271 Alfons Paquet for instance wrote: »On the hill stands the Governor's Palace, which in its challenging stature is reminiscent of the Imperial Palace in Posen.« Paquet, Alfons, loc cit., p. 297.
272 Cf. Hobow, Junichi, *Tsingtao. The Riviera of the Far East*, Tsingtao 1922.
273 He considers the »unpermissible pressure of time, which made it impossible to produce a cost estimate« responsible for the increased cost. »The extra costs incurred are not due to the facade,« at the time the granite cladding cost in Qingdao only a fifth of the normal price in Berlin. Cf. Bundesarchiv Freiburg, Kiautschou File RM3/v. 6995, Sheet 17f. A story about this villa is of interest here: the German Governor of Qingdao, Oskar Truppel, was in fact not dismissed by Kaiser Wilhelm II, because he had built himself a palace. Truppel took home leave in Germany for 22 months during the building period and did not return until September 1906.
274 Mahlke, Das neue Gouvernements-Dienstgebäude in Tsingtau (Kiautschou) in *Zentralblatt der Bauverwaltung*, Berlin, 17 August 1907, p. 444–447.
275 *Deutsch-Asiatische Warte. Amtlicher Anzeiger des Kiautschou-Gebietes*, Tsingtao, 20 April 1899, vol. 1, p. 1.
276 Cross vaults were an expression of the European architectural culture which was in competition here with Chinese culture. Simple barrel vaults were regularly used in Chinese architecture for gateway buildings, but cross vaults or intersecting barrel vaults were virtually unknown in China.
277 Nellist, George F., loc cit., p. 135f.
278 Reichsmarineamt, loc cit. *Denkschrift 1897–1898*, Berlin 1899, p. 12.
279 Nellist, George F., loc cit., p. 135f.
280 *Ostasiatischer Lloyd*, Shanghai, 29 May 1914, p. 485.
281 Paquet, Alfons, loc cit., p.297.
282 Prisoners who had sentences of over six months were taken to the Chinese gaol in the village of Licun (Litsun), 15 kilometres away. The plaque with the inscription »Chinese gaol« is still in the Qingdao museum. The prison for Europeans was in the eastern part of the European district and was completed as early as 1900. It was next to the former Chinese Yamen, in which the whole German administration had its offices in the early years.
283 Behme, Fr. and Krieger, M., *Führer durch Tsingtau und Umgebung*. 3rd edition, Wolfenbüttel 1906, p. 99.
284 Reichsmarineamt, loc cit. *Denkschrift 1902–1903*, Berlin 1904, p. 44.

285 *Ostasiatischer Lloyd*, Shanghai, 9 August 1907.
286 »The Germania engineering factory, the first company on the continent specialising in building breweries and maltings, has a large number of prospering breweries overseas equipped with modern German systems. For instance virtually all Japanese industrial breweries were built to their designs and fitted with their equipment.« *Ostasiatischer Lloyd*, Shanghai, 16 December 1904.
287 *Ostasiatischer Lloyd*, Shanghai, 2 September 1904, p. 402.
288 Cf. *Ostasiatischer Lloyd*, Shanghai, 1 March 1907, p. 367.
289 Wang Tan; Fujimori, Terunobu; Xü Feipeng, *The architectural heritage of modern China*: Qingdao, Beijing 1992, p. 59.
290 Reichsmarineamt, loc cit., *Denkschrift 1908–1909*, Berlin 1910, p. 54.
291 *Ostasiatischer Lloyd*, Shanghai, 19 January 1912, p. 56.
292 Ibid. This was a poem by Ernst von Wildenbruch (1845–1909).
293 *Deutsch-Asiatische Warte*, Tsingtao, 20 April 1899.
294 *Deutsch-Asiatische Warte*, Tsingtao, 20 November 1901.
295 Hugenin, C., *Geschichte des III See-Bataillons*, Tsingtao 1912, p. 128.
296 Reichsmarineamt, loc cit., *Denkschrift 1899–1900*, Berlin 1901, p. 37.
297 Cf. Kronecker, Franz, *Fünfzehn Jahre Kiautschou. Eine kolonialmedizinische Studie*, Berlin 1913, p. 15.
298 Ibid. p. 20f.
299 *Deutsch-Asiatische Warte*, Tsingtao, 4 September 1901.
300 Cf. Mohr, F.W., *Handbuch für das Schutzgebiet Kiautschou*, Tsingtao 1911, p. 392: »Schulordnung für die Kaiserliche Gouvernements-Schule in Tsingtau« of 24.7.1909.
301 Cf. *Ostasiatischer Lloyd*, Shanghai, 12 February 1909, p. 323.
302 Cf. ibid., 11 December 1914, p. 553.
303 On 29 September 1912 the reformist politician Sun Yixian (Sun Yat-sen) visited the college and gave a speech to the students. *Ostasiatischer Lloyd*, Shanghai, 11 October 1912, p. 331.
304 Rothkegel, Curt, »Evangelische Kirche für Tsingtau-Kiautschou«, in *Zentralblatt für das Deutsche Baugewerbe*, Berlin, 26 March 1909.
305 Ibid.
306 Cf. *Tsingtauer Missions Korrespondenz*, Tsingtao, vol. 3, 1 June 1933, H. 2, p. 31f.
307 *Steyler Missionsbote*, 1934, p. 146, »Kirchweih in Tsingtau.«
308 Cf. *Deutsch-Asiatische Warte*, Tsingtao, 20 April 1899.
309 Hartwich, Richard, loc cit., vol. 1, p. 472.
310 Lutschewitz planned the Christ Church which was consecrated in 1908 in the town of Jimo (Tsimo), 45 kilometres from Qingdao. Cf. *Ostasiatischer Lloyd*, Shanghai, 12 June 1908, p. 1121.
311 The two missions had very different philosophies: »The Protestant Berlin Mission carries out its mission in the way of missions down the ages. The missionaries try to reach the hearts of people by personal contact and charitable actions, such as running schools and hospitals. (…) Heathens who want to become Christians are taken in as candidates for baptism and during a Catechumenate usually lasting a year are instructed in the main points of the Catechism and after passing a test (…) are baptised.« Weicker, Hans, *Kiautschou, das deutsche Schutzgebiet in Ostasien*, Berlin 1908, p. 188.
312 Cf. Behme, Fr. and Krieger, M., loc cit., p. 71f.
313 Wilhelm, Richard and Blumhardt, Hanna, *Unsere Schulen in Tsingtau*, Berlin (year not given), p. 3f.
314 Cf. Mohr. F.W., loc cit., p. 451.
315 Richard Wilhelm lived until 1920 in Qingdao and founded the China Institute in Frankfurt in 1925.
316 Wilhelm, Richard, loc cit., p. 171f.
317 The site had been chosen so that it could be reached easily from the ships. However, when the large docks were opened in March 1904, the whole shipping activity moved from the business centre to the harbour district some 3 kilometres away.
318 Reichsmarineamt, loc cit., *Denkschrift 1901–1902*, Berlin 1903, p. 25.
319 *Nachrichten aus Kiautschou*, Shanghai, 28 October 1899.
320 The architect, Curt Rothkegel, had already built the German Concordia Club in Tianjin; one year later he completed the building for the Peking Club.
321 T. Warner archives, Darmstadt.
322 *Tsingtauer Neueste Nachrichten*, Tsingtao, 2 November 1913, p. 2.
323 Cf. Granet, Marcel, *Das chinesische Denken, Inhalt, Form, Charakter*, Frankfurt 1985.
324 During his 2-day visit to Qingdao, starting on 28 September 1912, the Chinese reformist politician, Dr. Sun Yixian (Sun Yat-sen, Sun Zhongshan; 1866–1925) stayed in the Strandhotel. He and his family and retinue occupied 16 rooms. Cf. *Ostasiatischer Lloyd*, Shanghai, 11 October 1912.
325 *Ostasiatischer Lloyd*, Shanghai, 18 November 1910, p. 498.
326 *Nachrichten aus Kiautschou*, supplement to the *Ostasiatischer Lloyd*, Shanghai, 30 September 1899.
327 Cf. *Adress-Buch des Deutschen Kiautschou-Gebietes für 1905*, Tsingtao, p. 21.
328 T. Warner archives, Darmstadt.
329 T. Warner archives, Darmstadt.
330 *Ostasiatischer Lloyd*, Shanghai, 18 November 1910, p. 498.
331 Falkenberg, Rainer, *Luis Weilers Briefe aus China*. In Kuo Heng-yü and Leutner, Mechthild, *Beiträge zu den deutsch-chinesischen Beziehungen*, München 1986, p. 123.
332 Bundesarchiv Potsdam, Gesandtschaft China, File 984, Sheet 54f.
333 Weicker, Hans, loc cit., p. 145.
334 Maercker, *Die Entwicklung des Kiautschougebiets*. Part 2. Berlin 1903. p. 62f.
335 Reichsmarineamt, loc cit., *Denkschrift 1903–1904*, Berlin 1905, fig. 6a.
336 Mohr, F.W., loc cit., p. 206.
337 Cf. Behme, F. and Krieger, M., loc cit., p. 42.
338 Cf. Wright, Arnold, loc cit., p. 614.
339 Wang Tan; Fujimori, Terunobu; Xü Feipeng, loc cit., p. 42.
340 *Adress-Buch des Deutschen Kiautschou-Gebietes für 1913–1914*, Tsingtao 1913.
341 Reichsmarineamt, loc cit., *Denkschrift 1901–1902*, Berlin 1903, p. 36.
342 In *Social Shanghai*, an illustrated magazine published monthly in Shanghai, these »Beautiful homes in Shanghai« were regularly featured.
343 The first inhabitant of this house, Captain Freiherr von Liliencron, was adjutant to the Governor from 1899 to 1902. He returned to Germany and was in Qingdao once more from 1912 to 1913, this time as commander of the 3rd Sea Batallion. Cf. Huguenin, C., loc cit., p. 58.
344 On the base of the building.
345 Cf. *Ostasiatischer Lloyd*, Shanghai, 29 May 1914.
346 Archives of Professor Dr. Matzat, Bonn.
347 T. Warner archives, Darmstadt.
348 In the Guide to Tsingtao of 1904 a walk around the city is described: »At Gouvernements Platz turn to the north-west and take Hohenlohe Weg towards the mission. On the way there one passes several pretty villas; the second of these, which enjoys a delightful view over the city and the harbour, is the home of the pastor to the German Administration.« In the next edition of the travel guide the house is no longer mentioned. Cf. Behme, F. and Krieger, M., loc cit., p. 44 and this *Führer durch Tsingtau und Umgebung*, 3rd edition, Wolfenbüttel 1906, p. 67.

LITERATUR/BIBLIOGRAPHY

Ungedruckte Quellen

Bautätigkeit der Firma F.H. Schmidt (Altona, Hamburg, Tsingtau) in Ostasien, Bayerische Staatsbibliothek München, Signatur Ana 517.

Deutsche Gesandtschaft China Akten, Bundesarchiv Potsdam, Signatur 266: Gesandtschaftviertel Peking, Ankauf und Tausch von Grundstücken.
  640: Deutsch-Chinesische Schule in Hankau.
  697: Sommerwohnung in Peitaiho.
  853: Reklamation der Firmen Telge & Schröter und Rothkegel & Co. wegen Nichteinhaltung des Vertrages zum Bau des Parlaments.
  918: Generalkonsulat Shanghai.
  984, 985: Konsulat Tsinanfu.
  1000: Settlement und Gemeindeordnungen in Shanghai.
  1015: Gemeindeordnung für Tientsin.
  1032, 1033, 1034: Deutsche Niederlassung in Hankau.
  1048, 1049, 1050, 1051: Deutsche Niederlassung in Tientsin. 1588: Sommerquartier Tjelaisze und Peitaiho.

Fischer, Hermann, Bahnhof Tsinanfu Central, Bayerische Staatsbibliothek München, Signatur Ana 517.

Gouvernement Kiautschou, Akten betreffend Garnisonsbauten, Juli 1908–April 1912, Bundesarchiv-Militärarchiv Freiburg, Signatur RM 3/v. 6995.

Nachlaß Admiral von Truppel, Bundesarchiv-Militärarchiv Freiburg, Signatur N 224.

Tätigkeit des Architekten Curt Rothkegel in China, Lichtenstein 1940, Sammlung T. Warner.

Periodika

Adressbuch des Deutschen Kiautschou-Gebiets für 1905–1914, Tsingtau 1905–1914.

Allgemeiner evangelisch-protestantischer Missionsverein, Missionsblatt des Allgemeinen evangelisch-protestantischen Missionsvereins, Heidelberg, 1898–1905.

Allgemeiner Evangelisch-Protestantischer Missionsverein, Jahresbericht, Heidelberg, 1903.

Der Auslandsdeutsche, Observatorium Tsingtau, Stuttgart, Juni 1912.

Bericht über die Deutsche Ingenieurschule für Chinesen in Schanghai für das zweite Schuljahr (1913/14), Schanghai 1914. (Tongji-Universität)

Bericht über die Deutsche Ingenieurschule für Chinesen in Schanghai für das dritte Schuljahr (1914/15), Schanghai 1915. (Tongji-Universität)

Bericht über die Deutsche Ingenieurschule für Chinesen in Schanghai für das vierte Schuljahr (1915/16), Schanghai 1916. (Tongji-Universität)

Bilder vom Auslanddeutschtum. Beilage des Auslanddeutschen, Die Tung-chi Technische Hochschule in Wusung bei Schanghai, Deutsches Ausland-Institut (Hrsg.), Stuttgart, August/September 1925, S. 30. (Tongji-Universität)

Bilder vom Auslanddeutschtum. Beilage des Auslanddeutschen, Ostasiatisches Liebesmahl in Hamburg am 5. März 1927, Deutsches Ausland-Institut (Hrsg.), Stuttgart, April 1927.

The China Year Book 1916, Montague Bell, H.T. und Woodhead (Hrsg.), London.

Desk Hong List. A general and business directory for Shanghai and the northern and river ports. 1902, 1904, 1910. Shanghai 1902, 1904, 1910.

Deutsch-Asiatische Warte. Wochenblatt des Deutschen Kiautschou-Gebiets, Tsingtau 1899–1903.

Deutsche Niederlassungs-Gemeinde in Tientsin, Protokoll über die jährliche Gemeindeversammlung der Deutschen Niederlassungs-Gemeinde in Tientsin am 26. Februar 1913 und Jahresbericht 1912, Tientsin 1913.

Deutsche Niederlassungs-Gemeinde in Tientsin, Abschluß und Jahresbericht 1916. Voranschlag 1917, Tientsin 1917.

The Directory & Chronicle for China, Japan, Corea, Indo-China, Straits Settlements, Malay States, Siam, Netherlands India, Borneo, the Philippines, &.c. for the year 1909, The Hongkong Daily Press Office (Hrsg.), Hongkong 1909.

The Directory & Chronicle for China, Japan, Corea, Indo-China, Straits Settlements, Malay States, Siam, Netherlands India, Borneo, the Philippines, &.c. for the year 1937, The Hongkong Daily Press Office (Hrsg.), Hongkong 1937.

The Directory of Peking and Tientsin, Tientsin Press (Hrsg.), Tientsin 1908.

The East of Asia Magazine. A non-political illustrated quarterly, Shanghai 1902–1905.

Far East Magazine, An international illustrated industrial, commercial and political review, Bartels, W. und Taylor, W.H.M. (Hrsg.), Shanghai und Tientsin 1934–1936.

The Far Eastern Review. Commerce, Engineering, Finance. Volume 8–14, 26–28 und 32, Manila, Shanghai, Yokohama 1911–1918, 1932–1934 und 1936.

Handelsnachrichten. Beilage zur Zeitschrift der Ostasiatische Lloyd, Shanghai 1914.

Huazhong Jianzhu (Huazhong Architecture), No.2, 1987, Zhongguo jindai jianzhushi yanjiu taolunhui lunwen zhuanji (Special Issue: Symposium of conference on Chinese Architecture 1840–1949), Wucang, Hubei 1987.

Huazhong Jianzhu (Huazhong Architecture), No.3, 1988, Di er ci Zhongguo jindai jianzhushi yanjiu taolunhui lunwen zhuanji (Special Issue: Symposium of conference on Chinese Architecture 1840–1949), Wucang, Hubei 1988.

The Maritime Customs (Hrsg.), Decennial reports on the trade, industries, etc. of the ports open to foreign commerce, conditon and development of the treaty ports provinces, 1902–11. Vol. 1. – Northern and Yangtze ports. Shanghai 1913.

Nachrichten aus Kiautschou, Beiblatt zum »Ostasiatischen Lloyd«, Shanghai 1898–1901.

Der Ostasiatische Lloyd. Organ für die deutschen Interessen im fernen Osten, Fink, C. (Hrsg.), Shanghai, 1898–1916.

Reichsmarineamt (Hrsg.), Denkschrift betreffend die Entwicklung des Kiautschou-Gebiets in der Zeit vom Oktober 1897 – Oktober 1909, Berlin 1898–1910.

Shanghai Municipal Council (Hrsg.), Report for the Year 1933 and Budget for the Year 1934, Shanghai 1934.

Shanghaier Nachrichten, Beilage zu Der Ostasiatische Lloyd, Fink, C. (Hrsg.), Shanghai, 1907–1915.

Social Shanghai. A Magazine for Men and Women, Shorrock, Mina (Hrsg.), Shanghai 1906–1912.

Steyler Missionsbote, Kirchweih in Tsingtau, Steyl 1934.

Tageblatt für Nordchina, Tientsin, 1. August 1907.

Tsingtauer Missions Korrespondenz, Plan der Michaelskirche in Tsingtau, Tsingtau, Juni 1933.

Tsingtauer Neueste Nachrichten, Tsingtau, 1909–1913.

Bibliografie

Arlington, L.C. und Lewison, William, In search of old Peking, Peking 1935, Reprint Hongkong 1991.

Arnold, J., Picturesque Hong Kong. A Handbook for Travellers, Hong Kong 1911.

Arnold, Julean, Commercial Handbook of China, Volume 1, (Miscellaneous Series No. 84), Washington 1919.

Arnold, Julean, China. A commercial and industrial handbook. Washington 1926.

Artelt, Jork, Tsingtau. Deutsche Stadt und Festung in China 1897–1914, Düsseldorf 1984.

Bach, Kurt, Vom Bau der Schantung-Eisenbahn, in: Zentralblatt der Bauverwaltung, Berlin, 16., 23. und 30. September 1905.

Bächer, Max; Hädler, Emil und Yu Lin, Innerstädtische Wohnquartiere in Shanghai. Eine DFG-Studie, Darmstadt 1988.

Baedecker, Karl, Russia with Teheran, Port Arthur and Peking. Handbook for Travellers, Leipzig 1914.

Behme, Fr. und Krieger, M., Führer durch Tsingtau und Umgebung, 2. Auflage, Wolfenbüttel 1904.

Behme, Fr. und Krieger, M., Führer durch Tsingtau und Umgebung, 3. Auflage, Wolfenbüttel 1906.

Bergmann, George von, Der Lao-shan bei Tsingtau als klimatischer Kurort, Tsingtau 1932.

Berrens, B.; Foethke; Schab, von, Die Entwicklung der deutschen Medizin- und Ingenieurschule Schanghai, in: Schüler-Liste 1916, Shanghai 1916. (Tongji-Universität)

Die Betheiligung der Deutschen Marine an den Kämpfen in China. Sommer 1900, (Sonderdruck aus Marine-Rundschau), Berlin 1901.

Betz, Heinrich, Die wirtschaftliche Entwicklung der Provinz Schantung seit der Eröffnung Tsingtaus (1898–1910), Tsingtau 1911.

Bland, J.O.P. und Backhouse, E., China under the Empress Dowager. Being the history of the life and times of Tzu Hsi, London u.a. 1911.

The little Blue Book of Shanghai, Shanghai 1932.

Bökemann, Über Wirtschaft und Verkehr in der Provinz Schantung, in: Koloniale Monatsblätter. Zeitschrift für Kolonialpolitik, Kolonialrecht und Kolonialwirtschaft, Deutsche Kolonialgesellschaft (Hrsg.), Berlin 1913.

Bökemann, Die Stadtanlage von Tsingtau, in: Koloniale Monatsblätter, Deutsche Kolonialgesellschaft (Hrsg.), Berlin, November 1913.

Boerschmann, Ernst, Baukunst und Landschaft in China. Eine Reise durch zwölf Provinzen, Berlin 1926.

Boerschmann, Ernst, Chinesische Architektur. Band 1 und 2, Berlin 1925.

Boerschmann, Ernst, Chinesische Pagoden, Berlin und Leipzig 1931.

Boy-Ed, Peking und Umgebung, Tientsin 1906.

Boy-Ed, Peking und Krieger, M., Peking und Umgebung nebst einer kurzen Geschichte der Belagerung der Gesandtschaften (1900), 2. Auflage, Wolfenbüttel 1910.

Bredon, Juliet, Peking. A historical and intimate description of its chief places of interest, 2nd Ed., Shanghai 1922.

Brooke, J.T.W. und Davis, R.W., The China Architects and Builders Compendium, 1st Ed., Shanghai 1924.

Brooke, J.T.W. und Davis, R.W., The China Architects and Builders Compendium, 10th Ed., Shanghai 1934.

Ce Shaozhen, Flaneur im alten Peking. Ein Leben zwischen Kaiserreich und Revolution, Köln 1987.

Chen Congzhou und Zhang Ming (Hrsg.), Shanghai jindai jianzhu shigao (Moderne Architektur in Shanghai), Shanghai 1988.

The Commercial Press, Views of Shanghai, Shanghai 1910.

The Commercial Press, Views of Shanghai, Shanghai 1925.

Crane, Louise, China in sign and symbol, Shanghai 1926.

Crow, Carl, Handbook for China (including Hongkong), 3rd Ed., Shanghai 1921.

Crow, Carl, Handbook for China, 5th Ed., Shanghai 1933, Reprint Hongkong u.a., 1986.

Darwent, C.E., Shanghai: A handbook for travellers and residents, 2nd Ed., Shanghai 1920.

Deimling, Die Kolonie Kiautschou in den ersten beiden Jahren ihrer Entwicklung, (Abteilung Berlin-Charlottenburg der Deutschen Kolonial-Gesellschaft. Verhandlungen 1899/1900, Heft 2), Berlin 1900.

Denkschrift aus Anlass der feierlichen Einweihung der Tungchi Technischen Hochschule in Schanghai-Woosung, Woosung 1924. (Tongji-Universität)

Deutsche Bauten in Kiautschou, in: Die Bauwelt, Berlin, 17. September 1914.

Deutsche Kulturarbeit in China. Die neue deutsche Ingenieurschule Dung-Chi in Schanghai, in: Berliner Illustrierte Zeitung, Berlin, 8. April 1923. (Tongji-Universität)

Dost, Paul und Hartwig, Werner, Deutsch-China und die Schantungbahn, Krefeld 1981.

Dukes, E.J. und Fielde, A., Alltagsleben in China. Bilder aus dem chinesischen Volksleben, Basel 1892.

Eckart, Wolfgang Uwe, Deutsche Ärzte in China 1897–1914. Medizin als Kulturmission im Zweiten Deutschen Kaiserreich, Stuttgart und New York 1989.

Englert, Siegfried und Reichert, Folker, Shanghai. Stadt über dem Meer, (Heidelberger Bibliotheksschriften 17), Heidelberg 1985.

Eitel, Ernest, Feng-Shui. The Science of sacred Landscape in old China, 1873, Reprint London 1984.

Erling, Johnny, Chinesische Töne im »Palais Willkommen«, in: Die Welt, 19. September 1992.

European Settlements in the Far East. China, Japan, Corea, Indo-China, Straits Settlements, Malay States, Siam, Netherlands India, Borneo, The Philippines, etc., London 1900.

Exner, A.H., China. Skizzen von Land und Leuten mit besonderer Berücksichtigung kommerzieller Verhältnisse, Leipzig 1889.

Fabritzek, Uwe, Gelber Drache – Schwarzer Adler, München u.a. 1973.

Falkenberg, Rainer, Luis Weilers Briefe aus China (Dezember 1897 – August 1901). Materialien zur Entwicklung in Qingdao und zum Bau der Shandong-Bahn, in Kuo Heng-yü und Leutner, Mechthild (Hrsg.), Beiträge zu den deutsch-chinesischen Beziehungen, (Berliner China-Studien 12), München 1986.

Fei-shi (Fischer, Emil), Guide to Peking and its Environs, Tientsin 1909.

Fei-shi (Fischer, Emil), Guide to Peking and its Environs near and far, Tientsin und Peking 1924.

Festschrift zum Gedenken des 20jährigen Bestehens der staatlichen Tung-Chi Universität Woosung, China, Shanghai 1928. (Tongji-Universität)

Festschrift anläßlich des 25jährigen Bestehens der Staatlichen Tung-Chi Universität zu Woosung, China, Shanghai 1932. (Tongji-Universität)

Fischer, Martin, Szetschuan. Diplomatie und Reisen in China während der letzten drei Jahre der Kaiserzeit, München und Wien 1968.

Forsyth, Robert Coventry, Shantung. The sacred province of China, Shanghai 1912.

Franke, Otto, Erinnerungen aus zwei Welten, Berlin 1954.

Franzius, Georg, Ein Ausflug nach Kiau-Tschou, (Deutsche Kolonial-Gesellschaft, Abteilung Berlin-Charlottenburg, Verhandlungen 1897/98, Heft 3), Berlin 1898.

Franzius, Georg, Kiautschou. Deutschlands Erwerbung in Ostasien, Berlin 1898.

Gao Zhonglin (Hrsg.), Tianjin jindai jianzhu (Moderne Architektur in Tianjin), Tianjin 1990.

Gensburger, F.M. (Hrsg.), Tsingtao – »The Riviera of the Far East«, Shanghai 1937.

Gerstenberg, Hans, Die Wegebauten in Tsintau, in: Beiträge zur Kolonialpolitik und Kolonialwirtschaft, Deutsche Kolonialgesellschaft (Hrsg.), Berlin 1899/1900.

Giordani, Paolo, The German Colonial Empire. Its Beginning and Ending, London 1916.

Godshall, Wilson Leon, Tsingtau under three Flags, Shanghai 1929.

Granet, Marcel, Das chinesische Denken. Inhalt, Form, Charakter, Frankfurt/Main 1985. (Die Originalausgabe erschien 1934 unter dem Titel »La pensée chinoise« in Paris)

Gründer, Horst, Geschichte der deutschen Kolonien, 2. Auflage, Paderborn u.a., 1991.

Grünfeld, Ernst, Hafenkolonien und kolonieähnliche Verhältnisse in China, Japan und Korea. Eine kolonialpolitische Studie, Jena 1913.

Hai-Ho Commission, Hai-Ho Conservancy Board 1898–1919, Tientsin 1919.

Hankow. Ancient and Modern, American Church Mission (Hrsg.), Hankow 1922.

Hartwich, Richard, Steyler Missionare in China, Band 1, Missionarische Erschließung Südshantungs 1879–1903, St. Augustin 1983.

Hartwich, Richard, Steyler Missionare in China, Band 2, Bischof A. Henninghaus ruft Steyler Schwestern 1904–1910, Nettetal 1985.

Hartwich, Richard, Steyler Missionare in China, Band 3, Republik China und Erster Weltkrieg. 1911–1919, Nettetal 1987.

Haupt, Adolf, Führer durch Tsingtau und Umgebung, Tsingtau 1927.

Haupt, Adolf, Guide to Tsingtao and its Environs, Tsingtao 1934.

Heide, Hermann auf der, Die Missionsgesellschaft von Steyl. Ein Bild der ersten 25 Jahre ihres Bestehens. Jubiläumsausgabe zum 8. September 1900, Steyl 1900.

Heeren, M., Einfamilienhaus in Tsingtau, in: Deutsche Bauhütte, S. 160–161, Hannover 1915.

Hesse-Wartegg, Ernst von, Schantung und Deutsch-China. Von Kiautschou ins Heilige Land von China und vom Jangtsekiang nach Peking im Jahre 1898, Leipzig 1898.

Heßler, Carl, Deutsch-Kiaotschau. Kurze Beschreibung von Land und Leuten unserer Besitzung von Kiaotschau, Leipzig 1898.

Heyking, Elisabeth von, Briefe die Ihn nicht erreichten, 5. Auflage, Berlin 1903.

Heyking, Elisabeth von, Tschun. Eine Geschichte aus dem Vorfrühling Chinas, Berlin und Wien 1914.

Hildebrand, Heinrich, Der Tempel Ta-chüeh-sy (Tempel des großen Erkennens) bei Peking, Berlin 1897, Nachdruck Peking 1943.

Hobow, Junichi, Tsingtao. The Riviera of the Far East, Tsingtao 1922.

Huguenin, C., Geschichte des III. See-Bataillons, Tsingtau 1912.

Imperial Japanese Government Railways, An Official Guide to Eastern Asia, Vol. IV, China, Tokyo 1915.

Kato, Yuzo, Ajia no toshi to kenchiku (A Guide to Shanghai's Modern Architecture), Kajima Shuppankai Verlag, Tokyo 1986, 2. Auflage 1992.

Kato, Yuzo, Asia no toshi to kenchiku, 29 exotic asian cities (Stadtarchitektur in Asien), Tokyo 1986, 3. Auflage 1992.

Kawata, T., Glimpses of China and Japan Trade Records 1919, Osaka 1919.

Kelling, Rudolf, Das chinesische Wohnhaus. Mit einem 2. Teil über das frühchinesische Haus unter Verwendung von Ergebnissen aus Übungen von Conrady im Ostasiatischen Seminar der Universität Leipzig von Rudolf Kelling und Bruno Schindler, (Supplementband 13 der Mitteilungen der Deutschen Gesellschaft für Natur- und Völkerkunde Ostasiens. Tokyo 1935.

Koberstein, F., Tientsin und Umgebung, Tientsin 1906.

Kreissler, Françoise, L'action culturelle allemande en Chine. De la fin du XIX siècle à la Seconde Guerre mondiale, Paris 1989.

Kronecker, Franz, Fünfzehn Jahre Kiautschou. Eine kolonialmedizinische Studie, (Sonderabdruck aus Deutsche Medizinische Presse), Berlin 1913.

Lao She, Rikscha Kuli, Frankfurt 1989. (Übersetzt von Florian Reissinger. Die Originalausgabe erschien 1937 unter dem Titel Luotuo Xiangzi.)

Lauber, Wolfgang, Deutsche Architektur in Togo, Stuttgart 1993.

Lin Wenbi und Xu Dongsheng (Hrsg.), Old Photos of Beijing, Beijing 1989.

Lin Yutang, Moment in Peking. A Novel of contemporary Chinese Life, o. Ort, 1939.

Linde, Max, Die Tung-Chi Universität in Schanghai-Woosung, (Deutschtum und Ausland, Heft 13, Hrsg. Georg Schreiber), Münster in Westfalen 1928. (Tongji-Universität)

Liu Jie, Occidental slice of Oriental city, in: China Daily, Beijing, 15. März 1989.

Loesch, Karl C., Deutsche Züge im Antlitz der Erde. Deutsches Siedeln, deutsche Leistung, München, o.J.

Luff, Reginald, Buildings in Shanghai, in: Social Shanghai, A Magazine for Men and Women, Shanghai, July 1908.

Macmillan, Allister, Seaports of the Far East. Historical and descriptive commercial and industrial facts, figures, & resources, London 1907.

Macmillan, Allister, Seaports of the Far East, 2nd Ed., London 1925.

Madrolle's handbooks, Shanghai and the valley of the Blue River, Paris und London 1912.

Maercker, Die Entwicklung des Kiautschougebiets, Erster und zweiter Teil, (Abdruck aus der Deutschen Kolonialzeitung), Berlin 1902 und 1900.

Mahlke, Das neue Gouvernements-Dienstgebäude in Tsingtau (Kiautschou), in: Zentralblatt der Bauverwaltung, Berlin, 17. August 1907.

Muramatsu, Noboru, Shanghai – toshi to kenchiku 1842–1949 (Die Architektur der Stadt Shanghai 1842–1949), Parco shuppan Verlag, Tokyo 1991.

Matzat, Wilhelm, Die Tsingtauer Landordnung des Chinesenkommissars Wilhelm Schrameier, (Studien und Quellen zur Geschichte Schantungs und Tsingtaus, Heft 2), Bonn 1985.

Maugham, W. Somerset, On a Chinese Screen, Hongkong 1986. (Die Originalausgabe erschien 1922 in New York)

Meid, Michiko, Europäische und nordamerikanische Architekten in Japan. Der Einführungsprozeß der europäischen und der nordamerikanischen Architektur in Japan seit 1542, (11. Veröffentlichung der Abteilung Architektur des Kunsthistorischen Instituts der Universität Köln), Dissertation, Köln 1977.

Meisner, Heinrich Otto, Denkwürdigkeiten des General-Feldmarschalls Alfred Grafen von Waldersee, Dritter Band, 1900–1904, Stuttgart 1923, Nachdruck Osnabrück 1967.

Mohr, F.W., Handbuch für das Schutzgebiet Kiautschou, Tsingtau 1911.

Mohr, F.W., Fremde und Deutsche Kulturbetätigung in China, (Deutschtum und Ausland, Heft 13, Hrsg. Georg Schreiber), Münster in Westfalen 1928.

Morton-Cameron, W.H. und Feldwick, W., Present Day Impressions of the Far East and Prominent & Progressive Chinese at Home and Abroad. The history, commerce, industries and resources of China, Hongkong, Indo-China, Malaya and Netherlands India, London u.a., 1917.

Müller, Alfred von, Die Wirren in China, und die Kämpfe der verbündeten Truppen, 2. Auflage, Berlin 1902.

Müller-Jabusch, Maximilian, Fünfzig Jahre Deutsch-Asiatische Bank 1890–1939, Berlin 1940.

Muthesius, Hermann, Die kleineren Bauwerke der Pariser Weltausstellung, in: Centralblatt der Bauverwaltung, Berlin, 8. September 1900.

Navarra, Bruno, China und die Chinesen, Auf Grund eines 20jährigen Aufenthaltes im Lande der Mitte, Bremen und Shanghai 1901.

Nellist, Georg F., Men of Shanghai and North China. A standard biographical reference work, Shanghai 1933.

Ostasiatischer Verein Hamburg-Bremen (Hrsg.), Ostasiatischer Verein Hamburg-Bremen zum 60jährigen Bestehen. 13. März 1900 – 13. März 1960, Hamburg 1960.

Pan Pen-zhi, Souvenir Photographs of the Restoration of Tsing Tao 1923, Shanghai 1924.

Paquet, Alfons, Li oder Im neuen Osten, Frankfurt/Main 1913.

Pfeiffer, M., Ein Deutscher Reiterposten in Schantung, Berlin 1909.

Pirazzoli-t'Serstevens, Michèle, China, München 1970.

Plüschow, Gunther, Die Abenteuer des Fliegers von Tsingtau. Meine Erlebnisse in drei Erdteilen, Berlin 1916.

Potsdamer Schlösser in Geschichte und Kunst, Staatliche Archivverwaltung der DDR (Hrsg.), Leipzig 1984.

Pott, Franzis Lister Hawks, A Short History of Shanghai. Being an account of the growth and development of the International Settlement, Shanghai 1928.

Preyer, Otto E., Das Eisenbahnwesen Chinas, in: Archiv für Eisenbahnwesen, S. 84–159, Berlin 1909.

Preyer, Otto E., Die Entwicklung des chinesischen Eisenbahnwesens in den letzten drei Jahren (1909–1911), in: Archiv für Eisenbahnwesen, S. 965–1003, Berlin 1913.

Rasmussen, O.D., Tientsin. An illustrated outline history, Tientsin 1925.

Review of Tsingtao. 1928–1929, The Tsingtao Times (Hrsg.), Vorwort: Chao Chi, Tsingtao 1928.

Rivinius, Karl Josef, Weltlicher Schutz und Mission. Das deutsche Protektorat über die katholische Mission von Süd-Shantung, Köln und Wien 1987.

Rohrbach, Paul, Die deutschen Kolonien. Ein Bilderbuch aller deutschen Kolonien, Dachau 1914.

Rohrbach, Paul, Deutschland in China voran?, Berlin 1912.

Rohrbach, Paul, Erwachendes Asien. Geschautes und Gedachtes von einer Indien- und Ostasienreise 1932, München 1932.

Rothkegel, Curt, Evangelische Kirche für Tsingtau-Kiautschou, in: Zentralblatt für das Deutsche Baugewerbe, Berlin, 26. März 1909, S. 157–160.

Salzmann, Erich von, Aus Jung-China. Reiseskizzen nach der Revolution. August bis Oktober 1912, Tientsin 1912.

Salzmann, Erich von, Das Revolutionäre China, Berlin 1913.

Salzmann, Erich von, Die deutsche Gesandtschaft in Peking, in: Die Woche. Moderne Illustrierte Zeitschrift, Berlin, Januar 1914, S. 24–29.

Samagalski, Alan und Buckley, Michael, China. A Travel Survival Kit, Victoria, Australia 1984.

Schab, von, Geschichte der Deutschen Medizin- und Ingenieurschule 1907–1919, in: Festschrift anläßlich des 25jährigen Bestehens der Staatlichen Tung-Chi Universität zu Woosung, China, Woosung 1932. (Tongji-Universität)

Scheibert, Justus, Der Krieg in China 1900–1901 nebst einer Beschreibung der Sitten, Gebräuche und Geschichte des Landes. 1. Band, Berlin 1901.

Schinz, Alfred, Cities in China. (Urbanization of the Earth 7, Wolf Tietze, Hrsg.), Berlin und Stuttgart 1989.

Schlubach, Eric W., Reisebriefe aus dem Fernen Osten 1903–1905, Hamburg, o. J.

Schmelzer, Mitteilungen über die Tientsin-Pukow-Bahn, in: Glasers Annalen für Gewerbe und Bauwesen, Berlin, September 1911, S. 96–117.

Schmidt, Vera, Die deutsche Eisenbahnpolitik in Shantung 1898–1914. Ein Beitrag zur Geschichte des deutschen Imperialismus in China, Wiesbaden 1976.

Schönsee, Über die Kaibauten an der deutschen Niederlassung in Hankau (China), in: Centralblatt der Bauverwaltung, Berlin, 20. Oktober 1900.

Schrameier, Wilhelm, Die Grundlagen der wirtschaftlichen Entwicklung in Kiautschou, (Abteilung Berlin-Charlottenburg der Deutschen Kolonial-Gesellschaft, Verhandlungen 1902/03, Band 7, Heft 2), Berlin 1903.

Schrameier, Wilhelm, Aus Kiautschous Verwaltung. Die Land-, Steuer- und Zollpolitik des Kiautschougebietes, Jena 1914.

Schrameier, Wilhelm, Kiautschou. Seine Entwicklung und Bedeutung. Ein Rückblick, Berlin 1915.

Schrameier, Wilhelm, Die Deutsch-Chinesischen Handelsbeziehungen, (Meereskunde, Heft 124), Berlin 1917.

Schweitzer, Georg, China im neuen Gewande. Kultur und Wirtschaft im fernen Osten, Berlin 1914.

Segalen, Victor, René Leys, Frankfurt 1982. (Die Originalausgabe erschien 1922 in Paris)

Seidel, Paul, Der Kaiser und die Kunst, Berlin 1907.

Sirén, Osvald, The walls and gates of Peking, London 1924.

Slovensky Biograficky Slovnik. (od roku 833 do roku 1990), Martin 1987.

Smith, Arthur H., Village Life in China. A study in sociology, New York u. a., 1899.

Stenz, Georg Maria, Der Kaiserkanal, in Beiträge zur Kolonialpolitik und Kolonialwirtschaft, Deutsche Kolonialgesellschaft (Hrsg.), Berlin 1903/04.

Stenz, Georg Maria, In der Heimat des Konfuzius. Skizzen, Bilder und Erlebnisse aus Schantung, Steyl 1902.

Stone, Albert H., Historic Lushan. The Kuling Mountains, Hankow 1921.

Stumpf, Richard, Neuzeitliches Hochbauen in Shanghai im Jahre 1932/33, in: Festschrift anläßlich des 25jährigen Bestehens der Staatlichen Tung-Chi Universität zu Woosung, China, Woosung 1932.

Tirpitz, Alfred von, Erinnerungen, Leipzig 1919.

Tsingtau Souvenir. Album mit 50 Ansichten. Verlag Adolf Haupt, Tsingtau o. J. (ca. 1909)

Uthemann, Walther und Fürth, Tsingtau. Ein kolonialhygienischer Rückblick auf die Entwicklung des Deutschen Kiautschougebietes, (Beihefte zum Archiv für Schiffs- und Tropenhygiene, Beiheft 4), Leipzig, Mai 1911.

Voh Kee Construction Co. (Hrsg.), The memorial supplement for the construction of 22-storied building for the Joint Savings Society, Shanghai 1934.

Wagner, Rudolf und Buchmann, E., Eine Reise durch die Deutschen Kolonien, VI. Band, »Kiautschou«, 2. Auflage, Berlin 1913.

Walters, Derek, Feng Shui. Perfect Placing of your happiness and prosperity, London u. a., 1988.

Wang und Meerscheidt-Hüllessem, In und um Peking während der Kriegswirren 1900–1901, Berlin 1902.

Wang Shaozhou, Shanghai jindai chengshi jianzhu (Shanghai Modern Architecture), o. O. 1989.

Wang Shaozhou, Zhongguo jindai jianzhu tulu (Bildband zur modernen Architektur Chinas), Shanghai 1989.

Wang Tan; Fujimori, Terunobu; Xu Feipeng; u. a., Zhongguo jindai jianzhu zonglan, Qingdao pian (The Architectural Heritage of Modern China: Qingdao), Beijing 1992.

Warner, Torsten, Shuoshuo Huayuan Fandian (Über den Deutschen Gartenclub in Shanghai, an dessen Stelle sich heute das Garden-Hotel befindet), aus dem Englischen übersetzt von Qian Zonghao, in Xinmin Wanbao, Shanghai, 30. Juli 1991, S. 7.

Warner, Torsten, Shanghai de jindai Deguo jianzhu (Modern German Architecture in Shanghai), aus dem Englischen übersetzt von Qian Zonghao, in Tongji Daxue Xuebao – Journal of Tongji University, Humanities and Social Science Section, Volume 3, No. 1, März 1992, Seite 15–21 und 116f, Shanghai 1992.

Warner, Torsten, Shanghai de Deguo jianzhu (German Architecture in Shanghai), aus dem Englischen übersetzt von Zhang Fuhe, in: Wang Tan und Zhang Fuhe (Hrsg.), Di si ci Zhongguo jindai jianzhushi yanjiu taolunhui lunwenji (Sammlung von Aufsätzen zum vierten Symposium für Chinesische Architektur des 20. Jahrhunderts), Seite 81–86, Beijing 1993.

Wassiljew, W. P., Die Erschließung Chinas. Kulturhistorische und wirtschaftspolitische Aufsätze zur Geschichte Ostasiens. mit Beiträgen von Prof. Dr. A. Conrady, Leipzig 1909.

Weale, B.L. Putnam, The Re-Shaping of the Far East, London 1905.

Weber, Dietrich, (Hrsg.), Kaiser-Wilhelm-Schule zu Schanghai. 40 Jahre Deutsche Schule in Schanghai. 1895–1935, Schanghai 1935.

Wegener, Georg, Zur Kriegszeit durch China. 1900/1901, Berlin 1902.

Weggel, Oskar, Geschichte Chinas im 20. Jahrhundert, Stuttgart 1989.

Weicker, Hans, Kiautschou. Das deutsche Schutzgebiet in Ostasien, Berlin 1908.

Wilhelm, Richard, Die Seele Chinas, Berlin 1926.

Wilhelm, Richard und Blumhard, Hanna, Unsere Schulen in Tsingtau, Berlin o. J. (ca. 1913)

Wilhelmy, Emil, China. Land und Leute. Illustrierte Geschichte des Reiches der Mitte, Berlin 1904.

Woas, Franz, Ostasiatische Architektur der neueren Zeit, in: Deutsche Bauzeitung, Berlin, 7. September 1904.

Woodhead, H.G.W., The truth about the Chinese Republic, London 1925.

Wright, Arnold und Cartwright, H.A., Twentieth Century Impressions of Hongkong, Shanghai and other Treaty Ports of China: Their history, people, commerce, industries and resources, London u. a. 1908.

Zhongyiyuan Gailan (The Parliament Compendium), o. O. 1919.

ABBILDUNGSNACHWEIS

Archiv der Steyler Missionare, Societas Verbi Divini (SVD), Rom: 171 o, 171 u, 175 o, 175 ul, 177 o, 177 u, 251 o
Bayerische Staatsbibliothek München, Signatur Ana 517, Bautätigkeit der Firma F.H. Schmidt (Altona, Hamburg, Tsingtau) in Ostasien: 49 u, 65 o, 67, 238, 270, 271 o, 289 o
Bundesarchiv Koblenz, Fotos aus China und Kiautschou: 43 u, 55 o, 55 u, 69, 79 o, 189 o, 211 o, 222, 231, 237 o, 263 o
Bundesarchiv Potsdam, Akten der deutschen Gesandtschaft Peking, Aktennummer 1000, Blatt 42 und 43: 91 o
Bundesarchiv-Militärarchiv Freiburg, Signatur: N 224/78: 169 ol; N 224/79: 269, 293 u, 295 o, 297 o, 301 o; N 224/80: 207 o, 266; N 224/82: 209 ol, 209 ml, 209 ul; N 224/84: 237 o; N 224/90: 293 o;
Küstenmuseum und Stadtarchiv Wilhelmshaven: 205, Umschlag
Rothkegel, Helmuth, Republik Südafrika: 37 u, 39 u
Schwarzenbach, Beat, Jinan und Frauenfeld/Schweiz: 223 u
Shanghai Local History Museum: 99
Warner, Torsten, Hamburg: 19, 20, 21, 29 u, 33 r, 41 o, 41 u, 45 u, 48, 51, 54, 64, 65 u, 71, 73 o, 73 u, 75, 77 o, 77 u, 109, 113 u, 115, 117 r, 118, 119 o, 119 u, 121 u, 123, 125 l, 125 r, 137, 138, 147 u, 151 u, 152, 153 o, 153 u, 161 o, 161 u, 163 o, 163 u, 172 r, 172 l, 173 r, 173 l, 181 o, 181 u, 182, 183 u, 185, 187, 189 u, 191, 192 l, 192 r, 193 l, 193 r, 207 u, 208, 209 or, 211 u, 212, 213, 215, 216, 217, 219, 221 o, 221 u, 223 o, 225 u, 227 u, 229, 233 u, 235 u, 237 u, 239 u, 241 u, 243, 245 u, 246 l, 246 r, 248, 249 l, 249 r, 251 u, 253 u, 255 u, 257 u, 260, 261 u, 263, 265 o, 265 u, 267 u, 271 u, 273, 275, 276, 277 u, 279 u, 281 u, 283 u, 285 u, 287 u, 288, 289 u, 291, 295 u, 297 u, 299, 301 u, 303 u

Periodika

Adressbuch des Deutschen Kiautschou-Gebiets und der Provinz Schantung, Tsingtau 1913-14: 290
Allgemeiner Evangelisch-Protestantischer Missionsverein, Missionsblatt des Allgemeinen evangelisch-protestantischen Missionsvereins, Heidelberg, November 1903: 257 o
Centralblatt der Bauverwaltung, 14. Jahrgang, Berlin 1894: 35
Centralblatt der Bauverwaltung, 19. Jahrgang, Berlin 1899: 92
Far East Magazine, Shanghai und Tientsin 1934: 132, 133
Far East Magazine, Shanghai und Tientsin 1936: 167 u
The Far Eastern Review, Volume 9, Manila, Shanghai, Yokohama 1912–13: 165 or, 165 lu
The Far Eastern Review, Volume 10, Manila, Shanghai, Yokohama 1913–14: 37 o, 39 o
The Far Eastern Review, Volume 12, Manila, Shanghai, Yokohama 1915–16: 31, 33 lo, 33 lu
Huazhong Architecture, No.2, 1987, Symposium of conference on Chinese Architecture 1840–1949, Wucang, Hubei 1987: 74 Der Ostasiatische Lloyd, Shanghai, 6. Juli 1900: 175 ur
Der Ostasiatische Lloyd, Shanghai, 10. Juli 1908: 149
Der Ostasiatische Lloyd, Shanghai, 19. Februar 1909: 151 o
Quack. Sporadic Not Periodical, Shanghai 1912: 53
Reichsmarineamt (Hrsg.), Denkschrift betreffend die Entwicklung des Kiautschou-Gebiets in der Zeit vom Oktober 1900 bis Oktober 1901, Berlin 1902: 168, 239 o
Reichsmarineamt (Hrsg.), Denkschrift betreffend die Entwicklung des Kiautschou-Gebiets in der Zeit vom Oktober 1901 bis Oktober 1902, Berlin 1903: 253 o, 303 o
Reichsmarineamt (Hrsg.), Denkschrift betreffend die Entwicklung des Kiautschou-Gebiets in der Zeit vom Oktober 1903 bis Oktober 1904, Berlin 1905: 283 o
Reichsmarineamt (Hrsg.), Denkschrift betreffend die Entwicklung des Kiautschou-Gebiets in der Zeit vom Oktober 1905 bis Oktober 1906, Berlin 1907: 225 o, 298
Shanghai Municipal Council, Report for the Year 1933 and Budget for the Year 1934, Shanghai 1934: 139 o, 139 u
Shanghaier Nachrichten, Beilage zur Zeitschrift Der Ostasiatische Lloyd, 8. Jahrgang, Shanghai, 12. Juni 1914: 121 o
Social Shanghai, A Magazine for Men and Women, Shanghai 1907: 91 u

Bibliografie

Arnold, Julean, Commercial Handbook of China, Volume 1, (Miscellaneous Series No. 84), Washington 1919: 93, 272
Bach, Kurt, Vom Bau der Schantung-Eisenbahn, in: Zentralblatt der Bauverwaltung, Berlin, 30. September 1905. 169 or, 169 ul, 169 ur
Behme, Fr. und Krieger, M., Führer durch Tsingtau und Umgebung, 3. Auflage, Wolfenbüttel 1906: 154
Boerschmann, Ernst, Chinesische Architektur. Band 1 und 2, Berlin 1925: 162
Boy-Ed und Krieger, M., Peking und Umgebung, 2. Auflage, Wolfenbüttel 1910: 45 o
Bredon, Juliet, Peking. A historical and intimate description of its chief places of interest, Shanghai 1922: 22
The Commercial Press, Views of Shanghai, Shanghai 1910: 101
The Commercial Press, Views of Shanghai, Shanghai 1925: 111
Denkschrift aus Anlass der feierlichen Einweihung der Tungchi Technischen Hochschule in Schanghai-Woosung, Shanghai 1924: 124, 129 u
Festschrift zum Gedenken des 20jährigen Bestehens der staatlichen Tung-Chi Universität Woosung, China, Shanghai 1928: 127, 129 o, 136
Forsyth, Robert Coventry, Shantung. The sacred province of China, Shanghai 1912: 178
Imperial Japanese Government Railways, An Official Guide to Eastern Asia, Vol. IV, China, Tokyo 1915: 56, 84, 140
Lin Wenbi und Xu Dongsheng (Hrsg.), Old Photos of Beijing, Beijing 1989: 47
Linde, Max, Die Tung-Chi Universität in Schanghai-Woosung, (Deutschtum und Ausland, Heft 13, Hrsg. Georg Schreiber), Münster (Westfalen) 1928: 103 o, 135
Maercker, Die Entwicklung des Kiautschougebietes, Erster Teil, (Abdruck aus der Deutschen Kolonialzeitung), Berlin 1902: 233 o
Pan Pen-zhi, Souvenir Photographs of the Restoration of Tsing Tao 1923, Shanghai 1924: 241 o
Plan von Tsingtau und Umgebung, Maßstab 1 : 12 500, Tsingtau o.J. (um 1913): 194
Postkarte vom japanischen Klub in Qingdao (um 1920): 261 o
Rasmussen, O.D., Tientsin. An illustrated outline history, Tientsin 1925: 70
Rohrbach, Paul, Die deutschen Kolonien, Dachau 1914: 165 ol, 183 o
Rohrbach, Paul, Deutschland in China voran?, Berlin 1912: 259 o, 259 u
Rothkegel, Curt, Evangelische Kirche für Tsingtau-Kiautschou, in: Zentralblatt für das Deutsche Baugewerbe, Berlin, 26. März 1909: 247
Schmelzer, Mitteilungen über die Tientsin-Pukow-Bahn, in: Glasers Annalen für Gewerbe und Bauwesen, Berlin, September 1911: 165 ur, 167 o
Tsingtau Souvenir. Album mit 50 Ansichten, Verlag Adolf Haupt, Tsingtau o.J. (ca. 1909): 235 o
Wagner, Rudolf und Buchmann, E., Eine Reise durch die Deutschen Kolonien, VI. Band, »Kiautschou«, 2. Auflage, Berlin 1913: 227 o, 245 o, 267 o, 277 o, 281 o, 285 o
Wang und Meerscheidt-Hüllessem, In und um Peking während der Kriegswirren 1900–1901, Berlin 1902: 42, 43 o
Weber, Dietrich, (Hrsg.), Kaiser-Wilhelm-Schule zu Schanghai, Shanghai 1935: 103 u, 105, 131
Weicker, Hans, Kiautschou. Das deutsche Schutzgebiet in Ostasien, Berlin 1908: 225 o, 253 o, 279 o
Wilhelmy, Emil, China. Land und Leute. Illustrierte Geschichte des Reiches der Mitte, Berlin 1904: 255 o
Wright, Arnold und Cartwright, H.A., Twentieth Century Impressions of Hongkong, Shanghai and other Treaty Ports of China, London 1908: 49 o, 79 u, 83, 95 o, 95 u, 97, 107, 113 o, 117 l, 287 o

SACHREGISTER/INDEX

Afrika 16
Allgemeiner Evangelisch-Protestantischer Missionsverein 256, 258
American Lutheran Mission 254
Amerika 26, 114
Anglo-German Brewery Company 226
Apotheke 280, 288
Arnhold, Karberg & Co. 114
Astorhaus 120
Australien 94, 114
Auswärtiges Amt 42, 52, 61, 66, 78, 100, 146, 186

Bahnhof 72, 159, 160, 162, 164, 168, 180, 184, 222
Bahnhofshotel 159, 184, 264
Bank of China 130
Bauordnung 14, 20, 204, 282
Bauverwaltung 236, 240, 270, 300
Belgien 26, 58
Berliner Mission 254
Bismarck-Kaserne 202, 206, 234, 244
Bodenpolitik 198
Boxer 24, 25, 174
Boxerkrieg 25, 27, 28, 38, 50, 59, 60, 62, 174
Brandenburger Tor 19
Brauerei 226
Buchheister & Co. 118

Carlowitz & Co. 11, 112, 286
Ch'ien men, s. Qianmen
China Export, Import, Banking Company 116
Chinese Government Railways 72, 160, 162, 164, 166, 180, 182
Chow Soey Kee, Baufirma 120
Christuskirche, Qingdao 14, 240, 244, 288
Club Concordia, Shanghai 13, 48, 87, 88, 90, 96, 98, 116, 118, 130, 188
Club Concordia, Tianjin 15, 50, 64, 288
Club Germania, Hongkong 11, 82
Comprador Stil 11, 82
Country Club, Shanghai 96
Country Hospital, Shanghai 134, 136

Deutsch-Asiatische Bank 13, 46, 48, 59, 70, 94, 110, 148, 188, 276, 278
Deutsch-Chinesische Hochschule, Qingdao 122, 240, 242, 256
Deutsch-Chinesische Ingenieurschule, Wuhan 18, 62, 94, 122, 145, 152
Deutsch-Chinesische Mittelschule, Tianjin 62
Deutsch-Chinesisches Seminar, Qingdao 256
Deutsch-Evangelische Kirche, Shanghai 88, 89, 100, 102, 130, 132
Deutsche-Hankau-Niederlassung-Gesellschaft 144
Deutsche Ingenieurschule, Shanghai 62, 89, 94, 122, 152
Deutsche Medizinschule, Shanghai 89, 122, 134
Deutsche Niederlassungsgemeinde Hankau 150
Deutscher Evangelischer Kirchenausschuß 244
Deutscher Gartenclub Shanghai 13, 89, 94, 130
Deutsches Eck, Koblenz 15
Deutsches Eck, Shanghai 130
Deutsches Gemeindehaus, Shanghai 89, 130
Deutsches Gouvernement Kiautschou 206, 210, 214, 220, 224, 228, 232, 234, 236, 238, 240, 292, 294, 300
Diederichsstein 98, 230
Donghua Men, Beijing 19
Dung-hua-men, s. Donghua Men

Ehrenbogen 44
England 23, 26, 58, 59

Faber-Hospital, Qingdao 17, 256

Fachwerk 17, 18, 52, 260, 292
Fangtse-Revier 278
Fechner & Kappler, Baufirma 146
Feld-Artillerie-Kaserne 240
Fengshui (Geomantik) 17, 18, 152, 156, 160, 238, 296
Fertighaus 292
Forth Bridge, Schottland 166
Frankreich 23, 26, 58, 59, 60, 142
Franz-Xaver-Kolleg 174
Franziskaner 155, 156, 179, 190
Franziskanerinnen Missionarinnen Mariens 252

Garden Bridge, Shanghai 100
Geistermauer 18, 262
Generalkonsulat, deutsches 11, 88, 100, 102, 106, 130
Generalkonsulat, russisches 100, 102, 120
Geomantik, s. Fengshui
Gerichtsbarkeit 86, 89, 214
Germania Brauerei, Tsingtau 226
Gesandtschaft, deutsche 24, 38, 42, 50
Gesandtschafts-Sommerhäuser 52
Gesandtschaftsviertel 23, 25, 26, 27, 44, 46, 48, 60
Gouvernements-Dienstgebäude 14, 20, 210, 214, 276, 300
Gouverneurswohnhaus 14, 15, 17, 20, 200, 206, 244, 292, 294, 300
Green Line Building 100
Grundstückspreise 87, 199

Hai He-Fluß 57, 59, 72, 78
Hai-Ho, s. Hai He
Hamburg-Amerika-Linie 284, 302
Han-Fluß 141
Heilig-Geist-Kloster, Qingdao 238, 250, 252
Himmelstempel 24, 28
Historismus 106
Holland 26
Holy Trinity Cathedral School, Shanghai 104
Hua Dong Hospital, Shanghai 136, 138
Huang He Eisenbahnbrücke 166
Huang He-Fluß 159, 166
Huangpu-Fluß 85, 88, 89, 94, 100, 120, 126, 130
Hungshan-Revier 278
Hygieneausstellung, Dresden 32

Iltis, Kanonenboot 98, 228
Iltis-Denkmal, Shanghai 88, 89, 98, 130
Iltis-Kaserne, Qingdao 202, 232, 234, 300
Iltisbrunnen, Mineralwasser 226
Institut Technique Franco-Chinois 122
International Club, Beijing, s. Peking Club
Italien 26, 58

Japan 26, 58, 59, 62, 146, 197
Jugendstil 15, 50, 76, 78, 180, 182, 206, 218, 240, 244, 262, 270, 272, 288

Kaiping-Bergwerke 58
Kaiser-Wilhelm-Schule, Shanghai 89, 100, 102, 104, 130, 132, 138
Kaiser-Wilhelm-Schule, Tianjin 62
Kaiserkanal 57, 72, 155, 156, 159, 174
Kaiserlich Chinesische Universität 242
Kaiserliche Stadt, Beijing 23, 32, 34
Kang-You-wei-Museum, Qingdao 294
Kathedrale 112, 170, 190, 248, 250
Ketteler-Denkmal 44
Kiautschou-Vertrag 196
Kirche 14, 62, 68, 102, 132, 145, 174, 176, 244, 248, 250
Kloster Jietai Si 27
Kommunalverband 61, 66
Konfuziusvereinigung 258
Konsolenkapitell 17, 162

Konsulat, deutsches 15, 32, 59, 61, 66, 145, 146, 148, 179, 186, 188, 276
Kriegerdenkmal 68

Landordnung 81, 85, 203
Laoshan-Wasser 226
Lazarett, deutsches 46, 48, 134, 236
Lilong-Häuser 86, 144

M.A.N. Augsburg-Nürnberger AG 166
Mandschustadt, Beijing 23, 24, 27, 28, 34, 42
Mannschaftskasino, Shanghai 100, 102
Margaret Williamson Hospital, Shanghai 134
Martin & Pillzing, Gießerei 98
Maschinenfabrik Germania, Chemnitz 226
Me-I-Schule 258
Mecklenburghaus, Laoshan 198
Moltke-Kaserne, Qingdao 202
Mondtor 76, 78
Moore Memorial Church, Shanghai 132
Mow Kee, Baufirma 126

Neorenaissance, deutsche 13, 20, 46, 48, 70, 88, 90, 118, 188, 220, 222, 284, 302
Neorenaissance, italienische 70, 108, 110, 148, 188
Neoromanik 15, 20, 64, 248
Neues Palais, Potsdam 15
New Garden Hotel, Shanghai 96

Observatorium, Beijing 25
Observatorium, Qingdao 228
Opiumkrieg 23, 58
Ostasiatische Besatzungs-Brigade 46, 48, 68
Österreich-Ungarn 26, 58, 89

Paifang, s. Ehrenbogen
Pailou, s. Ehrenbogen
Parkhotel, Shanghai 132
Parlament, chinesisches 18, 30, 34, 38, 40
Paulun Hospital, Shanghai 134
Peiho, s. Hai He-Fluß
Peking Club 50, 296
Pension Luther, Qingdao 274, 288
Polizei 142, 150, 220
Post, chinesische 106, 280
Post, deutsche 100, 106, 280
Postmoderne 19
Preußische Maschinenbauschule 122
Preußisches Kultusministerium 238
Prinz-Heinrich-Hotel, Qingdao 268, 270, 272, 288

Qianmen, Stadttor 27, 28, 30
Qing-Dynastie 38, 63, 78, 203
Qingdaoer Renaissance 20

Reichsmarineamt 61, 186, 228, 232, 282
Reichstag, Berliner 18, 34, 36, 66
Republik China 38, 40, 203
Rickscha 87, 220
Rokoko 15
Rolandsäule 15, 68
Russisch-Chinesische Bank 108, 148
Rußland 26, 58, 60, 142

St. Francis Xavier School, Shanghai 104
St. Luke's Hospital, Shanghai 134
St. Michaels Kathedrale, Qingdao 248, 250
St. Michel Kirche, Beijing 26
St. Joseph Kirche, Shanghai 102
Sanssouci, Potsdam 10
Schantung-Bergbau-Gesellschaft 157, 158, 278
Schantung-Eisenbahn 159, 164, 179, 188, 197, 224, 286
Schantung-Eisenbahn-Gesellschaft 168, 184, 222, 278

319

Schlachthof 224
Schmidt, F.H., Baufirma 48, 64, 66, 70, 188, 210, 214, 218, 226, 234, 244, 270, 280, 292
Schu-Fan-Schule, Qingdao 258
Schule 62, 89, 100, 102, 104, 122, 126, 130, 145, 152, 174, 238, 242, 256, 258
See-Bataillon III 203, 234
Seebad 27, 52, 54, 197, 202, 294
Seemanshaus 17, 260
Seezoll, chinesischer 218, 286, 296
Seidenspinnerei 158
Selberg & Schlüter, Baufirma 106, 146
Shanghai Animal Hospital 132
Shanghai Club 94
Shanghai Municipal Council 138
Shanghai Mutual Telephone Company 114
Siemens und Halske 27
Sietas Plambeck, Firma 272
Slowakei 132
Social Shanghai, Illustrierte 203
Sommerfrische 19, 143, 202, 203
Stadtmauer 27, 28, 42, 57, 87, 156
Stahlbeton 114, 120, 138
Steyler Missionsgesellschaft 17, 155, 156, 160, 170, 174, 176, 250
Strandhotel, Qingdao 203, 266
Straßenbahn 27, 28, 57, 87
Suzhou-Creek, Shanghai 88, 100, 120

Ta-chüeh-sy, s. Tempel Dajue Si
Tageblatt für Nordchina, Tianjin 78
Taiping-Revolution 85
Tatarenstadt, s. Mandschustadt
Telge & Schroeter, Firma 34, 118
Tempel Dajue Si 11, 26
Tientsin-Baugesellschaft 74
Tientsin-Pukow Eisenbahngesellschaft 17, 72, 159, 160, 162, 164, 179, 180, 182
Tippelskirch & Co., von, Firma 280
Tje-tai-tze, s. Kloster Jietai Si
Tongji-Universität 89, 126, 128
Transsibirische Eisenbahn 142, 198
Trinity Cathedral, Shanghai 112
Trussed Concrete Steel Co., Detroit 114
Tsingtao-Beer 226
Tsingtau-Klub 18, 262
Tsingtauer Hotel Aktiengesellschaft 266
Tung-chi Hospital 134
Tung-chi Technische Hochschule, s. Tongji-Universität

Verband Deutscher Flottenvereine 228
Verband für den Fernen Osten 126
Verbotene Stadt, Beijing 23
Vereinigung zur Errichtung deutscher technischer Schulen in China 122, 152
Versailler Vertrag 25
Victoria Brauerei, Shanghai 226
Victoria-Nurses Home, Shanghai 138
Voh Kee Construction Co., Baufirma 134

Warenhaus Max Grill 290
Wasserwerk 87
Weimarer Mission 17, 254, 256, 258
Whangpoo, s. Huangpu-Fluß

Yangzi-Strom 85, 89, 126, 141, 143, 146
Yongding Men, Stadttor 27
Yuanming Yuan 23, 58
Yung-ting-men, s. Yongding Men

Zoll 81, 218, 296
Zhengshi Tang, Krönungspalais 32

PERSONENREGISTER/INDEX: NAMES

Adalbert von Preußen, Prinz 90
Anzer, Joh. Bapt. von, Bischof 155, 170, 174, 196, 250, 252

Bach, Bauinspektor 162
Baedecker, Carl, Architekt 18, 90, 94, 122, 152
Bartels, Franz, Pater 248, 250, 252
Becker & Baedecker, Architekten 48, 70, 100, 116, 118, 145, 188, 276
Becker, Heinrich, Architekt 13, 90, 94, 96, 102, 106, 108, 110, 148
Begas, Reinhold, Bildhauer 98
Bernatz, Regierungsbaumeister 238, 250, 252
Bernick, H. & Pötter 274, 298
Bernick, Hermann 298
Bialucha, Arthur, Architekt 248
Boerschmann, Ernst, Regierungsbaumeister 11
Borkowetz, Ingenieur 166
Busch, E., Architekt 130, 148, 150

Ch'ing, Prinz, s. Qing
Chen-han-pu, Reichsbankdirektor 18
Chou-fu, Gouverneur 292
Chun, Prinz 44
Cixi, Kaiserinwitwe 18, 36
Corbinarius, Pater 190, 192

Dennison, Ram & Gibbs, Architeken 82
Diederichs, von, Admiral 196, 230
Dörffel, A., Architekt 90
Dorpmüller, Julius 166
Dowdall & Moorhead, Architekten 102

Eckhardt, Th. 96
Eggebrecht, Gouvernements-Tierarzt 224
Erlemann, Heinrich, Pater 170, 174, 176, 248

Faber, Ernst, Missionar 258
Faust, J. 78
Fischer, Hermann, Architekt 180
Fischer, Martin, Gesandter 12
Fittkau, Hans, Architekt 214, 218
Fräbel, Alfred, Pater 248
Franzius, Georg, Hafenbaudirektor 68, 80, 143, 195
Friedrich der Große 10

Gaedertz, Alfred 222
Gong, Prinz 204
Grill, Max, Kaufmann 290
Guo Moruo, Dichter 44

Hackbarth, Bauassistent 162
Hamburger, Architekt 138
Heinrich von Preußen, Prinz 98, 230
Hempel, G.L., Architekt 146
Henle, Richard, Pater 176
Henn 284
Hennighaus, Augustin, Bischof 248
Herold, E., Architekt 52
Hildebrand, Heinrich, Regierungsbaumeister 11, 142, 186, 222, 276
Hudec, Ladislaus Edward, Architekt 132, 134, 136

Jaeschke, Paul, Gouverneur 198, 276
Jandl, Abteilungsbaumeister 160

Ketteler, Clemens von, Gesandter 25, 44
Knipping, Konsul 63
Konfuzius 155, 160, 170
Kraus, August, Bildhauer 98
Krieg, Martin 118
Kung, Herzog 160

Kung, Prinz, s. Gong
Kunze, Missionar 254

Lange, Konsul 186
Larz, Apotheker 288
Lazarowicz, Werner, Architekt 262
Lieb, Hans Emil, Architekt 104, 120
Linow, Ingenieur 182
Ludwig, Garnisonsbauinspektor 46, 52
Lundt, R.H. 118
Luther, Helene 274

Mahlke, Regierungsbaumeister 206, 210
Mao Zedong 208
Marcks, Lothar, Architekt 130, 234
Marcks, Lothar & Busch, Architekten 148, 150
Martwig, R. 264
Mauerer, Franz Xaver, Architekt 256
Meyer-Waldeck, Alfred, Gouverneur 208
Mittag, Max 118
Moorhead, R.B., Architekt 102
Müller, Georg Alexander, Korvettenkapitän 98
Müller, Hauptmann, Ingenieuroffizier 232
Müller, Pionierhauptmann 230
Mumm, von, Gesandter 54

Neumann, Richard, Schlachtermeister 100
Nies, Franz X., Pater 176

Oberlein, Erich, Regierungsbaumeister a.D. 126
Ohlmer, Ernst, Seezolldirektor 42, 200, 218, 296

Paget, Charles, Architekt 114
Paquet, Alfons, Schriftsteller 15, 142, 220
Paulun, Erich, Arzt 134
Phillips, G.W., Ingenieur 114
Pötter, Ingenieur 298
Purnell, Arthur, Architekt 114

Qing, Prinz 78

Raffelt, Regierungsbaumeister a.D. 232
Ram, E.A., Architekt 82
Rex, Graf von, Gesandter 52
Richter, Paul Friedrich, Architekt 186, 228, 262, 272, 290
Richthofen, Ferdinand von, Geograph 157
Rothkegel, Curt, Architekt 18, 19, 26, 28, 30, 34, 38, 40, 50, 64, 76, 244, 262, 270, 274, 288
Rothkegel, Gertrud 28, 32

Saarinen, Eliel, Architekt 180
Schab, Oskar von, Arzt 134
Schaffrath, Architekt 150
Schrameier, Wilhelm 200, 203
Schwechten, Franz, Architekt 15
Seel, Richard, Architekt 108
Segalen, Victor 12
Stenz, Georg, Pater 156
Stoessel, Regierungsbaumeister 224
Strasser, Hochbaudirektor 206, 218
Suhr & Woserau, Architekten 104
Suhr, Karsten Hermann, Architekt 70, 104, 122, 152

Truppel, Oskar, Gouverneur 14, 208
Tsai-hsün, Prinz, s. Zaixun
Tsai-lun, Prinz, s. Zailun
Tschang, General, s. Zhang
Tschun, Prinz, s. Chun
Tz'u-hsi, Kaiserinwitwe, s. Cixi

Uechtritz, Freiherr von, Bildhauer 68

Waldersee, Alfred Graf von, Generalfeldmarschall 48, 60
Wallot, Paul, Architekt 34

Weig, Georg, Bischof 248
Weiler, Luis, Ingenieur 222, 276
Wentrup, Regierungsbaumeister 220
Wilhelm, Richard 10, 204, 256, 258
Wilhelm I., Kaiser 15
Wilhelm II., Kaiser 14, 15, 64, 90, 98, 155, 196
Wutzler, W., Architekt 106, 146

Yuan Shikai, Präsident 32
Yung-tao, Taotai 18

Zailun, Prinz 78
Zaixun, Prinz, Marineminister 18, 32
Zhang, General 196

ORTSREGISTER/INDEX: PLACES

Altona 48, 64, 66, 70, 188, 210, 214, 218, 226, 234, 244, 270, 280, 292
Amoy, s. Xiamen

Beidaihe 27, 52, 54, 294
Beijing 11, 12, 13, 23–50, 52, 54, 57, 58, 60, 70, 142, 143, 242, 248, 296
Berlin 34, 48, 68, 70, 100, 106, 146, 148, 188, 198, 244, 276
Bohai-Meer 52, 166
Boshan 157, 278
Budapest 132

Cangkou 158
Cangzhou 164
Caozhou 155
Chemnitz 226
Chemulpo, s. Inch'ön
Chengdu 12
Chi-kung-shan, s. Jigong Shan
Chicago 142
Chin Chow, s. Jinzhou
Chou-tsun, s. Zhoucun
Chufou, s. Qufu

Dabaodao 179, 200, 220, 250, 254, 268, 284
Dagu 57
Daijia Zhuang 176
Dairen, s. Dalian
Dalian 197, 203, 248
Dalny, s. Dalian
Danzig 282
Dä-tja, s. Daijia Zhuang
Detroit 114
Dezhou 164
Dresden 32
Düsseldorf 190

Formosa, s. Taiwan

Gaomi 168, 202
Guangzhou 85, 114
Guling 143
Guodian 168
Gustavsburg 166

Hamburg 34, 48, 64, 66, 70, 116, 188, 210, 214, 218, 226, 234, 244, 270, 280, 292
Hankou, s. Wuhan
Hanyang, s. Wuhan
Hebei 60
Helsinki 180
Hildesheim 296
Hongkong 11, 80, 82, 85, 203, 228, 276, 286

Inch'ön 228

Jendschofu, s. Yanzhou
Jiangsu 166
Jiaozhou 13, 143, 155, 158, 170, 196
Jigong Shan 143
Jinan 13, 16, 17, 72, 156, 158, 164, 168, 179–192, 197, 218, 222, 248, 276, 280
Jining 155, 174, 176
Juye 155

Kairo 94
Kanton, s. Guangzhou
Kaumi, s. Gaomi
Kiautschou, s. Jiaozhou
Koblenz 15
Köln 94
Kotien, s. Guodian
Küfu, s. Qufu
Kuling, s. Guling
Küyeh, s. Juye
Kwantung, s. Liaodong

Laoshan-Berge 14, 198
Lei-chou-fu, s. Leizhou
Leizhou 190
Licun 216, 254, 280
Litsun, s. Licun
Lungschan, s. Pinglingcheng
Luokou 166
Lushan 143
Lüshun 142, 197

Majiapu 27
Manila 228
Matschiapu, s. Majiapu
Mukden, s. Shenyang
München 94, 226, 250, 252
Münster in Westfalen 44

Nan-hsia-kou, s. Nanxiakou
Nanhai 18
Nanjing 17, 58, 62, 72, 126, 159, 162, 180, 198, 214
Nanxiakou 164

Paris 90
Peitaiho, s. Beidaihe
Peking, s. Beijing
Ping-yuan-hsien, s. Pingyuan
Pinglingcheng 168
Pingyuan 164
Port Arthur, s. Lüshun
Po-shan, s. Boshan
Posen 15
Potsdam 10, 15, 25
Pukow, s. Nanjing

Qingdao 11, 12, 13, 15, 19, 20, 32, 61, 80, 98, 106, 130, 157, 158, 159, 168, 179, 184, 186, 188, 195–302
Qufu 155, 160, 170
Schanghai, s. Shanghai
Schantung, s. Shandong
Schwerin 94
Shandong 17, 155–176, 195, 292
Shanghai 13, 48, 59, 85–138, 141, 146, 152, 188, 195, 196, 203, 226, 228, 286, 292
Shenyang 32, 57, 58, 130
Shimonoseki 60, 142
Sichuan 12
Sikawei, s. Xujiahui

Tai'an 17, 162
Tai-an-fu, s. Tai'an

Tai hsi tschen, s. Taixi Zhen
Tai tung tschen, s. Taidong Zhen
Taidong Zhen 200, 201, 202, 254
Taikia, s. Daijia Zhuang
Taishan 155, 162
Taixi Zhen 201
Taku, s. Dagu
Tangshan 58
Tapautau, s. Dabaodao
Te-chou, s. Dezhou
Tetschow, s. Dezhou
Tianjin 15, 19, 23, 26, 32, 50, 54, 57–78, 141, 145, 159, 162, 164, 195, 198, 203, 244, 248, 274, 286, 288
Tientsin, s. Tianjin
Tokio 230
Tsang-chou, s. Cangzhou
Tsangkou, s. Cangkou
Tschoutsun, s. Zhoucun
Tsimo, s. Jimo
Tsinanfu, s. Jinan
Tsingtau, s. Qingdao
Tsining-tschou, s. Jining

Wei-hsien, s. Weifang
Weifang 157, 179, 278
Westberge, Beijing 26, 204
Woosung, s. Wusong
Wuchang, s. Wuhan
Wuhan 18, 27, 59, 72, 94, 130, 141–152, 195
Wusong 89, 124, 126, 128

Xiamen 30
Xujiahui 228

Yanzhou 155, 160, 170, 174
Yen-chou-fu, s. Yanzhou
Yentschoufu, s. Yanzhou

Zaudschofu, s. Caozhou
Zhoucun 168, 179

1. 理夏德‧衛禮賢(Wilhelm, Richard)《中國之魂》(Die Seele Chinas)柏林，一九二六年，第二六六頁。理夏德‧衛禮賢於一八八九年至一九二零年僑居青島，一九二五年在法蘭克福創辦了中國文化歷史研究所。
2. 海因丁‧菲舍爾巴(Hildebrand, Heinrich)《北京城郊的名勝－大覺寺》(Der Tempel Ta-chüeh-sy. Tempel des großen Erkennens) bei Peking)柏林，一八八七年，一九四三年在北京再版。
3. 恩斯特‧比希曼(Boerschmann, Ernst)《中國的建築藝術》(Chinesische Architektur)，柏林，一九二五年；《中國的寶塔》(Chinesische Pagoden)柏林，萊比錫，一九三一年第五十三年。
4. 維克多‧賽加倫(Segalen, Victor)：《萊納‧雷斯》Ren Leys法蘭克福，一九八二年，第四十三頁。作者在一九一三年到一九一四年在北京撰寫了此書，一九二二年第一次出版。
5. 馬丁‧菲舍爾(Fischer, Martin)《清末三年在四川的社交及旅遊雜記》(Diplomatie und Reisen in China während der letzten drei Jahre der Kaiserzeit)慕尼黑，維也納，一九七八年第五十三頁。
6. 十九世紀末二十世紀初，西洋建築對中國傳統建築手法的影響在中國沿海城市已初見端倪。由外國建築師其中一部分為德國人設計的西式樓房也是中國現代建築的一部份。中國建築史學者把這些建築看作是中國近代建築史的研究對象。羅小末，上海同濟大學建築系教授，一九九二年四月五日。
7. 赫爾曼‧穆特西吾斯(Muthesius, Hermann)引自《建築管理匯報》(in Centralblatt der Bauverwaltung)柏林，一九〇〇年九月八日，第四二九頁。
8. 見《德文新報》(Ostasiatischer Lloyd)，上海，一九一二年九月十三日，第二三二頁。
9. 參見《青島快報》(Tsingtauer Neueste Nachrichten)，青島，一九一三年十二月十六日，第二頁。
10. 阿爾豐斯‧派克韋斯(Paquet, Alfons)：《禮儀還是立憲？》(Li oder Im neuen Osten)，法蘭克福，一九一三年，第二九七頁。派克韋斯是德國工廠聯合會董事會成員。
11. 威廉二世當時對建築很感興趣，也通曉設計制圖的技能。他的風格對德意志帝國時期的建築形式頗有影響。參見保羅‧賽德爾(Seidel, Paul)：《皇上與藝術》(Der Kaiser und die Kunst)柏林，一九〇七年，第三六頁。
12. 參見沃爾夫岡‧勞貝爾(Lauber, Wolfgang)：《多哥的德國建築》(Deutsche Architektur in Togo 1884-1914)，斯圖加特，一九九三年。
13. 保羅‧羅爾巴赫(Rohrbach, Paul)《德國的殖民地》(Die deutschen Kolonien)，達豪，一九一四年。
14. 《德文新報》(Ostasiatischer Lloyd)，上海，一九〇五年一月十三日，第八二頁；一九一〇年五月九日八日，四五九頁。
15. 庫爾特‧羅克格(Rothkegel, Curt)：《建築師庫爾特‧羅克格在中國的建築設計活動》(Tätigkeit des Architekten Curt Rothkegel in China)，利希滕施泰因，一九四〇，尚未發表的手稿。
16. 維克多‧賽加倫(Segalen, Victor)：《萊納‧雷斯》(René Leys)法蘭克福，一九八二年，第二頁。
17. 北京舊城牆於一九五八年被拆毀，以修建環城路，現今僅在北京火車站後還有一些斷垣殘壁尚存。保存下來的城門寥寥無幾。
18. 《德文新報》(Ostasiatischer Lloyd)，上海，一九一一年九月十五日，第二二二頁。
19. 里夏德‧衛禮賢(Wilhelm, Richard)：《中國之魂》(Die Seele Chinas)，柏林，一九二六年，第二十五頁。
20. 埃米爾‧威廉密(Wilhelmy, Emil)：《中國的風土人情》(China. Land und Leute)，柏林，一九〇四年，第五四八頁。
21. 《波茨坦宮殿的歷史及其藝術價值》(Potsdamer Schlösser in Geschichte und Kunst)，萊比錫，一九八四年，一五二頁。
22. 《德文新報》(Ostasiatischer Lloyd)，上海，一九〇三年五月二十八日，第五七七頁。
23. "在大清帝國的京都生活了一段時間的外國人都會感到，北平的外國僑民除了那些乏味的社交聚會和招待會外再沒有什麼娛樂消遣了。" 見《德文新報》(Ostasiatischer Lloyd)，上海，一九〇二年十二月十六日，第五六〇頁。
24. 海因里希‧錫樂巴(Hildebrand, Heinrich)《北京城郊的名勝－大覺寺》(Der Tempel Ta-chüeh-sy bei Peking)柏林，一八八七年。
25. 波茨坦聯邦檔案館檔案(Bundesarchiv Potsdam)‧中國公使館(Gesandtschaft China)，第一五八八卷，第四十四，七十四頁。
26. 《上海社會－大眾雜誌》(Social Shanghai. A Magazine for men and Women)一九〇六年六月。
27. 一八九六年到一九〇七年，德國政府工程師海因里希‧錫樂巴受中國工部左侍郎，會辦商業大臣盛宣懷之托編制並規劃了北京至武漢約一千五百公里長的鐵路路線。一八九八年到一九〇四年錫樂巴還主持了青島至濟南的鐵路鋪設工程。參見格奧爾格‧弗蘭茨吾斯(Franzius, Georg)《膠州。德國在東亞的保護地》(Kiautschou. Deutschlands Erwerbung in Ostasien)，柏林，一八九八年，第六十八頁及下頁。
28. 《德文新報》(Ostasiatischer Lloyd)，上海，一九一四年二月十三日，一九一四年六月五日。
29. 《東亞畫報》(The East of Asia Magazine)，上海，一九〇二年，第五頁。
30. 《遠東時報》(The Far Eastern Review)，馬尼拉，上海，橫濱，一九一五年七月，第六十四頁及下頁。
31. 奧斯瓦德‧西雷(Sirén, Osvald)：《北平的城門和城牆》(The Walls and gates of Peking)，倫敦，一九二四年，第一七一頁。
32. 每隔十六級台階都設有一休息平台，共有五個休息平台。這樣，人們在登高時就不會太吃力。每一台階高十五厘米，寬三十厘米。
33. 裝飾線高四十三厘米，厚約三十厘米。
34. 奧斯瓦德‧西雷，同〈31〉，第一七五頁。人們對改建前門一事都深感遺憾："給城門前裝上裝上不倫不類的裝飾線，並在城門周圍建了平台及通向平台的造價昂貴而不實用的階梯。想以此來裝扮孤零零的外城門。然而這又有什麼用？北京最雄偉狀觀的城門已永遠不存在了。" 《德文新報》(Ostasiatischer Lloyd)，上海，一九一五年九月十七日。
35. 見《德文新報》(Ostasiatischer Lloyd)：上海，一九一一年七月七日，第十七頁。
36. 參見庫爾特‧羅克格：同十五。
37. 參見庫爾特‧羅克格：同十五。
38. 《建築管理匯報》(Centralblatt der Bauverwaltung)，柏林，一八九四年，第四四三頁。
39. 羅克格後來寫道："國會主席認為建築局規定的四百五十名下議院議員數額太少……希望增加到約六百個席位。" 參見波茨坦聯邦檔案館檔案(Bundesarchiv Potsdam)：中國公使館(Gesandtschaft China)第八五三卷，第十三頁。後來羅克格又修改了設計圖。
40. 《德文新報》(Ostasiatischer Lloyd)上海，一九一〇年十二月九日，第五六五頁及下頁。
41. 見H.G.W.伍德黑迪(Woodhead, H.G.W.)：《中華民國紀實》(The Truth About the Chinese Republic)，倫敦，一九二五年，第十七頁。奧斯卡‧韋格爾(Weggel, Oskar)：《二十世紀的中國歷史》(Geschichte Chinas im 20. Jahrhundert)，斯圖加特，一九八九年，第廿八頁。
42. 波茨坦聯邦檔案館檔案(Bundesarchiv Potsdam)中國公使館，第八五卷，第一〇五頁。
43. 《德文新報》(Ostasiatischer Lloyd)，上海，橫濱，一九一〇年十一月八日，第四六三頁。
44. 《遠東時報》(The Far Eastern Review)，馬尼拉，上海，橫濱，一九一三年九月，第一二二頁及下頁。
45. 波茨坦聯邦檔案館檔案(Bundesarchiv Potsdam)中國公使館，第八五三卷，第九十二頁到九十三頁。
46. 庫爾特‧羅克格：同〈15〉。
47. 《德文新報》(Ostasiatischer Lloyd)，上海，一九一三年四月十八日，第三七五頁。
48. 《德文新報》(Ostasiatischer Lloyd)，上海，一九一四年五月廿九日，第四五二頁。
49. 埃里希‧馮‧薩爾茨曼(von Salzmann, Erich)，《北平的德國公使館》(Die deutsche Gesandtschaft in Peking)，登載於《每周評論》，柏林，一九一四年一月至三月卅一日，第十四至十九頁。
50. 飛石(FEI-SHI. Fischer, Emil)《北京及近郊旅遊指南》(Guide to Peking and its Environs)，天津，一九〇九年，第十九頁。
51. 《德文新報》(Ostasiatischer Lloyd)，上海，一九一一年二月十七日，第一七八頁。
52. 北京昌平縣明十三陵前第一座石牌坊，規模造型與"保衛和平"牌坊相似，但十三陵的石牌坊面闊五間，較之"保衛和平牌坊"更寬些。
53. 飛石：同〈50〉，第六十六頁。《德文新報》於一九〇二年十一月廿八日在九八三頁上刊登了拉丁語的碑文。見正文圖文。
54. 《德文新報》(Ostasiatischer Lloyd)，上海，一九〇二年十一月八日。
55. 里夏德‧衛禮賢(Wilhelm, Richard)同〈1〉，第卅頁和第二六三頁。
56. 波茨坦聯邦檔案館檔案(Bundesarchiv Potsdam)，中國公使館，第一〇四八卷，第二二一頁。
57. 波茨坦聯邦檔案館檔案(Bundesarchiv Potsdam)，中國公使館，第二六六卷，第六七二頁。
58. 《德文新報》(Ostasiatischer Lloyd)，上海，一九〇四年五月二十一日，第八七二頁。
59. 卡爾‧C‧略施(Loesch, Karl C.)《外國人看德國人和德國文化》(Deutsche Züge im Antlitz der Erde)，慕尼黑，第一七二頁。
60. 卡特賴特‧阿諾德‧賴特(Wright, Arnold, Cartwright)：《二十世紀的香港、上海及中國其它通商口岸之觀感》(Twentieth Century Impressions of HongKong, Shanghai, and other, Treaty Ports of China)，倫敦，一九〇八年，第六〇三頁。
61. 波茨坦聯邦檔案館檔案(Bundesarchiv Potsdam)中國公使館，第一〇四八卷，第一九三頁。
62. 《德文新報》(Ostasiatischer Lloyd)，上海，一九一二年十二月廿日，第五六〇頁。
63. 波茨坦聯邦檔案館檔案(Bundesarchiv Potsdam)，中國公使館，第六九七卷，第一一六頁。
64. 參見波茨坦聯邦檔案館檔案(Bunde-sarchiv Potsdam)中國公使館，第一五八八卷，第一一三頁(一九一五年地圖)。
65. 《德文新報》(Ostasiatischer Lloyd)，上海，一九〇八年六月廿六日，第一〇九七頁。
66. 《上海社會》(Social Shanghai)，上海，一九〇六年，第一二五頁。
67. 《海河管理局一八八八至一九一九年工作備忘錄》，一九一九年，第卅七頁(Hai-Ho Conservancy Board 1898-1919)。海河是天津與大海相連的通道，冬天海河結凍，貨物運輸也因此停滯。
68. 一八九四年鐵路鋪至山海關，即長城終點臨海之處；一八九九年錦州通車。參見O.D.拉斯姆森(Rasmussen, O.D.)《天津簡史》(Tientsin. An Illustrated Outline History)，天津，一九二五年，第九十五頁及下頁。
69. 中國鐵路局為業主。該鐵路線在大連河以東與其並行至德州，在濟南附近繞過黃河再往南直抵長江。此線長六百二十五公里的北段由德國工程師承攬鋪築。
70. O.D.拉斯姆森，同〈68〉，第廿七頁。
71. 一九〇二年美國租界並入英國租界。參見波茨坦聯邦檔案館檔案(Bundesarchiv Potsdam)中國公使館第一〇一五卷，第三一四頁。
72. 一千七百二十名日本人、一千五百卅名英國人、七百五十三名德國人、五百四十二名美國人、二九四名法國人、一百五十四名俄國人、九十三名意大利人、八十五名端士人、七十名丹麥人、十二名奧地利人等。參見日本皇家鐵路局(Imperial Japanese Government Railways)《關於東亞的官方資料》(An Official Guide to Eastern Asia)一九二〇年。
73. 一九〇二年在英國租界內有二百五十五名英國人、一百四十五名日本人、一百零四名德國人、三十五名俄國人、十五名丹麥人、十二名奧地利人和廿六名歐洲其它國家的人。住在英國租界的約四千三百名個中國人中有一千八百名左右受僱於外國人。參見《德文新報》(Ostasiatischer Lloyd)，上海，一九〇二年十一月八日，第九七七頁。
74. 參見布魯諾‧納瓦拉(Navarra, Bruno)《中國和中國人》(China und die Chinesen)，不萊梅，上海，一九〇一年，一〇七頁三。埃米爾‧威廉密(Wilhelmy, Emil)：《中國的風土人情》(China a. Land und Leute)，柏林，一九〇四年，第六二頁及下頁。
75. 一九〇二年駐紮在華北的官兵數字如下：一千九百廿名法國人、一千六百名英國人、一千六百名德國人、四百八十名日本人、四百八十名俄國人、一千九百五十名意大利人、一百五十名美國人，總計約為八千七百人。
76. 駐紮在天津的軍隊有英國兵一千二百人、日本兵四百廿人、意大利兵二百廿八人、美國兵一百七十人、俄國兵一百廿八人以及德國兵一百名。
77. 《德文新報》(Ostasiatischer Lloyd)，上海，一九一二年十二月十日，第五五六頁。
78. 中國在一八九四至一八九五年的中日甲午戰爭中敗北。台灣島及附屬各島嶼歸屬日本，可是其後歸還所占領的東北地區，歸還華北的重要的軍港旅順，參見埃米爾‧威廉密。同〈20〉，第五一六頁以及下凡頁。
79. O.D.拉斯姆森，同〈68〉，第九十五頁。
80. 波茨坦聯邦檔案館檔案(Bundesarchiv Potsdam)中國公使館，第一〇五卷，第五十五頁。
81. 租界的稅額取決於租界代表大會代表的票數。每個代表最高能投十二票。因而一九一一年天津建築公司和隸屬德華銀行的德國租界協會就占了一半的選票。參見波茨坦聯邦檔案館檔案(Bundesarchiv Potsdam)中國公使館，第一〇五卷，第十一頁，第一〇四八卷，第九十九頁及一一〇頁。
82. 一九一三年在德國租界作了一次人口普查，其結果為：一千二百零五名中國人、二百八十四名歐洲人、美國人和日本人。其中有一百一十七名德國僑民及三百零四名德國士兵。當時約有七百名德國人僑居天津。參見《德文新報》(Ostasiatischer Lloyd)，上海，一九一三年五月卅日；日本皇家鐵路局(The Imperial Japanese Government Railways)同〈72〉，第廿五頁。
83. 波茨坦聯邦檔案館檔案(Bundesarchiv Potsdam)中國公使館，第一〇五〇卷，第一八四頁及下頁，第三一〇頁。
84. 波茨坦聯邦檔案館檔案(Bundesarchiv Potsdam)中國公使館，第一〇五〇卷，第二二〇頁(一九一二年五月七日的函件)。
85. 引文同上。
86. 波茨坦聯邦檔案館檔案(Bundesarchiv Potsdam)中國公使館，第一〇五〇卷，第四五四頁(一九一二年八月十五日的函件)。
87. 當時的海關總督、慶親王的兒子載倫、載洵、載濤(音譯)以及江南提督張勳任進租界並購地買房。"張勳與袁世凱勢均力敵，可謂中國極有權勢貴力的人。"參見波茨坦聯邦檔案館檔案(Bundesarchiv Potsdam)中國公使館，第一〇五卷，第一九〇頁以及下頁，第二七四頁。
88. 《天津近代建築》。
89. 阿諾德‧賴特(Wright, Arnold)同〈60〉，第七三〇頁。
90. 波茨坦聯邦檔案館檔案(Bundesarchiv Potsdam)中國公使館，第一〇五卷，第九十八頁。
91. 波茨坦聯邦檔案館檔案(Bundesarchiv Potsdam)中國公使館，第一〇五〇卷，第一九三頁。《華中日報》(Tageblatt für Nordchina)，天津，一九零七年八月一日。
92. 《中國時報》(China Times)一九〇七年八月一日；"同心同德則盛，離心離德則衰"。參見波茨坦聯邦檔案館檔案(Bundesarchiv Potsdam)中國公使館，第一〇五一卷，一九五頁。
93. 《德文新報》(Ostasiatischer Lloyd)上海，一九〇八年四月三日，第六三九頁。
94. 《德文新報》(Ostasiatischer Lloyd)上海，一九一三年六月十五日，第六十一頁。
95. F.科貝爾施泰因(Koberstein, F.)，《天津及其近郊》(Tientsin und Umgebung)天津，一九〇六年，第三十八頁。
96. 十四世紀到十八世紀在德國的北部城市建起這種象徵著市

97. 民人權和自由的騎士雕像。參見阿諾德、賴特,同〈60〉,第七二六頁。
《德文新報》(Ostasiatischer Lloyd),上海,一九〇三年十一月六日,第七二七頁。這裡所指的是格奧爾格·弗蘭茨吾斯所著的《膠州,德國在東亞的領地》一書。此書一八九八年在柏林出版。
98. 阿諾德、賴特:同〈60〉,第六〇四頁。
99. 波茨坦聯邦檔案館檔案(Bundesarchiv Potsdam)中國公使館,第一〇五一卷,第五〇頁。
100. 《德文新報》(Ostasiatischer Lloyd)上海,一九一〇年四月八日。
101. 參見《華中建築》,湖北武昌,一九八七年第二期,在《中國近代建築史研究討論會論文專輯》中,這幢建築被誤認為德國領事館。
102. 波茨坦聯邦檔案館檔案(Bundesarchiv Potsdam)中國公使館,第一〇四卷,第七十六頁。
103. 參見恩斯特·比希曼(Boerschmann, Ernst)《中國的建築》(Chinesische Architektur),柏林,一九二五年,第一集第十五頁。
104. 參見阿諾德、賴特:同〈60〉,第七四六頁;F.科貝爾施泰因:同〈95〉,第四十頁。
105. 波茨坦聯邦檔案館檔案(Bundesarchiv Potsdam)中國公使館,第一〇五卷,第五十九頁。
106. 格奧爾格·佛朗求斯(Franzius, Georg),柏林,一八八八年同〈27〉,第十七頁。
107. 阿諾德、賴特:同〈60〉,第五十九頁。
108. 阿諾德Arnold:《秀麗的香港》(Picturesque Hong Kong),香港,一九一一年,第十五頁。
109. 《德文新報》於一九〇一年九月日發表文章,對幾個城市的人口密度作了比較:"在倫敦一英畝的土地上居民人數為六十六人,在格拉斯哥為六十一人,在香港為六十六人。人口高度集中往往導致諸如瘧疾和其它傳染病的滋生和蔓延。"在倫敦每平方公里有居民一萬四千八百人,在格拉斯哥為一萬五千零七十四人,香港的人口密度最高,每平方公里三萬一千人。
110. 單威廉(Schrameier, Wilhelm)《膠洲行政》(Aus Kiautschous Verwaltung),耶拿,一九一四年,第廿八頁。
111. 同上,第十八頁及下頁,第四十三頁及下頁;阿諾德:同〈108〉,第五十九頁。
112. 《德文新報》(Ostasiatischer Lloyd),上海,一九一四年五月十九日,第四八五頁。
113. 阿諾德:同〈60〉,第一七〇頁。
114. 《青島快報》(Tsingtauer Neueste Nachrichten)青島,一九一三年十二月十六日,第二頁。
115. 僅因後德國康科迪婭總會在上海落成,該建築為典型的德國文藝復興式復古風格。
116. 《德文新報》(Ostasiatischer Lloyd),上海,一九〇三年一月廿三日,第一五八頁。
117. F.L.H.波特(Pott. F.L.H.):《上海簡史》(A Short History of Shanghai),上海,一九二八年,第五十一頁、七十九頁。
118. 《德文新報》(Ostasiatischer Lloyd),上海,一九〇六年九月七日,第四六〇頁。
119. 《德文新報》(Ostasiatischer Lloyd),上海,一九〇六年九月廿一日,第五五五頁。
120. 《德文新報》(Ostasiatischer Lloyd),上海,一九〇六年九月七日,第四六一頁。
121. 《德文新報》(Ostasiatischer Lloyd),上海,一九〇六年九月十四日,第五〇八頁。
122. 《德文新報》(Ostasiatischer Lloyd),上海,一九〇六年八月卅日,第四一五至四一六頁。
123. 一八四三年英國首先在上海劃定租界。一八六二年至一八六三年中國界和美租界合并。稱作公共租界。一八四八年在華人城區和公共租界之間劃出了自行其政的法國租界。一八九九年公共租界由七點五平方公里擴展到廿二點八平方公里,一九一四年法國租界也擴大了地盤。
124. 《德文新報》(Ostasiatischer Lloyd),上海,一九〇四年一月八日,第四十頁。
125. 從以下的數據可以看出地價增長的幅度:一八四三年每平方米零點三金馬克,一九〇三年每平方米四馬點五金馬克,參見弗蘭茨·沃阿斯(Woas, Franz《東亞近代建築》(Ostasiatische Architektur der neueren Zeit),登載於《德國建築》(Deutsche Bauzeitung),柏林,一九〇四年九月七日,第四五一頁。
126. 雷金納德·盧夫(Luff, Reginald):《上海的建築》(Buildings in Shanghai)引自《上海社會》(Social Shanghai),上海,一九〇八年七月,第廿六頁。
127. 《德文新報》(Ostasiatischer Lloyd),上海,一九〇四年十二月十六日,第四〇三頁。
128. F.L.H.波特:見〈117〉,第二三二頁。
129. 《遠東雜誌》(Far East Magazine),上海、青島,一九三四年十二月。
130. 參見《建築管理匯報》(Centralblatt der Bauverwaltung),柏林,一八八九年,第五一五頁。
131. 《上海新聞》(Shanghaier Nachrichten)《德文新報》的副刊,上海,一九〇七年一月十八日,第十頁及下頁。
132. 《上海社會》(Social Shanghai),一九〇七年上半年合刊,第二八頁至二九五頁。
133. 為建造新廈,總會自籌白銀二萬兩,通過會員購買7.5%股有價證券籌集一萬兩,另以7%的利息向德華銀行貸款的八萬銀子。一兩銀子約等於二點七金馬克。
134. 《上海社會》(Shanghaier Nachrichten),上海,一九〇八年二月八日,第廿七頁。
135. 阿諾德、賴特,同〈60〉,第三七八頁。

136. 關於這兩位建築師的情況請參見《上海新聞》(Shanghaier Nachrichten),上海,一九一一年三月十日(登載兩名建築師的相片);《上海社會》(Social Shanghai),上海,一九〇七年,第二九四頁。
137. 《上海社會》(Social Shanghai),上海,一九〇六年上半年合刊,十七至二十頁。
138. 七十一名遇難的海軍官兵被葬在黃海岸邊的"伊爾蒂斯墓"。每年七月廿三日人們在紀念碑前獻花圈。參見《德文新報》(Ostasiatischer Lloyd),上海,一九〇三年七月卅日,第一六八頁。
139. 《上海新聞》(Shanghaier Nachrichten),上海,一九〇八年九月十一日,第一九七頁。
140. 波茨坦聯邦檔案館檔案(Bundesarchiv Potsdam)中國公使館,第九一八五卷,第九四九至九五五頁。
141. 奧托·弗蘭克(Franke, Otto)《來自兩個世界的回憶》(Erinnerungen aus zwei Welten),柏林,一九五四年,第六十二頁。
142. 《德國僑民》(Der Auslandsdeutsche),斯圖加特,一九一二年第六期,第三頁。
143. 《德文新報》(Ostasiatischer Lloyd),上海,一九〇三年十二月四日,第八九七頁;阿諾德·賴特:同〈60〉,第六六六頁。
144. 《德文新報》(Ostasiatischer Lloyd),上海,一九〇一年四月五日,第二八三頁。
145. 《德文新報》(Ostasiatischer Lloyd),上海,一九〇〇年五月十一日,第二九五頁。
146. 《德文新報》寫道:"一樓有兩間教室,每間可容納學生三十名。二樓也有兩間教室,以推拉門相隔。如果將推拉門拉開便成為一間寬敞的可容一百多人的禮堂。《德文新報》(Ostasiatischer Lloyd),上海,一九〇一年九月十三日,第七九〇頁及下頁。
147. 參見《德國僑民》(Der Auslands-deutsche),斯圖加特一九一二年六月。
148. 喬治·內利斯特(Nellist, George),《上海人與北方人》(Men of Shanghai and North China),上海,一九三三年,第三七五頁。
149. 《上海新聞》(Shanghaier Nachrichten),上海,一九一一年四月十日,第二二九頁。
150. 參見《上海新聞》(Shanghaier Nachrichten),上海,一九一一年七月七日,《公共租界教育局工作報告》。
151. 關於威廉學堂的情況參見迪特里希·韋伯(Weber, Dietrich):《上海威廉學堂》(Kaiser-Wilhelm-Schulezu Schangai),上海,一九三五年,第十七頁。
152. 《德文新報》(Ostasiatischer Lloyd),上海,一九〇五年五月十二日,第八六五頁。
153. 參見米歇科·麥德(Meid,Michiko),《日本的歐洲和北美建築》(Europäische und Nordamerikanische Architekten in Japan),博士論文,科隆,一九七七年,第二六頁及下頁。
154. 關於這幢樓的外觀和內部設施的詳情參見《德文新報》(Ostasiatischer Lloyd)上海,一九〇二年十月十四日,八六五至八七二頁。
155. 參見C.E.達爾溫特(Darwent, C.E.):《上海導游手冊》(A Handbook for Travellers and Residents),一九二〇年第汪頁:"華俄道勝銀行大廈具有意大利建築風格。門楣上都有人物或動物雕飾。中國人誤將這些雕像當作外國人的家神。"
156. 參見《德文新報》(Ostasiatischer Lloyd),上海,一九一一年三月十日,第一七一頁及下頁。
157. 參見《德國建築報》(Deutsche Bauzeitung),柏林,一九〇四年九月七日,第四五〇至四五二頁。
158. 《德文新報》(Ostasiatischer Lloyd),上海,一九〇二年八月一日,六一六至六一七頁。
159. 弗蘭茨·沃阿斯(Woas, Franz):《東亞近代建築》(Ostasiatische Architektur der neueren Zeit),見《德國建築報》(Deutsche Bauzeitung),柏林,一九〇四年九月七日,第四五二頁。
160. 這座位於漢口路與江西路口的五層大樓是由和怡公司設計,瑞新公司營造的。參見《上海新聞》(Shanghaier Nachrichten),一九〇七年三月廿二日。
161. 《上海新聞》(Shanghaier Nachrichten),一九〇七年三月十二日,第六四頁。
162. 《上海新聞》(Shanghaier Nachrichten),一九〇八年一月三日,三至四頁。
163. 阿諾德、賴特:同〈60〉,第七九四頁。
164. 阿諾德、賴特:同〈60〉,第六〇四頁。
165. 《上海新聞》(Shanghaier Nachrichten),一九〇八年一月三十一日,第三十三頁。
166. 一九〇四年阿瑟·沃阿斯寫道:"由於上海市區地皮價格昂貴,人們只得把住宅建到市郊。"久而久之便形成了"上海西城"。許多歐洲人喜歡住在此區域內,有錢的中國人也在此置地建房。後期建起的別墅模仿英國或美國的建築形式沒有什麼特色。而那些在"上海西城"初斯建造的古樸的西式別墅倒別有風味。上海西城的樓房大部是磚木結構,外牆用嵌白灰縫的清水牆砌築。"參見弗蘭茨·沃阿斯(Woas,Franz):《近代東亞建築》(Ostasiatische Architektur der neueren Zeit)刊登於《德國建築報》(Deutsche Bauzeitung),柏林,一九〇四年九月七日,第四五一頁。
167. 阿諾德、賴特:同〈60〉,第六〇四頁,在六五六頁上登載著一張"維爾弗里德"住宅的相片。
168. 參見《上海社會》(Social Shanghai),一九〇七年上半年合訂本,第二九四頁。
169. 《上海建設》(Building Activities of Shanghai)刊登於《遠東時報》(The Far Eastern Review)馬尼拉、上海、橫濱,

170. 一九一六年九月十日,第一四四頁和第一八一頁及下頁。
171. 參見《上海新聞》(Shanghaier Nachrichten)上海,一九一四年六月十二日,第一九四至一九五頁。
172. 參見《吳淞同濟大學十五周年校慶專輯》(Festschrift anlässlich des 25jährigen Bestehens der Staatlichen Tung-Chi Universität zu Woosung)吳淞,一九三二年,第四頁。
173. 參見B·貝雷倫(Berrens, B.):《德國工程及醫學院的發展軌跡》(Die Entwicklung der deutschen Medizin-und Ingenieurschule Schanghai),引自《中學生報考高校指南》(In Schülerverzeichnis),上海,一九一六年,第廿七頁及下頁。
174. 《上海新聞》(Shanghaier Nachrichten),上海,一九一四年五月五日,第一八一頁及下頁。
175. 《同濟工學院第二學年(一九一四一一九一五)工作報告》(Bericht über die Deutsche Ingenieurschule für Chinesen in Schanghai für das dritte Schuljahr),上海,一九一五年,第十六頁。
176. 《柏林畫報》(Berliner Illustrierte Zeitung),柏林,一九二三年四月八日,第二六四頁。
177. 《慶祝同濟工業大學在上海吳淞重建專輯》(Denkschrift aus Anlass der Feierlichen Einweihung der Tungchi Technischen Hochschule in Schanghai-Woosung),吳淞,一九二四年,第廿七頁。
178. 關於同濟大學發展史請參閱《慶祝同濟工業大學在上海吳淞重建開業專輯》(Denkschrift aus Anlass der Feierlichen Einweihung der Tungchi Technischen Hochschule in Schanghai-Woosung),吳淞,一九二四年;《吳淞同濟大學十五周年校慶專輯》(Festschrift anlässlich des 25jährigen Bestehens der staatlichen Tung-Chi Universität zu Woosung),吳淞,一九三二年。
179. 迪特里希·韋伯斯:同〈151〉,第廿四頁。
180. 參見《中國工商行名錄及編年史》(The Directory & Chronicle of China),日本、朝鮮、印度支那、香港,一九三七年,第八十三頁。
181. 迪特里希·韋伯斯:同〈151〉,第廿六頁。
182. 鄔達克生平詳情請參閱《斯洛伐克名人傳記》(Slovensky Biograficky Slovnik),馬爾提,一九八七;喬治·內利斯特:同〈148〉,第一八二頁及一八七頁。
183. 參閱馮·沙伯(von Schab)《同濟大學一九〇七年至一九一九年發展史》(Geschichte der Deutschen Medizin-und Ingenirsschule 1907-1919)發表於《同濟大學廿五周年校慶專輯》(Festschrift anlässlich des 25jährigen Bestehens der Staatlichen Tung-Chi Universität zu Woosung),吳淞,一九三二年,第一頁。
184. 參見《同濟大學十五周年校慶專輯》(Festschrift anlässlich des 25jährigen Bestehens der Tung-Chi Universität zu Woosung),吳淞,第二至三頁。
185. 參見里夏德·施圖烈夫(Richard Stumpf)《一九三二年至一九三三年上海的近代高層建築》(Neuzeitliches Hochbauen in Shanghai im Jahre 1932/33)引自《同濟大學廿五周年校慶專輯》(Festschrift anlässlich des 25jährigen Bestehens der Staatlichen Tung-Chi Universität zu Woosung),吳淞,一九三二年,第一六六頁及下頁。
186. 漢口有人口八十五萬,漢陽四十萬,武昌五十萬。
187. T·卡沃達(Kawata, T.):《中國和日本貿易港口城市掠影》(Glimpses of China and Japan Trade Records),大阪,一九一九年,第一七三頁。
188. 《德文新報》(Ostasiatischer Lloyd),上海,一九一三年五月卅日,第五二二頁。
189. 格奧爾格·佛朗求斯(Franzius, Georg):《膠州,德國在東亞的領地》(Kiautschou, Deutschlands Erwerbung in Ostasien),柏林,一八九八年,第六十九頁。
190. 阿利斯特·麥克米倫(Macmillan, Allister):《遠東的海港》(Seaports of the Far East)倫敦,一九二五年,第一六九頁。
191. 阿爾韋斯·派克韋特(Paquet, Alfons):《禮儀還是立憲制》(Li oder Im neuen Osten)法蘭克福,一九一三年,第二三二頁。
192. 格奧爾格·佛朗求斯(Franzius, Georg):《膠州,德國在東亞的領地》(Kiautschou, Deutschlands Erwerbung in Ostasien),柏林,一八九八年,第七十頁及下頁。
193. 同上。
194. T·卡沃達:同〈186〉,第一七六頁。
195. 波茨坦聯邦檔案館檔案(Bundesarchiv Potsdam)中國公使館,第一〇三卷,第四卷。
196. 波茨坦聯邦檔案館檔案(Bundesarchiv Potsdam)中國公使館,第一〇五卷,第五〇頁。
197. 《德文新報》(Ostasiatischer Lloyd),上海,一九一〇年十月廿一日,第四〇二頁。
198. 一九〇五年臨江大道沿線每平方米地價為十八金馬克,離漢江較遠的地段每平方米地價為十一金馬克,一九一二年江邊的地價每平方米四十三金馬克,離開江岸的地價每平方米十七到廿一金馬克。租界附近的居住區每平方米八點五到十五金馬克,工程技術學院的校園離租界稍遠一些,每平方米的價格為零點九金馬克,參見波茨坦聯邦檔案館檔案(Bundesarchiv Potsdam)中國公使館,第六四〇卷,第四一六頁及下頁,第四二五頁,第一〇三二卷,第二六七頁。
199. 參見《德文新報》(Ostasiatischer Lloyd),上海,一九〇五年五月五日,第八一六頁。
200. 《德文新報》(Ostasiatischer Lloyd),上海,一九〇五年

323

200. 參見《德文新報》(Ostasiatischer Lloyd)，上海，一九〇八年七月十日，第八十八頁及下頁。
201. 《上海新聞》(Shanghaier Nachrichten)，上海，一九一一年三月十七日，第七十二頁及下頁。
202. 《德文新報》(Ostasiatischer Lloyd)，上海，一九〇七年三月廿九日，第五七七頁及下頁。
203. 《德文新報》(Ostasiatischer Lloyd)，上海，一九〇二年二月十九日，第三七三頁。
204. 同上。
205. 武漢的德國建築師把他們煞費苦心地繪制的設計寄到北京德國公使館，然而沒有得到答復，此事就不了之。參見波茨坦聯邦檔案館檔案(Bundesarchiv Potsdam)中國公使館，第六四〇卷，第四〇四至五〇五頁。
206. 關於風水理論參閱德里克・沃爾特斯(Walters, Derek)《風水－保證您生活安逸,富裕,幸福的參謀》(Feng Shui. Perfect Placing of your Happiness and prosperity)，倫敦、新加坡，一九八八年，喬治・內利斯特，同〈148〉，第一八二和第一八七頁。
207. 青島的情況是由私營公司開發的，所以情況不同，總督把此地產無償贈給學校和教會組織。
208. 詳見格奧爾格・瑪麗亞・斯丹資(Georg Maria Stenz)，《大運河》(Der Kaiserkanal)引自《殖民地政治經濟文》(Beiträge zur Kolonialpolitik und Kolonialwirtschaft)，柏林，一九〇三至一九〇四年。
209. 埃米爾・威廉密(Emil Wilhelmy)，同〈20〉，第三五頁。
210. E.J.杜科恩(E.J.Dukes)、A. 菲沃特(A. Fielde)，《中國的日常生活》(Alltagsleben in China)，巴塞爾，一八九二年，第一四九頁。
211. 參見德里克・瓦爾特斯(Derek Walters)同〈206〉；布魯諾・納瓦拉(Bruno Navarra)，同〈74〉，第四九頁及下頁。
212. "教堂設塔樓，工廠煙囱是不可饒恕的罪孽，因為這擾壞了仙界的靈氣。" E.J.杜科特(E.J. Fiel de)《中國的日常生活－中國民俗生活掠影》(Alltagsleben in China .Bilder aus dem chinesischen Volksleben)，巴塞爾，一八八二年，第一四六至一五〇頁。
213. 格奧爾格・瑪麗亞・斯丹資(Georg Maria Stenz)《大運河》(Der Kaiserkanal)引自《殖民地政治經濟文業》(Beiträge zur Kolonialpolitik und Kolonialwirtschaft)，柏林，一九〇三至一九〇四年，第一三〇頁。
214. 博克曼(Bökemann)，《山東省的經濟與交通》(Über Wirtschaft und Verkehr in der Provinz Schantung)，引自《殖民地周刊》(Koloniale Monatsblätter)，柏林，一九一三年，第一三二頁。
215. 《德文新報》(Ostasiatischer Lloyd)，上海，一九一二年十一月十日，第三九七頁。
216. 博克曼(Bökemann)，同〈214〉，第九十六頁。
217. 參見《德文新報》(Ostasiatischer Lloyd)，上海，一九〇三年九月十五日，第四七六頁。
218. 參見庫爾特・巴赫(Kurt Bach)，《論山東鐵路的建設》(Vom Bau der Schantung-Eisenbahn)，同《建築管理匯報》(Zentralblatt der Bauverwaltung)，柏林，一九〇五年九月十六日，第四九三頁。
219. 參見保爾・多斯特(Paul Dost)，《德國與中國及山東鐵路》(Deutsch-China und die Schantungbahn)，克雷費爾德，一九八一年，第五三頁。
220. 黃河並非重要水路。其下游有大量泥沙淤積而幾乎無法行船。一八五二年的特大洪災後，黃河最後一次改道，其入海口北移四百公里。
221. "佔領行動便捷是保障殖民地安全的首要條件。" 見漢斯・格斯登貝格(Hans Gerstenberg)，《青島的道路建築》(Die Wegebauten in Tsintau)，引自國殖民地貿易公司(Deutsche Kolonialgesellschaft)編：《殖民地政治經濟文業》(Beiträge zur Kolonialpolitik und Kolonialwirtschaft)，柏林，一八九九至一九〇〇年，第一二八頁。
222. 關於建築規定參見海因里希・拜茨(Heinrich Betz)：《山東省之經濟發展》(Die wirtschaftliche Entwicklung der Provinz Schantung)，青島，一九一一年，第六〇頁及下頁。
223. 《一九一一至一九一二年德國膠澳保護地姓名地址錄》(Adressbuch des Deutschen Kiautschou-Gebiets für 1911-1912)，青島，一九一一年，第七十五頁。
224. 《德文新報》(Ostasiatischer Lloyd)，上海，一九一二年九月十日，第二六二頁。
225. 卡爾・克魯(Carl Crow)：《中國全書》(Handbook for China)，上海，一九一二年，第二七六頁。
226. 《德文新報》(Ostasiatischer Lloyd)，上海，一九〇九年五月廿八日，第一〇七三頁。
227. 同〈223〉，一九一一至一九一二年，第七十五頁及下頁。
228. 恩斯特・比希曼(Ernst Boerschmann)：《中國建築》(Chinesische Architektur)，第一卷，同三插圖冊三（磚砌山牆），：插圖冊七（磚石建築）。
229. 恩斯特・比希曼(Ernst Boerschmann)：《中國的建築藝術與風景》(Baukunst und Landschaft in China)，柏林，一九二六年，第七八頁。
230. 《德文新報》(Ostasiatischer Lloyd)，上海，一九〇九年十一月四日，第六十七頁。
231. 《遠東時報》(The Far Eastern Review)，馬尼拉，上海，橫濱，一九一三年一月，第三四一頁。
232. 格奧爾格・佛郎求斯(Georg Franzius)：

233. 《德文新報》(Ostasiatischer Lloyd)，上海，一九一二年十至十一月。
234. 慕尼黑巴伐利亞國家圖書館，第Ana517號。
235. 盡管山東鐵路的另一終點站—青島火車站，在規模上比濟南火車站更近似於一座小火車站，但卻未予擴建。這一事實充分說明了山東鐵路與津浦鐵路在濟南的競爭。
236. 參見庫爾特・巴赫(Kurt Bach)，《論山東鐵路的建設》(Vom Bau der Schantung – Eisenbahn)，同〈218〉，第四九二頁及下頁。
237. 波茨坦聯邦檔案館(Bundesarchiv Potsdam)，中國公使館(Gesandtschaft China)，第九八五卷，第一五二頁。
238. 波茨坦聯邦檔案館(Bundesarchiv Potsdam)，中國公使館(Gesandtschaft China)，第九八四卷，第一九六及第二二六頁。
239. 波茨坦聯邦檔案館檔案((Bundesarchiv Potsdam)，中國公使館(Gesandtschaft China)，第九八五卷，第三卅七頁。
240. 阿諾德・賴特(Arnold Wright)，同〈60〉，第六〇四頁。
241. 《德文新報》(Ostasiatischer Lloyd)，上海，一九一三年六月十五日，第一六十七頁。
242. 羅伯特・科文萊・福塞斯(Robert CoventryForsyth)：《山東－中國的神密省份》(Shantung. The Sacred Province of China)，上海，一九一二年，第一六五頁。
243. 《德文新報》(Ostasiatischer Lloyd)，上海，一九〇八年六月廿六日。
244. 艾倫・薩瑪加斯基(Alan Samagalski)、邁克・巴克雷(Michael Buckley)：《中國一旅遊生活指南》(China. A Travel Survival Kit)，澳大利亞維多利亞，一九八四年，第四七九頁。
245. 中國建築中極少使用十字拱，但墓穴和門洞建築則常呈圓拱狀。
246. 《德文新報》(Ostasiatischer Lloyd)，上海，一九〇〇年七月六日，第五〇九頁。
247. 《德文新報》(Ostasiatischer Lloyd)，上海，一九〇四年十月十五日，第六十七頁。
248. 格奧爾格・瑪麗亞・斯丹資(Georg Maria Stenz)：《在孔夫子的家鄉》(In der Heimat des Konfuzius)，斯泰爾，一九〇二年，第六十七頁。
249. 理夏德・哈特維希(Richard Hartwich)，《斯泰勒修士在中國》(Steyler Missionare in China)第一卷，《一八七九至一九〇三年山東南部的教務開發》(Missionarische Erschliessng Südshantungs 1879 – 1903)，至奧古斯汀，一九八三年，第一九八頁及下頁、第三一九頁及第三四八頁。
250. 參見《德文新報》(Ostasiatischer Lloyd)，上海，一九一四年三月十三日，第二三二頁及下頁。
251. 參見理夏德・哈特維希(Richard Hartwich)，同〈249〉，第一卷，地形圖，第五二六頁及下頁。
252. 參見〈249〉，第三卷，《中華民國與一九一一至一九一九年的第一次世界大戰》(Republik China und der Erste Weltkrieg 1911 – 1919)，第二六頁及第二九頁。
253. 同〈249〉，第一卷，第五五百及下頁。
254. 譯自《香港每日新聞》(Hongkong Daily Press)，引自《青島時報》(Tsingtauer Neueste Nachrichten)，一九一三年九月五日。
255. 參見格奧爾格・佛郎求斯(Georg Franzius)，《膠州》(Kiautschou)，同〈106〉，第九十八頁及下頁。
256. 參見C．胡格寧(C. Huguenin)，《第三海軍管理歷史》(Geschichte des III. See – Bataillons)，青島，一九一二年，第三至八頁。
257. 這一條約成了英國租借香港 "新界" 的樣板，租期亦為九十九年，將於一九九七年到期。對歸還英國皇家殖民地的討論使人聯想起其仿效對象—前德國殖民地青島。
258. 例如：天津依傍於大運河、海河。上海落在黃浦江畔，緊靠長江口及長江入海口。武漢位於長江上游一千一百公里處。廣州僅依於珠江江畔。珠江江口一帶則是英國殖民地香港和葡萄牙殖民地澳門。與中國內地唯一類似於青島情況的新建歐洲城市是自一八八八年起由俄國工程師開辟的大連市。俄國佔領遼東半島前，島上亦無基礎設施。一九〇一至一九〇二年、西伯利亞聯軍鐵路開工至一九〇一年十一月三日竣工。它溝通了莫斯科、海參崴、哈爾濱和大連之間的聯系，並在大連市大規模的城市建設及鐵路東南端不凍港的規劃建設中提供了可能。
259. 魯道夫・瓦格納(Rudolf Wagner)、E・布赫曼(E. Buchmann)，《德國殖民地之旅》(Eine Reise durch die Deutschen Kolonien)，第六卷，《膠州》(Kiautschou)，柏林，一九一三年。
260. 參見帝國海軍部(Reichsmarineamt)編，《一九零四年十月至一九零五年十月膠澳保護區發展情況備忘錄》(Denkschrift betreffend die Entwicklung des Kiautschou – Gebiets in der Zeit vom Oktober 1904 bis Oktober 1905)，柏林，一九〇六年，第一〇七頁。
261. 單威廉(Wilhelm Schrameier)，《膠州行政》(Aus Kiautschous Verwaltung)，耶拿，一九一四年，第五十二頁。
262. 威廉・馬察特(Wilhelm Matzat)：《單威廉與青島土地法規》(Die Tsingtauer Landordnung des Chinesenkommissars Wilhelm Schrameier)，波恩，一九八五年，第廿七頁及下頁。
263. 《德屬膠州官報》(Deutsch–Asiatische Warte)，青島，一八九九年四月廿日。
264. 自一八四二年起，英國人設立了第一批外國租界。外國人只能在與現有中國港口城市毗鄰的特定區域內購地。在北京的外國人只許住在外國公使區內。唯一例外的是傳教士。

265. 漢斯・魏克爾(Hans Weicker)：《膠州，德國在東亞的保護地》(Kiautschou. Das deutsche Schutzgebiet in Ostasien)，柏林，一九〇八年，第六七頁。
266. 威爾遜・利昂・戈德謝爾(Wilson Leon Godshall)《三面旗幟下的青島》(Tsingtau under three Flags)，上海，一九二九年，第一三〇頁。
267. 關於青島的發展參見帝國海軍部於一八九七至一九〇九年編寫的備忘錄。
268. 《上海社會》(Social Shanghai)，上海，一九〇六至一九一二年。
269. 單威廉(Wilhelm Schrameier)：《膠州行政》(Aus Kiautschous Verwaltung)，耶拿，一九一四年，第三十二頁。
270. 衛禮賢(Richard Wilhelm)，同〈1〉，第一八八頁。
271. 阿爾豐斯・派克韋特(Alfons Paquet)這樣寫道："總督公館以威儀四方的氣勢座落在坡頂，不禁使人聯想到波茲南皇宮那宏偉之狀。"引自阿爾豐斯・派克韋特(Alfons Paquet)，同〈10〉，第二九七頁。
272. 賈尼奇・霍布(Junichi Hobow)：《青島，遠東的里維埃拉》(Tsingtao. The Riviera of the Far East)，青島，一九二二年。
273. 他認為："由於時間緊迫而無法預算建造費用，"最後勢必提高造價。"花崗石砌立面並非產生額外費用的原因。"當時，用花崗石砌面牆的費用在青島只相當於柏林的普通價格的五分之一。參見弗賴堡聯邦檔案，膠州卷，第RM3/V.6995號，第十七頁及下頁。另有必要說明一下有關這座別墅的小史：德國駐青島總督沛綠文並非由於大興土木而被威廉二世親自罷職。總督私宅建造期間，他回國休假長達十二個月，而並非六月才返華。
274. 邁克(Mahlke)：《青島（膠州）的新總督官署》(Das neue Gouvernements-Dienstgebäude in Tsingtau, Kiautschou)，引自《建築管理匯報》(Zentralblatt der Bauverwaltung)柏林，一九〇七年八月十七日，第四四四至第四七七頁。
275. 德屬膠州官報(Deutsch-Asiatische Warte. Amtlicher Anzeiger des Kiautschou-Gebietes)，青島，一八九九年四月廿日。
276. 十字拱是歐洲建築文化和建築技術的表現，與當地的中國文化相競爭。中國幾乎沒有十字拱或交叉圓拱。中國的門洞建築一般采用簡單的圓拱。
277. 格奧爾格・F・內利思特(George F. Nellist)，同〈148〉，第一三五頁及下頁。
278. 帝國海軍部(Reichsmarineamt)，同〈267〉，《一八九七至一八九八年備忘錄》(Denkschrift 1897/98)，柏林，一八九八年，第十二頁。
279. 格奧爾格・F・內利思特(George F. Nellist)，同〈148〉，第一三五頁及下頁。
280. 《德文新報》(Ostasiatischer Lloyd)，上海，一九一四年五月十九日，第四四五頁。
281. 阿爾豐斯・派克韋特(Alfons Paquet)，同〈10〉，第二九七頁。
282. 判刑六個月以上的囚犯被解往青島十五公里遠的李村華人監獄。上書"華人監獄"的門牌現保存青島市博物館内。歐洲人的監獄於一九〇〇年完工。它位於歐洲的東部，旁邊原是清朝衙門。德國佔領青島初期，其行政部門皆設置於此。
283. Fr．貝默爾(Fr. Behme)、M．克里格爾(M.Krieger)：《青島及其郊區導游》(Führer durch Tsingtau und Umgebung)，第3版，沃爾芬比特爾，一九〇六年，第九十頁。
284. 帝國海軍部(Reichsmarineamt)，同〈260〉，《一九零二至一九零三年備忘錄》(Denkschrift 1902-1903)，柏林，一九〇四年，第四十四頁。
285. 《德文新報》(Ostasiatischer Lloyd)，上海，一九〇七年八月九日。
286. "德國機械廠是一家建造啤酒廠和麥芽作坊的歐洲專業廠。它按照現代化的德國體系裝備了海外許多欣欣向榮的啤酒廠。例如：幾乎所有的日本大啤酒廠是按照德國機械廠的圖紙建造，並用其機器裝備的。"引自《德文新報》(Ostasiatischer Lloyd)，上海，一九〇四年十二月十六日。
287. 《德文新報》(Ostasiatischer Lloyd)，上海，一九〇六年九月二日，第七〇二頁。
288. 參見《德文新報》(Ostasiatischer Lloyd)，上海，一九〇七年三月一日，第三六七頁。
289. 汪坦(Wang Tan)、藤森照信(Terunobu Fujimori)、徐飛鵬(Xü Feipeng)：《中國近代建築總覽，青島篇》(The architectural heritage of modern China : Qingdao)，北京，一九九二年，第三十六頁。
290. 帝國海軍部(Reichsmarineamt)，《一九〇八至一九〇九年備忘錄》(Denkschrift für 1908-1909)，柏林，一九一〇年，第五十四頁。
291. 《德文新報》(Ostasiatischer Lloyd)，上海，一九一二年一月十九日，第五十六頁。
292. 同上，這是恩斯特・馮・維爾登布魯赫(Ernst von Wildenbruch)(一八四五至一九〇九年)的一首詩。
293. 《德屬膠州官報》(Deutsch-Asiatische Warte)，青島，一八九九年九月十七日。
294. 《德屬膠州官報》(Deutsch-Asiatische Warte)，青島，一九〇〇年十一月廿日。
295. C．胡格寧(C. Huguenin)：《第三海軍軍歷史》(Geschichte des III.See – Bataillons)，青島，一九一二年，第一二八頁。
296. 帝國海軍部(Reichsmarineamt)，同〈287〉，《一八九九至一九零零年備忘錄》(Denkschrift 1899-1900)，第三十

297. 參見弗蘭茨·克勞奈克爾(Franz Kronecker),《膠州十五年.殖民地醫學研究》(Fünfzehn Jahre Kiautschou. Eine Kolonialmedizinische Studie),柏林,一九一三年,第十五頁。
298. 同上,第廿頁及下頁。
299. 《德屬膠州官報》(Deutsch-Asiatische Warte),青島,一九○一年九月四日。
300. 參見F.W.默爾(F.W.Mohr),《青島全書》(Handbuch für das Schutzgebiet Kiautschou),青島,一九一一年,第三九二頁:"青島德國總督府學校校規",訂於一九○九年七月廿四日。
301. 參見《德文新報》(Ostasiatischer Lloyd),上海,一九○九年二月十二日,第三二三頁。
302. 參見《德文新報》(Ostasiatischer Lloyd),上海,一九一四年十二月十一日,第五五三頁。
303. 一九一二年九月廿九日,改良政治家孫逸仙參觀該校,並對學生發表演說。參見《德文新報》(Ostasiatischer Lloyd),上海,一九一二年十月十一日,第三三一頁。
304. 庫爾特·羅克格(Curt Rothkegel),《青島,膠州的基督教堂》(Evangelische Kirche für Tsingtau-Kiautschou),引自《德國建築行業報》(Zentralblatt für das deutsche Baugewerbe),柏林,一九○九年三月廿六日。
305. 同上。
306. 參見《青島傳教通訊》(Tsingtauer Missions Korrespondenz),一九三三年六月一日,第二期,第卅一頁及下頁。
307. 《青島的教堂落成典禮》(Kirchweih in Tsingtau)引自《斯泰勒傳教信使》(Steyler Missionsbote),一九三四年,第一四六頁。
308. 參見《德屬膠州官報》(Deutsch-Asiatische Warte),青島,一八九九年四月廿日。
309. 理夏德·哈特維希(Richard Hartwich),同〈249〉,第一卷,第四七二頁。
310. 一九○八年,即墨縣城新落成的基督教堂也是由路徹維次(Lutschewitz)設計的。即墨距青島四十五公里。參見《德文新報》(Ostasiatischer Lloyd),一九○八年六月十二日,第一一二頁。
311. 這兩所傳教會在實質上有很大區別。"天主教柏林傳教會沿用自古以來的傳教方式開展教務活動。傳教士通過個人交往和慈善事業如學校、醫院來努力深入人心。(......)欲皈依基督教的異教徒先申請受洗,接受為期一年的洗禮教育,學習基督教教義,經考試之後,方可受洗。"引自漢斯·魏克爾(Hans Weicker),《膠州,德國在東亞的保護地》(Kiautschou, das deutsche Schutzgebiet in Ostasien),柏林,一九○八年,第一八八頁。
312. 參見Fr.貝默爾(Fr. Behme)M.克里格爾(M. Krieger)同〈283〉,第七十一頁及下頁。
313. 衛禮賢(Richard Wilhelm)、漢娜·希盧姆哈特(Hanna Blumhardt):《我們在青島的學校》(Unsere Schulen in Tsingtau),柏林,無出版年代,第三頁及下頁。
314. 參見F.W.默爾(F.W. Mohr),同〈300〉,第四五一頁。
315. 衛禮賢在青島生活至一九二○年。一九二五年,他在法蘭克福(美因河畔)建立了中國問題研究所。
316. 衛禮賢(Richard Wilhelm),同〈1〉,第一七一頁及下頁。
317. 水師飯店的基址選在船隻易於到達的位置。一九○四年三月大港啟用後,所有海運業務遷至距商業中心三公里遠的港區。
318. 帝國海軍部(Reichsmarineamt),同〈267〉,《一九零一至一九零二年備忘錄》(Denkschrift 1901/02),柏林,一九○三年,第廿五頁。
319. 《膠州消息》(Nachrichten aus Kiautschou),上海,一八九九年十月十八日。
320. 建築師羅克格在天津曾參與修建德國康科迪亞總會。一年後,他又完成了北京總會的建築。
321. 達姆施塔特T.華納(T.Warner)檔案。
322. 《青島時報》(Tsingtauer Neueste Nachrichten),一九一三年十一月二日,第二頁。
323. 參見馬塞爾·格拉奈特(Marcel Granet),《中國人之思維,內容,形式與性格》(Das chinesische Denken, Inhalt, Form, Charakter),法蘭克福,一九八五年。
324. 中國的改良政治家孫逸仙博士(一八六六至一九二五年)一九一二年九月廿八日在青島停留兩天,下榻於海濱旅館。孫先生及其家眷、隨從人員共占用客房十六間。參見《德文新報》(Ostasiatischer Lloyd),上海,一九一二年十月十一日。
325. 《德文新報》(Ostasiatischer Lloyd),上海,一九一○年十一月十八日,第四九八頁。
326. 《膠州消息.德文新報副刊》(Nachrichten aus Kiautschou, Beiblatt zum Ostasiatischen Lloyd),上海,一八九九年九月卅日。
327. 參見《一九零五年德國膠澳保護地姓名地址錄》(Adress-Buch des Deutschen Kiautschou-Gebietes für 1905),青島,第廿頁。
328. 達姆施塔特T.華納(T.Warner)檔案。
329. 同上。
330. 《德文新報》(Ostasiatischer Lloyd),上海,一九一○年十一月十八日,第四九八頁。
331. 賴訥·法爾克恩貝格(Rainer Falkenberg):《路易斯·魏爾勒寄自中國的書籍》(Luis Weilers Briefe aus China);引自郭恆昱(音譯)(Kuo Heng-yü)、梅希蒂爾德·洛伊特納(Mechthild Leutner):《中德關系文叢》(BeitägeEzuEden deutsch-chinesischen Beziehungen),柏林,一九八六年,第一二三頁。
332. 波茨坦聯邦檔案館檔案(Bundesarchiv Potsdam),中國公使館(Gesandtschaft China),第九八四卷,第五四頁及下頁。
333. 漢斯·魏克爾(Hans Weicker),同〈256〉,第一四五頁。
334. 邁爾克爾(Maercker):《膠州地區之發展,第二部》(Die Entwicklung des Kiautschougebiets. Zweiter Teil.),柏林,一九○三年,第六十二頁及下頁。
335. 帝國海軍部(Reichsmarineamt),《一九零三至一九零四年備忘錄》(Denkschrift für 1903/04),柏林,一九○五年,圖六a。
336. F.W. 默爾(F.W.Mohr),同〈300〉,第二○六頁。
337. 參見Fr.貝默爾(Fr. Behme)M.克里格爾(M. Krieger),同〈283〉,第四十二頁。
338. 參見阿諾德·賴特(Arnold Wright),同〈60〉,第六一四頁。
339. 汪坦(Wang Tan)、藤森照信(Fujimori Terunobu)除飛鵬(Xü Feipeng),同〈289〉,第四十二頁。
340. 《一九一三至一九一四年德國膠州保護地姓名地址錄》(Adressbuch des Deutschen Kiautschou-Gebietes für 1913-1914),青島,一九一三年。
341. 帝國海軍部(Reichsmarineamt),同〈267〉,柏林,一九○三年,第卅六頁。
342. 每月在上海出版的畫刊《上海社會》(Social Shanghai)定期介紹"上海美居"。
343. 這幢房屋的第一位主人是上尉弗賴海爾.利利恩可龍。他於一八九九至一九○二年任總督副官。此後返回德國。一九一二至一九一三年,利利恩可龍重返青島,任第三海軍營營長。參見C.胡格寧(C. Huguenin),同〈256〉,第五十八頁。
344. 此篇誌文刻於阿里文住宅的牆基上。
345. 參見《德文新報》(Ostasiatischer Lloyd),上海,一九一四年五月十九日。
346. 波恩馬察特(Matzat)教授檔案。
347. 達姆施塔特T.華納(T. Warner)檔案。
348. 一九○四年版本的《青島導游》(Führer durch Tsingtau)描述了市區游覽景點:"由總督府廣場向西北方向拐入傳教站後的霍恩洛厄路,可見幾處漂亮的別墅。第二幢是總督牧師的住宅。由此可遠眺城市和港灣的風景。"這本導游書的續版卻對比建築隻字未提。參見Fr.貝默爾(Fr. Behme).M.克里格爾(M. Krieger),同〈283〉,第四十四頁。另見該作者《青島及其郊區導游》(Führer durch Tsingtau und Umgebung),第三版,沃爾芬比特爾,一九○六年,第六十七頁。

標題索引

澳大利亞 95, 115
奧格斯堡－紐倫堡 M.A.N. 有限公司 167
奧匈帝國 26, 58, 89
保安 141, 151, 221
寶隆醫院 135
北京俱樂部 51, 297
俾斯嗟兵營 202, 207, 235, 245
比利時 26, 58
伯恩尼克＆波特爾公司 275, 299
勃蘭登堡門（柏林）19
柏林國會大廈 18, 35, 37, 67
柏林傳教會 255
長江 85, 89, 127, 141, 143, 147
巢絲廠 157
車站飯店 159, 185, 265
城牆 27, 29, 43, 57, 87, 156
"出口房" 293
大覺寺 11, 26
大禮拜堂學校（上海）105
大清郵局 107, 281
大上海 131
大運河 57, 73, 155, 156, 159, 175
德國工學院教學樓，武漢 18, 62, 95, 123, 145, 153
德國海員俱樂部（上海）101, 103
德國花園俱樂部，上海 13, 87, 95, 131
德國技術工程學院 62, 89, 95, 123, 153
德國膠州總督府 207, 211, 215, 221, 225, 229, 233, 235, 237, 239, 241, 293, 295, 301
德國領事館 15, 33, 58, 61, 67, 145, 147, 149, 179, 187, 189, 277
德國啤酒廠 227
德國使館別墅 53
德國文藝復興式復古風格 13, 20, 47, 49, 71, 88, 91, 119, 189, 221, 223, 285, 303
德國新福音教堂 88, 89, 101, 103, 131, 133
德國醫學院（上海）89, 123, 135
德國郵政局 101, 107, 281
德國總領事館 11, 88, 101, 103, 107, 131
德一漢租界公司 143
德華工業大學 123, 241, 243, 257
德華銀行 13, 47, 49, 59, 71, 95, 111, 149, 189, 277, 279
德華中學（天津）60
德意志之角落・科布倫芝 15
德語報（天津創刊）79
德中工程學院 18, 60, 95, 123, 144, 153
地方協會 59, 67
帝國大廈（柏林）18, 35, 37, 67
帝國海軍部 59, 187, 229, 233, 283
狄特立克斯（紀念碑）99, 231
電車 27, 29, 57, 87
東華門（北京）19
東亞戰領軍兵團 47, 49, 69
董家渡天主教堂學校 105
斗拱 17, 163
俄國 26, 58, 60, 142

俄國總領事館 101, 103, 121
發電廠 86
法國 23, 26, 58, 59, 60, 142
法律 85, 89, 215
凡爾賽條約 25
坊子煤礦 279
非洲 16
費希納和卡普勒 147
風水 17, 18, 153, 156, 161, 239, 297
婦孺醫院 135
風水 17, 18, 153, 156, 161, 239, 297
婦孺醫院 135
福斯灣大橋（蘇格蘭）167
福音堂（青島）14, 241, 245, 289
格瑪妮俱樂部，香港 11, 83
公使館區 23, 25, 26, 27, 45, 47, 49, 60
公使館（德國的）24, 39, 43, 51
觀象臺（北京）25
觀象臺（青島）229
國際飯店 133
海濱旅館（青島）203, 267
海濱浴場 27, 53, 55, 197, 202, 295
海關 81, 219, 297
海河 57, 59, 73, 79
漢口德國租界工部局 151
荷蘭 26
桁架結構建築 17, 18, 53, 261, 293
亨利王子飯店（青島）269, 271, 273, 289
后現代主意思潮 19
華東醫院 135, 137
華俄道勝銀行 109, 149
花之安醫院（青島）17, 257
皇城（北京）23, 33, 35
黃河 159, 167
黃河鐵路大橋 167
黃蒲江 85, 88, 89, 95, 101, 121, 127, 131
混凝土 115, 121, 139
火車站 73, 159, 161, 163, 165, 169, 181, 185, 223
基督教堂 14, 60, 69, 103, 133, 145, 175, 177, 245, 249, 251
建築法規 14, 20, 204, 283
建築管理局規劃處 237, 241, 271, 301
膠州租條約 196
戒臺寺 27
津浦鐵路 17, 73, 157, 161, 163
警察 142, 151, 221
開平煤礦 58
康科迪亞總會（上海）13, 49, 87, 88, 91, 97, 99, 117, 119, 131, 189
康科迪亞總會（天津）15, 51, 65, 289
康有為紀念館（青島）295
克林德級念碑 45
克姆尼茨市德國機械廠 227
來泰公司 35, 119
嶗山礦泉水 35, 119
雷州大理石 191
禮查公園（上海）121
禮合公司 11, 113, 287

禮合商業大樓 11, 113, 287
里弄樓房 86, 144
洛可可風格 15
羅馬式復古風格 15, 20, 65, 249
羅蘭德雕像 15, 69
馬丁＆皮爾率聯（合鐵造廠）99
馬關條約 59, 142
買辦建築風格 11, 83
滿月門 77, 79
茂記建築公司 127
美國 26, 115
美國底特律綱筋混凝土建築公司 115
美國路德傳教會 255
美懿書院（青島）259
梅克倫堡之家（嶗山）198
米歇勒天主教堂 26
沫恩堂 123
內城（滿族地區）23, 24, 27, 29, 35, 43
牌坊 45
普魯土皇家機械學校 123
普魯土文化部 239
騎士雕像 15, 69
前門 27, 29, 31
清朝（政府）39, 60, 79, 203
青島德國俱樂部 18, 263
青島俱樂部 263
青島尊孔文社 259
青年派風格 15, 51, 77, 79, 181, 183, 207, 219, 241, 245, 263, 271, 273, 289
日本 26, 58, 59, 62, 147, 197
人力車 86, 221
瑞記商行 115
山東礦務公司 157, 158, 279
山東鐵路 159, 165, 179, 189, 197, 225, 287
上海道達洋行 103
上海德僑活動中心 89, 101, 103, 105, 131
上海電話局辦公樓 115
上海花園飯店 97
上海社會（文化雜志）200
上海市政府 139
施密特, F.H.公司 49, 65, 67, 71, 189, 211, 215, 219, 227, 235, 245, 271, 281, 293
生瑞公司 119
聖方濟各沙勾略修院 175
聖彌愛爾大教堂 249, 251
聖三一教堂 113
聖心修道院（青島）239, 251, 253
聖言會 17, 155, 161, 171, 175, 177, 251
聖約瑟夫教堂 103
獸醫站 133
水師飯店 17, 261
斯泰爾修會聖言會 17, 155, 156, 161, 171, 175, 177, 251
蘇州河（上海）87, 101, 121
太平天國革命 85
特格°施洛特公司 35, 119
天津建築公司 75
天浦線鐵路公司 17, 73, 159, 161, 163
天壇 24, 29

326

天主大教堂 113, 171, 191, 249, 251
天主教聖言會 155, 156, 179, 191
鐵路通車 142, 198
同濟大學 87, 127, 129
同濟醫學堂 89, 123, 135
同仁醫院 135
土地法規 81, 85, 203
屠宰場 225
外白渡橋（上海）101
外交部（德意志帝國的）43, 53, 61, 67, 79, 101, 147, 187
維克多利亞護士宿舍（上海）139
威廉學堂（上海）8, 9, 101, 103, 105, 113
威廉學堂（天津）60
魏瑪傳教會 17, 255, 257, 259
西門子公司 27
西塔斯°普拉姆拜克公司 273
香港德國總會 11, 83
祥泰商行 117
新羅馬主義 15, 20, 65, 249
學校 62, 89, 101, 103, 105, 123, 127, 131, 144, 153, 175
雅片戰爭 23, 57
野戰醫院 47, 49, 135, 237
意大利 26, 58
意大利文藝復興復古風格 71, 109, 111, 149, 189
伊爾帝斯兵營（青島）199, 233, 235, 301
伊爾帝斯號炮艦 99, 229
伊爾帝斯青銅雕紀念碑（上海）87, 89, 99, 131
義和團 24, 25, 175
義和團運動 25, 27, 29, 39, 51, 59, 60, 62, 175
怡泰大樓 101
醫藥商店 281, 289
醫院（德國的）47, 49, 135, 237
醫療衛生展覽會（德累斯頓）33
英國 23, 26, 58, 59
英國斜橋總會 97
永定門 27
圓明園（北京）23, 58
運東聯合會 127
照壁 18, 263
政事堂 33
中法通惠工商學校 123
中方企業皮káro公司 239
中國國會大廈 18, 31, 35, 39, 41
中國建造德國技術學校促進會 123, 153
中國鐵路局 73, 161, 163, 165, 167, 181, 183
中國銀行 131
中國政府鐵路局 73, 161, 163, 165, 167, 181, 183
中國海關 219, 287, 297
中華民國政府 39, 41, 203
紫禁城（北京）23
自來水廠 87
總督府邸／私邸 14, 15, 17, 20, 200, 207, 245, 293, 295, 301
總督府行政辦樓 14, 20, 211, 215, 277, 301
總督官署 14, 20, 211, 215, 277, 301

總會康科迪婭總會（上海）13, 49, 87, 88, 91, 97, 99, 117, 119, 131, 189
總會康科迪婭總會（天津）15, 51, 65, 289

人名索引

阿達爾貝特°普魯士王子 91
埃克哈德° Th. 97
安治泰° J.B.（主教）155, 171, 175, 196, 251, 253
奧伯業因°埃里希 127
奧爾默°恩斯特 43, 198, 219, 297
巴赫（建築總監）161
貝爾納茨（政府總建築師）239, 251, 253
貝加斯° R. 99
貝克°海因里希 13, 91, 95, 97, 103, 107, 109, 111, 149
貝克°培迪克（建築師）49, 71, 101, 117, 118, 145, 188, 276
比希曼°因斯特 11
午°里夏德 109
伯恩尼克°海爾曼 299
波特爾（工程師）299
布契°衛（建築師）131, 149, 151
陳漢樸（大清銀行總裁）18
淳（皇太子）45
慈禧太后 18, 37
狄特立克斯°馮·水師提督 195, 231
多普未勒°尤利烏斯 167
恩博仁（神甫）171, 175, 177, 249
菲列普斯° G.W. 115
菲舍爾°赫爾曼 181
菲舍爾°馬丁 12
弗蘭茨吾斯。格奧爾格 69, 80, 142, 195
弗萊波爾（神甫）249
弗里德里希一世 10
浮士德° J. 79
格德爾茨°阿爾弗雷德 223
郭沫若（作家）45
吉利°馬克斯 291
哈克巴爾特（建築助理）161
哈姆布子格 139
亨寶商業大樓 285, 303
亨利王子（普魯士）99, 231
亨姆普爾° G.L. 147
亨內舍 285
康裕科 91
科比那利烏斯°神甫 191, 193
克里格°馬丁 119
克林德 25, 45
克尼平（德國領事）60
克芬斯°奧克斯特 99
孔夫子 155, 163, 171
孔古爵 161
拉爾茨（藥劑師）289
拉姆° E.A.（建築師）83
朗格（領事）187
雷克斯伯爵°馮（公使）53

里勃°漢斯·埃米爾 105, 121
里諾（總工程師）183
里希特°保爾·弗里德里希罕 87, 229, 263, 273, 291
里希特霍分胺°馮·斐迪南 157
路德維希 47, 53
羅克格 18, 19, 26, 29, 31, 35, 39, 41, 51, 65, 77, 245, 263, 271, 275, 289
羅克格°格特魯德 29, 33
馬爾克（政府建築師）207, 211
馬爾克斯°洛塔爾 131, 235
馬特維希° R. 265
毛澤東 209
米勒°格奧爾木 99
米塔爾°馬克斯 119
莫赫德° R.B. 103
牧姆°馮（大使）55
諾伊曼°里夏德 101
帕格特°查爾斯 115
派克偉特°阿爾豐斯 15, 142, 221
培迪克°卡爾 18, 91, 95, 123, 153
沛祿文（總督都）14, 209
普爾耐爾°亞瑟 115
薩里寧°伊力爾 181
賽加倫°維克多 12
沙伯°馮 135
沙天拉特（建築師）151
施特拉塞爾（房建總監）207, 219
施偉希頓 15
蘇爾°卡斯泰赫爾曼 71, 105, 123, 153
蘇爾和瓦澤芬（建築師）
瓦德西（德國陸軍元師）49, 58
瓦洛特（建築師）35
魏爾勒°路易斯 223, 277
魏嘉碌（主教）249
衛禮賢 10, 204, 257, 259
威廉一世 15
威廉二世 14, 15, 65, 91, 99, 155, 196
烏茨勒° W. 107, 146
鄔達克 133, 135, 137
席阿密豁°威廉（中國事務特派員）198, 203
錫樂巴°海因里希 11, 142, 187, 223, 277
楊德爾（建築師）163
永滔 18
於希特利茨男爵°馮（教授）69
袁世凱 33
載洵（親王）18, 33
載倫（親王）79
章高元（清軍守將）196
周紹科 121

地名索引

阿爾托納區（漢堡）49, 65, 67, 71, 189, 211, 215, 219, 227, 235, 245, 271, 281, 293
巴黎 91
北戴河 27, 53, 55, 295
北京 11, 12, 13, 23-51, 53, 55, 57, 58, 60, 71,

142, 143, 243, 249, 297
波茨坦 10, 15, 25
波茨南 15
勃海 53, 167
柏林 35, 49, 69, 71, 101, 107, 147, 149, 189, 198, 245, 277
博山 157, 279
滄口城 157
滄州城 165
曹洲城 155
成都 12
大鮑島 178, 200, 221, 251, 255, 269, 289
大沽 57
大連 196, 203, 249
戴家莊 177
但澤一 283
德累斯頓 33
德州城 165
底特律 115
東京 231
杜塞爾多夫 191
高密城 169, 202
古斯塔夫堡 167
郭店 169
廣州 85, 115
漢堡 35, 49, 65, 67, 71, 117, 189, 211, 215, 219, 227, 235, 245, 271, 281, 293
漢口 〉武漢
漢陽 〉武漢
河北省 58
雞公山 142
濟南 13, 16, 17, 73, 156, 158, 165, 169, 179-193, 197, 219, 223, 249, 277, 281
濟寧城 155, 175, 177
江蘇省 167
膠州 13, 143, 155, 158, 171, 196
巨野城 155
開羅 95
科布倫芝 15
科隆 95
克姆尼茨市 227
牯嶺 142
崂山 14, 198
李村 217, 255, 281
盧山 142
旅順 141, 197
馬家鋪 27
馬尼拉（菲律島）229
明斯特爾城（在威斯特法倫）45
慕尼墨 95, 227, 251, 253
南海（北京）18
南京 17, 58, 62, 73, 127, 159, 163, 181, 198, 215
南霞口城 165
平陵城 169
平原城 165
青島 11, 12, 13, 15, 19, 20, 33, 61, 80, 99, 107, 131, 157, 158, 159, 169, 179, 185, 187, 189, 195-303

曲阜城 155, 161, 171
仁川（南朝）229
山東 17, 155-177, 195, 293
上海 13, 49, 59, 85-139, 141, 147, 153, 189, 195, 196, 203, 227, 229, 287, 293
什未林 95
沈陽 33, 57, 58, 131
四川省 12
蘇格蘭 167
泰安 17, 161
泰山 155, 163
臺東鎮 199, 201, 202, 255
臺西鎮 199, 201
天津 15, 19, 23, 26, 33, 51, 55, 57-79, 141, 145, 159, 163, 165, 195, 198, 203, 245, 249, 275, 287, 289
濰坊城 157, 179, 279
武昌武漢
武漢 18, 27, 59, 73, 95, 131, 141-153, 195
吳淞 88, 125, 127, 129
西山（北京）26, 201
廈門 31
香港 11, 81, 83, 85, 203, 229, 277, 287
逍遙官 10
徐家匯 229
兗州城 155, 161, 171, 175
芝加格 141
周村 168, 179